Marxist Theory of Economic Crisis and Cycles : Structure and Changes

by Liu Mingyuan

translated by Wang Lingling

CANUT INTERNATIONAL PUBLISHERS

Istanbul - Berlin - London - Santiago

本书受到"中华社会科学基金 (Chinese Fund for the Humanities and Social Sciences) 资助.

The publication is supported by Chinese Fund for the Humanities and Social Sciences.

Marxist Theory of Economic Crisis and Cycles : Structure and Changes
by Liu Mingyuan
translated by Wang Lingling
Chinese Title: 马克思主义经济危机和周期理论的结构与变迁
ISBN: 9787300106854
Copyright © 2009, China Renmin University Press, Beijing

Canut International Publishers

Canut Intl. Turkey, Teraziler Cad. No.29. Sancaktepe, Istanbul, Turkey
Canut Intl. Germany, Heerstr. 266, D-47053, Duisburg, Germany
Canut Intl. United Kingdom, 12a Guernsay Road, London E11 4BJ, England
Copyright © 2018, Canut International Publishers
ISBN: 978-605-9914-68-0

About the Author

Liu Mingyuan, associate professor of Renmin University of China, Ph.D. in Economics. His main research objects are the Marxist economic crisis and cycles theory; Marx's six books plan in his economic treatise; Marxist ecological economics. He teaches at the Renmin University of China since 1990. His representative papers are: The US Subprime Mortgage Crisis in the View of Political Economy; Acquaintance Society, Group Benefit and Stable Development of Chinese Private Finance

.

Preface by the Author

I

With the establishment of the capitalist system and the development of the industrial revolution, capitalism ushered in the era of machines. It happened that "the bourgeoisie, during its rule of scarce one hundred years, has created more massive and more colossal productive forces than have all preceding generations together." However, this momentum was increasingly constrained by capitalist relations of production, and the bourgeoisie was increasingly like the wizard who can no longer control the devil summoned by his magic. As a result, it had to suffer cyclical crises of overproduction. In these crises, a great part of the products as well as a large part of the productive forces has been destroyed. "In these crises, there breaks out an epidemic that, in all earlier epochs, would have seemed an absurdity."

During more than two hundred years since Britain had the very first economic crisis of overproduction in 1788 till 2008, there were a total of 28 economic crises of overproduction in the capitalist world, of which six occurred before 1825, namely crises in 1788, 1793, 1797, 1810, 1815 and 1819. As the crises in this period only occurred in some industries within Britain, the impact on the entire economy was quite small. The frequency of these crises was irregular, with a maximum interval of up to 13 years and a minimum of 4, so they should be referred to as local economic crisis of overproduction, which was an early form of capitalist economic crisis and cannot be regarded as typical. In some hundred years from 1825 to 1929, 13 economic crises occurred in the capitalist world, namely crises in 1825, 1836, 1847, 1857, 1866, 1873, 1882, 1890, 1900, 1907, 1914, 1921 and 1929. During this period, the crises essentially occurred and developed spontaneously in cycles, and the frequency was not only comparatively regular, but universal and worldwide, showing a trend of gradual intensification. The crises in this period were the typical form of capitalism in the period of free competition. From 1937 to 2008, 9 economic crises occurred in the capitalist world, namely crises in 1937, 1948, 1957,

1969, 1973, 1979, 1990, 1997 and 2008. Compared with those in the previous period, we see some new changes occurring in later crises. From the 1950s to the 1970s, due to the implementation of state's macro-economic control policies, the alternating process of the four-stage cycle of reproduction became more and more blurred; there was a gradually easing trend of the crisis; the synchronization and non-synchronization of the economic crisis in major capitalist countries took place alternately; there was a shortened trend of the cycle; and there was stagflation. However, since the early 1980s, governments adopted a policy of intervening in the economy as little as possible, which not only led to the frequency of crises repeating every decade or so, but also the extent of the crises has gradually increased, epitomized as cyclical financial crises. The crises have gradually moved towards a high degree of synchronization.

Before the 19th century, as the British Empire dominated the world economy, the vast majority of crises occurred first in England. When the United States dominated the world economy in the 20th century, of course the center shifted. Before the 1820s, the leading industry in England was the wool textile industry, and the phenomena of overproduction often occurred in this industry. When economic crises occurred, this industry was often hit hardest. After the 1920s, the cotton textile industry flourished and replaced wool textile as the leading industry. In the entire first half of the 19th century, the textile industry (including sectors which have direct contact with it) enjoyed an absolute advantage over all other industrial sectors, therefore the industry was always a major source of overproduction crises in that era, playing a leading role in the alternation between each stage of the economic cycle. It was always the first to face the crisis, and always the first to recover from the crisis. In the late 19th century, the development of the machinery industry and railway construction greatly stimulated the development of mining, metal smelting and machinery manufacturing, gradually raising these industries to become the leading industries that competed for leadership with the textile industry. They eventually replaced the textile industry in the late 19th century, and conquered the summit. Thus, these industries became the major source of the overproduction crisis, and played a dominant role in the development of the various stages of the economic cycle. Since the 20th century, the industries that played a dominant role in the national economy were mainly metallurgy, cement, machinery manufacturing and coal before World War II; the dominance then shifted to automobile manufacturing, shipbuilding, power generation, petroleum, chemicals, electrical appliances, electronics and other industries; since the 1980s, it has mainly shifted to real estate, financial services, IT industry and other newborn industries. With this change, the source of the overproduction crises has shifted to the respective sectors or industries.

Recalling the practice of capitalist economic crises in the past 200 plus years, each crisis has been unique and different from the others, however, their nature and characteristics were essentially the same. That is: The cyclical economic crises of overproduction were the inevitable companions of the capitalist mode of production. It is the chronic disease that capitalism cannot cure. Within its own scope, capitalism can only alleviate the crises, but is not able to eliminate them fundamentally; the foundation of economic crisis is overproduction; the financial crisis is often the precursor of the industrial crisis, and it is often accompanied by the economic activities of rampant speculation; mostly or generally the crises always break out first in those countries that have a dominant position in the world economy, specifically, in the sectors or industries that have absolute influence in its national economy.

II

Marx had experienced seven typical capitalist economic crises in his lifetime. In the crises of 1825 and 1836, Marx did not do a follow-up study, either because he was young or because his research had not yet shifted to the economic sphere. Later Marx experienced the crises of 1847, 1857, 1866, 1873 and the early phase of the 1882 crisis. Since Engels' studies on economic issues and capitalism had started earlier than Marx's, when Karl Marx began to study the capitalist economic crisis, Engels had already discovered, in a general sense, the nature and some of the laws of capitalist economic crisis, and accurately predicted that the 1847 crisis would be more violent, and longer than any previous crisis. It is because of his study that Marx and Engels were able to describe a series of conclusions on the roots, nature, consequence and orientation of the capitalist economic crises in the *Communist Manifesto* published in 1848. From 1849 on, as Marx turned his research largely to the economic sphere, they began to study the history of economic crises in details, and absorbed all economic literature on crises of their contemporaries. In the meantime, they took a lot of excerpts and notes on issues related to economic crises, and carefully reviewed the details of the previous crises since 1825, trying to grasp all the details of the process of a crisis in the industrial cycle. They made a careful distinction between the symptom and the cause, and various other components of a crisis (These components include excess speculation and stock market crisis, credit crisis and currency market crisis, the commercial crisis itself and financial crisis, foreign trade crisis and gold outflow, general commercial crisis and banking crisis), trying to grasp the links between currency, credit and crisis. Meanwhile, in order to examine the results of previous studies, so as to continue to develop and improve their theories, Marx and Engels not only paid great attention exploring theoretical aspects of the capitalist economic crisis, but also closely observed the actual development of the capitalist economy. They paid great attention to the fermenting economic crisis of 1857, and conducted a study for many years before it broke out. As a result, not only did they foresee its explosion a year before the great crisis, but they also achieved a series of important theoretical results. These results are reflected in the *Economic Manuscripts of 1857-1858*. Marx also asserted that there was a crisis potential in the simple commodity production, and such a potential could turn into a reality. This is because in the capitalist production, the contradiction between use value and the value of a commodity is the contradiction between the private labour and social labour components of productive labour, and furthermore it is the contradiction between large-scale socialized production and private ownership of the means of production in capitalism. This contradiction is concretely expressed through a number of limitations created by capitalist relations of production—which is based on private ownership of the means of production—to the development of socialization in large-scale production— the necessary labour is the limit of the exchange value of the capacity of the living labour or the limit of the wages of the industrial workers; surplus value is the limit of the surplus labour and development of labor's productive forces (productivity); money becomes the limit of production; the production of use value is restricted by the production of exchange value and causes contradictions and conflicts. As these contradictions and conflicts escalate, the potential possibility of crises gradually develops into reality of cyclical economic crises. Therefore, the root of the capitalist economic crisis is the capitalist system itself, not some artificial casual factors. On this basis, Marx creatively revealed that the renewal of the fixed capital is the material basis of the periodicity of capitalist economic crisis, and thus pointed to the root cause of the periodic cycle of capitalist economic crises.

III

In *Economic Manuscript of 1861-1863*, Marx's theory of economic crisis achieved further development. Marx thoroughly criticized people like Say and Ricardo once again, who erroneously denied the existence of widespread repeated capitalist economic crises, and he also pointed out that Sismondi and some other petty bourgeois economists had serious flaws in their arguments on the inevitability of capitalist economic crises. Through his criticism on the crisis theories of bourgeois political economy, he further elaborated and developed his theory of crisis, and thus drew a series of important conclusions, that is, that the capitalist economic crisis is the manifestation of all the contradictions of bourgeois economy, it is the result of the full expansion of various contradictions of capitalism, it is the really comprehensive and compulsory equilibrium of all the contradictions of the bourgeois economic relations. The capitalist economic crisis is a movement of the unity of opposites of an economic relation. The normal operation of an economy means that its inner elements are in a unified state, and once these elements become separate and independent of each other, this development trend forces these elements to evolve towards reunification. This process of unification is called crisis. This contradictory movement process of the unity of opposites appears as the movement of the one and same process passing through two opposite phases, and thus it is essentially the unity of the two phases. This movement is essentially the separation of these two phases and their becoming independent of each other. Since, however, they belong together, "the independence of the two correlated aspects can only show itself forcibly, as a destructive process. It is just the crisis in which they assert their unity, the unity of the different aspects. The independence which these two linked and complementary phases assume in relation to each other is forcibly destroyed. Thus the crisis manifests the unity of the two phases that have become independent of each other. There would be no crisis without this inner unity of factors that are apparently indifferent to each other." "Crisis is the forcible establishment of unity between elements that have become independent and is the enforced separation from one another of elements which are essentially one."

The cyclical capitalist economic crisis is cyclical and forcible recovery ensuing the cyclical disequilibrium of the proportional relation of the reproduction of social capital, because "all equalizations are accidental and although the proportion of capital employed in individual spheres is equalized by a continuous process, the continuity of this process itself equally presupposes the constant disproportion which it has continuously and often violently, to even out" (TSV2, 492).

Though Marx had not fully expounded on his research and conclusions, he was able to form the core of the Marxist theory of economic crisis.

After 1863, in his three-volume manuscripts of *Capital*, according to the principles of his original methodology, Marx discussed the process of economic crisis gradually transforming from potential possibility to reality. In *Capital* Volume I, in his analysis of means of circulation, of money and means of payment, Marx discusses the potential possibility of the crisis. In *Capital* Volume II, in his analysis of circulation of capital, turnover of capital and reproduction of social capital, Marx revealed a series of contradictions between production and consumption, between supply and demand and between the production and the realization of surplus value in the movement of the capitalist economy, and proved the intrinsic link between these contradictions and the economic crisis. Finally, in *Capital* Volume III, on the basis of revealing the law of accumulation and the law of the tendency of the rate of profit to fall in the capitalist economic movement, Marx thoroughly elaborated on the root cause of the capitalist economic crises and its impacts on the historical trend of the capitalist economic movement. Marx argued that the root cause of the capitalist economic crisis lay in the conflict between the development of the material production capacity and its social form in the capitalist economy movement: "The moment of arrival of such a crisis is disclosed by the depth and breadth attained by the contradictions and antagonisms between the distribution relations, and thus the specific historical form of their corresponding production relations, on the one hand, and the productive forces, the production powers and the development of their agencies, on the other hand. A conflict then ensues between the material development of production and its social form." No matter what form the emergence of the economic crisis assumes, it forcibly alleviates some of the contradictions inherent in the capitalist economic development through great damages on productive forces. However, "The crises are always but momentary and forcible solutions of the existing contradictions. They are violent eruptions which for a time restore the disturbed equilibrium." (C III, 244). When the development of the productive forces of a society can only continue relying on the violent destruction of these productive forces themselves, this society will certainly not be able to escape the historical destiny of final collapse.

In the process of writing *Economic Manuscript* of 1861-1863 and *Economic Manuscript* of 1863-1865, Marx also conducted follow-up studies on the crises of 1866, 1873, 1882. But he did not spend so much time and effort compared to the 1857 crisis. He probably believed that he had recognized the basic elements of the capitalist economic crisis, such as its essence, cause, characteristics and transmission process, and grasped the general law of the periodical emergence and movement of the capitalist economic crises. His follow-up study and observation of the crises were, on the one hand, to test his theory that was created, and, were to discover new facts and new problems in order to further improve his theory on the other hand. In fact, as he created the scientific theory of the economic crisis, revealed the law of the emergence and the development of the capitalist economic crisis, Marx became the prophet of the capitalist economic crises, and he has accurately predicted several crises of his era. Even before the crises emerged, he has made correct predictions on the sphere and the extent, depth of the approaching crisis.

Nearly one century after Marx died, the capitalist economic system was accompanied by partial adjustments, such as the gradual advancement from shareholder system to monopoly capitalism, state monopoly capitalism, state intervention economy, the welfare state economy, and recently the international regulation of economic relations. The economic crises of capitalism also experienced certain changes: the transition from gradual intensification to gradual alleviation, the appearance of the cyclical and non-cyclical intersection of economic cycles, the appearance of indistinctness in the alternating process of each stage of reproduction, the simultaneous coexistence of excessive productive forces and massive unemployment, as well as the appearance of the interwoven coexistence of economic crisis and inflation. Faced with these changes, the mainstream Marxist economics in general has achieved to keep up with the times. In carrying forward the Marxist theory of the economic cycle, Marxists have achieved theoretical innovations to a certain extent and in a certain range, during their in-depth studies of the realities of economic crisis, especially on The Great Depression of the 1930s. They have explored and offered several new interpretations complying with the tenets of Marxist economics. Moreover, some Marxist scholars have made systematic studies on the cyclical economic crises having occurred since the establishment of capitalism, summarized and reviewed the Marxist theory of the economic crisis, proposing the disequilibrium theory, the theory of contradiction between production and consumption, collapse theory, under-consumption theory, over-investment theory, and the long wave theory. I should also mention orthodox textbook crisis analysis framework which was developed in socialist countries. Scholars also conducted deeper studies in the spheres such as the reason of crises, their transmission mechanism, their durations, the characteristics of each phase in the cycle, intermediate crises, structural crises and the phenomenon of stagflation, and have put forward many valuable theoretical viewpoints. Of course, now and then some voices rebutting the Marxist economic cycle theory have also arisen among Marxist economists, triggering heated debates.

IV

Within the ranks of Marxist theorists since Marx, Rudolf Hilferding has recognized the inevitability of the economic crises, but he also argued that the advance of scientific and technological developments and the strengthening of the important role of monopolies, namely the emergence of organized capitalism would enable capitalism to be temporarily prolonged, crises to be alleviated, or at least the negative impacts of the crises on workers to be inhibited. Inheriting Marx's theory of economic crisis, Lenin criticized the non-Marxist thoughts related to economic crises, by pointing out that the very root of the capitalist economic crisis is the contradiction between the socialization of production and private ownership of capitalism. Since the basic contradiction is manifested as the contradiction between the organized production in individual enterprises and the anarchy of production in the whole industry, as well as the contradiction between the infinite expansion trend of production and the ever-diminishing purchasing power of the working class, the analysis of the capitalist economic crises was actually the analysis of these two contradictions, and many Marxist scholars, including Lenin, E. Varga, L.A. Mendelson, Jürgen Kuczynski and others have analyzed capitalist economic crises with this model, promoting the formation of a model with relatively sound structure, appropriate for the analysis of capitalist economic crises in their relations with war and revolution.

In China during the 1950s, this model above was absorbed by our textbooks and became the standard model for analyzing capitalist economic crisis. But in the following decades, countermeasures to the economic crisis have emerged, and correspondingly, the reformed textbook model or "the basic contradictions" model as we call it in Chinese academy has been gradually formed. Gradually, the focus of studies has shifted from the analysis of the basic contradiction to the analysis of the contradictions between the basic contradiction and the arising countermeasures to the economic crisis. The analysis method became also more diversified, which has greatly expanded the scope of analysis of capitalist economic crisis, enabled its application not only for the analysis of its essence, but also for the analysis of its economic operations.

Western scholars following the tenets of Marx's crisis theory introduced further factors to analyze capitalist economic crises. In addition to the promotion of the academic contention, these works have also expanded the scope of Marxist economic analysis and understanding of the capitalist economic crisis, offering a valuable contribution. But some of them have criticized Marx's theory of crisis by employing the erroneous methodology of non-Marxist economics. One can ask, what will be worth discussing if the methodology of bourgeois vulgar economics—a theory which generally ignored the bare fact:

cyclical capitalist economic crises—are employed to refute the methodology of Marxist political economy. If we review the existing research literature on the studies of the long-wave phenomenon, the differences are difficult to bridge, but they offer two advantages worthy of recognition: First, the existence of long waves has been proved by using empirical analyses: statistical data, statistical methods, and IT technologies; second, the reasons for the existence of the long-wave phenomenon have been revealed from the perspective of political economy. Though not mature enough, the long-wave theory has become an effective tool for many scholars to explain the historical development of the world economy and a tool to predict global economic trends, and it also influences the strategic decision-making and macroeconomic policy choices and decisions in many countries.

V

Chinese Marxist scholars have first started to explore the issue of economic crisis and its cyclic character in the 1930s after the Great Depression. Initial studies were deeply affected by the economic theories of the Soviet Union, which to some extent restricted creative theoretical exploration. Nevertheless they have made extensive research and held academic debates on major theories and practical issues related to economic crises, and have published abundant books and articles, among which many have achieved breakthroughs.

The fruits of their studies indicate that they have been successful in analyzing and understanding the capitalist economic crisis using the basic principles of the Marxist theory of economic crisis. They have kept pace with the times, actively observed new changes in the capitalist economic crisis, and interpreted the new phenomena and new features employing Marxist economics and basic methods of the Marxist economics. They have actively promoted and participated in academic debates on major new issues. They have also made positive innovations, and adopted new scientific methods to enhance theoretical analysis.

Innovatively employing the Marxist theory of economic cycle, Chinese scholars have established an entirely new field of study – the research of China's socialist economic cycles. Since China's socialist economic construction required the study of the fluctuations in the socialist economy initially the motive and purpose of the research contained strong practical features, namely to control the cycle. Accordingly when the research started, the scholars strived to prove the objectivity of cyclical fluctuations in the socialist economy with the basic principles of Marxism. Along with the deepening of the research, the scholars combined methodological innovations with theoretical innovations, introduced modern statistics, metrical, quantitative and other methods, while maintaining the traditional analysis of contradictions, which has greatly improved the analytical capacity and ability to explain the economic cycles. In the process of forming the socialist economic cycle theory, Deng Xiaoping's idea of "development in steps" has played an important supporting role. Today, I can say that the design of China's economic cycle study has already grown quite mature, that is: study of methodology → description of fluctuation → explanation of fluctuation → construction of theory → examination of reality → revision of methodology → revision of the explanation of the fluctuation and of the theory for the analysis of cycle. The achievements by Chinese scholars on socialist economic cycles have become an important foundation for macroeconomic management, and a specific discipline that closely combines theory and practice.

VI

Initially the writing of this book aimed to study the Asian financial crisis of 1997. The original motivation was to generalize a more comprehensive, effective and reasonable theoretical model of Marxist economic crisis and cycle for analysis and feasibility. As the study deepened, the author became increasingly aware that a lot of study was necessary for summarizing Marx's theoretical analytical model for economic crisis and cycle. To elucidate the origin and development of this model, as well as its development and evolution after Marx, it is apparent that even more time and study was necessary. It was difficult to complete in a short period.

In order to figure the problem out, and achieve substantive results, the author decided to conduct a research and to write on the special topics of the crisis theories of Marx and Engels. This needed revisiting its formation and its relationships with the analytical model of classical economists. This anterior part includes two topics. After that, the study includes the historical sequence starting with the Marxist theory of economic crisis and cycle, the evolution of economic thoughts and analytical models, and ends with the review and reflection on the issue of Chinese scholars' studies of socialist economic cycles, which involves a number of topics. When studying and writing on these topics, the author's short-term goal was to publish in academic journals and bring together a special book in the long-term, so some parts of the content in the book is already published. Due to this reason, each chapter of the book is a thematic paper, relatively independent in format and integral in content. Such a structure has both strengths and shortcomings. The strengths are that readers can have a more comprehensive understanding of the content offered under a topic, and the shortcomings are that there are partial crossovers in some chapters. It should be noted that, the book is to build a theoretical system in the form of topics, but it does not affect its logical structure. The unity of logic and history is invariably followed, and the chapters are unfolded in a smooth manner.

The author believes that this research topic has great theoretic and practical significance, but he has no idea of what the result will be. Due to limitations in his ability and other objective conditions, there might certainly be ample errors in the book, thus criticism is sincerely welcome.

Beijing, 2009

Introduction

The Significance of Independent Innovation in Chinese Economics and Studies on the History of Economic Thought[1]

In our view, as can be observed in the Western academia, the discipline of history of economic thought, although in equal footing with western economics and political economy has been seriously neglected when compared with the other disciplines of economics. Since the discipline is not getting any financial support, and receives the least funds, the brain drain seems extremely severe, thus the research and the teaching of the history of economic thought in some universities almost faces a standstill. Generally speaking at present, this discipline lacks successors in China.

How to revitalize the study of the history of economic thought? This is an important issue that cannot be ignored and must be tackled immediately in the development of economics in China. We believe that the independent innovation in Chinese economics could provide a historic opportunity for the revitalization and major innovation in the history of economic thought. Based on this consideration, we shall first discuss why we need to have independent innovation in Chinese economics, and then talk about the important effect of the study of the history of economic thought on the independent innovation in Chinese economics. Finally, we will offer a brief discussion on Jia Genliang's idea of new history of economic thought. Of course, our statements presented below are just our own understanding and perception, and these preliminary views are put forth in the hope of getting attention and correction from our colleagues.

---

[1] Co-authored by Jia Genliang and Yao Kaijian.

Why Innovation in China's Economics

Let's start with the first book of the series, "The International Movement of Reform in Economics", an academic movement which opposes the domination of Western "mainstream" economics in the academy, formerly called itself as the "post-autistic economics movement". In English, "autistic" is a psychiatric term, referring to "self-closedness", "fantastic" or "fictitious". When the French students launched the movement in 2000, they used this term to accuse Western mainstream economics as being "self-enclosed economics", which implies a strong criticism against those serious problems in economics education and study in Western countries. Some researchers have suggested that the rise of "the international movement of reform in economics" marks that the western economics is faced with the most serious crisis since the Great Depression.

However, unlike the rebellious movement by the economics students of France, Britain and the United States; since the mid-1990s, there occurred an idolatrous trend of Western mainstream economics which keeps rising in China's economics circles. If one reviews the literature of the international movement of reform in economics, it can be easily found that this dogmatism is no more than Western mainstream economics being pirated into China. Whether in China or in Western countries, such a dogmatism essentially regards the Western mainstream economics as the only scientific economics, and demands that this paradigmatic advocate and practice should be accepted as the "desired standard" which all economic disciplines need to follow. It encompasses all aspects of economics sphere, including the teaching, scientific research, personnel selection, etc. suggesting that the Western mainstream economics could systematically dominate the entire relevant sphere.

We believe that the Chinese economics circles should think carefully and inquire the issues addressed by "the international movement of reform in economics", but not ignore it. If we have not had the in-depth study of the scientific basis and crisis situations of the western mainstream economics, or not taken into account the economic type China needs, but stubbornly continue to implement the Chinese economics education system towards the entire Western mainstream economics on a large scale in accordance with the accepted neoclassical paradigm, it is undoubtedly irresponsible historically. We know that, economists believe in the rational concept of reflection or introspection as the first prerequisite, and it is said that they recently began a cutting-edge research on beliefs and cognitive patterns. However, they really should first look at their own rationality, beliefs and cognitive patterns, and the rationality, beliefs and cognitive patterns of economists are essentially constituted by the philosophical foundation or the world view of economics. Therefore, it is necessary for us to have a brief examination.

It is hard for economists to deny the decisive influence of the philosophical basis on the paradigms of economics; accordingly William Stanley Jevons and Léon Walras are widely recognized as the pioneers of modern western mainstream neoclassical economics. However, as for the philosophical foundation of Western mainstream economics, Nicholas Georgescu-Roegen once wrote the famous words, "When Jevons and Walras started the foundation for modern economics, and one amazing revolution in physics swept the mechanistic dogma in the field of natural science and philosophy. Curiously, architects of 'effectiveness and selfish mechanics', or even the more recent model designers do not seemed to notice this decline timely". Currently, the Western mainstream economics still adhere to the mechanical reduction theory as the fundamental rationality – individualism – a balanced view of the world, and never go one step further. This old-fashioned view of the world has increasingly shown its serious flaws in dealing with the increasing complexity of the modern economic life.

Because it is based on the establishment of the above-mentioned mechanical, static and closed worldview, the Western mainstream economics considered the mathematical formalization of economics as a universal, or even the only scientific method, and therefore established an academic norm. However, examining its scientific and philosophical base, we will find that whether it is the assumption of the closed system or the standard of inner compatibility, the mathematical formalization of economics cannot guarantee its real relevance to mathematical methods because of its own shortcomings. The mathematical formalization of economics has largely driven economics away from the reality and away from the science increasingly, and this is because science cannot be divorced from reality. As for the point of view that Western mainstream economists believe the science of economics depends on mathematical formalization, French economists who support the economic reform movement pointed out that it is childish and ridiculous to link science and the use of mathematics, and it is a deception to limit the controversy on scientific status of economics in the issue of whether to use mathematical or not. (Edward Fullbrook, 2004).

3

Thus, for a long time, many economists including some Nobel Economics Prize winners had fierce criticism on the mathematical formalization attitude, because mathematical formalization is institutionalized in the economic circle in the West, it has become a chronic malady that cannot be eradicated. When talking about the issue in *Economics in the 20th Century: A Century of Lost Opportunity*, Geoffrey Hodgson once noted very pessimistically that the formalistic approach does not require knowledge of the history of economics, nor even need to understand the history of actual economics. Formalism is growing and self-reinforcing, just like bad money drives out good money. If economics were not dead, it is dying. Whether economics is left to rot or beyond cure, within the current framework of prevailing economic system, the hope for recovery is extremely slim (Geoffrey Hodgson, 1999).

However, if we look closely, we will find two very interesting phenomena. First of all, there are some defects or others in various study traditions of Western heterodox economics thought, its intuitive sense suits the new world-view of the modern natural science, and it also eliminates the scientific thinking of the mathematical formalism in understanding the nature. However, various schools of Western heterodox economics have also created a strong sectarianism in the long process of development, tending to overestimate themselves but to belittle others, or even having the dogmatism towards its own ideological traditions, such as Paul Davidson, the Post-Keynesian school representative, who asserted that *The General Theory of Employment, Interest and Money* by John Maynard Keynes is the only real alternative to the neo-classical theory. Second, the keen interests on economic issues from other disciplines in social science are being rapidly developed. Currently, many scholars of School of Business, Department of Sociology, and other departments or even institutions of the public policy are engaged in economic research, which is reality-oriented and public-oriented, and its excellent research is mainly found in the publications of School of Business, Technology Policy, Public Policy and International Relations, or published as a book, rare to be found in the authoritative *Journal of Economics* (Hodgson, 1999). However, studies on economic issues beyond economics faculties are often not recognized as a proper economics study by Western mainstream economics.

However, these economic studies beyond the Western mainstream economics, especially the study of evolutionary economics are, in fact, the components of the new paradigm of the evolutionary science, a potential tide widely surging in various disciplines of social science. The evolutionary social science is the trend in the future development of disciplines of social science, while the Western mainstream economics has been locked in the traditional paradigm of economics and cannot escape. Thus, it is not a disaster, but an opportunity for China's economics to be behind the West in the development of the old paradigm of Western mainstream economics, because the observation of the history of economic thought confirms the "allopatric speciation" in evolutionary biology: the formation and evolution of a new species will move away from regions of a huge number or being competitive of the original species, and a new economics is most likely to achieve a more complete development in outlying semi-edge areas where the original paradigm of economics is locked through the "punctuated equilibrium". In this case, it is a real case that China must have an in-depth study of economics of innovation in the following issues: how to avoid repeating the mistakes of Western mainstream economics, and absorb a useful gain from Western heterodox economics but avoid its sectarianism, while incorporating the economics studies in which the scientific community in Western society are engaged beyond economics faculties into our system of teaching and research in economics.

However, China's independent innovation in economics did not just eventuate from observing the trend of Western social science development, but more from the awareness of The China question. At present, in less developed countries the theories of economic development still lags behind and as the world's largest developing country, China should make an important contribution to this in the process of achieving economic take-off. China has achieved remarkable success before entering the new century, but as alerted by many serious difficulties faced in the recent years, past success does not guarantee future to be the same, and currently we still do not have a deeper understanding of our past successes. Many serious difficulties we currently encounter suggest that, the economic development mode based on comparative advantage, relying on foreign investment and external demand, and lacking the effective protection of the national industry and the majority of workers cannot sustain, especially in the face of the challenge of the new techno-economic paradigm revolution, China's future economic development is still a major and pending issue of economic theories. With regard to solving these problems, the failure of "Washington Consensus" marks that there is a serious flaw in the western mainstream economics, and the current Western heterodox economics fails to cope with this challenge. In this case, China's economics has no other way but develop independent innovation based on the China question, and thus achieve the strategic objective of serving China's economic development.

The Significance of the History of Economics and the Independent Innovation of Chinese Economics

The main objective of the independent innovation of Chinese economics is to solve the China question, and to develop the new paradigm of evolutionary science. In this case, we must always keep acute problem awareness in mind. However, whether we can raise the special and specific, but original theoretical propositions on the China question as well as find a strong and creative answer through the evolution of a new paradigm of scientific development, depend on the profound subsidiary awareness obtained by Chinese scholars through a variety of ways imperceptibly. The subsidiary awareness is what Michael Polanyi called the tacit knowledge inherited from the scientific tradition or cultural traditions. Therefore, the question is what types of subsidiary awareness does Chinese economics need for independent innovation? First of all, as for the less developed countries, since they encountered some important theoretical propositions quite different from the developed economies, the subsidiary awareness generalized by the contemporary and historical experiences and theories on the historic transformation from the less developed economies to the developed economies is essential. Second, the new paradigm of evolution is in some way behind the modern natural sciences in economics, or even in the whole social sciences, and therefore, absorbing nutrients from a wide range of philosophy and modern natural sciences became the basic precondition of the independent innovation in Chinese economics. Finally, the evolution of a new paradigm of science has affulent pioneering thoughts in the history of Western economic thought, and it has also some amazing similarity with Chinese philosophical tradition (Jia Genliang, 2004). Therefore, it has become a basic theoretical work in the independent innovation efforts of Chinese economics to give answers on the issue of the creative transformation in the subsidiary awareness extracted from the knowledge of history of thought with a new vision.

With the above-mentioned subsidiary awareness, studies on the history of economic thought will undoubtedly provide an important source of inspiration for the innovation of economics, and it is especially true nowadays when the new paradigm of the evolution science is unfolding in economics. The history of scientific development tells us that at the critical moment when a crisis occur a revolution of paradigm brews in a discipline, it is essential to reflect the history of the discipline itself. Thus, the famous physicist Jules Henri Poincaré wrote between the early 19th century and the 20th century when the revolution in physics occurred, "in order to foresee the future of mathematics, the correct approach was to study its history and status quo."

Similarly, if we do not know the history of economic thought, we will not know where to inject the innovation. George Lennox Sharman Shackle, the economist influenced by Austrian economics, said it well: "The theorists of creation need ruthless self-confidence. They must overthrow the understanding of hundreds of people, and their first instinct is to resist and counterattack. However, the reconstruction of the theory should inevitably use many of the old material. The sincerity about the theory of the past is not only respectable, but essential. The invention without the reference to the tradition will be very difficult" (Hodgson, 2008). Well, in terms of the independent innovation of China's economics, what significance does the history of Western economic thought have?

First, it helps to develop pluralistic thinking in economics, and hinders the dominance of the Western mainstream economics. Pluralism in economics is one of the core aims of the "International Movement of Economics Reform", which advocates the formation of intellectual pluralism pattern within the internal economics, promote competition among different approaches, theories and paradigms on an equal basis, and oppose the dominance of Western mainstream economics. The so-called pluralism in economics is, in Uskali Mäki's words, "a world with more than one theory" (Uskali Mäki, 2005): the objective world is exclusively unique, but it is composed of numerous things, complex evolution and uncertain future, and therefore, since observers have different angles, the world will demonstrate its diversity, and the interpretation will also possess diversified, mistakable and deficient features. In accordance with this view of pluralism in economics, the simple and static study paradigm of the Western mainstream economics is fundamentally flawed. Nonetheless, it is still a method to study the real world. The independent innovation of Chinese economics does not deny its value, but commits itself to the development of a more complex and dynamic new paradigm of evolutionary science.

The study of the history of Western economic thought can provide a wide field of view for such kind of pluralistic thinking. There is a basic fact in the history of development of economic thought: There has always been different research traditions within economics, and even within the same study tradition, there are different study methods and paradigms; Moreover, mainstream and non-mainstream are not static in their status, a heretic trend in a country or in a certain historical period is likely to become a mainstream doctrine in another country or in another historical period. For example, while the classical political economics and neoclassical economics dominating the development of British economics, the German Historical School and the old American school were once the mainstream economics of Germany and the United States between 1840 and 1940 and in the early 20th century respectively. On the other hand, the mainstream neoclassical economics earned the mainstream status in the United States and Continental Europe only after World War II, but was still rejected by a number of Western heterodox schools.

Ignoring these basic facts in the history of economic thought, our economists had once popularized the dogmatic point of view that "there is only one economics" assuming the principles of economics to be unitary and unified, economics should not have national differences, meaning that there is only one real economics in the world, the "modern economics" represented by the neoclassical mainstream economics. Even there is a famous economist who argues that the theories of the mainstream and non-mainstream economics are the same, since both the current mainstream economics, and the most basic theory of economics still advocates the general equilibrium theory, or known as the modern concept of general equilibrium theory by Gérard Debreu. It has a very solid foundation, and there is no other set of logic developed to replace it, but to supplement, amend and develop on its basis (Jia Genliang, 2006). These views are clearly untenable, and invalidate the need for the independent innovation of China's economics. As for the status quo, the study of the history of economic thought has to assume the fundamental function of emancipating the mind.

Secondly, according to research report published by Gulbenkian Commission on the Restructuring of the Social Sciences, " The conceptual framework offered by evolutionary complex systems as developed by the natural science presents to the social sciences a coherent set of ideas that matches long standing views in the social sciences, " (quoted from Wallerstein, 1997), we believe that the evolutionary thought in the history of Western economic thought is the most abundant in the history of Western social sciences, and the study of the history of economic thought can make three fundamental contributions to the development of the new paradigm of evolutionary science in economics, and even in social sciences as a whole: To provide essential supplies; to provide historical experiences and lessons for the success in theoretical innovation; to provide new ideas and sources of inspiration for important theoretical issues which is not well attended or even neglected in the current development, thus new theories can be built upon the solid foundation of the history of thought.

In the history of Western economic thought, pioneer ideas in evolutionary economics can be traced back to philosophy and economics in the Renaissance period, including historical school and Marxist economics, but the modern evolutionary economics is the product of Darwinian revolution. Affected by the Darwinian revolution, in his classic essay *"Why is Economics not an Evolutionary Science?"* in 1898, Thorstein Veblen created the term "evolutionary economics". Moreover, he proposed an ambitious research program, trying to turn economics into an evolutionary social science. Between the late 19th century and World War I, the evolutionary thought was quite popular in the economic circles, and Alfred Marshall once wrote that: "The Mecca of the economist lies in economic biology rather than in economic dynamics" (Alfred Marshall, 1897). However, as the development of the evolutionary doctrine fell into its "dark age" between the early 20th century and 1940s, the evolutionary paradigm in economics was ignored and was no longer popular after the 1920s. After World War II, as the neo-classical economics became increasingly dominant in the western economic circles, the evolutionary paradigm in economics was caught in a state of silence. Only after the 1980s, the evolutionary economics began to revive. Currently, the concept of evolution has become such a popular term in economics that the evolutionary game theory and economic theory of complex systems are claiming to be part of the evolutionary paradigm in economics.

However, according to modern cosmology of open systems and the specific nature of social sciences, evolutionary game theory and economic theory of complex systems cannot be classified under evolutionary economics, and they also do not belong to the early attempts and try its early pioneer thought of the new paradigm of evolutionary science in the history of Western economic thought. From this perspective, the study of the history of Western economic thought is the basic approach to the insight into the future development of economics, and the evolutionary economics in particular. Because Thorstein Veblen had provided one of the earliest and most profound Darwinian explanations of the evolution of the society – economic system, Geoffrey Hodgson has pointed out: "in order to reconstruct the development of institutional economics, and avoid redundant discovery in science, we had to make backtrack in large span of time, revisiting the controversies that occurred on evolution in 19th century and early 20th century, and revisit the intelligence world of Charles Sanders Peirce, William James, Thorstein Veblen and John R. Commons, and discovered that what we want to say has been much talked about in the past" (Geoffrey M. Hodgson, 2005).

Because rich ideas were created on evolutionary thought in the history of Western economic thought, for future development of the new paradigm of the evolutionary science, revisiting the history of Western economic thought has become a fundamental theoretical work. If we review the two books by Geoffrey M. Hodgson on the history of economic thought published recently (i.e., *How Economics Forgot History: The Problem of Historical Specificity in*

Social Science in 2001 and *The Evolution of Institutional Economics: Agency, Structure and Darwinism in American Institutionalism* in 2004), we can conclude that these works include the following three basic constructive roles on the development of the new paradigm of the evolutionary science.

Firstly, as Hodgson pointed out in the preface of his book in 2004, the purpose of studying the history of economic thought "is to regain materials from the past and to build something new." For example, issues about the relationship between activity and structure have not been completely resolved yet in current economics or even in social sciences as a whole. Hodgson believes that the answer to some of the unresolved issues seems to be found mainly in some American literature (basically from the 1890s to the 1920s), and it will give us valuable intellectual inspiration and guidance to re-examine these literature, which is probably the motive that Hodgson conducted specific study on agency, structure and Darwinism in American institutionalism.

Secondly, the study on the history of economic thought can provide valuable experiences and lessons for the new development of the evolutionary paradigm in order to avoid detours. For example, through his study on the history of thought of American institutionalism, Hodgson reveals why the old American institutionalism deviated from its original Darwinian vision in its later development, the lesson of which is still worth pondering and drawing today.

Thirdly, the study on the history of economic thought can discover important theoretical issues which are not well attended or are neglected in the current development of the new paradigm of evolutionary science. For example, situational and context-specific theories and methods (historically specific issues) were just being taken seriously in the past few years, which had in fact been recognized by Karl Marx and other German historical scholars as early as in the 1840s, and had once become the central issue of the theory in the past hundred years. Hodgson's book in 2001 will undoubtedly promote the evolutionary economists to pay more attention to this important theoretic issue, and learn many lessons from studying the history of thought as well.

The last but most important issue of the study on the history of economic thought on Chinese economic innovation is: To explore policy tools, institutional measures and the "development strategy" the current developed countries took when they were in a poor status, so as to achieve the goal of getting rich; as the foundation of these policy tools, institutional measures and "development strategy", how the economics proceeded discussion; in the era of economic globalization and the revolution in information, are still valid. Through this study, the history of economic thought can provide a reference to solving the China question directly. In this regard, Xiazhun Zhang, a development economist at the University of Cambridge and Norwegian economist Erik S. Reiner had made outstanding contributions, in which their study on how the developed countries were developing in the history had posed a serious challenge to western mainstream economic theory and to "Washington

Consensus", providing an alternative idea for developing countries to devise a development strategy.

Through the in-depth study of the history of Western economic thought, economists, especially represented by Erik S. Reinert, proposed the "knowledge and production-based alternative economics of canons" (Erik S. Reinert, Jia Genliang, 2007), which had been existing in the economic thought of mercantilism, American School, the German Historical School, American institutionalism and Schumpeterian economics, and has been extended to the modern times since the Renaissance. This is an economics which considers production, knowledge, innovation, collaboration, thus increasing returns and the consequently institutional change as the core mechanism of the economic development. The reason that the United Kingdom, Germany, the United States, Japan and South Korea have been rising is because they accepted the basic rule of the alternative economics of canons when they were in a poor status. Now, it can still provide an important theoretical and historical experience of thought for us in building an innovative country, and provide an important source of ideas for the innovation of Chinese economics as well, which constitutes an important part of the study of the so-called "New History of Economic Thought".

Preliminary Ideas for the Study of the "New History of Economic Thought"

10

Since the study of the history of economic thought has very important significance to the Chinese economic innovation, how do we engage in this study? We believe that, according to the two main goals of the independent innovation in Chinese economics, we are faced with two new tasks in the study of the history of Western economic thought. The first task is to rethink the architecture and the evolution of the history of Western economic thought from a philosophical basis and in accordance with the modern cosmology, sorting out the history of evolution in economic thought and making new exposition. This can only be done by having a profound insight to the essence of the modern cosmology and to its embodiment in the new paradigm of social science on the philosophical basis. Generally speaking, in stark contrast to the Newtonian time-reversible typological thinking, static, atomistic, closed worldview and mechanical determinism, the modern cosmology is characterized by the Darwinian time-irreversible, population thinking, dynamic, organic, open and uncertain worldview. However, the current education of economics cannot meet the study needs of this "new history of economic thought", and therefore, the "new history of economic thought" itself must bring up a large number of well-trained economists from a philosophical basis, especially the philosophy of social science in the latest progress.

However, the relationship between the history of economic thought itself and the modern cosmology is definitely not in a passive position and studying the history of economic thought has roles of initiative inspiration and promotion in understanding the embodiment of the modern cosmology in the new paradigm of evolutionary social sciences. The reason is that, as the Nobel Prize winner Ilya Prigogine has sharply pointed out, the classic (natural) science does not recognize the evolution and diversity of nature; the modern cosmology was born in the great revolution in biology in the second half of the 19th century and in physics in the late 19th century and the early 20th century, while the revolution of complexity in the natural sciences further enriched this new cosmology in the second half of 20th century. However, if we have some basic knowledge of this modern cosmology, we will find that the modern evolutionary economics, by the intuitive sense of many western pioneers in the history of economic thought, is somehow consistent with the cosmology provided by modern natural science, and the theoretical work has simple elements of modern cosmology. We can even say that they have some ideas of modern cosmology pioneers.

It is because of these reasons, when we re-determine the direction of development of the modern economics in accordance with the new paradigm of the evolutionary science, the history of economic thought must be rewritten. For example, as the revolution of the complexity in natural sciences was accepted by some economists, they took a new vision to re-examine the history of economic thought, which is illustrated by the fact that in 1998 the History of Economic Thought Society of the United States had a special discussion on the complexity theory in the history of economic thought, and published a book (David Colander, ed., 2000). According to the study of these scholars, when we look through the lens of complexity theory, some economists who had originally high position in the history of economic thought, such as David Ricardo, had their status greatly declined, and scholars who were neglected or not even being considered as economists, such as Charles Babbage quickly rose from obscurity to a prominent position. David Colander, the chief editor of this book also pointed out that in the history of economic thought the most interesting stories about the view of complexity have something to do with the heretical economists, many of whom have some ideas approaching to the conception of complexity. In fact, the heretical economists David Colander talked about here are basically what we call pioneers of the evolutionary economics. However, compared to the rich evolutionary thought in the history of Western economic thought, we can only get a very partial understanding at most by observing the history of economic thought according to the complexity theory.

However, if we re-observe the history of Western economic thought by modern cosmology, we will find that since the Renaissance, there had been two very different economics study traditions in the history of Western economic thought: One is the study tradition dated from Mercantilism, American School, the German Historical School, Schumpeterian economics and even Marxist economics until the modern evolutionary economics, while the other is the one dated from physiocratism, David Ricardo, "vulgar economics" and Marginal Revolution, etc. until the modern neoclassical economics. The former tradition is, in the eyes of the Western mainstream economists, the heretic and subjected to denigration, while the latter is regarded as orthodox and respected. However, if the study is from the perspective of the "new history of economic thought," we'll come to an exact opposite view: The heretical economics study tradition in the eyes of the Western mainstream economists represents the future of economics. Therefore, the first important task for the "new history of economic thought" to re-sort the history of economic thought following these revolutionary ideas, providing an ideological source for the independent innovation of China's economics. For example, in the economic system of some very important economists, such as Adam Smith, Karl Marx and Alfred Marshall, these two study traditions coexist. However, the current textbook on the history of economic thought neglected seriously, or even completely the economic evolution ideas of these economists, and did not discuss them at all. Therefore, if we rethink of and further explain the theoretical system of these economists according to two major study traditions in economics, we can obtain important innovative results from the study of the history of economic thought.

What we discussed above is the first task for the study of the "new history of economic thought". Therefore, what is the second task for the study raised by the independent innovation in Chinese economics? We have already pointed out, for the independent innovation in Chinese economics, the significance of studying the history of economic thought is that, it can solve the China question and propose special and specific theoretical propositions to support subsidiary awareness. Therefore, the second task raised by the "new history of economic thought" is to take the awareness of the China question as the core, studying the relevant history of economic thought on the successfully historic transformation of the current developed countries from an underdeveloped economy to a developed economy, studying the relevant history of economic thought on the successful settlement of challenges similar to the ones we facing currently in the development process; combining with the technology revolution of information and communication, China's national conditions and major changes in the international environment in which our country is facing, studying to what extent these historical economic thoughts are still valid; studying whether these economic thoughts need to be discarded, or corrected and developed under the new conditions. Through these studies, the discipline of the history of economic thought can provide important subsidiary awareness for solving the China question.

To achieve this goal, the scope of studying the history of economic thought must be expanded. In addition to the study of the history of economics or the history of economic thought, both of which are comparatively systematic, we must also study the "history of economic policy thought" in combining the history of economics and the "history of economic policy". The history of economics and the "history of economic policy" do not belong to the scope of the history of thought, but there is no reason for us to exclude the "history of economic policy thought" from the study of the history of economic thought.

However, the current focus of the study of the history of economic thought is on the history of economics as a system, with the emphasis on the abstract economic theory based on the particular assumption while ignoring those economic thought of lower abstraction, which are based on practical observation and historical experience, and which sometimes may not be regarded as an economic theory. Particularly, we tend to ignore those economic thought which had once had a significant and practical influence on economic policies and economic management but was not a system, or even the ones to be summarized. However, when facing with very difficult major problems in the process of catching up with the developed countries, and trying to seek to learn from the solutions of developed countries at a similar stage of development, the underdeveloped countries need in particular, the latter two types of study which are ignored or even not existed in the current study of the history of economic thought. It is because of this reason, the economic theory based on practical observation and historical experience, together with the "history of economic policy thought", constitute the important content of studying the "new history of economic thought".

Due to space limitations, we only take *The Great Transformation: The Political and Economic Origins of Our Time* (1944) by Karl Polanyi as an example to illustrate the importance of the economic theory based on practical observation and historical experience. With its emphasis on the economy in Western Europe, the book by Karl Polanyi analyzes the process of how the socio-economic status in which the market was severely regulated in the 18th century, transformed into the uncontrolled market economy in the 19th century, and then how it transformed into one in which the market economy was constrained and the state intervention was implemented. The latter transformation is referred to as the "great transformation". Based on the history of Western economics from the 19th century to the 1940s, Karl Polanyi proposed a theory: ... a self-adjusting market implied a stark utopia. Such an institution could not exist for any length of time without annihilating the human and the natural substance of society; it would have physically destroyed man and transformed his surroundings into a wilderness. Therefore, the society is bound to take measures to protect itself. From the date of birth of the self-adjusting market system, the social security will inevitably become its accompaniment."The social history in the 19th century is the result of a double movement": On the one hand, market expansion extended around the world, and the number of goods involved grew to an incredible size; but on the other hand, at the same time there is a backlash with the purpose of fighting against the harmful effects of the market economy. Karl Polanyi noted that social protection which avoids the inherent risk of self-adjusting market system is the most inclusive characteristics in the history of this era.

However, despite the free market and social protection go hand in hand, the trade-off between these two forces has presented as a long-term cyclical movement: If the laissez-faire movement ignores the polarization, unemployment and the state of social unrest it has caused, it will eventually and necessarily trigger a countermovement of social protection in order to counter its serious harms. Especially when a state goes further with the free-market economy, the recoil of the society will be more powerful. However, as Karl Polanyi pointed out that any measures taken will harm the self-adjustment of social market, destroy the organization of industrial life and therefore harm the society in another way. Karl Polanyi's implication is that such long-term "double movement" of free market and social security has not been able to maintain a non-pendulum balance, and sometimes it can even lead to major social disaster. For example, as the reaction to the laissez-faire movement in the late 19th century, the different intensity of reversal social protection campaign produced four different types of society, namely welfare state, Soviet socialism, German fascism and South-eastern Asian developmental state, in which the fascism caused unprecedented disaster for the human beings and society.

The famous book by Karl Polanyi is "unknown" in the history of Western economic thought, but his theory mentioned above (we can call it theory of socioeconomic history) provided a sharp scalpel for us to understand various theories of economics from the 19th century to the 20th century, as well as a profound insight into recognizing serious socioeconomic problems contemporary China is facing. In commemoration of the 30th anniversary of reform and opening up, we can clearly see that China is currently in a turning point far more serious than the social protection emphasized in Karl Polanyi's "double movement". Serious social polarization, domestic demand not started for a dozen years, failure in health care and social security reform, immoral behaviour of the market (such as 2008 Chinese milk scandal and a series of events), "three rural issues", and the destruction of resources, environment and ecology, as well as a large part of the Chinese economy controlled by foreign investors, etc., all of which suggests that a "great transformation" is needed in China's reform and opening up in the future.

Consistent with Karl Polanyi's "great transformation", if China's reform and opening up is placed under the international backdrop of periodic alternation between free trade and trade protection (state intervention) in the history of economic thought, we can also observe that, since the rise in the 1970s, the neo-liberalism had its development momentum decayed when entering the new century, since when the pendulum of periodic alternation began to swing to state intervention and the protection of national industry in the developing world (Jia Genliang, Huang Yanghua, 2008). Currently, the process of economic globalization has come to a halt, and the collapse of the Doha Development Round Negotiations and the outbreak of the U.S. economic crisis is an important signal that the process of economic globalization may reverse. The core of our current great transformation is to curb the devastating effects of the free market economy and to put Chinese economic reform back on the healthy track of the independence and prosperity through a series of institutional construction and policy measures such as social protection, protection of national industry and environmental protection, etc. However, our mainstream media still pro-pagandizes the clichés of the so-called "firmly adhering to the market-oriented reforms" by the agent of neo-liberalism in China, and one of the important reasons is the lack of knowledge of the history of economic thought, especially not understanding the results of economic theory which is based on practical observation and historical experience in the history of economic thought.

We believe that the study of the "new history of economic thought" has broad prospects in China, and it is an endeavour worth efforts for the Chinese economic circles. Currently, the foreign studies on the history of economic thoughts has accumulated a lot of new ideas and new materials, and began to overturn the traditional ideas and theories in the aspects of dominant mercantilism, physiocratism, Adam Smith, the German Historical School and the neo-classical economics, etc. However, these new ideas and new materials are still excluded by the mainstream Western economics from the textbook on the history of Western economic thought. In this case, the current textbooks on the history of Western economic thought have largely become the tool to maintain the dominance of the Western mainstream economics. Therefore, guided by the Marxist philosophy of science as well as new developments in the philosophy of science under critical realism, taking the tough challenges China is facing as the core, re-sorting and rewriting the history of economic thought in accordance with the two study traditions in economics has become a cutting-edge issue in the development of China's economics. It can vigorously promote the independent innovation in China's economics, and more importantly, it can make a positive contribution in solving many important and practical issues in China's economic development.

15

References:

Georgescu-Roegen, N. *The Entropy Law and the Economic Process*, 1971, pp. 2-3.

David Colander (ed.).*Complexity and the history of economic thought*, Routledge, 2000, pp. 35-36, p. 41.

Edward Fullbrook (ed.). *The Crisis in Economics: The post–autistic economics movement: the first 600 days.* Beijing: Higher Education Press, 2004.

Immanuel Wallerstein, et al. *Open the Social Sciences: Report of the Gulbenkian Commission on the Restructuring of the Social Sciences.* Beijing: SDX Joint Publishing Company, 1997.

Erik S. Reinert, Jia Genliang (eds.). *The Wealth of Poor Nations: A Selection of Essays on Evolutionary Economics.* Beijing: Higher Education Press, 2004.

Geoffrey Hodgson. *Economics of the 20th Century: The Century of Lost Opportunity*. China Education and Research Network of Political Economy.

Geoffrey Hodgson. *How Economics Forgot History: The Problem of Historical Specificity in Social Science*. Beijing: China Renmin University Press, 2008.

Uskali Mäki. *The one world and the many theories*. In Geoffrey Hodgson (ed.). *A Modern Reader in Institutional and Evolutionary Economics: Key Concepts*. Beijing: Higher Education Press, 2005.

Alfred Marshall. *Principles of Economics*. Beijing: Commercial Press, 1997.

Karl Polanyi. *The Great Transformation: The Political and Economic Origins of Our Time*. Taiwan: Yuan-Liou Publishing Co. Ltd., 1989.

Jia Genliang. *Chinese Economic Revolution*. In *Social Science Front*, 2006(1).

Jia Genliang, Huang Huayang and Yang Hutao. *New Debate of Evolutionary Economics of Development and Trade Policy*. In *Comparative Economic & Social Systems*, 2008(5).

Contents

CHAPTER II

The Classical Form of
the Economic Crisis Theory

I. Introduction

In the late 18th and early 19th century, the strong growth in the capitalist production and the emergence of cyclical fluctuations in the economy became the two extraordinary economic phenomena after the industrial revolution. This raised more and more concerns: there were some inherent scales in the growth of the production, and if these scales were exceeded, the product could not be sold out. Some even asserted that unless certain policies and measures were implemented to ensure that there would be sufficient income to purchase those products, it would be impossible to create enough purchasing power to absorb the growing industrial production output spontaneously and automatically. This was a very serious issue placed in front of the bourgeois economists, and the society was looking forward to a reasonable explanation. To answer the call of the times, those economists who "failed in their mission" launched an unprecedented large-scale discussion. Besides the most influential economists such as Say, Ricardo, Sismondi, Malthus, John Ramsay, McCulloch, John Stuart Mill and James Mill, the debate also included Robert Torrens, Samuel Bailey, Thomas Chalmers and others. Even some economists who were quickly forgotten or rarely remembered in the history of economics were involved in the debate. In the debate over the possibility of occurrence of the crisis of universal overproduction in capitalist economy, these economists were divided into two groups. One was the group of Say and Ricardo, including John Ramsay,

McCulloch, James Mill, and a large number of Ricardo's followers. The other was the group of Sismondi and Malthus, whose followers were mostly some unknown figures. The possibility of the economic crisis due to the universal overproduction in the real economy was the topic of their debate. Those who believed that the capitalist economic crisis was unlikely to happen were keen to prove that there was a mechanism of automatic maintenance of balance between production and consumption, as well as between supply and demand, i.e., thus imbalance would never happen. And those who believed that the capitalist economic crisis was inevitable were anxious to prove that there was a mechanism of imbalance. As can be seen from the debate, they have not found the nature of the crisis, but their conclusions already implied that the crisis was the imbalance of the equilibrium relationships. Therefore, they well understood each other about where the focus of the debate lied and what its essence was. Both were also aware that it was their common task to prove that there was a mechanism of imbalance between production and consumption, as well as between supply and demand.[1]

II. The Metaphysical Equilibrium of Say's Law

Say, an important figure in the classical school had restored the "commodity – money – commodity" formula to "commodity – commodity", and proposed that commodity exchange is actually "purchasing products by products", and money was only "the great wheel of circulation, the great instrument of commerce"[2]. The purpose of putting forward this view was to prove that wealth does not come from circulation, which opposed to the misunderstanding of mercantilism on the source of wealth. By the early 19th century, such point of view had become a fundamental basis to deny the possibility of overproduction.

Perhaps due to the sense of responsibility of an economist, or in order to eliminate fears, Say consciously assumed the "responsibility" of explaining why the capitalist crisis of universal overproduction would not occur, and therefore gained fame. Soon after he became famous, he confidently suggested that the reason why the crisis of universal overproduction would not occur in capitalist economy was that the production of merely one product could open the way for the selling of other products. As to the production of the entire society, the production of one product could create the demand for another product.

1   Since the 1820s, Ricardo, Malthus, James Mill, McCulloch, and Sismondi et al. gradually walked together and became good friends. They conducted wide academic exchanges through various means such as writings, correspondences and visits and had more than one decade's fierce debate on value, wage, profit, land rent, production, and consumption and so on, among which the debate over the possibility of an universal overproduction crisis was the most fierce and notable. Since the debate was conducted in an honest and friendly atmosphere, although their arguments stood in sharp opposition to each other, all of them could speak out freely and express their honest opinions about problems. We can see some details of the whole debate from the *Works and Correspondence of David Ricardo*.

2   Adam Smith. *An Inquiry into the Nature and Causes of the Wealth of Nations* (Vol. 1).Beijing: The Commercial Press, 1972, p. 267.

"there must needs be some violent means, or some extraordinary cause, a political or natural convulsion, or the avarice or ignorance of authority, to perpetuate this scarcity on the one hand, and consequent glut on the other."[3] Say said. The reason was that in the process of two exchanges; product for money and money for product, money worked only in the moment, and at the end of the transaction, money is always expressed as an exchange of goods for other goods. Here, although Say was referring to the commodity exchange by means of money, which actually reflects barter, later economists have grasped this common-sense error, and Say had to face merciless ridicule and criticism. However, Say had begun to evaluate the issue of the macro-operation of the economy from the aspect of the equilibrium relationships of the total national economy, which was ignored by other economists.

With Say's view widely accepted, some advocates summed it up as a "Law", that commodity exchange is the exchange of product for products, and each seller is the buyer while each buyer is the seller, which was then commonly called "Say's Law". James Mill even called it "the metaphysical equilibrium of purchases and sales", despite the fact that he had advocated the same argument published in the booklet of "Commerce Defended" six years earlier (1808) than "Say's Law", namely that "Whatever... be the amount of the annual produce, it never can exceed the amount of the annual demand.... Of two men who perform an exchange, the one does not come with only a supply, the other with only a demand; each of them comes with both a demand and a supply... The supply which he brings is the instrument of his demand and his demand and supply are of course exactly equal to one another. It is, therefore, impossible that there should ever be in any country a commodity or commodities in quantity greater than the demand, without there being, to an equal amount, some other commodity or commodities in quantity less than the demand."[4]

27

---

3 Say. *A Treatise on Political Economy*. Beijing: The Commercial Press, 1995, p.144.
4 Marx & Engels Collected Works, Vol.13, 1st Ch. edition, Beijing: People's Publishing House, 1962: 87. In the footnote for Mill's opinions above, Malthus pointed out, "if it is assumed that everyone's demand is always equal to his supply in a precise sense, he will have to sell his commodities as per the production cost that contains normal profit forever; thus, once the production is excess, the assumption will be untenable. This argument has been proved for many times. However, it seems that Mr. Mill does not know this evident thing, i.e. the supply must be in proportion to the quantity forever while the demand must be in proportion to the value forever." He further pointed out, "Mr. Mill used the term 'demand' in the following sense: the total expense that the purchaser can pay in order to obtain the sold commodity, or in the words of Mill, his means of purchase. However, it's very clear that his means of purchase of other commodities is not in proportion to the quantity of commodities he produces and would like to sell, but in proportion to the exchange value of the latter; unless the exchange value of a commodity is in proportion to the quantity of the commodity, it is impracticable to consider that everyone's demand is always equal to his supply. According to the acknowledged law of demand and supply, the increase in the quantity of a commodity often results in the decrease in the value of the commodity and the actual decrease in the means of purchase of other commodities." (Beijing University. The Collection of Malthus' Reactionary Opinions. Beijing: The Commercial Press, 1960: 91.) From here we can see that Malthus found the mistake contained in Mill's opinion, but he did not know the nub of the problem and the solution.

The equilibrium relationship in Say's Law is based on the barter exchange, despite the fact that there is no such equilibrium relationship in the economic society. But why were Say's views widely respected by economists, and called "Law"? Besides having met the special needs for non-crisis "proof", some deceptive assumptions contained therein had also played an important role, because these assumptions were concerning men's real economic activities and had clearly contributed to the understanding of the phenomenal form, so that they formed a barrier which could prevent people from understanding the essential relations. These assumptions are, in Say's words, that: (1) "Its whole utility has consisted in conveying to your hands the value of commodities, which your customer has sold, for the purpose of buying again from you; and the very next purchase you make, it will again convey to a third person the value of the products you may have sold to others. So that you will have bought, and everybody must buy, the objects of want or desire, each with the value of his respective products transformed into money for the moment only."[5] (2) "When the producer has honoured the finishing hand to his product, he is eager to sell it immediately, lest its value should diminish in his hands. Nor is he less anxious to receive the money he may get for it; since the value of money is also perishable. But the only way of getting rid of money will be the purchase of some product or other."[6] (3) "They (the sellers) would not ask for money…, since the only use they could make of it would be to convert it forthwith into articles of their own consumption."[7]

From his view of "supply creating its own demand", Say deduces four conclusions: (1) In every community the more numerous the producers are, and the more various their productions will be, together with the more prompt, numerous, and extensive products; and, by a natural consequence, the more profitable they will be for producers; since price rises with demand. (2) Each individual is interested in the general prosperity of all, and the success of one branch of industry promotes that of all others. In fact, whatever profession or line of business a man may devote himself to, he is the better paid and he more readily finds employment, in proportion as he sees others thriving equally around him. (3) It is no injury to the internal or national industry and production to buy and import commodities from abroad; for nothing can be bought from strangers, except with native products, which find a vent in this external traffic. (4) The encouragement of mere consumption is no benefit to commerce; for the difficulty lies in supplying the means, not in stimulating the desire of consumption; and we have seen that production alone, can furnish those means. Thus, it is the aim of good government to stimulate production, but bad government to encourage consumption.[8] In barter, the four conclusions are correct as well, but in real society, it is the exchange of commodities with currency as the means.

---

5 Say. *A Treatise on Political Economy*, Beijing: The Commercial Press, 1995, p. 143.
6 Ibid., p. 144.
7 Ibid..
8 Ibid., pp. 147-148. The conclusion (3) refers to: Luxemburg, *A History of Political Economy*, Vol. 2, Beijing: Joint Publishing Press, 1958, p. 40.

First of all, it is necessary to mention the intention of Say's metaphysical equilibrium. Say's conclusion is derived from the proof of an argument: the difficulty in the exchange of commodities does not lie in therein that the United Kingdom produced too many commodities, but in the estimation that too few countries bought these products. In Brazil, for example, the British producers cannot dispose the goods they try to export to Brazil, because either the British exporters made a wrong estimation of goods that the Brazilians need, or the Brazilians have nothing to export to the United Kingdom or to a third country to exchange for money to pay the British producers. In fact, Say's argument is also drawn from a more general principle that occurs in domestic trade. In the division of labour, a person wants to get commodities and services he needs, the general means is to produce something equivalent which will match the price of those commodities and services. It can be deduced that the production increases are formed not only by the supply of goods in the market, but usually also by the demand for commodities. In this sense, the production did create its purchasing power, and did form demand for the product, thus whether from the perspective of domestic trade or of international trade, it can easily be concluded that the product is finally paid by the product. If that what Say suggests is considered from the aspect of the barter in all production sectors, it is obviously correct. That is because, in the case of barter, if supply increases, demand will increase; if the supply decreases, demand will decrease.

Since supply will create its demand, there are in reality dull sale or oversupply of certain products. Say was not only aware of the existence of such logical problems , but also that a logical explanation for this was needed. To those who attribute the dull sales of a certain products to "the scarcity of money", he asserted that supply creates its demand: "To say that sales are dull, owing to the scarcity of money, is to mistake the means for the cause", "money is the agent", "sales cannot be said to be dull because money is scarce, but because other products are so. There is always money enough to conduct the circulation and mutual interchange of other values, when those values really exist."[9] Therefore, a country should do its best to develop production instead of worrying about overproduction, because the mere circumstance of the creation of one product immediately opens the market for other products. "One kind of production would seldom outstrip every other, and its products be disproportionately cheapened, were production left entirely free". Moreover, Say also believed that the more production increased, the more likely that economy will be running smoothly. He said when debating with Sismondi: "If the productive powers increase, then rapid production methods will increase, in a word, if products are rich, then supply in the country will be more complete and more general." The reason is that "In countries with fast production such as Britain, America, Belgium, Germany, and France and so on, which are the most developed industrial countries and occupy most prosperous regions or they are in less poor areas."[10] These arguments are undoubtedly beneficial to "Say's Law".

9   Say, A Treatise on Political Economy. Beijing: The Commercial Press, 1995, p. 144.
10   Sismondi, New Principles of Political Economy. Beijing: The Commercial Press, 1977, p. 530.

Say's Law built a model of the aggregate social demand being always roughly equal to the aggregate social supply. Its implicit assumption is that the cyclic process can be automatically in the equilibrium at the full employment. If unemployment occurs in some sectors due to the shift of social demand, the wage elasticity will increase the labour supply in these sectors, thus the wages will decrease so that labour demand equals to labour supply, achieving market clearing. Meanwhile, in some other sectors, as the labour supply decreases, the wages will raise, which will also results in the market clearing. In short, even if there is a temporary unemployment, it will eventually achieve the market equilibrium through wage adjustment. The assumptions of the model are: The production of the products itself can create its own demand; it is not able to spread to a universal overproduction across all sectors of the national economy, the phenomenon disequilibrium of demand and supply only occurs in certain individual departments of the national economy, which is also temporary even if it exists; money merely the agent of circulation, and purchase and sale of commodities will not separate.

Since there is imbalance in the labor and money markets during the recession, mass unemployment will continue, and regarding the exchange with money which is used as a agent for barter, the model of the aggregate social demand being always equal to the aggregate social supply based on Say's Law is hard to hold water owing to the fact that its hypothetical condition does not hold.

"Say's Law" reflects that Say does not understand the difference between barter and exchange with money as the agent. Marx's assessment exactly pointed out where the errors of "Say's Law" lay: "If this means that the number of actual sales is equal to the number of purchases, it is mere tautology. But its real purport is to prove that every seller brings his buyer to market with him... But no one is forthwith bound to purchase, because he has just sold. Circulation bursts through all restrictions as to time, place, and individuals, imposed by direct barter, and this it effects by splitting up into the antithesis of a sale and a purchase, the direct identity that in barter does exist between the alienation of one's own and the acquisition of some other man's product."[11] Say only saw the aspect of identity in purchase and sale but failed to see aspect of the possible separation of the two in time and space.

Although bourgeois economics later ultimately abandoned Say's Law, economists have always considered this law contains some meaningful elements, and they have tried to give multi-angle explanation of it and supported some views in it, giving a certain position of Say's Law in the history of economic doctrines. Since Schumpeter, such efforts have almost become a tradition. Schumpeter had commented: "Say showed successfully that, however large the phenomenon of overproduction may loom in the historical picture of individual

11   Karl Marx and Frederick Engels (Chinese Version I), Vol. 23, Beijing: Peoples Publishing House, 1972, pp.132-133.

crises, no causal explanation can be derived from it: there is no sense in saying that there is a crisis because 'too much' has been produced all round. Though negative, this contribution was very important. It may be said to stand at the fountainhead of the scientific analysis of cycles and to mark the point at which the latter broke away from pre-analytic thought." Here, Schumpeter clearly values the method and original work of Say, and as long as the topic is concerned, Say's Law "is a negative contribution."[12]

Since Say inherited and systematically exposed J.S. Mill's viewpoint, Mill had fully embraced the result of Say's viewpoint and formulated it as "Say's Law." As mentioned above, before "Say's Law" was put forward, J.S. Mill had tried to prove that the aggregate demand and supply are always equal, that is, the oversupply of certain commodities must always be balanced in proportion by the undersupply of other commodities, and general excess is impossible. With Mill's own words, "...anything produced by an individual and not to set aside his own consumption is the inventory that he can use to exchange for other goods. His desire to purchase and means of purchase, or his demand is just equal to the number of products that he has produced but he is not willing to consume."[13] and "...the production of commodity creates its own market...a country is likely to have an overproduction of commodities, but there will never be a general commodity surplus."[14] Marx had wisely analyzed and criticized these views, and he commented, "Mill establishes equilibrium by reducing the process of circulation to direct barter, but on the other hand he insinuates buyer and seller, figures derived from the process of circulation, into direct barter. ... The metaphysical equilibrium of purchases and sales is confined to the fact that every purchase is a sale and every sale a purchase, but this gives poor comfort to the possessors of commodities who unable to make a sale cannot accordingly make a purchase either."[15]

III. Ricardo's Support of "Non-Crisis Theory"

In addition to James Mill, Ricardo not only acknowledged Say's Law with satisfaction, but also accepted other views. Its reason seems to be simply that it is because Ricardo accepted the economic equilibrium relationships and the rules of behaviour of producers and consumers established by Say. For example, "M. Say," writes Ricardo in Chapter XXI ("Effects of Accumulation on Profits and Interest"), "has most satisfactorily shown, that there is no amount of capital which may not be employed in a country, because demand is only limited by

12   Joseph Schumpeter, History of Economic Analysis, Vol. 2, Beijing: The Commercial Press, 1992, p. 540.
13   Beijing University, The Collection of Malthus' Reactionary Opinions, Beijing: The Commercial Press, 1960, p.91.
14   Chen Daisun, From Classical Economics to Marx, Beijing: Beijing University Press, 1996, p.222.
15   Karl Marx and Frederick Engels, 1st Chinese edition, Vol. 13, Beijing: People's Publishing House, 1962, pp.87-88.

production. No man produces, but with a view to consume or sell, and he never sells, but with an intention to purchase some other commodity, which maybe immediately useful to him, or which may contribute to future production. By producing, then, he necessarily becomes either the consumer of his own goods, or the purchaser and consumer of the goods of some other person. It is not to be supposed that he should, for any length of time, be ill-informed of the commodities which he can most advantageously produce, to attain the object which he has in his view, namely, the possession of other goods; and, therefore, it is not probable that he will continually" (the point in question here is not eternal life) "produce a commodity for which there is no demand." Of course, the following propositions that Say has repeatedly emphasized have also appeared in Ricardo's writings, e.g. "too much of a particular commodity may be produced, of which there may be such a glut in the market, as not to repay the capital expended on it; but this cannot be the case with respect to all commodities" and "productions are always bought by productions, or by services; money is only the medium by which the exchange is affected."[16] Ricardo has not only repeatedly reaffirmed the correctness of these propositions, but even made a further demonstration for some propositions. While Say put emphasis on the operation of national economy in a closed state, Ricardo considered the operation of various national economies in the context of world economy. He thought that, not only in a nation which is in a closed state, supply will create its own demand, but also that in an open state, because when people created goods for exchange, they created trade, thus also created consumption. That is to say, even if there is foreign trade, it will in no way disturb the equilibrium between production and consumption. It only introduces equal but more diverse values into the market, in order to meet consumers' various preferences. Ricardo once gave this example: If the British cloth production increased 100,000 bales per year, then all what the foreign trade does is not to make the British consumption become these 100,000 bales of cloth, but the corresponding value of wine, spices, or the foreign trade that can provide them with all other forms of commodities. In analyzing the reason why trade between Britain and Brazil was not enough, he thought it was the flaw in social system, resulting in product circulation being impeded as well as the heavy duties hindering the circulation of commodities. That is because at that time all things in Brazil were grasped by monopoly, and property was not exempt from the invasion of the government. In England, the heavy duties were a serious obstruction to foreign trade of the nation, inasmuch they circumscribe the choice of returns.[17]

Originally, in Ricardo's old age, there was not only developed commodity production and circulation, but large-scale machine production had also become a normal production condition. Although the cyclical economic crises in the capitalist world still did not have regular manifestation, local crises had

16   Karl Marx and Frederick Engels, 1st Chinese edition, Vol. 26 (2), Beijing: People's Publishing House, 1973, p. 570.

17   Sismondi, New Principles of Political Economy, Beijing: The Commercial Press, 1977, p. 502.

become increasingly frequent. No matter from which perspective to look at these contexts, Ricardo should not have accepted Say's Law, or easily denied the existence of the crisis of general overproduction, but he has unexpectedly accepted And many reasons found for this error. (1) "Ricardo himself did not actually know anything of crises, i.e. the general crises of the world market, arising out of production process itself."[18] This is because the first economic crisis of general overproduction of the capitalist economy broke out in 1825, and Ricardo's *On the Principles of Political Economy and Taxation* was only published in 1817, but he regretfully died in 1823. (2) Ricardo did not realize that the purpose of capitalist production did not aim at use values, but aimed at gaining surplus value; he did not realize that the capitalist commodity exchange was not the exchange of products of labour among producers any longer, but the exchange of capital goods. (3) Ricardo turned the commodity containing exchange value and use value which were opposite to each other into the mere product and turned the exchange of commodities into the exchange of use value. (4) "Forgetting or denying the basic elements of capitalist production: the existence of the product as a commodity, the duplication of the commodity in commodity and money, the consequent separation which takes place in the exchange of commodities and finally the relation of money or commodities against wage labour."[19] (5) Ricardo did not understand that purchase and sale, as morphological change motion of commodity, was not only the unity of two stages but also the opposition between them. Under the capitalist mode of production, the opposition between them is manifested as a destructive process during the formation of a crisis, while the unity of them is also manifested as a process that the opposition is forcefully eliminated during the formation of a crisis. In short, whatever reason may be brought forward, Ricardo's support of Say's Law is inconsistent with his theory, his times and his social status. This support obviously played a very important role in promoting Say's Law to the creed of mainstream economics in that era, but because, just because of Ricardo's reputation, economists could not dare to deny Say's Law.

IV. Sismondi's Debate with Say and Ricardo

Sismondi's debate with Say and Ricardo was mainly focused on "Say's Law". The theoretical proposition of Sismondi, a petty-bourgeois economist, was basically opposite to that of Say, Mill and Ricardo. Sismondi insisted that the produce in each year was purchased with the produce of the previous year, and only with this purchasing power the produce newly produced this year can be purchased; therefore, just because the first had purchasing power, i.e. the demand, the production, i.e. the supply, will become possible. Moreover, proceeding from Adam Smith's doctrine, Sismondi thinks that in the capitalist society—since the value of commodities is decomposed into three types of

18 Karl Marx and Frederick Engels, 1st Chinese edition, Beijing: People's Publishing House, 1973: 567, Vol. 26 (2).
19 Ibid., p. 572.

income, that is wages, profits and rents—the so-called "purchasing commodities by commodities" is actually "purchasing commodities by income", and "production is subject to consumption" is actually "the scale of production is subject to the scale of social income", because only then can the increase of consumption determine the expansion of reproduction, while the consumption can only be adjusted to the income of consumers. Proceeding from these ideas Sismondi had obtained a conclusion completely opposite to Say, Mill, Ricardo, namely that the income determines production or in other words production is determined by demand, "The total amount of annual income is determined to be exchanged with the total amount of annual production, ... if the total amount of annual income cannot buy the total amount of annual production, then one part of this production will be unsold, and be piled up in the producers' warehouses, cripple their capitals, and bring the production to a standstill."[20] But, the product is still purchased by income, and when production exceeds income, i.e. the product exceeds the consumption, the conflict between production and consumption will inevitably lead to economic crisis. This conclusion is the negation of Say's Law, namely that it will be not correct to assume that to produce commodities for exchange is equivalent to creating exchange, or to creating consumption, and that Say's theory cannot prove that the production and consumption in the entire world market or in all those countries that have no trade relations with other countries are in equilibrium. As explained above the theoretical proposition of Sismondi stands in fundamental opposition to Ricardo, Say, etc. Thus a heated debate was inevitable.

34

"Say's Law" was established on the basis of two false premises, namely: (1) Any increase of production is the increase in income. (2) Any increase of income determines the increase of consumption. Sismondi had discovered these two defects, and used it as a weapon to launch a debate against Ricardo and Say. He believed that the increase of production would often only cause losses, while the increase of income—in most cases—only determines that the consumption prices rise. As to the relationship between production and consumption, he believed that the consumption plays a decisive role in the development of production, not only within the scope of one country, but in the world market as well. Sismondi reasoned as follows:

"All nations whose production exceeds their consumption, turn their attention equally to foreign markets eagerly, and since its limits are unknown, its extent appears unlimited. However, since navigation has been improved, trade routes have opened and safety has been better assured, it has been discovered that the world market was circumscribed in the same way as previously each national market; that the general optimism of all producers who sold abroad has everywhere raised production above demand; ... No matter what kind of industry, agriculture, or industry, in all the countries of Europe, they are subjected to market stagnation alternately, unable to sell or to sell at a loss. They have overproduction or lack coordination between production and consumption. When

20   Sismondi, New Principles of Political Economy, Beijing: The Commercial Press, 1977, p.76.

the market is congested, and when the goods produced cannot find the market, the whole business falls into agony. At this time, no matter which businessman or industrialist you ask, he or she will confirm that this is true. ...... Just casually taking a look If we glance at trade news, the newspapers, stories of travellers, we see everywhere proofs of that superabundance of production which exceeds consumption; of a manufacture that does not proportion itself at all to demand, but to capitals which seek employment; of the efforts of merchants which brings them to throw themselves in a mass into every new market, exposing them in turn to ruinous bankruptcies in every trade from which they expected profits. We have seen commodities of all kinds, but above all those from England, that great manufacturing power, abound in every Italian market, in amounts which so greatly exceeded demand that the merchants, in order to recoup a part of their capital, were obliged to give the goods away with a quarter or a third loss, instead of a profit. The torrent of trade, repulsed from Italy, has spilled over into Germany, Russia, and Brazil, and soon has encountered the same difficulties there."[21] He added, "We have seen that the domestic market cannot expand except through national prosperity and increases in national income, comes to be true again of the world market for every nation that sends its goods to foreign nations and participates in world trade; an increase in global sales can only come from world prosperity. It is only when men acquire new incomes that they can satisfy new needs and buy what we want to sell them."[22]

Following the view that consumption determines production, Sismondi further pointed out that since commodity is purchased by commodity, the buyer must first have his commodity before he purchases another person's commodity. Therefore it is not the supply that creates its own demand, on the contrary, it is the demand that makes supply possible. Under the conditions of capitalism, the contradiction between production and consumption is manifested as the contradiction between the unlimited expansion of production and the underconsumption caused by the shortfall of income. Its concrete manifestation is: on the one hand, what the producers are faced with is that they are unable to grasp the demand situation in the broad market. Due to new inventions and use of new technologies, the big machine production, the continuous concentration of companies and capital, particularly, the increasingly intensified free competition and blind expansion of production leads to a situation where production is for production. On the other hand, affected by the unfair capitalist distribution system, the expansion of production cannot increase social income correspondingly but only reduces it, that is, while the income of the vast majority of labouring people who have nothing in the world steadily decreases, this polarization in the society compels many small producers to go bankrupt, subsequently small producers' sales incomes fall down. This unlimited expansion of the capitalist production and the corresponding reduction in income and consumption is first manifested as the shrinking of the domestic market. In order

---

21 Ibid., p. 219.
22 Ibid., p.218.

to remedy the shrinking domestic market, the capitalist production increasingly feels the necessity of opening to foreign markets, which causes a hard competition in the world market, finally also increasingly shrinking the world market. Therefore, whether it is domestic or foreign, the market is reduced accordingly, and the slackness of sales in capitalism becomes an insurmountable difficulty. The contradiction between the expansion of production and the underconsumption caused by the shortfall of income makes the economic crisis inevitable.

Sismondi tried to prove his above views by analyzing 1818 and 1825 economic crises, and he believed that these two crises were caused by that production which was not replied by any demand, or that the production had exceeded consumption,[23] instead of other reasons. During the crisis, "the factories have no orders, there is no sales, workers have not enough wages and countless workers are totally unemployed; the productive side of the huge capital is used to produce excess products and these products are completely piled up in the warehouses, which is the sign of the resulting panic and poverty, day by day growing severity of the disequilibrium between production and consumption. Today people suffer more seriously and live pains because the illusion of prosperity prevalent last year has made the economic difficulties in Britain extremely serious. Though some factories still have some orders and show some improvement in the market, it will be a failure to follow last year's optimism. Britain once provided a loan of 40 million Pounds (1 billion francs) in advance to each country, and similarly advanced a huge sum of money to those companies engaged in lucrative big business deals. Not only these 2 billion francs expended to them during the past two or three years will be hard to be recollected in the next two to three years, but also the interest of this venture capital invested needs a long time to be recollected. Therefore, due to relation of the amount of consumption and the illusory prosperity caused by the huge amount of advanced capital, a huge deficit will emerge. However, I would never say that such a disaster is irreparable: Britain has abundant resources and the British government has accumulated rich financial experience. The lessons withdrawn from this huge capital injection will certainly let us see through everything. The past experience has shown: consumption is by no means the inevitable result of production; conversely, market saturation is the inevitable result of the mode of production people follow."[24] Sismondi also particularly emphasized that regardless of how great a market the American continent offers, it still cannot absorb all British goods, because the British production far exceeds the consumption demand. Therefore the British government hopes that the loans by new republics (in the North American continent) will greatly increase the purchasing power of consumers in these countries.

As to the above criticisms made by Sismondi, Say complained that Sismondi misinterpreted his "principles", namely that nothing is more favourable to the demand of one product than the supply of another. Say argued: By pointing

---

23 Ibid., p. 221.
24 Ibid., p. 223.

to the example of massive flow of English manufactured products into foreign markets causing an inventory glut, Sismondi has proved the possibility of excessive expansion of productive forces of manufacture, which is a misunderstanding. In fact, this phenomenon of inventory glut is nothing but the proof that the production in those countries that have been glutted with British manufactured products is too feeble. Was Brazil rich in production, the British manufactured products exported to Brazil would be certainly sold off, without glutting the Brazilian market. Therefore, the solution to this problem should of course be that as to the concerned countries, for example the legislative bodies of Brazil and England, the one should allow free production, the other should permit free importation.

Sismondi put great emphasis of his views based in reality. In the debate with Say and Ricardo, he emphasized that although numerous economists support the assertions of Say and Ricardo that production determines demand, almost all capitalist entrepreneurs acknowledge the proposition that demand determines production. This is not only because the direct cause that determines production expansion or reduction seems to be the market demand in industry or agriculture, but also because entrepreneurs hope to determine their production according to the market demand, though they do not often achieve success.[25] In terms of the relationship between demand and production, Sismondi emphasized that the increase in demand and production originated from two unrelated causes, which sometimes were even completely opposite to each other. If there is no demand for labour and the entrepreneur insists that the production is determined by the demand for labour, the market will go out of action and the production will become the cause to go bankruptcy.

If we say that Say and Ricardo fabricated the balance between production and demand, between production and consumption, and between production and income, we can say that Sismondi failed to discover that peoples' demand was dependent on their ability to pay or buy, and consumption is what is established on the basis of income. He just realized that consumption was not the inevitable result of production, and although the needs and desires of human beings were unlimited, such needs and desires could be satisfied through consumption only when human beings had enough means of exchange.

Sismondi placed great emphasis on the importance of the establishment of equilibrium relationships between production and demand, between production and consumption, as well as between production and income and believed that the increase in production should be consistent with the increase in demand, income, and consumption. He said, "If demand, income and consumption requires additional products, it will be a good thing to increase production; if there is no increase in demand and producers rely entirely on depriving consumers of competitor's products, it will be a bad thing to increase production."[26]

25 Ibid., pp. 501-502.
26 Ibid., p. 530.

However, due to institutional and legal reasons, on the one hand the labouring classes are deprived of all property and security, and on the other hand they are pushed produce blindly. Such imbalance between production and demand, as well as imbalance between demand and purchasing power makes the labouring classes poorer. Therefore, in the path towards prosperous development, it is particularly necessary for countries to gradually increase production in accordance with the needs for new products and also carefully consider the increase in purchasing power among people.

For this reason, Sismondi advocated that political economy should regard the balance between production and consumption as its fundamental question, rather than just focus on the production of wealth as Say and Ricardo thought or just consider that the greatest prosperity of a country always consists in continuous production. In his opinion, political economy should support the idea of Malthus and some European scholars, not regarding consumption as the inevitable result of production. Although the needs and desires of human beings are unlimited, such needs and desires can be satisfied through consumption only when human beings have enough means of exchange.

Sismondi believed that it was impossible to transfer wealth to people with desires or needs just by increasing the means of exchange, because the following case had often happened. The means of exchange in the society is increased while the demand for labour or the wage is reduced. As a result, some people's desires and needs cannot be satisfied, so that the consumption is reduced. Thus, the symbol of social prosperity is not the growing production of wealth, but the growing demand for labour or in other words the rising of wage as labour remuneration.

On the equilibrium mechanism of production and consumption, Sismondi accepted Malthus' opinion. That is to say, in his opinion, each worker's production is sure to outstrip his or her consumption, which is an inevitable outcome of development of technology, industry and human civilization; thus, if all of human beings are producers, they will be unable to consume all of products, accordingly resulting in an imbalance between production and consumption. To achieve a balance between production and consumption, a class not involved in productive activities or people involved in the production of non-commodity items are indispensable, because these people will consume the products beyond the scope of consumption of producers, accordingly achieving a balance between production and consumption. The equilibrium mechanism of production and consumption means that it is required to make the class not involved in productive activities or people involved in the production of non-commodity items boost their consumption accordingly whenever improving the labour productivity. In Principles of Political Economy published in 1820, Malthus presented an idea that the government spending sometimes could also promote the growth of public wealth, because it created an idle consumer class, and without this class, the production will be suspended very soon due to market congestion. Sismondi was very interested in this idea and paid adequate attention to it. He even further proved the importance of "the consumption of the third group of people" to avoid market consumption on the basis of the fact that the modern British Government and the vaunted Athenian model had adopted Malthus's idea[27].

From the debate of Sismondi, it can be seen that, in relation to the source of economic crises, he is not only an advocate of "the under-consumption theory", but also an advocate of "the disproportionality theory of crisis" and "the overproduction theory of crisis". The viewpoint that he was an advocate of "the under-consumption theory" was early accepted by Malthus. As to the viewpoint that he is an advocate of "the disproportionality theory of crisis" and "the overproduction theory of crises", we can find an authoritative saying from Schumpeter. Schumpeter said, "Sismondi presented so many factors of crises, so that he couldn't tell people exactly which theory he advocated. Undoubtedly, he advocated the excessive saving theory. This argument is the core of his analysis of the imbalance between production and consumption. However, the under-consumption caused by the low wage is more prominent. On one hand, the low wage is caused by the 'vicious' income distribution; on the other hand, it arises from the underemployment caused by labour-saving machines. Besides, there is an idea concerning to the sequence of his analysis, i.e. the growing output will meet the total purchasing power and the latter depends on the income earned from the participation in the production with a smaller output in the past. In addition, Sismondi attached adequate importance to all random variations. Just through these variations, theorists saw a steady and long-term normal state. In this way, he became the guardian of all 'explanations'. These explanations rest on talking about the anarchy of capitalistic production and rest on talking about that producers do not understand what others are doing and what purchasers want, though those rough and immature things that can be found in such literatures should not be attributable to him."[28] However, even so, from the exposition of Sismondi, we can see that the real economic life is an organism consisting of multiple equilibrium relationships. Sismondi misconstrued some equilibrium relationships while discovering some equilibrium relationships, so that his conception of the imbalance of these equilibrium relationships and deeper causes thereof is rather vague. Lenin gave a comment on Sismondi's "under-consumption" theory of crises, which was regarded as an authoritative argument by many economists. In the eyes of Lenin, the major

---

27 Both the British government and the Athenian government adopted Malthus's advice that the following measures must be taken to maintain the social balance and the balance between production and consumption, i.e. first, utilizing surplus products ready to sell to support unemployed workers and having them construct secular or religious public buildings; second, encouraging the rich to lead a luxurious life, accordingly consuming the poor's labour; third, providing one kind of mental work or patriotic work for the public in order that they can kill the time saved due to technological progress. Sismondi, New Principles of Political Economy, Beijing: The Commercial Press, 1977, p. 518.

28 Joseph Schumpeter, History of Economic Analysis, Vol. 2, Beijing: The Commercial Press, 1992, p. 542.

mistake in Sismondi's theory of crises is shown in the following aspects. First, he equated the realization problem with the personal consumption problem from the perspective of "Smith's Dogma" and forgot the realization problem of means of production. Second, he failed to put foreign trade aside and enlarged the scope of the problem from one country to many countries. Third, the expansion of capitalistic production, i.e. the expansion of domestic market, depends less on consumption goods than on means of production, or in other words, the growth of means of production outstrips the growth of consumption goods. It's thus clear that the expansion of domestic market of a capitalistic country, to some extent, does not depend on the growth of personal consumption, but depend mostly on the growth of productive consumption. Fourth, the saying that the development of production (i.e. the development of domestic market) mainly depends on means of production seems to be incredible and obviously paradoxical. This saying refers to the real "production for production". That is to say, the production is expanded while the consumption is expanded accordingly. However, this is not a theoretical contradiction, but a contradiction in the real life. This is just a contradiction that is compatible with the nature of capitalism and other contradictions in this socio-economic system.[29] Lenin's comment made the defect in Sismondi's theory clearer.

V. The Debate between John Ramsay McCulloch and Sismondi

In order to defend Ricardo's theoretical proposition, McCulloch, as one of main members of the Group of Ricardo, debated with Sismondi. McCulloch published an article in Edinburgh Review to refute Sismondi and said that his theoretical proposition was a thoroughly false theory. In his opinion, "the consumption capacity must often increase as the production capacity increase"[30] and "demand" and "production" are two inter-convertible nouns. The production of one kind of wealth is the demand for another kind of wealth. The exchange of a certain amount of industrial products for a certain amount of agricultural products with the same value will form the demand for a certain amount of agricultural products. When the cost of the consumed agricultural products is equivalent to the cost required in the production of a certain amount of industrial products, the actual demand for a certain amount of industrial products will come into being. In the words of McCulloch, "as long as the commodities are always going on the market in this proportion and the exchanged commodities are equivalent in the production cost, i.e. the value, the increase of production of one kind of commodities will provide equivalents to purchase the commodities arising from the increase of production of another kind of commodities."[31] Obviously, these opinions of McCulloch are explanations of "Say's Law", but they contain a new element. In his opinion, for commodity

29 Collected Works of Lenin, Vol. 3., Beijing: People's Publishing House, 1984, p. 40.
30 Sismondi, New Principles of Political Economy, Beijing: The Commercial Press, 1977, p. 482.
31 Ibid., p. 486.

buyers, the buying behaviour is determined by two reasons that have nothing to do with the production cost, i.e. the need and the capacity to pay. This fatally flawed idea was easily rejected by Sismondi. Sismondi pointed out that the selling of a thing would not necessarily mean the buying of another thing if the two reasons above did not exist. Provided that people have possessed many products of one kind, when they do not need them any longer regardless of the increase in the quantity of such products, it will be difficult to achieve a balance between exchange and production.

When responding to the refutation of Sismondi et al., McCulloch was always able to apply "Say's Law" to actively coping with challenges. As to the issue of crises, he disagreed with the idea of Sismondi et al., i.e. using lack of demand to explain crises. As pointed out by him, if some people believed that there would be no crisis as long as the demand increased in proportion to the increase of production, they would be unable to explain the surplus and stagnation phenomenon arising from commercial activities in anarchy. In the opinion of McCulloch, surplus refers to a phenomenon that the production of one kind of commodities is increased while another kind of commodities equivalent in value to such commodities, of which the production is increased in proportion, do not exist. In order to explain his opinion and make readers agree with him, he gave such an example, "when 1,000 farm owners and 1,000 factory owners exchange their products and provide markets for each other, 1,000 new capitalists come to involve in their activities and each of them employs 100 farm workers. Undoubtedly, the new capitalists will immediately result in the overproduction of agricultural products, because the output of industrial products that should be used to exchange agricultural products is not increased in proportion. However, if half of the new capitalists become factory owners, the industrial products produced by them will be enough to exchange the products produced by the other half of the capitalists that need to be processed. In this way, the balance will be restored. The 1,500 farm owners and the 1,500 factory owners will easily exchange their products just as the 1,000 farm owners and the 1,000 factory owners in the past."[32] Obviously, this example quite fits the meaning of "Say's Law", so that it is appropriate to regard it as the popular form of "Say's Law".

The above explanation of McCulloch about the reason of overproduction and economic crises was attacked by Sismondi. He said, "The explanation makes people not surprised at the unreality of the way of solving all difficulties put forward by them later. Capitalists suddenly double the arable area, the number of farm workers, and the total output of land of a civilized country and new people appear out of nowhere. All of these are the things that could only happen in a wonderland. Even if people admit the possibility of this assumption, they will feel difficult to restore the balance and object this practice, because half of the capitalists and half of the workers appearing out of nowhere must be forced

---

32   Ibid., p. 495.

to give up agriculture and engage in crafts."[33] From the sharp words, we can see that, in the eyes of Sismondi, the balance relationship mentioned by McCulloch is imaginary and there is no such a balance in reality. "The fact is not always that the output of agricultural products outstrips that of industrial products. The stagnation phenomenon that makes the business community pour out endless grievances is not caused by agricultural products. At least nowadays, what we see more is that many factories throw products well beyond the purchasing power of the public into the market regardless of the need and demand of the public, although the purchasing power that limits the demand is indeed not in proportion to the consumption need. Just imagine, is it an easy job to invest all superfluous industrial capital in the land and further reclaim new land to restore the balance in a country where all of the land has already been cultivated? It is a thorough change of the industrial structure of a country that needs nearly a century. Can it timely remedy the turbulence every year? When the stagnation and surplus phenomena occur in an industrial sector in succession, can this measure stand up to the surplus arising from the condition that the production constantly outstrips the demand?"[34] The answer can only be that the supply will not create the equivalent demand on itself.

As a complement to the opinion stated above, McCulloch put forward that one kind of commodities would be unsalable when the production of such commodities was expanded regardless of the production of other kinds of commodities. However, when the production of all kinds of commodities is expanded simultaneously, various kinds of commodities will purchase each other and the expansion of production would be aligned with the increase in demand. Sismondi considered that this opinion of McCulloch was incorrect, because it was possible in the real economic life that all kinds of commodities were unsalable. Sismondi required McCulloch to face reality, because the actual situation is "all cities on the Old Continent generally get into a panic, so do all villages on the New Continent. The business around the world gets into depression and encounters poor sales. This disaster has been lasting for at least five year. Instead of coming to a stop, this disaster appears to become increasingly severe as the time goes by."[35] In the face of the fact cited by Sismondi, McCulloch was speechless.

In this controversy, Sismondi and McCulloch were inconsistent in the starting point. McCulloch made up a real case from the perspective of "Say's Law" while Sismondi refuted McCulloch's argument from the perspective of the real case.

---

33 Ibid., pp. 495-496.
34 Ibid., p. 497.
35 Ibid., p. 498.

VI. The Debate between Malthus and Say

Sismondi's criticism of Say and Ricardo et al. was supported by Malthus. In 1820, Malthus published *The Principles of Political Economy*. The book questions "Say's Law" in the same manner while completely accepting Sismondi's opinions.[36] In this book, he mentioned "Say, Mill and Ricardo et al. made some fundamental mistakes" and "they regarded the commodity as a few figures, among which the relationships need to be compared, other than the consumer goods that must involve the number and desires of consumers."[37] Malthus denied "Say's Law" in a more straightforward and determined way. He wrote, "The saying 'the increase in supply is the only reason for the increase in effective demand' is far away from the truth. If this saying is correct, it will be very difficult for a society where food and clothing are temporarily reducing to restore balance. However, due to the kind-hearted preparation of the nature, this reducing within certain limits will not reduce, but increase effective demand."[38]

The joining of Malthus promoted the strength of the Group of Sismondi. They echoed each other and launched attacks against the Group of Ricardo one after another. Sismondi highly appreciated the good performance of Malthus. He used to appraise Malthus with the following glowing words, "as an economist Malthus has great thinking and talent. If he did not often involve his enemies in the depth of metaphysics or excessively apply the sophisticated and scientific computing method to spiritual strength, he could have quicken the development of science, because he saw the necessity to maintain an appropriate balance between production and consumption and he was quite sure that consumption is not an inevitable outcome of production. He found that the possible market congestion made the production activity become one of reasons for the producer's bankruptcy. However, both Malthus and the school derived from him believed that a huge and effective origin of wealth was continuous expansion and acceleration of production and each country should do its best to speed up the development of its industry. He drew an odd conclusion that the promotion of consumption was also important, the responsibility of the rich is to enjoy themselves as they wish and annihilate building commodities rapidly, and those who had to earn their living by hard work, both the wasteful spending of both the rich and the government was a good thing."[39]

As scholars of the same times, the academic discussion and argument between Malthus and Ricardo lasted for a long time. Due to their reputation and influence, various ideas and arguments contained in the correspondences between them resulted in the emergence of many critical books and articles in

---

36 Afterwards, Marx described this book of Malthus as the English version of the book of Sismondi.

37 Beijing University, The Collection of Malthus' Reactionary Opinions. Beijing: The Commercial Press, 1960, p. 82.

38 Ibid., p. 92.

39 Sismondi, *Studies on Political Economics*, Vol. 1, Beijing: The Commercial Press, 1960, pp.46-47.

the 1920s. The debate over the problem of excess supply lasted for more than a decade. It did not only involve major economists at that time, including Say, Ricardo, Malthus, Sismondi, Torrens, McCulloch, John Stuart Mill and James Mill, but also involve Samuel Bailey, Tomasi Chalmers, and other forgotten or rarely mentioned people in the history of economic theories. There were controversies between Sismondi and Say, between Sismondi and Ricardo, between Malthus and Say, and between Malthus and Ricardo in various forms, including correspondences and publications.

Malthus also considered that the crisis caused by universal overproduction was inevitable. Nevertheless, his debate with Say, Mill and Ricardo was different from Sismondi. Although he plagiarized a full set of grounds for Say's Law from Sismondi as usual,[40] his theoretical starting point was the defect existing in Ricardo's theoretical system.

Malthus found the basis for the establishment of a proposition from Adam Smith's system of economic thoughts, i.e. the price of every commodity is considered to be equivalent to the sum of the value of the commodity and an "excess", namely, the profit. Here, he regarded the profit as the excess of the selling price of a commodity over the production cost of the commodity in terms of labour and believed that the profit was generated in the exchange process. In order to get more profit, capitalists always accumulate their income and transform the accumulated income into capital. When the accumulation outstrips which is required to provide effective demand for products, a part of the accumulated income will become useless very soon and it will not be of the same nature as wealth. The working class will lose jobs and a significant extension on poverty decline in wealth, and population, will follow. For this reason, he warned the bourgeoisie that to continue to transform income into capital for the purpose of a continuous increase in wealth without sufficient demand for capital goods was as futile as to continue to encourage marriage and birth without demand for labour and increase in support fund.[41] He said, "We have already seen that the productive force existing in whatever scope is insufficient to independently achieve an increase in wealth at a corresponding level. In order to drive the force, another thing seems to be necessary. That is the effective and unlimited demand for all products. The key to achieve this goal is the product distribution that can constantly increase the exchange value of all

44

---

40 "At first glance, no one will believe that Principles of Political Economy of Malthus is nothing but Malthus' translation of New Principles of Political Economy of Sismondi. However, that is the truth. The book of Sismondi was published in 1819. One year later, Malthus' lame imitation in English was published. Just as he plagiarized Townsend and Anderson, he found theoretical pillars for his own book on economics from Sismondi. Besides, he utilized a new theory learned from Ricardo's book named 'On the Principles of Political Economy and Taxation'. " Karl Marx and Frederick Engels (1st Chinese edition), Vol. 26 (III), Beijing: People's Publishing House, 1974, pp. 51-52.

41 Beijing University, The Collection of Malthus' Reactionary Opinions. Beijing: The Commercial Press, 1960, p.84.

products and the adaption of a product to its consumer's desire."[42] This was the initial embryo of "Theory of Insufficient Effective Demand" and Keynes made the most of it in his books.

In that way, how can we continue capital accumulation under the capitalist condition? Malthus believed that, it was difficult to achieve this just relying on producers, because producers always saved a huge proportion of their income; if they did not increase consumption, it would be impossible to realize profit. Thus, there must be a group of people who are just consumers, not producers. Where are these consumers from? Malthus said, "They should be the people who are willing to and able to consume the material wealth more than what they have produced. Among the people in this class, there is no doubt that the landlord ranks the first. Not only that, but a large number of servants supported them are also indispensable, because their own consumption is insufficient to support and increase the value of products or make the increase in the quantity of products exceed the offset arising from the decline in the price of products. In this case, capitalists cannot continue capital accumulation as usual in an effective way either."[43] Why not promote capital accumulation through increasing the consumption of the worker class? To this question that must be answered, Malthus answered, "This way is the most promising if the worker class is well paid. However, the significant increase in the consumption of the worker class will inevitably result in the significant increase in the production cost, accordingly resulting in the decline in profit. Thus, before agricultural, industrial and commercial prosperity reaches a considerable degree, capitalists should reduce or suspend capital accumulation."[44] In this answer, Malthus saw the contradiction and development trend of capital accumulation, but he considered this is not the result of capital accumulation, but the result of the increase in the income of the worker class.

45

After excluding the productive class and the working class, Malthus concluded that the consumption of the unproductive class was the major factor promoting capital accumulation. Malthus once made such explanations on the conclusion: Their (a bunch of unproductive consumers) specific use in encouraging wealth is, to maintain such a balance between produce and consumption as will give the greatest exchangeable value to the results of national industry. If such consumers were to predominate, the comparatively small quantity of material products brought to market would keep down the value of the whole produce, from the deficiency of quantity. If, on the other hand, the productive classes were in excess, the value of the whole produce would fall from excess of supply. There is therefore a certain proportion between the two which will yield the greatest value, and command for a continuance the greatest quantity of domestic and foreign labour, and we may safely conclude that, among

---

42 Ibid., p. 85.
43 Beijing University, The Collection of Malthus' Reactionary Opinions. Beijing: The Commercial Press, 1960, p.86.
44 Ibid..

the causes necessary to that distribution, which will keep up and increase the exchangeable value of the whole produce, we must place the maintenance of a certain body of unproductive consumers. This body, to make it effectual as a stimulus to wealth, and to prevent it from being prejudicial, as a clog to it, should vary in different countries, and at different times, according to the powers of production; and the most favourable result evidently depends upon the proportion between productive and unproductive consumers, being best suited to the natural resources of the soil, and the acquired tastes and habits of the people.

As for the accumulation of capitalists, Malthus opposed to its extreme form; the excessive accumulation. As for the proper accumulation, he still holds a positive attitude. He believes that savings and temporary reduction in consumption often helps the proliferation in wealth in the highest degree, and sometimes is absolutely necessary for the progress of wealth."A state may certainly be ruined by extravagance; and a diminution of the actual expenditure may not only be necessary on this account, but when the capital of a country is deficient, compared with the demand for its products, a temporary economy of consumption is required, in order to provide that supply of capital which can alone furnish the means of an increased consumption in future."[45] However, the capitalist accumulation always appears in an extreme form; limitless accumulation of capital. In the capitalist world, "there is no nation short of capital, and most of them are extremely insufficient". Therefore, in such a society, the increase in capital is extremely necessary, and at the same time, the increase in wealth will inevitably be limited. This is because, first of all, "no nation can possibly grow rich by an accumulation of capital, arising from a permanent diminution of consumption."[46] Second, in the case where commodity demand can only provide profits far less than the usual for producers and where capitalists feel confused where and how to use their capital effectively, the accumulated income which intends to increase capital can only prematurely weaken the motivation for accumulation and further increase the difficulty of the capitalists, but rarely can add useful and effective capital. Malthus concluded if there is indefinite transformation of income to capital by capitalists, the capitalist economic crisis of widespread overcapacity is inevitable.

Malthus's widespread overproduction crisis is inevitably built on the negation of the theory that "supply creates its own demand" as Say, Mill, and Ricardo et al. insisted. He opposes to the view, considering that desires of mankind are easy to satisfy in a short term.. Since desire for consumption is greatly limited in the short term, if the ability to produce goods progresses consumers will be fully satisfied and then refuse to buy more goods. The drop in sales caused by the refusal to buy will lead to fall in profits, resulting in widespread stagnation and declining in the commodity accumulation initiative. That is to say, when the increase in the supply of goods is rendered as continuous process

45   Beijing University, Selections of Malthus' Reactionary Remarks, p. 86.
46   Ibid., p.83.

of self-promotion, due to lack of a similar mechanism which will keep consumption desire up with the times, the prospects of lucrative sales will look bleak. Malthus disputed that the technological advance in supply will ensure the increasing amount of commodity. However, is there any market to ensure the absorption of these products with the technological advance in supply? Obviously, it is impossible. Therefore, Malthus pointed out, against the view by Say et al, that "What an entirely false view, does it give of the real state of things, what a complete obscuration instead of illustration of the subject is it, to represent the demand for shoes as determined by the supply of hats, or the demand for hops by the supply of cloth, cheese, or even corn. In fact, the doctrine that one half of the commodities of a country necessarily constitute an adequate market or effectual demand for the other half, is utterly without foundation. The great producers who are the great sellers, before they can venture to think about, the supplies of hats, shoes, and cloth, on which they may perhaps expend a tenth part of what they have brought to market, must first direct their whole attention to the replacing of their capital, and to the question whether, after replacing it, they will have realized fair profits. Whatever may be the number of intermediate acts of barter which may take place in regard to commodities – whether the producers send them to China, or sell them in the place where they are produced: the question as to an adequate market for them, depends exclusively upon whether the producers can replace their capitals with ordinary profits, so as to enable them successfully to go on with their business."[47]

Since the general overproduction mainly occurs because of the saturation of the short-term demands, Malthus focuses on improving the short-run marginal propensity to consume. He also believes that one way to achieve this is to allow workers to participate in the redistribution of income, because the poor encounters fewer difficulties in spending than the rich. Thirty or forty owners with the annual income of 1,000 to 5,000 pounds, compared with a single owner with the annual income of 100,000, will have more effective demand on necessities, conveniences and luxuries. Yet, his final treatment plan for overproduction is that there is large group of the "unproductive consumers", that is to say, they have income but do not produce commodities to supply the market. Pastor is a good example in which he is able to provide total demand without increasing the group of market supply.

In order to prove the possibility of capitalist overproduction, Malthus proposed a model of general overproduction,: Assume there are only three classes in an economy, tenant farmers, capitalists and workers. In order to make this model work, Malthus assumed that workers are always obtain subsistence income. The rest of the produce is exchanged between tenant farmers and capitalists, and they form the complementary market between them. Or else, if tenant farmers and capitalists decide to reduce their consumption in order to accumulate at the same time, then the product market wills disappear rapidly. Items cannot be sold, profits falls, and widespread overproduction occur. Verily,

47　Ibid., p. 83.

accumulated desires will initially create demand for investment. However, investment is the appendage of consumption, and thereof after all used to supply consumption. If the product cannot be sold in the end, why do people invest? Malthus believes that, his argument is complete, self-consistent, and do not need to resort to monetary factors.

Malthus embarked on such a defense in the theoretically unconvincing cases. He argued that the productive class has the ability to consume all products they produced and if this strength is properly used, then from the point of view of wealth, it is no longer necessary for unproductive consumers to exist. However, experience shows that even there is such a power there is no such a desire. In order to nurture this desire, it must have a number of unproductive consumers.

VII. Debate between Ricardo and Malthus

Ricardo and Malthus had multi-round confrontation up to dozen years with broad topic of debate, among which the most compelling argument is the economic crisis. The argument began with the exploration of the reasons for the decline in margins. Ricardo insists that there is no other reason for the decline in profit margins except the decreasing land revenue and the increasing in wage that leads to profit margins to fall, . But Malthus disputes that if there is no adequate product market, it would cause a decline in profit margins. In October 1820, Malthus wrote to Ricardo that he found "if there is not an adequate taste for luxuries and conveniences, or unproductive labour, there must necessarily be a general glut."[48] Ricardo did not accept Malthus' view, and he replied to Malthus saying "I can see no soundness in the reasons you give for the usefulness of demand, on the part of unproductive consumers."[49] Then the two people gradually went into the intense debate. What they argued revolved mainly around the following issues: (1) What is cause for wealth growth? (2) Whether the general glut of production will occur? (3) Whether a special class for unproductive consumption was needed in the development of social production? If yes, what kind of people should they be? (4) Whether is the great manufacturing beneficial to the society?

Malthus believes that if there is not adequate unproductive consumption, the commodity production of a society will be unsalable, profits will fall, production will lack motivation, and the whole economy will stagnate. Therefore, the unproductive consumption of landlords and capitalists are very necessary. "An appropriate share of products should belong to those who promote the production", and this is one of the most important one in the various production motivations. The study of the direct cause of growth in wealth is to study the motivation. If the actual product is misallocated, there is no adequate motivation to continue producing. Such kind of a strong accumulation behaviour will

---

48 The Works and Correspondences of David Ricardo, Chapter 8, p. 259. Beijing: Commercial Press. 1987.
49 Ibid., p. 273.

inevitably lead to a large reduction in unproductive consumption, thus further damaging the production motivation seriously, and prematurely hindering the growth in wealth. More specifically, that is "under all common circumstances, if an increased power of production is not accompanied by an increase in unproductive expenditure, it will inevitably lead to lower profits and throw labourers into unemployment. But on the other hand, if it is accompanied by a proper proportion of unproductive expenditure it will certainly raise both profits and wages and greatly advance the wealth of the country."[50] Ricardo resolutely disagreed about it. Ricardo refused to recognize that the capitalist mode of production will have a general glut of overproduction, and he did not admit that there will be stagnation. He thinks that stagnation is a proper term to be applied to a state of things in which there is no motivation to a further increase of production for a time. When there is a great accumulation of capital, and a want of means of providing food for an increasing population profits shall be so low and all the motivation for further savings will cease, but there will be no stagnation—all that is produced will be at its fair relative price and will be freely exchanged. Surely, the word stagnation is improperly applied to such a state of things, for there will not be a general glut, nor will any particular commodity be necessarily produced in greater abundance than the demand shall warrant. Ricardo is so convinced, and this is because he was convinced that "supply will create its own demand". However, he also had to consider whether it is possible that glut of production gradually develop into a general glut of overproduction. He almost admitted that there is a trend for the unlimited development of production, but he did not think such a development would bring catastrophic consequences. In his own words, "I believe it might possibly be pushed so far, but we have never witnessed it in our days, and I feel quite confident that however injurious such a state of things may be to the capitalist, it is so only because it is attended with disproportionate and unusual benefits to the labourers. The remedy, and the sole remedy therefore is a more just distribution of the produce…This can be brought about only, …, by increasing the numbers of workers or on the part of the capitalist by more liberal unproductive expenditure."

49

In short, "surplus of capital" and the general "have-never-witnessed" glut of overproduction are the two important bases for Ricardo to deny the possible occurrence of the crisis of general glut of overproduction. Denying the possibility of a general glut of overproduction, Ricardo acknowledges that capitalism lacks production regularly, the reason of which comes mainly from the insufficient allocation, that is, the improper distribution of actual products has led to insufficient motivation to continue production, leading to a huge production capacity which is kept idle around the world, as people see it.

50　The Works and Correspondences of David Ricardo, Chapter 9, pp.17-18. Beijing: Commercial Press. 1986.

In such a way, Ricardo and Malthus had a direct confrontation in their views. Malthus wrote to remind Ricardo that "production can go on so far without an adequate motive, which is what actually happened lately. Huge production capacity is put in use, and that we are now suffering the consequences of it in fall in profits, in stagnation of trade, in a want of employment for our labourers, etc. In the face of overproduction, the remedy mankind finds is either a reduction of production, or an increase of consumption. Because of the ongoing capital accumulation and expansion in the scale of production by capitalists, the reduction of production cannot be realized. Moreover, because the accumulation limits their own consumption, and therefore, an increase of consumption can only be achieved by the increase of unproductive class in unproductive consumption. Ricardo retorted this that "I acknowledge there may not be adequate motives for production, and therefore things will not be produced, but first I should say that commodities will continue produced with these inadequate motives, and secondly if their production is attended with the loss of the producer, it is not any other reason than given a great proportion to the labourers."[51] Even if there is a partial overproduction, Ricardo thinks that is caused due to the faulty distribution, and "the real cause of this faulty distribution would be found in the inadequate quantity of labour in the market." Increase the number of labourers employed, and the nature of the evil points out the remedy; "it would be effectually cured by an additional supply of it".[52]

Ricardo and Malthus agree that the unproductive consumption boosts the development of production, but they differ on the question of who should bear the unproductive consumption. Ricardo considers that unproductive consumers should be labourers, "because all that fund which should, and in ordinary cases, does, constitute profit, goes to wages, and immoderately swells that fund which is destined to the support of labour. The labourers are immoderately paid for their labour, and they necessarily become the unproductive consumers of the country."[53] Different from Ricardo, Malthus thinks these unproductive consumers should be consumers rather than producers, and they should be landlords, officials, priest, annuitant, army, etc.

Based on his profit upon alienation theory, Malthus still emphasizes that "this certain proportion of unproductive consumption varying according to the fertility of the soil, etc. is absolutely and indispensably necessary to call forth the resources of a country."[54] He also believes that if an increased power of production is not accompanied by an increase of unproductive expenditure it will inevitably lower profits and throw labourers out of employment. Ricardo has different views, and he stressed that with the development of production, it must be accompanied with an increase either of productive or of unproductive expenditure. "If the labourer receives a large proportion of the produce as wages, all that he receives more than is sufficient to prompt him to the necessary exertions

---

51   Works and Correspondences of David Ricardo, Chapter 9, p.23.
52   Ibid.
53   Ibid., p. 29.
54   Ibid., p. 27.

of his powers, is as much unproductive consumption as if it were consumed by his master, or by the state—there is no difference whatsoever."[55] From repeated experience, Malthus believes that "the money price of labour never falls till many workmen have been for some time out of work. And the question is, whether this stagnation of capital, and subsequent stagnation in the demand for labour arising from increased production without an adequate proportion of unproductive consumption on the part of the landlords and capitalists, could take place without prejudice to the country, without occasioning a less degree both of happiness and wealth than would have occurred if the unproductive consumption of the landlords and capitalists had been so proportioned to the natural surplus of the society as to have continued the motives to production in an uninterrupted manner, and prevented first an unnatural demand for labour, and then a necessary and sudden diminution of such demand. But if this is so, how can it be said with truth that parsimony, though it may be prejudicial to the producers cannot be prejudicial to the state; or that an increase of unproductive consumption among landlords and capitalists may not sometimes be the proper remedy for a state of things in which the motives to production fail."[56] Malthus's rebuttal is clearly directed at the key point of the Ricardo and Say.

As a representative of the interests of the petty bourgeoisie, Malthus opposed to great machinery production, and he considers that the capitalist overproduction disaster comes from the great machinery production, which provides a lot of excess commodities, lowers the price, and leads to the low profit margins. With very low profits the motives for saving would cease, and therefore the motives for increased production would also cease. This can be seen from the question of Ricardo to Malthus that "Is it not your objection to machinery that it often produces a quantity of commodities for which there is no demand, and that it is the glut which is the consequence of quantity which is unfavourable to the interests of mankind."[57] Ricardo thought Malthus was wrong, but actually he was the one who who argued for the wrong.

Malthus blames excess savings for the stagnation of production and fall in profits, and he also blames it for stagnation of trade, which is clearly opposed to Ricardo's view. What Ricardo believes is that "I should not make a protest against an increase of consumption, as a remedy to the stagnation of trade, if I thought, as you do, that we were now suffering from too much savings. As I have already said I do not see how stagnation of trade can arise from such a cause."[58] "In my opinion increased savings would alleviate rather than aggravate the sufferings of which we have lately had to complain. Stagnation is a derangement of the system, and not too much general production, arising from too great an accumulation of capital."[59]

---

55   Ibid., p. 23.
56   Ibid., p. 26.
57   Ibid., p. 29.
58   Ibid., pp. 30-31.
59   Ibid., p. 32.

In the debate, Ricardo also made clear the principle that savings and invest-ment are consistent, and linked with his arguments that production could never be excessive. Based on the fundamental assumption that the entire productive costs will be certainly used, directly or indirectly, for product purchase, thus the supply creates its own demand, Ricardo considered that the saving behaviour of any one will inevitably lead to that the labour and goods originally provided for consumption will be invested in the production of the means of production and raw materials. Therefore, no matter how much the accumulated capital is, it will never be used favourably."[60] Savings and investment are unified. Since the result of the whole production equals consumption plus saving, while sav-ing equals investment, the total demand for commodities must be equal to the total supply of goods. Therefore, no matter how production increases, the mar-ketability of the product will not be a problem. After that, the consistency of savings and investment has become an important tenet of bourgeois economics.

In the debate with Malthus, Ricardo's followers were also actively involved in it. However, they focused only on issues of demand other than production, and do not even understand Malthus' view that the "consumption of unproductive class" is the stable economic development. They thought that it is tantamount to hand money to others by the producer, and it is by no means different than producers burning out their own goods. Therefore, Ricardo's followers believe that Malthus' presump-tion has no sense, and therefore it is not going to happen. It is the production itself other than the consumption of unproductive class that realizes the balance between capital and income, supply and demand, as well as production and consumption.[61]

VIII. Conclusions

The big prehistoric debate on cyclical economic fluctuations can be seen as an event with far-reaching effects in economics. It has a long period of time, a large number of participants, broad range of debate, sharp and profound views, heated debate, and it is a relatively rare event in the history of economics. The focus of the debate is whether the economic crisis of general glut will occur or not.

Those who advocate there is no crisis of general glut proposed only one ana-lytical model, which can be called Say-Ricardo model. The basic structure is:

Assumptions: (1) Transaction is always shown as an exchange of one good for another. Supply creates its own demand, and buying and selling is consistent; (2) The revenue of all production = consumption + savings; (3) savings = investment.

Fundamental equilibrium: total social demand of a commodity = total so-cial supply of a commodity

---

60 The Works and Correspondences of David Ricardo, Chapter 1, p. 247. Beijing: Commercial Press. 1991.
61 See Marx and Engels Collected Works, Volume 26 (II), pp. 59-60, Beijing, People's Publishing House, 1974.

Conclusion: The more the producers are, the more diversified the products are, and the more easily the sales are. Due to the faulty distribution of capital, it would cause a temporary and partial overproduction of a certain commodity. However, the general overproduction and the economic crisis caused by the overproduction both are impossible.

Crisis of general glut advocated by some proposed two analytical models, namely the Sismondi's Model and Malthusian Model.

The basic structure of the Sismondi's model is:

Assumptions: (1) Product are always bought with income; (2) Production is subject to consumption; (3) In a "normal" society, production that is not subject to consumption with unlimited development will inevitably lead to the alienation of production from consumption.

Fundamental equilibrium: social production = social consumption

Realistic conditions: On the one hand there is a trend of infinite expansion of capitalist production, and on the other hand the share of the total working masses continues to decline in the total income of the society.

Conclusion: Capitalist economic crisis of overproduction is not only inevitable, but continuous. Capitalism can only rely on small commodity producers and foreign non-capitalist market to overcome the crisis.

The basic structure of the Malthusian model is: 53

Assumptions: (1) The value of commodities is determined by the labour it can exchange in the market. (2) Labour for exchange = live labour + profits; effective demand = value of means of production + wages + profits.

Fundamental equilibrium: total value of social goods = effective demand

Basic conclusion: The mutual dealings between capitalists and the inadequate expenditure of workers' wage constitute a sufficient "effective demand". If we only depend on the demand of these two types of classes, the total value of social commodities cannot be achieved. There has to be a third type, "unproductive consumers", whose purchase and consumption will offset the glut of oversupply in the market. Therefore, in order to ensure the smooth development of capitalism, and to eliminate the danger of capitalist economic crisis from possibility to reality, it is necessary for unproductive consumers to exist and expand.

Either the opposite debating side is convinced, but its theoretical model has had a profound impact. Some of the ingredients are absorbed by the model of bourgeois economics, becoming the dominant theory creed of mainstream economics. For example, "Say's Law" had been used till the Great Depression in 1930s, while Keynesian "Insufficient Effective Demand" theory became the basic proposition of neoclassical economics, and is still a central credo till now. Some scientific components of these models were critically absorbed by Karl Marx, becoming the scientific elements of Marx's analytical model of the economic crisis.

CHAPTER II

The Development of Marx's Thought on Economic Crisis and Cycles, and Classical Models

I. Introduction

In *Theories of Surplus Value*, Marx criticized Ricardo's crisis theory, which is normally seen as an important symbol of the formation of his crisis theory. It is based on: (1) *Theories of Surplus Value* in *Capital* Volume IV, which is among the mature writings of Marx, basically including his main economic theories. (2) The premise when criticizing a theory with another theory is that the latter should be more mature and more scientific, otherwise the critique cannot be accomplished. Like in Marx's other theories, the foundation of his crisis theory was firstly based on the critique of the past classical theory of economic crisis and the contemporary theories as well, then Marx strives to build a new crisis theory on the basis of critically absorbing the achievements and studies made on the real crisis.

Theories of Surplus Value was written in the early 1860s (see Marx's Manuscripts 1861-63), and it basically summed up the research and critique achievements of the previous 20 years or so. Many of Marx's previous critiques were scattered in his notebooks, particularly in his London Notes from 1849 to 1856, in which he excerpted and reviewed almost all the important materials and documents on economic crisis written by his contemporaries. If we examine Marx's notebooks of different periods together with his books, articles and correspondence in the corresponding period, we can find the relationship between Marx's criticism process on others crisis theories and creation of his own ideas.

It is well known that Marx failed to complete all his future writing plans in economics, and further deeper examination of the crisis theory was only one part of his complete study goal. The necessary theoretical speculation based on the theoretical structure and prompts in the existing literature, so as to reveal the basic outline or even the full view of Marx's crisis theory, should also become an integral part of his complete goal.

Previous studies on Marx's theories have all addressed this fact but generally lack an accurate analysis on this issue, they have concluded that Marx's works have not developed enough theoretically, and have argued that the remarkable study results he reached were only limited.

The analytical models related to economic crises we find in Marx's existing literature are the ones that he elaborated with a special chapter, but these chapters were written in the process of his critique on the classical economists crisis theory of and of his other contemporaries, besides these texts were written when he observed the actual crises. We might say that this could be the disposal of these theoretic elaborations

Hence, firstly, I suggest that Marx's crisis theory needs an urgent improvement, and secondly it should be evaluated as a theory to be developed. Whether for its improvement or development, we need to examine its structures, and development trend, in a certain theoretical pattern, (theoretical situating).

II. Exploring the Historical Process of Economic Crisis

Marx and Engels did not focus on the capitalist economic crisis until 1844. Originally, in *The Condition of the Working Class in England* written by Engels, where he described how the individual and small-scale crises get centralized and gradually develop into a series of crises with periodic recurrence in the industry. Engels also gave a brief description of the various stages of the economic cycle: "This is the beginning of the crisis, which then takes precisely the same course as its predecessor, and gives place in turn to a season of prosperity. So it goes on perpetually, prosperity, crisis, prosperity, crisis, and this perennial round in which English industry moves is, as has been before observed, usually completed once in five or six years. Engels also especially focused on the effects of the above process for the working class. He believed the cycle was "usually completed once in five or six years"; and "the intensity of the crisis increases with each repetition." He also successfully predicted the next (crisis)… may be expected not later than 1847, will probably be still more violent and lasting."[1] In *The Principles of Communism* published in 1847, Engels also mentioned that commercial crises were occurring in a cycle of every five to seven years, noting that: "Ever since the beginning of the 19th century, the condition of industry has constantly fluctuated between periods of prosperity and periods of crisis; and nearly every five to seven years, a fresh crisis has intervened, always bringing the greatest hardships for workers, and always accompanied by general revolutionary stirrings and direct peril to the whole existing order of things. He wrote: "To what extent want and suffering prevail among these unemployed during such a crisis, I need not describe." (*The Condition of the Working Class in England*, by Engels, 1845) Engels evaluated this commercial crisis as the one caused by big industry and free competition since the crisis arising from industrial overproduction. "It lies in the nature of industrial competition and the commercial crises which stems from it." "In the present unregulated production and distribution of the means of subsistence, which is carried on not directly for the sake of supplying needs, but for profit, in the system under which every one works for himself to enrich himself, disturbances inevitably arise at every moment?" However, "so long as big industry remains on its present footing, it can be maintained only at the cost of general chaos every seven years, each time threatening the whole of civilization and not only plunging the proletarians into misery but also ruining large sections of the bourgeoisie; hence, either that big industry must itself be given up, which is an absolute impossibility, or that it makes unavoidably necessary an entirely new organization of society". (*The Condition of the Working Class in England*, by Engels, 1845) From the above critique we can see that Engels has recognized the cycle, trends and consequences of the capitalist economic crisis, though, it was still in its preliminary form, thus he has linked the crises and the fate of the capitalist system. So we can say that in this stage, Marx and Engels have grasped the nature and cause of the capitalist economic crisis; on the other hand, they have collected and examined some factual or phenomenal materials related to crises. But, they hadn't yet built a theoretical system for its realization mechanism, or brought a systematic theoretical explanation.

In the 1840s, in his first book related to political economy – *The Poverty of Philosophy*, Marx mentioned on the features of cycles in capitalist production, he wrote: "This true proportion between supply and demand, ...ceased long ago to exist. It has passed into the stage of senility. It was possible only at a time when the means of production were limited, when the movement of exchange took place within very restricted bounds. With the birth of large-scale industry this true proportion had to come to an end, and production is inevitably compelled to pass in continuous succession through vicissitudes of prosperity, depression, crisis, stagnation, renewed prosperity, and so on."[2] At the same time, he had begun to explore the sources of the crisis. He has found

---

1 See *Marx and Engels Collected Works*, Volume 2, 366–372, Beijing, People's Publishing House, 1957.

2 *Marx and Engels Collected Works*, Volume 4, p.109, Beijing: People's Publishing House, 1958.

that "the anarchy of production", was "the source of so much misery…" A year later, in his other article, , Marx continued to explore and express his ideas on the phases of capitalist production cycle as: "We see the various phases of prosperity, overproduction, stagnation, crisis", as a repeated cycle. In this speech, he had already cognized overproduction as the major phenomenon and characteristics of the crisis. In the Speech, *Wage Labour and Capital* at Brussels German Workers' Association, Marx made comments on the issues of crisis. He analyzed the links between the crisis and the accumulation of capital, talked on how the accumulation of capital needs to expand markets: "In short, the crises increase. They become more frequent and more violent, if for no other reason, then for this alone, that in the same measure in which the mass of products grows, and there the needs for extensive markets, in the same measure does the world market shrink ever more, and ever fewer markets remain to be exploited, since every previous crisis has subjected to the commerce of the world a hitherto unconquered or but superficially exploited market." He also pointed out to the destructive phenomena of the crises related to wealth, products, and productive forces. Not only the productive forces were destroyed, but a large number of workers were forced to illness and death, and they become the funerary of capital . As he described, "in the same measure in which the capitalists are compelled, by the motion described above, to exploit the already existing gigantic means of production on an ever-increasing scale, and for this purpose to set in motion all the mainsprings of credit, in the same measure do they increase the industrial earthquakes, in the midst of which the commercial world can preserve itself only by sacrificing a portion of its wealth, its products, and even its forces of production, to the gods of the lower world – But capital not only lives upon labour. Like a master, at once distinguished and barbarous, it drags with it into its grave the corpses of its slaves, whole hecatombs of workers, who perish in the crises."[3]

58

Herein we see Marx emphasizing the inevitability of the crises and proposing the theory of ever shrinking realization of markets in economic crisis, which is consistent with the view he advocated in the *Communist Manifesto*. The capitalist economic crisis was a disaster caused by overproduction, as well as a disaster absolutely unavoidable, during which the bourgeois tried to get over these crises by enforced destruction of a mass of productive forces; and by the conquest of new markets, and by the more violent exploitation of the older ones.

Examining the fate of capitalist system together with the commercial crisis, had been a study subject before Marx and Engels, but other researchers were unable to discover the true intrinsic links between the two. One of the examples was the theory of "impossible crisis" represented by Say, and another being the crisis theory advocated by Sismondi. Marx and Engels began to focus on the relationship between commercial crisis and the capitalist economic system in

---

3 *Selected Works of Marx and Engels*, Volume 1, p.363, Beijing: People's Publishing House, 1995.

the early 1840s, and their preliminary findings have appeared in the *Communist Manifesto* published in the early 1848. Their conclusions were: Cyclical commercial crisis of overproduction is the product of the contradictory motion of the capitalist mode of production, which is increasingly threatening the existence of bourgeois society. The bourgeoisie is unable to overcome the commercial crisis of overproduction within its own scope because "the conditions of bourgeois society are too narrow to comprise the wealth created by them", and "they bring disorder into the whole of bourgeois society; endanger the existence of bourgeois property." (*Communist Manifesto*, Chapter I) The bourgeoisie tried measures to get over these crises, such as "on the one hand by enforced destruction of a mass of productive forces; on the other, by the conquest of new markets, and by the more thorough exploitation of the old ones." However, "That is to say, by paving the way for more extensive and more destructive crises, and by diminishing the means whereby crises are prevented."[4] It is obvious that at this stage Marx's research had a lot of limitations or flaws. He pointed out the objective necessity of periodic commercial crises, but he believes the crisis is the result of the revolt of modern productive forces against modern production relations, against the bourgeois and the ownership relationship of the existence conditions for its rule. This has not yet been rising from general reasons to specific, or not yet studied the periodic commercial crises at the level of the basic contradiction of capitalism. However, there are some scholars who believe that the *Communist Manifesto* has laid the main line of Marx's discussion on economic issues crisis which is the contradictory motion between productive forces and production relations, as well as its temporary solutions. The various crisis theories are the development of this mainline.[5]

After the *Communist Manifesto* was published, Marx and Engels obviously increased their concerns about the capitalist commercial crisis, and they published a series of reviews in Neue Rheinische Zeitung: *Review of Political Economy*, recalling in detail the history since the industrial cycle in 1837, distinguishing between signs and causes of the crisis, as well as its various manifestations and factors. Such as excessive speculation and stock market crisis, credit crisis and currency market crisis, commercial crisis and financial crisis, foreign trade crisis and gold outflow, general commercial crisis and banking crisis, and so on. Stock market crisis caused by excessive speculation and credit crisis caused by excessive expansion of credit, are only a symptom of crisis in their view, and the real cause of the crisis is the industrial overproduction and the correspondingly excessive expansion of foreign trade.[6]

While conducting such studies, Marx and Engels were always attaching their attention on the economic crisis as well as revolution. They have had a clear understanding that the periodical commercial crisis is a crisis of the

---

4   Ibid., p.278.

5   See Zhu Zhongdi, *The Study of Western Scholars on the Marxist Theory of the Economic Crisis*, Shanghai: Shanghai People's Publishing House, 1991, p. 269.

6   See *Marx and Engels Collected Works*, 1st Chinese edition, Volume 10, Beijing: People's Publishing House, 1962, pp. 575-583.

industrial capitalism in England that threatening the Continental Europe, which triggered the European Revolution of 1848; world trade and world communications gained new direction and new centres due to the development of the emerging industries in England. The world market adapted the large industrial production which has began to develop and the industry of several countries were competing in this market. "Given this general prosperity…a real revolution is out of the question…A new revolution is only a consequence of a new crisis. The one, however, is as sure to come as the other."[7] The review predicted: The impact of the next crisis will probably be still more violent than any time in the past, because England is experiencing at the same time the *dual crisis*; an industrial and an agricultural crisis. Germany represents England's biggest continental market and foremost cotton and wool supplier, and therefore no European country will be hit so directly, to such an extent and with such intensity as Germany. We can see from Marx's *London Notes* that, when writing this note, Marx had examined in detail issues on currency, credit and crisis. When a lot of works blamed the outbreak of the crisis in 1847 for the wrong monetary policy and credit policy, it prompted Marx to connect the study of the crisis with the study of money and credit. He pointed out that "gold and silver are in the form of medium with their own currency properties. The exchange behaviour is decomposed into purchase and sale, demand and supply. Hence, the inevitable result of money is the separation of these two behaviours, which must eventually balance each other but may be inconsistent or imbalance at each given time. Therefore, money has laid foundation for crisis."[8] Herein Marx had already seen the possibility of the economic crisis from money as a means of the circulation. In the manuscript *Reflection*, he pointed out in the analysis of trade between industrialists as well as between industrialists and consumers that in times of crisis, capital exists in the form of goods and cannot be exchanged into money; it lacks circulation means rather than capital. In London Notes, Marx regarded economic crisis as a harbinger of revolutionary upsurge. Believing that the outbreak of commercial crisis and the revolution will take place concurrently. Since 1850 Marx began to predict the outbreak of the next crisis, and tried to explain why its delayed. In his article *The Class Struggles in France* written in 1850, Marx analyzed the relationship between crisis and revolution, and pointed out the second great economic event that hastened the outbreak of the revolution, which was a general commercial and industrial crisis in England. A new revolution was only a consequence of a new crisis. The one, however, was as sure to come as the other. The study on the economic crisis of 1857 also showed his concern for the relationship between crisis and the revolution. With regard to his works, the first crisis he carefully studied was the crisis of 1857 to 1858. In the fall of 1857 when the crisis broke out in the United States, Marx expressed his feelings in a letter to Engels, "the

60

7 *Marx and Engels Collected Works*, 1st Chinese edition, Volume 7, Beijing: People's Publishing House, 1962, p. 114.
8 Central Compilation and Translation Bureau, *Study of Marx and Engels*, 1st Series, Unpublished , pp. 2-3.

U.S. crisis is terrific. (We have predicted that it will break out in New York in the review of November 1850.)" In the subsequent letters he expressed his concern about the crisis, "I myself suffering economic difficulties but I have never felt so comfortable for the outbreak of this crisis since 1849."[9]

Marx looked forward to the outbreak of new crises, to bring once again a revolutionary motion after a long pause, which prompted him to make every effort to "conclude my studies in economics", "to finish the *Principles of Political Economy*". The revolution floods he expected have come now, and he had only a little time for his theoretical writings.[10] In addition, he also collected material about "the present crisis", and took notes. He told Engels that "I have started three large record books– England, Germany, and France". In his letter written on 18 December 1857 to Engels, he said, "All the material on the American affair is available in the *Tribune*". He also told Ferdinand Lassalle that "The present commercial crisis has impelled me to set to work seriously on my outlines of political economy and also to prepare something on the present crisis".[11] "Prepare something" is mainly the process of the economic crisis of 1857. In short, these studies are an important stage of Marx's writings, which enabled him to have a better understanding of the contents that a crisis theory should have, or should be expected of. Furthermore, it is also worth noting that Marx and Engels accurately foresaw the arrival of the crisis of 1857, which shows that they have a clear understanding of the mechanism of the capitalist economic crisis.

In the early stage of their theoretical creation, Marx and Engels believed that capitalist crisis was systemic and cyclical. Any crisis is likely to be triggered by a special event suddenly; such as crop failure, trade interruption caused by political changes or a war; bankruptcy fraud and financial corporations Hence, the crisis seemed to be an accidental phenomenon, which was exactly what the bourgeoisie explained, because they believed a moderate reform could eliminate the risk of these crises, so that the prosperity of capitalism would continue to increase. Therefore, in England of 1840s, the liberal economics said the past crises were caused by the restrictions of Corn Laws and by the inadequate control over currency. Thus, till 1844, the implementation of the Banking Act and the abolition of the Corn Laws were declared as measures to eliminate general crisis pathogens forever. However, it seemed to Marx and Engels that the crisis was no accident, and it was the superficial and necessary presentation of the contradictions of capitalist mode of production.

The *Economic Manuscript* (1857-1858) explored issues on economic crisis. In January 1857 when Marx began to write *A Contribution to the Critique of Political Economy* after an in-depth study for a dozen years, he had a clear understanding of the periodic modern crisis. The outbreak of the crisis in 1857 to

9   *Marx and Engels Collected Works*, 1st Chinese edition, Volume 29, Beijing: People's Publishing House, 1972, p. 198.
10   *Ibid.*, p. 219, p. 226.
11   *Ibid.*, p. 527.

1858 also provided Marx an excellent opportunity for testing the result of the past research and exploring new issues. During the crisis, Marx had collected a lot of data and done a thorough and detailed follow-up study. These researches helped Marx have a clearer statement of the concept of economic crisis, and he also had a more explicit understanding of its position in the system; scope and content of the general theory of periodic crisis. Therefore, the research at this stage is generally regarded as the initial formation of the Marxist crisis theory, and has a significant impact on the future study. The recurring materials, or with different use in the manuscript of 1860s included a lot of research in this period.

The manuscripts of *Introduction, Bastiat and Carey, the Critique of Political Economy (Rough Draft of 1857-58)*, typifies his research on the economic crisis. In *Introduction*, Marx put crisis as the last chapter of the planned five-work program structure of economics works, which is the *World Market and Crisis*. This shows that Marx already had a better understanding of the structural logic of capitalist economic crisis, and began to figure out its theoretical content and scope. In the second and the third programs of the five-work structure in *the Critique of Political Economy (Rough Draft of 1857-58)*, the position was the same. Crisis should be put in the last chapter with the world market in the theoretical system of the planned economics works. Despite the six-book, structure plan did not explicitly list the World Market and Crisis, according to the elaboration to the nature of the crisis in *the Critique of Political Economy (Rough Draft of 1861-63)*, we can infer that the contents of the world market, as well as the crisis, are in the same category. Or we can put international trade and world market in the front, but it must be linked to crisis. The reason that Marx's emphasis on putting the crisis as last one in the theoretical system for elaboration is because the economic crisis is an overall concept and the result of the full development of various contradictions of capitalism; the world market constitutes the last chapter. In the last chapter, the capitalist production was set to be the general one, and all the contradictions were fully developed. Therefore, in such a theoretical system, the planned elaboration on crisis was part of the full development of various contradictions of capitalist mode of production. Marx believed that the economic crisis in such a theoretic narration should play a determining role: The whole capitalist mode of production in which the crises were generally beyond the premise, reproduced in the theory at the end of the discussion, was forced to adopt a new form of history.[12] Or as said in the third program of the five-work structure, the narration on the world market ought to state "encroachment of bourgeois society over the state", and the elaboration on economic crisis theory should explain "dissolution of the mode of production and form of society based on exchange value".[13] In *the Critique of Political Economy (Rough Draft of 1857-58)*, Marx's discussion

---

12   Marx and Engels, *Collected Works*, Volume 46a, Beijing: People's Publishing House, 1979, p. 178.
13   Ibid., p.220.

for the first time touched the overall process of capitalist production. Since the prerequisite is that the value and surplus value produced by reproduction and accumulation of capital was realized in circulation, and capital encountered boundaries in the process of circulation, that is, the society had boundaries required by the ability to pay over commodities produced in capitalism: The infinite desire for increasing value added was restricted by the dual limits, that is, restricted by value in use, as well as restricted by value. These were its own boundaries, and because in a pure capitalist economy, the exchange subject was capitalists or labour workers, while the exchange object was commodities produced in capitalism. Therefore, Marx attempted for the first time to clarify the nature provisions, which is how the inherent contradictions find expression in external boundaries, conflicts and crises in the process of capitalist reproduction. Hence, he began to explore the possibilities and impossibilities of universal overproduction. He accused Ricardo and his school with not understanding the true essence of the modern crisis. According to Marx's point of view, what they lacked was the proper understanding of the inherent contradictions of the capitalist mode of production What Marx emphasized, was to explain the "base of overproduction", the "bud of overproduction" included in the inherent contradictions of capital relationships, "not in the description of overproduction prescriptions"[14]. In spite of this still the crisis was further defined as "universal overproduction."[15]

When writing *the Critique of Political Economy (1857-58)*, Marx began a systematic critique of the erroneous views of Ricardo. With respect to Ricardo's denial of the possibility of widespread crisis, he pointed out that even in a simple commodity economy there was a possibility of widespread crisis, and Ricardo's practices were, in essence, an attempt to deny the inevitability of the capitalist economic crisis by negating product attributes of capitalist production. This is because, in barter, purchase and sale were connected in time and space, and it was possible there was overproduction of a commodity and underproduction of another, so, under such conditions Ricardo was correct. However, the exchange of commodities was an exchange with money as the medium, which made the inherent contradictions conceived within the commodity, takes the form of external opposition, and the exchange of commodities split into the phase where purchase and sale could be separated in space and time. People could only buy without selling, or sell without buying. Thus, "in the splitting of exchange into two acts, there lies germ of crises, or at least their possibility." However, the possibility is far from reality, and it "cannot be realized, except where the fundamental preconditions of classically developed, conceptually adequate circulation are present."[16] Therefore, Marx revealed the first possibility of the crisis in the analysis of the function of currency circulation means. Then, he revealed the second possibility of the crisis in the analysis

---

14 See *Marx and Engels Collected Works*, Volume 46a, pp. 396-403. The exposition on issues of reproduction, accumulation and overproduction of capital.

15 Ibid.

16 *Marx and Engels Collected Works*, Volume 46a, p. 147.

of the function of currency payment means. It seemed to Marx that in commercial credit, as the value of general commodities changed, the value of currency would also change. "To money as measure, this change is irrelevant, for 'in a changing medium, two different relations to the same thing can always be expressed, just as well as in a constant medium'. As medium of circulation it is also irrelevant, since its quantity as such is set by the measure. But as money in the form in which it appears in contracts, this is essential, just as, in general, its contradictions come to the fore in this role."[17] As changes in the value of the currency will cause difficulties for the debtor in the exchange activities based on credit to repay the debt, and he could not sell his goods in the corresponding period. If it was so, bankruptcy was sure to come, causing massive economic crisis. Later, in the draft of *the Critique of Political Economy* Volume I, Marx further developed this idea, arguing that if this balance and the credit payment, the basis for such balance, were destroyed, money would appear in its realistic form or it would cause a crisis. Marx even had recognized the relation between the two possibilities of the crisis, i.e., the second possibility of crisis was the development of the first one, and in the absence of the second, the first might also exist; if there was not the first, the second would not emerge.

In the in-depth critique of the Ricardo's view, Marx also initially revealed the objective economic conditions of the crisis which transformed it from an abstract possibility to reality. The objective economic conditions are the formation and development of all the contradictions of the capitalist economic crisis. In the *Economics Manuscript* (1857-1858), Marx had detailed analysis of these contradictions as well as their restrictions on the development of capitalist production, and he believed that with the development of these contradictions, restrictions and conflicts, the abstract possibility of the crisis lain in commodity production and exchange would then gradually develop into the reality of crisis. These restrictions are mainly that the following: The restriction on capitalist production is mainly from consumption, and the conversion of commodity capital to money capital is also one of the restrictive factors; surplus value is the restriction on the development of productivity. Marx believed that these restrictions of the capitalist system on production were not always seen in the general production. Since contradictions, conflicts and periodic economic crisis caused by such restrictions are indications of basic capitalist contradictions, therefore, Marx considered that, "[i]t is enough here to demonstrate that capital contains a particular restriction of production—which contradicts its general tendency to drive beyond every barrier to production—in order to have uncovered the foundation of overproduction, the fundamental contradiction of developed capital; in order to have uncovered, more generally, the fact that capital is not, as the economists believe, the absolute form for the development of the forces of production—not the absolute form for that, nor the form of wealth which absolutely coincides with the development of the forces of production".[18]

---

17   Ibid., p.188.
18   *Marx and Engels Collected Works*, Volume 46a, p.399.

Against, the view arguing that universal overproduction is impossible, Marx made an effort to refute it and attempted to explain that the overproduction was possible and was inevitable under the inherent conditions of specific capitalist mode of production. In the Manuscript Marx proposed the concept of balanced capitalist reproduction for the first time, and analyzed as well how various contradictory elements of capital necessarily became independent and formally unrelated economic magnitudes in the exchange process, he wrote: "purchase and sale are equally essential but there must come a moment when the independent form is broken and when their inner unity is established externally through a violent explosion…there lies the germ (Ed. possibility) of crisis". However, the external motion manifested, as well as its inner unity manifested, are part of the concept of capital. Therefore, the proper concept of a modern crisis can also be clarified based on capital and through capital. Hence, the external motion demonstrated by this inner unity, namely the kind of crisis cycle on which is acted again and again by the inner unity of various factors independent from each other in the process of capitalist reproduction can only be examined when discussing the reality of capital which is competition and credit. Here, in fact, what Marx meant was that all of these needed a further explanation.

When writing the *Economics Manuscripts of* (1857-1858), Marx began to pay attention to the basis for the industrial cycle. In the letter to Engels on 2 March 1858, he asked "Can you tell me how often machinery has to be replaced in, say, your factory?" This is because "The average period for the replacement of machinery is one important factor in explaining the multi-year cycle which has been a feature of industrial development ever since the consolidation of big industry."[19] Engels wrote him back on 4 March 1858, and informed him about the common practice of machinery replacement, as well as the cycle of new and expanding investments in the cotton and textile industry in Manchester.[20] Marx expressed his best thanks for Engels' **éclaircissements** (clarification) to the machinery, and he stressed that "The figure of 13 years corresponds closely enough to the theory, since it establishes a unit for one epoch of industrial reproduction which plus **ou moins** (or less) coincides with the period in which major crises recur". Their course is also determined by factors of a quite different kind. But for him "the important thing is to discover, in the immediate material postulates of big industry, one factor that determines cycles."[21] This explanation also appeared in the *Economics Manuscript* (1857-1858) again: To discover a unit to measure the turnovers of capital through fixed capital and its reproduction, and the reproduction of capital "is now not merely externally, but rather necessarily connected with this unit". "There can be no doubt whatever that the cycle which industry has passed through since the development of fixed capital on a large scale, at more or less 10-yearly intervals, is connected with this total reproduction phase of capital. We shall find other determinant

65

---

19 *Marx and Engels Collected Works*, Volume 29, p. 280. Beijing: People's Publishing House, 1972.
20 Ibid.
21 Ibid., p.284.

causes as well. But this is one of them".[22] This indicates that Marx's study on economic cycle has in fact touched its essence.

In the *Economics Manuscript* (1857-1858) published earlier (the first part for the early part of *the Critique of Political Economy*), some elements of the crisis theory re-emerged, in a position where it was correct and necessary in the system. Marx stressed that in the analysis of circulation of commodity and circulation of money, it had already contained a general possibility of crisis, that is, the circulation of commodities with money as the medium would inevitably split into two separate and independent acts —purchase and sale. In *Chapter on Money*, Marx explicitly stated that "… the quality of money as a medium in the splitting of exchange into two acts" was "germ of crises, or at least their possibility", and described crisis as "a violent explosion". Thus, the crisis manifests the unity of the two phases which have become independent of each other. There would be no crisis without this inner unity of factors that are apparently indifferent to each other."[23] In the analysis of money as a means of payment in the first part of *the Critique of Political Economy*, Marx revealed the second possibility, the possibility in the form of a currency crisis.

In *Chapter on Money* of *the Critique of Political Economy* (Rough Draft of 1857-58), in analysis of the possibility of the split into purchase and sale in the simple circulation, Marx had proposed the concept of "abstraction" of crisis. "In so far as purchase and sale, the two essential moments of circulation, are indifferent to one another and separated in place and time, they by no means need to coincide. Their indifference can develop into the fortification and apparent independence of the one against the other. But in so far as they are both essential moments of a single whole, there must come a moment when the independent form is violently broken and when the inner unity is established externally through a violent explosion. Thus already in the quality of money as a medium in the splitting of exchange into two acts, there lies germ of crises…"[24] He also had a systematic elaboration of the concept of "abstraction" in the *Economics Manuscript* (1857-1858), and expounded on that in almost each of his later manuscripts. Hence, the abstract concept of economic crisis that the inner unity of elements within a whole but independent of each other (such as purchase and sale, production and consumption, etc.) was restored through violence was consistent with the explanation of Marx's economic crisis theory. If there was a change, it was mainly shown in the requirements on the content of various processes that caused the economic crisis, as well as in the operational implications of economic crisis for bourgeois economics.

In the original initial debates related to the capitalist economic crisis, based on the argument that the underconsumption by the working class may lead to the trend of general excessive production, the group of economists led by Heinrich

---

22   Marx and Engels, *Collected Works*, Volume 46b, p. 235. Beijing: People's Publishing House, 1980.

23   Marx and Engels, *Collected Works*, Volume 46a, p. 147. Beijing: People's Publishing House, 1979.

24   Ibid., pp. 146-147.

Friedrich von Storch, Sismondi, and Malthus et al. refuted the proposition by Jean Baptiste Say and David Ricardo that negated the possibility of universal overproduction.[25] In the beginning of writing the *Economics Manuscripts of* (1857-1858), Marx not only basically agreed the argument of under-consumption theory for overproduction advocated by Malthus and Sismondi, but he also gave it a try personally.[26]

Malthus stressed that premise to the existence of profits was that there were other demands in addition to the demand for labour, and Marx wrote accordingly that "production itself posits drives it forward, and must drive it forward beyond the proportion…if the demand exterior to the demand of the labourer himself disappears or shrinks up, then the collapse occurs."[27] Marx realized that there were demands among individual capitals, but he thought this was secondary because in his opinion the personal consumption was the ultimate limit of production. However, he soon changed his view on Malthus' theory of "underconsumption".[28] When he was criticizing Proudhon's demonstration of overproduction, Marx pointed out that Proudhon thought the worker could not buy back his product with his wages, which was an entirely complete misunderstanding of the value theory. "Thus, out the window goes Mr. Proudhon's discovery that the worker cannot buy back his product. The basis on which this rests is that he (Proudhon) understands nothing, either about value-determination or about price-determination. But, furthermore and regardless of that, his conclusion that this is why there is over production is false in this abstraction."[29]

This critique on Proudhon was once understood as the critique of principle on the argumentation of underconsumption theory for overproduction, and this understanding was not appropriate. Marx considered Proudhon's argument made in this abstraction was false because people could get such a conclusion: This argument could be another meaning in another expression.

The worker could not buy back his product—which was never going to happen in the capitalist relationship—and this argument was not sufficient to demonstrate overproduction because not only the worker had needs, so did the capitalist. Marx vaguely felt that, Sismondi's argument was that the capitalist production had the tendency of limitless development, but the likelihood of the consumption of the working class continued to be restricted, and therefore the demand of the capitalist should fill a growing gap which was impossible anyway. Marx was not like Proudhon, not because of the view of underconsumption theory itself, but he dynamically examined the capitalist mode of production based on such a view while Proudhon was still limited to examine

---

25 See above pp.389-401 the elaboration by Marx on issues of reproduction, accumulation and overproduction.

26 Ibid.

27 Ibid.

28 See related argumentation in *Marx and Engels Collected Works*, 1st Chinese edition, Volume 46a, pp.405-410.

29 Ibid., pp. 423-424.

the relationship of exploitation statically, and basically concluded that overproduction was also related to exploitation.

In the *Economics Manuscript* (1857-1858), other specific causes of the crisis are also being suggested. For example, it is written that "general overproduction would take place…, not too much for consumption, but too much to retain the correct relation between consumption and realization".[30]Naturally, views like this were not further expanded in the *Economics Manuscript* (1857-1858), but underconsumption theory was mainly demonstrated.

Determining the position of the economic crisis in the theoretical architecture is one of the major achievements of the *Economics Manuscript* (1857-1858). The content and format of Marx's economic theory is unified, and Marx not only focused on the study of the former, he had also given enough attention the latter. One of the important evidence is that Marx spent a lot of energy on handling the structure of *Capital*. When he began writing the book on economics in 1857, he did not have a full-fledged structure. However, Marx tried to create such a structure. He presented the structured program of his economic writings in the *Introduction* in 1857, and the structure reflected the logical order of development from abstraction to concreteness, the most specific part of which was "the world market and crisis".[31] In the structure of two more specific programs in the main body of the *Economics Manuscript* (1857-1858), the economic crisis was placed in the last and examined together with the world market, where Marx certainly articulated more clearly the characteristics and significance of the economic crisis. The revised structure program during this period, namely the six-book plan, did not explicitly tie the world market to the economic crisis and raise them up, but there was no indication that the economic crisis was not in the final part.

The possibility and reality of the economic crisis, which had been repeatedly distinguished by Marx during 1857-1863, was raised and further extended in the *Economics Manuscript* (1861-1863). This is part of *Theories of Surplus-Value*, titled Ricardo's Theory of Accumulation and a Critique of it. (The Very Nature of Capital Leads to Crises).[32] In this part, combining the critique of Ricardo's theory with the theoretic narration, Marx discussed the crisis issue with more concentration. On the one hand, he criticized Ricardo's theory of no crisis, and on the other, he described his theoretic views on issues of crisis. With regard to the methodological issues of the economic crisis, Marx made a clearer explanation: "The world trade crises must be regarded as the real concentration and forcible adjustment of all the contradictions of bourgeois economy." It is the result of all the contradictions being fully developed. "The individual factors, which are condensed in these crises, must therefore emerge and must be described in each sphere of the bourgeois economy and the further we advance

---

30   *Marx and Engels Collected Works*, 1st Chinese edition, Volume 46a, p.437.

31   Ibid., p.46.

32   *Marx and Engels Collected Works*, 1st Chinese edition, Volume 26b, p.537. Beijing: People's Publishing House, 1973.

68

in our examination of the latter, the more aspects of this conflict must be traced on the one hand, and on the other hand it must be shown that its more abstract forms are recurring and are contained in the more concrete forms."[33] This clearly expressed the study method of the crisis theory and its corresponding narrative approach. In the meantime, it also made specific instructions on the prescriptions of the concept of the crisis, that is, it was a multi-prescription, multi-layered structure. The crisis theory could be explained further through various connections between simple prescriptions and complex prescriptions of capital. In the final part of the theoretical description, there was a full chapter devoted to the description of crisis, which would discuss manners of "generalizing" and "equalizing" in the crisis of various factors which contradicted each other in the capitalist production. According to the narrative form, the crisis and the cyclical movement of capitalist economics from one crisis to another could not "generalize" all the contradictions of the capitalist mode of production until then.

Marx also described the relationship between the description of abstract theory and that of the reality of the crisis. Unlike the description of abstract theory of the crisis, the reality of the crisis could only be introduced from the capitalist real movement, competition and credit. We must describe the real crisis after we finished describing capital—capital and profits. Before that, the germ of crisis and the form of crisis, which were described when examining the process of simple production, reproduction, cycle and reproduction. However, the real movement of capital did not mean the obvious, daily or empirical reality of capitalism in a particular historical moment but rather a theoretical stage, that is, "the real movement denotes developed capitalist production, which starts from and presupposes its own basis", a stage of the overall process.[34] Besides, in the final part of the six-book structure, when finishing describing competition, credit, stock system, wage labour, land ownership, nation, and foreign trade, it reached this stage, the world market.

In order to achieve this program, it requires us to carefully and consciously carry out the description in accordance with the methodology. In each of the analysis level, we need to clearly show what new crisis factors are added, what new forms of crisis are introduced, and how to extend the prescription of the content of the crisis.[35] Marx was not clear at all in this manuscript that how various factors of real crisis was connected with the requirements and forms of the general concept of crisis, which could be distinguished in the analysis. For example, the specific factors of money crisis learned from every crisis in the history, could not be fully understood through the first or second prescription of forms which might appear in simple circulation, and it needed further supplementary prescriptions. However, those prescriptions could only be obtained through analysis of the modern credit system.

---

33   Ibid., p.582.
34   *Marx and Engels Collected Works*, 1st Chinese edition, Volume 26b, p.586. Beijing: People's Publishing House, 1973.
35   Ibid. pp. 583, 586, 591.

Marx was very clear that, it was necessary to have an overall summary and general thinking of varied prescriptions of forms and requirements for the content of crises, and it was also needed to study how the general possibility of crises would become a certainty. It meant that under which condition of the whole movement of the capitalist mode of production would be in periodic crisis. It also required theoretical discussion of "the general possibility of crisis", that is, the common conditions that all periodic world market crises had in modern capitalism, were connected with the general conditions of the capitalist production.[36] In order to understand these conditions it was also required to have a clear understanding of the history of economic crisis. If guided by theory, it is certainly helpful to have known or estimated what might appear or break out in the economic crisis, but we still must understand how the economic crisis emerges.

It should be noted that, issues on economic crisis expounded in *Capital* was in line with the idea of Marxist economic theory, that is, to expound "crisis in general sense" and "cycle of crisis". In *Capital*, Volume 3, Part III: The Law of the Tendency of the Rate of Profit to Fall, Marx connected its result with capitalist economic crisis, but it was not where Marx had a possible, systematic, and overall examination over the general conditions of the economic crisis in the capitalist mode of production. The discussion and interpretation of the law of the tendency of the rate of profit to fall, as well as the basic law of the possible economic crisis, could and must be conducted separately with complete independence. However, in this Chapter, Marx, for the first time, made a general discussion of the overall process of capitalist production. Abstract as it was though, he still made a necessary and systematic review of the inherent contradictions and regularity of capitalist mode of production at his previous analysis level. Hence, Marx's discussion of economic crisis at the overall level was complied with the normal development of logic, and that was also reasonable expansion of the theory In order to understand the form and the content regulation of the economic crisis, as well as to complete the task laid down before, Marx had studied out the logical end of capitalist development, that is, the concept of absolute overproduction or excessive accumulation of capital. But he soon realized that the actual surplus of capital and absolute overproduction were two different things. Overproduction was relative, and the further studies of it was part of the examination of the surface movement of capital, that is, the part "further expounding interest-bearing capital, credit, etc."Therefore, Marx's existing economic system was far from being expanded.

The Further Exploration of the Issues on Economic Crisis in the *Economics Manuscript* (1861-1863)

In the *Economics Manuscript* (1861-1863), when he criticized Ricardo's theory of accumulation, Marx spent a certain length of pages devoted to the economic crisis, which had never been seen in the *Economics Manuscript*

36 *Marx and Engels Collected Works*, 1st Chinese edition, Volume 26b, p.588. Beijing: People's Publishing House, 1973.

(1857-1858). In this part of the discourse, while he was criticizing Ricardo's and Say's points of views, Marx focused on expounding the results of studying the capitalist economic crisis. In comparison, in this manuscript, Marx expounded in detail two of the most abstract forms of the economic crisis and their relationship, and put forward a series of important points in the following two aspects.

First of all, Marx made a more in-depth exposition of the attribute of the economic crisis, and he regarded the economic crisis as an inevitable trend of opposite and unity acts of actual economic relations, and the capitalist economic crisis as the separation and independence from the unity in essential, which was the result of all kinds of contradictions fully developed and the inevitable companion of the capitalist system. He considered that the most abstract form of the economic crisis was the metamorphosis of commodities itself, that is, W-G and then G-W, in which the difficulty of converting the commodity into money, of selling it, only arising from the fact that the commodity must be turned into money but the money need not be immediately turned into commodity. This form contains the possibility of crisis, that is to say, "the possibility that elements which are correlated, which are inseparable, are separated and consequently are forcibly reunited, their coherence is violently asserted against their mutual independence. Crisis is nothing but the forcible assertion of the unity of phases of the production process which have become independent of each other."[37] For this understanding, Marx pointed out in describing the general circulation of commodity, "If, for example, purchase and sale—or the metamorphosis of commodities—represent the unity of two processes, or rather the movement of one process through two opposite phases, and thus essentially the unity of the two phases, the movement is essentially just as much the separation of these two phases and their becoming independent of each other. Since, however, they belong together, the independence of the two correlated aspects can only show itself forcibly, as a destructive process. It is just the crisis in which they assert their unity, the unity of the different aspects. The independence which these two linked and complimentary phases assume in relation to each other is forcibly destroyed. Thus the crisis manifests the unity of the two phases that have become independent of each other. There would be no crisis without this inner unity of factors that are apparently indifferent to each other."[38] In explaining the unity of the production process and the circulation process, he further pointed out that, "The mere (direct) production process of capital in itself, cannot add anything new in this context." "This can only emerge in the circulation process which is in itself also a process of reproduction."[39] "The circulation process as a whole or the reproduction process of capital as a whole is the unity of its production phase and its circulation phase, so that it comprises both of these processes or phases. Therein lays a further developed possibility

71

37 *Marx and Engels Collected Works*, 1st Chinese edition, Volume 26b, p. 581. Beijing: People's Publishing House, 1973
38 Ibid., p.571.
39 Ibid. pp. 585-586.

or abstract form of crisis... If they were only separate, without being a unity, then their unity could not be established by force and there could be no crisis. If they were only a unity without being separate, then no violent separation would be possible implying a crisis. Crisis is the forcible establishment of unity between elements that have become independent and the enforced separation from one another of elements which are essentially one."[40] From a historical point of view the development of Marxist economics, these conclusions basically laid the foundation of Marx's theory of economic crisis.

The unity of opposites in the social capital movement was also the unity of its quantity equalization and continuity. This is because the realization condition of the reproduction of the total social capital includes the relation of quantity equalization and proportion coordination, as well as the continuity relation of the process of the reproduction of the social capital. When the reproduction is running smoothly, the production phase and circulation phase maintain continuity, otherwise, they will be at an interrupted status. In the status of continuity, various stages of reproduction are in a unified state, otherwise, they will be at an interrupted status.

In the *Economics Manuscript* (1861-1863), Marx continued to criticize those bourgeois theories which attempted to attribute the root causes of the crisis to some occasional human factors, and at the same time, he exposed the nature of apologists. Say et al. always attributed the causes of the crisis to the rise in grain prices due to poor harvests, and explained the causes of the crisis as the devaluation of banknotes, devaluation of colonial commodities and excessive floating capital, against which Marx pointed out incisively, "The constant recurrence of crises has in fact reduced the rigmarole of Say and others to a phraseology which is now only used in times of prosperity but is cast aside in times of crises."[41] He believed the essence that Say et al. negation of the crisis of general overproduction was to defend the capitalist system. "Instead of investigating the nature of the conflicting elements which erupt in the catastrophe, the apologists content themselves with denying the catastrophe itself and insisting, in the face of their regular and periodic recurrence, that if production were carried on according to the textbooks, crises would never occur. Thus the apologetics consist in the falsification of the simplest economic relations, and particularly in clinging to the concept of unity in the face of contradiction."[42] Or, "Because there is this unity, there can be no crises."[43] Or, from another aspect, "The apologetic phrases used to deny crises are important in so far as they always prove the opposite of what they are meant to prove. In order to deny crises, they assert unity where there is conflict and contradiction. They are therefore important in so far as one can say they prove that there would be no crises if the contradictions which they have erased in their imagination, did

---

40   *Marx and Engels Collected Works*, Volume 26b, p.586.
41   Ibid., p. 570.
42   Ibid., pp. 570-571.
43   Ibid., p.571.

not exist in fact. But in reality crises exist because these contradictions exist. Every reason which they put forward against crisis is an exorcised contradiction, and, therefore, a real contradiction, which can cause crises. The desire to convince oneself of the non-existence of contradictions, is at the same time the expression of a pious wish that the contradictions, which are really present, should not exist."[44]

The use of analytical method of contradiction to analyze the nature of capitalist economic crisis is also an equalization approach in nature. What Marx said "The world trade crises must be regarded as the real concentration and forcible adjustment of all the contradictions of bourgeois economy" was also from the perspective of equalization relation of the social capital reproduction. Marx viewed the disproportion of social production as the imbalance of equalization relation of social capital reproduction. Because of the unity of opposites in the capital movement, on the one hand it was manifested as the equalization between the opposing sides, and on the other hand it is manifested as the continuity between various stages of the movement. Hence, from the perspective of the unity of the continuity in social capital movement and the equalization in reproduction, Marx explained the realization mechanism of economic crisis from possibility to actuality. Marx created the theory of social capital reproduction in the *Economics Manuscript* (1861-1863), in which he had already regarded the process of social reproduction as the process of dialectical development, the successful running of social capital as the satisfaction of a series of proportionality and equalization, and the movement of social capital as the process of dialectical development where equalization went towards imbalance, and then imbalance towards a new equalization. Therefore, as an inevitable trend, when he was criticizing Ricardo's metaphysical equalization, Marx pointed out that, "all equalisations are accidental and although the proportion of capital employed in individual spheres is equalised by a continuous process, the continuity of this process itself equally presupposes the constant disproportion which it has continuously, often violently, to even out." This violent equalization is economic crisis.

Second, Marx made some suggestive description of the logical sequence of the crisis converting from a general possibility to the actual possibility, and he further explored the intermediate link of the crisis converting from possibility to actuality. The possibility of crisis existing in the simple commodity economy, also existed in the developed commodity economy, but they are still the abstract forms of crisis, "These forms alone, therefore, do not explain why their crucial aspect becomes prominent and why the potential contradiction contained in them becomes a real contradiction."[45] This is because, "now the further development of the potential crisis has to be traced—the real crisis can only be deduced from the real movement of capitalist production, competition and credit—in so far as crisis arises out of the special aspects of capital which

---

44 *Marx and Engels Collected Works*, Volume 26b, p.593.
45 Ibid., p. 585.

are peculiar to it as capital, and not merely comprised in its existence as commodity and money."[46] Therefore, to examine the capitalist economic crisis, it must be based on the movement of both the unity of opposites in the capitalist commodity economy and capital relations. For example, "The mere (direct) production process of capital in itself, cannot add anything new in this context. In order to exist at all, its conditions are presupposed. The first section dealing with capital—the direct process of production—does not contribute to any new element of crisis. It does contain such an element, because the production process implies appropriation and hence production of surplus-value. But this cannot be shown when dealing with the production process itself, for the latter is not concerned with the realisation either of the reproduced value or of the surplus-value."[47]"This can only emerge in the circulation process which is in itself also a process of reproduction."[48] "The circulation process as a whole or the reproduction process of capital as a whole is the unity of its production phase and its circulation phase, so that it comprises both these processes and phases. Therein lies a further developed possibility or abstract form of crisis."[49] "The process of reproduction and the predisposition to crisis which is further developed in it, are therefore only partially described under this heading and require further elaboration in the chapter on 'Capital and Profit'."[50] Even so, the crisis is still manifested in its abstract form, because "the real crisis can only be deduced from the real movement of capitalist production, competition and credit."[51] Therefore, "There are, besides, a large number of other factors, conditions, possibilities of crises, which can only be examined when considering the concrete conditions, particularly the competition of capitals and credit."[52]

74

According to the tips above, we can roughly deduce the logical order unfolded in Marx's theory of economic crisis. That is: as a means of circulation and a means of payment, money contains the most abstract and the most general possibility; it has been further developed in the process of production and circulation, and through separation and independence of continuity, imbalance and violent recovery of equalized, it reveals the occurrence mechanism of crisis; in the unity of production process and circulation process, through the elaboration of the law of the tendency of the rate of profit to fall and its internal contradictions, it unfolds the inevitable trend for the capitalist economic crisis to occur and its causes. On such basis, with the theory gradually expounded from the abstract to the concrete, factors like competition, credit, stock system, wage labour, land ownership, national and foreign trade world market are gradually coming into range of examination. And after the examination of these factors, it has a last summative elaboration on crisis. At this point, the crisis has become

46 Ibid..
47 Ibid..
48 Ibid., p.586.
49 Ibid..
50 Ibid..
51 Ibid., p. 585.
52 Ibid., p. 609.

an actual world market crisis, and an integral concept. The process of expounding the above-mentioned logic of the development of capitalist economic crisis is, in Marx's words, "In world market crises, all the contradictions of bourgeois production erupt collectively; in particular crises (particular in their content and in extent) the eruptions are only sporadically, isolated and one-sided."[53] "The world trade crises must be regarded as the real concentration and forcible adjustment of all the contradictions of bourgeois economy. The individual factors, which are condensed in these crises, must therefore emerge and must be described in each sphere of the bourgeois economy and the further we advance in our examination of the latter, the more aspects of this conflict must be traced on the one hand, and on the other hand it must be shown that its more abstract forms are recurring and are contained in the more concrete forms."[54] Such sequence of theoretic development is the logical reflection of the six-book structure of Marxist economics.

III. Critique of the Classical Model

To Reveal the Nature of Crisis in Critique

It has been mentioned in earlier chapters that due to various reasons, Ricardo lacked his own insights into the issues of crisis. He was trying to go along with Say, James Mill, who believed that "there is no amount of capital which may not be employed in a country, because demand is only limited by production. No man produces, but with a view to consume or sell, and he never sells, but with an intention to purchase some other commodity, which may be immediately useful to him, or which may contribute to future production. By producing, then, he necessarily becomes either the consumer of his own goods, or the purchaser and consumer of the goods of some other person. It is not to be supposed that he should, for any length of time, be ill-informed of the commodities which he can most advantageously produce, to attain the object which he has in view, namely, the possession of other goods; and, therefore, it is not probable that he will continually" (the point in question here is not eternal life) "produce a commodity for which there is no demand."[55] Under the conditions of not being fully proven by the practice, the fundamental basis for Ricardo to accept the view of Say et al. was obviously just logical speculation, so in his lifetime he in fact did not understand the point of view that Say had made, how it was right, and how it was wrong.

The reason that Ricardo accepted Say's view was that he lacked a proper methodology of the capitalist mode of production, which was prominently manifested in the fact that he did not understand the relation between production in general and the capitalist production specifically, regarding the equalization between production and consumption as a common feature of all social

---

53 *Marx and Engels Collected Works*, Volume 26b, p.610.
54 Ibid., p.582.
55 *Marx and Engels Collected Works*, 1st Chinese edition, Volume 26b, p. 610.

production. Marx discovered this weak link in Ricardo's theory of crisis, using it as a breakthrough, and then he had a systematic and profound critique against it. With regard to the perception on production and consumption by Ricardo et al., Marx pointed out that the most prominent feature of the capitalist production was that the motive and purpose of production was "not the immediate use-value but the exchange-value and, in particular, the expansion of surplus-value".[56] "The criterion of this expansion of production is capital itself, the existing level of the conditions of production and the unlimited desire of the capitalists to enrich themselves and to enlarge their capital, but by no means consumption, which from the outset is inhibited, since the majority of the population, the working people, can only expand their consumption within very narrow limits, whereas the demand for labour, although it grows absolutely, decreases relatively, to the same extent as capitalism develops."[57] So in capitalism, the equalization between production and consumption was accidental. Although both had a trend of mandatory equalization regularly, its precondition was a recurring imbalance. Such inconsistency of capitalist production and consumption illustrated that the capitalist mode of production was not the general form of social production but rather one of its special forms. The error in this methodology is rooted in that "they regard bourgeois production either as a mode of production in which no distinction exists between purchase and sale—direct barter—or as social production, implying that the society, as if according to a plan, distributes its means of production and productive forces in the degree and measure which is required for the fulfillment of the various social needs, so that each sphere of production receives the quota of social capital required to satisfy the corresponding need. This fiction arises entirely from the inability to grasp the specific form of bourgeois production and this inability in turn arises from the obsession that bourgeois production is production as such."[58]

76

Ricardo's errors in methodology was also reflected in the fact that he did not regard capitalist production as a dialectical movement, and what he saw was only the unity of process rather than its opposites. It was because of this error, he asserted that the economic crisis of general overproduction would not occur in capitalism. Unlike Ricardo, in Marx's vision, the capitalist production was both a process of unity and of opposites. "If, for example, purchase and sale—or the metamorphosis of commodities—represent the unity of two processes, or rather the movement of one process through two opposite phases, and thus essentially the unity of the two phases, the movement is essentially just as much the separation of these two phases and their becoming independent of each other. Since, however, they belong together, the independence of the two correlated aspects can only show itself forcibly, as a destructive process. It is just the crisis in which they assert their unity, the unity of the different aspects.

---

56   Ibid., pp. 564-565.
57   Ibid., p.562.
58   Ibid., p.604.

The independence which these two linked and complimentary phases assume in relation to each other is forcibly destroyed. Thus the crisis manifests the unity of the two phases that have become independent of each other. There would be no crisis without this inner unity of factors that are apparently indifferent to each other."[59] Hence, if the process of capitalist production was not viewed in the unity of opposites, there was no way for us to understand the inevitability of the capitalist economic crisis. The critique of Ricardo's methodology was a very critical link. In this part, Marx regarded economic crisis as a trend of separation and unity of interrelated and complementary economic factors, as well as the process of its forcible recovery—forcible separation and independence by unity, and forcible recovery of unity by separation and independence. When economics ran normally, it meant that the intrinsic factors were in a state of unity or separation—if the essentially unified factors had not yet been independent and separated, or the essentially independent and separated factors had not yet been unified. On the contrary, when economics ran abnormally, "crisis is the forcible establishment of unity between elements that have become independent and the enforced separation from one another of elements which are essentially one." Of course, "If they were only separate, without being a unity, then their unity could not be established by force and there could be no crisis. If they were only a unity without being separate, then no violent separation would be possible implying a crisis."[60] This is the core of Marx's analytic model of the economic crisis, which at this point forms a fundamental difference between Marx's model and the classical model.

In the critique of Ricardo's opinion on the rate of profit to fall, Marx had further understanding of the nature of crisis. He found that the rate of profit to fall was the law of the development of productive forces in capitalism, which contained basic contradictions of capitalism internally. Through the law of the rate of profit to fall and the volume of profit to rise, the basic contradictions of capitalism developed to contradictions between production and realization of surplus value, between production expansion and value proliferation, as well as between excess population and excess capital. The intensification of these contradictions was reflected in the outbreak of a crisis. The crisis could only temporarily overcome these contradictions, but made them more profound and expansive. Thus, the conclusion is that "The crises are always but momentary and forcible solutions of the existing contradictions. They are violent eruptions which for a time restore the disturbed equilibrium."[61]

The Possibility and Reality of the Crisis

For John Stuart Mill et al. who tried to use the possibility of crisis contained in the morphological changes of commodity to illustrate the crisis, Marx did not believe that their situation was something even better. This is because those provisions instructing the possibility of crisis is far from being able to explain

59　*Marx and Engels Collected Works*, 1st Chinese edition, Volume 26b, p. 571.

60　Ibid., p.586.

61　*Capital*, Volume III, Beijing: The People's Publishing House, 1975, p.278.

the reality, and how it would have such contradictions in different stages of reproduction process, so that only through crisis and through a mandatory process their inner unity can be in action. Despite the fact that the separation of purchase and sale was manifested in a crisis, this was only the crisis in the form of elements. To describe crisis with its element form was the description of a crisis with its most abstract form, that is, to explain the crisis with a crisis. The process and realization mechanism of the crisis converting from possibility to reality, was another key link in the creation of Marx's theories of economic crisis. Whether the link can break through or not was related to whether we could separate the capitalist economic crisis and other types of economic crisis, and was related to whether we could reveal the profound root of capitalist economic crisis in the system.

The economic crisis was not a phenomenon unique to the capitalist society, but capitalism evolved the crisis of overproduction into an inevitable periodic phenomenon. What is the internal mechanism of this evolution? The classical model almost bypassed the entire intermediate link. Therefore, In his critique of Say and Ricardo's model, Marx not only needed to point out the inevitability of the capitalist crisis of general overproduction, he also needed to address factors such as conditions and relations, of which the crisis was converting from the most general possibility to reality.

It is also necessary to elaborate the possibility and reality of the crisis, because it relates to the determination of the starting and ending points of the theoretical system. The scope of the starting point should be the most general, simplest and most common one in the form of factor, which should contain the germ of all crises forms. It is not which other form, but the most general possibility of a crisis. Marx believed that the possibility of a crisis lied in the forms of two different functions of money: "It can therefore be said that the crisis in its first form is the metamorphosis of the commodity itself, the falling asunder of purchase and sale." "Its second form is the function of money as a means of payment, in which money has two different functions and figures in two different phases, divided from each other in time."[62] "The general possibility of crisis is given in the process of metamorphosis of capital itself, and in two ways: in so far as money functions as means of circulation, [the possibility of crisis lies in] the separation of purchase and sale; and in so far as money functions as means of payment, it has two different aspects, it acts as measure of value and as realisation of value. These two aspects [may] become separated."[63] With respect to the relation between the two forms of the possibility of crisis, Marx considered that the second form was more specific than the first one, and in case that there was not the second possibility, the first possibility might emerge. That is to say, in the absence of credit, and in the absence of money functions as means of payment, the crisis might occur. However, in the absence of the first possibility, namely in the absence of separation of purchase and sale, there could not be the

---

62   *Marx and Engels Collected Works*, 1st Chinese edition, Volume 26b, p. 582.
63   Ibid., p.587.

second possibility. So we say the crisis occurs due to the separation of buyers and sellers, and when money functions are as means of payment, the crisis will develop to money crisis. In this case, as long as the first form of crisis emerges, the second form of crisis will naturally emerge. Marx added, "if we say that the simple form of metamorphosis comprises the possibility of crisis, we only say that in this form itself lies the possibility of the rupture and separation of essentially complimentary phases."[64] "That is to say, the possibility that elements which are correlated, which are inseparable, are separated and consequently are forcibly reunited, their coherence is violently asserted against their mutual independence. Crisis is nothing but the forcible assertion of the unity of phases of the production process which have become independent of each other."[65] The potential crisis formed with the separation of purchase and sale is the most abstract form of crisis.

Of course, "[i]f purchase and sale do not get bogged down, and therefore do not require forcible adjustment—and, on the other hand, money as means of payment functions in such a way that claims are mutually settled, and thus the contradiction inherent in money as a means of payment is not realised—if therefore neither of these two abstract forms of crisis become real, no crisis exists. No crisis can exist unless sale and purchase are separated from one another and come into conflict, or the contradictions contained in money as a means of payment actually come into play; crisis, therefore, cannot exist without manifesting itself at the same time in its simple form, as the contradiction between sale and purchase and the contradiction of money as a means-of payment. But these are merely forms, general possibilities of crisis, and hence also forms, abstract forms, of real crisis. In them, the nature of crisis appears in its simplest forms, and, in so far as this form is itself the simplest content of crisis, in its simplest content. But the content is not yet substantiated. Simple circulation of money and even the circulation of money as a means of payment—and both come into being long before capitalist production, while there are no crises—are possible and actually take place without crises. These forms alone, therefore, do not explain why their crucial aspect becomes prominent and why the potential contradiction contained in them becomes a real contradiction."[66]

The scope of the ending point is world market crisis, which is the actual capitalist economic crisis. From the form of factors to the world market crisis, it was manifested in the expansion of the theoretical system as follows: With the elaboration of the capitalist economic relations expanded from the abstract to the concrete, "the more aspects of this conflict must be traced on the one hand, and on the other hand it must be shown that its more abstract forms are recurring and are contained in the more concrete forms." Or, in the world market crisis, "The individual factors, which are condensed in these crises, must therefore emerge and must be described in each sphere of the bourgeois

---

64 Ibid., p.580.
65 Ibid., p.581.
66 *Marx and Engels Collected Works*, 1st Chinese edition, Volume 26b, pp. 584-585.

economy."[67] So, the description of the crisis in the elementary form, namely the possibility of a crisis has been the starting point of the theoretical narrative.

Marx believed that the investigation of the potential crisis in a further developed form, namely the real crisis, could only be deduced from the real movement of capitalist production, competition and credit. The further development of the potential crisis can only be investigated thoroughly by the investigation of the special aspects of capital which are peculiar to it as capital, and not merely comprised in its existence as commodity and money. In the writings of Marxist economics architecture, this process was apparently after total circulation process, or total reproduction process of capital.

Deepening the Theory in Critique

Since he only experienced the capitalist economic crisis between 1800 and 1815, Ricardo did not find the generality of economic crisis in capitalism, but talked about its specificity. So, Ricardo and his disciples naturally interpreted capitalist economic crisis as an accidental phenomenon, and they explained the reasons for the crisis with the rise in grain prices caused by poor harvests, with the devaluation of bank notes, with the decline in the value of colonial goods, failing to look for the root of periodic crisis. Despite the real crisis emerging regularly and periodically, the perspective of Ricardo and his disciples was "in fact reduced ... to a phraseology which is now only used in times of prosperity but is cast aside in times of crises."[68] However, they still believed that they were correct.

The interpretation on the cause of crisis by Ricardo and his disciples was shown in the nature of antagonism, so was it on other issues. Ricardo and his subsequent James Wilson, John Fullarton, Wilhelm Roscheret et. al. had described the crisis with excess capital, while denying the overproduction of commodities. Marx wrote that "the entire phenomenon resolves into one of over-production of commodities which they admit under one name and deny under another."[69] He believed that the argument of using "excess capital" to replace "overproduction of commodities" was a subterfuge, and an unconscionable rash. On the contrary, the argument from "overproduction of commodities" to "excessive capital" was actually an improvement. Because it implied the recognition of commodity producers not as mere commodities owners, but as capitalists opposing each other.

The reason that Ricardo denied the general overproduction and did not recognize the possibility of crisis contained in the inherent contradictions in the commodity and money, was because he regarded the capitalist commodity production as simple barter, and in his words, "[p]roductions are always bought by productions, or by services; money is only the medium by which the exchange is effected... Too much of a particular commodity may be produced, of which

---

67   Ibid., p. 582.
68   Ibid., p. 570.
69   *Marx and Engels Collected Works*, 1st Chinese edition, Volume 26b, p.569.

there may be such a glut in the market, as not to repay the capital expended on it; but this cannot be the case with […] all commodities."[70] When Ricardo aired this view, the capitalist economic crisis had not yet exhibited strict periodicity, but had frequently occurred, with some regularity, expansion in range and strengthening in degree. When it came to an era in which Ricardo's disciples were active in the field of economics, the periodic world economic crisis had been more amply demonstrated. So, while they still insisted on the Ricardo's view, their antagonism was even more pronounced.

In the writings of discussion on the crisis by the classical economists, the following propositions are seen as the core of the antagonism:

"There cannot, then, be accumulated in a country any amount of capital which cannot be employed productively, until wages rise so high in consequence of the rise of necessaries, and so little consequently remains for the profits of stock, that the motive for accumulation ceases."

"There is no limit to demand—no limit to the employment of capital while it yields any profit, and that however abundant capital may become, there is no other adequate reason for a fall of profit but a rise of wages, and further it may be added, that the only adequate and permanent cause for the rise of wages is the increasing difficulty of providing food and necessaries for the increasing number of workmen."[71]

"It is, however, always a matter of choice in what way a capital shall he employed, and therefore there can never, for any length of time, be a surplus of any commodity; for if there were, it would fall below its natural price, and capital would be removed to some more profitable employment".

"Productions are always bought by productions, or by services; money is only the medium by which the exchange is affected."

"Too much of a particular commodity may be produced, of which there may be such a glut in the market, as not to repay the capital expended on it; but this cannot be the case with […] all commodities".

"Whether these increased productions, and consequent demand which they occasion, shall or shall not lower profits, depends solely on the rise of wages; and the rise of wages, excepting for a limited period, on the facility of producing the food and necessaries of the labourer".[72]

Marx believed that the basic characteristics of apologists was that "instead of investigating the nature of the conflicting elements which erupt in the catastrophe, the apologists content themselves with denying the catastrophe itself… [They] consist in the falsification of the simplest economic relations, and particularly in clinging to the concept of unity in the face of contradiction."Its

---

70   Ibid., p.570.
71   Ibid., p.567.
72   *Marx and Engels Collected Works*, 1st Chinese edition, Volume 26b, p.570.

essence lies in that "[]n order to prove that capitalist production cannot lead to general crises, all its conditions and distinct forms, all its principles and specific features—in short capitalist production itself—are denied. In fact it is demonstrated that if the capitalist mode of production had not developed in a specific way and become a unique form of social production, but were a mode of production dating back to the most rudimentary stages, then its peculiar contradictions and conflicts and hence also their eruption in crises would not exist."[73] That is to say, they only recognized the unity of opposing factors but in order to exclude their opposites.

Marx regarded crisis as a movement of the unity of opposites in economic relations. The normal functioning of the economy meant that both parties of contradictions was in the quantitative accumulation process, and in the process, those elements of unity in essence were gradually separated and independent, and once the separation and independence was beyond a certain barrier, the forcible unity would occur, the process of which was the crisis. This movement of contradictions in the unity of opposites was manifested in reality as that, it represented a movement through two opposing phases, and if this process was also a unity of the two phases, then the movement was also essentially the separation and independence of the two phases. "However, they belong together, the independence of the two correlated aspects can only show itself forcibly, as a destructive process. It is just the crisis in which they assert their unity, the unity of the different aspects. The independence which these two linked and complimentary phases assume in relation to each other is forcibly destroyed. Thus the crisis manifests the unity of the two phases that have become independent of each other. There would be no crisis without this inner unity of factors that are apparently indifferent to each other."[74]

"Productions are always bought by productions, or by services; money is only the medium by which the exchange is effected", which was proposed by Say and acknowledged by Ricardo. Marx believed that this view by Ricardo et al. was false because commodity became mere product, the exchange of commodities was transformed into mere barter of products, of simple use-values. This was a return not only to the time before capitalist production, but even to the time before there was simple commodity production; and the most complicated phenomenon of capitalist production—the world market crisis—was flatly denied, by denying the first condition of capitalist production, namely, that the product must be a commodity and therefore expressed itself as money and underwent the process of metamorphosis. Instead of speaking of wage-labour, the term "services" was used. This word again omitted the specific characteristic of wage-labour and of its use, and it disregarded the specific relationship through which money and commodities were transformed into capital. Therefore, the approach by Ricardo et al. to argue that it was impossible for the crisis to occur was that, "crises are thus reasoned out of existence

---

73   Ibid., p.571.
74   Ibid., p.571.

here by forgetting or denying the first elements of capitalist production: the existence of the product as a commodity, the duplication of the commodity in commodity and money, the consequent separation which takes place in the exchange of commodities and finally the relation of money or commodities to wage-labour."[75]

As the continuation of methodological critique, Marx had practical critique of the economic crisis theory, the object of which was still the famous words by Ricardo: "No man produces, but with a view to consume or sell, and he never sells, but with an intention to purchase some other commodity, which may be immediately useful to him, or which may contribute to future production. By producing, then, he necessarily becomes either the consumer of his own goods, or the purchaser and consumer of the goods of some other person. It is not to be supposed that he should, for any length of time, be ill-informed of the commodities which he can most advantageously produce, to attain the object which he has in view, namely, the possession of other goods; and, therefore, it is not probable that he will continually produce a commodity for which there is no demand."[76]

Marx believed that Ricardo's views were contrary to the following facts, namely: (1) No capitalist produces in order to consume his product. (2) A man who has produced, does not have the choice of selling or not selling. He must sell. (3) In capitalist production revenue, appears as the result and not as the determining purpose. Everyone sells first of all in order to sell, that is to say, in order to transform commodities into money. (4) The immediate purpose of capitalist production is not "the possession of other goods", but the appropriation of value, of money, of abstract wealth. It seems to Marx that, contrary to such simple facts, "this is the childish babble of a Say, but it is not worthy of Ricardo".[77]

The reason for Ricardo to deny the possibility of a general glut in the market was that, "[t]oo much of a particular commodity may be produced, of which there may be such a glut in the market, as not to repay the capital expended on it; but this cannot be the case with respect to all commodities; the demand for corn is limited by the mouths which are to eat it, for shoes and coats by the persons who are to wear them; but through a community, or a part of a community, may have as much corn, and as many hats and shoes, as it is able or may wish to consume, the same cannot be said of every commodity produced by nature or by art. Some would consume more wine, if they had the ability to procure it. Others having enough of wine, would wish to increase the quantity or improve the quality of their furniture. Others might wish to ornament their grounds, or to enlarge their houses. The wish to do all or some of these is implanted in every man's breast; nothing is required but the means, and nothing can afford the means, but an increase of production"[78].

75 *Marx and Engels Collected Works*, 1st Chinese edition, Volume 26b, p.572.
76 Ibid., p.563.
77 Ibid., p. 573.
78 David Ricardo, *On The Principles of Political Economy and Taxation*; Chapter 21.

Marx believed that the recognition of a glut in the market formed only by particular commodities, and not by all kinds of commodities, is a poor way out. In the first place, if we consider only the nature of the commodity, there is nothing to prevent all commodities from being superabundant on the market, and therefore all falling below their price. We are here only concerned with the factor of crisis. That is all commodities, apart from money [may be superabundant]. [The proposition] the commodity must be converted into money, only means that: all commodities must do so. And just as the difficulty of undergoing this metamorphosis exists for an individual commodity, so it can exist for all commodities. The general nature of the metamorphosis of commodities—which includes the separation of purchase and sale just as it does their unity—instead of excluding the possibility of a general glut, on the contrary, contains the possibility of a general glut. Ricardo's and similar types of reasoning are moreover based not only on the relation of purchase and sale, but also on that of demand and supply, which we have to examine only when considering the competition of capitals. As Mill says purchase is sale etc., therefore demand is supply and supply is demand. But they also fall apart and can become independent of each other. At a given moment, the supply of all commodities can be greater than the demand for all commodities, since the demand for the general commodity, money, exchange-value, is greater than the demand for all particular commodities, in other words the motive to turn the commodity into money, to realise its exchange-value, prevails over the motive to transform the commodity again into use-value.

84

If the relation of demand and supply is taken in a wider and more concrete sense, then it comprises the relation of production and consumption as well. Here again, the unity of these two phases, which does exist and which forcibly asserts itself during the crisis, must be seen as opposed to the separation and antagonism of these two phases, separation and antagonism which exist just as much, and are moreover typical of bourgeois production.

With regard to the contradiction between partial and universal over-production, in so far as the existence of the former is affirmed in order to evade the latter, the following observation may be made: Firstly: Crises are usually preceded by a general inflation in prices of all articles of capitalist production. All of them therefore participate in the subsequent crash and at their former prices they cause a glut in the market. The market can absorb a larger volume of commodities at falling prices, at prices which have fallen below their cost-prices, than it could absorb at their former prices. The excess of commodities is always relative; in other words it is an excess at particular prices. The prices at which the commodities are then absorbed are ruinous for the producer or merchant. Secondly: For a crisis (and therefore also for over-production) to be general, it suffices for it to affect the principal commercial goods.[79]

---

79   See *Marx and Engels Collected Works*, 1st Chinese edition, Volume 26b, pp.575-577.

The reason Ricardo denied the universal overproduction is that he did not understand the demand in capitalism is the demand backed by ability to pay. Overproduction in capitalism is only concerned with demand backed by the ability to pay, other than absolute demand or desire to possess goods. In times of over-production, the very commodities which glutted the market were consumer goods, of which were in need by their producers. Therefore, it could not be said that these commodities glutted the market because no one was in want of them, but because the mass of the producers remained to be tied to the average level of needs. "If over-production could only occur when all the members of a nation had satisfied even their most urgent needs, there could never, in the history of bourgeois society up to now, have been a state of general over-production or even of partial over-production."Of course, it could not be said here that they should produce things in order to obtain them, for they had produced them and yet they had not got them. Nor could it be said that a particular commodity glutted the market, because no one was in want of it. "If, therefore, it is even impossible to explain that partial over-production arises because the demand for the commodities that glut the market has been more than satisfied, it is quite impossible to explain away universal over-production by declaring that needs, unsatisfied needs, exist for many of the commodities which are on the market."[80] Marx once pointed out on this issue that: "The capitalist system does not know any other modes of consumption than effective ones, except that of sub forma pauperis or of the swindler. Those commodities are unsalable means only that no effective purchasers have been found for them, i.e. consumers (since commodities are bought in the final analysis for productive or individual consumption)."[81] Therefore, if we raised the wages of the working class, and the working class got a larger portion of their products, could the crisis be avoided? Marx believed that this was impossible, because "crises are always prepared by precisely a period in which wages rise generally and the working-class actually gets a larger share of that part of the annual product which is intended for consumption."[82] However, the crisis has not been removed. "It appears, then, that capitalist production comprises conditions independent of good or bad will, conditions which permit the working-class to enjoy that relative prosperity only momentarily, and at that always only as the harbinger of a coming crisis."[83]

Sismondi thought that—basing himself on Adam Smith's dogmatic view— in the capitalist society, because the value of goods was decomposed into three types of income, that is, wages, profits and rents, then the so-called "to buy commodity with commodity" actually meant "to buy commodity with income", and "production subject to consumption" was actually "the scale of production subject to the scale of social income". This was because "only increase in consumption can determine the expansion of reproduction, while the consumption

80 *Marx and Engels Collected Works*, 1st Chinese edition, Volume 26b, p.578.
81 *Capital*, Volume III, Beijing: The People's Publishing House, 1975, p.456.
82 *Capital*, Volume III, p.457. Beijing: The People's Publishing House, 1975.
83 Ibid., p.457.

can only be adjusted based on the income of the consumers".[84] Sismondi had obtained a completely different conclusion compared to Say, Mill, Ricardo et al. On the contrary, Sismondi believed that income determined production or in other words production determined demand, "The total amount of annual income must be used to be exchanged with the total amount of annual production,...... if the total amount of annual income cannot buy the total annual product, then part of the products will not be sold, and have to be piled up in the producers' warehouses, backlogging the capital of producers, and even causing the production activity to a standstill."[85] The product was again purchased by income, and when production exceeded consumption or the income exceeded the product, the conflict between production and consumption would inevitably lead to economic crisis. This conclusion by Sismondi was undoubtedly correct, but the theoretical basis from which the conclusions were derived was wrong. What was wrong was that he established his own underconsumption theory based on "Adam Smith's dogma", following Smith to attribute the production of social products as a whole to a personal consumption. Just like Adam Smith, Sismondi also attributed the production of social products as a whole to the production of personal consumption, thus he ignored an extremely important channel for consumption—the consumption of means of production by the society for producing means of production and consumer goods, and thereby artificially reduced, to a great extent, the existing, regular and increasing demand for national products and its important parts.

86

Sismondi further considered that, in capitalism, the contradictions between production and consumption were manifested as the contradictions between unlimited expansion of production and underconsumption caused by insufficient income. In terms of unlimited expansion of production, in the capitalist system, producers faced a vast market in which they could not grasp its demand, because of invention and adoption of new technologies, large machinery manufacturing, increasingly intensified corporate and capital, especially increasingly contentious free competition with blind expansion of production, it formed a situation of producing for the sake of producing. For underconsumption that is caused by insufficient income, Sismondi argued that in an unfair distribution system in capitalism, the expansion of production could not increase the social income correspondingly but reduce it. This was firstly shown in the declining revenues of the majority working people with nothing, followed by the bankruptcy of small producers caused by the polarization, and consequently the reduction in the income of small producers.

Sismondi believed that unlimited expansion of capitalist production and the corresponding reduction in income and consumption, was shown as the shrinking domestic market. To remedy it, the need to seek foreign markets was increasing, resulting in the competition on the world market, and consequently the world market was getting smaller and smaller. Therefore, whether it was

---

84 Sismondi, *New Principles of Political Economy*, Beijing: The Commercial Press, 1977, p.62.
85 Ibid., p.76.

domestic or foreign market, it was correspondingly reduced, and the unsalable capitalist commodity became an insurmountable difficulty. The contradiction of underconsumption caused by expansion in production and insufficient income made the economic crisis inevitable. Sismondi's views were clearly correct, because overproduction and underconsumption were the endogenous economic contradictions within the capitalist society, nature, and in the institutional structure where the capitalist economy ran, there was naturally insufficient aggregate demand, because there was not enough endogenous force to pull or drive itself to generate sufficient aggregate demand so as to solve the problem of excessive production capacity. While capital could select international markets, expanding foreign markets through the early colonial manner or by the later encouragement of direct foreign investment and expansion of exports, this would only lead to conflicts between production and the market within a larger scope, instead of solving the problem of capitalist accumulation mechanism fundamentally. Once the overproduction was formed worldwide, the world market crisis would come.

Projecting himself into the petty-bourgeois' situation, Sismondi revealed the basic contradictions of capitalism, which was his most valuable contribution. Marx gave him a fair and reasonable assessment, saying that Sismondi was profoundly conscious of the contradictions in capitalist production; "he is aware that, on the one hand, its forms—its production relations—stimulate unrestrained development of the productive forces and of wealth; and that, on the other hand, these relations are conditional, that their contradictions of use-value and exchange-value, commodity and money, purchase and sale, production and consumption, capital and wage-labour, etc., assume ever greater dimensions as productive power develops. He is particularly aware of the fundamental contradiction: on the one hand, unrestricted development of the productive forces and increase of wealth which, at the same time, consists of commodities and must be turned into cash; on the other hand, the system is based on the fact that the mass of producers is restricted to the necessaries. Hence, according to Sismondi, crises are not accidental, as Ricardo maintains, but essential outbreaks—occurring on a large scale and at definite periods—of the immanent contradictions. He wavers constantly: should the State curb the productive forces to make them adequate to the production relations, or should the production relations be made adequate to the productive forces? He often retreats into the past, becomes a *laudatory temporis acti* (praiser of time past), or he seeks to exorcise the contradictions by a different adjustment of revenue in relation to capital, or of distribution in relation to production, not realising that the relations of distribution are only the relations of production seen from a different aspect. He forcefully criticizes the contradictions of bourgeois production but does not understand them, and consequently does not understand the process whereby they can be resolved. However, at the bottom of his argument is indeed the inkling that new forms of the appropriation of wealth must correspond to productive forces and the material and social conditions for the production of wealth which have developed within capitalist society; that the bourgeois forms are only transitory and contradictory forms, in which wealth attains only an antithetical existence and appears everywhere simultaneously as its opposite. It is wealth which always has poverty as its prerequisite and only develops by developing poverty as well."[86]

Marx believes that underconsumption was only the "final cause" of crisis, but not the direct cause. Because the history of periodic crises was less than a hundred years and underconsumption of the mass had already existed since the antagonisms occurred between the exploiting class and the exploited class. Before the emergence of industrial capitalism, exploitation almost exclusively served for the purpose of consumption, and what was blackmailed from workers had been completely squandered. Let alone of the overproduction generated by social causes. In a capitalist society, it was completely a different case. Capitalist society was built on the basis of the advanced commodity production, and production was directly for the market. In a free competition, those who won were producers of commodities of the lowest and cheapest price in the market. Here, the enhancement of technology and improvement of machines had decisive significance.

IV. Conclusions

The original form of Marxist analytic model of crisis theory is on the contradictory motion of productive forces and production relations, and the cause of the crisis is the conflict between the unlimited development trend of productive forces and the relatively small market. Solutions to the crisis are, forcible destruction of massive productive forces, by the conquest of new markets, and by the more thorough exploitation of the old ones, and such solutions are only ones to prepare for a more comprehensive and more violent crisis.

Later Marx gradually explored the relations of production as the fetters to the development of productive forces ; namely barrier of the relations of production is the material basis for periodic economic crises; the possibility of the economic crisis and the conditions to transform the crises into reality; the risk factors in the imbalance of various equalized relations and in interruption of the continuous relations; accumulation, organic composition of capital to increase, rate of profit to fall, expansion of contradictions, and the root cause of the capitalist economic crisis; the impact of competition, credit, stock system on the crisis. On this basis, Marx revealed the nature of the economic crisis—the capitalist economic crisis is the performance of all contradictions of bourgeois economy, it is the result of all contractions of capitalism being developed, and it is the complex of reality and the forcible adjustment of all the contradictions of the bourgeois economic relations.

---

86 *Marx and Engels Collected Works*, 1st Chinese edition, Volume 26c, p. 55.

Marx regarded the capitalist economic crisis as a movement of the unity of opposites in economic relations. The normal operation of the economy meant that its inner factors were at a unified status and once these factors were separated from and independent of each other, the development trend was bound to make these elements tend to be reunified, the process of which was called crisis. This contradictory movement process of the unity of opposites was shown as a process of movement through two opposite phases, and if the process was essentially the unity of the two phases, the movement was essentially just as much the separation of these two phases and being independent of each other. Since, however, they belonged together, "the independence of the two correlated aspects can only show itself forcibly, as a destructive process. It is just the crisis in which these correlated two aspects assert their unity, the unity of the different aspects. The independence which these two linked and complimentary phases assume in relation to each other is forcibly destroyed. Thus the crisis manifests the unity of the two phases that have become independent of each other. There would be no crisis without this inner unity of factors that are apparently indifferent to each other."[87]

By the critique of Say-Ricardo's model, Marx elaborated the possibility of the economic crisis, and revealed that the developed economies, large machinery manufacturing were both conditions of the capitalist mode of production and the conditions of the capitalist economic crisis. By the critique of Sismondi's model, he absorbed the scientific factors of his model in practical conditions, namely: On the one hand there was a trend of infinite expansion of capitalist production, and on the other hand the share of the total working masses continued to decline in the total income of the society, as well as the scientific factor in Sismondi's "conclusions", namely: the capitalist economic crisis of overproduction was inevitable.

Of course, by contrast with the Marxist theory of crisis, the non-scientific factors of the classical economics models are shown clearly. The error of Say-Ricardo's model is to regard "production in general" as capitalist production, the production of capitalist commodity as barter, and thus make a wrong assumption and derive a wrong equilibrium relation, and finally arrive at the wrong conclusions. Sismondi's model has also made the same mistake of a wrong assumption. Based on Adam Smith's dogma, Sismondi decomposed the value of goods into three types of income, that is, wages, profits and rents, and he proposed incorrect assumptions that products were bought with income and production was subject to consumption. Although the conclusions he deduced had scientific factors, there were also serious deficiencies that capitalist crisis would occur continuously, only small commodity producers and foreign non-capitalist market could be the fundamental solutions to save capitalism. In Marx's vision, elements of Malthus' model were almost dross, and there was nothing to be learned from.

---

87 *Marx and Engels Collected Works*, Volume 26 (II), Beijing, People's Publishing House, 1973, p. 571.

CHAPTER]|[]|[

Structure, Content and Features of Marx's Analytic Model of the Economic Crisis

I. Introduction

Marx does not have specific distinct texts which elaborated on the economic crisis issues, which is one reason why his ideas on the crisis has become the subject of the controversial debate and attention. In the field of economics, whether from Marxist or non-Marxist economists, Marx's theories of the crisis attract abundant attention. Researchers have offered different opinions, and a variety of viewpoints. Among them, relatively typical ones include: 1) Some argue that Marx did not have a systematic and comprehensive crisis theory, instead he only wrote a few unsystematic ideas and elaborations in *Capital*, *Theories of Surplus Value*, and in his relevant letters. 2) Others argue that Marx provided a complete, self-contained theory, which not only included the reason, performance, results and the trends in the formation of the economic crisis, but also includes the abstract possibility, actual possibility, necessity, periodicity, essence and significance of the formation of the crisis, besides he provided critiques of a variety of flawed theories on economic crisis. However, these theories were not included in a specific distinct text but were dispersed in *Capital*, *Theories of Surplus Value* and his relevant letters, "if all his important arguments and ideas are studied in an integrated manner, the crisis theory will show its systemacity and integrity.[1] 3) Some scholars argue that Marx obviously established his systematic crisis theory, but it is only the general theory of economic crisis, in the most abstract sense. Compared to his world market crisis theory, his economic crisis theory was far from being elevated to a concrete level, meaning Marx's theory of crisis needs to be further developed and refined.[2] To what extent do these views reflect the true status of Marx's crisis theory is a difficult question to answer from a single point of view. For example, if it is argued that Marx's theory only consisted of a few scattered fragments of ideas and discussions, it would mean that he was not able to offer a complete explanation on the capitalist economic crisis. That said, his descendants could not further develop his ideas and complete them coherently unless his theories were well developed. If Marx's views and ideas on crisis that are scattered in *Capital*, *Theories of Surplus Value*, and in his relevant letters are assembled ably, it may seem to form a "complete system", but it is quite hard to explain why Marx expounded his crisis theory in the last part of his entire theoretical system in economics, and it is also quite difficult to explain the relation between his ideas and the crisis theory expounded in the last part, as well as to explain what the difference it has in the content and the logical structure within the whole system. If Marx only had the general theory of crisis, then it could only offer a general explanation on crisis, meaning it has a general rather than a specific significance, and cannot explain a specific crisis. The advocates of this third thesis offer several similar other views in which they explicitly or implicitly point that that Marx's theory of crisis is an imperfect system, its logical structure needs to be fully expounded, meaning it needs to be further developed and improved.

From the existing literature, I can say that there is one universal perspective deficit problem in how the academic community understands Marxist crisis theory, and in outlining its model. Whether in the model outlined by Hilferding, or in the textbooks[3], or models proposed by other Marxist economists, all models have somehow failed to wholly absorb the key ideas discussed in Marx's texts related to economic crisis, that is, the capitalist economic crisis is the performance of all contradictions of bourgeois economy, it is the result of all contradictions of capitalism being developed, they are part of a complex chain of causation, and the forcible adjustment of all contradictions inherent in bourgeois economic relations.

---

1   Hu Daiguang, Wei Xun, *Contemporary Western Scholars' Study of Marx's 'Capital'*, Beijing: The Economic Press of China. 1990, , pp.327-328.
2   See Tang Zaixin, *Exploration of the Sequel of Marx Leading to Capital*, Beijing: China Financial Publishing House, pp. 536-568.
3   Textbooks here refer to teaching materials used by universities and party schools in socialist countries.

The capitalist economic crisis is a movement of unity of opposites in an economic relation. The normal operation of the economy means that its inner elements are in a unified state, and once these elements dispel and get separated and become independent of each other, the development trend is to lead these elements to reunification, the process of reunification (unity)is called crisis. This contradictory movement process between opposition and unity is demonstrated as the movement of one single process appearing as two opposite phases. Marx writes: "...represent the unity of two processes, or rather the movement of one process through two opposite phases, and thus essentially the unity of the two phases the movement is essentially just as much the separation of these two phases and their becoming independent of each other. Since, however, they belong together, the independence of the two correlated aspects can only show itself forcibly, as a destructive process. It is just the crisis in which they assert their unity, the unity of the different aspects. The independence which these two linked and complimentary phases assume in relation to each other is forcibly destroyed. Thus the crisis manifests the unity of the two phases that have become independent of each other. There would be no crisis without this inner unity of factors that are apparently indifferent to each other."[4]"All equalisations are accidental and although the proportion of capital employed in individual spheres is equalised by a continuous process, the continuity of this process itself equally presupposes the constant disproportion which it has continuously, often violently, to even out."[5] Due to the above incomplete understanding, it becomes hard to have a comprehensive and scientific inquiry on Marx's analytical model. Hence, we need to have a complete and accurate understanding of Marx's theory of crisis, and on the basis, draw a complete and accurate Marxist analytical model of economic crisis, so as to develop and improve Marx's theory of crisis.

However, the premise of this task is to first figure out the methodology of Marx's crisis theory, and based on it as a tool, analyze the content, structure and characteristics of the theory. Only on such basis and properly positioning it in his entire theoretical system in economics, can we hypothesize on the content, structure and characteristics it should have.

II. The Methodological Features of Marxist Crisis Theory

Marx regarded crisis as the unity of the two phases that had become independent of each other, and regarded the capitalist economic crisis as the real concentration and forcible adjustment of all the contradictions of bourgeois economy, the result of all the contradictions being fully expounded. This is an overview of the nature of crisis, or even the capitalist economy from

---

4   *Marx and Engels Collected Works*, Volume 26 (II), Beijing, People's Publishing House, 1973, p.571.
5   Ibid., p.562.

a methodological point of view. If Marx's theory of crisis is not approached from this perspective, it is impossible for us to truly understand and master the structure, content and characteristics of this theory. Denial and distortion of Marx's crisis theory by those kinds of arguments which are related to the methodological defect usually ignore the essence of Marx's crisis theory. We can argue from a methodological point of view that the object of study of Marxist economics is the capitalist relations of production, and with the development of the theoretical system where it comes back from the abstract to the concrete, contradictions unfold step by step. When the system is fully back from the abstract to the concrete, the various contradictions will fully expound. At this time, what the theoretical work needs to do is to make a final and total generalization. Therefore, in understanding Marx's theory of crisis from a methodological point of view, it tends to come to this conclusion: The entire theoretical system in Marxist economics works which expound on the crisis theory and throughout the unfolding of its system is carried out together with the development of the theory.

To understand the methodology of Marxist economics works by examining the Capital is undoubtedly important, but there are limitations of it as well. According to Marx's writing program raised in the late 1850s and early 1860s, what *Capital* has described is only "Capital in General", which is only a part of research of capital in the "six-book structure". Therefore, to understand the methodology of Marxist economics within the framework of the "six-books structure" is the way which can accord with Marx's intent.

Marx's analysis of capitalist economic relations is unfolded in such a logical order, from the abstract to the concrete, from essence to phenomenon, from simplicity to complexity, from the general to the particular and then to the individual. In adaption of these analytical methods, he designed his own writings in economics as a system composed of six books. Namely: "Capital", "Landed Property", "Wage Labour"; "the State", "International Trade", "World Market." The first book above "Capital" is divided into four parts, namely capital in general, competition, credit, and share capital. Among these four parts, "Capital in General" consists of the following chapters: 1. Commodity, 2. Money or simple circulation, 3. Capital. The "Capital" section also includes three parts: 1) The Process of Production of Capital, 2) The Process of Circulation of Capital, 3) The Process of Capitalist Production as a Whole, or Capital and Profits. The six-books structure includes a way (Ger. Weise) which marches from the abstract to the concrete and to an highly complete scientific system. Here, the starting point of analysis is capital, "the overarching economic rights in bourgeois society" and before it, this abstract general relations between commodity and money are investigated in the introduction part. The first three volumes with "Capital" as the core analyzes the internal structure of capitalist society, and reveals the relationship among the three social classes, which lay the foundation for investigating the state in the fourth volume. The fourth volume aimed the generalization of studying the bourgeoisie society at the single state level, namely, to fully and comprehensively examine the domestic relations of capitalist production. The last two volumes are a transition from domestic to international relations of production, and finally rise to the world market, the specific bearer of capitalist production with the highest encompassing which gives a comprehensive description of how the actual production in the capitalist world is carried out in the capitalist relations and its historical movement. In these six books, Marx made the outlining and integration of issues on crisis in the last book. The reason for this arrangement is that: It seems to Marx that, the capitalist economic crisis is the performance of all contradictions of bourgeois economy, it is the result of all contractions of capitalism being developed, and it is the complex of reality and the mandatory balance of all contradictions of the bourgeois economic relations. And all of this can only be fully demonstrated in the world market. "The world trade crises must be regarded as the real concentration and forcible adjustment of all the contradictions of bourgeois economy."[6] "In world market crises, all the contradictions of bourgeois production erupt collectively; in particular crises (particular in their content and in extent) the eruptions are only sporadic, isolated and one-sided."[7]

Due to various reasons, Marx failed to complete his ambitious writing project on economics, and *Capital*, the economics works he actually completed is roughly equivalent to the scope and the content of "capital in general". This means that Marx in fact also failed to have a comprehensive integration and summarization of the crisis in the stage that all the contradictions of capitalism are fully expounded. The elaboration on crisis theory in *Capital* is inadequate or incomplete, and it is still at an unfinished stage. There are, besides, a large number of other factors, conditions, possibilities of crises, which can only be examined when considering the concrete conditions.[8] However, Marx, after all, has completed the basic theoretical narrative of his writings on economics, so Marx's theory of the economic crisis and the economy writings which have been completed are compatible in logical hierarchy, and are also manifested to a certain degree.

In Marx's economic system, the crisis is both in an abstract and a specific category, and in a specific category in a general sense. It has both very abstract provisions and specific contents, and in the capitalist mode of production, the economic crisis is manifested as the separation, division and independence of two aspects of opposition and unity within the economic relations, and it is manifested as forcible unity of the two. So, the contradictions of capitalist economic relations, from essence to appearance, from the abstract to the concrete, from the simple to the complex, are factors, conditions and possibilities of the existence of a crisis. In this sense, the analysis of every contradiction of bourgeois economics is to analyze the regularity that forms a crisis and determines the manifestations of a crisis; all Marx's theories of the capitalist economy are in fact the crisis theory.

---

6 *Marx and Engels Collected Works*, 1st Chinese edition ,Volume 26 (II), p. 582.
7 Ibid., p.610.
8 See *Marx and Engels Collected Works*, 1st Chinese edition, Volume 26 (II), p.609.

Features of Marx's theory of economic crisis and methods of Marxist economics are linked. The most basic and general approach of Marxist economic theory is dialectical materialism, but it is also specifically expressed in two categories: One is how it is manifested; such as the unity of logic and history, from the abstract to the concrete, systematic approaches, etc. The other one is in what it is manifested; such as contradictory analysis, equilibrium analysis, static and dynamic analysis, empirical and normative analysis, etc. The approach of how it is manifested provides the logical sequence and development trend of the crisis theory; the approach of in what it is manifested provides how it is developed and what the realization conditions are in theory of economic crisis.

Based on the critique of the methodology of bourgeois political economy, Marx determines that, only the approach "from the concrete to the abstract" is how the political economy should be described scientifically. Following this approach, he built the logical structure system of his own economic writings at different levels. For example, in terms of the whole economics works, he arranged a "six-book structure" system; in *Capital*, he arranged "The Process of Production of Capital", "The Process of Circulation of Capital", and the unity of the two;"The Process of Capitalist Production as a Whole". Thus, Marx's economics works are, actually an organic writing as a whole, on the basis of the approach from the abstract to the concrete, in overall built on a series of writings at different levels. Only through writing as a whole, can the overall capitalist economic relations be reproduced completely and accurately in the process of thinking. The reproduction process, as Marx described: "The individual factors, which are condensed in these crises, must therefore emerge and must be described in each sphere of the bourgeois economy and the further we advance in our examination of the latter, the more aspects of this conflict must be traced on the one hand, and on the other hand it must be shown that its more abstract forms are recurring and are contained in the more concrete forms."[9]

Marx regarded crisis as a movement of the unity of opposites in economic relations. The normal functioning of the economy meant that both parties of contradictions were in the quantitative accumulation process, and in the process, those factors of unity in essence were gradually separated and independent, and once the separation and independence was beyond a certain barrier, the forcible unity would occur, the process of which was called crisis. This movement of contradictions in the unity of opposites was manifested in reality was that, it represented a movement through two opposing phases, and if this process was also a unity of the two phases, then the movement was also essentially the separation and independence of the two phases. "However, they belong together, the independence of the two correlated aspects can only show itself forcibly, as a destructive process. It is just the crisis in which they assert their unity, the unity of the different aspects. The independence which these two linked and complimentary phases assume in relation to each other is forcibly destroyed. Thus the crisis manifests the unity of the two phases that have

---

9 *Marx and Engels Collected Works*, 1st Chinese edition, Volume 26 (II), p.582.

become independent of each other. There would be no crisis without this inner unity of factors that are apparently indifferent to each other."[10] Therefore, in this sense, factors of all the contradictions of the capitalist economic relations are factors of the economic crisis, the accumulation of contradictions is the accumulation of crisis, the further development of contradictions is the development of crisis, and the analysis of contradictions is the analysis of crisis.

However, there are significant differences between contradictions and crisis, and the contradiction that exists and develops in the unity of opposites is constantly in the process of quantitative and qualitative changes. Contradictions in quantitative changes contain only the potential possibilities of a crisis, but contradictions in qualitative changes will turn the potential possibilities of a crisis into reality. Therefore, the economic crisis is the result of both the development of contradictions, and basic form of solution to contradictions. In other words, the development of capitalist contradictions contains factors that overcome itself, and when contradictions are developing to a stage where they must be resolved by forcible adjustment, the economic crisis breaks out. Therefore, the economic crisis can also be seen as a way of sharpening the contradictions of capitalism, or the concentrated manifestation of the contradictions of capitalism. The development of crisis is the cause, and the breakout of crisis is the result. This causation determines the theory to be expressed in a particular way, that is, the main line of theoretical analysis is the development of contradictions, and only when contradictions are developing at a stage of gradual unfolding, the sequence manifested in the contradiction itself is the possibility, cause and essence of the intensification of contradictions, as well as the performance in different levels of contradictions being unfolded.

With regard to Marx's theory of economic crisis later scholars summarize it as follows: 1) Each crisis is derived from the insurmountable contradictions of capitalist accumulation; 2) Overcoming each crisis can only take ways that will inevitably lead to a new, routinely more serious crisis; 3) When capitalism develops to a certain stage, the crisis on a world scale must necessarily be repeated at every regular interval.[11]

III. Crisis Theories in *Capital*

The law of the unity of opposites is expressed in the capitalist economy as: Factors with inner unity are in the process of periodical movement, separation, independence and forcible unity. Overproduction and economic crisis is the development trend and internal regulatory mechanism of the capitalist economy. Overproduction is the performance of economic imbalance, and the economic crisis is the coercive power to form a new equilibrium. We can see these relations from the lines of Marx's crisis theory.

---

10   Ibid., p.571.
11   See Stanislaw Mendelson, *Theory and History of the Economic Crisis and its Cycle*, Beijing: Joint Publishing, p.184

In the existing Marx's analytic models of economic crisis, factors of the model exist in such relations and contradictions in *Capital*: There might be the equalization of disproportionality; there might be the disproportionality of equalization; there might be the continuity relation of factors of independence and separation; there might be continuity status of independent factors and separated relations. The specific forms of the internal contradictions of the law of the rate of profit to fall being fully expounded – contradictions between production and realization of surplus value, between production expansion and value self-expansion, as well as between excess population and excess capital, etc. *Capital* was one of Marx's mature writings, but because it only expounded "capital in general", the crisis theory involved was only relatively abstract theory, which did not include all the contents of Marx's crisis theory. This was reflected in the determination for the nature of the crisis, as well as in the methodology of Marx's crisis theory. Some tips scattered in Marx's writings were also a very strong evidence. For example, the kind of crisis that arise from "the disproportion in the distribution of social labour between the individual spheres of production", "can only be dealt with in connection with the competition of capitals."[12] Examining the possibility of crisis contained in the process of circulation of capital, Marx pointed out: "There are, besides a large number of other factors, conditions, possibilities of crises, which can only be examined when considering the concrete conditions, particularly the competition of capitals and credit."[13]

According the elaboration on the nature of the crisis by Marx, we cannot summarize and generalize the crisis theory in *Capital* just by looking for the word crisis in those paragraphs from the index, but by looking for "equalization" and "continuity" relations because only in these relations it contained the factors of crisis. Whenever the theory expounded in these spheres, namely: Interrelated and mutually complementary economic factors had the tendency of forcible separation from each other or independence from unity; Interrelated and mutually complementary economic factors had the tendency of forcible recovery of unity from independence and separation, the economic crisis would occur. When economics ran normally, it means that the intrinsic factors were in the status of unity or separation – if the essentially unified factors had not yet been independent and separated, or the essentially independent and separated factors had not yet been unified. On the contrary, when economics ran abnormally, "crisis is the forcible establishment of unity between elements that have become independent and the enforced separation from one another of elements which are essentially one." Of course, "If they were only separate, without being a unity, then their unity could not be established by force and there could be no crisis. If they were only a unity without being separate, then no violent separation would be possible implying a crisis."[14] This is the core of Marx's analytic

12 *Marx and Engels Collected Works*, 1st Chinese edition, Volume 26 (II), p.595.
13 Ibid., p.609.
14 Ibid., p.586.

model of the economic crisis. Hence, Marx's analytic model of economic crisis is not the textbook model, nor the model generalized by the existing references like "underconsumption" or "imbalance", but in a way that various contradictions being fully expounded, in a way of unity of factors independent of each other, the real concentration and forcible adjustment of all the contradictions.

The most appropriate way for us to summarize and generalize the crisis theory in *Capital*, as well as to outline Marx's analytic model of the economic crisis is, in a certain logical structure system, to extract the relations of "equalization" and "continuity" from the theoretical system, to arrange them in a certain logical structure, and to describe the transformation trend of factors that constitute them towards separation and independence from unity.

The Process of Production of Capital, the Process of Circulation of Capital, the Process of Capitalist Production as a Whole, and the Possibility of Crisis

What *Capital* described only included the most general possibility and the most abstract form of the crisis, and the possibility of crisis which acquired further development or the abstract form of crisis which acquired further development. The two forms of the crisis described in Volume I, namely the possibility of crises contained in the metamorphosis of the commodity itself, and the possibility of crises contained in the function of money as a means of payment, were the most general possibility or the most abstract form of crisis. Besides, it did not contribute any new factors to the crisis, though it did contain such factors, because "these factors which explain the possibility of crises, by no means explain their actual occurrence. They do not explain why the phases of the [reproduction] process come into such conflict that their inner unity can only assert itself through a crisis, through a violent process."[15] In addition to this factor, it is also "because the production process implies appropriation and hence production of surplus-value. But this cannot be shown when dealing with the production process itself, for the latter is not concerned with the realisation either of the reproduced value or of the surplus-value."[16] In Volume II which explained the process of circulation of capital, the possibility of crisis which became apparent in the simple metamorphosis of the commodity in Volume I was once more demonstrated in a further developed form, in the real movement based on the capitalist production, which started from and presupposed its own basis, and in the circulation or reproduction process in which it denoted how capital was produced,. As soon as these processes did not merge smoothly into one another but became independent of one another, the crisis was there. However, the process of reproduction and the predisposition to crisis which was further developed in it, were therefore only partially described under this heading and required further elaboration in the chapter on "Capital and Profit".[17] In Volume III that described of the Process of Capitalist

99

---

15 Marx and Engels, Collected Works, 1st Chinese edition, Volume 26 (II), p.572.
16 Ibid., p.585.
17 Ibid., p.586.

Production as a Whole, because the reproduction process of capital as a whole was the unity of its production phase and its circulation phase, "[t]herein lies a further developed possibility or abstract form of crisis".[18] Therefore, in the theoretical system of *Capital,* the possibility of crisis included in Volume II was the manifestation of the forcible separation of the factors from one another which were essentially one; the possibility of crisis included in Volume III was the manifestation of the forcible establishment of unity between elements that have become independent. But these are only factors of crisis when regarding the process of capitalist production process as a whole, and there were more factors related to the crisis included in the specific aspects of its logical development. That is "[t]he circulation process as a whole or the reproduction process of capital as a whole is the unity of its production phase and its circulation phase, so that it comprises both these processes or phases. Therein lies a further developed possibility or abstract form of crisis. The economists who deny crises consequently assert only the unity of these two phases. If they were only separate, without being a unity, then their unity could not be established by force and there could be no crisis. If they were only a unity without being separate, then no violent separation would be possible implying a crisis. Crisis is the forcible establishment of unity between elements that have become independent and the enforced separation from one another of elements which are essentially one."[19]

100 The transformation of the general possibility of the economic crisis to the possibility of the capitalist economic crisis was realized in the transformation of commodity production into capitalist commodity production. Marx pointed out that at the very beginning the capitalist production of commodity was the developed production of commodity, which would make various forms of the inherent contradictions of commodity be fully reflected, while the development of contradictions of capitalist mode of production could only be realized in there where contradictions of commodity were able to be fully expounded.

Large machinery industry was the material basis for the possibility of crisis to transform into reality. This is because when large machinery industry took place, the expansion force of capital suddenly increased. "As the general conditions requisite for production by the modern industrial system have been established, this mode of production acquires an elasticity, a capacity for sudden extension by leaps and bounds that finds no hindrance except in the supply of raw material and in the disposal of the produce."[20] "When the machinery industry is so ingrained that it had an absolute influence over the entire national product... the repeated cycles began to appear, whose respective successive stages last few years, and in the end they are always in a widespread outbreak of a crisis."[21]

18   Ibid., p.586.
19   *Marx and Engels Collected Works*, 1st Chinese edition, Volume 26 (II), p.586.
20   *Capital*, Volume I, Beijing: People's Publishing House. 1975, p.494
21   Ibid., p.695.

The general, abstract possibility of crisis denotes no more than the most abstract form of crisis, without content, without a compelling motivating factor. Therefore, in the reproduction process of capital, or the movement of capital from the moment in which it leaves the production process as a commodity in order once again to emerge from it as a commodity, that is C'-M'-C-P-C', that only here they receive a content, a basis on which to manifest themselves.

First of all, If we abstract here from all the other factors determining its content, then the total commodity capital and each individual commodity of which it is made up, must go through the process C—M—C, the metamorphosis of the commodity. The general possibility of crisis, which is contained in this form— the falling apart of purchase and sale—is thus contained in the movement of capital, in so far as the latter is also commodity and nothing but commodity. From the interconnection of the metamorphoses of commodities it follows, moreover, that one commodity is transformed into money because another is retransformed from the form of money into commodity. Furthermore, the separation of purchase and sale appears here in such a way that the transformation of one capital from the form commodity into the form money, must correspond to the retransformation of the other capital from the form money into the form commodity. The first metamorphosis of one capital must correspond to the second metamorphosis of the other; one capital leaves the production process as the other capital returns into the production process. This intertwining and coalescence of the processes of reproduction or circulation of different capitals is on the one hand necessitated by the division of labour, on the other hand it is accidental; and thus the definition of the content of crisis is already fuller.

Secondly, with regard to the possibility of crisis arising from the form of money as means of payment, it appears that capital may provide a much more concrete basis for turning this possibility into reality. For example, the weaver must pay for the whole of the constant capital, such as cotton, flax, weaving machines, wood, coal, etc., but weaver now sells the cloth to the merchant and in return for a bill of exchange, and if the merchant does not pay at maturity, there comes a universal crisis. This is nothing other than the possibility of crisis described when dealing with money as a means of payment; but here—in capitalist production—we can already see the connection between the mutual claims and obligations, the sales and purchases, through which the possibility can turn into reality.

"If purchase and sale do not get bogged down, and therefore do not require forcible adjustment—and, on the other hand, money as means of payment functions in such a way that claims are mutually settled, and thus the contradiction inherent in money as a means of payment is not realised—if therefore neither of these two abstract forms of crisis become real, no crisis exists. No crisis can exist unless sale and purchase are separated from one another and come into conflict, or the contradictions contained in money as a means of payment actually come into play; crisis, therefore, cannot exist without manifesting itself at the same time in its simple form... But these are merely forms, general possibilities of crisis, and hence also forms, abstract forms, of real crisis. In them, the nature of crisis appears in its simplest forms, and, in so far as this form is itself the simplest content of crisis, in its simplest content. But the content is not yet substantiated. Simple circulation of money and even the circulation of money as a means of payment—and both come into being long before capitalist production, while there are no crises—are possible and actually take place without crises. These forms alone, therefore, do not explain why their crucial aspect becomes prominent and why the potential contradiction contained in them becomes a real contradiction."[22] The contradictions developed in the circulation of commodities and the circulation of money, including the possibility of crisis, as well as the further development of the potential crisis, are bound to be manifested in capital relations, because in fact only on the basis of the development of capital relations can there be the developed circulation of commodity and circulation of money. Therefore, the real crisis can only be deduced from the real movement of capitalist production, competition and credit.

However, with the direct production process of capital in itself, the further development of the potential crisis cannot be reflected. This is because although it does contain such an element, it does not contribute any new element of crisis, but production of surplus-value. The latter is not concerned with the realisation either of the reproduced value or of the surplus-value. This can only emerge in the circulation process which is in itself also a process of reproduction, because the process of circulation then is complementary to the process of production, a process of reproduction of separation and independence of each other. In the unity of the circulation process as a whole or the reproduction process of capital as a whole, therein lies a further developed possibility or abstract form of crisis.

Continuity, Coexistence, Unity and the General Conditions for Their Destruction

Conditions for the normal operation of the capitalist real production are the satisfaction of a series of relations of continuity, coexistence and equalization. This objective requirement from the production itself becomes the natural condition of production in the abstract large socialized production and non-confrontational society, but in capitalism, the relations of continuity, coexistence, unity and equalization of the real production movement become the condition of capital movement. However, due to the presence of a series of antagonistic contradictions of capitalism, the continuity, coexistence, unity and equalization of the production cannot be achieved through human consciousness but the spontaneous acts of the market mechanism. As a result, the movement of a series of antagonistic contradictions makes capital movement difficult to be run smoothly due to the interruption in continuity, the absence of coexistence, the splitting in unity, the imbalance of equalization, and when these relations are "interrupted", "absent", "split" and "imbalanced", the internal expansion

---

22 *Marx and Engels Collected Works*, 1st Chinese edition, Volume 26 (II), pp.584-585.

force of the capitalist economy will inevitably be recovered by way of a violent outbreak. The way of this violent outbreak is the economic crisis. Specifically, in terms of several stages that must be gone through, and if there is a continuity essentially, when they appear in a row, its development will contain the trend of a phase of separation or independence; when several stages are in a separate or independent state, it would contain the development trend of forced recovery of continuity, so the crisis occurs. In a continuous process, if the several elements have the unity essentially, its movement contains a trend of separation, and when they are at a status of splitting, the movement itself will contain a trend that forces them to move towards unity, so the crisis is about to occur. In terms of the organism constituted by a number of economic variables, if it is in an essentially equalized trend, it means that it has the equilibrium law. When variables are in equilibrium, its development will have a trend towards non-equilibrium status; when this non-equilibrium status reaches its limit, it will restore the equilibrium in a forcible way, then the crisis occurs. In *Capital*, whenever Marx basically elaborated on these relations, there must be urgency for their development –the economic crisis.

In the methodology of the Marxist economics, the development, intensification and mitigation of the crisis, as long as the actual capitalist production operation is concerned, is a movement from equalization to imbalance, and then back to equalization through a compelling force. Because this movement continues to repeat itself in a periodic manner, as long as the production process as a whole does not stop, the equilibrium and imbalance is always in a process of mutual transformation, and as an aspect of the law, where "all equalisations are accidental and although the proportion of capital employed in individual spheres is equalised by a continuous process, the continuity of this process itself equally presupposes the constant disproportion which it has continuously, often violently, to even out."[23]

103

The continuity, unity, coexistence, equalization in of capital movement is the mutual relations between factors in the process of capital movement. Therefore, fundamentally they are unified, and the inconnection of each of them presupposes the existence of other relations, which are intertwined, mutually inclusive, and interacting. From a different angle and side, they show conditions that need to be met in order to have a smooth movement of capital. However, continuity and equalization are the most basic relations in capital movement, while unity and coexistence are the derived forms of continuity and equalization, and the associated characteristics of continuity and equalization in the deployment process. Unity is the manifestation of continuity, and coexistence is the manifestation of equalization.

23   *Marx and Engels Collected Works*, 1st Chinese edition, Volume 26 (II), p.562.

The Unity of Continuity and Coexistence

The premise for capitalists to invest a small quantity of money and to gain a large quantity of money is: The money must be capital; the money must be exchanged with labour; the money must go through a complete cycle. A complete cycle includes three stages of purchase, production and sale, and they have continuity in nature. As capital has a general and a specific form, the continuity of capital movement is accordingly manifested in its general form and specific form.

The general form of continuity, namely M-C-M', which is adapted to all specific forms of capital, therefore an abstract, is a general from of capital movement. The continuity in the general form is manifested in: M-C is the initial, and then it is C-M'. If not for such a continuity, there can be real capitalist production. The unity of the general form is manifested in that it is constituted of purchase and sale, the two phases that complement each other and its opposition is manifested in that the two phases can be separated from each other in time and space, but as the movement of capital, the separation of the two phases must eventually move towards unity, otherwise it would mean the end of capital. Here, no matter what kind of specific form capital takes, they are always manifested as the unity of M-C and C-M', although "in the case of interest-bearing capital, the circulation M-C-M' appears abridged. We have its result without the intermediate stage, in the form M-M', "en style lapidaire" so to say, money that is worth more money, value that is greater than itself."[24] But it is just an abbreviated form of capital movement, a form eliminating the middle part. The general form of the continuity is manifested as purchase to be supplemented by sale, and also the unity of purchase and sale.

The special form of continuity is in the category linked with the specific form of capital. The continuity of industrial capital movement is: M-C...P... C'-M'. This form of movement is special because: there is a new production phase added in between purchase and sale, the two phases that complement each other, in addition to the symmetry of starting and ending points, as well as the correspondence of purchase and sale, the continuity of the process is manifested as that capital movement must go through three phases successively, take three forms of functions respectively, and finally go back to the original starting point to achieve the self-expansion of the value. Therefore, the continuity of industrial capital cycle is manifested in the successive loops of three phases of industrial capital cycle, in the successive transformation of three forms of functions, as well as in the unity of the process of production and the process of circulation.

The form of the continuity of commercial capital movement is the general form of capital movement, namely: M-C-M'. The purchase of M-C is for sale, a necessary preparation for sale; the sale of C-M' is the realization of the motive and purpose of purchase, an indispensable complement of purchase. The form of continuity of loan capital movement is: M-M-C-P-C'-M'-M' or

---

24   *Capital*, Volume I, Beijing: People's Publishing House, 1975, p. 177.

M-M-C-M'-M'. The loan capital loops twice in spending, twice in reflux, and the process of production or the process of circulation of commodity as a medium in the middle. If considered only from the perspective of investment and recovery of loan capital, namely: M-M', the form of functional capital movement is its intermediary. Whether the prepaid value can be successfully recovered and can achieve growth, the key lies in whether the movement of functional capital can maintain continuity. If the continuous movement of functional capital is not interrupted, it will lay a solid foundation for loan capital to maintain continuity, however, it does not mean that there is no barrier in the continuity of loan capital movement, because as long as functional capitalists[25] do not repay the debt on time and in full, the continuity is difficult to maintain. If the loan capital is carried out with bank as the intermediary, its circulating form is M-M-M-C-P-C'-M'-M'-M', and despite its movement will undergo three times of payment and three times of reflux, it does not change the basic relation, but increases levels and links of the movement and increases the possibility of continuity to be damaged. Once the continuity is destroyed, purchase cannot be supplemented by sale, and it will also cause the interruption of a range of payment chain. Speculative capital is different with loan capital. The intermediary in speculative capital movement is a variety of securities and real estate, as well as options, exchange rates, stock indexes and other derivative financial assets in the form of fictitious capital. Continuity of speculative capital movement is in the form of: M-M-C-M'-M'.

This form has the meaning of: The venture capitalists obtain money capital through credit, and invest money capital into these securities, options, futures, foreign exchange, and real estate. In a transaction, speculators recover the money capital which is increased in value, and repay principal and interest. Whether the whole cycle is carried out smoothly, whether it can maintain the continuity of the cycle, a critical phase lies in C-M'. The three results of the phase will bring the other three joint results. If C-M' does not bring changes in the market value, debt service is still difficult, and the possibility for the chain of debt to interrupt still exists; If C-M' causes loss of value, debt service is more difficult, and the chain of debt has partially or completely interrupted. If C-M achieves appreciated value, the manifestation of movement becomes C-M', and the subsequently all joint payment activities can be carried out smoothly.

The purpose of capital circulation is to exchange value, which determines that it is a never-ending course of movement. The recycling chain formed in this process contains the cycle of three functional forms of industrial capital. Therefore, the condition which is a must for the capitalist to make endless profit necessitates continuous cycles of his capital. This continuity in itself is manifested as a state when meeting the following two conditions, namely: (1) Capital cannot take only one functional form, but should be divided into

---

25   Karl Marx has analyzed dual character capitalist: (i) the functional capitalist, the business administrator of the means of production namely "the effect of the social mechanism, of which he is but one of the wheels."

appropriate parts according to certain proportions, thus they coexist in three forms: as money capital, production capital and commodity capital, that is, the three functional forms of capital coexist in space. Otherwise, the process of production and the process of capital circulation will alternately interrupt. In other words, the three forms of capital are arranged in sequence, and must be equalized in number. If all the capital is invested in the form of only one functional form of capital, it is hard for the capital movement to achieve the consequentiality in time, and the process of production will be interrupted. Of course, if all capital is disproportionately allocated to the three functional forms, the circulation of capital cannot be carried out smoothly, and the process of reproduction will be interrupted. This relation shows the equilibrium relations between production and circulation in the process of reproduction. (2) Capital must have to go through the three phases of the cycle in succession, namely the consequentiality of the three functional forms of capital in time. The relationship between these two conditions is: Consequentiality is the precondition for and basis of the form of coexistence, and vice versa. There will be no consequentiality without coexistence; if consequentiality is interrupted, coexistence will be destroyed. Coexistence makes consequentiality a reality, and consequentiality makes coexistence to be maintained.

Equilibrium in Reproduction: Continuity and equalization reflects the development and the relative stabilization of contradictions. Without continuity, there will be no development of contradictions, which is inevitably manifested as continuity. The existence of contradictions is always manifested as that both contradictory parties move towards imbalance from equalization, and then towards a new equalization from imbalance. The intensification of contradictions is that the imbalance of opposing parties breaks the boundary in degree, and the resolving of contradiction is to form a new equilibrium. The trend of imbalance in equilibrium is the possibility of crisis.

In Marx's model of the reproduction of social capital as a whole, whether the reproduction of social capital as a whole can proceed smoothly lies in whether the social product as a whole can achieve bodily renewal and replacement of value smoothly. The total value of social product is composed of three parts, c, v, m in value form, it is also composed of means of production and means of subsistence in physical form, and the corresponding social production is also divided into two major departments. Department I is the production of means of production, and Department II is the production of means of subsistence. If the society is carrying out the simple reproduction, the equilibrium that the two major departments must maintain is:

$$I_{(v+m)} = II_c$$

$$I_{(c+v+m)} = I_c + II_c$$

$$II_{(c+v+m)} = I_{(v+m)} + II_{(v+m)}$$

If the society is carrying out the expanded reproduction, the equilibrium that the two major departments must maintain is:

$$I_{(v+\Delta v+m/x)} = II_{(c+\Delta v)}$$

$$I_{(v+m)} = II_c + I_{\Delta c} + II_{\Delta c}$$

$$I_{(c+m-m/x)} = I_{(v+m/x)} + I_{\Delta v} + II_{\Delta v}$$

In the two equilibrium relations, $I_{(v+m)} = II_c$ and $I_{(v+\Delta v+m/x)} = II_{(c+\Delta v)}$ are the basic realization conditions for simple reproduction and expanded reproduction respectively, and the rest is derived conditions. Whether it is simple form or expanded form, social reproduction must first meet the above realization conditions. However, even if these conditions are satisfied, it does not mean that social production can be successfully carried out, because these conditions simply indicate the proportion between the two major departments. In order for the reproduction of social capital as a whole to be carried out smoothly, the two major departments need to maintain appropriate proportion between each other, besides, they need to maintain appropriate proportion within themselves. In *Capital*, Marx took the second department as an example, and he described its internal equilibrium relations, as well as the realization conditions related to reproduction. Marx divided the production within Department II into two subdivisions of II_a (consumer necessities) and II_b (consumer luxury). Products of II_a meet the consumption demand of the working class, and also become part of the consumption of the bourgeois; Products of II_b only meet the consumption demand of the bourgeois. Equilibrium condition is described by the formula:

$$II_{a(c+v+m)}$$

$$II_{b(c+v+m)}$$

Assume all surplus value is for personal consumption of capitalists, of which 2/5 is for luxury consumption, 3/5 for necessities consumption. The exchange within Department II is as follows:

$$II_{a[c+v+(3/5+2/5)m]}$$

$$II_{b[c+v+(3/5+2/5)m]}$$

In which, the physical form of $v+3/5m$ in II_a are consumer necessities, and is realized within II_a. The physical form of $2/5m$ in II_b is consumer luxury, and is realized within II_b. $2/5m$ in II_a is for luxury consumption of the capitalists, but its physical form is consumer necessities; $v+3/5m$ in II_b is consumer necessary for the workers and the capitalists, but it is in itself articles of luxury. Hence, the part that needs to be exchanged between II_a and II_b, as well as its equilibrium equation is:

$$II_{a(m*2/5)} = II_{b(v+m*3/5)}$$

$$II_{a(c)} + II_{b(c)} = I_{(c+v+m/x)}$$

The proportion within departments will affect that between departments, because the proportion within departments would affect production of departments, will affect the proportion between departments. Relations between the two major departments are the overall equilibrium, and the economic crisis caused by the imbalance between them tends to be the universal crisis. Relative to the relations between departments, the equilibrium within departments is the partial equilibrium. Its imbalance normally causes partial economic crisis, or structural economic crisis.

The total product of society is realized through circulation of commodity, for which, there are always two things necessary, that is commodities thrown into circulation and money thrown into circulation. In the realization of the total capital of society, commodities are invested by capitalists, so is money.

In the realization of the total product of society, it contains exchanges between numerous individual capitalists. And these exchanges are conducted in such a successful equilibrium; money thrown as the intermediary for the exchange of commodities, under circumstances of the normal circulation of commodities, would return to him who advanced it in accordance with their respective advance, that is there is an equilibrium between advance and reflux of money in quantity.

This equilibrium is known as the general law of money as the intermediary of circulation. "From this it incidentally follows that if any money-capitalist at all stands behind the producer of commodities and advances to the industrial capitalist money-capital (in the strictest meaning of the word, i.e., capital-value in the form of money), the real point of reflux for this money are the pocket of this money-capitalist. Thus the mass of the circulating money belongs to that department of money-capital which is organised and concentrated in the form of banks, etc., although the money circulates more or less through all hands. The way in which this department advances its capital necessitates the continual final reflux to it in the form of money although this is once again brought about by the reconversion of the industrial capital into money-capital."[26] In a commodity economy, this is the fundamental equilibrium of social reproduction and circulation for demand and supply of money, and the crisis caused by the imbalance of it is normally payment crisis.

The use-value of fixed capital generally can continue to play the role in the reproduction process for many years, and its value is gradually replaced through the form of depreciation, but fixed capital is renewed for one time. These characteristics have determined that when recovering the value of fixed capital, the capitalists continuously extract the value from circulation in the form of money. They settle down beside the productive capital, and have the replacement of the substance of fixed capital. Money plays a unique role, and by the means of sinking fund, it has made a necessary preparation for the reproduction of fixed capital.

---

26 *Capital*, Volume II, Beijing: People's Publishing House. 1975, p.459.

The replacement of fixed capital requires capitalist to have an advanced accumulation of money. Capitalists hoard the money withdrawn from sinking fund, the way of which is actually selling without buying, making the exchange proportion of the two major departments become imbalanced, as well as a corresponding number of means of production and means of subsistence become surplus products, and thus money advanced cannot achieve normal reflux. The replacement of the substance of fixed capital requires objectively the existence of such equilibrium: the total value of fixed capital renewed in a year must be equal to the total sinking fund hoarded in the same year, or money used for the actual renewal is equal to money of sinking hoard. It is called the equilibrium of quantity between the renewed value of fixed capital and sinking fund hoarded. This equilibrium reflects the value equilibrium in reproduction, and in the real economy, it is manifested specifically as the equilibrium of money and the equilibrium of supply and demand.

Taking the second department as an example: The second department is composed of many individual capitals, and in the process of social reproduction, the fixed capital of each capitalist can be at different stages. The fixed capital of some capitalists is withdrawing sinking fund to accumulate money, thus not buying temporarily. The fixed capital of another part of the capitalists has been completed in the wear and tear, and the money accumulated can be used to renew the fixed capital. Assume: Capitalists of the second department are divided into two categories, namely $II_{c(1)}$ and $II_{c(2)}$, when $II_{c(1)}$ throws the hoarded sinking fund into circulation for buying new means of production to renew the fixed capital, $II_{c(2)}$ have saved the money in the form of sinking fund. Thus, the equilibrium model between the two is:

$$II_{c(1)} = II_{c(2)}$$

In the case that they are equal, money and commodity reach equilibrium, and reproduction can be carried out smoothly. When $II_{c(1)} > II_{c(2)}$, there would be excess money and inadequate commodity; when $II_{c(1)} < II_{c(2)}$, there would be inadequate money and excess commodity. In order for the reproduction to be carried out smoothly, when $II_{c(1)} > II_{c(2)}$, it needs to import commodities from abroad; when $II_{c(1)} < II_{c(2)}$, it needs to export commodities. Marx believed, both cases can be remedy through the development of foreign trade, foreign trade, however it is not always the essential element of remedy, but only expands and worsens the crisis even more.

In the capital accumulation process, there are always such two opposite situations: some capitalists only sell without buying, hoarding money; the other only buy without selling, throwing money into circulation. Marx called the behaviour of the former the accumulation of money, and the latter actual accumulation. In the reproduction of total social capital, there is an equilibrium between the two, namely: money thrown into the market must be equal to the accumulation of money. The premise of such equilibrium is: in quantity the value of the one-sided purchases and that of the one-sided sales tally. Its realization mechanism is: the value used for the accumulation is part of surplus value, capitalists engaged in the accumulation of money withdraw money by the sale of surplus products from circulation, holding on to it and impounding it. The formation of a hoard is no production at all, hence not an increment of production. This operation is carried on not alone by A, but at numerous points along the periphery of circulation by other capitalists, A', A", A'", all of them working with equal zeal at this sort of hoard formation. These numerous points at which money is withdrawn from circulation and accumulated in numerous individual hoards or potential money-capitals appear as so many obstacles to circulation, because they immobilise the money and deprive it of its capacity to circulate for a certain length of time. Capitalist A is able to hoard money, because he himself is the seller of surplus product, rather than appearing as a buyer. Thus, that although withdrawing money to the quantity of his surplus-value from circulation and hoarding it, A on the other hand throws commodities into it without withdrawing other commodities in return. The capitalists B, B', B", etc., are thereby enabled to throw money into circulation and withdraw only commodities from it. When capitalists B, B', B" continue to transform a considerable number of potential money-capital into productive capital, and capitalists A, A', A" are still engaged in the hoard of a possible monetary capital. Therefore, capitalists of these two categories are often transposed: One is the buyer, and the other is the seller, with each party playing only a role of the two. Moreover, no matter how position is interchangeable, the equilibrium of 110 the quantity has always been the premise of such act to carry out normally.

From the social point of view, for fast turnover department, variable capital is fast in withdrawing products from the society, and it is fast in throwing products into circulation. By contrast, for low turnover department, variable capital withdraws means of subsistence constantly from the market, but only throws money equivalents. If these two departments are disproportionate, especially in the case that departments of slow turnover in variable capital with long turnaround are higher in proportion, it will increase the needs of society that has the ability to pay, so that the price of means of subsistence and means of production will hike. The increase in price will stimulate speculation, and the prevalence of speculation would lead to a massive shift of capital. Some speculators get rich, and this arouses strong consumer demand on the market, causing an increase in the input of foreign goods and articles of luxury, resulting in the excess input; on the other hand the increase in price attracts a lot of potential relative excess population, even employed workers, to new industrial sectors, resulting in blind socio-economic expansion and false prosperity. Therefore, the smooth reproduction of social capital needs to maintain a reasonable equilibrium of variable capital between long turnaround and short turnaround. Marx believes that this is an accompanying phenomenon in the period of full capitalist expansion, and a prelude to the crisis of overproduction.

In terms of social capital, of a certain commodity in the total social product, its supply and demand has the equilibrium in use value, and in value as well. Since in a period of time the society has a certain demand for a certain commodity, and if its total output exceeds the social demand, the excess part will not be accepted by society, because whether this commodity has use value depends not only on whether its ability can meet the needs of society, but also on whether its number can be suitable for specific needs of society. If the commodity does not have social use value, its value cannot be achieved, the labour spent to produce these commodities cannot be achieved, and the labour spent to produce these commodities will not become socially necessary labour.

The principle suggests that: In the equilibrium between total supply and total demand, the yield of a certain commodity and all the labour time it contains is a quantity that can be recognized by society, that is to say, it is a quantity that can be achieved in value. The quantity of the value can be achieved. This quantity may be considered as the sum of value of a series of individual commodities which contain necessary social labour time, and it is an equilibrium quantity with inherent measurement. If the necessary social labour contained in the total supply of a certain commodity is less than this quantity, society would admit it in accordance with the "objective quantity", and if it is more than this "objective quantity", there would be a part that cannot be recognized by society, and correspondingly a portion of use value will become surplus. This is the realization of the law of value in the aggregate sense, or the law of socially necessary labour time determining the value of commodities. The "socially necessary labour time" in the aggregate sense can be applied to explain the role of law of value in the closed economy of a state, as well as to explain the role of law of value on the world market in the open economy. In the condition of the production of commodity as the production of capital, dominated by the law of the pursuing maximized surplus value of the capital mode of production, the production and supply of a certain type of products is often seriously imbalanced with its social demand, and this imbalance is structural with respect to all kinds of products in the whole society. But when this structural imbalance develops to the overall imbalance from the complex state, the capitalist crisis of universal overproduction will be there.

The socially necessary labour time in the aggregate sense is actually "only the necessary part of the total labour-time of the society that is used in the particular sphere, only the labour-time which is required for the satisfaction of social need (demand)".[27] Comparing the socially necessary labour time in this sense with that in individual commodity, both of them have the immanent measure determined by value, and for individual commodity, the measure is the average labour time in producing it; it is, for the socially necessary labour time in the aggregate sense, the product the demand of the use value for the product in a particular sphere for production in the society, and the socially necessary labour time of the individual product in this sphere. The requirements of the

---

27 *Marx and Engels Collected Works*, 1st Chinese edition, Volume 26 (II), p.595.

socially necessary labour time in the aggregate sense have determined the realization of the law of value on this level: "Just as it is a condition for the sale of commodities at their value, that they contain only the socially necessary labour-time, so it is for an entire sphere of production of capital, that only the necessary part of the total labour-time of society is used in the particular sphere, only the labour-time which is required for the satisfaction of social need (demand). If more is used, then, even if each individual commodity only contains the necessary labour-time, the total contains more than the socially necessary labour-time; in the same way, although the individual commodity has use-value, the total sum of commodities loses some of its use-value under the conditions assumed."[28] If the situation is reversed, even if each unit commodity contains only the necessary labour time, the aggregate quantity of value of these unit commodities represents "the labour-time which is required for the satisfaction of social need (demand)".[29]

It can be inferred from the determination and realization of the socially necessary labour time in the aggregate sense, the ideal condition for the production is that the labour time spent in a particular sphere of production is equal to the labour-time which is required for the satisfaction of social need (demand). If this quantity appears to be unequal, the social production will be disproportionate, and the more spheres of inequality are, the greater the range of disproportionate production is. In capitalist commodity economy, this ideal production condition is difficult to achieve, and the actual condition is that the ideal production does not become the normal condition for production. On the contrary, the normal condition for production is then an-ideal condition for production. Capitalist production is always from the proportionate production to the disproportionate and then to the proportionality of a newer and higher level, the driving force of this movement is the competition among "a lot of capital," which is exactly that "proportionate production is, however, always only the result of disproportionate production on the basis of competition".[30]

Disproportionate production has two levels objectively: First, disproportion among production sectors; Second, disproportion within the production sectors. The reason for the formation of the former is that the total quantity of labour in society as a whole has inconsistent configuration in particular sectors with the objective proportion; the reason for the formation of the latter is that the quantity spent in labour is inconsistent with "the labour-time which is required for the satisfaction of social need (demand)."Despite some differences in the specific reasons, both of them are essentially consistent, and the former is caused by the latter.

The connection between disproportion and crisis is that: If disproportion occurs within some production sectors, crisis is partial; if disproportion occurs in the chain of the whole society, the crisis may be universal.

---

28   Ibid.
29   Marx Capital III: p.620-21.
30   *Marx and Engels Collected Works*, 1st Chinese edition, Volume 26 (II), p.595.

In the commodity economy, the condition for the commodity capital to be sold "for an entire sphere of production": "Only the necessary part of the total labour-time of society is used in the particular sphere, only the labour-time which is required for the satisfaction of social need (demand)." This is "Just as it is a condition for the sale of commodities at their value, that they contain only the socially necessary labour-time."[31]

The realization form of the law of value in the total quantity of a particular sphere of production: the value is determined by "the necessary part of the total labour-time of society", "the labour-time which is required for the satisfaction of social need (demand)." The function of the law of value is that the market value fluctuates around "the labour-time which is required for the satisfaction of social need (demand)". When the labour time of social labour distributed in a certain sphere of production is greater than "the labour-time which is required for the satisfaction of social need (demand)", the market value lowers; when the labour time of social labour distributed in a certain sphere of production is less than "the labour-time which is required for the satisfaction of social need (demand)", the market value increases.

The result of law of value is that: the market value fluctuates around "the labour-time which is required for the satisfaction of social need (demand)", and the functioning mechanism as a force of resource allocation, "results in the withdrawal of capital from one branch of production and its transfer to another, the migration of capital from one branch of production to another", making the distribution of social labour in production spheres moving close from imbalance to harmony. This is an equilibrium form. Marx believes that, "This equalisation itself however already implies as a precondition the opposite of equalisation and may therefore comprise crisis; the crisis itself may be a form of equalization."[32]"The disproportion in the distribution of social labour between the individual spheres of production" is related to the competition of capitals, and it can be said to be the result of the competition of capitals. Therefore, for the disproportion in the distribution of social labour between the individual spheres of production, this can only be dealt with in connection with the competition of capitals.[33]

Reasons for Law of Continuity and Equilibrium to be Destroyed

It seems to Marx that the economic crisis is the result of all contradictions of capitalism being fully expounded, and the influences of these contradictions may, "at one time operate predominantly side by side in space, and at another succeed each other in time. From time to time the conflict of antagonistic agencies finds vent in crises. The crises are always but momentary and forcible solutions of the existing contradictions. They are violent eruptions which for

---

31 Ibid.
32 *Marx and Engels Collected Works*, 1st Chinese edition, Volume 26 (II), pp. 595-596.
33 Ibid., p.595.

a time restore the disturbed equilibrium."[34] Although these propositions are answers to the nature and occurrence of the capitalist economic crisis, it has features of high generality and abstraction, and people cannot find a specific and clear exposition on such propositions from the existing Marx's references, so that people cannot accurately answer what these contradictions are, how they expand, how they are solved, how the equilibrium is restored, and so on.

In the current study, the conclusions of mainstream Marxist economics are: As capitalist mode of production has many insurmountable contradictions, the proportion needed for the reproduction of social capital is often destroyed, and thus there must be all sorts of problems and difficulties in the production process of social capital: there are contradictions between the realization condition and the realization format in the reproduction of social capital; there are contradictions between reproduction and consumption in the reproduction of social capital. The root of these contradictions is the basic contradiction of capitalist society, the contradiction between the organized nature of individual enterprises production and the anarchy of production in the whole society; the contradiction between the infinite widening trend of the production and the working people reduced ability to pay. Since there are a series of insurmountable contradictions in capitalism, it is difficult for the realization condition and the realization form in the reproduction of social capital to adapt to each other, so that the proportion of reproduction can only be achieved spontaneously with the functioning of the market mechanism. In general, the mainstream economics regarded the contradictions between the realization condition and the realization form, and the contradictions between production and consumption as a specific form of contradiction, as a contradiction on the level of being fully expounded.

In the mainstream Marxist political economy, there is another interpretation that is, based on *Capital* Volume III, *Part III: The Law of the Tendency of the Rate of Profit to Fall*, to explain the capitalist economic crisis. The exposition of the internal contradictions of the law of the rate of profit to fall is regarded as all kinds of capitalist contradictions being fully expounded, the intensification of the basic contradiction is seen as the root cause of the crisis, and the crisis itself is seen as a solution to the contradiction. To understand how reasonable this explanation is, the key is to figure out the relation between contradictions expounded in the rate of profit to fall and "all kinds of contradictions being fully expounded" in capitalism. If they are referring to the same thing, this interpretation is reasonable, and if not, it is the opposite.

In the Chapter on "[t]he Exposition of the Internal Contradictions of the Law", Marx mainly described some of the following issues: the basic contradiction of capitalism expounded as the contradiction between the production and realization of surplus value, between production expansion and value augmentation, as well as between excess population and excess capital by the law of the rate of profit to fall and the mass of profit to increase. The intensification

---

34 *Capital*, Volume III, Beijing: People's Publishing House, 1975, pp. 277-278.

of these contradictions was reflected in the outbreak of a crisis. The crisis could only temporarily overcome these contradictions, but make them more profound and expansive. Specifically:

Firstly, it seemed to Marx that, the contradictions between the production and the realization of surplus value was originating from the essence of the capitalist production. This production includes producing commodities with surplus value, as well as selling them. If they cannot be sold, or can only be partially sold, or only sold at prices below the prices of production, the labourer has been indeed exploited, but his exploitation is not realised as such for the capitalist, and this can be bound up with a total or partial failure to realise the surplus-value pressed out of him, indeed even with the partial or total loss of the capital. The reason is that "the conditions of direct exploitation, and those of realising it, are not identical. They diverge not only in place and time, but also logically. The first are only limited by the productive power of society, the latter by the proportional relation of the various branches of production and the consumers' power in the society. But the latter is not determined either by the absolute productive power, or by the absolute consumer power, but by the consumer power based on antagonistic conditions of distribution, which reduce the consumption of the bulk of society to a minimum varying within more or less narrow limits. It is furthermore restricted by the tendency to accumulate, the drive to expand capital and produce surplus-value on an extended scale".[35] The contradictions between production and realization of surplus value cause contradictions between production and consumption."The more productiveness develops, the more it finds itself at variance with the narrow basis on which the conditions of consumption rest".[36] The market must be continually extended, so that its interrelations and the conditions regulating them assume more and more the form of a natural law working independently of the producer, and become ever more uncontrollable.

Secondly, Marx also believed that the contradiction between production expansion and value augmentation was actually the contradiction between the ends and means of capitalist production. With the development of productive forces, some factors increase the rate of profit, some decrease them, but factors that increase the rate of profit is so overwhelming over the other, so there is still a trend of rate of profit to fall. In the interaction of the trend between rising and falling of rate of profit, it shows the capitalist mode of production is in the development of contradiction: when productive forces develop, the rate of profit will fall, and the total quantity of capital will increase; the increase in the quantity of capital will lead to depreciation; the devaluation of capital will result in the rise in the rate of profit, and also stimulate the accumulation of capital, thus the devaluation has become a means of direct self-expansion; in the meantime, the use value as the material factors of capital also increases, becoming a means of indirect capital self-expansion; the accumulation of capital

---

35 *Capital*, Volume III, Beijing: People's Publishing House, 1975, pp. 272-273.
36 *Ibid., p.* 273.

will stimulate the increase of labour force, while by increasing organic composition of capital, creates an artificial excess population. These contradictions in capitalist mode of production are the result of the constraints of capitalist relations of production on productive force. "The contradiction, to put it in a very general way, consists in that the capitalist mode of production involves a tendency towards absolute development of the productive forces, regardless of the value and surplus-value it contains, and regardless of the social conditions under which capitalist production takes place; while, on the other hand, its aim is to preserve the value of the existing capital and promote its self-expansion to the highest limit (i.e., to promote an ever more rapid growth of this value). The specific feature about it is that it uses the existing value of capital as a means of increasing this value to the utmost. The methods by which it accomplishes this include the fall of the rate of profit, depreciation of existing capital, and development of the productive forces of labour at the expense of already created productive forces."[37] This means that capitalism cannot overcome these contradictions, but overcomes them only by means which again place these barriers in its way and on a more formidable scale

Thirdly, Marx also deduced excess capital accompanied with excess population from the law of rate of profit to fall. He believed that the excess of capital always applied essentially to those for which the fall in the rate of profit was not compensated through the mass of profit, or to those which placed capitals incapable of action on their own at the disposal of the managers of large enterprises in the form of credit. The excess of capital and the relative overpopulation are the same, caused by the accumulation of capital, and are, therefore, a phenomenon supplementing the latter, although they stand at opposite poles — unemployed capital at one pole, and unemployed worker population at the other. The excess of capital causes the contradictions within capitalists. In the case of the equalisation of the general rate of profit, competition affects an operating fraternity of the capitalist class, so that each shares in the common loot in proportion to the size of his respective investment. But as soon as it no longer is a question of sharing profits, but of sharing losses, everyone tries to reduce his own share to a minimum and to shove it off upon another. The excess of capital will cause competition and encourage overproduction of commodities, and thus it has to be forcibly resolved temporarily by the economic crisis. In a crisis, a large number of capitals are withdrawn, or even partially destroyed. Prices fall generally, the process of reproduction is in stagnation and chaos. On the other hand, the crisis leads to massive unemployment, forcing decline in workers' wages. Thus, the constant depreciation of capital and falling wages also means the increase in the rate of profit. So they prepared for the future expansion of production. In the expansion of production and market, as well as the improvement of productive forces, the same vicious circle will appear again, so that the crisis shows periodicity. However, the absolute excess capital does not mean the absolute excess of production and means of subsistence in a general sense, but that they cannot achieve self-expansion based

---

37   Ibid., p.278.

on the exploitation which the development of capitalist production needs. The development of social productive forces, on the one hand will cause excess capital, and on the other hand, will cause a relative overpopulation, an over-population of labourers not employed by the surplus-capital owing to the low degree of exploitation at which alone they could be employed, or at least owing to the low rate of profit which they would yield at the given degree of exploita-tion. Capital consists of commodities, and therefore over-production of capital implies over-production of commodities. The production process of capital is absolute in terms of its scope. Therefore, overproduction of commodities does not refer to the partial overproduction in one or several production sectors, but rather a universal, general overproduction. The excess capital and excess popu-lation, as well as the overproduction of commodities are relative to the capital which augments in its value. Therefore, they are also relative. (1) There are not too many necessities of life produced, in proportion to the existing popula-tion, but too little.(2) There are not too many means of production produced to employ the able-bodied portion of the population. Quite the reverse, there are too little. (3) Not too much wealth is produced. But at times too much wealth is produced in its capitalistic, self-contradictory forms. The historical mission of capitalism is to develop the productive forces, production for the sake of production, and thus promote the development of the productive forces of la-bourers. But its immediate goal is the self-expansion of capital, and while the improving productive forces are confronted with this mission, it would impede the development of productive forces.

117

Based on all these contradictions of the capitalist mode of production, Marx concludes that the capitalist mode of production has its own barriers on its development, namely: (1) In that the development of the productivity of labour creates out of the falling rate of profit a law which at a certain point comes into antagonistic conflict with this development and must be overcome constantly through crises. (2) The motive and purpose of capitalist production is the appro-priation of unpaid labour, a definite rate of profit, rather than to meet the needs of the society. With these limitations, capitalist production seeks continually to overcome these immanent barriers, but overcomes them only by means which again place these barriers in its way and on a more formidable scale. The real barrier of capitalist production is capital itself. Capital and its self-expansion is the purpose and motive of production, and production is only production for capital. This limited purpose within which the preservation and self-expansion of the value of capital rests on the expropriation and pauperisation of the great mass of producers, come into conflict with the unconditional development of the social productivity of labour. "The means—unconditional development of the productive forces of society—comes continually into conflict with the limited purpose, the self-expansion of the existing capital."[38] Therefore, if the capitalist mode of production was a historical means of developing the produc-tive forces, then the capitalist relations of production, at the same time, come into conflict with the developing productive forces. This is reflected in: (1) The

38 *Capital*, Volume III, Beijing: People's Publishing House, 1975, p. 279.

limitation to use new machines by capitalism. Only through a saving in the paid portion of living labour, as compared to labour expended in the past, the machine is used by capitalism. So far as capital is concerned, productiveness does not increase through a saving in living labour in general, but only through a saving in the paid portion of living labour, as compared to labour expended in the past. (2) The limitation to use labour forces by capitalism. "The development of productivity concerns it only in so far as it increases the surplus labour-time of the working-class, not because it decreases the labour-time for material production in general."[39] Therefore, as the capitalist is concerned, he only cares about whether he can appropriate the surplus labour time of workers, and if not, he will let these workers become relative surplus population. (3) The development of productive forces is subject to the law of the rate of profit to fall. No capitalist ever voluntarily introduces a new method of production, no matter how much more productive it may be, so long as it reduces the rate of profit. (4) The contradictions between the capitalist relations of production and productive forces lead to the outbreak of the crisis. (5) The development of productive forces are restrained by the relations of production. The development of capitalist production increasingly leads to the three cardinal facts: 1) "Concentration of means of production in few hands, whereby they cease to appear as the property of the immediate labourers and turn into social production capacities. Even if initially they are the private property of capitalists."[40] 2) Organisation of labour itself into social labour: through co-operation, division of labour, and the uniting of labour with the natural sciences.[41] 3) Creation of the world-market. The socialized production developing under the capitalist mode of production creates the stupendous productivity, but it is also limited by the capitalist private ownership, which is the basic contradiction of capitalism, and the intensification of the contradiction will lead to a crisis. Therefore, the economic crisis lies in the fundamental contradictions of capitalism.

These contradictions that Marx reveals in "Exposition of the Internal Contradictions of the Law" are clearly not the contradictions in the overall sense. This is because, even if some elements in the sense of "capital in general" have not been introduced into the process of theory exposition, such as the stock system. With regard to factors of other levels of wage labour, land ownership, nation, foreign trade, the world market and ?so on, there is no trace at all. Therefore, in *Capital* Volume III, the so-called "Exposition of the Internal Contradictions" is just the summary and generalization of contradictions in the sense of "capital in general", lacking many elements in multiple links of the exposition of contradictions in the overall sense. The exposition of contradictions mentioned here is only relative exposition in abstraction, where the crisis is not a crisis in the overall sense.[42]

39   Ibid., p.294.
40   Ibid., p. 296.
41   Ibid.. .
42   See Tang Zaixin et al., *Exploration of the Sequel to Capital*. Beijing: China Financial Publishing House. Yang Guochang et al.: *Inheritance and Innovation of Marxist Economics System*. Beijing: Beijing Normal University Press, 2004.

IV. The Economic Cycle and its Operating Mechanism

Continuity and equilibrium of the capital movement are the normal conditions that capital movements should satisfy for its normal operation, and they are periodically destroyed and restored in the complex contradictory movement of capitalist mode of production. The whole process is manifested as: The opposite elements of the old continuity and equilibrium gradually acquire uneven quantity, asymmetrical distribution and partial interruption of continuity, and when changes in the quantity is accumulated to a certain extent, it will cause a qualitative change in the old continuity and equilibrium. This kind of qualitative change is manifested, in the process of capital movement, as reaching a new continuity and equilibrium with the massive destruction of productive. But the process does not end, the creation and development trend of the new equilibrium and continuity is a destruction of the new equilibrium and continuity. This is an infinite evolution cycle, from lower to higher, from simple to complex. The driving force and source of this evolution comes from the basic contradiction of capitalism, namely, the contradiction between production socialization and the private ownership of means of production.

Corresponding to the intensification of the basic periodic contradiction of capitalism, the reproduction of capitalism is also shown in a periodical process. Each process is manifested as the destruction of equilibrium and continuity which enables reproduction to be carried out, as well as the creation of an equilibrium and continuity. Such periodicity "[a]s the heavenly bodies, once thrown into a certain definite motion, always repeat this, so is it with social production as soon as it is once thrown into this movement of alternate expansion and contraction. Effects, in their turn, become causes, and the initially irregular, and superficially accidental changes, have increasingly been becoming the form of a normal period. However, when the machine industry is so ingrained that it had a decisive impact on the entire national product; when foreign trade began to surpass domestic trade due to the machine industry; when the world market was gradually appropriating vast regions of the New World, Asia and Australia; Finally, when the industrial countries embarking on the playing field became numerous; from this time onwards, the cycle repeatedly began to appear, with successive stages in the last few years, and always ending with a widespread outbreak of crisis, which is both an end of a period, and another starting point for a new cycle."[43]

Imbalance and then the new equilibrium formed, interruption and restoration of the continuity, being repeated about 10 years on the average in Marx's time. This is a circulation with rules, the results of Marx's study suggest that it coincides in line with the life with fixed capital broadly.

---

43 *Capital*, French Version, Volume I, Beijing: China Social Sciences Press, 1983, p. 675.

"As the magnitude of the value and the durability of the applied fixed capital develop with the development of the capitalist mode of production, the lifetime of industry and of industrial capital lengthens in each particular field of investment to a period of many years, say of ten years on the average... the cycle of interconnected turnovers embracing a number of years, in which capital is held fast by its fixed constituent part, furnishes a material basis for the periodic crises. During this cycle business undergoes successive periods of depression, medium activity, precipitancy, and crisis. True, periods in which capital is invested differ greatly and far from coinciding in time. But a crisis always forms the starting-point of large new investments. Therefore, from the point of view of society as a whole, more or less, a new material basis for the next turnover cycle takes place."[44]

The material basis for the capitalist economic periodicity to lose balance and to recover is the renewal of fixed assets. When the economy entered a phase of stagnation, out of competition, capitalists began a new round of investment, which drove economy to grow, so that the production could get out of the crisis. However, with the economic recovery, investment was carried out in an accelerated manner, driving the economy quickly to the limit of prosperity, and thus created conditions for the next round of economic imbalances. In respect to the periodicity of the economic crisis, as well as the manifestation of each stage of the periodicity, in *Capital*, Marx took the cotton industry in England in 1825-1873, for example, and made a more detailed description: The cotton industry in England was always in the stages of getting better or recovering (i.e., moderately active), prosperity, crisis and stagnation, with periodic changes. In the general case, the various stages of the production cycle had the following characteristics: After the crisis, when the decline in production had reached rock bottom and had experienced a period of stagnation, when surplus commodities had been cleared in the market, when vendors of poor competitiveness and poor economic strength disappeared due to bankruptcy or being merged, the market (domestic and foreign) demand for commodities began exposing the increasing trend. In this way, the business surviving the crisis and being adjusted began to resume production, and some even expanded the production. Employment was gradually increasing, with the demand for means of production (including labour tools and raw materials) increasing as well. As the crisis caused a large number of loan capital to be withdrawn, then the interest rate was very low, it provided a favourable condition for capitalists to have massive new investment. With the economic growth driven investment expansion, the economy gradually transformed from the phase of crisis and stagnation to the recovery. With the development of the market towards a more favourable direction, there were more companies that expanded production capacity to increase production, so as to meet increasing market demands. At this time, the demand for additional production and demand for additional labour would be further expanded. This interaction between the various sectors

44   *Capital*, Volume II, Beijing: People's Publishing House, 1975, pp. 206-207.

further expanded the market demand for various products. As the market had become increasingly active, the price of commodities began to rise, profits increased, the stock market became active, interest rate rose, and the employment increased. At this time, the economy was moving from recovery (i.e. moderate activity) to the phase of prosperity.

"In times of prosperity, intense expansion, acceleration and vigour of the reproduction process, labourers are fully employed. Generally, there is also a rise in wages which makes up in some measure for their fall below average during other periods of the business cycle. At the same time, the revenues of the capitalists grow considerably. Consumption increases generally. Commodity-prices also rise regularly, at least in the various vital branches of business. Consequently, the quantity of circulating money grows at least within definite limits, since the greater velocity of circulation, in turn, sets up certain barriers to the growth of the amount of currency."[45]

In times of prosperity, money reflux is unobstructed and quick. Thus, the financial market is active, credit is expanded, securities price rises, stock market is active, and interest rate has gone up, but only rises slowly. Since the whole production process is showing the momentum of prosperity in both purchase and sale, it induces capitalists to push the increase in production to excitement. "But this state of excitement itself, is only the precursor of the state of convulsion."[46]From prosperity to crisis, it often comes all of a sudden.

Under normal circumstances, so long as the products are sold, everything 121 takes its regular course from the standpoint of the capitalist producer.. Whether the producer decides to change the scale of production is mainly based on product sales. The smoother the product is sold, the more likely the producers will expand production scale.

Capitalist socialized production enables the commodity capital to function independently, so that the commodity capital becomes the form opposite to that of commercial capital, and the circulation becomes a relative independent phase of the capital cycle. In this case, as long as the producer sells the commodity to the wholesaler at the ex-factory price, the commodity is considered to have already been sold, and then he can rely on the credit system to obtain funds, and to continue production or expand production. But the reality is often: "a large part of the commodities may have entered into consumption only apparently, while in reality they may still remain unsold in the hands of dealers, may in fact still be lying in the market. Now one stream of commodities follows another, and finally it is discovered that the previous streams had been absorbed only apparently by consumption. The commodity-capitals compete with one another for a place in the market. Late-comers, to sell all, sell at lower prices. The former streams have not yet been disposed of when payment for

45 *Capital*, Volume III, Beijing: People's Publishing House, 1975, p.505.
46 *Marx and Engels Collected Works*, 1st Chinese edition, Volume 8, Beijing: People's Publishing House, 1961, p. 422.

them falls due. Their owners must declare their insolvency or sell at any price to meet their obligations. This sale has nothing whatever to do with the actual state of the demand. It only concerns the demand for payment, the pressing necessity of transforming commodities into money. Then a crisis breaks out."[47]

"In spite of its independent status, the movement of merchant's capital is never more than the movement of industrial capital within the sphere of circulation. But by virtue of its independent status it moves, within certain limits, independently of the bounds of the reproduction process and thereby even drives the latter beyond its bounds. This internal dependence and external independence push merchant's capital to a point where the internal connection is violently restored through a crisis.

Hence the phenomenon that crises do not come to the surface, do not break out, in the retail business first, which deals with direct consumption, but in the spheres of wholesale trade, and of banking, which places the money-capital of society at the disposal of the former."[48]

Therefore, the movement of commercial capital has a direct impact on accelerating or retarding the continuity of the capital movement. During the crisis, the general case is the drop in prices, a large part of commodities stacked in the warehouse, difficult to sell. As the interruption in the transformation process of C'-M', thereby the production of commodities is also forced to curtail, the result is that companies of weak strength are bankrupt, massive unemployment is seen, and there is a significant decline in the wages of workers. The hindered production and circulation further causes the destruction of the credit relations. From the enterprise to the bank, the debt chain is destroyed, and "once the crisis has broken out, it becomes from then on only a question of means of payment. But since everyone is dependent upon someone else for the receipt of these means of payment, and no one knows whether the next one will be able to meet his payments when due, a regular stampede ensues for those means of payment available on the market, that is, for bank-notes. Everyone hoards as many of them as he can lay hand on, and thus the notes disappear from circulation on the very day when they are most needed."[49] Meanwhile, in the crisis, fictitious capital, interest-bearing paper, its price falls with rising interest. It falls, furthermore, as a result of the general shortage of credit, which compels its owners to dump it in large quantities on the market in order to secure money. In particular, the stock price will double drop, which is due to: (1) the increase in interest rate; (2) securities owners are in pursuit of money and sell stocks; (3) the reduction in dividend income. This market crash fuelled speculation that if buying a lot of cheap securities when prices fall, once the storm has passed, prices rise, huge profits can be made. At the same time, by such gambling, the capital ownership is highly concentrated in the hands of the big financiers. "In a period of crisis, the circulation of bills collapses completely;

47 *Capital*, Volume II, Beijing: People's Publishing House, 1975, p.89.
48 *Capital*, Volume III, Beijing: People's Publishing House, 1975, p.340.
49 Ibid., pp.598-599.

nobody can make use of a promise to pay since everyone will accept only cash payment..."[50] Because of the debt chain being broken, as well as the shock wave of a run, banks, stock exchanges, etc. were merged or went bankrupt.

After a heavy blow in the phase of the economic crisis, the economy is gradually dropped to the bottom. At this point, a lot of capital loan is borrowed with low interest rates. Industrial capitalists begin large-scale of equipment renewals, and this leads to the increase of production, making the economy begin recovering gradually. Thus a new cycle begins again.

V. The Realization Mechanism of the World Market Crisis

According to the nature of the crisis elaborated in *Capital*, the crisis is the manifestation of all the contradictions of capitalism, it is the result of the contradictions of capitalism being fully expounded, the real concentration and forcible adjustment of all the contradictions of bourgeois economy, and therefore, the crises manifested in these characteristics are world market crises. The development process of the crisis in the history started as a partial crisis, and eventually evolved into the world market crisis. The existing Marxist economics books only describe the capitalist economic crisis of nation-states, revealing its nature, causes, manifestations and realization mechanisms, while elaboration on the world market crisis, like that on credit issues, is left with only some fragments of the views; suggestive descriptions and general expositions. These achievements could suggest that Marx has made intensive research on the world market crisis, and achieved breakthroughs in almost all the major issues. However, after all, it failed to give a systematic elaboration. Marx's existing writings about crisis theory have answered the question of what the fundamental root of capitalist economic crisis is, and it also answered the system of periodic intensification of basic contradictions in a closed economy mechanism, but he did not put forward what the realization mechanism for the intensification of basic contradictions in the global market crisis is, and what its conduction mechanism is. Marx has found elements that promote the creation of the world market, but he did not elaborate how these elements are to play a role. Therefore, the lack of theoretical systematization and completeness of the contents, is the prominent feature of the Marxist theory of economics on the world market crisis.

The Basic Points of Views

Marx's theory of crisis regards the world market crisis as the form in which the economic crisis has been fully expounded, because the world market is the sum of bourgeois society formed on the basis of bourgeois society in all countries, and it is an international society of bourgeoisie developed on a global scale which extends beyond the barriers of nations. It is the largest overall

---

50 *Capital*, Volume III, Beijing: People's Publishing House, 1975, p.613.

category, but also the most complex, the most specific category. In such a totality, not only native relations of production is included, but also "secondary and tertiary matters, in general, derivative, inherited, non-original relations of production, which influence the international production relations."[51] In here, the production and circulation of capital, as well as each element is manifested as the overall, and all the contradictions of capital relations are expounded. "The world market is the basis and the vital element of capitalist production".[52] That being the case, the world market crisis is a concept linked to the world market in general.

How is the world market in general created? What characteristics does it have? Marx believes that the world market is the result of the development of the capitalist mode of production on its own. This proposition is based on: Capital is the value that can bring surplus value, capital maintains its survival and development (accumulation) by constantly appropriating surplus value. Capital's innate and uncontrollable motive for surplus labour and its unstoppable urge to expand causes constant expansion of capital and pushes capital-based production as an ever growing movement. With the development of the capital and its gaining dominance in the domestic economic life, the domestic market is becoming increasingly narrow and then an obstacle for the accumulation of capital. Thus, according to the logic of its own development, capital breaks the barrier of nations and goes onto the world stage. Until one day when it blew out the Great Wall of narrow and closed natural economy in all the backward countries, when it spread the mode of production adapted with itself throughout the world, it would develop its own as the world market in general, and establish its own millennium kingdom. Marx pointed out that "just as capital has the tendency on one side to create ever more surplus labour, so it has the complementary tendency to create more points of exchange; … i.e. at bottom, to propagate production based on capital, or the mode of production corresponding to it. The tendency to create the world market is directly given in the concept of capital itself."[53] So, capital opens up the international market for its own development, and it is the inevitable result of the development of the capital itself.

Marx believes that capital opens up the international market starting from the field of circulation, and then progresses to production. When the circulation and production of capital is throughout the world, and when the process of internationalization of its various elements and aspects is being fully expounded, and then the unified world market is established and the economy of each country is joined as a whole, resulting in the internationalization of economic life, the world market in general will eventually be created. In the creation of the world market in general, the international division of labour is an important promoting factor. The international division of labour digs up the

51 *Marx and Engels Collected Works*, 1st Chinese edition, Volume 46 (I), p.47.
52 *Capital*, Volume III, Beijing: People's Publishing House, 1975, p.127.
53 Marx and Engels, *Collected Works*, 1st Chinese edition, Volume 46 (I), p.391.

national basis of industry, resulting in internationalizing the commodity production process, as well as that the process of capitalist production transforms form the partial development within a country to the overall development on a global scale. The reality of this development is "industries that no longer work up indigenous raw material, but raw material drawn from the remotest zones."[54] Status of resource allocation can be "the spinner can live in England while the weaver resides in the East Indies... division of labour was about to assume such dimensions that large-scale industry, detached from the national soil, depends entirely on the world market, on international exchange, on an international division of labour."[55] Similarly, the consumption determined and constrained by the production, has also become an international process, which is manifested as the main body, and "industries whose products are consumed, not only at home, but in every quarter of the globe. In place of the old wants, satisfied by the production of the country, we find new wants, requiring for their satisfaction the products of distant lands and climes."[56]

In the world market in general, all economic factors and links are also similarly expressed as in general, gaining the full demonstration of its nature. For example, products develop into commodities in general, and the remnants of the natural economy has been cleaned up and exhausted; Meanwhile, the value also develops into the international value. In the international exchange of commodities which enjoys full development, and in an infinite series of products created in the most extensive range of the world and in every country, commodities in general show their value. Thus, in the international value formed with the global labour in the world, value truly becomes the undifferentiated crystalline of human labour, so that the concept of value has pure manifestation and gets universal significance. Relative to the world labour, the national labour is manifested in individual labour, having a nature of "private labour"; relative to the international value, the national value is shown as individual value. Similarly, money also develops into the universal money, and only in the form of universal money, money really gets full development, or put it this way, "money acquires to the full extent the character of the commodity whose bodily form is also the immediate social incarnation of human labour in the abstract. Its real mode of existence in this sphere adequately corresponds to its ideal concept."[57] In the world market in general, "the entanglement of all peoples in the net of the world market, and with this, the international character of the capitalistic regime."[58] Marx also believes that the development of the whole social organism, does not indicate the end of the development process, but "that it becomes the general because it is an element of its process, or its

125

---

54 *Marx and Engels Collected Works*, 1st Chinese edition, Volume 4, Beijing: People's Publishing House. 1958, p.470.
55 Ibid., pp.168-169.
56 Ibid., p.470.
57 *Marx and Engels Collected Works*, 1st Chinese edition, Volume 23Beijing: People's Publishing House. 1972, p.263.
58 Ibid., p.831.

development." That is to say, its development into the general is only part of its overall development process, and it must put the general as an element of its own development and continue to move forward, so as to complete its own development as a whole. The same is true for the capitalists. When the capital develops into the world market in general, "the world market constitutes a prerequisite and taker of the general." This means that capital will also take the world market as its carrier in general to continue its movement. With the creation of the world market in general, the crisis has become the world market crisis, a world market crisis that erupts periodically. "As the heavenly bodies, once thrown into a certain definite motion, always repeat this, so it is with social production as soon as it is once thrown into this movement of alternate expansion and contraction. When the machine industry is so ingrained that it had a decisive impact on the entire national product; when foreign trade began to surpass domestic trade due to the machine industry; when the world market was gradually appropriating vast regions of the New World, Asia and Australia; Finally, when the industrial countries embarking on the playing field became numerous; from this time onwards, the repeated cycle began to appear, with successive stage of each last few years, and always ended with a widespread outbreak of crisis, which is both an end of a period, and another starting point for a new cycle."[59] Here, the necessity of the formation of the world market in general is derived from the contradictory movement of the productive forces and relations of production, which is consistent with the reason for the forma-

126 tion of the crisis.

In Marx's theory of economic crisis, in addition to discussion of the creation process of the world market in general, as well as its characteristics, it also investigated the realization mechanism of the world market crisis, and revealed it. Since Marx believed that "The world trade crises must be regarded as the real concentration and forcible adjustment of all the contradictions of bourgeois economy."[60] Therefore, obviously, the fundamental root for the global capitalist crisis is caused by the intensification of basic contradictions of capitalism at the world scale. In addition to these most basic elements, Marx also referred to the non-essential elements of the world market, international credit, international trade, international flows of energy resources and trade tariff policies. These elements have different functions, which play different roles in the creation of the world market crisis. From some of Marx's discussions and tips, we can summarize the effects of these factors on crisis listed as below .The world market is functioning as the economic condition. Its effects in the creation of the crisis are mainly manifested as follows: (1) The world market is the basis and living condition of the capitalist mode of production, and therefore it is also the basis and condition of the formation and development of the world market crisis. (2) The world market exists in all domestic markets linked to the foreign markets rather than the mere domestic market, and at the same time

59 *Marx and Engels Collected Works*, 1st Chinese edition, Volume 49, Beijing: People's Publishing House. 1982, pp. 240-241.
60 *Marx and Engels Collected Works*, 1st Chinese edition, Volume 26 (II), p. 582.

as an integral part of the domestic market, all domestic markets in the foreign market. As an extension and supplement to the domestic market, the world market can alleviate the relatively small contradictions with a certain degree between the capitalist production and domestic market. However, this effect is very limited. (3) The market has an external geographical barrier. "In the same measure in which the mass of products grows, and therefore the needs for extensive markets, in the same measure does the world market shrink ever more, and ever fewer markets remain to be exploited"[61], the crises becomes more frequent and more violent. The bourgeoisie gets over these crises "by the conquest of new markets", "that is to say, by paving the way for more extensive and more destructive crises"[62]. (4) "The spatial distance of the place between market and production of commodities (i.e. investigating the market from the point of view of location), within the scope of one country, then outside the country, constitutes an important factor, especially on the basis of the capitalist production, because for most of the products of capitalist production, the capitalist market is the world market."[63] The increase in market distance, on the one hand separates the buyers, as well as production and circulation even more, and on the other "with it therefore grows, both absolutely and relatively, that part of social capital which remains continually for long periods in the stage of commodity-capital, within the time of circulation",[64] thus contributing to the expansion of credit and extension of credit period. In this way, the originally potential abstract possibility of the crisis in the commodity money relations has the access to the full development and realization.

127

Influence of the international credit in the world market crisis is mainly shown in: (1) It prompted most of the exchange activities to be concentrated in businessmen. The huge merchant capital engaged in the bulk import and export trade, which is established on the basis of world market and credit, will break the limitations of reproduction process even more, and promote the process of reproduction beyond its various limitations. Commodities may still be in the changing hands of the importers and exporters, or be stranded on the world market without actually entering in the cost of living, but merchant capital is able to run the production process on the same or expanded scale within certain operational boundaries, enabling this process to be at the most prosperous state on the surface. "The crisis occurs when the returns of merchants who sell in distant markets (or whose supplies have also accumulated on the home market) become so slow and meagre that the banks press for payment, or promissory notes for purchased commodities become due before the latter have been resold. Then forced sales take place, sales in order to meet payments. Then

---

61 *Marx and Engels Collected Works*, 1st Chinese edition, Volume 6, Beijing: People's Publishing House. 1961, p. 506.

62 *Marx and Engels Collected Works*, 1st Chinese edition, Volume 4, p.472.

63 *Marx and Engels Collected Works*, 1st Chinese edition, Volume 49, p. 312.

64 *Marx and Engels Collected Works*, 1st Chinese edition, Volume 24, Beijing: People's Publishing House. 1972, p. 279.

comes the crash, which brings the illusory prosperity to an abrupt end."[65](2) In the international credit, "the capitalist mode of production creates a necessary form for their production process to a suitable scale, to shorten the process of circulation, and the world market simultaneously formed with this production, helps to cover up the role of this form in each individual occasion, and provide a very broad scope for this form to expand."[66] Thus the crisis in germ erupts more violent. (3) The period of the international credit will be prolonged with the increasing distance of the market. (4) With the market away from the production site and the extension of the international credit period, elements of speculation will become increasingly dominant over transactions.

The impact of international trade can be broadly summarized as follows: (1) At a certain stage in the development of world capitalism, the dominant industrial power in international trade forms the source and center of the world market crisis. (2) The impact of the intensity of the crisis in the center countries over other countries depends on the tightness between their trade links. (3) The international trade is the main channel for the spread of the crisis. (4) Excessive international trade is one of the reasons leading to the world market crisis. Credit expansion and blind expansion of production makes a country's foreign trade in extreme expansion, resulting in both too much exports and imports. If there is excessive exports, commodities cannot find sales in other importing countries, and commodity capital cannot be converted into money capital; if there is excessive imports, difference due at maturity is a deficit for a country, although the total trade balance may be a surplus. "What appears in one country as excessive imports, appears in the other as excessive exports, and vice versa. But over-imports and over-exports have taken place in all countries." "The balance of payments is in times of general crisis unfavourable to every nation, at least to every commercially developed nation, but always to each country in succession, as in volley firing, i.e., as soon as each one's turn comes for making payments; and once the crisis has broken out, e.g., in England, it compresses the series of these terms into a very short period. It then becomes evident that all of these nations have simultaneously over-exported (thus over-produced) and over-imported (thus over-traded), that prices were inflated in all of them, and credit stretched too far. And the same break-down takes place in all of them."[67](5) The establishment of a universal system of free trade promotes the open world market, thus easing this contradiction and the crisis generated on this basis. However, on the other hand, the establishment of the world market and the intensification of competition in the world market promoted by free trade intensifies the contradictions in a wider range, resulting in the outbreak of the widespread world market crisis in the true sense.

128

---

65   *Marx and Engels Collected Works*, 1st Chinese edition, Volume 25, Beijing: People's Publishing House. 1974, p.341.

66   *Marx and Engels Collected Works*, 1st Chinese edition, Volume 49, p.292.

67   *Marx and Engels Collected Works*, 1st Chinese edition, Volume 25, p. 557.

The influence of the international flow of precious metals is mainly shown in: (1) The flow of precious metal in the industrial cycle. Generally, an import of precious metal takes place mainly during two periods. On the one hand, it takes place in the first phase of a low interest rate, namely the phase of recession; and then in the second phase, when the interest rate rises, but before it attains its average level, namely the phase of recovery. This period, in which precious metals constantly outflow on a large scale, precedes the crash, or vice versa, "the real crisis always broke out only after a change in the rates of exchange, that is, as soon as the import of precious metal had again gained preponderance over its export."[68] (2) The outflow of precious metal accelerates the crisis. As the capital in the form of money, even a feather is enough to make the scale fall, the outflow of precious metal will increase the interest rate, and fuel the demand for loan capital which is already extremely tight; . Thus, it accelerates the outbreak of the crisis. (3) The outflow of precious metal occurring in each country in turn heralds the arrival of universal world market crisis. On the eve of crisis, the overproduction occurs in a country, resulting in excessive export and import on foreign trade, and deficit in the balance of payments, causing the outflow of precious metals. The outflow of precious metals in a country prompts the outbreak of the crisis, which would cause the rebound in the flow of precious metals, thus it re-inflows. The inflow of precious metal in a country is manifested as the outflow of precious metals in another country, so the crisis repeats itself in another country. For example, "In 1857, the crisis broke out in the United States. A flow of gold from England to America followed. But as soon as the bubble in America burst, the crisis broke out in England and the gold flowed from America to England. The same took place between England and the old continent (Europe)."[69]

The system of protecting tariff in a certain period of time can become a means of ensuring its monopoly in the domestic market, but on the other hand, it intensifies the contradictions between the huge development of production and relatively small sales market. "The results are a general chronic overproduction, depressed prices, falling and even wholly disappearing profits."[70] Then a more serious crisis will come.

The above remark includes almost all the aspects of the Marxist perspective of the world market crisis. Marx's ideas about the formation of the world market in general, the realization mechanism of the world market have provided the basic theoretical tool and analytical model for the analysis of the capitalist world market crisis, and these achievements undoubtedly play an important academic role in the Marxist economic system. Quoting these theoretical achievements is the need to explore the development of the theory and logic of the topic, and more importantly, it is the need to analyze and solve practical problems. To analyze the world market crisis, we must first understand its

---

68   Ibid., p. 643.
69   Ibid., p.557.
70   Ibid., p. 495.

nature. Marx regards the world market crisis as a result of the contradictions of capitalism being fully expounded, and it is the real concentration and forcible adjustment of all the contradictions of bourgeois economy. The essential prescription on the world market crisis has determined that the analytical method of contradiction must be used in the study, analysis and interpretation of the world market crisis should be done, so as to analyze the issues on the role of basic contradictions relevant to the nature of the crisis, and to study the issues on the role of non-basic contradictions not directly related to the nature of the crisis. The capitalist world system has already become a general system, but as an element of its own development, the whole system is always in the midst of continuous development. The world market crisis always occurs in the world market in general which is linked with a specific time, place and condition, and therefore, the study of the history of the crisis should be put into the context of its corresponding world market in general, and the study of the real world market crisis must also be put into the context of the world market in general, otherwise we cannot understand the reason for crises fundamentally. The occurrence of the world market crisis cannot leave out the role of a series of its realization mechanism, and naturally the study of the world market crisis cannot leave out the investigation of these factors.

VI. Crisis in General, Crisis in Special, Crisis in Individual

The possibility of the crisis, the nature of the crisis, the continuity and equilibrium in relation of productions, the tendency of rate of profit to fall and the exposition of contradictions, etc., are all the factors of the economic crisis. *Capital* describes the "capital in general", in other words, the three volumes are thought to correspond to "capital in general" within Marx's plan (see his April 2, 1858; letter to Engels). And since the above-factors of the crisis are expounded throughout the chapters of *Capital*, we can conclude that they are the general provisions of the crisis. This simple reasoning has its basis, the key lies in, which point of view could be the most appropriate when inquiring into Marx's theory of crisis. If it is reviewed within the "six books structure"[71] system, this reasoning will be correct; if it is reviewed from the aspect of Marx's statements on the nature of his crisis theory, as well as the real crisis theory he described, this reasoning will also be reasonable. However, if it is viewed from the perspective of modern Western economics, this reasoning will be meaningless, because there are fundamental differences in the methodologies of the two.

71 In his letter written to Lasalle on February 22, 1858, where Marx mentioned his six-book plan to complete his economic studies: "The whole is divided into 6 books: 1. On Capital (contains a few introductory Chapters). 2. On Landed Property. 3. On Wage Labor. 4. On the State. 5. International Trade. 6. World Market, generally speaking the critique and history of political economy and socialism would form the subject of another work and, finally, the short historical outline of the development of economic categories and relations yet a third." (Collected Works, vol. 40).

Since the crisis theory has its "general form", that means it also has its "special form" and "individual form." The development of its concept will go through three aspects of the general, special, and individual, which is the basic methodology that Marx adopted when realizing his theoretical illustration. If we say, what *Capital* illustrates belongs to "capital in general", then his several later texts or books illustrate the "capital in special" and the "capital in individual" aspects. That he had planned to write on the issues of crisis in his final book, does not mean that the crisis only has its "individual form" rather than other forms. The crisis is the manifestation of all the contradictions of capitalism, it is the result of the contradictions of capitalism being fully expounded, and it is the real concentration and forcible adjustment of all the contradictions of the bourgeois economy. These propositions by Marx illustrate the nature of the crisis, as well as the form of existence and conditions for its occurrence. And such conditions can only exist in the world market.

As the social relations of production as a whole have a very wide range of content, and is in a distribution of multi-level structure, including "secondary and tertiary matters; in general, derivative, inherited, not original relations of production."[72] Apart from domestic relations, there are also "influence here of international relations."[73] How could such a whole of the objective specification be scientifically reproduced as the thought in general? Marx believed that only the method "from the concrete to the abstract" could be the scientific method in order to achieve this purpose. The development of the concept from abstract to the concrete should proceed from the general, to the special and further to the individual.

In Marx's theoretical system of economics, the development of the concept is a spiral process of affirmation (positive), negation (negative), negation of the negation, and the corresponding concepts are manifested as three links: The general, special and individual. It is not a theoretical system of single structure and single level, but a complex whole of the organic combination of composite structures and multi-level structures. For example, in terms of the concept of the economic crisis, in *Capital*, the crisis can be decomposed as three levels, namely, crisis in general, crisis in special and crisis in individual, with causes corresponding to these three levels to be: The disjunction of buying and selling relation which is related to functions as the means of circulation and the means of payment- of money-, as well as the interruption of credit relations; the intensification of the basic contradiction of capitalism, that is, the contradiction between socialized production and private ownership of the means of production; between the anarchy in the whole socialized production and the relative contraction in the purchasing power of the masses of people. But in the study of the system of economic theory in "the whole bourgeois economic system", the concept reflects the provisions or laws at the most abstract and most general

---

72 *Grundrisse: Foundations of the Critique of Political Economy.*
73 *Selected Works of Marx and Engels*, 2nd Chinese edition, Volume 2, Beijing: People's Publishing House, 1995, p. 27.

level. Therefore the concept can explain the origins of the economic crisis, as well as the root causes of capitalist economic crisis, but it cannot explain the more specific reasons for capitalist economic crisis.

The "six-book structure" of Marx's economics texts and the logical evolution of the three aspects in the concept development have played a decisive impact on Marx's crisis theory. Here, we can make this inference: Marx's entire economic writing system delves into the discussion of economic crisis, because the full form of the theoretical system of Marx's economics is the full illustration of various contradictions of the capitalist mode of production. In fact, in Marx's theoretical system of economics, the crisis concept is both handled as an abstract and as a specific category. His concept includes both very abstract provisions and specific contents, and in capitalist mode of production, the economic crisis is manifested as the separation, division and independence of two aspects: Opposition and unity within the economic relations, and it is manifested as forcible unity of the two. So, the contradictions inherent in capitalist economic relations, from their essence to appearance, from the abstract to the concrete, from the simple to the complex, are all factors, conditions and possibilities of the existence of a crisis. In this sense, the analysis of every contradiction of bourgeois economy is at the same time the analysis of the regularity that forms a crisis and determines the manifestations of a crisis; therefore the entirety that Marx's theories related to capitalist economy are in fact the elements of the crisis theory.

132

We can further make this inference: As Marx reveals capitalist economic relations starting from the general, to the specific and further to the individual, the economic crisis as a concept as a whole has also experienced a logical evolution from the general, to the specific and further to the individual, and correspondingly, causes of the crisis also include three levels of the general, the special and the individual. The reason is that the concept is the unity of essence and phenomenon; in the evolution from the general, the special to the individual, includes the gradual increase in the provisions of its quality, the morphological phenomenon (aspect) of the concept also shows diversity and multilevel qualities. Correspondingly, causes for the phenomenon also show diversity and multilevel qualities. For example, the capitalist economic crisis, the production of relative surplus value, the intensification of the basic contradictions of capitalism determine that the same thing is reflected in three aspects: As the phenomenon, the essence and the root in the general level. The capital flights and slump in exchange rate (as seen in 1997 Asian financial crisis), the interruption of credit relations, frenzied speculation by financial speculators also represent that the same thing is reflected as the phenomenon, the essence and the root throughout the certain (special) level.

The Economic Crisis in General

It reflects the most general prescription of the capitalist economic crisis — since the Marxist Economics is the study of capitalist economic relations, so in Marxist economics, the economic crisis means capitalist economic crisis, in fact, the universal outbreak of the economic crisis only becomes a reality in the capitalist society—. The prescriptions should be: The capitalist economic crisis is a crisis of the relative overproduction, and the conditions of its formation are the conditions needed for the crisis to transform from a possibility to reality. On the one hand, the increasing wealth created by labourers becomes the private property of capitalists, which is turned to means of further acquisition of wealth by capitalists, and the result is that capitalist production wildly grows like a snowball. On the other hand, the disposable income of workers is restricted within the range of labour value, and the result is that the capitalist production increasingly exceeds beyond the production which are divorced from the basis for demand. Hence, under capitalism, there is a built-in tendency for production to outstrip the market. As Marx argues, "since the aim of capital is not to minister to certain wants, but to produce profit...a rift must continually ensue between the limited dimensions of consumption under capitalism and a production which forever tends to exceed this immanent barrier." However, the motion or the struggle of the contradictions does not only appear in such a single way, and they also have another important supplementary conflict, that is, the pressure coming from competition and the inherent dynamic of capital expansion which force the individual capitalists to organize and manage production in accordance with the most scientific, the most effective ways, but when evaluated in terms of the social capital as a whole, it is in the state of anarchy. These two intertwined contradictions cannot be overcome within the range of the capitalist mode of production, because they are the concrete manifestation of the contradictions between the socialized capitalist production and private ownership of the means of production. In Marx's writings on economics, he has offered concentrated illustrations related to general provisions of the economic crisis, which was completed in his discussions on *The Law of the Rate of Profit to Fall*. He believed that the basic contradiction of capitalism demonstrates itself as the contradiction between expansion of production and the creation of surplus values, between expansion of production and the value augmentation, as well as the contradiction between growing excess population and excess capital which is determined by the law of the rate of profit to fall and the mass of profit to increase. The intensification of these contradictions is reflected as the outbreak of a crisis. The crisis can only temporarily overcome these contradictions, instead make them more profound and expansive. Within the capitalist scope, the economic crisis cannot be overcome. So, in a general sense of the crisis, "The crises are always but momentary and forcible solutions of the existing contradictions. They are violent eruptions which for a time restore the disturbed equilibrium."[74]

133

74 *Capital*, Volume III, Beijing: People's Publishing House, 1975, p.278.

The Economic Crisis in Special

It refers to its own provisions of (related to the economic crisis in partial form. With the general provisions as the premise, and on the basis of these general provisions, they are those provisions demonstrated during the forcible solutions related to various elements which are in mutual confrontation which are gradually expounded and constitute aspects of the whole or part, as well as the part imbalance and the forcible restoration of the continuity. In the logical development process from the abstract to the concrete, these provisions are distributed in all aspects from the "capital in general" to the capital before it becomes the concept as a whole, that is to say, when investigating the capital, we should in addition to the provisions of its pure form also investigate world market form of it, similarly there are provisions of the "crisis in special" as one aspect of it. Formally speaking, the crisis in special is manifested as the industry crisis (industrial crisis, agricultural crisis), business crisis and credit crisis (money crisis, banking system crisis, debt crisis, payments crisis, etc. are part of credit crisis), where industry crisis is manifested as production surpassing it needs, namely, the production of relative surplus; commercial crisis is manifested as a large backlog of commodities, difficult to realize the value; credit crisis is manifested as the interruption of debt chain, and so on.

The Economic Crises in their Specific Aspects

It refers to the prescription of the economic crisis in the overall form itself, a unity of generality and specificity of crisis, and the most concrete form of crisis in the thinking process. In the theoretical system of Marxist economics from the abstract to the concrete, the economic crisis is manifested in the overall category, the logic level of which is the world market, and therefore the crisis as the overall concept is the world market crisis, or the crisis as the world market crisis is the "economic crisis in individual" aspect. In Marx's economic system, the economic crisis in its individual aspect is manifested as the result of various contradictions of the world market being fully expounded, and because of this, he pointed out: "The world trade crises must be regarded as the real concentration and forcible adjustment of all the contradictions of bourgeois economy. The individual factors, which are condensed in these crises, must therefore emerge and must be described in each sphere of the bourgeois economy and the further we advance in our examination of the latter, the more aspects of this conflict must be traced on the one hand, and on the other hand it must be shown that its more abstract forms are recurring and are contained in the more concrete forms."[75] So, in the level of the economic crisis in individual, there is no need for the abstracted factors, because "the individual factors, which are condensed in these crises" have been "described in each sphere", all provisions of the contractions have been described been elucidated, and its more abstract forms contained in the more concrete forms have been described. Such a crisis is in fact a real form of crisis, or cyclical capitalist world economic crisis manifested in vastly different ways.

75 *Marx and Engels Collected Works*, 1st Chinese edition, Volume 26 (II), p. 582.

Corresponding to the logical structure of its concept, the economic crisis also shows features of multi-level causes.

The Cause in General (Root Cause of Crisis)

It is the most fundamental cause of the crisis phenomenon, the essential link between opposition and unity of various elements contained within the crisis, and the self-identity of the cause of crisis maintained in its own development. At this level, the factors investigated are: the basis of capitalist economic relations; the essential prescription of capital; the essence of capitalist production; capital accumulation and its historical trends; the increasing socialization of production and its driving force; the continuity and equilibrium conditions for the smooth operation of social reproduction and the general conditions for destruction. These factors determine the investigated contradictions that are confined to the range of the basic contradiction and its basic manifestation of capitalism, because they are the originating factors of the cause in general. The reason is generally that when the development of the productive forces is beyond the quantity boundary that production relations can tolerate, the driving factors of the forcible equilibrium are the driving forces when the anarchy of social production, the inconsistency of production and consumption tends to be intensified or alleviated, or the phenomenon caused by the conflict of the narrow basis between the development of the productive forces and the relations of consumption. The root causes that constitute the crisis and its internal relations are a contradictory system that prescribes the emergence, development and changes of the crisis, and their trend of interdependence, interaction and conflicting determines the objective necessity of the crisis. The root causes of the crisis have unity and interconnectivity; it is the only provision that maintains the quality of its existence, and it has always been throughout the theoretical development of the crisis. Since the factors that constitute the root cause of the crisis are also the basic factors that constitute the capitalist economic system, so the root cause of the crisis is always linked with the essential provisions of the capitalist economic system; within the limits of the system to maintain its quality, the root causes of the crisis have also maintained their qualitative provisions unchanged; the development of system promotes the crisis to break out periodically, and the periodic outbreak of the crisis continues to promote the system to have changes in quality and partially in quantity; because the root cause of the crisis is the most basic one to be caused it's development and changes prescribes and affects the development and changes in non-fundamental causes. The root cause of the crisis has certainty, relative stability and universality. For example, as long as it is the capitalist economic crisis, disregarding when and where did it occur, or why did it occur, or what specific form it had, we can trace its root reason back to the intensification of the basic contradictions of capitalism.

The Cause in Special (Indirect Cause of Crisis)

It is the non-root cause of the crisis, it is the partial form of the causes of the crisis, or the partial phenomenon that causes the crises; it is also the self-diversity of the causes of the crisis constantly shown in its development, as well as an external manifestation of different provisions contained within the causes of the crisis. Therefore, the causes here are manifested as many causes. Although the partial cause of the crisis will lead to the outbreak of the partial crisis, the general world market crisis is the inevitable result of the joint action (effect) of various multiple partial causes which will be sufficient to cause a qualitative change. Factors that constitute the indirect causes of the crisis are the primary factors that constitute or determine the social and economic systems, factors purely related with the operation of the economy and dominated and constrained by the elements of the basic social system, which are in a constant contradictory movement of—interaction, mutual promotion, mutual exclusion and mutual struggle—whose result would be that: the equilibrium of a series of quantitative indices that keep the normal operation of the social economy would tend to march to an imbalance, as well as whose result would be that: a series of continuity tends to be interrupted and to a greater extent makes the imbalance and interruption to arrive at a new equilibrium and continuity again. Such factors constitute the indirect causes of the crisis. As for the specific forms of indirect causes, some are the results of single factors, while others are the results of several factors working together. For example, the indirect causes of the Asian financial crisis were: imbalance in industry structure caused by the extensive business; uncollectible accounts caused by the burst of "bubble economy"; worsening of balance of payments caused by the decline in exports, etc., all of which are in the form of single factors. Means that have created conditions for the speculative acts of the international speculative capital, such as liberalization of capital markets, fixed exchange rate regime, and financial deregulation, are in a way of being effected by multiple factors. Compared with the root causes of the crisis, the indirect causes of the crisis have variability and uncertainty. Variability is manifested as follows: With the economic development and the increasing complexity of the economic relations, a number of factors which in the past contributed to the imbalance economic relations or interruption of the continuity gradually lose their role in functioning, and thus no longer constitute the indirect causes of the economic crisis; some did not exist in the past, and later factors which are formed with the economic development and the increasing complexity of the economic relations gradually transformed into the factors that cause the imbalanced economic relations or interruption of the continuity, and thus becoming the new indirect cause of the crisis; some of these factors may constitute indirect causes of the crisis, but through conscious policy adjustments, the ways of the interaction among these factors are changed, causing a change in the results, and thus they no longer are or delay to become the indirect causes of the crisis. Uncertainty is manifested in: those which may be the indirect causes of the crisis here and now have become factors conducive to the smooth development of the economy there and then; those which may be factors conducive to the smooth development of the economy there and then, have become the indirect causes of the economic crisis here and now; the contributing factors that may become the indirect causes of the economic crisis in one case, may not or does not become the contributing factors to the indirect causes of the economic crisis in another. For example, there is a lot of inconsistency in the indirect causes of the Great Depression in the 1930s and the Asian financial crisis, and many causes lead to the Great Depression in the 1930s are actually factors to get out of the Asian financial crisis and to promote the smooth development of the economy. The variability and uncertainty of the indirect causes of the crisis has determined that the general rules of the causes that lead to the economic crisis cannot be found on the level of indirect causes, and there are but only special, ever-changing, and specific factors that lead to economic crisis over and over again.

The Cause in Individual (Direct Cause of Crisis)

The direct causes of the crisis are the unity of opposites of the general and special causes of the crisis, and they are very specific causes among the rest, as well as a unity of the diversity of causes. For the causes in this part, the specificity and certainty has been fully and clearly displayed. If the indirect causes of the crisis are the driving factors that lead to the destruction of the equilibrium and continuity conditions needed for the smooth operation of the social production, the direct cause of the crisis is the factor or means of functioning to make the forcible adjustments to the equilibrium and continuity conditions that have been destroyed. Factors that constitute the direct cause of the crisis may be either single or diverse. For example, factors that have directly caused the the 1997 Asian financial crisis were diverse: (1) The crazy impact of the international hot money; (2) rapid exodus of foreign capital; (3) policy mistakes by the governments when responding to the crisis. As the direct cause of the crisis is the cause floating on the surface the crisis, it is associated with the morphological phenomena of the crisis, with the intuitive, perceptible, and receptive features. The direct cause of the crisis corresponds to the crisis in the form of individuality, so it is a concept associated with the general category, where all provisions and factors have been described, eliminating the need for any abstract form; everything is manifested as a living reality, as people can perceive. The direct cause also has the characteristics of variability, contingency, uncertainty, and diversity. The outbreak of the crises in different times, under different conditions has their own special direct causes, and therefore, it is impossible to find a universal direct cause. The above-mentioned features of the direct cause of the crisis show that: with the role of human factors, the crisis can be triggered in one way or another, the time of crisis can be advanced or delayed, and the intensity of the crisis can be mitigated or aggravated. For example, the international financial speculators triggered the Asian financial crisis in time and place that they deem appropriate and in an appropriate manner.

VII. Conclusions

Marx described two abstract possibilities of the economic crisis, how the possibility of the crisis could turn into a reality, causes of the crisis, the periodicity of the crisis, and other issues, but eventually he did not complete his elaboration on crisis theory, which can certainly be proved from the structure and methodology of Marx's works on economics. Understanding Marx's analytic model of the crisis theory from the perspective of methods and theories is clearly the right choice in methodology. Through methods, we can understand the content and structure of the crisis theory; through theories, we can understand the nature and manifestations of the crisis. The method of manifestation form determines that the entire theoretical system of Marxist economics works that is elaborating the crisis in theory, and all Marx's theories of the capitalist economy at the same time are the crisis theory; the method of content manifestation determines that Marx must reveal the occurrence mechanism of the crisis through the analysis of equilibrium and continuity. Marx used these methods to build the "six-book structure" system of his books on economics, and also built his theoretical system of the crisis. Since Marx failed to complete his books on economics, his theory of the crisis is not a completed system. Because *Capital* describes only the "capital in general", so the theory of crisis reflected in *Capital* also has the same nature, with a clear abstract and general characteristics. Relative to the other points of views, focusing on the "six-book structure" to investigate and to understand Marx's crisis theory can not only make a more reasonable explanation of the status quo of Marxist crisis theory, but also makes a reasonable speculation of the full picture of Marx's crisis theory by using the method of Marxist economics.

The existing Marxist analytic model of the economic crisis, which has a highly abstract characteristic, has determined that it has a powerful function of arguing the essential relations. Using this model to analyze the nature and the development trend of capitalist economic relations, will no doubt prove to be a very effective tool, but it does not mean that it cannot be used to analyze the non-essential causes for the real crises. Here, the key with regard Marx's analytic model of the economic crisis is not only a kind of tool, but a method as well. The analysis of the economic crisis is to analyze the development trend of equilibrium and continuity in the economic operation, and with regard to the specific tools for the analysis, we can use the empirical one, normative one and so on. In short, any analytic means discovered in the economic science can be applied. Here, the universal one is preferably the principle. Mathematical models, econometric methods, computer analysis models, statistical methods are widely used in modern economics to analyze the economic crisis and economic volatility, which is consistent with the basic means of Marx's economic crisis analytical model – the methodology, and there is not the so-called "substantive error", but rather a development. The modern western mainstream economics adopted various different models to analyze the economic cycle, but the "equilibrium" and "continuity" are the core elements of its methodology, which is worthy of consideration. It is believed that the use of the method of Marx's analysis of the economic crisis, to introduce more specific elements and to establish more specific analytic model of the theory is in line with the objective requirements for the development and innovation of Marxist economic theory. Meanwhile, to meet the requirements of the times, the introduction or the creation of a more effective analytical tool, or the establishment of more a powerful analytical model is also in line with the requirements for the development and innovation of Marxist economic theory.

The understanding of Marx's crisis theory must follow Marx's method as clue. A complete system of Marxist crisis theory should include three levels as: the crisis in general, in special and in individual, and Marx's existing books on economics only describes the contents of the first two levels. If we do not understand this situation of Marx's economic crisis theory, it is easy to conclude: that Marx's theory of crisis can only explain the general cause of the crisis but not its actual cause.

CHAPTER IV

The Structure, Elements and Mechanism of Marx's Analytic Model of the Financial Crisis

I. Introduction

The financial crises certainly have a longer history than that of overproduction crises and we know that before the crisis of overproduction the financial crises have occurred, which was often caused by commercial wars, or the excessive speculative activities by certain groups. The financial crises occurring in the era of the overproduction crises that are often caused by overproduction. Therefore, with the advent of the era of capitalist cyclical economic crises, the financial crises have also showed cyclical characteristics. The financial crisis often occurred before the crisis of overproduction, , and has become a signal of the crisis of overproduction. Of course, when we say the financial crisis occurs periodically, it does not means that the non-periodic, independent financial crisis which is based on wars or excessive speculation is came to an end, it means that it still occurs in accordance with its own law of development. As long as the condition for crisis is mature, it will erupt. For example, a series of financial crises that have occurred since the 1990s, are still strong evidence of this conclusion. In the era of Marx, financial crises have occurred regularly, resulting in the more typical manifestation of its essential characteristics, occurrence mechanism, and forms, and it has had the conditions for in-depth study. Marx had studied almost all materials and facts on financial crisis that can be found in the time, and also had an in-depth study of the financial crises occurring during and before his era. Thus, he established his own theory of the financial crisis, explaining its possibility and reality, as well as its nature, occurrence mechanism, relations with the credit, relations with the crisis of overproduction, and the performance in the economic cycle, etc., and furthermore, on this basis, he also described the international financial crisis. Due to the special nature of narrative methods we see in Marx's writings on economics, we do not have a special section or a special text expounding on the issues of financial crises, but his propositions are distributed in various texts. This chapter will summarize Marx's theory of the financial crisis, so that we can have a clear outline of its system and its structural patterns.

II. The Possibility of the Crisis Contains General Elements of the Financial Crisis

We can conclude from Marx's crisis theory that: No matter what specific forms financial crises take, they are directly caused by the interruption of the debt chain. Therefore, to explore the causes of the financial crises, we must start from the creditor-debtor relations in the economic activities. In the creation of the theory of the financial crisis, Marx had studied almost all references on financial crisis that can be found in the time based on the real financial crisis, and then created his own theory of the financial crisis. When having the narrative on theory, in accordance with the sequence of "crisis in general", "crisis in special", and "crisis in individual", Marx expounded the theoretical system of economic crisis. The financial crisis is a special form of economic crisis. So, before elaborating the content of the financial crisis, he had already had the description of the "crisis in general". The relation between "crisis in general" and "crisis in special" is that: "general crisis" has already contained the most general prescription of "crisis in special"; "crisis in special" is further expounded on the basis of the most general prescription of the economic crisis. According to such a sequence of development of the theoretical system, as well as the relations between each part of the theoretical system, if we want to grasp Marx's theory of the financial crisis as a whole, the starting point must be the elements of the financial crisis contained in the "crisis in general". In *Capital*, starting from the possibility of the crisis, Marx's exposition: on the "crisis in general" begins to investigate this possibility from the analysis of the commodity.

According to Marx's explanation in *Capital*, he analyzed the inner contradictions of commodities just from the emergence of commodities. The development of inner contradictions of commodity: that between the use value and value, as well as between the concrete labour and the abstract labour lead to the emergence of money, consequently the circulation of money becomes the metamorphosis of commodities with money becoming the medium. The exchange of commodities with money as the medium is different from barter; it can make the full exchange process of buying and selling achieve the separation in space and in time. This separation contains the possibility of crisis: First, the commodity which actually exists as the use value must be transformed into money, that is, C-M. If this difficulty, the sale, is solved then the purchase, M-C, presents no difficulty, since money is directly exchangeable against everything else. Secondly, it is further assumed that the individual value of the commodity is equal to its social value, that is to say, that the labour-time materialised in it is equal to the socially necessary labour-time for the production of this commodity. Therefore, "[t]he possibility of a crisis, in so far as it shows itself in the simple form of metamorphosis, thus only arises from the fact that the differences in form—the phases—which it passes through in the course of its progress, are in the first place necessarily complimentary and secondly, despite this intrinsic and necessary correlation, they are distinct parts and forms of the process, independent of each other diverging in time and space, separable and separated from each other."[1] Therefore, the possibility of crisis lies solely in the separation of sale from purchase that the commodity remains in the form of the commodity but cannot be transformed into money form. For such possibility of the crisis, Marx pointed out: "if we say that the simple form of metamorphosis comprises the possibility of crisis, we only say that in this form itself lies the possibility of the rupture and separation of essentially complimentary phases."[2] "That is to say, the possibility that elements which are correlated, which are inseparable, are separated and consequently are forcibly reunited, their coherence is violently asserted against their mutual independence. Crisis is nothing but the forcible assertion of the unity of phases of the production process which have become independent of each other."[3] The separation of sale from purchase forms the potentiality of the crisis, which is the most abstract form of crisis.

143

The development and increase of commodity exchange causes inconsistencies between use value and exchange value in the transfer of the commodity at the time, namely, the second metamorphosis is carried out on credit, and then the first metamorphosis is carried out to obtain money.

With such behaviour of purchasing on credit terms and postponing cash money payments money becomes a means of payment. The function of money in such a payment mode makes parties of buyers and sellers be called as the creditor and the debtor, so that the parties involved in social exchanges form a payment chain one after the other, and if anyone in this chain cannot fulfill his payment obligations, a series of parties in these chains also cannot fulfill payment of their debts. Therefore, everyone in the chain begins demanding to pay cash, and thus forms the money crisis. It should be noted that: the crisis occurring because of the interruption of the payment chain, "not only because

---

1   *Marx and Engels Collected Works*, 1st Chinese edition, Volume 26 (II), p.580.
2   Ibid.
3   Ibid., p.581.

the commodity is unsalable, but because it is not saleable within a particular period of time, and the crisis arises and derives its character not only from the unassailability of the commodity, but from the non-fulfilment of a whole series of payments which depend on the sale of this particular commodity within this particular period of time. This is the characteristic form of money crises."[4]

The inherent relations between the two formal possibilities of crisis are: "The form we have mentioned first is possible without the latter—that is to say, crises are possible without credit, namely without money functioning as a means of payment. But the second form is not possible without the first—that is to say, without the separation between purchase and sale." If the crisis appears, therefore, because purchase and sale become separated, it becomes a money crisis, as soon as money has developed as means of payment, and this second form of crisis follows as a matter of course, when the first occurs.

The two formal crises with money as means of circulation and the second as means of payment, is the general and abstract possibility of crisis, and Marx believes that it "denotes no more than the most abstract form of crisis, without content, without a compelling motivating factor." These possibilities, after all, are merely forms of the crisis, and the general possibilities of the crisis. Hence, they are also forms of the real crisis, and the abstract forms of the real crisis. In them, the nature of crisis appears in its simplest forms, and, in so far as this form is itself the simplest content of crisis, in its simplest content. But the content is not yet substantiated. These possibilities of economic crisis come into being long before capitalist commodity production had emerged, but these possibilities have not become reality. The reason is that there must also be a series of relations between the two, that is, a series of intermediate links in the transition from the potential crisis to the real crisis.

144

Marx believed that the investigation of the real crisis, which is the further developed form of the potential crisis, can only be deduced from the actual movement of capitalist production, competition and credit. The further development of the potential crisis can only be investigated thoroughly by the investigation of the special aspects of capital which are peculiar to it as capital, and not merely comprised in its existence as commodity and money.

III. The Possibility of Capitalist Economic Crisis Contains the Actual Elements of Financial Crisis

Historically the transformation of the general possibility of economic crisis towards the possibility of capitalist economic crisis is realized with the transformation from the commodity production phase to the capitalist commodity production phase. Marx has argued that the capitalist commodity production was the developed commodity production in the beginning, thus the capitalist commodity production caused various forms of contradictions inherent within

---

4 *Marx and Engels Collected Works*, 1st Chinese edition, Volume 26 (II), p.587.

the commodity fully expose themselves and the exposition of contradictions of the capitalist mode of production could only be realized in the place where the inherent contradictions of commodity can fully be expounded. If it is said that the general, abstract possibility of crisis is the most abstract form of crisis, without any content, and possesses no cause enabling its content become rich, then we can say the movement of capital C'-M'-C-P-C' in the reproduction process of capital, or from the moment in which it leaves the production process as a commodity in order once again to emerge from it as a commodity, the crises only here receive a content, a basis on which to manifest themselves. Therefore, first of all, if we abstract here from all the other factors determining its content, then the total commodity capital and each individual commodity of which it is made up, must go through the process C-M-C, through the metamorphosis of the commodity. The general possibility of crisis, which is contained in this form—the falling apart of purchase and sale—is thus contained in the movement of capital, in so far as the latter is also commodity and just nothing but commodity.

This external opposition between the use value of commodity and money, is bound to be manifested as money crisis where there is economic crisis of overproduction, that is "as long as the social character of labour appears as the money-existence of commodities, and thus as a thing external to actual production, money crises—independent of or as an intensification of actual crises—are inevitable".[5] Furthermore, the separation of purchase and sale appears here in such a way that the transformation of one capital from the commodity form into the money form, must correspond to the retransformation of the other capital from the money form into the commodity form. The first metamorphosis of one capital must correspond to the second metamorphosis of the other; one capital leaves the production process as the other capital returns into the production process. This intertwining and coalescence of the processes of reproduction or circulation of different capitals is on the one hand necessitated by the division of labour, on the other hand it is accidental; and thus the definition of the content of crisis is already more accurate. Secondly, however, with regard to the possibility of crisis arising from the form of money as means of payment, it appears that capital may provide a much more concrete basis for turning this possibility into reality. For example, the weaver must pay for the whole of the constant capital, such as cotton, flax, weaving machines, wood, coal, etc., but weaver now sells the cloth to the merchant and in return for a bill of exchange, and if the merchant does not pay at maturity, there comes a universal crisis. This is nothing other than the possibility of crisis described when dealing with money as a means of payment; but here—in capitalist production—we can already see the connection between the mutual claims and obligations, the sales and purchases, as well as the actual elements of financial crisis, through which the possibility can turn into reality.

145

5　*Capital*, Volume III, Beijing: People's Publishing House. 1975, p. 585.

Marx also pointed out the contradictions developed in the circulation of commodities and the circulation of money, including the possibility of crisis, as well as the further development of the potential crisis, are bound to be manifested in capital relations, because in fact only on the basis of the development of capital relations can there be the developed circulation of commodity and circulation of money. Therefore, the real crisis can only be deduced from the real movement of capitalist production, competition and credit. However, with the direct production process of capital in itself, the further development of the potential crisis cannot be reflected. This is because although it does contain such factors, it does not contribute any new factors to the crisis, but to the production of surplus-value. The latter is not concerned with the realisation either of the reproduced value or of the surplus-value. This can only emerge in the circulation process which is in itself also a process of reproduction. "The circulation process as a whole or the reproduction process of capital as a whole is the unity of its production phase and its circulation phase, so that it comprises both of these processes or phases. "Therein lies a further developed possibility or abstract form of crisis."[6] So, revealing the possibility of capitalist economic crisis is bound to examine the unity relations between the process of production and the process of circulation of the capitalist total process of production, because it contains the possibility of capitalist economic crisis, as well as the possibility of financial crisis.

146 IV. The Financial Crisis and Its Transmission Mechanism

Various schools of economics offer different interpretations for the financial crisis and their differences are mainly reflected in the level of their nature, while their descriptions in the level of phenomenal knowledge are basically the same. In the abundant literature of Marxist political economy, the financial crisis is defined as the severe turbulences and chaos in the capitalist money circulation and credit fields, and its main manifestations are: domestic commercial credit and bank credit is sabotaged, massive bank deposits are withdrawn, banks go bankrupt, the interest rate increases sharply, prices of commodity and equity tumble; international credits reduce greatly, international settlements require payments in gold, consequently the price of gold soars, and exchange rates become extremely volatile. Marxist political economy also argues that the financial crisis is generally caused by the cyclical crisis of overproduction, which in turn deepens the crisis of overproduction. In the boom phase of the production cycle, with the booming of production and inflation, as well as active business ventures, it leads to credit expansion. Through the issuance of securities, capitalists expand the production beyond the needs of the society in the ability to pay with bank loans and commercial credit, which leads to the overproduction crisis. With the advent of the crisis, a large number of commodities cannot be sold, price declines, market shrinks, business collapses, credit

6 *Marx and Engels Collected Works*, 1ˢᵗ Chinese edition, Volume 26 (II), p.586.

shakes, and a large number of manufacturers go bankrupt because they cannot repay the debt, which causes the chain reaction, so that the field of money and credit face turmoil and chaos. Under particular circumstances, events such as economy, politics and war will lead to financial crisis. In the literature of Western economics generally the financial crisis is concisely defined as the violent deterioration of all or most of the financial indicators temporarily, or beyond its cycle. These indicators include abnormality in short-term interest rates, price of assets (equities, real estate, and land), bankruptcy of companies, and bankruptcy of financial institutions. A considerable part of Western scholars believe that the financial crisis stems from the irrational economic expectations related to the economic boom, based on the expectations that the price of assets will continue to rise, and a lot of money rush into real estate or long-term financial assets. When the industrial crisis occurs, based on the expectation that the price of assets will decline, real estate or long-term financial assets are sold for money, which leads to the financial crisis. Those in early days, the credit expansion was extending the speed of the psychological expectation was towards the opposite direction; shaken confidence due to some financial events, as well as financial commitments, etc., are evaluated as determinant factors which cause the financial crisis. From the above two extremely opposite points of views we can extract a common conclusion that the financial crisis is shown as the disorder in credit relations.

The transmitting form of financial crisis appears in various forms, if summarized, we can say there are basically two forms: First, the financial crisis caused by the industrial crisis; Second, the financial crisis triggered by the crisis in exchange sphere. From Marx's numerous fragments of description, we can summarize the transmission mechanism triggering these two financial crises as follows:

1. The Transmission Mechanism of Financial Crisis Triggered by Industrial Crisis

The process triggered by industrial crisis must also start from the interest rate in the early prosperity phase. The interest rate is very low in this phase, and industrial capitalists take the opportunity to expand the scale of production with the use of credit funds. But with the development of prosperity, capital turnover rate decreases, the disproportionate production, product sales stagnate, circulation rate of credit money declines, etc. appear. Therefore, in order to maintain the requirements for production, industrial capitalists have urgent demand for bank credit. With the increase in bank credit, the industrial capital is increasingly relying on bank credit to maintain production, because the product they produced actually cannot be sold, and the prepaid capital cannot be recovered. At this point, the reality is that bank credit has created a false prosperity, overshadowing the disproportion at the beginning. At this time, due to the difficulties in product sales, business credit has been unable to be carried on, so the circulation means further appears inadequate. In order to maintain production, industrial capitalists are in urgent need that the banks can expand their lending capacity. But in this phase the lending capacity of the banking system falls to the minimum levels. Why does the lending capacity of the banking system fall to the minimum levels in this phase? Generally, there are three reasons:

(1) The system has provided a huge sum of loans to industrial capitalists; (2) It has provided a huge sum of loans to stock speculators; (3) Part of capital has flown abroad. The reasons for foreign capital outflows roughly are in four cases: (1) in countries where the upsurge is at its peak and thus the crisis is approaching, there is a trend of international deterioration of balance of payments. (2) the most important part of the international balance of payments is deteriorating, demanding plenty of gold to liquidate. (3) High interest rates at the prosperous heyday absorb a lot of foreign currency to flow into the country for the purchase of securities, causing the drain of money from other countries. (4) Deterioration in the trade balance results in the drain of gold. Because the bank reserves dropped to the limit, the central bank cannot stop its expansion of reserves. Then the commercial banks have to start tightening credit. This result, for the industrial capital, would mean that the interference produced by disproportionate investment can no longer be offset, because the moneyed capital needed cannot be supplied. So, what is followed are: The industrial capitalists are in the urgent need for means of payment, and in order to get the means of payment, they have to dump commodities. Everyone is dumping commodities, causing prices to fall. The industrial credit is thoroughly shaken, and is no longer able to obtain credit from banks. Due to the lack of means of payment, industrial capitalists are unable to repay their bank loans. Thus the banks lose their liquidity, namely payment difficulties, there are runs on the bank cashier, panic appears and begins to spread, and all banks cease their cash payments one after another. Thus, the banking system crisis erupts.

2. The Transmission Mechanism of Financial Crisis Triggered By Crisis in the Stock Market

Low interest rates in the early prosperity phase stimulate the price of fictitious capital market to rise, which in turn fuels rampant speculation. The expansion in speculative activities causes a further increase in demand for stocks, resulting in further boost in stock prices. The rise in stock prices promotes the development of entrepreneurial activity. The new holding companies have emerged, and the existing joint stock companies expand their own capital. So there is a significant increase in new stock issuance, and the stock prices are still in an upward trend. This is the phase in which the entrepreneurial activities are the most busy and the banks are those which gain the most profits through stock issuing deals. Driven by greater profit greed, speculators begin riskier speculations relying on bank loans. With a significant increase in the demand for credit, this increase in loan demand began to promote the rise in interest rates. With the prosperity entering its peak period, the stocks continue to shoot up, and speculators use stocks as collateral to obtain credit from banks, then even further speculate more rampantly, and consistent with this speculation, interest rates continue to rise. When interest rates reach the peak, speculators

148

have to stop the efforts of driving up the price, and instead withdraw part of the credit funds from the speculation. At the same time, the entrepreneurial profits are reduced to the minimum due to high interest rates, so that the issuance is handicapped. Speculation reaches the saturation point, because they face the risk that new shares cannot be sold or can only be sold at a lower price. Thus, speculation begins to tighten, and the stock begins to fall along. The fall of stock price makes the bank realize the danger of encouraging speculation, and therefore, begin the compulsory auctions of the pledged stock. Auction causes a sudden increase in supply of shares, and further leads to a more substantial decline in value of the securities market. At this point, some professional spec- ulators start wantonly selling shares, and the bank is also further engaged in auctions of the pledged stock. In the joint efforts of all forces, the stock market finally collapses, and an exchange crisis breaks out in this market. However, crisis in the stock exchange is not the end; it is merely a prelude to or a symp- tom of an industrial and commercial crisis. After the crisis in the exchange, the share price immediately drops to the lowest point. At this point, a lot of big capitalists and bankers begin to buy the devalued securities in order to throw them at a higher price when the panic passes and the market price rises. This situation continues until in the next cycle, the deprivation process of part of speculators and the concentration process of property on capitalists' hand restarts, and thus the exchange executes function of means to realizing prop- erty concentration through the concentration of fictitious capital. Marx saw the origin of fictitious capital in the development of the system and the joint-stock 149 system. "The formation of a fictitious capital is called capitalisation."(Marx, Capital, Vol. III, Part V, Division of Profit into Interest and Profit of Enterprise. Interest-Bearing Capital). It represents a claim to property rights or income. Such claims can take many forms, for example, a claim on future government tax revenue or a claim issued against a commodity that remains, as yet, unsold. The stocks, shares and bonds issued by companies and traded on stock markets are also fictitious capital.

From the transmission mechanism that triggers the financial crisis, there is an intrinsic link between the financial crisis and industrial crisis. Marx had a very detailed description of this relation: "In a system of production, where the entire continuity of the reproduction process rests upon credit, a crisis must obviously occur—a tremendous rush for means of payment—when credit sud- denly ceases and only cash payments have validity. At first glance, therefore, the whole crisis seems to be merely a credit and money crisis. And in fact it is only a question of the convertibility of bills of exchange into money."[7]

Financial crisis can either be a harbinger of an overproduction crises or can occur independently. If we say that the crisis of overproduction is the epiphe- nomenon born with the capitalist system, the financial crisis is the epiphenom- enon of exchange of commodities with money as the medium, and Marx once said: "As long as the social character of labour appears as the money-existence

---

7 *Capital*, Volume III, Beijing: People's Publishing House. 1975, pp.554-555.

of commodities, and thus as a thing external to actual production, money crises— independent of or as an intensification of actual crises—are inevitable."[8] The slump in securities of the financial market causes the collapse of banks and non-bank financial institutions, as well as the turmoil in financial markets, but the industrial sector has not been affected, with the reproduction still proceeding smoothly. At this time, the financial crisis has the characteristics of an independent occurrence. In Marx's time, the money crisis is generally accompanied by the overproduction crisis, and has periodicity. The independent money crisis often occurs due to the war, the speculative trade of some special commodities, the speculative operations on government bonds and listed stocks, as well as other factors, and Marx called it a special crisis, which is not caused by the industrial crisis, but it is counterproductive to industry and commerce. "The pivot of these crises is to be found in moneyed capital, and their sphere of direct action is therefore the sphere of that capital, viz., banking, the stock exchange, and finance."[9]

V. Capitalist Credit Relations and the Financial Crisis

Recognizing the crisis from the most general possibility to its reality, this thinking itinerary includes our understanding of the financial crisis. The thinking itinerary, at a certain point, has an entrance to our understanding of the financial crisis, which is the Marx's theory of credit. In Marx's theoretical system of economics, credit is seen as one of the three levels that drive the concentration of capital, together with the competition and the joint stock system, on which Marx intended to elaborate by special efforts. It was also one of the important aspects for his theoretical system to develop from the abstract to the concrete. Marx also regarded credit as a movement of the capitalist mode of production for capital creation. He said: "And this movement, disposing on condition of returning, constitutes per se the movement of lending and borrowing, that specific form of conditionally alienating money or commodities."[10] Obviously, for Marx, credit is "the movement of lending and borrowing"; it is a lending practice "disposing on condition of returning".

Originally, credit is an economic category subordinate to money relations, and the historical premise for its emergence was as follows: at least a part of the produced goods are transformed into commodities and various functions of money, especially its function as a means has developed to a certain level. Different conditions of production and sales capacity among the commodity producers, besides the uneven distribution of monetary assets among them prepares the basis for credit trading, thus forms mutual credit relations between the creditor and the debtor. Credit relations attain different characteristics under

---

8   *Marx and Engels Collected Works*, 1st Chinese edition, Volume 25, Beijing: People's Publishing House. 1974, p.585.
9   *Marx and Engels Collected Works*, 1st Chinese edition, Volume 23, Beijing: People's Publishing House. 1972, p.158.
10   *Capital*, Vol. III Part V. Division of Profit into Interest and Profit of Enterprise. Interest-Bearing Capital

different social conditions; therefore the same lending practice reflects different economic relations when occurring in different socio-economic conditions. Capitalist credit as one component part of it appears on the basis of capitalist relations of production, is a "unique" lending practice of capital goods with repayment as the condition, and embodies such relations that borrowing capitalists and functional capitalists divide the surplus value between them. As the capital can take both the form of money and the form of goods, the capitalist credit can be divided into commercial credit and bank credit, as the two basic forms. Commercial credits appear among capitalists in their trading activities.

In Marx's theoretical system of economics the crisis is both in an abstract and a specific category and in a specific category in the general sense. It has both highly abstract provisions and specific contents, and in the capitalist mode of production the economic crisis is manifested as the separation, division and independence of two aspects of opposition and unity within the economic relations, and it is manifested as forcible unity of the two. So, the contradictions of capitalist economic relations, from essence to appearance, from the abstract to the concrete, from the simple to the complex, constitute the factors, conditions and possibilities of the existence of a crisis. In this sense, the analysis of every contradiction of bourgeois economics is to analyze the regularity that forms a crisis and determines the manifestations of a crisis; all Marx's theories of the capitalist economy are in fact the crisis theory. Marx regarded crisis as a movement of the unity in opposites in the economic relations. The normal functioning of the economy means that its inner factors are in unity, and once these factors are gradually separate and independent, the developing trend would be that the separate and independent factors tend to be unified, the process of which is the crisis itself. In reality, this movement of the contradiction of the unity of opposites appears as a movement which develops through two opposing phases, and if this process is also a unity of the two phases, then the motion is also essentially the separation and independence of the two phases. Marx wrote: "However, they belong together; the independence of the two correlated aspects can only show itself forcibly, as a destructive process. It is just the crisis in which they assert their unity, the unity of the different aspects. The independence which these two linked and complimentary phases assume in relation to each other is forcibly destroyed. Thus the crisis manifests the unity of the two phases that have become independent of each other. There would be no crisis without this inner unity of factors that are apparently indifferent to each other."[11] Therefore, in this sense, factors of all the contradictions of the capitalist economic relations are factors of the economic crisis, the accumulation of contradictions is the accumulation of crisis, the further development of contradictions is the development of crisis, and the analysis of contradictions is the analysis of crisis. The aim of in-depth study of the capitalist credit relations by Marx is to reveal the crisis factors it contains, namely the "equilibrium" relation and "continuity" relation contained in the credit relations.

---

11   *Marx and Engels Collected Works*, 1st Chinese edition, Volume 26 (II), p. 571.

Commercial credit is the type of credit transaction between two entrepreneurial capitalists related to purchase and sales of commodities between them, which is the basis of the credit system. Commercial credit exchanges commodity capital and "commodities are not sold for money, but for a written promise to pay for them at a certain date."[12] This written promise, as commercial bills or promissory notes, can be used as means of payment and means of circulation to purchase commodities from or pay debts to other capitalists upon "endorsement", so they actually perform a certain functions as money. In a commercial credit transaction money undertakes the function as the means of payment. The commodity capital lent in the commercial credit is part of the industrial capital, and this close relationship between commercial credit and industrial capital makes it play the role of the medium, which is quite unique and hard to be replaced by other forms of credit, from commodity to money or from money to commodity. As Marx writes: "(commercial) Credit, then, promotes here 1) as far as the industrial capitalists are concerned, the transition of industrial capital from one phase into another, the connection of related and dovetailing spheres of production; 2) as far as the merchants are concerned, the transportation and transition of commodities from one person to another until their definite sale for money or their exchange for other commodities."[13]

Marx distinguished two types of capitalist or the dual character of a capitalist: (i) the functional capitalist, i.e., the business administrator (operator) of the means of production; and (ii) the rentier capitalist whose livelihood derives either from the rent of property or from the interest-income produced by finance capital, or both. Marx wrote: "But, so far as he is personified capital, it is not values in use and the enjoyment of them, but exchange-value and its augmentation, which spur him into action. Fanatically bent on making value expand itself, he ruthlessly forces the human race to produce for production's sake; he thus forces the development of the productive powers of society, and creates those material conditions, which alone can form the real basis of a higher form of society, a society in which the full and free development of every individual forms the ruling principle. Only as personified capital is the capitalist respectable. As such, he shares with the miser the passion for wealth as wealth. But that which in the miser is a mere idiosyncrasy, is, in the capitalist, the effect of the social mechanism, of which he is but one of the wheels."

This means that changes in motion scale of the commercial credit is inevitably affected and constrained by the cycle of industrial capital. The development of commercial credit is based on the development of production, and the expansion and contraction of commercial credit is consistent with the expansion and contraction of the reproduction process of industrial capital. There is a relation of interaction and mutual promotion between commercial credit and capitalist production, "the development of the production process extends the credit, and credit leads to an extension of industrial and commercial operations."[14]

---

12 *Marx and Engels Collected Works*, 1st Chinese edition, Volume 25, p. 450.
13 Ibid., p.546.
14 Ibid., p. 544.

This interaction mechanism promotes the unlimited expansion of capitalist production. "A large quantity of credit within the reproductive circuit does not signify a large quantity of idle capital, which is being offered for loan and is seeking profitable investment. It means rather a large employment of capital in the reproduction process."[15] "The maximum of credit is here identical with the fullest employment of industrial capital, that is, the utmost exertion of its reproductive power without regard to the limits of consumption."[16] The development of commercial credit on the one hand accelerates the transformation of commodities in the form of capital, on the other; it speeds up the circulation and turnover of capital, thus contributing to the expanded reproduction of capitalism. Thus the study of the intrinsic link between the commercial credit and the accumulation of real capital becomes the basic approach to reveal the intrinsic link between the industrial crisis, commercial crisis and financial crisis, through which we can see transmission mechanism from the industrial crisis to commercial crisis.

We have mentioned above that the commercial credit assumes the form of commodities, and has certain limitations: firstly it is restricted by the reserve that functional capitalists can dictate, and secondly, the conversion time from the commodity to money, thirdly it is vulnerable to changes in price levels. These limitations make the commercial credit unable to meet the needs for expanded capitalist reproduction, thus the bank credit must be a supplement. Bank credit is a credit that bank capitalists provide for functional capitalists in the form of money, which breaks all restrictions on commercial credit, and has more advantages than commercial credit: through the credit provided by the bank to the functional capitalists, it can put various idle funds concentrated in the society together to form a huge loan capital, provides more loan capital to functional capitalists, and thus it is not restricted by the quantity of individual capital and capital reflux; its object is the temporarily idle moneyed capital freed from the production process, and thus its range can be free from the direction of commodity circulation; it can be provided to any one of the functional capitalists by the bank. These advantages mean that it can adapt to the needs of expanded capitalist reproduction in a greater degree, and it is also able to meet the needs of capitalists to have speculative activities in capital operation. With the existence of bank credit, the bank concentrates a lot of temporarily idle moneyed capital in the society in the form of deposits, opposing to the functional capitalists as the representative of all lenders; on the other hand, and the bank lends the concentrated loan capital to functional capitalists, as the representative of all borrowers opposing to all lenders. In the special movement of bank capital (M-M-C-M'-M'), the link completed by the bank is M-M, among which the first M is equity capital and borrowed capital of the bank and the second M is the capital actually used for borrowings. In addition to the equity capital of the bank, the first M is the loans flowing to the

---

15 *Capital*, Vol. III, Part V, Chapter 30. Money-Capital and Real Capital I.
16 Ibid., p. 546.

bank through a variety of channels, and the second M is the loans flowing to functional capitalists through discount on exchange, credit loans, mortgages, deposit overdrafts and other channels. In order to achieve constant repetition of M-M, the premise is that functional capitalist can successfully perform promise of M'-M', namely the repayment of repay principal and interest. Otherwise, the volume of deposits and loans will be unbalanced, and the movement of M-M will be interrupted.

When explaining bank credit, Marx carefully examined credit given by a banker, which may assume various forms: bills of exchange on other banks, cheques on them, credit accounts of the same kind, and finally, if the bank is entitled to issue notes—bank-notes of the bank itself. Marx said: "A bank-note is nothing but a draft upon a banker, payable at any time to the bearer, and given by the banker in place of private drafts." A bank note is a credit tool issued to meet needs of discount on notes. Areal bank note can replace money of precious metals to perform the functions of the means of circulation and means of payment. As a form of credit, the bank note breaks out of the confines of mere commercial circulation into general circulation, and serves there as money. It actually has the national credit to back them, and is more or less a legal tender, and therefore it is the real credit money. A bank note is used for discount on commercial bills, which are caused by the credit in commodity exchange. Therefore, the circulation of bank notes is based on commercial credit, and the quantity of bank notes is adjusted through the need for transaction. If the quantity of commodity exchange expands, commercial bills increase, it requires a corresponding increase in discount on bills, and the amount of issuance by banks will increase correspondingly, otherwise it will reduce. The direct reason that this part has been able to enter Marx's study on credit issues is that, the bank note is a credit tool, and the deeper reason is that as the bank note is used for discount on commercial bills, it promotes the larger scale of expansion of the capitalist reproduction, and thereby it exacerbates the contradictions of capitalist production and circulation.

154

Marx also had a multi-aspect and multi-angle description of the law of changes in the constituent elements of the credit relation: (1) on the credit contraction and expansion trend. Marx pointed out: "These phases are, briefly, an utter contraction of credit in the year of panic, followed by a gradual expansion, which reaches its maximum when the rate of interest sinks to its lowest point; then again a movement in the opposite direction, that of gradual contraction, which reaches its highest point when the interest has risen to its maximum, and the year of panic has again set in."[17] (2) On the law of changes on interest rate in the industrial cycle Marx pointed out: "If we observe the cycles in which modern industry moves…, we shall find that a low rate of interest generally corresponds to periods of prosperity or extra profit, a rise in interest separates prosperity and its reverse, and a maximum of interest up to a point of extreme

17   *Marx and Engels Collected Works*, 1st Chinese edition, Volume 12, Beijing: People's Publishing House, 1962, p.346.

usury corresponds to the period of crisis. ......It is possible, however, for low interest to go along with stagnation, and for moderately rising interest to go along with revived activity."[18] (3) The movement of interest rates and industrial capital. Marx believed that the movement of interest rates in the opposite direction to that of industrial capital. "At the beginning of the industrial cycle, a low rate of interest coincides with a contraction, and at the end of the industrial cycle, a high rate of interest coincides with a superabundance of industrial capital."[19] (4) Means of payment and industrial cycle. With the outbreak of the credit crisis, the process of payment of the balance will be interrupted due to the sudden fluctuations in credit, and the payment mechanisms is also destroyed, so that people will suddenly require money to become a real general means of payment, as well as require that all the wealth to exist in the dual form. It is both commodity and money, and the existence of mutual consistence is manifested as that money is the only wealth. (5) Means of circulation and industrial cycle. "The demand for currency between consumers and dealers predominates in periods of prosperity, and the demand for currency between capitalists predominates in periods of depression. During a depression the former decreases and the latter increases."[20]

For the reason of credit contraction, Marx believes that it is but a symptom of changes in the industrial cycle[21], rather being caused by the changes in the industrial cycle. "The superficiality of political economy shown itself in the fact that it looks upon the expansion and contraction of credit, which is a mere symptom of the periodic changes of the industrial cycle as their cause."[22]

155

In Marx's theory of credit, Marx first regarded the credit relationship as the expansion factor of capitalist economic relations. The role of this factor is mainly reflected in that it can promote the accumulation, concentration and agglomeration of capital; it can promote averaging profits; it can save commercial capital, distribution costs and means of circulation volume; it can accelerate the process of reproduction; it enables individual capital to control social capital; it promotes the establishment of joint-stock companies. These effects reflect much the unity of capital on the one hand, where they can accelerate or delay the outbreak of the crisis, but it is not the root cause of the crisis itself.

Marx's credit theory reveals the relationship between the credit and the crisis from various aspects, and these relationships are manifested in the following areas:

(1) The credit relationship contains the general possibility of a crisis. The function of money as the means of payment is also the basic form of credit relationship. This form of the payment chain formed by the creditor-debtor

18 *Capital*, Volume III, Beijing: People's Publishing House. 1975, p.404.
19 Ibid., p.553.
20 Ibid., pp.509-510.
21 See *Capital*, Volume I, Beijing: People's Publishing House. 1975, p. 694.
22 Karl Marx, *Capital*, Vol. 1, Chapter 25: The General Law of Capitalist Accumulation.

relationship contains the possibility of money crises. The possibility has the premise of the possibility of separation of purchase from sale, but it is after all the second possibility in the existence of the first possibility (separation of purchase from sale). Especially in modern society, where the credit relationship has permeated all levels of social and economic life, the possibility of crisis reflected in the credit sometimes has relative independence, and its power of dissemination and destruction of crisis is greatly enhanced.

(2) Credit has a strong role in the outbreak of crisis. The expansion of credit on capital prompts each production sector to dominate the capital of the entire capitalist class, not in accordance with the amount of their own capital of capitalists in this sector, but in accordance with their production needs. This creates conditions for the blind expansion and over-expansion of capitalist production. Particularly in the industrial upsurge period, it results in that the development of production grow by leaps and bounds in spite of the demand with the ability to pay, so there has been a more serious crisis in the future.

(3) The independence of merchant capital and its tremendous development contributed by modern credit system, not only makes its own motion within certain limits of unrestricted reproduction process, but will even drive the process of reproduction to jump out of its various limitations. Thus, "aside from the separation of C-M and M-C, which follows from the nature of the commodities, a fictitious demand is then created."[23] The form of commercial credit has separated the production process from the circulation process, and the form of bank credit through discount on bills or through secured loans of goods that cannot be sold enlarges and aggravates this separation. Bank credit "creates a form for the commodity capital to achieve conversion in advance to money", or that "[c]redit renders the reflux in money-form independent of the time of actual reflux. both for the industrial capitalist and the merchant." However, in such times of prosperity, "the appearance of rapid and reliable refluxes always keeps up for a longer period after they are over. In reality by virtue of the credit that is under way, since credit refluxes take the place of the real ones."[24] In this way, the actual overproduction would be covered up.

(5) Credit As The Effective Tool of Speculation.

By making a difference between the nominal value and the actual value and then profiteering is one of the most common speculation tricks. Such speculation zealously aims to artificially expand the reproduction process. This expansion makes the production process reach a very serious level, and the speculation will not restrain itself but behave in an intensified manner, because this is the only way to create a more favourable condition for speculators. When the speculative basis suddenly collapses, the pursuit of the means of payment occurs. "At first glance, therefore, the whole crisis seems to be merely a credit and money crisis. And in fact it is only a question of the convertibility of bills

156

23 *Capital*, Volume III, Beijing: People's Publishing House. 1975, p. 340.
24 Ibid., p.507.

of exchange into money." ... "At the same time, an enormous quantity of these bills of exchange represents plain swindle, which now reaches the light of day and collapses; furthermore, unsuccessful speculation with the capital of other people; finally, commodity-capital which has depreciated or is completely un-salable, or returns that can never more be realised again." ... "Incidentally, everything here appears distorted, since in this paper world, the real price and its real basis appear nowhere, but only bullion, metal coin, notes, bills of ex-change, securities."[25] In conclusion, credit is an important leverage for over-production and excessive commercial speculation. (6) The dual nature of credit leverage can either alleviate or exacerbate the crisis under certain conditions. For example, when a financial panic occurs, "it is clear that as long as the credit of a bank is not shaken, it will alleviate the panic in such cases by increasing credit-money and intensify[ing] it by contracting the latter."[26] This mechanism has become the most basic form in the modern financial control system.

In addition to the above-mentioned relationship between credit and crisis, Marx also revealed the relationship between the credit crisis and industry cri-sis. He noted that despite credit has a significant impact on crisis, or even at first glance, "therefore, the whole crisis seems to be merely a credit and money crisis. And in fact it is only a question of the convertibility of bills of exchange into money. But the majority of these bills represent actual sales and purchases, whose extension far beyond the needs of society is, after all, the basis of the whole crisis."[27] In reality, the first outbreak of the credit crisis and money crisis is reflected as the inverted crisis. Originally the first is the capitalist overpro-duction, followed by commodity capital surplus and commercial crisis, leading to credit crisis and money crisis; however, the outbreak of crisis is precisely reversed, and the first is the outbreak of credit crisis and money crisis, then commercial crisis, and finally the production crisis. Therefore, money crisis and credit crisis is often the fuse or indication of a full outbreak of crisis.

In general, with regard to the development of the credit relations at that time, Marx had done the best study, because people before him, or even his contem-poraries had not done the similar thing yet, to say nothing of findings like his; his study results not only reflect the whole development of credit relations at that time, but are also somehow highly forward-looking.

VI. The Economic Cycle and Financial Crisis

Marx has studied the periodicity of economic crises, and also the perfor-mance of various elements in each sub-stage of every period: to explain these issues Marx gave a more detailed description in *Capital*, analyzing the practice of the textile industry in England in 1825-1873 for example. We can find the changing trend of some elements of the financial crisis from various stages of

---

25 *Capital*, Volume III, Beijing: People's Publishing House. 1975, p. 555.
26 Ibid., p. 585.
27 Ibid., p. 555.

the production cycle, as well as the law of crisis occurrence. Based on multiple texts from Marx, we can make the following summary:

After the crisis when the decline in production has reached rock bottom and has experienced a period of stagnation and when the excess commodity has been cleared from the market, companies of poor competitiveness or with weak economic strength disappear due to bankruptcy or being acquired, the demand for commodities in (domestic and foreign) markets began showing the increasing trend. Thus, companies surviving the crisis and adjusted to begin to recover production, and some even expanded production. Employment is gradually increased up and the demand for means of production (including labour tools and raw materials) are also gradually increased up. In general, the moneyed capital originally used in the production and commercialization is extracted from business by capitalists, and deposited in the bank on a large scale, and banks convert them to loan capital, this fact largely increases the supply of loan capital. At the same time, due to the recession of production and commercialization, the demand for loan capital is reduced, and thus the interest rate is very low. This provides favourable conditions for capitalists to engage in massive new investment. Due to the economic growth driven by the expansion of investment, the economy gradually changes from the crisis and stagnation to recovery.

In the recovery phase, the demand for discount on bills and bank loans is still small. At this stage, because there is a large number of idle capital available, the bank can easily expand its deposit liabilities, and it can also safely ensure its reserves relying on the repayment of their loans on a regular basis and easier borrowing from the money market. In maintaining adequate reserves and the proportion of liabilities, the central bank is also in a very advantageous position. Under the combined effect of these factors, the rate of interest is at a low state, and this promotes the renewal of fixed capital on a large scale.

In the early stages of prosperity, the scale of industrial production gradually expands, and commercial credit will also be active and will be greatly expanded, because at this stage, the expansion of commercial credit and the smooth capital refluxes are combined together regularly, thereby it expands the lending of commodity capital, and does not need to retain huge reserves for the payment of bills on maturity, thus ensuring the supply of loan capital. At the same time, as the development of production, a large number of commodities are produced in a steady stream, thus the commodity trading tends towards prosperity, with the gradually increasing social wealth, and it also brings an increase in loan capital. At the same time, due to the commercial discount, credit loans, a substantial increase in the scale of fixed capital renewal, the demand for loan capital has increased significantly. Marx wrote: specially, "In times of prosperity, intense expansion, acceleration and vigour of the reproduction process, labourers are fully employed. Generally, there is also a rise in wages which makes up in some measure for their fall below average during other periods of the business cycle. At the same time, the revenues of the capitalists grow considerably. Consumption increases generally. Commodity-prices also rise regularly, at least in the various vital branches of business. Consequently, the quantity of circulating money grows at least within definite limits, since the greater velocity of circulation, in turn, sets up certain barriers to the growth of the amount of currency."[28]

In times of prosperity, money reflux is unobstructed and quick. Thus, the financial market is active, credit is expanded, securities prices are in the rise, stock market is active, and interest rate level has increased, but still its rise is slow. Since the whole production process shows the momentum of prosperity in both purchase and sale, it induces capitalists to push the increase in production to excitement. As Marx wrote: "But this state of excitement itself, is only the precursor of the state of convulsion. Excitement is the highest apex of prosperity; it does not produce the crises, but it provokes its outbreak"[29]

The crisis phase of capitalist economic cycle in general began when the speculative hoarding of commodities by the wholesaler collapsed. The rise in the rate of interest and the reduction in effective demand forced the speculative hoarding commodities to be on sale, which will lead to the collapse of the price, making it extremely difficult for debt liquidation. The bankruptcy of those wholesalers will have negative impact on banks that have provided a large amount of loan for speculation. Because, the emergence of the situation of "inability to pay" greatly hinders new commercial credit transactions among capitalists. Banks greatly limit their transactions related to discounting of bills or promissory notes, because banks need to ensure their own safety, keep their savings and avoid bankruptcy. With the emergence of this credit crisis, the central bank is put into a very difficult situation: It faces the increased demand for loans, but cannot determine the creditworthiness of assets held for sale, and at the same time, it is also reducing its own reserves. Therefore, the interest rate reaches the highest point...when there is a new crisis, sudden interruption of credit, payment freezing, and paralysis of the reproduction process. There is a serious shortage of loan capital alongside the rest of the untapped industrial capital. At the same time, there is a sharp decline in the rate of profit, and often it becomes negative. The fundamental changes in profits are expected, and the rise in the rate of interest will lead to the transformation from the speculative prosperity into crisis in the capital markets. If speculative stocks transaction during the last stage of the rise relies on credit, then the capital market crisis will throw those speculators who cannot liquidate their debentures into a sudden wave of bankruptcies.

The capitalist socialized production makes functions of the commodity capital independent, thus the commercial capital becomes the form of capital opposed to the industrial capital, and the circulation becomes a relatively independent stage of the circulation of capital. In this case, as long as the commodity

---

28   *Capital*, Volume III, Beijing: People's Publishing House. 1975, p. 505.
29   Marx, *Pauperism and Free Trade*, The approaching commercial crisis, First published in the New-York Daily Tribune, No. 3601, November 1, 1852.

producers sell the commodity to the wholesalers at the producer prices, the commodity is considered to have already been sold, thus the producer thinks he can continue production or expand production relying on the funds from the credit system. But as Marx states the reality is often different: "A large part of the commodities may have entered into consumption only apparently, while in reality they may still remain unsold in the hands of dealers, may in fact still be lying in the market. Now one stream of commodities follows another, and finally it is discovered that the previous streams had been absorbed only apparently by consumption. The commodity-capitals compete with one another for a place in the market. Late-comers, to sell at all, sell at lower prices. The former streams have not yet been disposed of when payment for them falls due. Their owners must declare their insolvency or sell at any price to meet their obligations. This sale has nothing whatever to do with the actual state of the demand. It only concerns the demand for payment, the pressing necessity of transforming commodities into money. Then a crisis breaks out."[30]

The credit crisis is firstly because of the difficulties for the liquidation of commercial debt during the end of the upswing stage. Because of the loss of credit, the issuance of new commercial credit is virtually impossible. It cannot be sustainable to get the means of payment by a loss of sales. To pay the debt, the liquidation on a mass scale is also to be paid through sales of a large number of commodity inventories, which will lead to the alleviation of the pressure to access to the means of payment and then cause depression in the beginning stage.[31]*

160

In spite of its independent status, the movement of merchant's capital is never more than the movement of industrial capital within the sphere of circulation.

"By virtue of its independent status it moves, within certain limits, independently of the bounds of the reproduction process and thereby even drives the latter beyond its bounds. This internal dependence and external independence push merchant's capital to a point where the internal connection is violently restored through a crisis." In the next paragraph Marx goes on: "Hence the phenomenon that crises do not come to the surface, do not break out, in the retail business first, which deals with direct consumption, but in the spheres of wholesale trade, and of banking, which places the money-capital of society at the disposal of the former."[32] (See Marx: *Capital*, Vol. III Part IV, Conversion of Commodity-Capital and Money-Capital into Commercial Capital and Money-Dealing Capital (Merchant's Capital)).

Therefore, the movement of commercial capital has a direct effect on accelerating or delaying the continuity of capital movement, and making it from equilibrium to destruction as well. During the crisis, the general situation is that

30   *Capital*, Volume II, Beijing: People's Publishing House. 1975, p.89.
31   Marx also calls Money-Dealing Capital as Merchant's Capital.
32   *Capital*, Volume III, Beijing: People's Publishing House. 1975, p.340. See Marx: Capital Vol. III Part IV, Conversion of Commodity-Capital and Money-Capital into Commercial Capital and Money-Dealing Capital (Merchant's Capital).

the prices go down, and a large number of commodities are accumulated in the warehouses in the cycle of sales and become difficult to sell. Because of the interruption of the conversion process from C'-M' the production of commodities thus are forced to diminish, and those enterprises with weaker strength go bankrupt along with massive unemployment, and there is a significant decline in the wages workers. Crises hindered in the production and circulation phases, it further causes the damage of the credit relationship. From the enterprise to the bank, the debt chain is destroyed, and "Once the crisis has broken out, it becomes from then on only a question of means of payment. But since everyone is dependent upon someone else for the receipt of these means of payment, and no one knows whether the next one will be able to meet his payments when due, a regular stampede ensues for those means of payment available on the market, that is, for bank-notes. Everyone hoards as many of them as he can lay hand on, and thus the notes disappear from circulation on the very day when they are most needed."[33]

Meanwhile, in the crisis, the price of fictitious capital, i.e. the price of interest-bearing notes falls with the rising interest rates. The price of fictitious capital falls, furthermore, as a result of the general shortage of credit, which compels its owners to dump it in large quantities on the market in order to secure cash money. In particular, the stock price will drop, which is due to: (1) the increase in interest rate; (2) securities owners are in pursuit of cash money and try to sell their stocks; (3) the reduction in dividend income. This market crash fuels a lucrative speculation: big financiers buy a lot of cheap securities when prices fall, once the storm has passed and securities prices rise, then huge profits can be made. At the same time, by such gambling, the capital ownership is highly concentrated in the hands of the big financiers. "In a period of crisis, the circulation of bills collapses completely; nobody can make use of a promise to pay since everyone will accept only cash payment..."[34] Because of the debt chain being broken, as well as the shock wave of a run, banks, stock exchanges, etc. initiate mergers or go bankrupt.

After a heavy blow in the phase of the economic crisis, the economy is gradually dropped to the bottom. At this point, a lot of capital loan is withdrawn, with low interest rate. Industrial capitalists began large-scale equipment renewal carefully and thus led to the development of production, making the economy begin to recover slowly. Another new cycle begins again.

VII. Fictitious Capital and Financial Crisis

From the writings by Marx, we can see that the asset forms of bank capital basically include two categories: cash and securities. Securities can also be divided into two types, commercial securities and public securities. Commercial securities are mainly drafts or promissory notes. Public securities include

---

33 *Capital*, Volume III, Beijing: People's Publishing House. 1975, pp. 598-599.
34 Ibid, p. 613.

government bonds, treasury bills, mortgages of a variety of stock and real estate, and so on. In the narrow sense, public securities can be traded, being part of the securities; commercial securities cannot be traded, these latter are priceless securities. In Marxist political economics, commercial and public securities are called fictitious capital. When he was investigating bank capital in *Capital*, Marx has focused on this feature. Various public securities, as a debt obligation or securities of ownership, not only bring regular incomes for their holders, but can be traded as a commodity, with a unique method of price determination. From the phenomenon, it seems that the securities itself is capital in reality, but in fact it is not the real capital, it is "paper replica "of capital. Marx believes that fictitious capital is formed based on the interest-bearing capital, and in essence is the capitalization of income. "The form of interest-bearing capital is responsible for the fact that every definite and regular money revenue appears as interest on some capital, whether it arises from some capital or not. The money income is first converted into interest, and from the interest one can determine the capital from which it arises." Therefore, fictitious capital" is and remains a purely illusory conception."[35] The fictitiousness of bank capital is also evidently manifested in the deposits. After the depositor deposits funds in the bank, the bank will immediately change these deposits into interest-bearing capital and loan them out, and to form the real capital of the functionalist capitalists, while deposits of the depositor becomes the capital of a "written book of the bank." In addition, the derived function of deposits of the bank can create deposits on bank account, and which is several times more than the original ones. Therefore, from this perspective, most of the bank's capital is composed of illusory fictitious capital.

162

The price of securities in nature is capitalised income. "Their value is always merely capitalised income, that is, the income calculated on the basis of a fictitious capital at the prevailing rate of interest."[36] The fictitious capital existing insecurities can have capital gains in the effective duration, and they are also traded; their market value or price will change with the size and reliability of profits, and when the expected revenue has been set, price fluctuation and interest rate are inversely proportional. **The current price on market of securities = revenue of securities / lending interest rate.** In addition to the two decisive factors in the equation that affect the current price on market of securities, there are also other factors like the supply and demand for securities, real economic development, the economic cycle process and so on. Generally, the volatility of securities is always associated with the various stages of the production cycle. In the phase of prosperity, as companies are operating in good condition, with improved profitability, increasing investment, low interest rates, and the idle moneyed capital is turning to the securities market for a way out, thus making the price of stocks and other securities rise again. When the crisis comes and hits, the production will stagnate, expected income will be reduced, the

---

35   *Capital*, Volume III, Beijing: People's Publishing House. 1975, p. 526.
36   Ibid., p.530.

money market will be tight, with inadequate money causing the interest rate to rise, and due to the widespread need of cash, securities are sold out, thus making the market value or price of securities decline significantly. The unique movements and determination method of the market value or price of securities make them become the object of speculation, especially the equities, which are the main target for speculative activities. The primary purpose of speculation with securities is to earn the difference between the market price, and the reason that such speculation has been able to be achieved is because the market value of securities "is determined not only by the actual income, but also by the anticipated income, which is calculated in advance"[37]. Securities speculation is mainly traded with option and whether the trading parties can make money depends on the fact that whether the actual changes in market price of the securities are consistent with the expectation of speculators. As the purpose of buyers and sellers is to earn the difference of fluctuations in the market price of securities, they are often the fictitious bargain, and it ends the transaction by paying the difference from one party to another at the settlement.

These securities transactions make securities trade become a big gamble. Those monopolist capitalists or financial speculators who are abundant in capital, familiar with insider trading often cause or initiate waves with their large number of securities and moneyed capital, artificially creating fluctuations in market prices, and thus making the fluctuations in market price consistent with the expected upward or downward trend, thus profiteering from the "price fluctuation difference." The price of securities is often inflated due to the manipulation of speculators, and small investors generally could not withstand the temptation of huge profits and have followed. When the price reaches a certain level and the bubble suddenly bursts, the speculators have already had clearance and exited, but small investors who are firmly trapped, have to bear the loss of the slump in market price. As Marx said: "A result of gambling on the stock exchange, where the little fish are swallowed by the sharks and the lambs by the stock-exchange wolves."[38] This artificial volatility in securities trading markets, tend to make translocation of the creditor and the debtor, so that the original creditor-debtor relationship is destroyed, and caused a chain reaction, leading to bank credit crisis. As already said, in the condition that crisis does not occur in the industry, the financial crisis can occur independently. This mechanism of independent occurrence exists in the special movement of the fictitious capital.

Before Marx, economists had different views on the fictitious capital, but none of them had explored its theoretical significance. Marx was the first to notice its significance in the mature capitalist economy, and tried to bring a theoretical explanation on its association with independent monetary and financial crisis. Marx believed that as the fictitious capital; on the one hand it does not correspond to the real capital, or even does not represent the real capital, but

163

---

37   *Capital*, Volume III, Beijing: People's Publishing House. 1975, p.530.
38   Ibid., p.497.

represents the right of profit or the claim for money; on the other hand, the fictitious capital has its market value, which has basically nothing to do with the real movement of capital, because the fictitious capital itself has become a commodity, whose market value is mainly determined by the supply and demand for moneyed capital and fictitious capital on the capital markets, and thus its market value fluctuates, so that the trade of such financial instruments is more of speculation and expectation. Compared with general merchandise, fictitious capital and general commodities also have the risk of separation of purchase from sale, but it represents a greater fictitious wealth and more claims for money, and hence the risk is greater. In addition, it in itself is a credit instrument, so as to establish a broader credit-debt relationship.

The fictitious capital has completely separated the value and the price, and the non-labour items have prices, and then turn into value along with the money exchange. It is here that the capitalist economy has changed. In addition to the production, this change is resulting in a fictitious capital market. The fictitious capital market attracts the idle money capital in the society and forms another round of the rise and volatility in market prices. Its contact with the self-expansion of practical value is wiped clean, leaving not a trace. In the meantime, bank financial institutions are involved, whether it is the purchase of stocks, bonds by banks, or credit operations with stocks, bonds as collateral. In short, much of the capital banker is purely fictitious, which are composed of a claim for debt, national bonds and stocks. In addition, the use of fictitious capital to issue and carry out mortgages, makes the speculation in the fictitious capital market more prevalent, because speculators are holding other people's capital for gambling, which is commonly known as "moral trap" today. Thus, centered by the fictitious capital, it forms a self-circulation market composed of the wealthy class, banks, speculators and owners of small capital to have conversion of trading with each other between fictitious capital of securities and credit money, and thus the credit (instrument) and credit money are accelerating expansion here. Everything here appears distorted, since in this paper world, the real price and its real basis appear nowhere. There is no problem of production or commodity here. If the emergence of money makes the price of money deviate from its value, then the emergence of fictitious capital makes credit gain tremendous development, enabling financial movement to deviate extremely from the actual production movement, so that the credit money greatly deviates from gold money, and the issuing of the bank credit money deviates from the rule of the metal currency.

It is in the process of self-circulation in which the fictitious capital deviates from the actual economy, money has revealed the opposition with fictitious capital commodities, as well as with credit money, and as a general form of value, money accumulates its contradiction with the market value of fictitious capital, as well as with the denomination value of credit money, waiting for a mandatory uniform and overlap—a money crisis. It seems to Marx that, money becomes into commodity and is opposed to all other commodities, which is bound to show up, and especially in the developed capitalist commodity economy, on the one hand has largely been replaced by the credit operation, and on the other hand, in countries where it has been replaced by credit money, it is especially so. First of all, in times of emergency when credit is shrunk or completely stopped, money will be suddenly regarded as the only means of payment and the actual value, absolutely in opposition to all commodities. Secondly, only when its value represents the absolute real money, the credit money is the money. The developed capitalist economy is a credit economy, which is the expanded development movement of the fictitious capital, namely the fictitious economy. Because credit and credit money is not real money, nor real wealth, and like the general commodities, it will ultimately turn into money. Thus, in the crisis, the demand is made that all bills of exchange, securities and commodities shall be simultaneously convertible into bank money, and all this bank money, in turn, into gold. As long as the social character of labour appears as the money-existence of commodities, and thus as a thing external to actual production, money crises—independent of or as an intensification of actual crises—are inevitable.

According to Marx's analysis, the over-excessive expansion in the fictitious capital market and the over-excessive growth in bank credit, namely the extraordinary development of the financial system, are the basis and condition for the independent monetary and financial crises to occur. That is to say, compared with the non-independent monetary and financial crises, the financial expansion required is much higher. In the extraordinary development of the financial system, as long as the capital injected in the stock market is stalled, or bank credit is contracted, or financial speculators or financial institutions fail, this development will directly trigger a financial crisis.

It must be seen that the development of the fictitious capital market may bring mitigation of overproduction, and once it goes in front, it will withdraw the moneyed capital from the production process, or attract the financial resources, resulting in the rapid development of fictitious capital markets or even the whole financial system, so that the growth of commodity production is relatively backward. Hence, when an independent monetary and financial crisis occurs, the commodity production may not have reached the critical state of surplus, although it is affected, and it does not necessarily produce economic crisis.

Overall, in Marx's views: (1) The financial crisis is essentially money crisis, although it is shown as the liquidity crisis of companies and banks, debt payment crisis, and the pursuit of money is the most basic feature of the financial crisis; (2) Excess production and surplus finance are two conditions of financial crisis, and the financial crisis can either break out in the economic crisis because of overproduction, or erupt in chaos of the extraordinary development of the financial system with the representative of the fictitious capital. The self-expansion movement of fictitious capital is the main mechanism for the formation of the independent monetary and financial crisis.

165

VIII. Types of Financial Crisis

In the era Marx lived, the development of the financial industry in general was still relatively low, and types of financial crisis were still largely confined to the bank crisis, the stock market crisis, debt crisis, and money crisis. In Marx's writings, only credit crisis and money crisis are mentioned, and there is no such concept as financial crisis. Among them, the credit crisis includes all the crises caused by the interruption of the debt chain; the money crisis basically means the universal pursuit of means of payment during the crisis, with a lot of customer deposits withdrawn from the bank, a large number of borrowers going bankrupt, a large number of banks failing, commercial credits reduced, the demand for loan greatly exceeding the supply of capital, and a sharp rise in the rate of interest. In his writings, Marx had described different types of financial crises; however, he did not focus on the field where the crisis occurred but focused on the mechanism of the crisis. Therefore, in order to understand Marx's theory of the financial crisis, it is necessary to summarize types of financial crisis from this point of view, so as to understand Marx's theory of crisis from different aspects. Such aspects include:

1. **Manipulation.** Big scale moneyed capitalists profiteer by manipulating the money market: "they are strong enough to disrupt the whole money-market at any given moment and thereby bleed white the smaller money-dealers..... There were several such money sharks, who could considerably intensify a stringency by selling one or two million's worth of consols and thereby withdrawing an equal amount of bank-notes from the market. The joint action of three large banks would suffice to transform a stringency into a panic by a similar manoeuvre."[39]

2. **Precious Metal Drain.** If the reduction of a country's precious metal becomes a trend and the metal reserves of the bank fall to a level significantly below the median, it will endanger the domestic credit. People will lose confidence in the form of the domestic money, thus exacerbating the eruption of the crisis. This is because at this time, everyone wants to get more cash and dominates as much credit means as possible. But it does not. At this time, the market is surplus, with extreme contraction of credit, the discount rate raised by bank, coupled with the drain of precious metals, which intensified this conflict even more. Thus, in general, the number of drain of gold might even be as tiny a number in a country's gold reserves, but in the period that precedes the crisis, "by acting like a feather which, when added to the weight on the scales, suffices to tip the oscillating balance definitely to one side."[40]

3. **Credit Expansion.** Since the misleading information stimulates the business speculation, which stimulates credit expansion, which in turn fuels the business speculation, resulting in surplus of commodities and thus triggering crisis.

166

---

39 *Capital*, Volume III, Beijing: People's Publishing House. 1975, p. 613.
40 Ibid., p. 647.

4. **Credit Contraction.** Continuous circulation takes place between constant capital and constant capital (even regardless of accelerated accumulation). Since constant capital is never produces for its own sake but solely it is needed in spheres of production, stimulated by prospective demand, therefore, the business of merchants and industrialist goes briskly forth. "The crisis occurs when the returns of merchants who sell in distant markets (or whose supplies have also accumulated on the home market) become so slow and meager that the banks press for payment, or promissory notes for purchased commodities become due before the latter have been resold. Then forced sales take place, sales in order to meet payments. Then comes the crash, which brings the illusory prosperity to an abrupt end."[41] In short, "in a system of production, where the entire continuity of the reproduction process rests upon credit, a crisis must obviously occur—a tremendous rush for means of payment—when credit suddenly ceases and only cash payments have validity."[42]

Marx also discussed the relationship between the central bank system and the crisis, and argued that "the central bank is the pivot of the credit system. And in turn, the metal reserve is the pivot of this bank." The reason that the metal reserve has such a sensitive effect is because: "The development of the credit and banking system, which tends, on the one hand, to press all money-capital into the service of production (or what amounts to the same thing, to transform all money income into capital), and which, on the other hand, reduces the metal reserve to a minimum in a certain phase of the cycle, so that it can no longer perform the functions for which it is intended—it is the developed credit and banking system which creates this over-sensitiveness of the whole organism."[43]However, in the simple commodity economy, due to the simplicity of credit relations (here mainly usurious credit is prevalent); "this over-sensitiveness of the whole organism" is generally difficult to occur.

167

Marx also explained from another perspective; the credit itself contains certain elements to ease the crisis. For example, when the crisis arrives, issuing bank notes with state credit as the guarantee can achieve the purpose of easing the crisis. Here, Marx's correct observation of his time is proven with the later practice, that capitalism generally uses fiscal policies to ease crises.

IX. International Credit, Liquidity of Precious Metals and Financial Crisis

Marx also pointed out that the capitalist countries not only apply the credit and fictitious capital domestically, but also on an international scale as a means to break through the limit of production. And the international expansion of this credit will promote expansion of exports and imports of all countries, as well as overproduction. Capitalist world trade and international market is also

---

41   Ibid., p. 341.
42   Ibid., pp. 554-555.
43   *Capital*, Volume III, Beijing: People's Publishing House. 1975, pp. 647-648.

built on the basis of the credit system. Similarly, the expansion of commodities and debt supported by credit still needs money to achieve. The international credit expansion and national overproduction enables all countries to have the conditions for the financial crisis to occur. Therefore, when the crisis occurs in a country, countries that already possess conditions for a crisis will face it one after the other. As the crisis realization mechanism, the "international credit" has its influence on the world market crisis mainly in: (1) International credit prompted most of the exchange activities to be concentrated in businessmen. The huge merchant capital engaged in the bulk import and export trade, which is established on the basis of world market and credit, will break the limitations of reproduction process even more, and promote the process of reproduction beyond its various limitations. Commodities may still be in the changing hands of the importers and exporters, or be stranded on the world market without actually entering in the cost of living, but merchant capital is able to run the production process on the same or expanded scale within certain operational boundaries, enabling this process to be at the most prosperous state on the surface. "The crisis occurs when the returns of merchants who sell in distant markets (or whose supplies have also accumulated on the home market) become so slow and meager that the banks press for payment, or promissory notes for purchased commodities become due before the latter have been resold. Then forced sales take place, sales in order to meet payments. Then comes the crash, which brings the illusory prosperity to an abrupt end."[44] (2) In the international credit, "the capitalist mode of production creates a necessary form for their production process to a suitable scale, to shorten the process of circulation, and the world market simultaneously formed with this production, helps to cover up the role of this form in each individual occasion, and provides a very broad scope for this form to expand."[45] Thus the crisis in germ erupts more violently. (3) The period of the international credit will be prolonged with the increasing distance of the market. (4) With the market away from the production site and the extension of the international credit period, elements of speculation will become increasingly dominant over transactions.

168

Marx's analysis of the financial crisis is based on the domestic system, but not limited to it. In the mid-19th century before the international gold standard was established, the international capital flow has been relatively free and frequent. Marx noted in particular the role of capital flows on the financial crisis in the capitalist world, and he pointed out that the European financial crises in 1847 and 1857 were caused first by capital flows, and then by the economic crisis. In *Capital* Volume III, Marx studied the general condition of the financial crisis, and in Chapter 35, he was devoted to the impact of capital flows on capitalist economy and finance. As the realization mechanism of the world market crisis, the "International Flows of Precious Metals" has the influences as follows: (1) the flows of precious metals

44 *Marx and Engels Collected Works*, 1st Chinese edition, Volume 25, Beijing: People's Publishing House, 1974, p. 341.
45 *Marx and Engels Collected Works*, 1st Chinese edition, Volume 49, Beijing: People's Publishing House. 1982, p. 292.

in industrial cycle. Before the economic crisis, there will always be the massive export of precious metal, but after the crisis there will be massive imports. This regular change of export and import with the reproduction cycle explains that there are intrinsic connections between export and import of the precious metal and the production cycle. This connection is manifested in that, the production cycle affects and restricts the export and import of precious metals, which in turn reflects changes in the production cycle. Under normal circumstances, the inflow of precious metals occurs mainly in two phases. First, it is the first phase in which the rate of interest is slightly low, namely the phase of depression, and then it is the second phase in which the rate of interest is raised but not yet reaches the average level, namely the phase of renewed activity. This is because in these two phases, the price of means of production is relatively low, and the rate of deposit is also low, both of which are conducive to commodity exports, as well as to attracting foreign investment. Marx discovered the law: "The inflow of bullion goes hand in hand with flourishing trade, prices not yet high but rising, a surplus of capital, and excess of exports over imports."[46] As in the phases of depression and renewed activity, loan capital is relatively abundant, and the inflow of precious metals in the first place only exists as the surplus loan capital, which also facilitates the supply of loan capital, limits the rise in the rate of interest, and is conducive to the recovery and prosperity of business. However, the drain of precious metals is continuous on a large scale, in the period of which precedes the crash. At this time, there is overproduction, and an illusory prosperity is maintained only by means of credit. As commodities are difficult to sell, returns no longer flow, but raw materials are required to be purchased into on a large scale, therefore, the demand of entrepreneurs for loan capital is increasingly intense. "A drain, a continued and heavy export of precious metal, takes place…as soon as a greatly increased demand for loan capital exists and the interest rate, therefore, has reached at least its average level."[47] The continuous drain of precious metals means the great withdrawal of loan capital, reducing the supply of loan capital, and further raising the interest rate. The raise of the interest rate does not restrict the continuous expansion of credit, but prompts it of over-expansion. (2) The drain of precious metals accelerates the outbreak of the crisis. The drain of precious metals as the capital in the form of money will raise the interest rate, and fuels the already extremely tense demand for loan capital. Under normal circumstances, the amount in the drain of gold is only a relatively small part of a country's gold reserve, but in the period preceding the crisis, "by acting like a feather which, when added to the weight on the scales, suffices to tip the oscillating balance definitely to one side."[48] That is to say, in the case that the credit has been shaken, compared with all the gold reserve in banks, the drain of precious metals, even in small quantity, will fluctuate the entire economy, prompting a violent crisis to erupt. The reason that the drain of precious metals can bring such a result is because the capital, as the moneyed capital, performs both the function of money,

169

46 *Marx and Engels Collected Works*, 1st Chinese edition, Volume 27, Beijing: People's Publishing House, 1972, p. 193.
47 *Marx and Engels Collected Works*, 1st Chinese edition, Volume 25, p. 646.
48 Ibid., p. 647.

and the function of capital. As the capital, the drain of precious metals will affect the supply and demand of domestic loan capital, thereby affecting changes in the interest rate, as well as the entire credit relationship. Before the crisis, a drain of gold will reduce the bank reserve, and the turnover will be difficult, causing widespread panic; withdrawals are increased, deposits are reduced, credit is contracted, and the bank is forced to raise the discount rate, leading to a shaken credit, triggering a credit crisis and a currency crisis, until finally evolving into a comprehensive economic crisis. The over-sensitiveness of capitalist economy is caused by the developed banking system and credit system, and occurs in the urgent period of industrial cycle. If the production is not developed enough, or not in the crisis phase of the industrial cycle, even there is the import and export of precious metals, which makes the amount of the domestic gold reserve above or below its average level, it will generally and not necessarily have the effect in this special occasion on domestic money liquidity, loan capital, and rate of interest, etc. (3) The drain of precious metals occurs in various countries, indicating the advent of the widespread crisis in the world market. When a country has overproduction before the crisis, there are excessive export and imports in foreign trade, and balance of payments is unfavourable, causing the drain of precious metals. The drain of precious metals prompted the crisis in the country, which would cause the rebound in flow of precious metals and re-inflows. Marx said: "It should be noted in regard to imports and exports, that, one after another, all countries become involved in a crisis."[49] All of countries have exported (this is, traded too much) and imported (that is, produced too much) too much. Credit has expanded in all of the countries. And all countries have the same crash to ensue. "The phenomenon of a gold drain then takes place successively in all of them and proves precisely by its general character that the sequence in which it hits the various countries indicates only when their judgement-day has come, i.e., when the crisis started and its latent elements come to the fore there."[50] The inflow of precious metals in a country is shown as the drain in another country, so the crisis will repeat itself in another country. For example, in "1857, the crisis broke out in the United States. A flow of gold from England to America followed. But as soon as the bubble in America burst, the crisis broke out in England and the gold flowed from America to England. The same took place between England and the continent."[51] The phenomenon of the drain of precious metals will occur in turn in all countries, and this universal phenomenon indicates that the drain of the precious metal is just the phenomenon of the crisis, rather than the cause. Therefore, the sequence of the drain of precious metals in different countries is the information at what time a crisis will occur in these countries.

Marx's analysis clearly shows that in the global expansion of the capitalist economy, the world's financial, trade and production are closely related, and financial system is particularly vulnerable. On the one hand, it is that the production is particularly vulnerable to excess, and on the other hand, the finance is

---

49   *Capital*, Volume III, Beijing: People's Publishing House. 1975, p.556.
50   Ibid., p.557.
51   Marx and Engels, *Collected Works*, 1st Chinese edition, Volume 25, Beijing: People's Publishing House. 1975, p. 557.

particularly vulnerable to expansion, while the capital movement is extremely sensitive, so that the financial crisis is particularly prone to occur, and it is destined to be an international and global financial crisis.

X. Conclusions

The structure, contents and system of Marx's theory of the financial crisis contain the basic model for us to analyze the financial crisis. The model itself is divided into two types: (1) The model used to analyze the financial crisis triggered by overproduction crisis; (2) The model used to analyze the financial crisis triggered by the war, political events, and excessive speculation.

The basic structure and elements of Model (1):

Assumptions: (1) The world economy dominated by free competition; (2) The capitalist economy in pursuit of profit maximization as the goal; (3) The developed commodity economy; (4) The existence of well-developed credit relationships.

Continuity: Includes the continuity of cycling chain of credit M_1-M_2-M_3-C-p-C'-M_1'-M_2'-M_3' (M_1 represents depositors funds, M_2 bank credit funds, M_3 moneyed capital of the functional capitalist, M_1' sales income of the functional capitalist, M_2' principal and interest of bank capital, M_3' principal and interest of depositors.)

Equilibrium:

$$M_1' - EI = M_2' \qquad [1]$$
$$M_2' - BI = M_3' \qquad [2]$$
$$(S–I) + (T–G) = CA \qquad [3]$$
$$CA + FA + \Delta R = 0 \qquad [4]$$
$$BM = DC + R \qquad [5]$$

Nominal value of fictitious capital = Actual value of fictitious capital [6]

Liabilities = Payments of debt [7]

In formula [1], [2], [3], [4] and [5], EI represents revenue of the business owner, BI banks' profits, S private savings, I investment, T government taxes, G government spending, CA current account balance, FA capital account balance, ΔR net change in state reserves, BM[52] high-powered money (base money), DC domestic credit assets, R assets of foreign currency reserves .[53]

---

52 In economics, the monetary base (also base money, money base, high-powered money, reserve money, or, in the UK, narrow money) in a country is defined as the portion of the commercial banks' reserves that are maintained in accounts with their central bank plus the total currency circulating in the public (which includes the currency, also known as vault cash, that is physically held in the banks' vault).

53 Formula [1] indicates that: the principal and interest of credit recovered by the banker shall be equal to the functionalist capitalists' sales revenue minus the revenue of business

Root Cause: The basic contradiction of capitalism.

Transmission mechanism includes: credit → extreme expansion of production → commercial crisis → interruption of debt chain → financial crisis → full-blown crisis.

Variables: the stock market, the size of credit, foreign exchange rate, interest rate, discount rate, social retail price, export and import of precious metals, capital turnover rate, commercial inventories, sales rate.

Conclusions: capitalist financial crisis is the chaos caused by the overproduction crisis in the financial sector.

In capitalism, Model [2] is derived form of Model [1], and its basic structure and elements of are basically the same with Model [1], except that the model is more adapted to the stock market, foreign exchange market, and there are some changes in the transmission mechanism. The transmission mechanism of Model [2] is: vigorously speculate fictitious capital products like stocks, bonds and foreign exchange → boom of fictitious capital products and foreign exchange market → large clearance → collapse of fictitious capital products and foreign exchange market → interruption of credit relationship → the financial crisis breaks out. The independent financial crisis is not necessarily related with the basic contradictions of the capitalist system, and in most cases, it is only related with the failures in system arrangements.

172 Marx's analytic model of the financial crisis has certain limitations when analyzing the contemporary financial crisis, which is mainly reflected in the specific level, but it has still the validity when analyzing its nature, thus has a valuable practical significance.

---

owners. Formula [2] indicates that: the principal and interest revenue of depositors should be equal to the principal and interest revenue of bank credit minus bank profits. Formula [3] indicates: the gap of a country's savings and investment tends to be remedied by the stock of net foreign assets, namely the difference of current account balance; the gap of government savings and investment is actually the fiscal surplus or deficit; the unfavorable foreign trade is, from the macroeconomic structure point of view, the reflection of insufficient savings, excessive investment, and government budget deficits. Formula [4] indicates that: the current account deficit needs foreign capital inflows (including borrowing from banks, foreign governments and international organizations, as well as capital inflows of direct investment and portfolio investment), or to make use of official foreign exchange reserves, so the long-term, sustainable and stable capital account surplus is the precondition to ensure the transfer of net foreign assets in order to support domestic economic growth. Formula [5] indicates that: when maintaining monetary base unchanged, the domestic credit expansion will lead to the loss of foreign exchange reserves. Formula [6] indicates that: when the nominal value is deviated from the real value, especially when it is much higher than the real value, it is necessary to achieve balance through a mandatory approach. Formula [7] indicates that: when the ability to pay is far less than the liabilities, once the debt needs to be settled, the credit crisis will erupt.

CHAPTER V

Questions and Controversy over the Necessity of the Capitalist Crises

- Views Advocated by the Second International Theorists

I. Introduction

On the capitalist economic crisis, some important figures of the Second International era, such as Eduard Bernstein, Karl Kautsky, Rosa Luxemburg, Rudolf Hilferding and several others have formed influential theories and certain approaches which have aroused extensive attention and debate in the academy and politics. However, as some of their theoretical ideas were evaluated as ignoring or opposing the basic principles of Marxism, they were strongly critiqued by the Marxist camp represented by Lenin, who regarded them as revising Marxist theories. Due to the socio-historical limitations, the economic and social development at the time could not fully test their theories and perspectives with practice. Therefore, it is difficult to make a scientific judgment, and which be it, there are only one-sided views. With the advance in history, there are more practical tests on controversies of the past in the development of the capitalist mode of production, and we have condition to make a more objective evaluation with more scientific criteria on academic points of views once hotly debated over, thus drawing a more just and reasonable conclusion.

Objectively, the figures I have mentioned above, have discussed the issue of the capitalist economic crisis essentially within the scope of Marx's relevant theories. Among them, Eduard Bernstein has pointed to certain "contradictions" in the Marx's theory of crisis, intending to demonstrate that it lacked scientific proof, on the other hand he negated the cyclical economic crises of capitalism, and obviously he meant to prove that the Marxist theory of economic crisis is outdated.

Karl Kautsky negated Marx's theory of disproportion and the decisive role of underconsumption in the crisis of overproduction, and M.I. Tugan-Baranovsky (1865-1919) has radically critiqued the underconsumption theory and emphasized the decisive role of disproportionality in the crisis of overproduction. They all abandoned the fact that the basic contradiction of capitalism was the root of the capitalist economic crisis. Rudolf Hilferding has made an in-depth study of the relationship between the law of the rate of profit to fall and the capitalist economic crisis, and analyzed the new factors added to capitalist economic crises with the emergence of monopoly capitalism and financial capital assuming the dominant status under the circumstance of monopoly, he specifically focused on the mechanisms of the financial crisis. Hence, if we say that Marx's theory of economic crisis had achieved some progress in the era of Second International, it is mainly manifested in Hilferding's theories and works.

174 II. The Crisis Can Be Overcome – Bernstein's View

Amongst the theoreticians of the Second International, the veteran Eduard Bernstein was a close friend and collaborator to Friedrich Engels for many years, and was widely seen as an orthodox Marxist and an outstanding representative of the German Social Democratic Party. After the death of Engels, he published a series of papers in Die Neue Zeit (The New Time) Magazine in 1896-1897, which were later edited and published in his book titled The Preconditions of Socialism in 1899.

Karl Kautsky who followed Marxism in those days criticized this book and wrote: "Bernstein's is the first truly sensational (Ed. exaggerated or false) book work in German socialist literature." (see, Kautsky's book, Bernstein and the Program of the Social Democratic Party of Germany) and it was for the first time that Marx's crisis theory was knowledgeably defended by a famous Marxist. In the same year, Lenin wrote a praising review on Kautsky's defence.

Paul Sweezy also wrote: "'Revisionism,' applied to the works of Bernstein, is an extreme euphemism. His real aim, though he may not have been fully conscious of it, was to eradicate Marxism, root and branch, from the socialist movement."[1]

---

1   Paul M. Sweezy, *The Theory of Capitalist Development*. Beijing: Commercial Press. 1997, p.214.

Bernstein has also put forward many controversial ideas on the economic crisis, which were deemed as "revisionist remarks" or "fallacy" by the mainstream Marxist economists. In the following we will review various arguments advocated by Marxist economists against these remarks of Bernstein: Firstly, by citing casually the discussion by Marx and Engels on the issues of capitalist economic crisis, Bernstein was trying to prove that Marx and Engels' understanding of the root cause of capitalist economic crisis is poor, or contradictory. Bernstein concluded that Marx and Engels sometimes strongly opposed to explaining the root of the capitalist economic crisis with the theory of underconsumption, but sometimes regarded under-consumption as "the ultimate reason" of all real crises. For example, in Capital, Marx said: "The ultimate reason for all real crises always remains the poverty and restricted consumption of the masses…"[2] Some scholars have argued that this is a deliberate attempt of Bernstein to confuse the two different levels in Marx and Engels' analysis of the capitalist economic crisis. In Anti-Dühring, when analyzing the issue of capitalist economic crisis, Engels clearly revealed the root cause of the capitalist economic crisis, namely "the incompatibility of socialised production with capitalistic appropriation". When this contradiction "ends in a violent explosion," it will lead the economic collision to achieve "its apogee". Secondly, Engels analyzed two specific causes which trigger the economic crisis, first the antagonism between the planned character of production in single enterprises, and the anarchy of production in the whole society, second the antagonism between the ever expansion of production and the contraction of the consumer demand due to decrease in purchasing power of the masses. These two specific causes are the manifestation of the contradiction between socialized production and the private capitalist ownership of the means of production. Apparently, the distorted allegations by Bernstein on Marx and Engels' theory of the capitalist economic crisis, was a call to abandon the analysis of the basic contradiction of capitalism and its hostile nature between the ever increasing of socialized production and the private capitalist ownership of the means of production, and aimed to stir confusion on the distinction between the root cause and the immediate cause of the economic crises.

175

Secondly, Bernstein has obviously exaggerated the role of some new developments in the capitalist economy in order to negate the real possibility of economic crises. He has argued that the new and the increasingly sophisticated credit system, the advances in transport and communication such as post, telegraph, passenger transport and commodity freight, the enhancement of business statistics and economic information departments, as well as expansion of industrialist organizations, trusts, cartels, etc.. These factors greatly streamline the "relationship between production and marketing processes ", and thus it is "very likely that, as the economic modernization moves forward, in general we will simply no longer have to experience the kind of business crisis".[3] Bernstein

2   *Capital*, Volume III, Beijing: People's Publishing House, 2004, p.548.
3   Eduard Bernstein, *History and Theories of Socialism*, Beijing: Oriental Press. 1989, pp. 188-189.

denied characteristics of the capitalist development in a new era, and he also denied the real possibility of the capitalist economic crisis, thus claiming that Marx's theory of capitalist economic crisis has become an "outdated" theory.

Thirdly, Bernstein caught some misunderstandings of Rosa Luxemburg related to the effect of credit system on the capitalist economics and used it as a pretext of attack, but in this critique he drew two conclusions contrary to Marx's theory of capitalist economic crisis:

1) In the name of the "double nature" of capitalist credit system raised by Marx, he made a big fuss on the positive effects of the credit system, believing that the credit system is able to change the nature of private ownership of the capitalist on its own. "We are only expressing a fact frequently attested in reality when we say that credit abolishes the contradiction between property relationships and the relationships of production in that, by uniting many small capitalists, it transforms vast productive forces into collective property. We have studied this in the section on the distribution of income, indeed this is the case with joint-stock companies, in their simple and advanced forms." Therefore, "the contraction that the credit system has withstood and that led to the general paralysis of production today is not more than ever before, but fewer. Therefore, within this limit, factors for it to form the crisis have been relegated to a subordinate status."[4] 2) Bernstein asserted that with competition and technological advance in the capitalist economy, the phenomenon of "the absolute control of the market" by individual capital has been "precluded"; Thus, the overproduction in individual companies is not insufficient to cause other companies to have the same overproduction; the paralysis on credit in individual companies is also impossible to simultaneously spread to other companies, let alone to cause similar paralysis in credit of the whole society. Therefore, "overproduction is to a certain extent unavoidable. However, overproduction in individual industries does not mean general crises." Thus, the evidence of the inevitability of capitalist economic crisis by Marx and Engels, in fact, "is floating in the air of abstract speculation."[5] Moreover, Bernstein also stressed that the formation of cartels, trusts and other monopolistic organization enhanced the ability of capitalism to adapt, thus making it able to avoid the crises.

Fourthly, Bernstein's denial of Marx's crisis theory starts by mechanically emphasizing that the crisis is not always like what Marx said, regularly occurs in every 10 years, and therefore, he believes that the cyclical crisis does not exist.

On the issue mentioned in Article One, in fact, it has been the one being struggled in the academic community, and Bernstein's argument is just an academic point of view only. We can see from his view that, he knew nothing

---

4   Eduard Bernstein, *The Preconditions of Socialism*. Beijing: Joint Publishing. 1973, pp.132, 136.
5   Ibid., p.133, p.136.

about the multilevel nature in the cause of the economic crisis of capitalism, and he knew nothing about the distinction between the root cause and the specific reasons. Bernstein denied the possibility and reality of the capitalist economic crisis to occur periodically, and denied the universality of the capitalist economic crisis, thus claiming that the monopoly can overcome the capitalist economic crisis, and Marx's theory of capitalist economic crisis has become an "outdated" theory. Bernstein's extreme views reflect that he did not understand the law of development of capitalist mode of production, and he regarded some factors that are likely to ease the capitalist economic crisis as factors that can overcome the economic crisis of capitalism fundamentally.

III. The Contradiction between Production and Consumption Determines that the Crisis is Unavoidable – Kautsky's Logic of Reasoning

Karl Kautsky criticized Bernstein's views, but because he was not able to fully and correctly understand Marx's theory, there were some obvious errors in his criticism. When facing the denial of periodicity of the economic crisis by Bernstein, as a famous Marxist economist, Kautsky politely affirmed some of Bernstein's points of views. On issues of the periodicity of the economic crisis, he had argued that, the crisis cycle of every 10 years was not Marx's theory, but merely a confirmation of the empirical fact. Marx did not invent the periodicity of crises, observed and illustrated the periodicity of crises. The 177 key issue is not that the crisis will repeat every 10 years, but whether the crisis will recur regularly. For the latter, Kautsky replied with certainty, factors of crises exist among the commodity economy at the outset, and commodity production is the production performed by each independent producer for the market. This regulating factor in the production system of anarchy is price volatility. If production exceeds demand, prices will fall; if the production is less than demand, prices will rise. Hence, that the commodity cannot be sold at the production price is a phenomenon that commodity production is bound to occur on a regular basis, and it is precisely this phenomenon that forms the basis of the crisis. This is, nevertheless, only a possibility, and other conditions are required to bring the real economic crisis. It is the development of capitalism that creates conditions for the transformation of the possibility of crisis into the reality of crisis. The capitalism is turning the socialized production as a whole to become more and more the production of commodity, so that the survival of the majority in the society who are dependent on the product of their own is unhindered to be achieved. At this time, due to the development of the social division of labour and credit, the dependencies between each producer become closer and closer, so that any unsalable product in one place will cause confusion elsewhere. However, with the development of production and circulation of commodity, the small local market is turning into the huge global market, with an increasing number of intermediate links between producers and consumers, and producers are increasingly unable to understand the comprehensive market situation. As the modern scientific and technological advance and the development of credit, especially as there are a lot of industrial reserve armies, this makes capitalist production to have a greater likelihood of scalability and jumping development. But this does not eliminate the crisis, because any substantial increase in the demand will lead to the rapid expansion of production, resulting in overproduction. Finally, competition has led to that the continued production expansion has become conditions for its own existence in the capitalist mode of production. The conditions for expanding production are the corresponding expansion in the market, not only the expansion in the desire of the use the value of the product in need, but more importantly, the expansion in the effective demand of the purchasing power accordingly. In this way, it is in a contradiction with the other trend of capitalist development, namely the trend of the labour force value of workers which is more and more beaten down. Therefore, the expanding market is the biggest problem of the capitalists. In addition, any expansion of the market will play a catalytic role for production, driving it into surplus and crisis. Conversely, any crisis would strongly urge capitalists to seek new markets. When the market can no longer be expanded at the speed of production expansion, the desperate moment for capitalist mode of production will finally arrive. As long as there is economic development, this situation occurs because the domestic market is ultimately limited. Of course, this pole, this limit is not dead, but elastic. However, it is inevitable that the road gets narrower. The growth rate of world capitalism is at a fast growing pace, and the world market is difficult to expand for a long term accordingly. Once the possibility of expanding the market is lost, people will not tolerate the existence of the capitalist mode of production.

178

We can see from Kautsky's criticism against Bernstein that he actually attributed the root of the crisis simply to the contradiction between the possibility of unlimited expansion of production and the limited consumer market, but failed to explain the issue from another side of the basic contradiction of capitalism – the organisation of production in the individual workshop, and the anarchy of production in society generally. This can be attributed to both the theoretical bias, and contention within the academic scope. What is worthy of recognition is that Kautsky's understanding of the contradiction between production and consumption is consistent with Marx's discourses. He said the underconsumption is a common phenomenon that existed in the past class society, but the crisis of overproduction caused by it is something that appears only in modern times. Only in place to sell and produce, can overproduction be formed into crisis, which means crisis is associated with the production of commodity. As a result of commodity production, the concept of overproduction itself has a new meaning. In the past, overproduction is linked to production that exceeds the existing consumption possibility. Now, in a society of commodity economy, regardless of whether the consumption of residents is really met, production that exceeds consumer demand in possession of money is overproduction. This excess is a very relative concept. Inadequate consumption should not be understood from the physiological significance as nutritional deficiency, but should be understood in the sense of a social class that consumption lags behind its production. Not only when the production is unchanged or increasing, the limitation of consumption will result in insufficient consumption, and when the consumption is unchanged or increasing, this increase is more slowly compared with the growth in production, which can also lead to insufficient consumption.

If what Kautsky explained basically and correctly illustrates the relationship between capitalist production and consumption, he went astray in the following analysis, and fell into the pit of economic romanticism of the petty-bourgeois. He said: "Capitalists and workers they exploited, with the increase in the wealth of the former and the number of the latter, provide a growing market, which is not growing as quickly as the growth of capital accumulation and labour productivity, and is not enough for the means of consumption created by large-scale industry of capitalism. Large-scale industry of capitalism must be looking for complementary markets outside its field, in industries where the capitalist mode of production conducts production, and it found the market, and also was expanding the market. However, the expansion is quick enough, because the complementary market does not have the flexibility and the ability to expand in the process of capitalist production. As long as the capitalist production developed into a large industry… it is possible to develop such a leap, that in the short term it may exceed any expansion of the market. Therefore, each boom with the emergence of a significant expansion of the market was decided to be short-lived from the outset, and the crisis is the inevitable outcome."[6] Kautsky stressed that this view is the "orthodox" Marxist view, but it is not completely true, which is Sismondi's views, not the views of Marx. Marx's view is, of course, the development of capitalism is inseparable from foreign markets, but this is not because the value of commodity cannot be achieved, but because they need to obtain greater profits for higher profit rate. Kautsky's wrong ideas at the time had created a very negative impact in the team of Marxism. Obviously, Luxembourg was wrong on the issue of capital accumulation that because is affected by Kautsky.

From Robert Owen and onwards, many economists regard insufficient consumption as causes of the crisis. Marx and Engels argued that insufficient consumption is only "the ultimate reason" of crisis, but not the direct reason. This is because the history of cyclical crises only has the history of less than a hundred years, and the insufficient consumption of the masses had already existed in the antagonism between the exploiting class and the exploited class. Before the emergence of industrial capitalism, exploitation served almost exclusively for the purpose of consumption, and what is blackmailed from workers is completely squandered. The overproduction generated by the social causes simply does not apply here. In a capitalist society the situation is completely different. The capitalist society is built on the basis of the developed commodity

---

6   Karl Kautsky, *Theory of Crisis*. In *Die Neue Zeit*. 1902(4).

production, and the production is directly for the market. In free competition, those who won in the market are people with the lowest production costs and the cheapest selling price. Here, the technological advance and machinery improvement has a decisive significance. To this end industrial capitalists will not be able to consume the entire profit, and they must limit their spending, increase accumulation and capital, and introduce new technologies in order to remain competitive. This will inevitably lead to the continuous increase of production and improvement of labour productivity. Insufficient consumption of the exploited can no longer be compensated according to the growth of consumption of the exploiters. This is the reason for the emerging overproduction in the capitalist society.

Mikhail Tugan-Baranovsky was wrong not because he directly attributed the reason of crisis to the contradiction between production and consumption, but that he completely denies the existence of this contradiction and he believes that the crisis is not due to underconsumption, but merely due to the unplanned nature of capitalist production, the anarchy. He believes that the various sectors of capitalist production are necessarily in a certain proportion, and any significant disruption to this proportion will lead to stagnation, thus causing crisis. Therefore, the occurrence of the widespread crisis does not require the universal overproduction of various production sectors, and as long as the production development of a sector is beyond the scope determined by the proportion, it will interfere with the normal order of the entire production, causing serious confusion and widespread crisis. Kautsky believes that there is no doubt a component of truth in Tugan-Baranovsky's views. As widespread overproduction does not require the general overproduction, as long as there is overproduction of a commodity dominated in the world market, it may induce the widespread crisis. It is beyond doubt that the destruction of the proportion in various sectors of production can become the cause of crisis, but it should be noted that the destruction of the proportion will not only be caused by overproduction, but also by insufficient production. However, Marxists do not deny the contact of the unplanned nature with the crisis, but that, the intensification of unplanned nature of capitalist production is one of the prerequisites of crisis, and sometimes it can also separately lead to a crisis or intensify a general crisis. What Marxists deny is that it is regarded as the only reason of crisis, and that it does not recognize the insufficient consumption to be most fundamental reason of crisis. Kautsky believes that it is absurd for Tugan-Baranovsky to deny the existence of contradictions between production and consumption, which is a "strange theory." This is because Tugan-Baranovsky has completely severed ties between production and consumption, and the relative independence became the absolute, which ended up being the completely unrelated factors. His absurd belief is that in the capitalist economy, the demand for commodities is not affected by the total social spending, and the total social spending could be reduced, while the social demand for commodities may increase. The accumulation of social capital will inevitably lead to restrictions on the demand for means of consumption, while the aggregate demand for commodities will increase. This occurs because the means of production plays a growingly important role in the production process and in commodity markets, and workers and machines are retreated to the secondary position in comparison. At the same time, in comparison of the demand formed by the productive consumption of means of production and the demand formed by consumption of workers; there is a growing proportion of the former, while the latter is relegated to a subordinate status. The whole mechanism of the capitalist economy can be said to have taken a "self-existence" form, in which, the consumption of people is expressed as a simple element of capital reproduction and distribution process. For this "strange theory" by Tugan-Baranovsky, Kautsky argued that the production was, is and will be carried out for the consumption of people. The production of commodities for direct consumption of people declines continuously in the proportion of total production, while the production, in a direct or indirect way, to provide them with tools, machines, and transportation services is increasing. Regardless of how many intermediary links are needed for the products of these production sectors to ultimately become the consumer goods, that is to say, regardless of how indirect its consumer services for people are, their ultimate goal is always that the production is providing means of consumption for the consumption of people. As long as this ultimate goal cannot be achieved, this entire production activity will ultimately and inevitably be in stagnation. Kautsky pointed out that in the international division of labour, the situation is more complicated. The production for the consumption of people 181 in individual old industrial countries is often expanded very slowly, while the production of the means of production develops very rapidly, and the production of the means of production has a greater decisive significance for the entire country's economic pulse beating. Anyone who views it only from the standpoint of the countries concerned, it is easy for them to come to such a conclusion: The production of means of production can be prolonged faster than the growth of the means of consumption, and the former is not constrained by the latter. But this is a bias, and if the British textile machines are produced much faster than yarn, it must be the reason that new textile factories are established outside Britain, and the machineries these new factories are using supplied by Britain. If difficulties occur in the sale of yarn, it is bound to affect the establishment of the new plant, which will affect the production of textile machines. Thus Kautsky says: "Production is the one for the means of production for the consumption of people. This fact can only be concealed or restricted by the advance of division of labour, but cannot be eliminated."[7]

From the above it can be seen that, when he was criticizing Tugan-Baranovsky's crisis theory and expounding Marx's real theory, Kautsky had made many sound advices, but there were serious flaws. One of the flaws is that when he was explaining the significance of the foreign market on the realization of capitalist commodity, he fell into a morass of economic romanticism.

7   Karl Kautsky, *Theory of Crisis*. in *Die Neue Zeit*. 1902(4).

Another one of his flaws is that when he was exploring the reasons for the crisis of capitalism, he gave a more full illustration of the contradictions between production and consumption in the capitalist reproduction process, and it is necessary to do so in order to criticize the error of Tugan who denied the contradiction between production and consumption. However, he ignored the elaboration of the fundamental reason that formed the crisis –the basic contradiction of capitalism. Moreover, he failed to explain the sharp trend of this contradiction as the development of capitalist production and credit. Therefore, he was not able to fully and correctly describe the occurrence mechanism of the economic crisis in Marxist crisis theory.

IV. Monopoly Does Not Eliminate the Crisis – Hilferding's Views

Rudolf Hilferding had a profound study of the impact of the formation of the financial capital on the capitalist economic crisis. The initial motivation for his study of this problem is also related with Karl Kautsky. Therefore, what he has to prove is that Marx's theory of crisis is also applicable to the capitalism in the new development stage with the emerging problems. On the basis of studying Marx's theory of crisis, Hilferding put forward three "general conditions" of the economic crisis, which reflected his understanding on the general conditions of the economic crisis, different from Marx's. He believes that the likelihood of a crisis emerged with the commodity becoming both commodities and money. Money as the means of circulation has already had the possibility to store up money thus resulting in the disjunction of purchase and sale, but as long as money is the means of circulation, this disjunction can only be an isolated phenomenon. Historically as the money assumes its new function, namely becomes the means of payment, the disjunction of purchase and sale at one link may spread to several other links. Payment method strengthens the links between the different production sectors, resulting in the possibility of a partial disjunction to evolve in to a general disjunction. However, these two points are just the first "general condition" of crisis, which is far from causing the real crisis. With the generalization of commodity production, the already existing independence and irregularity of private production in the simple commodity production has developed into anarchy of production, which is the second "general conditions" of crisis. The third "general condition" of crisis is the separation of production and consumption caused by capitalist production. The three "general conditions" are brought about by Hilferding based on the Marxist two "general conditions".

As the capitalist production causes the separation of producer from his product, the consumption of the direct producer is only limited to those equivalents equal to the value of labour in the value of commodity, and therefore the consumption of the whole class of producers is not directly associated with the aggregate products, but with those product equal to wages in the aggregate products, while the production is not subject to consumption but for profit. Hence, under capitalist circumstances, consumption is determined by the scale of production, and production is subject to the possibility of self-expansion of capital and its degree. Based on these facts, Hilferding believes that the reason that the narrow basis provided by the capitalist relations of consumption constitutes the general condition of crisis is because in capitalism it is impossible to expand this basis. If the consumption can be expanded at will, it is impossible to have overproduction. However, the expansion of consumption means the reduction in profit and the rate of profit. Therefore, under capitalism, if the accumulation requires workers to increase consumption, resulting in the rate of profit to fall, so that the increased capital cannot produce the corresponding profits at the original profit rate, then the accumulation is bound to come to a halt. It is precisely here that a prerequisite for the accumulation – the expansion of consumption, is in conflict with another prerequisite – self-expansion of capital, the condition of which is against the expansion of consumption. Since the former is decisive, the contradiction is often upgraded to a crisis. Here we can see that Hilferding has repeatedly claimed that the root cause of the crisis cannot be attributed to "under-consumption", but he still made the same mistake as Luxembourg did, boiling consumption down to the consumption of the means of subsistence, and attributing the root cause of the crisis to the accumulation of surplus value that cannot be achieved.

Generally speaking, crisis is the interference in circulation, and it is manifested as that there is no demand for a lot of commodities, while the value of commodity cannot be realized as money. Therefore, it can only be explained from the special capitalist conditions of commodity circulation, rather than from the circulation of simple commodity. The special capitalist nature of commodity circulation determines that commodity must be produced as the product of capital, and to be realized as commodity capital, so this realization includes conditions for self-expansion of capital peculiar to the capital itself. Hilferding wrote that what Marx had studied in the second volume of *Capital* is exactly this condition, "from the standpoint of pure economic reasoning"; the study by Marx is "the most brilliant among other remarkable researches."[8]

183

Marx proposed and demonstrated in detail the realization of the conditions of simple reproduction and expanded reproduction of capitalism for the first time ever, and he clearly illustrated that there is a necessary proportion in industrial sectors that produce means of production and industrial sectors that produce means of consumption. Only if this proportion is maintained can capitalist reproduction proceed smoothly. If the proportion is destroyed, even under conditions of simple reproduction, the crisis may also occur. So, in a capitalist economic system, who can assume this function, and who can maintain this complex proportion?

---

8   Rudolf Hilferding, *Finance Capital*, Beijing: Commercial Press. 1994, p. 273.

For Hilferding this function could only be undertaken by the law of value. This is because for the expansion or the contraction of production, or for the establishment of new businesses and the bankruptcy of existing businesses, changes in price will be the decisive factors. The law of value is only possible regulator of the capitalist economy, and the destruction of the normal proportion among various social production sectors, must be from the interference in the special regulation of such special production, the interference in the price formation. The cyclical crisis suggests that such interference is bound to be cyclical. Due to the limitations of history, Hilferding did not see the intervention of state monopoly capitalism on the national economy, nor realized that as a "total capitalist", the state would safeguard the interests of the bourgeoisie and would intervene in the economy. It should be noted that this is a deficiency of Hilferding.

Hilferding had much more detailed and complex study on business cycle than it was in Capital. This is because, on the one hand, Hilferding who lived in a later era, was able to observe the abundant new developments and new expression forms in the real business cycle; on the other hand, Hilferding has studied the development law of the business cycle more specifically. Marx had already pointed out that the material basis for the capitalist business cycle is massive renewal of fixed capital, but he did not explain what the implementation mechanism of this renewal is. On this issue Hilferding thinks every industrial cycle starts from the expansion of production. The specific reasons for the expansion of production at different times may vary, but in general there is nothing more than some of the following reasons: the increased demand caused by exploitation of new markets, establishment of new productive sectors, adoption of new technologies and population growth. The increased demand for certain products leads to the rise in profits and expansion of production in sectors that produce these products, and it also means the development of those sectors which provide equipment and materials to these production sectors, and ultimately bringing comprehensive upsurge. Hence, the periodicity of business cycle starts from the renewal and increase of fixed capital, which is the main motivation for prosperity to arrive. Hilferding considers that combination of the expansion of production and the renewal of fixed capital should be at a right angle.

Hilferding is the first one to use the law of the tendency of the rate of profit to fall to explain the capitalist economic crisis in succession of Marx. On the basis of Marx's explanation, he had the elaboration on the law of the tendency of the rate of profit to fall in more detailed and comprehensive manner, developing and improving this principle. Hilferding actually thinks the rate of profit to rise and economic prosperity are mutually promoted, and in addition to improving demand, there are other factors that will promote the rate of profit to rise in times of prosperity. The first factor is that the turnaround of capital is shortened due to the increase in demand, as well as the acceleration in commodity realization. Due to the use of new technology, acceleration of the operation of the machine, overtime and other reasons, labour time is shortened. Goods sell well, and the time of circulation is often equal to zero because the production is based on ordering, which will certainly increase the annual rate of profit. The second factor is that with the turnaround time being reduced, the advanced moneyed capital by industrial capitalists is reduced as compared with the capital of production. The acceleration of machinery operation and the reduction of working hours make the existing factors of production be utilized more intensively and more efficiently. As the time of circulation is reduced and the circulation of money is accelerated, the amount of money held by the capitalist for realizing the circulation of commodities is also reduced. All of this makes the amount of capital for circulation purposes but not for production use; in comparison with the same money directly to create profit it is relatively reduced. The shortening of time of circulation and the acceleration of turnover rate reduces the capital which idles up as a commodity reserve and can only increase the non-productive cost. All of this will increase the rate of profit. However, the factors that promote the acceleration of the self-expansion of capital during the time of prosperity contributed to the potential factors which cause a decrease in investment and unmarketable commodity. This is primarily manifested in the emergence of a large number of new investments in times of prosperity, and these new enterprises are bound to adopt the latest technology in order to reap excessive profits, but the adoption of the latest technology means the increase of the organic composition of capital. When the new technology is promoted and the organic composition of capital is increased, it will inevitably result in the decline in the rate of profit and deterioration in conditions of asset growth, because the increase in the organic composition will make the same rate of surplus value show itself as a smaller rate of profit; on the one hand, the increase in the organic composition also means the increase in the fixed capital compared with working capital, and the turnaround time is bound to be extended, resulting in the decrease in the rate of profit. Secondly, in time of prosperity, the increased demand for labour and the increase in wage in turn means the decrease in the rate of surplus value and the rate of profit. While the investment is increasing in times of prosperity, speculation is also prevalent and there is a significant increase in the demand for credit, resulting in an increase in interest rates, an increase in bank profit, reduction in industrial profit and the deterioration of conditions for capital growth. Hilferding feels that there are two problems: how do these trends become the crisis during the competition? Why do these trends take the form of a sudden outbreak of realization, rather than gradual sharpening? Hilferding tries to find answers to these two questions through the differences in the organic composition of the production sector, as well as through the differences in law of price change. He believes that the decisive factor affecting the distribution of capital among the various productive sectors is the change in price and profit. During the time of prosperity, the price of commodity rises generally, and if this rise is balanced, then this rise is purely nominal. This change in price will not have any impact on production, and the proportion among various sectors will not undergo any changes. However, if the rise in prices of various commodities is not balanced, the situation is completely different. Disproportionate changes in price will inevitably lead to changes in the proportion among different production sectors, causing changes in the relationship between capital allocations.

The increase in the organic composition of capital is a prerequisite for the tendency of the rate of profit to fall. From the logical relationship, in the discussion of the law of the rate of profit to fall, it is the implementation mechanism of the increase in the organic composition of capital that need to be first noted, and on this basis, the implementation mechanism from the rate of profit to fall to the outbreak of the crisis also needs to be noted. Hilferding also made a more detailed discussion in these areas, and furthered Marxist theory. His contribution is mainly manifested in two aspects: (1) describe such a cycle from the technical progress –the increase in the organic composition of capital – the decline in the rate of profit – new technological advances. He believes that technological changes often occur most frequently in those places where machines are most used with the highest organic composition. The higher the degree of mechanization is, the greater the rationalization of equipment and the possibility of technical improvement are, which will quickly raise the organic composition. The higher organic composition is nothing other than the economic manifestation of a higher productivity (higher level of productive forces). The improvement of labour productivity means the reduction in cost price and the generation of excess profit. This will continue to promote the capital to flow into this area, and till new businesses are set up, a large number of new products go into the market to reduce the price, factors that correct the large capital inflows will appear in these sectors, but it is often too late. The decline in the rate of profit and the outbreak of crisis create conditions for new technological advances. (2) Put forward the thesis that sectors of high organic composition are often hit hardest by the crisis. With the development of capitalist production, the organic composition is increasing, as well as the fixed capital. But the more advance the technology develops the more the fixed capital increases and, the longer the time needed to manufacture these fixed capital; and the greater the difference in time of various sectors to produce and to expand . The longer the time required to create new equipment, the more the supply lagged behind demand and the more difficult for the commodity produced in the sector to adapt to consumer needs, and therefore the fiercer price increases here, while there is more intense and the more common the impulse to invest in these sectors. Hence, it is in the beginning of prosperity when the price of commodity produced by sectors with high organic composition of capital increase, sectors of high organic composition has the tendency of over-investment and over-accumulation over sectors of low organic composition. This also explains that in the early development of capitalism, the textile industry had the most serious crisis, and later it shifted to the heavy industry.

On the relationship between the economic disproportion and the crisis, Hilferding also had unique insights. He asserted that the relationship between changes in production and consumption often interfere with the normal proportion among various industrial sectors. In time of prosperity, the consumption increased absolutely, because the consumptions of both the capitalists and consumer workers have increased. However, the accumulation definitely increases faster because high profits had a strong stimulus to accumulation, while the growth of consumption and production are not synchronized, which will result in disproportion. Therefore, the disproportion in time of prosperity is generated by the interference of changes in the price. The reproduction of fixed capital will also interfere in the normal proportion among various industrial sectors in the capitalist reproduction process. Because under conditions of simple reproduction, the fixed capital consumed must be equal to the new fixed capital invested; under conditions of expanded reproduction, the latter is greater than the former. However, in the actual process of the development of production, these conditions are very hard to be achieved. In order to ensure the smooth production, companies must have a certain amount of commodity reserve and money reserve. Otherwise, production will continue to fall at a standstill. The abuse of commodity reserves and money reserves during the time of prosperity weakens the company's anti-jamming capability. Especially on the eve of the crisis, the reduction of all kinds of reserves is absolute. Once the reflux of capital credit and circulation credit started sluggish for some reason, it will result in the need for a large number of money as means of payment, and there will be 187 bankruptcy and then it will lead to massive crises.

In *Capital*, Marx explained the relationship between credit and capitalist economic crisis in a general sense, namely that "[h]ence, the credit system accelerates the material development of the productive forces and the establishment of the world-market. It is the historical mission of the capitalist system of production to raise these material foundations of the new mode of production to a certain degree of perfection. At the same time credit accelerates the violent eruptions of this contradiction—crises—and thereby the elements of disintegration of the old mode of production."[9] In comparison, Hilferding had a much more specific study, and he examined in detail the credit relations in capitalist business cycle, and its manifestations in different stages of the business cycle. The followings are descriptions by Hilferding:

In early time of prosperity, the expansion of production and increase in circulation increases the demand for loan capital. But at that time it was still relatively easy to meet this demand. The reason is that a lot of idle capital in the Depression can be utilized; with the increase in the circulation of commodity, the circulation of credit money is also increasing; the circulation of commodity speeds up, and the turnaround time is shortened, saving money in circulation. As the prosperity moves forward, the accumulation of contradictions is stepping towards acute. In the early days of prosperity, it can be seen there was a slow

---

9   *Capital*, Volume III, Beijing: People's Publishing House. 2004, p.500.

rise in interest rate, the turnaround time of capital is prolonged and the relationship between the different production sectors appeared to be in disharmony. All of this has been reflected in that sales of commodity are not so smooth, so that it will result in that a part of commercial bills cannot be cashed in on time, and thus it had to resort to bank credit. Credit provided among industrial capitalists is not enough, and the demand for bank credit increases. This in turn causes an increase in the demand for cash and the increase in interest rate. But this time the price of commodity remains high and lucrative. Therefore, capitalists are struggling through a variety of credit so that production can still continue at the original size even on a larger scale. They are completely unaware that the moneyed capital they used is no longer a transformation of the commodity of their own, and in fact, their commodities were not sold at all. The commodity reserves are increasing. It is just because the moneyed capital put in that it prevents the pressure of commodity on market and the decline in price. This illusion masks the contradiction between supply and demand, as well as the imbalance among various production sectors, which the producer sees everything to be normal. Moreover, in the early days of prosperity, the interest rate was low, and if the other conditions remained unchanged, this phenomenon would cause to the rise in the price of fictitious capital. At the same time, the speculation that people use the rising market price of securities to profit becomes rampant, and due to the surge in demand, the price of the stock remains at a higher level. High profits lead to frequent entrepreneurial activities, and the existing enterprises are soaring. Banks are actively involved in the activities of the stock issuance. Due to bullish practice, purchase is more than sale, so that the difference is expanded at the settlement, which will increase the demand for money and credit, and which in turn will directly affect the increase in interest rate. In commodity speculation, there are also the same problems.

188

When entering the heyday of prosperity, the price of commodity and the profit have reached the highest level. Higher yields make stock price soar, ordinary citizens participating in securities trading activities are increasing, which provides a good opportunity for the speculator to increase speculative gains at the expense of public interest. However, it is often ominous at this time. In the industry, despite the profit being still high, it is unable to maintain a higher price for sale. Once the bank realizes the danger of this situation, it is more difficult to borrow money. The result will be the rise in interest rate and the decline in share price, and eventually when speculators feel there would be no result in price gouging and want to throw inventories as soon as possible to recover the original investment capital, it is close to collapse.

Under the conditions of the expanding power of financial capital and part of the funds required by the industry to be provided by the bank, the increase in the interest rate depresses the industrial profit. In addition, the circulation slows and the credit squeezes, while the industry actually increases demand for credit, the more the credit provided by banks to industry is, the fewer the loans for speculations are, which means the reduction in the demand for securities and the fall of securities market price, followed by the big auction of stock. When they are aware of the danger, the professional speculators will quickly adopt the sell-off policy, and the results will be a disaster. Evidently, changes in money market and changes in credit relationship is the direct cause of the stock exchange crisis. Since the stock exchange crisis has a direct relationship with the interest rate, it will break out prior to the normal commercial crisis and industrial crisis, and becomes a precursor to the latter. Changes in money markets really depend on changes in production, and therefore, production leads to crisis.

Speculation in commodities will also have these circumstances. Speculation in commodity has closer relationship with changes in the production area. The rise in the interest rate and the credit crunch restrict commodity hoarding, although the initial price of commodity only stops rising, and the price remains at a high level. Production continues to expand, and imports are still increasing. High price suppresses consumption. Once the large speculators are aware that continuous hoarding will be very dangerous, commodity will flock into the market together, resulting in the collapse of the market.

Changes in both stock exchanges and commodity markets will also affect the bank. In the early time of prosperity, the interest rate is low, and capital issue has big profits. In the process of development of the cycle, both of them are changing in the opposite direction. As interest rates rise, the bank capital improves its profits at the expense of more entrepreneurs. With the prosperity continues, the share of industry profits banks occupy become greater. On the other hand, the expansion of production leads to the expansion of circulation, thereby the means of circulation needs to be increased. Bank reserves are consumed a lot, and it can only turn to the central bank, resulting in the excessive use of bank reserves to issue bank credit. When the bank credit cannot meet the need of circulation, it turns to the demand for cash. Cash increases in circulation, and again the reserves are reducing, forcing banks to tighten credit again. This situation means that the industry is unable to adjust the confusion-caused imbalance, because they have nothing to add money sources. Commodities on the market are forced to be dumped, the price of commodities begins to fall, and the ability of the industrial capitalists to repay the loan is under suspicion. If the bank lends the money to the insolvent capitalists, then the bankruptcy of the latter will be implicated in the bank. People will have to run on the bank, and thus lead to the banking crisis.

With credit crunch and bank failures, cash becomes the only means of payment that can be accepted. The existing means of circulation cannot meet the need, especially due to the unrest, large amounts of cash are hoarded, resulting in cash discount, the intrinsic value of money is gone, and the value of money is determined by the socially necessary value needed in circulation.[10]

189

---

10   Rudolf Hilferding, *Finance Capital*, Beijing: Commercial Press. 1994, p.310.

On the whole, the detailed description on the effects of credit in various stages of capitalist business cycle by Hilferding is a direct development of the Marxist theory. He also had creative answers to questions like how the possibility of crisis conceived in the commodity economy develops into a reality, as well as why the crisis will take the form of a sudden outbreak as its manifestation. At the time, such an analysis was made for the first time in the history of Marxist economics, and its groundbreaking significance is obvious. But, here again, it exposed the error in the value of Hilferding's theory, namely, he believed that in the period of crisis, "the intrinsic value of money is gone," and the value of money was "determined by socially necessary value needed in circulation."[11] This is a dualistic theory of value, namely that under normal circumstances, the value of monetary is determined by the self-contained socially necessary labour; in times of crisis, it is determined by the socially necessary value needed in circulation. In the meantime, this view also confuses differences between value and price.

After studying the direct reasons to form the crisis, Hilferding further studied the issue of the capitalist economic recovery, especially the role of moneyed capital in the recovery. He said that if we look at the reproduction of capitalism after the crisis, we will see that it is carried out on a reduced scale, and the accumulation of productive capital is completely stopped. If we look at the situation of individual capitalists and certain production sectors, it can be found that the scale of production has been reduced, but the production still continues. These enterprises have more advanced technology and equipment, and engaged in the production of the necessities of life. Because of advanced technology, the former is in a favourable position in the competition, so that it is able to sustain; because there cannot be excessive reduction in consumption commodity, the latter can still get some profit from manufacturing. These two kinds of companies still have part of the profits for the accumulation, although the rate of profit is low profit margins and the rate of accumulation are impossible to be high. However, this is only the accumulation of moneyed capital, and cannot be used for expanded reproduction. In time of depression, the scale of the production of the whole society is narrowing, or remains unchanged at best, and therefore, at this time there cannot be any accumulation on the social scale, but only the accumulation of individual capitalists. A producer makes a successful sale and the accumulation becomes possible, and it is only the result that the product of other producers cannot be sold. Therefore, this accumulation does not indicate the increase in the total social capital, and it just changes the allocation of moneyed capital among capitalists only. Hence, from the point of view of the whole society, this is only because the tightening of production separates a part of money from the capital turnover process, and it then becomes the excess capital. The idleness of moneyed capital means that of capital production. Due to production constraints and underemployment, the fixed capital produced has been put on hold, and cannot be put into production.

11   Rudolf Hilferding, *Finance Capital*, Beijing: Commercial Press. 1994, p. 211.

The potential of moneyed capital and credit system is widening due to the narrowing of circulation, and money is idle in the bank, waiting to be utilized. Therefore, it is wrong to say that the idle capital in times of depression is the accumulation of moneyed capital.

Those points of view holders who believe that the existence of a lot of idle moneyed capital is the driving force to promote the recovery of production are quite wrong. It is a direct violation of Marx's theory that production determines circulation. In fact, in times of crisis, on the one hand there is a lot of idle productive capital, and on the other hand there is a lot of idle moneyed capital, both of which are caused by the same reason. The reason that the moneyed capital suspends flows and no longer functions lies in the stagnation of production, as well as in the industrial downturn. Capitalism has completely proved Marx's theory that production status determines the circulation of money based on the reality of the development of the business cycle. In times of prosperity, the production expands, the demand for moneyed capital increases, and the attendant interest rate rises. Until the end, the moneyed capital is insufficient, high interest rate swallows production profit, new investment is aborted, and then the crisis comes. In times of depression, moneyed capital is accumulated, and is no longer used for new investment. The idea that no machines, docks, and railways can be produced without gold is unjustified. With the decline in interest rate, money capitalists began to be unsatisfied with low interest rates, so again, they put moneyed capital back into production. However, active investment must be based on the improvement in the rate of profit, as well as the recovery of the economy, that is, based on the better production conditions, without which the idle money capital will continue to stay in the bank vault, and will not be re-used in production.

The development of capitalism will undoubtedly make changes in the form of crisis. In the early stage of the capitalist economy, the capitalist production coexisted with a lot of craft production. Then a crisis occurring must be localized, and in general, it will only impact the individual capitalist enterprises. With the development of capitalist production, a large number of handicraft production and cottage industries were eliminated, and then the crisis would certainly impact the entire production system. However, at this time, the tightening of production is restricted in large part by the demand to meet the consumption of the society on a larger scale. With the growth of production, the socially necessary production is also expanding, and the smooth production of this part stops the complete disruption of the production and distribution process, then it is important to reduce the impact of the crisis. In a crisis, industries that produce commodities most needed in people's daily lives are less impacted, and it just proves the point.

With the development of capitalist production, the concentration of capital is also moving forward, which makes some features of the crisis be changed. First, in general, the viability of individual companies differs according to their size. In a crisis, small companies will collapse soon because of having no market for their product, credit interruption and insolvency, while large enterprises are likely to remain part of the production in times of crisis, so that the entire enterprise is able to be maintained. The more concentrated it is, the greater this ability of companies is. It needs specially mentioning that is a form of business organization such stock companies has great significance to prevent the outbreak of the crisis. Stock companies can also make production continue under circumstances of low profitability, because they only bear the responsibility for the payment of dividends to shareholders. Even in the case of losses, stock companies can survive, because their financing is more easy, and they can attract more capital. Stock companies accumulate wealth in good years to prepare for famine harvest. The form of organization of stock companies facilitates the implementation of banking for supervision, and thus can avoid difficulties of business operations caused by failures in speculation. Secondly, the concentration of bank capital has an impact. The increase in bank capital enables banks more likely to replace commercial credit with bank credit, thus avoiding the crisis due to the shortage of the means of payment. The key issue here is that the issue of bank credit is to be strictly limited within the scope in need of the actual circulation of money, and to adopt appropriate restrictive policies to prevent excessive demand for bank credit. For this reason, the policy must be implemented that those who hold very reliable collaterals can exchange bank notes. The avoidance of money crises can prevent the total collapse of the credit, so it can effectively prevent the outbreak of the banking crisis. Therefore, the development of capitalism will inevitably reduce the impact

192 of the crisis. The roles of banks and big monopolies in inhibiting crisis are also reflected in that; it makes the amount of speculation on commodities and securities greatly reduced. This is because the development of large monopolies make more direct transactions between producers and consumers, and a large number of businessmen are, in fact, transforming to agents of trust into syndicate, who work for the commission to prevent the hoarding of commodities and price gouging, and to avoid remaining an illusion of prosperity in the decline in the effective demand. Of course, wholesale trade has not lost its traditional position. But even in this area, speculation is increasingly dominated by the banks, because growth of bank credit has given the bank the power to control all the moneyed capital. In addition, the development of transport also mitigates commodity speculation. The modernized transport has shortened the distance between commodities and markets; the development of communication enables the market to spread information rapidly. All of this can dramatically curb speculation, and weakens the impact of the crisis. Finally, the speculation in stock exchange is an important reason to cause the crisis, especially the banking crisis. With the expansion of bank capital and concentration of financial forces, the status of the exchanges is declining, and banks' ability to control speculation is increasing, which also weakens the factors that exacerbate the crisis. However, these factors can only delay the outbreak of the crisis and curb its impact, but does not prevent the crisis from the root. The idea is unfounded that since monopolies can adjust production as well as supply and demand, thus

it will be able to completely eliminate the crisis. Hilferding believes that this view completely ignores the inherent nature of the crisis. This is because the crisis is by no means simply due to the lack of a comprehensive understanding of the market, and thus it is caused by the overproduction of commodities. The crisis is the overproduction of commodities, which is beyond reproach. However, the product of capitalist enterprise is not just an ordinary commodity, but a product of capital. The overproduction during the crisis is not merely an excess of commodity production, but the overproduction of capital, that is, the so-called excess here lies solely with that the product sales can no longer bring in enough profit for the capitalist. The regulation of price by cartel exacerbates the confusion. This is because the role of cartel is to eliminate competition within specific production sectors, to prevent the decline in commodity prices in these sectors, so that the rate of profit of cartelized corporations will be much higher than non-cartel sectors. Thus it cannot eliminate competition among sectors, nor change the impact on the price structure brought about by accumulation. On the contrary, it can only determine its own business activities following the changes in the price structure, so it cannot put an end to the disproportion among the production sectors. Anarchy of production cannot be eliminated by reducing the number of individual businesses while enhancing their strength. Planned and unplanned production are not opposite in quantity. A conscious economic system does not stand out from the anarchy because of more and more individual plans. Only when the entire production is subject to conscious regulation will this shift occur. Here, Hilferding criticized the fantasy of "ultra-imperialism", and he said: "In itself, a general cartel which carries on the whole of production, and thus eliminates crises, is economically conceivable, but in social and political terms such an arrangement is impossible, because it would inevitably come to grief on the conflict of interests which it would intensify to an extreme point."[12]

Cartels cannot eliminate the crisis, nor can they escape the effects of the crisis. Only when crisis and overproduction of commodities are confused with, can it be considered that cartels can quickly tackle the crisis by a very simple way of compressing production. Economic recovery requires two conditions: First, the coordination of proportion, second, the expansion of production which are necessary condition for the end of the depression.. There will be no prosperity where there is an expansion without production. The policies of reducing production and maintaining high price level that cartels take in times of crisis cannot achieve their goals. It can only pass to some extent the damages caused by the crisis onto those of non-cartel corporations, and ease the impact of the crisis on their own.

In his book *Financial Capital*, Hilferding had revealed the idea of "organized capitalism". He asserted that the ultimate result of the development of monopolies would produce an overall cartel, and the entire capitalist economy will have to be consciously adjusted by a competent body, thus ending the

12 Rudolf Hilferding, *Finance Capital*, Beijing: Commercial Press. 1994, p. 310.

anarchy of capitalist production. During World War I, especially in the post-war years, he further developed this idea, and clearly put forward the perspective that the time of "organized capitalism" has come. Then in May 1927, at the Kiel Congress of the Social Democratic Party of Germany, he made a report titled "The Role of Social Democratic Party in the Republic and its Tasks", where he made a systematic exposition of his "organized capitalism" theory, in its full-fledged form.

In 1924, in the first issue of Social Democratic Party of Germany Monthly edited by Hilferding, he published an article entitled The Time Question, which is actually the foreword of the publication. In this article, he pointed out that, the war and the post-war era means that the trend of capital accumulation is greatly enhanced. The development of cartels and trusts had a strong impetus. The era of free competition comes to an end. Large monopolies become masters of the economy, binding more and more closely together with the bank. Banks accumulate social capital, and dominate the entire economy. Formerly independent form of industrial capital, commercial capital and bank capital are increasingly unified in the form of financial capital. This means the transition from the capitalism of free competition to the organized capitalism. Labour socialization within the large enterprise has developed into a socialization in the labour process of the entire industrial sectors, as well as the mutual joint unification among the socialized industrial sectors. At the same time, it has formed a conscious economic order and the operating system in an attempt to overcome the inherent anarchy of free capitalist competition on the basis of capitalism. If this trend can continue to develop with no barrier, it will form an organized, albeit an organized economy with antagonism and hierarchy. Here, Hilferding regarded the "organized capitalism" as the inevitable result of the development of socialized production, and the result that the capitalist socialization of labour within the enterprises further extends to the entire industrial sector, or even the socialization of the entire national economy. In other words, he thinks that it is purely a matter of development of productive forces for capitalism of free competition to transit to the organized capitalism, regardless of the socio-economic nature. In fact, he also treated the issue in this way. This is because he had explicitly declared in this article that this is a regulation conducive to the owner class of the means of production, as well as an attempt to organize social productivity, so as to maintain their decisive influence on production leadership and social product distribution. It extended capitalism temporarily, mitigated the crisis, or at least suppressed the negative impact of the crisis on workers.

How did the bourgeoisie realize organization of the capitalist economy? Hilferding argued that these policy measures are mainly through large trusts to allocate new planned investments; in times of prosperity, properly compress new investment in fixed capital and in times of sluggish business, add new investment; in support of the central bank, largest banks implement appropriate credit adjustment. In order to adjust the relationship between the bourgeoisie and the working class, in an organized capitalist economy, there is a widespread use of the labour insurance system. This reduces the threat of unemployment and consequences that unemployment causes; adapting the increased mechanization, "scientific" method of business organization and method of operation are promoted, thereby increasing the labour intensity. However, due to the implementation of the pension system and the disability insurance system, as well as the labour time limitations, workers can do the job and adapt to stressful work caused by the implementation of "scientific" method of labour.

In May 1927, at the Kiel Congress, Hilferding further systematically discussed this problem in his report. He said, "[w]hat is decisive is that we are now at this stage of capitalism, in which capitalism is purely overcome by the era of free competition dominated by the blind laws of the market, and we have reached the economy where capitalism has the economic organization, that is, the economy of free competition of different forces has reached the organized economy."[13] He believes this change is first caused by the progress of science and technology. In addition to the widely use of steam and electricity in production, what is more important is that the development of synthetic chemistry can be applied directly to factory production. As a matter of principle, the application of such chemistry means something new. Due to this technological advancement, it can artificially create important raw materials from a large number of inorganic matters which exist everywhere, so that the capitalist economy is not dependent on the output of some important raw materials, which can enable us to avoid world war caused by competion for these materials. In the meantime, these advances in technology enable us to create expensive organic matters from very cheap inorganic compounds, which are bound to change the technology base of capitalist production with great explosiveness. Secondly, based on this brand-new technology, the emerging industry of all capitalist countries is not established on a huge scale in accordance with the technical requirements from the outset, but based on a very organized manner. Hilferding thinks, the development of cartels and trusts is the first great achievement brought about by the emerging industry. Finally, huge scale enterprises set up on the basis of this new technology naturally produce an intention that unites cartels and trusts in the international community. He cited an example of the rayon industry, saying that the rayon industry, is not only a monopoly industry for Germany, but is a concern of international monopoly fundamentally. The trusts of rayon industry in Germany are closely linked to that in England.

195

---

13 Peking University, *Rhetoric on Imperialism by Second International Revisionists* (Internal Data), p. 221.

V. The Contradiction Between Production and Market Determines that the Crisis is Unavoidable – Luxembourg's Point of View

In Rosa Luxemburg's theory, there is a very important part which aims to prove that the accumulation of capital would be impossible in a closed capitalist system. She thought that she had an important task, namely to complete Marx's theory, which Marx had failed to complete. By patching this missing proof, she would bridge a significant gap in the Marxist theoretical system and explain a hitherto unexplained phenomenon: modern imperialism. Luxembourg believed that the completion of this work is her bounden duty.

According to Rosa Luxemburg, the core issue is to explain capital accumulation, i.e., accumulation of surplus value. In simple reproduction age, the realization of surplus value (commodities) is not difficult to explain: they are all sold to capitalists for their own consumption. However, in expanded reproduction age, the situation is different. The value of all commodities, and thus the value of all social products are made of constant capital plus variable capital plus surplus value. Constant capital is achieved by capitalists when they buy the renewal supplies of their own; while variable capital is achieved by workers when they spend their wages, which is crystal clear. However, how about surplus value? Who will consume it? Some part is used (bought) by capitalists

for their own consumption and the other part is used for capital accumulation, but difficult question lies here. She asks: "Then, who can be the buyer and consumer of that portion (surplus value) of commodities whose sale is only the beginning of accumulation?"[14] So far as we have seen, it can be neither the workers nor the capitalists. Certainly surplus value (products) cannot be sold to the workers to realize accumulation which capitalism needs, because workers have exhausted their wages in the realization of variable capital. Surplus cannot be sold to capitalists themselves for their consumption since this will lead us to return back to the simple reproduction age. "But today, for capitalists as a class, the total consumption of the surplus value as luxury is economic suicide, because it is the destruction of accumulation. "Then, who can be the buyer and consumer of that portion (surplus value) of commodities whose sale is only the beginning of accumulation?"[15] Rosa Luxemburg goes on her analysis: "Perhaps the capitalists are mutual customers for the remainder of the commodities - not use them carelessly - but use them for the extension of production, or accumulation.Then what else is accumulation? It is not more than the extension of capitalist production?"…" If we assume that accumulation has started and that the increased production brings an even bigger amount of commodities on to the market in the following year, the same question arises again:

14 Rosa Luxemburg, *The Accumulation of Capital: A Contribution to an Economic Explanation of Imperialism*, Beijing: SDX Joint Publishing Company, 1959, p. 114.
15 Rosa Luxemburg, The Accumulation of Capital – An Anti-critique: in Imperialism and the Accumulation of Capital, Harbin: Heilongjiang People's Publishing House, 1982, p.16.

where do we then find the consumers for this even greater amount of commodities? There will be no solution, "then we have the roundabout that revolves around itself in empty space. That is not capitalist accumulation, i.e. the amassing of money capital, but it's contrary: producing commodities for the sake of it; from the standpoint of capital an utter absurdity."[16] Through the above reasoning, Rosa Luxemburg concluded: This question raised cannot be solved and the only way out is to abandon the original assumption, a closed system assumption, a system which is solely constituted of capitalists and workers. After she abandoned this assumption she then said that part of surplus value which is needed for accumulation can only be fulfilled by selling it to non-capitalist consumers, that is, selling it to consumers who live in the country where capitalism has not touched or belong to the population (e.g. peasants) who are still at the level of simple commodity production, and therefore are completely outside of the capitalist system. However, it is this expansion process that drags those backward countries and their residents into the track of capitalism, and the result is that they are all inside. When this happens, the closed capitalism which could not exist in theory will appear in practice, and the system itself will collapse. Based on this theory, the emergence of imperialism indicates that all the capitalist countries desperately want to win as much control as they could over the existing non-capitalist world; high protective tariff is manifested as a means of each country's attempt to block other countries' access to their own non-capital markets. Therefore, some of the most remarkable phenomena in the final stages of capitalist development are interpreted as becoming depleted due to the non-capitalist market; accordingly, they are also interpreted as a harbinger of the imminent collapse of capitalism, which can be prevented by no force in the world.

197

Rosa Luxemburg's theory has been criticized by orthodox Marxist economists. The reason is that she has a particularly prominent error, that when discussing the expanded reproduction, she secretly retained the assumption of simple reproduction. Workers' consumption cannot fulfil surplus value, which is the dogma she never doubted, and the dogma means that the total value of variable capital – therefore the consumption of workers – must be like it is in the simple reproduction, always remaining unchanged. In fact, the typical accumulation contains additional variable capital, and when the additional variable capital is spent by workers, it has fulfilled part of the surplus value in the physical form of consumer goods. Rosa Luxemburg does not understand this, and therefore, it seems to her that, the consumption within the capitalist system will not grow. From that point, she can immediately draw the following conclusions: The additional production reserves cannot play any role. If the premise she established that consumption is constant, then the following is undoubtedly correct that only those who believe in the theory of production and consumption are irrelevant to each other like Tugan-Baranovsky and his school will deny that the continuously adding to means of production is indeed

16   Ibid., p.17.

"the roundabout that revolves around itself in empty space." However, since the theory of consumption being unchanged is based on the stiff logic of Rosa Luxemburg which is extremely unreliable, so the whole theory goes downfall like a house of paper strips. Bukharin's bright pamphlet remains the most vivid criticism of her theoretical system: "If, however, one has excluded expanded reproduction from the start in one's logical proof, it naturally becomes easy to let it disappear at the end of it, for here one is dealing with the simple reproduction of a simple logical error."[17]

Other shortcomings and confusions in Rosa Luxemburg's thought are secondary compared with the fundamental error involving them in understanding and abuse of reproduction. Currently, it needs to point out that even this analysis is correct in negating the possibility of accumulation within a closed system, but her non-capitalist consumers cannot change this situation as well. It is impossible to sell something to a non-capitalist consumer without buying anything from him. In terms of the circulation process of capitalism, the surplus value cannot be handled in this way, which at best can only change its form. Who will buy the commodity "imported" from a non-capitalist neighbor? In principle, if it really needs nothing from the "exported" commodity, then it would have no demand for the "imported" commodity as well. All boundaries between "capitalism" and "non-capitalism" are completely irrelevant at this point. If this dilemma is true, then it would exceed her expectations to prove something more: it will prove that it is not that capitalism is increasingly collapsing, but capitalism cannot exist. Unlike the Russian Populists of 15 years ago, Rosa Luxemburg had a keen sense of economic and political realities, therefore she did not arrive at such an absurd romantic conclusion, forced by her false logic. She had never positioned herself in romantic fantasies, as Lenin once warned in his critique. However, she just used a doubtful expedient, to invent a false answer to a false questioning so as to avoid the above "romantic fantasy".

Luxembourg's views attracted a lot of criticism inside the Second International. Bauer pointed out in an article entitled *The Accumulation of Capital* that the issue raised by Luxembourg is the problem of the relationship between accumulation and consumption. The contradiction between the trend of infinite expansion of capital and social spending power is regarded as an insurmountable contradiction within the range of capitalism, which was proposed by Sismondi and becomes a major theoretical basis for him to criticize the capitalism. This view was inherited by Thomas Malthus and Johann Karl Rodbertus. In these people's view, in order for the capitalist society to be able to sell all the goods, there must be the presence of third persons who only consume but does not produce. Its error has been criticized by Marx systematically. Since Marx has correctly classified the social production as two major categories of the production of the means of production and that of the means

---

17 Nikolai Bukharin, *Imperialism and the Accumulation of Capital.* in *Selected Works of Bukharin* (Volume II), Beijing: People's Publishing House, 1981, p. 20.

of consumption, and put forward that the value of commodity is constituted of three parts, constant capital, variable capital and surplus value, it enables him truly and completely to solve the issue of the relationship between accumulation and consumption.

A. Pannekoek criticized Rosa Luxembourg. Pannekoek, argued: If we examine Marx's expanded reproduction schema carefully, we can see that the problem is not here or there is no difficult problem in this domain.[18] Pannekoek described his own view with this quote: "It's like what was described on page 33 of Kautsky's book Marx's Economics. The shoemaker, tailor and baker respectively own their goods which each of them need in order to live. Here money must appear in the scene in order to break the magic circle. As long as the circulation can be continued, wherein both the capitalists of the department I and II can get also eventually need unsold merchandise from each other. Consequently, capitalists will not wait till they sell out all their stock and till they pocket the surplus value which has become the money, instead they will not hesitate to start a new business cycle."[19] After these words, Pannekoek concluded: "As long as there is correct proportion, even in the expanded capitalist production, to find markets would not be difficult. However, this proportion will vary with different levels of production scale".[20] When criticizing Rosa Luxembourg, he added: "Capitalism would only come to an end - 'collapse' if you like - through the conscious action of the working class." F.A. Eckstein's criticism of Luxembourg is mainly concentrated in methodology. He believes that the relationship between production and demand is the most complex economic issue in the society of commodity production, which involves the most basic questions of political economy, and its properly resolved needs to be based on the knowledge of the law of value. One of Marx's most remarkable achievements is that he correctly solved this problem in *Capital* Volume II, Chapter 3. Eckstein pointed out, in this part of *Capital* that Marx successfully used the "abstraction", and had the correct and detailed analysis of dependence of production and demand. Based on the use of the products, Marx first divided the whole complex social production into two major categories, the production of means of production and the production of means of consumption; in accordance with the basic principles of the labour theory of value, commodity value can be divided into three parts, constant capital, variable capital and surplus value. In this way, Marx can explain the interdependencies between the value produced by the whole society and different parts of the total social products. The famous formula on the simple reproduction of total social capital is the scientific result summarized by this study. Eckstein believes that it is an extremely rare exception in the capitalist society that the capitalists spend the entire surplus value, but it is the only scientific way to solve the issue of the reproduce of social capital. Because only when the science first attributes this complex

199

---

18   Antonie Pannekoek, *Theories about the Cause of the Crisis*, in *Die Neue Zeit*, 1913(22), p.784.

19   Ibid., pp.784-785.

20   Ibid., p.786.

phenomenon to its most simple basis, and then furthers the study, after thoroughly sorting out these simple relationships, can we examine the factors which were not intended to note initially. Based on the detailed analysis of simple reproduction, Marx had the further analysis of the issue on accumulation of capital and expanded reproduction. The expanded reproduction is a typical form of capitalist production, and therefore the progress in the analysis has been closer to the realities of capitalism, but here Marx also used the "isolation method", which is to say that Marx analyzed the capitalist expanded reproduction here in the purest and the simplest case, so as to reveal the intricate relationship of circulation among various production sectors in the accumulation process. Hence, the analysis here does not directly and exactly match with the reality of capitalism. However, this study has a huge significance in understanding the reality, and the foundation to recognize the reality. Luxembourg's attack on Marxist theories and formulas of expanded reproduction is largely based on her misunderstanding of Marx's methods of study. She criticized that Marx failed to see where the growing demand which constitutes the basis of the further expansion of capitalist production came from. Eckstein believes that this attack is clearly and totally unjustified, because in *Capital* Volume II, Chapter 3 it is precisely to reveal the law that this exchange can be carried out and production and consumption can be equalized among a variety of different value groups and product groups. Luxembourg made various comments of mocking style on Marx's analysis, but in fact, it is her who is wrong. The reason she would think

that the surplus value used for accumulation cannot be achieved is because in the analysis she actually forgot the productive consumption in the process of expanded reproduction. Luxembourg also attacked Marx's schema that it could not expose the real purpose of the expanded reproduction of capitalism, in which it seems that they expand the production for the expanded reproduction, and Eckstein thinks it is even untrue because the pursuit of profit dominates the behaviour of all the capitalists, and also dominates the expanded reproduction, which is clearly illustrated in Marx's formula. His elaboration on the exchange process of the two major categories not only set forth who is the producer of the commodity, but also who is the buyer of the commodity. This exchange process of commodity is not only the realization process of the value of commodity, but also the implementation process of the surplus value. The purpose of capitalist production is to gain profit, which is precisely the process represented in the formula by Marx. Finally, Eckstein noted that Luxembourg was not satisfied with Marx's analysis, considering that Marx did not solve the problem of capital accumulation. She tried a different approach. She attempted the exchange with the third persons of non-capitalists to illustrate the implementation issue for the accumulation of surplus value. But she was not able to achieve her goal. Greedy capitalists shipped the goods to the colonies in order to plunder the wealth of the nation, and in this international trade, there were more of barter, and only a few differences were settled with gold. Thus, Luxembourg failed to solve the problem she raised, and she just threw the question from one country to the international context, but stood still in solving it.

Bukharin completely decried Luxembourg's erred remarks against Marx's theory of expanded reproduction and the formula for its realization. He stressed that Marx's schema of expanded reproduction shows that with the increase in production, the market is expanding, and while the market for means of production is expanding, the consumption demand is also growing, because in the case of the expansion of production, the absolute number of the consumption of capitalists or that of workers have increased, which make it possible to achieve equilibrium among various parts of the total social production, as also make it possible to achieve equilibrium between production and consumption. Meanwhile, Bukharin also pointed out that in Marx's analysis of the proportion between the two major categories in the expanded reproduction process of social capital, he set aside a number of factors unique to capitalism, and thus the analysis is in the most abstract stage. If you stay that at this stage, it will come to a negative conclusion for the contradictions of capitalism. As Marx would put it, "'the abusive swaps with the scientific language' of crisis, overproduction, mass poverty, and so on".[21] Nevertheless, the most abstract analysis at this stage is the essential premise. This is because if it is impossible for this accumulation, as well as the expanded reproduction of social capital at the most abstract stage, then, after taking some more specific factors, such as monetary factors into account, it is even more impossible. Luxembourg denies the possibility of such an abstract analysis, which suggests that she did not understand Marx's methodology.

After Bukharin pointed out Luxembourg's errors in methodology, he carried out a detailed error analysis on her theory of expanded reproduction. Finally, he concluded that: "Ergo: Rosa Luxemburg's basic mistake is that she takes the total capitalist as an individual capitalist. She underrates this total capitalist. Therefore, she does not understand that the process of realization occurs gradually. For the same reason she portrays the accumulation of capital as an accumulation of money capital. …Indeed, if the total capitalist is equated with the typical individual capitalist, the first of course cannot be his own consumer. Furthermore, if the amount of additional gold is equivalent to the value of the additional number of commodities, this gold can only come from abroad; if all capitalist have to realize their surplus value at once, they need 'third persons', etc."[22]

Bukharin's criticism on Luxembourg is completely different from Bauer's. He not only pointed out that it is wrong for Luxembourg to deny the possibility to fulfil the accumulation in a purely capitalist condition, he also pointed out the inevitability of contradictions in the process of expanded reproduction of capitalism and the periodic economic crises. He pointed out that the accusation by Luxembourg on Marxist formula of expanded reproduction is, in fact, to confuse Marx's vies with Tugan-Baranovsky. When studying the issue of expanded reproduction, Marx criticized Adam Smith's doctrine of neglecting

21   Nikolai Bukharin, *Imperialism and the Accumulation of Capital*. in *Selected Works of Bukharin* (Volume II), p.258.
22   Ibid., p.299.

constant capital, and he expounded the replacement of the original constant capital and the presence of the additional new constant capital is the most important part of the process of expanded reproduction. This discovery by Marx has great significance to solve the issue of expanded reproduction, and also to solve the issue of market. This is because, it indicates that, in addition to the consumer market, there are still markets for capital goods, which will expand at a faster rate with the expansion of production scales. Tugan-Baranovsky distorted Marx's theory completely, and he completely ignored the link between the two markets, believing that production is not affected by consumer market. He even developed such an error theory to its limits, considering that even due to the extensive use of the machine, all the workers have been replaced by machines, leaving only one worker to start all machines where there is no difficulty with capitalist production. However, in a capitalist society, the production of means of production has become independent due to the anarchy of market, but it is eventually linked with the production of consumer goods through many intermediate links, and cannot fail to be linked together. This is bound to generate conflicts, creating difficulties that the capitalist system cannot overcome. Here, production is not regulated; the stimulus of accumulation is the pursuit of more and more profit, as well as of the increasing scale of production, which is bound to make production beyond the bound of its due proportion, thus having conflict with social spending. Bukharin noted that in criticizing Marx, Luxembourg said that if it is possible to achieve in a pure capitalist society, then the productivity would surely grow unhindered. This is certainly not Marx's intention, and on the contrary, Marx believes that the development of capitalist production is carried out in contradictions. Although there is no continuous overproduction, cyclical overproduction is inevitability; although that the long-term and continuous product cannot be achieved does not exist, it is inevitable to achieve difficulties cyclically; although inherent contradictions of capitalist production cannot be completely solved within itself, the contradiction is temporarily delayed, and therefore there is a solution to contradictions relatively. Hence, capitalism can be developed, but it is impossible for it to have unhindered development. While conflicts can be eliminated periodically, but it is constantly being reproduced on a larger scale, and erupts with greater force periodically, the development of which in the breadth and depth will inevitably lead to the collapse of the capitalist system. The development of capitalism is the process of expanded reproduction of various contradictions of capitalism, Luxembourg criticized Tugan-Baranovsky's error of denying the contradiction between production and consumption, but it does not prove that her own point of view is correct, because criticism can come from various aspects. The mistake by Tugan-Baranovsky is not that he thinks it is possible to achieve, but that he separates the inevitable link between production and consumption, and that he denies the inherent contradictions of capitalist reproduction. Luxembourg's mistake is not that she insisted on the relationship, but that she thinks such a link in a capitalist society cannot be achieved, that is, that she thinks that the accumulated surplus product cannot be achieved.

Against Luxembourg's errors, Bukharin first illustrates the general causes of the external expansion of capitalism from the two aspects, and then further clarifies the economic roots of imperialism. Bukharin believes that in the first external expansion of capitalism, "it lies in the difficulties which result, if not from an absolute and constant over-production, then nonetheless from crises, including all their consequences".[23] He said that there needs to be no more explanation, because when a crisis occurs periodically, it is very natural to pursue the objective existence of a "new market". The second reason is a more important, more fundamental and more permanent reason, which is the possibility to obtain greater profits from non-capitalist environment, because in the exchange with the non-capitalist and poorer countries which are lagging behind, the "richer" capitalist countries can get extra profits. He pointed out that in *Capital*, Marx had done detailed instructions on this point. This is because the highly developed capitalist countries in the competition of the international trade are far superior to those backward non-capitalist countries. This is because the developed capitalist country has high productivity, thus resulting that even if its commodities are sold at the price far below that of the competitors', the price may still be considerably higher than the value, thus making the real profits considerably higher than that sold in its own country. Here, the labour in relatively developed capitalist countries is paid as a complex labour of high quality, and thus it can obtain excess profits. The obtaining of excess profits is also realization, but this is not the realization of general profits, but the realization of excess profits, which is a phenomenon closely linked with the external expansion of the capitalism. If you do not understand this then you cannot understand the real cause of capitalist expansion, but just like Luxembourg who could not explain why in the initial stages of the capital development the "third person" such as peasants and small handicraftsmen and as many as one can imagine around it, and when they are enough to achieve the object of surplus production, it has been starting madly external expansion and implementing the colonial policy.

Bukharin believes that what is talked about above is just the general problem of capitalist expansion, and he also needs to talk more specifically about the issue of the economic roots of imperialism. In this regard, there are also many errors with Luxembourg, and she once had hoped that her book *The Accumulation of Capital* can have some sense in the actual struggle against imperialism, but her writings were not able to solve this problem. As she revealed the roots of imperialism from the real problems of the accumulation of capital, she made imperialism "the specific traits of a specific, historically demarcated epoch disappear behind general observations on the expansion of capital".[24]

In the final part of *Imperialism and the Accumulation of Capital*, Bukharin

---

23 Ibid., p.338.
24 Ibid., p.384.

criticized Rosa Luxemburg on the political conclusions based on the accumulation theory, as well as on issue of the so-called "objective limit" of capitalism. Bukharin considered that Luxembourg's theory is very simple and plain, and it can be summarized as follows: "Capitalism is possible to the extent that it is 'impure', in other words, to the extent that a periphery of 'third persons' exists alongside the 'capitalist productive' centre. The third persons' constitute a premise of the process of the realization of surplus value, hence also a necessary condition of the process of expanded reproduction. Nonetheless, the movement of capital is, according to its tendency, a movement towards 'pure' capitalism, as to a certain mathematical limit of development. If, according to this theory, the solution of the contradiction between the process of the production of surplus value and its realization takes place at the expense of the 'third persons', the solution cannot be repeated forever, since the number of third persons is decreasing relatively. Here we come up against the objective-economic limit of capitalism as a specific, historically limited mode of production. Capitalism becomes an economic impossibility. This historical-economic necessity breaks through in the workers' revolution."[25] This theory by Luxembourg fully embodies the "economic determinism", and is full of the character of "revolution", but it is still wrong. First, Bukharin pointed out that out of the 1,700 million people population of our planet, 900 million (over half) live in Asia, where peasants and small handicraftsmen form the majority of the world population, and even nearly 50 per cent of the population of Europe is rural. This means that the vast majority of people in the world belong to the so-called "third persons" category by Luxembourg. If the collapse of capitalism has to wait until the "third persons" are destroyed, or until they are fully capitalized. So, the situation of the revolution cause would be very serious. However, in fact, in the era that Luxembourg lived, there has been a contradiction of capitalism which is extremely sharp, extremely nervous, extremely catastrophic and explosive, and the capitalism starts to collapse, while the proletarian dictatorship is built up in the Soviet Union. Since Luxembourg had almost completely set aside the issue of profit transfer in her studies, set aside special form of excess profits, which makes it difficult for him to see the nature of imperialism and where its contradictions lies, although he would very much like to make a revolutionary conclusion, the result turned out exactly the opposite. Secondly, Bukharin also believes that the root cause of the error in Luxembourg is that she does not know the dialectical nature of social contradictions, does not know the dialectical nature of the society as a whole and the law of its movement. "Capitalist society is a 'unity of contradictions'. The process of movement of capitalist society is a process of the continual reproduction of the capitalist contradictions. The process of expanded reproduction is a process of the expanded reproduction of these contradictions. If this is so, it is clear that these contradictions will blow up the entire capitalist system as a whole. We have reached the limit of capitalism."[26] As for to what extent can

25   Ibid., p.354.
26   Ibid.

the tension of this contradiction put capitalism in trouble, the answer should be looked for in the reproduction conditions of labour, and when the economic damage and the decreased productivity is caused by the outbreak of the capitalist contradictions, when the reproduction of labour one day becomes impossible, the production structure of society will burst, and the antagonistic classes will resort to arms.

Bukharin criticized Luxembourg's errors on the issue of capital accumulation and imperialism, but he did not take the attitude to beat her to death. In the last part of his article, he made a summary of Luxembourg's study of the issue of capital accumulation and imperialism, evaluating the merits and demerits, and he said: "The biggest theoretical merits of Rosa Luxemburg are that she raised the question of the relation between the capitalist and the non-capitalist milieu. But she only raised it. She silently or almost silently evaded the specific questions concerning this extensive problem (the question of the character of exchange, structural variation, modifications in the law of value, extra profit, the increased accumulation at the expense of third persons', etc., etc.). But doubtless the mere question deserves great respect. Comrade Rosa Luxemburg did not gain less merit for stressing the question of reproduction. … But Rosa Luxemburg has overlooked the fact that the extended reproduction of capitalist conditions at the same time is the extended reproduction of all capitalist contradictions. Had she seen that clearly, she would not have bothered with the problem of the 'objective limits' of capitalism. Another of Rosa Luxemburg's extraordinary theoretical merits is that she raised the question 205 of the historical necessity of imperialism. Opposed to the reformists, who had betrayed Marxism with open cynicism, and opposed to the quasi orthodox à la Kautsky, who was at that time already starting to stutter about the possibilities of an 'English style' reformed 'ideal capitalism', Rosa Luxemburg sharply raised the question of imperialism as the unavoidable 'immanent appearance' of capitalism at a certain stage of development. At any rate, she was not able to understand the problem theoretically as the specific problem of our time. She did not try to find the basis of imperialism in the hunt for larger monopoly profits and in the necessary movement of finance capital in that direction, but in the absolute impossibility of the existence of capitalism 'without third persons'. Nevertheless, she has raised the question about the necessity of imperialism and in general answered it properly, although her answer was based on theoretically wrong arguments. Rosa Luxemburg's work rose high above the bungling efforts and the miserable chattering of the reformists of directions, the open revisionists as well as the Kautskyans. It represents a daring theoretical attempt; it is the deed of a brilliant theoretical intellect. We do not have to mention especially that the historical part of the work has remained unsurpassed until today in its description of the history of the colonial conquests of capitalism."[27]

27　Nikolai Bukharin, *Imperialism and the Accumulation of Capital*. In *Selected Works of Bukharin* (Volume II), pp. 363-364.

The debate triggered by *The Accumulation of Capital* went on many years. History has shown that those who made a correct understanding of the issue of imperialism are scholars insistent on Marxist basic economic theory led by Lenin, rather than those critical attitudes towards the Marxist theory of social reproduction about the issue of capital or those who want to determine this theory. This again tells us that today, it is only by upholding of the basic tenets of Marxism we can have a proper understanding of the new developments of contemporary capitalism, and scientifically understand the new development of capitalism in order to creatively develop Marxist theory.

VI. Conclusions

In Marx's times, the cyclical economic crises occurring periodically in about every 10 years had become a reality. The occurrence of this reality which is directly related with the business cycle, has once again proved the correctness and accuracy of the theories and predictions put forward in the Marxist theory of business cycles. Thus, with the passage of time and repeated crises, people regard the cyclical economic crisis as an inevitability of the development of the capitalist economic system, even the arrival of the crisis on time is also seen as inevitability. If this crisis does not come on time, or that there are periodic irregular movements, people would question the periodicity of crises. Alternatively, the capitalist economic crisis is regarded merely as the product of the anarchy of production, and as long as plan and proportionality of production can be achieved, the cyclical economic crises can be avoided. Bernstein is aware that monopoly discarded the free competition of capitalism, and it is able to achieve the plan and proportionality of production and circulation on a certain scope and to a certain extent. Therefore, it can relieve the capitalist economic crisis to some extent, but it also means that the cyclical capitalist economic crisis is an occasional phenomenon. From the historical point of view, in the period of free competition of capitalism, crisis can basically come in time regularly in about 10 years. When it comes to the period of state monopoly capitalism, the periodic crises are disrupted, the extent of the industrial crisis is greatly reduced, and the financial crisis occurs frequently with the strengthening in degree. This shows that the periodicity of economic crisis in Marx's era is actually a natural frequency for the crisis to occur under conditions of no interference, and that this frequency is disrupted under monopoly conditions is because factors of government intervention are added in the operation of economy.

Bernstein denied the inevitability of periodic crises, because he saw the contingency of the crisis, and he says the inevitability of the crisis does not exist. Hilferding recognizes the inevitability of the economic crisis, but considers that with the advance of science and technology and strengthening of the role of monopoly, the organized capitalism emerges, which extended capitalism temporarily, mitigated the crisis, or at least suppressed the negative impact of the crisis on workers. Kautsky, Luxemburg and Tugan saw the inevitability of the crisis, but they only see a certain aspect of the roots of this inevitability, while ignoring the other. If these famous theorists of the Second International had any contribution to Marx's analysis model of economic crisis, it is that they saw the planning of the allocation of resources in the monopoly capitalist economy, as well as its effects on capitalist economic crisis. The debates around the development trend of the crisis are, in essence, an argument between the defence of Marx's analysis model of the economic crisis and the attempt to break the model.

CHAPTER VI

Political Economy Model of the Business Cycle

I. Introduction

It has been an important area of study in Marxist political economy to reveal the roots of cyclical volatility of capitalist economy and to describe the trend of each stage of the cycle and its characteristics, because the relevant study has both the important theoretical significance, and the important practical significance. In the history of the formation of Marxist economics, the cyclical volatility of the capitalist economy is an important basis for the creation of historical materialism by Marx, and also the fundamental basis for revealing the historical status and trends of the capitalist mode of production. Marx's pioneering study in this field laid the foundation for the future generations. From the existing references, Marx's study has achieved the following results: it reveals that the root of the capitalist business cycle lies in the basic contradiction of capitalist production, it is the result of all contractions of capitalism being developed; the length of the cycle is generally about 10 years, and there is a short-cycle interval of about 3 to 5 years; the material basis of the business cycle is the renewal of fixed capital; each cycle consists of several stages, in which the crisis is both the ending point of the previous cycle and the starting point of the next; specific crises are always caused by some specific reasons, and each crisis has its own specific reasons; cyclical fluctuations in the economy is an inevitable trend, capitalism is unable to overcome the crisis within its own scope, and methods that attempt to overcome the crisis only make the crisis arrive more violently. In the process of obtaining the conclusions, Marx examines a series of factors that impact and constrain the business cycle, such as cycling and turnover of capital, the realization conditions for social capital reproduction, the law of the trend of the rate of profit to fall, competition, credit, stock system, nations, foreign trade, world markets and etc. Overall, his outstanding study won him important discovery far more than his contemporaries. In the years of revolution and war, these findings are undoubtedly important theoretical weapons, playing a huge role in promoting the success of the revolution. But in the years centered by economic construction, the traditional textbook model of Marxist theory of business cycle has, in fact, become an abstract model unable to serve the reality. Western business cycle theory flew in, and became the dominant theory. Marxist economics uses the traditional analytical model when it is as a course of political theory, and uses the non-Marxist theory of business cycle when it is as a major course in economics, and which is much like the non-Marxist economics, taking the specific reason as the root reason, as well as taking the description of phenomena as the analysis of constitutive relations. In the real economic life, the use of the analytic model in the existing textbook to analyze the contemporary capitalist economic crisis has been feeble, seems at a loss when analyzing the socialist business cycle. Facing the embarrassing situation, there was a thinking that Marxist theory of business cycle was "outdated" thrown in desperation in academics. In this chapter, it argues that a comprehensive and profound study, understanding and uncovering the deep meaning of the Marxist theory of the business cycle is important to promote the Marxist theory of the business cycle, but if we do not expand the perspective of Marxist theory of the business cycle, but confine the exploration of the business cycle to constitutive relations and reject the investigation of specific reasons, it will be difficult to become an effective theoretical tool to analyze the real business cycle. Of course, fundamentally speaking, uncovering, sorting and developing Marxist theory of the business cycle is the fundamental way to solve the problem no matter in the past, present or future.

II. Formation of the Theory

In the beginning of exploring capitalist economic relations, Marx and Engels had paid more attention on the business cycle fluctuation. In the 1840s and early 1850s, they found the periodic feature of capitalist reproduction, and considered that the length of the period should be five to seven years. Engels wrote in *Outlines of the Critique of Political Economy*: "… trade crises, which reappear as regularly as the comets, and of which we have now on the average one every five to seven years."[1] Ina number of later writings, he sometimes said the length to be five years, sometimes five or six years, and sometimes to

---

1 *Marx and Engels Collected Works*, 1ˢᵗ Chinese edition, Volume 1, Beijing: People's Publishing House, 1956, p. 614.

be seven years, but the basic idea has not changed. In the early 1850s, Marx and Engels also held the same view that "[m]odern industry and commerce, it is well known, pass through periodical cycles of from 5 to 7 years."[2] But in the late 1850s when he began writing books in economics, he had a new view of the length of the cycle, which can be seen from the correspondence between Marx and Engels on the renewal of the fixed capital.

In a commentary[3] written in October 1850, Marx and Engels had a detailed review of the history of the industrial cycle since 1837, and although they did not fully describe the history between 1843 and 1844 in the article, they summarized in detail the process of an industrial cycle, made a careful distinction between symptoms and reasons of a crisis, as well as the various factors of the crisis. For example, excess speculation and stock crisis, credit crisis and money market crisis, commercial crisis itself and financial crisis, foreign trade crisis and gold outflow, general commercial crisis and banking crisis. The stock crisis caused by excessive investment and credit crisis caused by excessive credit expansion seem in their eyes only symptoms of the crisis, and the real reason of the crisis is industrial overproduction and the related expansion of foreign trade. Marx and Engels have clearly recognized that this is a crisis threatening the European continent by the British industrial capitalism, "the process of crises and prosperity originated in England, which is the demiurge of the bourgeois cosmos."[4] During this period, they studied the business cycle to the conclusion that: "The years 1843-5 were years of industrial and commercial prosperity, a necessary sequel to the almost uninterrupted industrial depression of 1837-42. As is always the case, prosperity very rapidly encouraged speculation. Speculation regularly occurs in periods when overproduction is already in full swing. It provides overproduction with temporary market outlets, while for this very reason precipitating the outbreak of the crisis and increasing its force. The crisis itself first breaks out in the area of speculation; only later does it hit production. What appears to the superficial observer to be the cause of the crisis is not overproduction but excess speculation, but this is itself only a symptom of overproduction. The subsequent disruption of production does not appear as a consequence of its own previous exuberance but merely as a setback caused by the collapse of speculation."[5] Marx and Engels put these as "only the most significant of these symptoms of overproduction[6] (As for the speculation in the years of prosperity, they thought "it was based upon a real demand", which means that there is no fixed form. For example, from 1843 to 1845, speculation was concentrated principally in railways; in corn, as a result of the price rise of 1845 and the potato blight, in cotton, following the bad

---

2 *Marx and Engels Collected Works*, 1st Chinese edition, Volume 8, Beijing: People's Publishing House, 1961, p. 416.

3 *See Marx and Engels Collected Works*, 1st Chinese edition, Volume 7, ,Beijing: People's Publishing House, 1959, p. 492.

4 *Marx and Engels Collected Works*, Volume 7, p.113.

5 Ibid., p. 492.

6 Marx and Engels Review: May-October 1850.

crop of 1846, and in the East Indian and Chinese trade, where it followed hard on the heels of the opening up of the Chinese market by England.[7] The above facts show that Marx and Engels had begun to pay close attention to some of the details of the development of the business cycle in the early 1850s, trying to accurately and completely reveal the law of the development of the business cycle. In fact they had given great attention to the 1857–1858 economic crises, and carried out extensive study, which laid a solid foundation for the creation of the crisis theory.

When writing the *Economics Manuscript* (1857-1858), Marx began to pay attention to the material basis for the industrial cycle. In the letter to Engels on 2 March 1858, he asked "Can you tell me how often machinery has to be replaced in, say, your factory?" This is because "The average period for the replacement of machinery is one important factor in explaining the multi-year cycle which has been a feature of industrial development ever since the consolidation of big industry."[8] Engels wrote him back on 4 March 1858, and informed him about the common practice of machinery replacement, as well as the cycle of new and expanding investments in the cotton and textile industry in Manchester.[9] Marx expressed his best thanks for Engels' **éclaircissements** (clarification) about machinery, and he stressed that "[t]he figure of 13 years corresponds closely enough to the theory, since it establishes a unit for one epoch of industrial reproduction which **plus ou moins** (more or less) coincides with the period in which major crises recur". Their course is also determined by factors of a quite different kind. But for him "the important thing is to discover, in the immediate material postulates of big industry, one factor that determines cycles".[10] This explanation also appeared in the *Economics Manuscript* (1857-1858) again: To discover a unit to measure the turnovers of capital through fixed capital and its reproduction, and the reproduction of capital "is now not merely externally, but rather necessarily connected with this unit". "There can be no doubt whatever that the cycle which industry has passed through since the development of fixed capital on a large scale, at more or less 10-year intervals, is connected with this total reproduction phase of capital. We shall find other determinant causes as well. But this is one of them".[11] Soon, Engels' understanding of the length of the business cycle was gradually consistent with Marx, and he wrote this change in *The Condition of the Working Class in England*: "The recurring period of the great industrial crisis is stated in the text as five years. This was the period apparently indicated by the course of events from 1825 to 1842. But the industrial history from 1842 to 1868 has shown that the real period is one of ten years; that the intermediate revulsions were

7　*Marx and Engels Collected Works*, Volume 7, p. 493.

8　*Marx and Engels Collected Works*, 1st Chinese edition, Volume 7, p. 493.

9　*Marx and Engels Collected Works*, 1st Chinese edition, Volume 29. Beijing: People's Publishing House, 1980, p. 280.

10　Ibid., p. 284.

11　*Marx and Engels Collected Works*, 1st Chinese edition, Volume 31. Beijing: People's Publishing House, 1980, p. 117.

secondary, and tended more and more to disappear."[12] Engels also mentioned the capitalist economic crisis at more or less 10-year intervals in many of his writings.

Marx and Engels' ideas have gradually converged on the duration of the business cycle, i.e., at more or less 10-year intervals, besides they also agreed on the existence of short-term fluctuations. Marx once pointed out: "For Modern Industry with its decennial cycles and periodic phases, which, moreover, as accumulation advances, are complicated by irregular oscillations following each other more and more quickly."[13] This means that among the 10-year cycle, there are still irregular short-term fluctuations. When describing the history of the British textile industry crisis in *Capital* Volume I, Marx summed up the cycle of 10 year and short-term fluctuations. He put years of 1825, 1837, 1838, 1847 and 1857 into category of "crisis", while years from 1831 to 1833 are called "continued depression"; 1840 "great depression"; 1842 "the manufacturers lock the hands out of the factories in order to enforce the repeal of the Corn Laws. The operatives stream in thousands into the towns of Lancashire and Yorkshire, are driven back by the military, and their leaders brought to trial at Lancaster". 1851 "falling prices, low wages, frequent strikes"; 1855 "news of failures stream in from the United States, Canada, and the Eastern markets"; 1861 "cotton famine"; 1862 to 1863 "complete collapse".[14] This shows that Marx adheres to the 10-year cycle theory and acknowledges the existence of short-term fluctuations, and he no longer calls the trough of the short-term fluctuations crisis, but refers to them as "depression" and so on. It is worth noting that, 1842 which Engels repeatedly called, 1851 which Marx intended it to be the commercial crisis and 1855 the large industrial and commercial crisis, are not to be called crisis again, but replaced with another expression. It also further illustrates, after the 10-year cycle theory produced by Marx, the shortwave movement was included among the 10-year cycle theory.

213

After entering the 1870s, the capitalist economy has undergone major changes, resulting in a number of new features shown in the crisis and its cycle. During this period, the discussion of the length of the cycle by Marx and Engels can be summarized as follows: (1) Theory of shortening crisis cycle raised by Marx around 1875. Marx pointed out in the letter to Pyotr Lavrov on 18 June, 1875 that "general crisis is shortening in the cycle time".[15] In *Capital* French Version Volume I published in separate sections between 1872 and 1875, Marx inserted the following statement: "The duration of this period is ten or eleven years, but this number should never be seen as fixed. On the contrary, according to the various laws of capitalist production we have described above, we

12 *On Economic Crisis by Marx, Engels, Lenin and Stalin*, Beijing: Science Press, 1958, p. 95.
13 *Marx and Engels Collected Works*, 1st Chinese edition, Volume 23, Beijing: People's Publishing House, 1972, p. 699.
14 See *Marx and Engels Collected Works*, 1st Chinese edition, Volume 23, pp. 498-499.
15 *Marx and Engels Collected Works*, 1st Chinese edition, Volume 34, Beijing: People's Publishing House, 1972, p. 139.

are bound to arrive at this conclusion: This figure is variable, and the cycle time will be gradually shortened."[16] In *Socialism: Utopian and Scientific* published in 1880, Engels also expressed a similar view. (2) During 1882 and 1883, Engels proposed the theory of "intermediate crisis". "Now, when the United States, Britain, France and Germany began to break the monopoly in the world market, and thus, as before 1847 overproduction began to appear more quickly, there is an intermediate crisis with a period of five years."[17] "Intermediate crisis must be paid attention to …Before 1847, these crises were regular intermediate links."[18] Please note that it is the regular intermediate links that were mentioned here. Actually it is admitted that it is a short-term fluctuation of regularity. (3) From the years 1885 to 1895, Engels repeatedly expounded the theory of long-term depression, and he said: "a change has taken place here since the last major general crisis. The acute form of the periodic process with its former ten-year cycle, appears to have given way to a more chronic, long drawn out, alternation between a relatively short and slight business improvement and a relatively long, indecisive depression-taking place in the various industrial countries at different times. But perhaps it is only a matter of a prolonging of the duration of the cycle."[19] Engels argued that since 1868, the 10-year cycle was broken; the infinite depression is often the characteristic of this period, which might extend the cycle. But at the same time, he also believes that in this phase there are still small crises, and in 1886 he wrote: "The collapse of England's monopoly on the world market has caused the crisis to continue unbroken since 1878."[20] In short, Marx, and Engels in particular had undergone a process of change in understanding the length of the cycle after the 1870s, in which we can see that there is such a side of thought that the business cycle in this period is attributed to long-term depression as well as the short-wave movement it contains.

214

In summary, Marx and Engels not only raised the five-year cycle theory, but also proposed the 10-year cycle theory and the theory of long-term of depression, although Marx and Engels are trying to find a business cycle length to summarize the capitalist economic fluctuations, although after the 10-year cycle theory is put forward, the five-year cycle is no longer focused on, although the five-year cycle is only regarded as intermediate fluctuations, Marx and Engels have discussed the existence of a variety of cycles on different occasions creatively, and they already have a clear outline of the concept of business cycle.

---

16 *Marx and Engels Collected Works*, 1st Chinese edition, Volume 23, p. 695 footnote.
17 *Marx and Engels Collected Works*, 1st Chinese edition, Volume 36, Beijing: People's Publishing House, 1975, p. 26.
18 *Marx and Engels Collected Works*, 1st Chinese edition, Volume 35, Beijing: People's Publishing House, 1971, p. 259.
19 *Marx and Engels Collected Works*, 1st Chinese edition, Volume 25, Beijing: People's Publishing House, 1974, p. 554.
20 *Marx and Engels Collected Works*, 1st Chinese edition, Volume 36, p. 436.

III. The Primary Cycle and the Short Cycle

In the process of studying the business cycle, Marx had done detailed study and distinction of each phase of the cycle, and we can find the relevant descriptions of his works in different periods. In *The Poverty of Philosophy*, Marx had such a description of the business cycle: "Production is inevitably compelled to pass in continuous succession through vicissitudes of prosperity, depression, crisis, stagnation, renewed prosperity, and so on."[21] In the ensuing *Pauperism and Free Trade*, Marx also pointed out: "In regular succession, go through the different states of quiescence next improvement growing confidence activity prosperity excitement over-trading convulsion pressure stagnation distress ending again in quiescence."[22] In *Capital* Volume 1, Marx succinctly summarized each phase of the cycle as follows: "The life of modern industry becomes a series of periods of moderate activity, prosperity, over-production, crisis and stagnation."[23] In *Capital* Volume 3, there is also the same description: "State of inactivity, mounting revival, prosperity, over-production, crisis, stagnation, state of inactivity".[24] In *Capital* Volume 2, Marx made the simplest statement of each stage of the 10-years cycle: "During this cycle business undergoes successive periods of depression, medium activity, precipitancy, crisis."[25] Later, Marxist political economy simplifies the concept of the business cycles as crisis, stagnation, recovery, and upsurge, four stages, and puts particular emphasis on the phase of crisis in the cycle, considering that crisis is the decisive stage of the business cycle in capitalism, the ending point of the previous cycle and also the starting point of the next. Therefore, Marx took the study of the crisis phase as the focus of studying the cycle.

The theory of four stages of the cycle in Marxist economics then gradually became the formulation consistent with the business cycle theory in Western Economics. During the 100 years from the economic crisis in 1825 to the eve of the World War II, the performance of the primary cycle is very obvious. The sudden contraction of the primary cycle is presented as the universal economic crisis, which intensifies the contradictions, often leading to war and revolution. During this period, compared with the primary cycle, the short cycle is only shown as the relatively minor fluctuations. Generally, a primary cycle is said to include two short cycles, and sometimes include three. In two short cycles, the contraction phase of a short cycle coincides with the primary cycle. This is also the reason to strengthen the primary cycle fluctuation. But the other short cycle occurs in the recovery phase or the upsurge phase of the primary cycle.

21 *Marx and Engels Collected Works*, 1st Chinese edition, Volume 4, Beijing: People's Publishing House, 1958, p. 109.
22 *Marx and Engels Collected Works*, 1st Chinese edition, Volume 8, Beijing: People's Publishing House, 1961, pp. 416-417.
23 *Marx and Engels Collected Works*, 1st Chinese edition, Volume 23, Beijing: People's Publishing House, 1972, p. 497.
24 *Marx and Engels Collected Works*, 1st Chinese edition, Volume 25, p. 404.
25 *Capital,* Volume 2, Beijing: People's Publishing House, 1975, p.207.

This will inevitably break the process of the primary cycle, and results in the emergence of a small fluctuation in the expansion process of the primary cycle, showing the process of a smaller contraction and the re-expansion. The business cycles that Western economists are talking about are usually short cycles. They also generally divided the cycle into four phases, which is very natural, because there will be four stages of upsurge, contraction, trough, and expansion, as long as there is fluctuation. As the primary cycle is very obvious before World War II, short-cycle is relatively weak. Hence, from the perspective of the primary cycle, there are movements mixed in the short cycle in the intermediate links, but generally we can still see the process in which the economy goes from crisis to depression, from depression gradually to recovery, and then goes into the upsurge. As Marx pointed out, "[t]he course characteristic of modern industry, viz., a decennial cycle (interrupted by smaller oscillations), of periods of average activity, production at high pressure, crisis and stagnation, depends on the constant formation, the greater or less absorption and the re-formation of the industrial reserve army or surplus-population.""[26] If look at it from the point of view of the short cycle, despite the fluctuation being not great, we still can see four stages. That is, in some stages of the primary cycle, there is a fluctuation process superimposed in the short cycle.

After World War II, in a series of new conditions, such as state monopoly capitalism, the business cycle has undergone huge changes. The primary cycle is largely weakened, and the short cycle is to some extent strengthened. Therefore, phases of the primary cycle have disappeared: a primary cycle is divided into two or three substantially the same short cycle distinctly. Phases of the short cycle are manifested as two phases of peak and trough, as well as two turning points of expansion and contraction. Sometimes the short cycle is also rendered as cycle of the growth rate, and despite that the performance will be a lower rate of economic growth, the whole upsurge phase is especially long. In 1980s, Chinese scholar Wu Dakun believed that the reason of cycle contraction is that the advance in science and technology shortens the renewal cycle of the fixed capital.

It needs to particularly note that the history of the cycle to date indicates that the previous business cycle is not identical with one another at all. The length of each cycle is not identical, nor is the process of each cycle, which is particularly and prominently manifested in the transition of this cycle from upsurge to trough, and some transition is manifested extremely violent, and some more relaxed. This involves the concept of crisis, which is necessary for further instructions. The textbook of Marxist political economics generally thinks that, the so-called capitalist economic crisis is the crisis of overproduction, where commodities produced cannot be achieved. It is expressed as the flood in market, decline in price, sluggish sales, decrease in production, credit destruction, bankruptcy, unemployment and etc. This definition is summarized from the economic phenomena. Marx and Engels had described the short cycle

26 *Marx and Engels Collected Works*, 1st Chinese edition, Volume 23, p. 694.

of the crisis in this way, but later this definition in the textbook is designed to illustrate the primary crisis cycle. However, in fact, this definition is not only in line with the reality of the economic crisis of primary cycle, it is also consistent with the reality of the economic crisis of short cycle. The performance of the post-war economic crisis has changed a lot, but this definition is, to some extent, broadly appropriate for the primary cycle and the short cycle. Here, from the perspective of the business cycle theory, we can also give the economic crisis another generalization, that is the economic crisis is the transition of the whole economy from the phase of upsurge to depression, or continued decline from upsurge to trough. We can say that this definition is both the attribution of the primary cycle, and of the short cycle, which can be used for summing up history and generally suitable for the present. These two definitions can be established and applied, and of course, used for different definitions in different places. In a more general sense, when exploring the laws of the business cycle, it seems better to use the latter. Marx and Engels had a variety of formulations of the economic crisis, in which they also called the economic crisis the economic panic, and sometimes the economic collapse. For the economic crisis, it is sometimes labelled with terms like universal, general, large, serious, most serious, most profound, small, intermediate, and etc. We borrow some of the wording by Marx and Engels, and an economic crisis of primary cycle can be called a major economic crisis. For the purpose of simplicity and distinguish easily , and trying to be consistent with the current academic term, this article also called the economic crisis of primary cycle, the economic crisis, and the economic crisis of short cycle, the economic recession. This means that the economic crisis in the broad sense refers to the economic crisis of fluctuation cycle; and the economic crisis in the narrow sense is specifically the economic crisis of primary cycle.

IV. Characteristics of Each Stage of the Business Cycle

In respect to the periodicity of the economic crisis, as well as the manifestation of each stage of the periodicity, in *Capital*, Marx studied the British cotton industry between 1825-1873, and made a more detailed description. These descriptions reflect the situation of British cotton industry – is always in the stages of getting better or recovering (i.e., moderate active), prosperity, crisis and stagnation, with periodic changes. But because of the typicality of British capitalist economy, to some extent it has the characteristic of generality. The existing references has a very detailed description on the business cycle of that period, but because of Marx's authority, it is more conducive to our description of the problem by quoting his description. Marx's descriptions are scattered in many places in his writings, and according to Marx's description, we have the following sub-descriptions:

"In times of prosperity, intense expansion, acceleration and vigour of the reproduction process, labourers are fully employed. Generally, there is also a rise in wages which makes up in some measure for their fall below average during other periods of the business cycle. At the same time, the revenues of the capitalists grow considerably. Consumption increases generally. Commodity-prices also rise regularly, at least in the various vital branches of business. Consequently, the quantity of circulating money grows at least within definite limits, since the greater velocity of circulation, in turn, sets up certain barriers to the growth of the amount of currency."[27] The financial market is active, credit is expanded, securities price rises, stock market is active, and interest rate has gone up, but only rises slowly. Since the whole production process is showing the momentum of prosperity in both purchase and sale, it induces capitalists to push the increase in production to excitement. "But this state of excitement itself, is only the precursor of the state of convulsion."[28]

From prosperity to crisis, it often comes all of a sudden. Under normal circumstances, so long as the product is sold, everything is taking its regular course from the standpoint of the capitalist producer. Whether the producer decides to change the scale of production is mainly based on product sales. The more smoothly the product is sold, the more likely the producers will expand production scale. Capitalist socialized production enables the commodity capital to function independently, so that the commodity capital becomes the form opposite to that of commercial capital, and the circulation becomes a relative independent phase of the capital cycle. In this case, as long as the producer sells the commodity to the wholesaler at the ex-factory price, the commodity is considered to have already been sold, and then he can rely on the credit system to obtain funds, and to continue production or expand production. But the reality is often: "a large part of the commodities may have entered into consumption only apparently, while in reality they may still remain unsold in the hands of dealers, may in fact still be lying in the market. Now one stream of commodities follows another, and finally it is discovered that the previous streams had been absorbed only apparently by consumption. The commodity-capitals compete with one another for a place in the market. Late-comers, to sell at all, sell at lower prices. The former streams have not yet been disposed of when payment for them falls due. Their owners must declare their insolvency or sell at any price to meet their obligations. This sale has nothing whatever to do with the actual state of the demand. It only concerns the demand for payment, the pressing necessity of transforming commodities into money. Then a crisis breaks out."[29]

Even if "[t]he manufacturer may actually sell to the exporter, and the exporter, in his turn, to his foreign customer; the importer may sell his raw materials to the manufacturer, and the latter may sell his products to the wholesale merchant, etc. But at some particular imperceptible point the goods lie unsold, or else, again, all producers and middlemen may gradually become overstocked.

27 *Capital*, Volume III,, Beijing: People's Publishing House, 1975, p.505.
28 *Marx and Engels Collected Works*, Chinese Version 1st Ed., Volume 8, Beijing: People's Publishing House, 1961, p. 422.
29 *Capital*, Volume II, Beijing: People's Publishing House, 1975, p. 89.

Consumption is then generally at its highest, either because one industrial capitalist sets a succession of others in motion; or because the labourers employed by them are fully employed and have more to spend than usual. The capitalists' expenditures increase together with their growing income. Besides, as we have seen (Book II, Part III), continuous circulation takes place between constant capital and constant capital (even regardless of accelerated accumulation). It is at first independent of individual consumption because it never enters the latter. But this consumption definitely limits it nevertheless, since constant capital is never produced for its own sake but solely because more of it is needed in spheres of production whose products go into individual consumption. However, this may go on undisturbed for some time, stimulated by prospective demand, and in such branches; therefore, the business of merchants and industrialists goes briskly forth. The crisis occurs when the returns of merchants who sell in distant markets (or whose supplies have also accumulated on the home market) become so slow and meagre that the banks press for payment, or promissory notes for purchased commodities become due before the latter have been resold. Then forced sales take place, sales in order to meet payments. Then comes the crash, which brings the illusory prosperity to an abrupt end."[30]

"Hence the phenomenon that crises do not come to the surface, do not break out, in the retail business first, which deals with direct consumption, but in the spheres of wholesale trade, and of banking, which places the money-capital of society at the disposal of the former."[31] During the crisis, the general case is the drop in prices, a large part of commodities stacked in the warehouse, difficult to sell. As the interruption in the transformation process of W'-G', thereby the production of commodities is also forced to curtail, resulting in that companies of weak strength are bankrupt, massive unemployment is seen, and there is a significant decline in the wages of workers. The hindered production and circulation further causes the destruction of the credit relations. From the enterprise to the bank, the debt chain is destroyed, and "once the crisis has broken out, it becomes from then on only a question of means of payment. But since everyone is dependent upon someone else for the receipt of these means of payment, and no one knows whether the next one will be able to meet his payments when due, a regular stampede ensues for those means of payment available on the market, that is, for bank-notes. Everyone hoards as many of them as he can lay hand on, and thus the notes disappear from circulation on the very day when they are most needed."[32] "In a period of crisis, the circulation of bills collapses completely; nobody can make use of a promise to pay since everyone will accept only cash payment..."[33] Meanwhile, in the crisis, fictitious capital, interest-bearing paper, its price falls with rising interest. It falls, furthermore, as a result of the general shortage of credit, which compels its owners to dump it in large quantities on the market in order to secure money. In particular, the stock price will double drop,

219

30 *Capital*, Volume III, Beijing: People's Publishing House. 1975, pp. 340-341.
31 *Capital*, Volume III, Beijing: People's Publishing House, 1975, p. 340.
32 Ibid. pp. 598-599.
33 *Capital*, Volume III, Beijing: People's Publishing House, 1975, p. 613.

which is due to: (1) the increase in interest rate; (2) securities owners are in pursuit of money and sell stocks; (3) the reduction in dividend income. This market crash fuelled speculation that if buying a lot of cheap securities when prices fall, once the storm has passed, prices rise, huge profits can be made. At the same time, by such gambling, the capital ownership is highly concentrated in the hands of the big financiers. Because of the debt chain being broken, as well as the shock wave of a run, banks, stock exchanges, etc. were merged or went bankrupt.

When the decline in production has reached rock bottom and has experienced a period of stagnation, when surplus commodities have been cleared in the market, when vendors of poor competitiveness and poor economic strength disappear due to bankruptcy or being merged, the market (domestic and foreign) demand for commodities began exposing the increasing trend. In this way, the business surviving the crisis and being adjusted began to resume production, and some even expand the production. Employment is gradually increasing, with the demand for means of production (including labour tools and raw materials) increasing as well. As the crisis caused a large number of loan capital to be withdrawn, then the interest rate is very low, it provides a favourable condition for capitalists to have massive new investment. With the economic growth driven investment expansion, the economy gradually transforms from the phase of crisis and stagnation to the recovery. With the development of the market towards a more favourable direction, there are more companies that expand production capacity to increase production, so as to meet increasing market demands. At this time, the demand for additional production and demand for additional labour will be further expanded. This interaction between the various sectors further expands the market demand for various products. As the market has become increasingly active, the price of commodities began to rise, profits to increase, the stock market active, interest rate to rise, and the employment to increase. At this time, the economy is moving from recovery (i.e., moderate active) to the phase of prosperity.

At each stage of the business cycle, the law of changes in financial markets is: "… a low rate of interest generally corresponds to periods of prosperity or extra profit, a rise in interest separates prosperity and its reverse, and a maximum of interest up to a point of extreme usury corresponds to the period of crisis. … It is possible, however, for low interest to go along with stagnation, and for moderately rising interest to go along with revived activity. The rate of interest reaches its peak during crises, when money is borrowed at any cost to meet payments."[34]

"The demand for currency between consumers and dealers predominates in periods of prosperity, and the demand for currency between capitalists predominates in periods of depression. During a depression the former decreases, and the latter increases."[35]

---

34   *Capital*, Volume III, Beijing: People's Publishing House. 1975, p. 404.
35   Ibid., pp. 509-510.

Compared with modern business cycle, the business cycle that Marx and Engels described during the free competition of capitalism has more regularity, with greater degree of volatility and more clear characteristics.

V. Reasons and Realization Mechanism of the Fluctuations in the Business Cycle

We can verify the cyclical phenomenon in economic development, by confirming to the statistical data of economic development, and also confirming by following-up and investigating certain economic phenomena. We can observe directly the direct reason that triggers the cyclical fluctuation, but it is difficult to find the root reason in the depths of the cyclical fluctuation, which is the basic view of Marxist political economy on the cyclical fluctuation in capitalist economy, as well as one of the fundamental differences between Marxist theory of business cycle and bourgeois theory of business cycle. Marxist political economy is committed to exploring the root reasons of the business cycle, but also puts great emphasis on investigation of the specific reasons. It considers that the specific crises at different times and under different circumstances are always caused by a variety of specific reasons, which is important to understand the reason at this level, but this is not enough to halt it, and we should understand the nature of the crisis and reveal the underlying reasons of the crisis through new change in the form of the crisis, or explore various specific reasons of the crisis from its fundamental reasons.

In respect to the root reason of cyclical fluctuations in the economy, it has been one of problems that economists of various types are trying to solve. Marxist political economics considers that the cyclical fluctuations in the economy are rooted in the basic contradictions of capitalism. When explaining in *The Law of the Tendency of the Rate of Profit to Fall*, Marx had clearly stated that: "Three cardinal facts of capitalist production:1) Concentration of means of production in few hands, whereby they cease to appear as the property of the immediate labourers and turn into social production capacities. Even if initially they are the private property of capitalists. These are the trustees of bourgeois society, but they pocket all the proceeds of this trusteeship. 2) Organisation of labour itself into social labour: through co-operation, division of labour, and the uniting of labour with the natural sciences. In these two senses, the capitalist mode of production abolishes private property and private labour, even though in contradictory forms.3) Creation of the world-market. The stupendous productivity developing under the capitalist mode of production relative to population, and the increase, if not in the same proportion, of capital-values (not just of their material substance), which grow much more rapidly than the population, contradict the basis, which constantly narrows in relation to the expanding wealth, and for which all this immense productiveness works. They also contradict the conditions under which this swelling capital augments its value. Hence the crises."[36]

---

36 *Capital*, Volume III, Beijing: People's Publishing House. 2004, pp. 295-296.

When explain the principles of Marxist political economy in *Anti-Dühring*, Engels had done a brilliant exposition, and he said: "In these crises, the contradiction between socialised production and capitalist appropriation ends in a violent explosion. ... The economic collision has reached its apogee. The mode of production is in rebellion against the mode of exchange, the productive forces are in rebellion against the mode of production which they have outgrown."[37] He also described the concrete manifestation of the basic contradiction of capitalism as "an antagonism between the organization of production in the individual workshop and the anarchy of production in society generally".[38] Later, Stalin again described the manifestation of the basic contradiction of capitalism as "contradictions between the tremendous growth in capitalist productivity and the relatively contraction of the demand of millions of working people to have the ability to pay."[39] At this point, when the textbook expounds the crisis theory, the specific forms of basic contradictions described by Engels and Stalin are collected together, and are called the two specific forms of the basic contradiction. Some textbooks also said that the contradiction between the socialization of production and of capitalist private ownership is the root reason of the capitalist economic crisis, while two specific forms of manifestation of the basic contradiction is the direct cause of the capitalist economic crisis.

Continuity and equilibrium of the capital movement are the normal conditions that capital movements should satisfy for its normal operation, and they are periodically destroyed and restored in the complex contradictory movement of capitalist mode of production. The whole process is manifested as: The opposite elements of the old continuity and equilibrium gradually have uneven quantity, asymmetrical distribution and partial interruption of continuity, and when changes in the quantity is accumulated to a certain extent, it will cause a qualitative change in the old continuity and equilibrium. In the process of capital movement, reaching a new continuity and equilibrium this kind of qualitative change is manifested as the massive destruction of productivity. But the process does not end, the creation and development trend of the new equilibrium and continuity is a destruction of the new equilibrium and continuity. This is an infinite evolution cycle, from lower to higher, from simple to complex. The driving force and source of this evolution comes from the basic contradiction of capitalism, namely, the contradiction between socialization of production and the private ownership of means of production.

Corresponding to the periodic intensification of the basic contradiction of capitalism, the reproduction process of capitalism also shows a periodic nature. Each process is manifested as the destruction of equilibrium and continuity

37 *Marx and Engels Collected Works*, 1st Chinese edition, Volume 20, Beijing: People's Publishing House, 1971, p. 301.

38 *Marx and Engels Collected Works*, 1st Chinese edition, Volume 19, P235. Beijing: People's Publishing House, 1963.

39 USSR Academy of Sciences Institute of Economics, *Textbook of Political Economics*, p.229, Beijing, People's Publishing House, 1955.

which enables reproduction to be carried out, as well as the creation of an equilibrium and continuity. Such periodicity "As the heavenly bodies, once thrown into a certain definite motion, always repeat this, so is it with social production as soon as it is once thrown into this movement of alternate expansion and contraction. Effects, in their turn, become causes, and the initially irregular, and superficially accidental changes, have increasingly been becoming the form of a normal period. However, when the machine industry is so ingrained that it had a decisive impact on the entire national product; when foreign trade began to surpass domestic trade due to the machine industry; when the world market was gradually appropriating vast regions of the New World, Asia and Australia; Finally, when the industrial countries embarking on the playing field became numerous; from this time onwards, the repeated cycle began to appear, with successive stage of each last few years, and always ended with a widespread outbreak of crisis, which is both an end of a period, and another starting point for a new cycle."[40]

Imbalance and the new equilibrium formed, interruption and restoration of the continuity, repeat about 10 years on the average in Marx's time. This is a circulation with rules; the results of Marx's study suggest that it coincides in line with the life with fixed capital broadly.

"As the magnitude of the value and the durability of the applied fixed capital develop with the development of the capitalist mode of production, the lifetime of industry and of industrial capital lengthens in each particular field of investment to a period of many years, say of ten years on an average... the cycle of interconnected turnovers embracing a number of years, in which capital is held fast by its fixed constituent part, furnishes a material basis for the periodic crises. During this cycle business undergoes successive periods of depression, medium activity, precipitancy, and crisis. True, periods in which capital is invested differ greatly and far from coinciding in time. But a crisis always forms the starting-point of large new investments. Therefore, from the point of view of society as a whole, more or less, a new material basis for the next turnover cycle begins."[41]

The material basis for the capitalist economic periodicity to lose balance and to recover is the renewal of fixed assets. When the economy enters a phase of stagnation, out of competition, capitalists began a new round of investment, which drove economy to grow, so that the production could get out of the crisis.

For many years, the description on the root reason and specific reason of the periodic capitalist reproduction by the mainstream economics has not been widely recognized in the academic circle, but arousing a lot of contentions. Some scholars believe that the root reason of the crisis that Marx identifies is the poverty of the masses and their limited consumption, which is based

40 *Marx and Engels Collected Works*, 1st Chinese edition, Volume 49, Beijing: People's Publishing House, 1982, pp. 240-241.
41 *Capital*, Volume II, Beijing: People's Publishing House, 1975, pp. 206-207.

on such a sentence that Marx wrote in *Capital* Volume III that: "The ultimate reason for all real crises always remains the poverty and restricted consumption of the masses as opposed to the drive of capitalist production to develop the productive forces as though only the absolute consuming power of society constituted their limit."[42] Some scholars complain that, when describing the reason of the economic crisis, the textbook has not mentioned the relations between the rate of profit to fall and the economic crisis. Actually it is the rate of profit to fall that hinders the accumulation and investment of capitalists, resulting in the interruption of the reproduction process, so that the rate of profit to fall should become another reason of the economic crisis. Overall, scholars holding the above two views are many in numbers, and they also have a broad impact in the academia. Some scholars who are called Western Marxists have many claims of the reasons of the business cycle, among which there are the followings that are representative: 1) On the assumption that the technical composition of capital remains unchanged, the increase in organic composition of capital leads to the decrease in the rate of profit, thereby causing the investment rate to drop, so that the production declines, until the outbreak of the crisis. 2) When the economy enters into the times of prosperity where full employment is achieved, the bargaining position of workers is improved, so that the exploitation rate is reduced, the rate of profit is decreased, the investment drops, and the economy goes into recession. 3) When capitalist economy is turning from contraction into expansion, the rate of profit is rising rapidly, but the wage is pressed at a lower level, resulting in the relative decline in consumer demand, as well as limiting the growth of aggregate demand, thus leading to the crisis. 4) The active mechanism of the acceleration principle would lead to periods of particularly high and particularly low rate of investment, thereby showing inadequate cyclical investment and cyclical economic fluctuations. 5) The decentralized decision-making anarchy leads to an excess production capacity in some sectors and insufficient in others, and the combination of such an excess and shortage leads to a decline in the rate of utilization of the total production capacity and causes inflation. Chinese scholars believe that this view has certain one-sidedness, despite it plays a specific role in the Marxist theory of the cycle, and on the whole it is more superficial.

Engels once had a detailed description on the implementation mechanism of the business cycle in *The Condition of the Working Class in England*:

"In the present unregulated production and distribution of the means of subsistence, which is carried on not directly for the sake of supplying needs, but for profit, in the system under which every one works for himself to enrich himself, disturbances inevitably arise at every moment. For example, England supplies a number of countries with most diverse goods. Now, although the manufacturer may know how much of each article is consumed in each country annually, he cannot know how much is on hand at every given moment, much less can he know how much his competitors export thither. He can only

42   *Capital*, Volume III, Beijing: People's Publishing House, 1975, p. 548.

draw most uncertain inferences from the perpetual fluctuations in prices, as to the quantities on hand and the needs of the moment. He must trust to luck in exporting his goods. Everything is done blindly, as guess-work, more or less at the mercy of accident. Upon the slightest favourable report each one exports what he can, and before long such a market is glutted, sales stop, capital remains inactive, prices fall, and English manufacture has no further employment for its hands. In the beginning of the development of manufacture, these checks were limited to single branches and single markets; but the centralizing tendency of competition, which drives the hands thrown out of one branch into such other branches as are most easily accessible and transfers the goods which cannot be disposed of in one market to other markets, has gradually brought the single minor crises nearer together and united them into one periodically recurring crisis. Such a crisis usually recurs once in five years after a brief period of activity and general prosperity; the home market, like all foreign ones, is glutted with English goods, which it can only slowly absorb, the industrial movement comes to a standstill in almost every branch, the small manufacturers and merchants who cannot survive a prolonged inactivity of their invested capital fail, the larger ones suspend business during the worst season, close their mills or work short time, perhaps half the day; wages fall by reason of the competition of the unemployed, the diminution of working-time and the lack of profitable sales; want becomes universal among the workers, the small savings, which individuals may have made, are rapidly consumed, the philanthropic institutions are overburdened, the poor-rates are doubled, trebled, and 225 still insufficient, the number of the starving increases, and the whole multitude of "surplus" population presses in terrific numbers into the foreground. This continues for a time; the "surplus" exists as best as it may, or perishes; philanthropy and the Poor Law help many of them to a painful prolongation of their existence. Others find scant means of subsistence here and there in such kinds of work as have been least open to competition, are most remote from manufacture. And with how little can a human being keep body and soul together for a time! Gradually the state of things improves; the accumulations of goods are consumed, the general depression among the men of commerce and manufacture prevents a too hasty replenishing of the markets, and at last rising prices and favourable reports from all directions restore activity. Most of the markets are distant ones; demand increases and prices rise constantly while the first exports are arriving; people struggle for the first goods, the first sales enliven trade still more, the prospective ones promise still higher prices; expecting a further rise, merchants begin to buy upon speculation, and so to withdraw from consumption the articles intended for it, just when they are most needed. Speculation forces prices still higher, by inspiring others to purchase, and appropriating new importations at once. All this is reported to England, manufacturers begin to produce with a will, new mills are built, every means is employed to make the most of the favourable moment. Speculation arises here, too, exerting the same influence as upon foreign markets, raising prices, withdrawing goods from consumption, spurring manufacture in both ways to the highest pitch of effort. Then come the daring speculators working with fictitious capital, living upon credit, ruined if they cannot speedily sell; they hurl themselves into this universal, disorderly race for profits, multiply the disorder and haste by their unbridled passion, which drives prices and production to madness. It is a frantic struggle, which carries away even the most experienced and phlegmatic; goods are spun, woven, hammered, as if all mankind were to be newly equipped, as though two thousand million new consumers had been discovered in the moon. All at once the shaky speculators abroad, who must have money, begin to sell, below market price, of course, for their need is urgent; one sale is followed by others, prices fluctuate, speculators throw their goods upon the market in terror, the market is disordered, credit shaken, one house after another stops payments, bankruptcy follows bankruptcy, and the discovery is made that three times more goods are on hand or under way than can be consumed. The news reaches England, where production has been going on at full speed meanwhile, panic seizes all hands, failures abroad cause others in England, the panic crushes a number of firms, all reserves are thrown upon the market here, too, in the moment of anxiety, and the alarm is still further exaggerated. This is the beginning of the crisis, which then takes precisely the same course as its predecessor, and gives place in turn to a season of prosperity. So it goes on perpetually,– prosperity, crisis, prosperity, crisis, and this perennial round in which English industry moves is, as has been before observed, usually completed once in five or six years."[43]

The above description is repeatedly mentioned by those who explore the transmission mechanism of the business cycle, especially in the Western references on the business cycle.

VI. The Business Cycle and International Economic Relations

In the writing program of Marxist economics, the cyclical fluctuation in the economy is the subject for final inspection in the whole system, and when the theoretical explanation reaches this level, the basic aspects of international economic relations such as international trade and world market have become elements of the business cycle. In reality, the business cycles had exhibited the worldwide features in the early 19th century, and then it is more and more obvious, and has become a regular phenomenon. This is reflected in: On the one hand, it produced a number of new factors of the world market crisis; on the other hand, some factors of crisis which had played a role within a country in the past have more specific forms in the world market, and affect the world market crisis in its emergence and development, after the crisis occurring in one country, it spreads to others. For these relations, Marx had given due attention in the early studies on the capitalist economic relations, and in his *Wage Labour and Capital*,

---

43 *On Economic Crisis by Marx, Engels, Lenin and Stalin*, Beijing: Science Press, 1958, pp. 97-98.

Marx pointed out: "They become more frequent and more violent, if for no other reason, than for this alone, that in the same measure in which the mass of products grows, and therefore the needs for extensive markets, in the same measure does the world market shrink ever more, and ever fewer markets remain to be exploited, since every previous crisis has subjected to the commerce of the world a hitherto unconquered or but superficially exploited market."[44] In *Communist Manifesto*, Marx further asserted that the crisis of the capitalist mode of production is manifested in the crisis of overproduction. Overproduction is the result of the conflict between the unlimited development of productivity by each capitalist who is forced by competitive pressures and constrained world market. In his later writings, Marx's discussion involved a number of important factors related to the business cycle in international economic relations, such as the world market, international credit, international trade, international flows of money, tariff policy and etc. The most basic one of these elements is the world market, and Marx believed that it is the basis and living condition of the capitalist mode of production, and therefore it is also the basis and condition of the formation and development of the world market crisis. As an extension and supplement to the domestic market, the world market can alleviate relatively small contradictions with a certain degree between the capitalist production and domestic market, or further intensifies it, because the world market can potentially expand, it still has an external geographic barrier or is limited at every certain time. When the market is expanding, it can serve to alleviate the crisis in the short term, but with the expansion of the world market, production sites are farther away from the market, the period of credit is also extended or increased, resulting in a credit reflux mitigation and increased speculative activities.

It needs particularly noted that: the development of the credit in the world market is also an important factor in the formation of the world market crisis. "The maximum of credit is here identical with the fullest employment of industrial capital, that is, the utmost exertion of its reproductive power without regard to the limits of consumption."[45] "Credit renders the reflux in money-form independent of the time of actual reflux.", so that "in credit, the capitalist mode of production creates a necessary form for their production process to a suitable scale, to shorten the process of circulation, and the world market simultaneously formed with this production, helps to cover up the role of this form in each individual occasion, and provide a very broad scope for this form to expand."[46] Therefore, the credit can often bring an illusory prosperity. For example, the huge merchant capital engaged in the bulk import and export trade, which is established on the basis of world market and credit, will break the limitations of reproduction process even more, and promote the process of

44 *Selected Works of Marx and Engels*, 2nd Chinese edition, Beijing: People's Publishing House, 1995, p. 363.
45 *Marx and Engels Collected Works*, 1st Chinese edition, Volume 25, Beijing: People's Publishing House, 1974, p. 546.
46 *Marx and Engels Collected Works*, 1st Chinese edition, Volume 49, Beijing: People's Publishing House, 1982, p.292..

reproduction beyond its various limitations. Commodities may still be in the changing hands of the importers and exporters, or be stranded on the world market without actually entering in the cost of living, but merchant capital is able to run the production process on the same or expanded scale within certain operational boundaries, enabling this process to be at the most prosperous state on the surface. "The crisis occurs when the returns of merchants who sell in distant markets (or whose supplies have also accumulated on the home market) become so slow and meagre that the banks press for payment, or promissory notes for purchased commodities become due before the latter have been re-sold. Then forced sales take place, sales in order to meet payments. Then comes the crash, which brings the illusory prosperity to an abrupt end."[47] Hence, in fact, the credit is manifest as the major leverage of overproduction and exces-sive commercial speculation. This role of credit makes it to have a close rela-tionship with the industrial cycle. Marx had touched this issue from different perspectives in some places. Marx regarded the expansion and contraction of credit as signs of replacement in every stage of the industrial cycle. "These phases are, briefly, an utter contraction of credit in the year of panic, followed by a gradual expansion, which reaches its maximum when the rate of interest sinks to its lowest point; then again a movement in the opposite direction, that of gradual contraction, which reaches its highest point when the interest has risen to its maximum, and the year of panic has again set in."[48] In the analysis of the rate of interest, Marx pointed out: "If we observe the cycles in which modern industry moves..., we shall find that a low rate of interest generally corresponds to periods of prosperity or extra profit, a rise in interest separates prosperity and its reverse, and a maximum of interest up to a point of extreme usury corresponds to the period of crisis. ......It is possible, however, for low interest to go along with stagnation, and for moderately rising interest to go along with revived activity."[49] He also came to this issue from the perspective of the relationship between accumulation of borrowing money capital and ac-cumulation of realistic capital."The movement of loan capital, as expressed in the rate of interest, is in the opposite direction to that of industrial capital. The phase wherein a low rate of interest, but above the minimum, coincides with the "improvement" and growing confidence after a crisis, and particularly the phase wherein the rate of interest reaches its average level, exactly midway between its minimum and maximum, are the only two periods during which an abundance of loan capital is available simultaneously with a great expansion of industrial capital. But at the beginning of the industrial cycle, a low rate of interest coincides with a contraction, and at the end of the industrial cycle, a high rate of interest coincides with a superabundance of industrial capital."[50]

228

47   *Marx and Engels Collected Works*, 1st Chinese edition, Volume 25, Beijing: People's Publishing House. 1974, p. 341.

48   *Marx and Engels Collected Works*, 1st Chinese edition, Volume 12, Beijing: People's Publishing House, 1962, p. 346.

49   *Capital*, Volume III, Beijing: People's Publishing House. 1975, p.404.

50   Ibid., p. 553.

The basic form of economic relations between countries is international trade, so its impact on the world market crisis is also essential. The excessive international trade is often the direct cause of the world market crisis. If there are excessive exports, commodities could not find sales in other importing countries, and commodity capital cannot be converted into money capital; if there are excessive imports, the difference due at maturity is a deficit for a country, although the total trade balance may be a surplus. "What appears in one country as excessive imports appears in the other as excessive exports, and vice versa. But over-imports and over-exports have taken place in all countries."[51] At its root, trade imbalances – with deficits at one and surpluses at the other- are not the cause of the crisis, but are yet another manifestation of it. "The balance of payments is in times of general crisis is unfavourable to every nation, at least to every commercially developed nation, but always to each country in succession, as in volley firing, i.e., as soon as each one's turn comes for making payments; and once the crisis has broken out, e.g., in England, it compresses the series of these terms into a very short period. It then becomes evident that all these nations have simultaneously over-exported (thus over-produced) and over-imported (thus over-traded), that prices were inflated in all of them, and credit stretched too far. And the same break-down takes place in all of them."[52] The world market crises tend to occur in those industrial powers dominant in the international trade, and then spread in turn to other countries based on how they are affected by those powers, that is, when there is a crisis of overproduction in a developed capitalist country, the overproduction will be output to other countries through international trade, particularly by using domestic commodity prices plummeting to dump a large number of surplus commodities to the international market, causing outbreak of the overproduction crisis in other countries, and the crisis in other countries in turn prompts the crisis or intensifies it in the exporting country again.

In the gold standard era, when a drain of precious metals occurs in turn in each country, it often heralds the widespread crisis in the world market is about to occur in turn. "A drain of metal is generally the symptom of a change in the state of foreign trade, and this change in turn is a premonition that conditions are again approaching a crisis."[53] The drain of precious metals prompts the outbreak of crisis in the country, which will in turn cause the rebound of precious metal and flowing back; the inflow of precious metals in a country is shown as the drain in another country, so the crisis will repeat itself in another country. "Every reduction of this reserve by drain on gold increases the crisis."[54] Because the drain of precious metals will raise interest rate, the already extremely tight demand for lending capital will be fuelled, thus speeding up the outbreak of the crisis. Overall, there is a close relationship between flows of precious metals and industrial cycle. The inflow of precious metals occurs

51   Marx, *Capital: A Critique of Political Economy*.
52   *Marx and Engels Collected Works*, 1st Chinese edition, Volume 25, p. 557.
53   Ibid., p. 645.
54   Ibid., p. 610.

mainly in recession and recovery phases while the drain occurs mainly in the eve of the "collapse". The relations between international mobility of precious metals and the business cycle, is essentially that, as Marx put it: "1) that gold drain is just a phenomenon of a crisis, not its cause; 2) that the sequence in which it hits the various countries indicates only when their judgement-day has come, i.e., when the crisis started and its latent elements come to the fore there."[55] Like the free trade policies will make the crisis much more violent, "these protective tariffs are nothing but preparations for the ultimate general industrial war, which shall decide who has supremacy on the world-market. Thus every factor, which works against a repetition of the old crises, carries within itself the germ of a far more powerful future crisis."[56]

In the history of international economic relations of capitalism, the two policies of free trade and protective tariffs is always in interchangeably recurring state, and according to their own situation, countries sometimes take the policy of free trade in order to develop foreign trade, and sometimes take the policy of protective tariffs, attempting to avoid or mitigate the blow of the economic crisis by limiting foreign competition. But capitalism cannot escape the fate destined to combat the economic crisis. When the capitalist countries establish their own large industrial systems under the protective tariff system, the productive forces it creates and the narrow domestic market limited by protective tariffs will lead to conflict and thus to the crisis. Therefore, they will have to open their portals to establish a free trade system, expand the world market, and ease the contradictions and conflicts between production and market. However, the establishment of the world market and the intensification of competition driven by the free trade intensifies the conflict in a larger context, resulting in the outbreak of the widespread crisis in the world market. Then, a new round of protective tariffs and free trade policies has begun converting and alternating. The implementation of protective tariffs and free trade policies artificially increases the production capacity domestically. The result is a comprehensive and regular overproduction, decline in the price, decrease or even disappearance of the rate of profit, and the cyclical crisis erupts.

VII. The Non-Marxist Traditional Model of Business Cycle

The main difference between non-Marxist economics and Marxist economics in exploring the business cycle is the root reason, because many explorations at the level of specific reasons are coincident. Marxist economics believes that the root reason of the cyclical fluctuation in the capitalist economy is the basic contradiction of capitalism, so it denies all the practices that regard the specific reason as the root reason, insists in understanding the nature of the business cycle, and reveals the root reason of the business cycle. The direct

---

55   Ibid. , p. 557.
56   Ibid., p. 554, Note 8.

purpose of doing so is to reveal the law of the capitalist system in its production, development and moving towards the demise, and to provide a theoretical weapon for the proletarian revolutionary movement. The reason that Marxist economics lacks interests in the specific reasons of the fluctuation in the business cycle is because its task is not to make plans to save the capitalist system, and it is also impossible for it to find ways to mitigate the cyclical economic fluctuations for capitalism. This is because in his opinion those attempts to overcome the crisis is to make the crisis come more violently. With the development of society and the changes in clients of Marxist political economy, Marxist political economy must also turn the focus from the study of the root reason in the past to the study of the specific reasons. As in the study of the specific reasons, non-Marxists have the extensive study experience and abundant knowledge accumulation for many years, having raised a variety of specific reasons, with the argument having been mainly evidence-based, Marxist political economy should fully absorb the scientific factors with a positive attitude, enrich and develop itself, so that it can more effectively serve the running of socialist market economy. If the main reason raised by non-Marxist economics can be regarded as specific reasons, we can activate a considerable portion of non-Marxist theory of business cycle in the paradigm of the traditional Marxist economics.

1. The agricultural cycle theorists associate the cyclical fluctuation in agricultural production with the changing cycle of sunspots, which is due to some coincidences in the fluctuation cycle they found between the two. Then the reason that they gradually forget is that even though they are racking their brains to find any relevant data, they are unable to find all the corresponding periods and the relevant data, and it is difficult to make people believe in some causal relationship between the accurate sunspot cycle and the non-accurate business cycle. In modern society, the achievements of natural science studies gradually confirms that the dramatic changes in sunspots would lead to the Earth's climate anomalies, which can cause floods and volatility in agricultural production, which in turn will lead to fluctuation in the price of agricultural commodity. This volatility will ultimately lead to fluctuation in the national economy through certain transmission mechanism. This view which seems to have no reason in the past and then proved to be reasonable scientifically should be given adequate attention.

2. The impact of psychological factors also has a crucial role in the business cycle. Because of the uncertainty about the future and poor judgment, it tends to form such a mechanism: expansion generates optimism, which stimulates investment and enhances expansion; recession generates pessimism, which exacerbates recession. While no psychological factors can fully explain the instability in the modern market economy, many studies have emphasized the psychological factors in the economic theory. The expositions on the instability in macroeconomic activities by Keynes gave great emphasis on the important role of psychological factors, while behavioural economics has even

treated psychological factors as an essential element, focusing on the impact of expectations and forecast in economic decision-making. For how economic institutions respond to the concerns of uncertainty, in fact, it reflects the psychological aspects of economic problems. Thus, we can conclude that: how economic institutions react to various stimuli is important in many interpretations of cycle.

3. The reason that Ralph George Hawtrey's shock mechanism of pure money can have a profound impact is mainly because its description is based on a series of economic operation mechanism with conductivity. Hawtrey insisted that the upsurge of business cycle is caused due to credit expansion, and as long as credit expansion continues, the upsurge will continue as well. The credit expansion is caused by that the bank relaxes loans to customers. The credit expansion will cause a chain reaction, resulting in cumulative expansion. From a businessman's perspective: businessmen have a strong sensitivity on changes in the rate of interest, even if the rate of interest being slightly lower is enough to make traders increase the inventory. The increase in orders from businessmen to producers stimulates to the expansion of production. The expansion of production causes the increase in both income and spending of consumers, which in turn expands the number of commodity demand. The result is that there is a reduction in inventories of businessmen, further expansion of the number of orders to producers, further increase in production activities, consumer income and spending and the general demand, and inventories is further reduced. This acceleration is sufficient to increase demands, which is enough to stimulate the acceleration. This creates a vicious cycle phenomenon, so that production becomes cumulative expansion. The expansion of production is limited, and when the cumulative expansion process of production makes a variety of industrial productive forces reach its limit, the price will continue to rise. The rising prices stimulate businessman to increase borrowed funds. The rising prices and the falling interest play the same role: In order to reap a profit from further increase in price, the businessman will prepare more inventories. The rising price also stimulates commodity producers to expand production. In order to expand production, the producer borrows a loan even more boldly in order to raise funds for the production in growth. This cumulative expansion accelerates with the cumulative rise in prices. When prices rise and businesses are active, traders and producers will borrow more money, and try to take advantage of all the original idle balances which may be freely disposed by them. If the idle balances are so large, it may be able to increase the income and expense of the consumer and the existing bank credit does not have to expand, or just has a very limited expansion. This means that there is a destabilizing factor of the currency in circulation in the accelerated expansion of production. Like expansion process, the contraction is also cumulative. When prices begin to fall, traders would expect the price to fall further more, so they are trying to reduce inventories, to reduce orders from producers, or even completely stop orders. The income and spending of consumers is reduced, the demand

232

waned, and despite trying to reduce inventory, the results are that it is piling up, and the borrowing is further reduced; then a long and painful experience begins. The original factors which are enough to promote upsurge but now has been increasingly promoting the contraction process. This vicious, downward spiral elapse is the antithesis of the kind of vicious, upward spiral elapse in all respects.

4. Wesley Clair Mitchell and Allan H. Meltzer are seen as two important representatives of the unemployment cycle. Mitchell had a very brief description of his cycle theory: "It is the same condition which makes industry profitable that gradually becomes the condition to force the reduction in profits. The growth in economic activities is initially the reason for profit growth, and then it is both the reason for profit growth and its consequence. When this growth forms pressure on the production capacity of the existing industrial equipment, the drop in additional costs of the every initially single output will gradually be stabilized, while expectations for the desired profit lure the drive-up of the price of raw materials, labour and borrowing money ... therefore the major costs engaging in industry is high, and when such a process is accumulated to a certain point, it will be difficult for the profit to reduce through accelerating the increase in the price in order to avoid erosion."[57] This series of continued causes result in the increase and decrease in profitability, and entrepreneurs will react to this, thus causing economic fluctuations. According to Melzer, entrepreneurs have a fixed understanding of sales ratio to the inventory that they expect. When there is an increase in demand for their expansion, they found that reducing its inventory. The attempts to resume its inventory level to a predetermined ratio result in an increase in new orders, thereby increasing employment and income. Since the latter effect also increases sales, the sales ratio of inventory will continue to maintain the level of decline. Melzer believes that the upper turning point is the result of the marginal propensity to consume, which is positive but less than 1. Therefore, the increase in sales will be less than the increase in revenue. In the latter part of the expansion, the desired inventory-sales ratio can be gradually restored, and it eliminates to stimulate the economy by increasing inventory levels, resulting in that an imbalance of expansion was eventually ruled out. The opposite occurs in the process of contraction: entrepreneurs try to reduce their inventory levels, while its sales decline. The effort further decreases revenue and prevents the decline in the rate. However, the rate of decrease of sales is lower than the rate of decline in revenue, so after a period of time, entrepreneurs can reconfigure the desired inventory sales ratio. The result of is that the contraction period reaches its lowest point.

5. In summary, the overinvestment theory can be divided into two categories of monetary overinvestment theory and non-monetary overinvestment theory. Swedish economist Knut Wicksell had published an article in 1890, explaining

---

57   Wesley Clair Mitchell, *Business Cycle and Its Causes*, University of California Press. 1959, p.61.

the causes of prosperity and depression from the perspective of monetary investment, and he believes in the recovery process, with the rise in consumer demand, it lags behind the rate of expansion of productivity based on increase in capital. Therefore, the speed of capital formation caused by the recovery could not have been maintained, and to a certain extent, it will stop expanding, but steer towards contraction. Hence, he concluded that the prosperity and depression of economy is rooted in the fluctuation of capital formation. Later, Wicksell again had made insights of more theoretical basis on issues of economic fluctuations in his book *Interest and Prices*. He distinguishes between natural and real interest rates, and explains the movement process of the business cycle through the active mechanism of the real interest rate and the natural interest rate, suggesting that when the real interest rate is below the natural interest rate, investment by capitalists is profitable, and they will increase loans, expand investment and increase production, which results in both profits and wages tend to rise, increasing the demand for the ability to pay in production and consumption, thus pushing the price to go up. And vice versa, there will be opposite behaviour and results. When the actual interest rate is equal to the natural interest rate, the increase or decrease in investment neither increase nor decrease the profit, and the result is that investment neither increases nor decreases, production and income remain unchanged, and price is stable, forming equilibrium. The changes in the price of commodity caused by changes in the rate of interest are cumulative in nature. When the actual interest rate is below

234 the natural interest rate and there is an increase in investment, production, income and prices, capitalists will continue to increase borrowings and expand investment due to the good investment prospects, so that production and prices will continue to rise. And vice versa, it will have the opposite behaviour and results. Because of the existence of the interest rate brakes, when the investment and prices go up, bank deposits are dwindling, and investments continue to grow. When the savings are below the demand for investment, the bank will raise real interest rate, so that the difference between the real interest rate and the natural rate of interest will be narrowed. At this time, the driving force for capitalists to invest tends to weaken, and investment rate of price increases slowly. With the real interest rate close to the natural rate of interest, the rate for the increases in production and prices is increasingly attenuated, getting closer to the equilibrium. Conversely, when investment prices are going downward, as bank savings are increasingly greater than the demand for investment, and it is forced to lower the real interest rate, resulting in that it has a deterrent effect on the downward movement of investment prices. There is a saying that if the bank lowers the real interest rate below the natural rate of interest, the demand for credit will grow and exceed the savings, and the excess has to be supplemented by an increase in bank credit, thus forming inflation. Conversely, if the bank lifts the actual interest rate above the natural rate of interest, the demand for credit will be reduced, the excess of the savings against the demand for credit will not be in use, resulting in the reduction of credit and forming deflation. Wicksell believes that the cyclical fluctuations between prosperity

and depression are actually formed by the fluctuations of credit demand caused by the volatility in interest rate, thereby causing the contraction and expansion of currency.

Ludwig von Mises combined money with microeconomic theory, and demonstrated how the marginal utility of money, the utility of other commodities, as well as the supply of currency interacts to determine the currency price. Mises is the follower of the quantity theory of money, who agreed with the sole role of currency to be exchange, and the increase in the quantity of money just makes the purchasing power of each monetary unit reduced, and cannot bring about social benefits. Mises believes that the ideal banking system should be of 100% reserve, which should be standard gold and standard silver. If the bank is part of the reserve, it will cause inflation, resulting in the distortions and deformities of production and price. In the 1920s, in the absorption of Wicksell's theory of the difference in the natural interest rate and lending rate, Mises developed his own theory of the business cycle, and proposed the "improper investment theory of currency." This theory regards the cycle of prosperity and depression as an inevitable product of inflationary credit expansion. This expansion artificially lowers the rate of interest, leading to insufficient investment in production of consumer goods, as well as causing inappropriately excessive investment in the production of high levels of capital goods. The halt of any credit expansion is the result of improper investment and the lack of sufficient savings, and the ensuing recession eliminates the distortion of prosperity and restores a healthy economy.

The outbreak of the Great Depression in the 1930s had drawn a protracted debate on the business cycle. During the period, the sheer number of participants, the intense debates, and more works published, were rare in the history of economics. In these disputants, there are many people who considered that the economic cyclical fluctuation is due to the excessive investment. According to the induction by Gottfried Haberler, these overinvestment theorists can be divided into three groups. Namely, Group A is the monetary overinvestment theorists, who argued that "the production will take place in the imbalance between the higher phase and the lower phase is because of the active currency strength under some form of credit institutions." Group B the non-monetary overinvestment theorists, who attributed the cause of the business cycle to those environments that provide opportunities for new investments with the opening up of new inventions, new discoveries and new markets. Group C is the follower of the theory of "acceleration and expansion of derivative demand", who thought due to technical reasons, changes in subsistence production will cause more violent fluctuations in the production of the means of production.

Members under the Group A are mainly Friedrich Hayek, Fritz Machlup, Ludwig von Mises, Joan Robinson, Wilhelm Röpke, Strel and et al. Their works devoted to the economic fluctuations were mainly published between 1931 and 1934 when it coincided with the upsurge of the Great Depression. According to the summary and generalization by Haberler, these writers made essentially the same explanations on the upsurge and turning-down (crisis). However, they were not quite the same in the explanations on downcast and turning up (resuscitation).

Hayek first proposed an important issue, why the product industry showed greater leeway than the consumer goods industry in the cycle? The researchers of the business cycle had noted that many of production in the advanced stage had greater volatility. Hayek acknowledged Wicksell's view, but he also believes that when the economy is rising, as banks lend to entrepreneurs, the market interest rate falls below the natural rate of interest, but he adds that banks inject loans in the advanced stage of production, and therefore it allows it to expand. If bank credit leads resources from the lower stages of production to an advanced stage, especially when the economy is in a state of full employment, the expansion will result in the increase in revenue, but at the same time the production of consumer goods will not increase, or even decrease. This situation will inevitably lead to the rise in consumer goods. The demand for consumer goods may indicate that an increase in income of the same proportion will not change the demand for consumption. As a result, the consumer price will rise, and consumers cannot buy more beyond the normal level of income. It is not that consumers are willing to buy less, but are forced to buy less due to the rise in the price of consumer goods. In a given and normal income level, consumers can only buy relatively fewer consumer goods, and it in fact improve the actual savings rate mandatorily. Consumers want to buy as they did before, but the products available for purchase have declined. When this shortage leads to higher prices, the rate of profit in production sectors of consumer goods will likely increase, so that resources will again be led back to the original level by the lower stages of production. The rise in consumer prices can offset the cost advantage of the low interest rate in advanced stage, as long as the banking system is able to expand its credit scale, and this process may continue and attract resources to transfer between the two stages in production. Thus, the so-called prosperity by Hayek is actually an abnormally rapid capital formation with the artificial stimulation of new loans injected by the bank in the advanced stage of production. The generation of the upper turning point is partly due to the limit of the expansion of bank credit, and partly due to the collapse of the prosperity of capital expenditure in the state of the decline in the actual consumer demand caused by the rise in the price. In addition, the recession caused thereby restore the initial equilibrium between sectors of consumer goods and sectors of products, and such equilibrium was recognized by consumers before the increase in bank credit caused by the previous expansion.

This complex interpretation has its advantages, namely, it is trying to explain the differences of the actual and observable variability between the above-mentioned industry of products and industry of consumer goods. This theory is relatively complex, but it is based on the simplistic view of the bank operating mechanism. Its drawbacks include that it does not recognize that the real factors are the same with the monetary factors, and may incur the formation of capital.

In general, it is criticized for too much emphasis on the importance of monetary factors, as well as for the relatively unrealistic nature of investment process on the whole. In particular, Hayek did not pay attention at all to the effect of the change in expectations on entrepreneurial behaviours. We will see that when considering the contribution made by Keynes in understanding the instability, the most noteworthy is: the volatility of profit expected is in principle at least as important as cost fluctuations in explaining changes in the investment, and finally, Hayek can explain the upper turning point, even if his explanation is far from being sufficient, but he explained little in the lower turning point. Hayek's theory expounded the principle of fixed investment cycle, but it is not an appropriate interpretation for the modern business cycle, because it ignores too many critical factors. After all, the business cycle is too complex that there is no relatively simple theory that can explain it properly.

In Schumpeter's opinion, loan capital only allowed investment expansion rate to exceed the capacity in fact that the economy makes the resource used in sectors of producing consumer goods. If the resource is injected in consumption, the investment will grow too fast, which Kassel basically agrees with. Relative to the resources for consumption rather than savings, the investment rate is too high. Shortage of capital therefore become a real shortage in the late expansion, and the cause of the shortage is not a shortage of revenue, but rather the conflict with the demand for resources that should be used to increase the production of plants and equipment.

6. Joseph Schumpeter believed that the most basic type of innovation is the emergence of new products with the new production process, especially the construction of a new plant or equipment required to produce it. There are also other types of innovation, including new resources of raw materials, new markets of products, or new organizational methods in industry. No matter what types of innovation, in Schumpeter's view, its significance lies in the introduction of new thinking into the production processes, and causes a new round of investment. The innovation of an industry or a company often leads to the emulation of other companies that seize the opportunity, forming an "imitation boom". Therefore, the use of new technologies is often a series. Schumpeter once had this description on the clustering of innovation: "Progress—in the industrial as well as in any other sector of social or cultural life—not only proceeds by jerks and rushes but also by one-sided rushes productive of consequences other than those which would ensue in the case of coordinated rushes. In every span of historic time it is easy to locate the ignition of the process and to associate it with certain industries and, within these industries, with certain firms, from which the disturbances then spread over the system."[58]

58   Joseph A. Schumpeter, *Business Cycles: A Theoretical, Historical and Statistical Analysis of the Capitalist Process*, New York: McGraw-Hill Book Company, 1939, p. 102.

7. Keynesian and post-Keynesian theory of business cycle. Keynes argued that the income is always divided into two parts, consumption and savings, and as the income increases, the proportion of consumption tends to reduce while the proportion of savings tends to increase. Because of the diminishing marginal propensity to consume, the increasing share of income will turn into savings, resulting in insufficient "aggregate demand". If savings are not turned into demand, unemployment and crisis of overproduction is unavoidable. Due to the stability of the short-term propensity to consume, the attempts to turn savings into personal consumption are more difficult. Therefore, it needs trying hard to turn savings into investment. It is also due to the decreasing trend of marginal efficiency of capital, as well as the preference over the liquidity of money, the confidence in investment is insufficient, resulting in a phenomenon of the lack of social investment. The lack of consumption and investment indicates that the capitalist system cannot guarantee to determine the propensity to consume the amount of savings, or to determine the marginal efficiency of capital in the amount of investment, as well as the rate of interest maintaining at the value of full employment, and only in occasional cases, it can be so. Therefore, crisis and unemployment will often appear. The proposal that Keynes suggested to solve the problem is that the government should adopt four basic policies, namely tax bearing, fiscal deficit, inflation, and foreign expansion. In order to illustrate the importance of government investment in promoting economic growth, Keynes introduced the multiplier theory, using it to explain the impact of investment stimulus on the growth of the national economy. According to the multiplier principle, the increase in investment can increase the direct revenue, as well as a number of indirect revenues. Therefore, when lacking private investment, the increase in government spending and public investment, even if those investments are unproductive, can lead to the increase in a series of derived employment. Because of this, Keynes was trying to use the multiplier theory to explain the major role of the increase in investment on reducing unemployment and overcoming the economic crisis. Keynes believed that the business cycle is relevant to all factors that determine the amount of employment, but among which the most basic is the volatility of the marginal efficiency of capital. In the late prosperity, investors had an overly optimistic expectation on the future earnings of capital assets, and when these expectation sudden bursts, the crisis will occur. When the economy enters recession, the marginal efficiency of capital is very low, or even negative. The collapse of the marginal efficiency of capital often brings the associated rise in the rate of interest, which makes the investment decline more seriously. As the psychological factors that lead to the fluctuations in the marginal efficiency of capital cannot be changed in the short term, it is not expected to have the private to determine the current investment size, but to have the central government to carefully control and manage. The administration uses a proactive fiscal policy to expand investment and increase employment and income, thereby increasing the effective demand. Corresponding to the multiplier principle, disciple of Keynes raised the "acceleration principle" from the perspective of income

causing changes in investment, so as to supplement the deficiencies of "multiplier principle". They believe the multiplier principle only shows how a certain amount of new investment cause changes in income and employment, but do not specify how changes in income in turn lead to changes in investment. Based on the technical characteristics that the modern machine production applies a large number of fixed capital, they believe that changes in income and consumption will cause more intense changes in the volume of investment, and they also find that changes in this "induced investment" do not depend on the absolute amount of changes in income or consumption, but on the ratio (percentage) of changes in the amount of income and consumption.

The acceleration principle suggests that the intensification of changes in investment is often greater than that in consumer demand, and in terms of the timing of the changes, investment generally does not change after consumer demand changes, but often in advance. This feature is often one of the powerful factors causing economic instability. When corporate sales rise and fall, the acceleration can enhance their fluctuations. When economic activity increases, it results in a net positive investment, and it results in a net negative investment when economic activity declines. This means that, in order to make the investment to maintain a continued growth, the consumption must be maintained in rapid growth. If the pace of consumption is slowing down, or just stays at the previously high levels, then the investment growth will be greatly decreased, or even down to zero. Thus, just as the rapid growth of sales halts, the recession may come, although in this case, the sales volume does not decrease absolutely, it is staying at a higher level. This is a dilemma that capitalist economy can hardly escape.

8. The theory of neoclassical synthesis school of business cycle has the characteristics that there generally is a pattern of changes in the output and employment of the economy, and it can be predicted. The business cycle is originated from the economic infrastructure itself, and it is the structural problems of the economy that cause the economic fluctuations. Therefore, the traditional business cycle theory tends to believe that the business cycle is caused by the endogenous variables, in other words, the economic fluctuations is rooted in internal economic factors, so the fluctuations in the economy is largely predictable. The most famous representative theory of the traditional theory of the business cycle is the so-called the multiplier and accelerator model. According to this model, assuming that the economy is in recession, but output begins to increase, sales begin to increase. Greater sales make manufacturers begin to be optimistic about the investment prospects. In order to catch up with the pace of sales, they further increase investments that will produce more output. However, economic growth will eventually encounter some constraints so that the process of economic expansion stops. For example, there is a shortage of labour in the economy; thereby it will stop the expansion of the economy. But once the economy stops expanding, or the growth rate is slowed down, demand for investment will decline. At this time, multiplier will work in the opposite direction, greatly reducing the total demand, and the decline in the level of

economic activity begins. Since the output declines, the investment will slow down, causing further decline in the economy, and the investment activities come to a standstill. But the old machines will ultimately be damaged or outdated, so even if the yield is not high during the recession, new investment is still needed. New investment stimulates demand, and demand in turn stimulates investment, therefore, the economy begins to expand again. In the theory of neoclassical synthesis school of business cycle, the business cycle is considered to be rooted in structural problems within the economy, and therefore economists who hold this view emphasize endogenous factors arising from fluctuations in the economy, and the main objective of economic policy they developed is to identify endogenous factors that cause these fluctuations in the economy, to reduce the effect of these factors, so as to achieve the purpose of stabilizing the economy. Their policy is called the built-in stabilizer in economy. As the government plays a dual role in the macro economy: the growth in the government spending increases the aggregate demand in the economy; the tax revenue of government will reduce people's income. Since consumption depends on people's disposable income, so the government's tax revenue will reduce consumption, thereby reducing the aggregate demand in the economy. Those who hold the traditional view of business cycle think that because the tax system in general is taking a progressive tax system, and therefore when people's income increases, the applicable tax rate will increase correspondingly, and the result of improving the tax, as we have analyzed, will reduce the

consumption level, so that the multiplier value decreases, reducing the aggregate demand in the economy, as well as decreasing the level of economic activity. Conversely, when the economy is in recession, people's income drops, and the corresponding income tax rate will decline, while the decline in the income tax rate will increase the multiplier effect, so that the economic downturn gets stimulus. Since the rate of income tax determined by the level of economic activity plays an automatically stabilizing role in the regulation of the economy, proponents of the traditional theory of the business cycle of the economy call such an inherent mechanism of the tax system the automatic and inherent stabilizer in economy, because this regulating and stabilizing effect on the economy in the tax system does not need people to deliberately make any decisions in order to achieve it. The progressive income tax is not the only automatic regulator of the traditional theorists of business cycle. There are other policies and rules that play the role of the automatic stabilizer, such as unemployment insurance system, which is one of them. When the economy is in times of prosperity, those who are employed pay social security tax, resulting in that the consumption level drops, the multiplier effect is reduced, and the economy is free from overheating. When the economy is in times of depression, some people are unemployed, resulting in the decline in income, so the aggregate demand reduces and the overall economic activity declines. However, at the same time, due to the increase in unemployment, the unemployment insurance also increases, and the multiplier effect increases. So the unemployment insurance system also plays a role of automatically adjusting the economy. The traditional theorists of business cycle argued that, since the reason for fluctuations in the economy is the structural factors within the economy, in order to stabilize the economy, the government should seek and design some stabilizers within the economy, so as to automatically reduce or increase the effect of the structural factors that cause fluctuations in the economy, such as automatic lowering and raising the multiplier effect, to achieve the purpose of reducing fluctuations volatility and stabilizing the economy.

9. There is a point of view which is between the traditional business cycle theory and real business cycle theory, and it is called New Keynesian perspective. New Keynesian perspective believes that the reason for business cycle to occur is because there is an unpredictable mechanism of the external shock amplification and duration in the economy, so there is a greater economic fluctuation in the economy. New Keynesian economists believe that this mechanism existing in the economy increases the external shocks, and makes the impact caused by the shocks last for a long term. Even after the initial disturbance has disappeared for a long time, this impact may also exist. According to the views of New Keynesian economists, fluctuations in the economy are exogenous, but some endogenous factors that exist in the economy have increased the fluctuations in the economy and make it permanent.

New Keynesian economists include shocks from supply emphasized by real business cycle theorists and interferences from the monetary supply emphasized by monetarist and neo-classical economists into the potential impact. However, unlike the monetarist and neo-classical economists who believe that the market economy will always be able to mitigate and absorb external shocks and impact, and maintain full employment in the economy, instead, New Keynesian economists believe that the economy often increases the external shocks and impact, and makes the impact of such shocks lasting. For example, in a tight credit economy, due to the decline in sales, lower commodity prices, and decrease in cash reserves of manufacturers, the funding capacity of manufacturers to invest is reduced, and their desire to bear the investment risk is also reduced. Thus, the potential decline in business investment caused by the decline in volume of sales today will be greater than the corresponding reduction in sales, and such decline in investment would cause a greater impact on national output through the multiplier effect. The same process can also occur in the opposite direction.

The market economy will expand external shocks, and it is also likely to respond slowly to forces that could restore the economy to a normal state. For example, after experiencing the recession, firms tend to take a more conservative strategy towards production and investment, and the financial position of vendors will improve as the economy improves though, the process is gradual. Because over time, the machine will wear and tear and be in obsolescence at the end and the demand for investment will become increasingly urgent. Finally, the investment occurs, and the production increases. Due to an increase in output, the financial situation is further improved, the company's confidence for investment is gradually restored, and economy is recovered, but it often takes months or years. So, according to the interpretation of the New Keynesians on this business cycle, the price for a recession may not be the price to be paid just during a recession, and as there is a process that makes the economic recession last), the price to be paid is much higher than the initial loss.

New Keynesian economists oppose to any views of the intervention in the economy. They believe that the market is able to adjust changes in the economy, but it is often not rapid enough, and thus, there may be a widespread unemployment in the economy. The government cannot turn a blind eye to the depression in the economy and the pain during the crisis, and in the meantime, the government can and should take certain measures against economic fluctuations.

New Keynesian economic theory suggests that even in the presence of rational expectations, the government's economic policies can still achieve great results. They agree the view raised by neoclassical and monetarist economists that private behaviours may offset the impact brought about by the government's economic policies, and they also agree that when the government is formulating policies, it should take the reaction of private to its policies into account. Private actions may often partially offset the effect of government policies, and sometimes may even completely offset the effect of all government policies. However, the new Keynesians insist that it is not correct that they think they can always offset all government policies. First, they believe that the view that the private sector can completely offset the policy implications is built on such an assumption that prices and wages are now considered very flexible, and changes in the economy can be adjusted quickly. However, New Keynesian economists believe that this is far from being the truth. In the real economy, prices and wages have a strong rigidity. Secondly, they are also sceptical about the assumption in the theory of rational expectations that, families and vendors are able to respond quickly to the government's policies, and to resolve the impact of the economic policies. Many people feel that assuming that every family can quickly know what policy the government is now taking, and have proficient and enough knowledge of economics and the current structure of the economy, so they are able to resolve the economic policy and everyone is taking a similar approach. However, it seems impossible. Thirdly, they believe that even if people do offset some of the effects of economic policies, but the effects of many economic policies are manifold, and response measures taken cannot offset the impact of economic policies from various aspects. For example, increasing taxes on the interest income may directly stimulate more consumption, and this policy could increase government revenue and reduce the deficit. Thus, consumers feel that the tax burden they carry and are responsible for the budget deficit in the future may be reduced, so the consumption is increased. Therefore, the government's tax increasing policy may, in turn, stimulate the consumption.

New Keynesians view that the government's economic policy not only is effective, but also contributes to economic stability. Firstly, New Keynesians believe that, because the market cannot make a quick adjustment to maintain full employment in the economy, therefore, the government intervention in the economy is needed to a certain degree, and this intervention has been effective. Secondly, New Keynesians consider that the government should not act in compliance with the so-called policies and rules, but should take measures of economic adjustment according to the economic situation. Because the economic environment changes all the time, the economic situation that has changed requires a corresponding change in economic policies. It is impossible to determine in advance what economic policies to take, as well as which economic policy is appropriate and which is not. While the recession has many common forms, each of the economic crisis has its own characteristics, requiring to adopt different economic policies to deal with.

However, the view which neoclassical and monetarist economists assert that the government tends to deepen economic fluctuations has a profound impact on the New Keynesian economists. Unlike most of the Keynesians who believe that the government can have a "fine adjustment" of the economy, so the economy can remain on the level of full employment and of no inflation, New Keynesian economists generally agree with neoclassical and monetarist economists that if there is too much government intervention in the economy or excessively ambitious policies implemented, the economy is likely to be worse.

Moreover, they are like the traditional business cycle theorists, who believe the automatic regulator in the economy may reduce the fluctuation in the economy, and the negative effect of economic impact on the economy.

In general, we can summarize the features of the Western non-Marxist business cycle theory as follows:

1) To treat extrinsic factors as intrinsic factors. These theories generally understand capitalism as an eternal system, with the precondition that capitalist private ownership is inviolable, and it excludes the intrinsic link of the crisis with the capitalist property relations. They attribute the causes of the cycle to nature, politics, technology, psychology, humanity, and other external factors of the economies, and even if some of the schools even understand the problem from within the economy, at best they only attribute it to market imperfections. Some schools even think that the business cycle itself is seen as the fluctuations in an economic growth process are just the change in the market. Most schools believe that the crisis can be cured with the adjustment within the internal capitalist economic system, and even some schools consider that capitalism has achieved or is achieving development of no crisis. 2) General studies of relations focusing on the market economy. Based on the general relations of the market economy, in many aspects of the relations such as in production, distribution, exchange and consumption, the majority of schools emphasize the analysis of distribution, exchange and consumption, focusing on their decisive role on production, but ignoring the study of the production process. Some schools explore the causes of the cycle in the production area, but it is only the opposition of the superficial phenomenon that they grasp.

The economic relations they studied in most cases are only general relations in the market economy, rather than reflecting the social and economic relations of the fundamental capitalist system. 3) Attentions on the study of anti-crisis policies and measures. The purpose of their study on the cycle is to explore the movement in order to propose effective control measures. Therefore, no matter what the opposition the theoretical perspectives and policy advocates of each school in the Western cycle theory is, their ultimate goal is exactly the same. The bone of contention is the effectiveness of theoretical and policy advocate on the governance of cycle, and which school takes the mainstream does not depend on its degree in science, but on the degree of application of the government, namely the extent of its services. 4) The improvement of the theoretical value as the obvious feature. They paid attention to the analysis of the process of the running cycle, and in the analysis of the detailed market relations and operational mechanism, they attempt to discover the intrinsic link between them and the economic fluctuations, to indicate conditions for formation and reasons for alternation of economic prosperity and recession, as well as the contact and conduction mechanism of the various stages of the cycle, so as to provide targeted theoretic support for the specific and operational anti-crisis measures. They paid attention to empirical analysis, in an attempt to more accurately grasp the law of economic fluctuations through the systematic analysis of the statistics, with particular emphasis on the analysis of the wavelength and stage length of the cycle. Some schools paid attention to the study of prediction, and established a complete forecasting system of the fluctuations of the cycle, in an attempt to take effective regulations and precautions through reasonable predictions of the future.

Western non-Marxist business cycle theory is fundamentally flawed, but it also contains some realistic analyses and rational views, as well as some valuable technical analysis methods that can be absorbed and learned from by the Marxist theory of the business cycle. 1) To explain the business cycle from the perspective of productive force. For example, proponents and advocates of the innovation cycle attribute the reasons of cyclical economic fluctuations to technological innovation, which is close to the viewpoint of Marxist theory of the business cycle with regard to the material basis of the cycle. Since the 20th century, especially after World War II, the development of science and technology and its role in economic development has become increasingly prominent, and it promotes Western economists to pay more attention to the study of it, who explain the business cycle from the perspective of technological innovation, and some factors are relatively reasonable. Firstly, they had in-depth study of the situation and development trend of modern science and technology, which reflects the nature and the development of the productive forces of modern society. They recognized that the expertise has become a decisive factor in the success of modern business, and scientific and technological progress has become the key to social and economic development. Secondly, on the basis of understanding of role of science and technology in economic development, they recognized that scientific and technological developments and the current capitalist enterprise system is contradictory, because the production develops more rapidly due to the promotion of technological innovation, and it is more contradictory with the capital. This reflects the conflict between the development of the social productive forces and capitalist economic relations in a certain sense. And they made some reasonable propositions with regard to the changes in the capitalist enterprise system and the development of science and technology, which reflects the reality and the objective requirements of the development of social productivity to some extent. Thirdly, they are aware of the impact of the development of science and technology on changes in the social industrial structure, as well as the profound impact of fluctuations in labour productivity on economic development. Finally, they proposed the perspective that technological innovation is directly related to the length of business cycle. They believe that there is a difference in the significance of technological innovation, and it has different roles and impact on economic fluctuations, resulting in different wavelength of the business cycle. These perceptions have certain rationality. 2) The cyclical fluctuations in the economy are connected with the capitalist system. The western radical system school adheres to the view to have the structural analysis of the capitalist economic system, and attributes the fluctuations in the economy to the irrational structure of the current system, which is valuable. They believe that the current system of capitalism has created inequity in social power and extremely unequal distribution of social income, and it is the main cause of social and economic instability. Moreover, many schools also attribute the causes of the business cycle to some defects in the distribution system, and advocate eliminating the economic crisis by improving the distribution system. They do not understand that the distribution system of the government is determined by the ownership relations of the capitalist means of production, and it is impossible to change the irrationality of the distribution system under the condition of retaining capitalist ownership relations, it is also impossible to achieve the purposes of overcoming the crisis from some improvement. However, their analysis of the defects in the distribution system of capitalism, as well as the analysis of the contradiction caused by the distribution system and the socio-economic and political consequence, to a certain extent, exposes the internal contradictions of capitalist economic relations. It is difficult for the improved distribution system to change the basic development trend of the capitalist reproduction cycle radically, but we should hold a positive attitude towards any real sense of progress that is conducive to improving the working people within the scope of capitalist system. 3) The theoretic analysis and policy position by western economists on state intervention into the social economy so as to overcome the economic fluctuations contains certain reasonable factors. They believe that there is an internal defect in capitalist market economy, which is impossible to achieve the natural equilibrium and co-ordination of economic development, and thus the macro-regulation of the capitalist economy is essential. They criticize that classical economics had overly and narrow understanding of the economic process, and regard the market as the only means of regulating the economy, but ignoring the effect of other important factors. They criticize that the economic liberals are those who are eager to have capitalism perish. They discuss the dual role of the state plan, and on the one hand it provides information to the private sector, coordinates the economic behaviour of private companies and prevents the disproportion caused by serious anarchy; on the other hand, it plays an important role in economic resource development, science and technology advance, social production and consumption structure adjustment, planning the social macroeconomic development and etc. They stress that the economic plan is particularly important for the state-owned sector of the economy, and it is the necessary condition for these sectors to improve economic efficiency and to play its essential role in the national economy. They think the economic plan economy is an important means to meet the technical socio-economic and social issues, which also has a very important scientific value. 4) The analysis of the operation mechanism of business cycle has reasonable factors. For example, based on the premise that the capitalist market economy has inherent defects, New Keynesians analyzed that, under conditions of the existence of imperfect market, incomplete information and uncertainty, how the behaviour of corporate profit maximization would inevitably lead to wage and price rigidity, resulting in inefficient allocation of social resources and economic instability. Keynesians analyzed the cumulative process of the business cycle with the combining effect of multiplier and accelerator. Harold is the first to combine the multiplier and the accelerator to describe the business cycle. He

believes that under the condition of economic prosperity and rise in the rate of interest, most of the increase in profits is used in savings and turned into investment, rather than consumption. Therefore, the propensity to consume gradually slows down with economic growth. The decrease in the propensity to consume means the decline in multiplier effect, and it also causes a decline in investment growth by the accelerator. The combination of multiplier and accelerator affect the stimulus ability of investment to the national income, as well as the volume of investment itself. He uses the combined effects of multiplier and accelerator to illustrate the transmission mechanism among consumption, investment and national income: investment affects national income through the multiplier effect, national income affects consumption through the propensity to consume, and consumption affects investment through the accelerator. This is a cumulative process cycle. Paul Samuelson and Sir John Richard Hicks added that there were factors of time lag and asymmetry of acceleration effect into the analysis respectively, making the analysis more realistic. Hicks investigated the combination of the multiplier-accelerator of each phase of the cycle in the form and the extent, and he illustrated the problem of steering process of the accumulation. In addition, because of the differences on the basic theory among the major schools of the Western business cycle theory, they have different focuses on the analysis of cycle mechanism, and the analysis of one school tends to be one-sided, but indeed there are in-depth points. The traditional Keynesians emphasized the decisive role of insufficient effective demand on cycle, so they paid attention to the analysis of the transmission mechanism of the impact of

changes in demand on economic fluctuations; The new monetarism emphasizes the study of the connection relations and mechanism between the quantity
of money and other economic variables; neo-liberalism had a relatively full
analysis of the mechanism of competition and the willingness of consumers;
the supply school had a more profound understanding of the process how production determines consumption; the actual cycle theory had a more adequate
analysis of the transmission process of the technological impact through the
internal mechanism of the economic system. We should pay attention to the
in-depth points of all schools, and try to dig reasonable factors that may be
contained. 5) Some analytical methods are worth borrowing. For example the
empirical analysis and the forecasting analysis. The empirical analysis organized and analyzed the historical statistics, found some regular economic fluctuations, and explored the causes, which undoubtedly has an important methodological significance to form a scientific cycle theory. With the development
of social statistics and the application of computers, it provides a more conve-
nient condition for the empirical analysis. The empirical analysis has been
widely used in contemporary western cycle theory and Marxist economics. The
direct purpose of business cycle prediction analysis is to provide the basis for
overcoming the possible economic fluctuations in the future. The early economic forecasting in the West started from the late 19th century, with the prediction of technology being mainly the simple economic indicators and time
series analysis, is mainly forecasting based on the base number. During this
period, the economic forecasting was at the stage of individual study, and was
not valued by society. After World War I, the Western economy had developed
rapidly, but it was also accompanied by frequent fluctuations, and the economic forecast had aroused widespread attention. Many countries had established a number of economic forecasting organizations, and they have made
some contributions to the national and to the world economic forecasting.
However, the traditional forecasting techniques did not foresee the major world
crisis in 1929, the study of economic forecasting was under blame and criticism. In 1939, on the basis of modern economics and mathematical statistics,
Jan Tinbergen and Ragnar Frisch created econometrics, which has made great
breakthrough in economic forecasting methods. Later, the application of computer adds an effective tool for the predictive analytics, which has made considerable progress and forms an important foundation of modern information
consulting industry. The predictive analytics of business cycle is the process of
processing the specific cycle information with the use of predictive methods,
and therefore, the predictive methods are the core of predictive analytics. The
forecasting methodology of business cycle and techniques are based on the
development of modern science and technology, which takes all scientific and
technological achievements that are possible to serve the predictive analytics to
establish its own methodology. As the business cycle involves all aspects of
social and economic life, it is relative with a variety of economic forecasts, and
its methodology and techniques should be based on a variety of economic forecasting methods, reflecting the rule of the operating characteristics of the social

economy as a whole, as well as a method that can process information of the business cycle with integration. In the methodology system of qualitative analysis and quantitative analysis of economic forecasting, methods that are directly used in the early warning analysis of macro economy can be divided as the followings based on the early warning, the climate index, the climate warning index and short-term econometric model; the measuring methods of the cyclic fluctuations of economic variables include the direct method and the residual method. Since many economic forecasting methods cannot achieve longer-term forecast results, so some economists advocated recently changes in long-term forecast method, and they have made certain achievements. The changing trend of the cycle forecasting which is developing to a long-term one, to different cycles related so we need to pay special attention to the combination of global forecast and local forecasts

VIII. Conclusions

Marx and Engels has gone through a long process in exploring the business cycle, during which they gradually discovered the difference between primary cycle and short cycle, the various stages of the primary cycle and their main characteristics, the root causes of cyclical fluctuations in the economy and the transmission mechanism of the business cycle, etc. These findings were not elaborated in a concentrated way, and some of them were not even written in the works in time, but these do not affect the scientific feature of the existing achievements. Marx revealed the intrinsic relations of business cycles, and while he was stressing the root cause of cyclical fluctuations in the economy, he was also focusing on the exploration of the specific reasons, the foundation of which is that in many parts of his writings, he has mentioned the specific reasons for the economic crisis. The main difference between Marxist business cycle theory and non-Marxist business cycle theory is that the former reveals the root cause of the capitalist business cycle, while the latter regards the general reason as the root cause. In Marx's vision, the business cycle as the result of all contractions of capitalism being developed, the contradiction of social mode of production is an essential element of the business cycle, and these elements are embodied in competition, credit, stock system, agriculture, wage labour, world market, international credit, international trade, international flows of precious metals, tariff policy and other relations. The intensification of contradictions is both the flashpoint of crisis and turning point of the business cycle. Due to the limitations of time and practice, Marxists and non-Marxists later had a lot of study on business cycle, involving a large number of very detailed elements, building a large number of models, the findings of which could be an important material to enrich and develop the Marxist business cycle theory.

CHAPTER VII

The Breakdown Model
and Its Evolution

249

I. Introduction

According to Marx's crisis theory, when the development trend of an economic crisis is gets worse and when it reaches a certain level, it will endanger the survival of the entire bourgeois society. There is no way for the bourgeoisie to overcome the crises, it takes measures like "by enforced destruction of a mass of productive forces", "by the conquest of new markets" and "by the more thorough exploitation of the old ones", however, "[t]hat is to say, by paving the way for more extensive and more destructive crises, and by diminishing the means whereby crises are prevented."[1] That is to say, "[t]hus every factor, which works against a repetition of the old crises, carries within itself the germ of a far more powerful future crisis."[2] The capitalist economic crisis is not only unavoidable, but its development trend would inevitably lead to the revolution by the proletariat to overthrow the bourgeoisie. From this theoretical inference, it is natural to conclude that: the crisis is a symbol of death for capitalism, and the crisis will become increasingly acute, eventually causing the breakdown

---

1 *Selected Works of Karl Marx and Frederick Engels*, 2nd Chinese edition, Volume 1, Beijing, People's Publishing House, 1995, p. 278.
2 *Marx and Engels Collected Works*, 1st Chinese edition. Volume 25, Beijing, People's Publishing House, 1995, p. 554.

of the capitalist system. However, when capitalism enters the monopoly stage, the bourgeois government intervenes in the economy with the identity of a total capitalist, adjusting not only the macro-economic operation, but also the relationship between class interests in a certain extent, and the result is that the basic contradictions of capitalism is eased, and the capitalist economic crisis and class conflicts have the trend of gradual ease. As a result, people began to argue that whether the economic crisis is a symbol of the death for capitalism or not? Whether the crisis will become increasingly acute, resulting in the breakdown of the capitalist system itself? The controversy surrounding these issues has formed two schools of "breakdown" and "modification", which had the debate for a long time. Entering the mid-20th century, Stalin supported the view that capitalism has entered the phase of general crisis, and the breakdown theory has also naturally evolved as the general crisis theory of capitalism. For this reason, the modification theory received a heavy blow, and it did not have the chance to rise until after the 1980s. By reviewing this process, this chapter reveals the basic structure and composition elements of the economic breakdown model, in order to further illustrate the evolution of the Marxist analysis model of economic crisis.

II. Bernstein's Modification Theory

Eduard Bernstein is the founder of modification school, and during the period of 1896 and 1897, he published a series of articles in the *Die Neue Zeit* (*The New Time*) magazine to explain his point of view. He believes that after Marx, the world economy has undergone many new situations: the modern credit system is flexible, postal, telegraph, transport including passenger and freight, communications facilities, and etc. are enhanced, commercial statistics and intelligence agencies are improved, the business and industrial organizations are expensing as well, etc., which greatly affect the "relations of production activities and market conditions" and thus is very likely to avoid "the kind of business crisis that has always been so."[3] So, the capitalist catastrophic breakdown theory is untenable and should be abandoned. The breakdown of capitalism is not the product of the development of real capitalism, but an outdated theory. Under the new historical conditions, it is able to eliminate the ills of capitalism peacefully and gradually. To do so, is not only the best way politically, but morally justified. These remarks of Bernstein actually equally announced that Marx did not have the scientific economic crisis theory. In fact, Bernstein had already held sceptic view about Marxist analysis model of economic crisis, and from the writings by Marx and Engels, it seemed to Bernstein that Marx and Engels' elaboration on the root cause of the economic crisis of capitalism was self-contradictory, because sometimes they had fierce opposition to revealing the root of the capitalist economic crisis with inadequate consumption, and sometimes they regarded inadequate consumption as the "ultimate reason" of

3   See Eduard Bernstein, *Zur Geschichte und Theorie des Sozialismus* (*The History and Theory of Socialism*), Beijing: Joint Publishing, 1962, p. 192.

the real crisis. Therefore, in Bernstein's mind, Marx did not have a mature crisis theory. But Bernstein insisted that the possibility of a comprehensive eruption of devastating crisis is getting smallerThe reason is that: 1) the population of those of property owners are not reduced but increased; 2) small business does not decline. That is, the development trend of the basic contradiction of capitalism is not on the rise, but slowing down. That Bernstein can seize the point to deny the possibility of the devastating crisis indicates that he is fully aware of the root of the capitalist economic crisis. Because of this, some later critics argue that, the criticism of Marxist crisis theory by Bernstein is an issue in two different levels which deliberately confuses the analysis of the capitalist economic crisis by Marx and Engels, and he thinks that in Engels' explanation, the reason of the economic crisis falls into two level of the root cause and the direct cause. The root cause is "the incompatibility of social production and capitalist possession." an antagonism between the organisation of production in the individual workshop, and the anarchy of production in society generally, as well as an antagonism between the expansion of production and the contraction of the consumer demand that masses can afford to pay, are the manifestations of contradictions between socialized production and capitalist possession, both of which are the direct reasons of the crisis. Bernstein believes that Marx's two crisis theories have contradictions, which abandons the analysis of the contradiction and the nature of socialized production and capitalist possession, and also confuses the distinction between the root cause of the economic crisis and its direct cause.

251

Bernstein's misinterpretation of Marx's crisis theory is obviously deliberate. But his modification theory is a new judgement based on new situations and new problems after capitalism enters into monopoly stage from free competition, and it is strongly academic and prophetic. The arrival of monopoly capitalism did not lead to changes in the basic economic relations of capitalism, but it has partly qualitative changes in many places. The economic basis at free competition stage is private capital or individual capital, and the specific form of capitalist ownership at that time is individual private ownership of capitalists; while the economic base at the monopoly stage is social capital, and the specific form of monopoly capitalist ownership is the private ownership of monopolies based on shares of capital. In the stage of free competition, it is dominated by individual capital, and in the stage of monopoly, it is dominated by monopoly capital. The production and circulation within the monopoly has some planning, and with its advantages in obtaining monopoly profits, it is more conducive to technological progress and with its monopoly on the production and marketing, it improves the adaptability of the market, which has never been seen in times of free competition. These new phenomena and the development trends in the new historical stage show that under conditions of free competition, the analysis of the theory of capitalist economic crisis, its limitations and elements have undergone changes in different degrees, and in such conditions, the insistence of the original conclusions is obviously inappropriate. For example, the anarchy of production and the incomplete information have clearly causal relations, and changes in production organization, technical conditions, market development and etc. in monopoly stage have significantly improved collection as well as the number and speed of transmission of information, which makes the production organization capable of effective forecasting of the changing trends of the market demand, and has necessary adjustments to its production and circulation. Overproduction is the other side of the narrow market, and the monopolistic behaviour of monopolies opens up their own markets, while the overall expansion of monopoly capitalism has opened up the market for the capitalist production as a whole. Monopolies can adapt to market demand and have some degree of regulation over the production, so that the production within the production sectors of the monopolies has a certain degree of planning. The establishment of the central bank decreased the level of risk in the banking system, and the contraction and expansion of credit has increased the constraining factors. As the total capitalists, capitalist countries begin to exercise their function of regulating social and economic relations. When Bernstein made remarks against the breakdown theory, the above phenomena were still in the early stages of growth, some even in the early embryonic stages; Bernstein had made predictions based on the development trends, and drew the conclusion that the Marxist analysis model of the economic crisis had already been "outdated". Bernstein's conclusion is deemed to have revisionist rhetoric, and has been under severe criticism by the orthodox Marxists. In explaining why Bernstein denied the "breakdown" theory, there is a very representative view that deserves serious consideration, that is "due to the temporary prosperity of the capitalist economy, especially with the emergence of cartels, syndicates, trusts and other monopolistic organizations, it results in an illusion that the contradiction between the inherent socialization of production of the capitalist economic system and the capitalist private ownership of the means of production seems to have 'disappeared', so the Marxist theory on the historical trend in the capitalist era – the theory of the inevitability of capitalist cyclical economic crisis and the theory that the capitalist system will ultimately and inevitably 'breakdown', seem to be an 'outdated' 'hypothesis'."[4] If we take the real economic relations of capitalism in Marx's era or in Bernstein era as the basis, and consider that Bernstein's remarks are the result of being confused by the illusion, and then, if we focus on the development of capitalism in the 20th century and its development trends in the 21st century, Bernstein's remarks are not all the misunderstanding or "poisonous weeds" of the history, nor the revisionist remarks, but a rational prediction of the capitalist economic relations, with strong academic colours. Therefore, it requires not just simple criticism and negativity by economists or politicians, but also deserves serious in-depth study.

252

---

4   Liu Peixian and Ma Jianxing, *The Study on the Thoughts of the Second International*, Beijing: China Renmin University Press, 1994, p. 66.

III. Cunow and Schmidt's "Collapse" Theory

Bernstein's remarks had caused widespread debate within the Second International, and even some members not being in the Second International also joined the debate. Heinrich Cunow was the first to publish an article on the official organ of the Social Democratic Party, and he refuted Bernstein's remarks. Based on the viewpoint of Marx, Cunow considers that the capitalist economy is deteriorating, and no matter what new situations arise, the breakdown is unavoidable, because the development of the capitalist economy is going to deteriorate with the shrinking of the external market. The issues being debated within the Second International coincided with those which Tugan was interested in and put a lot of effort to study, so he was soon involved in the discussion. He claimed in his book that he had overturned Marx's two breakdown theories: one is based on the tendency of the rate of profit to fall, and the other is based on lack of consumption. Tugan believes that the breakdown of capitalism is by no means inevitability in the economy. "Mankind will never achieve socialism as a gift of blind, elementary economic forces but must, conscious of its goal, work for the new order – and struggle for it."[5] For this reason, Tugan asserts: "There must come a time when overproduction will become chronic, and the capitalist economic order will break down because of the impossibility of finding outlets for its newly accumulated capital."[6] After reading Tugan's writings, Conrad Schmidt found that Tugan's views were in conflict with his own perspectives, because Tugan ignored the related discussion by Marx. Marx not only had the breakdown theory, and based on the lack of consumption; he also carried out a special dissertation. To this end, he made such a wonderful description:

"Don't the capitalists, by their opposition to all wage increases, conduct a struggle which has the tendency to keep the income – hence also the purchasing power – of the masses as low as possible, while they, the capitalists, on the other hand, raise their own income – and therewith the mass of accumulated capital seeking productive investment – in rapidly increasing progression? Will, under such circumstances, the increase in consuming power … be able to keep step with the tempo of capital accumulation? And if not, must not then the sale of commodities become always more difficult the more consumption demand, the basis of production, lags behind the rapidly increasing accumulation of capital and expansion of production – with only export, unproductive state expenditures, etc., to slow down the process? In this way, then, capitalism would tend to create in and of itself a steadily growing state of overproduction. Intensified competition on the market as a result of the growing difficulty of sales would have a tendency to manifest itself in a growing pressure on prices and therewith in a fall of the rates of return or of the average rate of profit, a fall in consequence of which the capitalist mode of production becomes even for

5   Quoted by Paul Sweezy, *Theory of Capitalist Development*, Beijing: Commercial Press, 1997, p. 217.
6   Ibid., p. 223.

the majority of private entrepreneurs ever more unprofitable and risky, while at the same time the labour market gets progressively worse for the workers, and the ranks of the industrial reserve army swell ever more terribly. The path of development of capitalist society would thus be likewise the path to its own bankruptcy, the transition to a new socialist order would be prescribed by a forced situation [Zwangslage] of society itself."[7]

In Schmidt's description, there seems to be the collapse theory of the tendency of the rate of profit to fall, but in fact it does not exist, because the rate of profit to fall that he talks about is caused by the lack of consumption, rather than by technological progress, or the improvement of the organic composition. Based on his under-consumption theory, Schmidt recommended overcoming the trend of lacking consumption by accelerating the tendency of the rate of profit to fall.

IV. Kautsky's Theory of Collapse

Originally Kautsky was an active supporter of the collapse theory, and he had written many rebuttals against Bernstein's modification theory. Inspired by Marx's theory and the reality of capitalism, he saw the trends that deteriorated capitalism due to its crises, and advocated the theoretical postulate of the collapse theory. Different than his contemporaries who agreed with it, he criticized the collapse theory systematically and in a very delicate manner. When explaining his point of view, Bernstein once said "the population of those of property owners are not reduced but increased", trying to prove that capital is not increasingly concentrated in the hands of a few, and the basic contradiction of capitalism is not on the rise, but at ease. Taking data from Germany for example, Kautsky gave a firm rebuttal. He pointed out that the proportion of the owners and employees in Germany in 1882 was 1: 2, while the proportion in 1895 was 1: 3. He also cited data provided in *On the Boundaries that Large German Factories and Enterprises Continue to Form* written by Sinzheimer and proved that the value of industrial output of the large factory in 1882 accounted for only half of that in Germany, while it accounted for two-thirds the 1895, which suggested that the rapid concentration of the German capital was underway, and Bernstein's view of denying the concentration of capital was untenable. In order to enhance the credibility of the argument, Kautsky also cited the detailed figures, indicating that the concentration trend of capital, which can also be reflected through the growth of enterprises of different employment sizes, changes in the proportion of enterprises of different sizes in the total number of enterprises, as well as changes in the proportion of the number of employees hired in the enterprises of different sizes in the total number of workers in the country.

---

7   Quoted by Paul Sweezy, *Theory of Capitalist Development*, Beijing: Commercial Press, 1997, pp. 218-219.

Bernstein stressed that the formation of cartels, trusts and other monopolistic organizations enhanced the adaptability of capitalism, thus it can avoid crisis, while Bernstein's Russian follower Tugan-Baranovsky put more emphasis on internal coordination mechanism of capitalist production, denying the possibility of the widespread crisis by denying the conflict between production and consumption, and recognizing only partial structural crisis. Kautsky criticized both of these two erroneous tendencies. However, but because he was not able to fully and correctly understand Marx's theory, he also exposed his shortcomings, or even errors in criticism. Bernstein's denial of Marx's crisis theory starts by mechanically emphasizing that the crisis is not always like what Marx said that it regularly occurs in every 10 years, and therefore, he believes that the cyclical crisis does not exist. Therefore, Kautsky's rebuttal starts from here. He believes that the crisis cycle of every 10 years was not Marx's theory, but merely a confirmation of the empirical fact. Marx did not invent the periodicity of crises, observed and illustrated the periodicity of crises. The key issue is not that the crisis will repeat every 10 years, but whether the crisis will recur regularly. For the latter, Kautsky replied with certainty; factors of crises exist among the commodity economy at the outset, and commodity production is the production performed by each independent producer for the market. This regulating factor in the production system of anarchy is price volatility. If production exceeds demand, prices will fall; if production is less than demand, prices will rise. Hence, that the commodity cannot be sold at the production price is a phenomenon that commodity production is bound to occur on a regular basis, and it is precisely this phenomenon that forms the basis of the crisis. This is, nevertheless, only a possibility, and other conditions are required to bring the real economic crisis. It is the development of capitalism that creates conditions for the transformation of the possibility of crisis into the reality of crisis. Capitalism is turning the socialized production as a whole to become more and more the production of commodity, so that the survival of the majority in the society who are dependent on the product of their own is unhindered to be achieved. At this time, due to the development of the social division of labour and credit, the dependencies between each producer become closer and closer, so that any unsalable product in one place will cause confusion elsewhere. However, with the development of production and circulation of commodity, the small local market turns into the huge global market, with an increasing number of intermediate links between producers and consumers, and producers are increasingly unable to understand the comprehensive market situation. As the modern scientific and technological advance and the development of credit, especially as there is a lot of industrial reserve army, it makes capitalist production have a greater likelihood of scalability and jumping development. But this does not eliminate the crisis, because any substantial increase in the demand will lead to the rapid expansion of production, resulting in overproduction. Finally, competition has led to that the continued production expansion has become conditions for its own existence in the capitalist mode of production. The condition for expanding production corresponds to expansion in the market, not only the expansion in the desire of the use the value of the product in need, but more importantly the expansion in the effective demand of the purchasing power accordingly. In this way, it is in a contradiction with the other trend of capitalist development, namely the trend of the labour force value of workers which is more and more beaten down. Therefore, the expanding market is the biggest problem of the capitalists. In addition, any expansion of the market will play a catalytic role for production, driving it into surplus and crisis. Conversely, any crisis would strongly urge capitalists to seek new markets. When the market can no longer be expanded at the speed of production expansion, the desperate moment for capitalist mode of production will finally arrive. As long as there is economic development, this situation occurs because the domestic market is ultimately limited. Of course, this pole, this limit is not dead, but elastic. However, it is inevitable that the road gets narrower. The growth rate of world capitalism is at a fast growing pace, and the world market is difficult to expand for a long time accordingly. Once the possibility of expanding the market is lost, people will not tolerate the existence of the capitalist mode of production.

Kautsky gave a more complete description of the collapse mechanism, so we can see more clearly the outline of the collapse model. The contradiction between production and consumption is the basic anchor of the collapse theory, and the issue of market is the core of the collapse theory. So, Kautsky's inference basically unfolded along with the two basic contradictions of the capitalist economy, which are consistent with Marx's derivation.

In 1902, Kautsky published a review article criticizing Tugan's book *Theory and History of Commercial Crises in England*, and in this article he discussed the collapse theory comprehensively and systematically, asserting: "One can say in general that crises are becoming ever more severe and extensive in scope."[8] Under the prevailing historical conditions, it is more realistic. He also asserts that capitalism is headed for a period of chronic depression, "According to our theory this development is a necessity, and that this alone that the capitalist method of production has limits beyond which it cannot go. There must come a time, and it may be very soon, when it will be impossible for the world market even temporarily to expand more rapidly than society's productive forces, a time when overproduction is chronic for all industrial nations. Even then up and downswings of economic life are possible and probable; a series of technical revolutions, which devalue a mass of existing means of production and call forth large-scale creation of new means of production, the discovery of rich new gold fields, etc., can even then for a while speed up the pace of business. But capitalist production requires uninterrupted, rapid expansion if unemployment and poverty for the workers and insecurity for the small capitalists are not to attain and extremely high pitch. The continued existence of capitalist production remains possible, of course, even in such a state of chronic depression, but it becomes completely intolerable for the masses of the population;

---

8   Quoted by Paul Sweezy, *Theory of Capitalist Development*, pp. 220-221.

the latter are forced to seek a way out of the general misery, and they can find it only in socialism. ... I regard this forced situation as unavoidable if economic development proceeds as heretofore, but I expect that the victory of the proletariat will intervene in time to turn the development in another direction before the forced situation in question arrives, so that it will be possible to avoid the latter."[9]

In the process of criticizing Tugan-Baranovsky, Kautsky puts great emphasis on Marx discussion of the relations between inadequate consumption and crisis. This is because, on the one hand, Tugan completely denied the connection between inadequate consumption and crisis; on the other hand there are some other bourgeois scholars who attribute the direct reason of crisis to the lack of consumption. As the defender of the Marxist economic theory, Kautsky correctly pointed out, the lack of consumption was a common phenomenon that existed in the class society in the past, but the overproduction crisis caused by it is something that appears only in modern times. Only in a place to sell and produce, can overproduction be formed into crisis, which means crisis is associated with the production of commodity. As a result of commodity production, the concept of overproduction itself has a new meaning. In the past, overproduction is linked to production that exceeds the existing consumption possibility. Now, in a society of commodity economy, regardless of whether the consumption of residents is really met, production that exceeds consumer demand in possession of money is overproduction. This excess is a very relative concept. Inadequate consumption should not be understood from the physiological significance as nutritional deficiency, but should be understood in the sense of a social class that consumption lags behind its production. Not only when the production is unchanged or increasing, the limitation of consumption will result in insufficient consumption, and when the consumption is unchanged or increasing, this increase is more slowly compared with the growth in production, which can also lead to insufficient consumption.

If what Kautsky explained basically and correctly illustrates the relationship between capitalist production and consumption, he went astray in the following analysis, and fell into the pit of economic romanticism of the petty-bourgeois. He said: "Capitalists and workers they exploited, with the increase in the wealth of the former and the number of the latter, provide a growing market, which is not growing as quickly as the growth of capital accumulation and labour productivity, and is not enough for the means of consumption created by large-scale industry of capitalism. Large-scale industry of capitalism must be looking for complementary markets outside its field, in industries where the capitalist mode of production conducts production, and it found the market, and also was expanding the market. However, the expansion is quick enough, because the complementary market does not have the flexibility and the ability to expand in the process of capitalist production. As long as the capitalist production developed into a large industry... it is possible to develop

9   Ibid..

such a leap, that in the short term it may exceed any expansion of the market. Therefore, each boom with the emergence of a significant expansion of the market was decided to be short-lived from the outset, and the crisis is the inevitable outcome."[10] Kautsky stressed that this view is the "orthodox" Marxist view, but it is not completely true, which is Sismondi's views, not the views of Marx. Marx's view is, of course, the development of capitalism is inseparable from foreign markets, but this is not because the value of commodity cannot be achieved, but because they need to obtain greater profits for higher profit rate. Kautsky's wrong ideas at the time had created a very negative impact in the team of Marxism. Obviously, that Luxembourg's error on the issue of capital accumulation is affected by Kautsky.

Mikhail Tugan-Baranovsky is wrong not because he directly attributed the cause of crisis to the contradiction between production and consumption, but that he completely denies the existence of this contradiction, and he believes that the crisis is not due to lack of consumption, but merely the unplanned nature of capitalist production, the anarchy. He believes that the various sectors of capitalist production are necessarily in a certain proportion, and any significant disruption to this proportion will lead to stagnation, thus causing crisis. Therefore, the occurrence of the widespread crisis does not require the universal overproduction of various production sectors, and as long as the production development of a sector exceeds beyond the scope determined by the proportion, it will interfere with the normal order of the entire production, causing serious confusion and widespread crisis. Kautsky believes that there is no doubt a component of truth in Tugan-Baranovsky's views. As widespread crisis does not require the general overproduction, as long as there is overproduction of a commodity (It was the textile before, and then the steel industry and processing industry) that dominated in the world market, it may induce the widespread crisis. It is beyond doubt that the destruction of the proportion in various sectors of production can become the cause of crisis, but it should be noted that the destruction of the proportion will not only be caused by overproduction, but also by insufficient production. However, Marxists do not deny the contact of the unplanned nature with the crisis, but that, the intensification of unplanned nature of capitalist production is one of the prerequisites of crisis, and sometimes it can also separately lead to a crisis or intensify a general crisis. What Marxists deny is that it is regarded as the only reason of crisis, and that it does not recognize the insufficient consumption to be most fundamental reason of crisis. Kautsky believes that it is absurd for Tugan-Baranovsky to deny the existence of contradictions between production and consumption, which is a "strange theory." This is because Tugan-Baranovsky's complete severing of ties between production and consumption has made the relative independence between production and consumption the absolute independence, which ended up to be the completely unrelated elements. His absurd belief is that in the capitalist economy, the demand for commodities is not affected by the total

258

10 Quoted by Liu Peixian, Ma Jianxing, *The Study on the Thoughts of the Second International*, Beijing: China Renmin University Press, 1994, pp. 166-167.

social spending, and the total social spending could be reduced, while the social demand for commodities may increase. The accumulation of social capital will inevitably lead to restrictions on the demand for means of consumption, while the aggregate demand for commodities will increase. This occurs is because means of production plays a growingly important role in the production process and in commodity markets and workers and machines are retreated to the secondary position in comparison. At the same time, in comparison of the demand formed by the productive consumption of means of production and the demand formed by consumption of workers, there is a growing proportion of the former, while the latter is relegated to a subordinate status. The whole mechanism of the capitalist economy can be said to have taken a "self-existence" form, in which, the consumption of people is expressed as a simple element of capital reproduction and distribution process. For this "strange theory" by Tugan-Baranovsky, Kautsky argued that the production was, is and will be carried out for the consumption of people. The production of commodities for direct consumption of people declines continuously in the proportion of total production, while the production, in a direct or indirect way, to provide them with tools, machines, and transportation services is increasing. Regardless of how many intermediary links are needed for the products of these production sectors to ultimately become the consumer goods, that is to say, regardless of how indirect its consumer services for people are, their ultimate goal is always that the production is providing means of consumption for the consumption of people. As long as this ultimate goal cannot be achieved, this entire production activity will ultimately and inevitably be in stagnation. Kautsky pointed out that in the international division of labour, the situation is more complicated. The production for the consumption of people in the old industrial countries is often expanded very slowly, while the production of the means of production develops very rapidly, and the production of the means of production has a greater decisive significance for the entire country's economic pulse beating. For anyone who views it only from the standpoint of the countries concerned, it is easy to come to such a conclusion: The production of means of production can be prolonged faster than the growth of the means of consumption, and the former is not constrained by the latter.

To this end industrial capitalists will not be able to consume all the profits and they must limit their spending, increase accumulation and capital, and introduce new technologies in order to remain competitive. This will inevitably lead to the continuous increase of production and improvement of labour productivity. Insufficient consumption of the exploited masses can no longer be compensated by according to the growth of consumption of the exploiters. The reason for the emerging overproduction in the capitalist society is this.

But this is a bias, and if the British textile machines are produced much faster than that of yarn, it must be the reason that new textile factories are established outside Britain, and the machineries these new factories are using are supplied by Britain. If difficulties occur in the sale of yarn, it is bound to affect the establishment of the new plant, which will affect the production of textile machines. Thus Kautsky says: "Production is the one for the means of production for the consumption of people. This fact can only be concealed or restricted by the advance of division of labour, but cannot be eliminated."[11]

From the above it can be seen that, when he was criticizing the crisis theory of Tugan-Baranovsky and expounding Marxist real theory, Kautsky had made many sound advices, but there were serious flaws. One of the flaws is that when he was explaining the significance of the foreign market on the realization of capitalist commodity, he fell into a morass of economic romanticism. Another one of his flaws is that when he was exploring the reasons for the crisis of capitalism, he gave a more full illustration of the contradictions between production and consumption in the capitalist reproduction process, and it is necessary to do so in order to criticize the error of Tugan who denied the contradiction between production and consumption. However, he ignored the elaboration of the fundamental reason that formed the crisis –the basic contradiction of capitalism. Moreover, he failed to explain the sharp trend of this contradiction as the development of capitalist production and credit. Therefore, he was not able to fully and correctly describe the occurrence mechanism of the economic crisis in Marxist crisis theory.

For the long-term trend of depression, Kautsky believes that with the approaching long-term depression, countries want to expand their share in world trade at the expense of others, "to which end the chief means are colonial conquest, protective tariffs and cartels, and the result is a steady sharpening of the antagonisms among the great industrial states."[12] So the only way for the proletariat to go is class struggle.

V. The Collapse Theories of Luxembourg, Grossmann, Bauer and Sweezy

Luxembourg is also one of the supporters of the collapse theory, but her demonstration of the issue is neither regards the rate of profit to fall as a logical starting point, nor considers it to be based on the inadequate consumption, but takes the issue of capital accumulation as a starting point for investigation. She tried to prove that it is impossible for a closed capitalist system to carry out capital accumulation. Luxembourg considered that the surplus value for accumulation cannot be achieved in the range of workers and capitalists, but only by selling it to non-capitalist consumers, that is, selling it to consumers who live in the country where capitalism has not touched, or belong to the population (e.g. peasants) who are still at the level of simple commodity production, and therefore are completely outside of the capitalist system. However, it is this expansion process that drags those backward countries and their residents into the track of capitalism, and the result is that they are all inside. When this

---

11 Quoted by Liu Peixian, Ma Jianxing, *The Study on Thoughts of the Second International*, p. 169.
12 Quoted by Paul Sweezy, *Theory of Capitalist Development*, p. 222.

happens, the closed capitalism which could not exist in theory will appear in practice, and the system itself will collapse. Based on this theory, the emergence of imperialism indicates that all the capitalist countries desperately want to win as much control as they could over the existing non-capitalist world; high protective tariff is manifested as a means of each country's attempt to block other countries to access to its own non-capital market. Therefore, some of the most remarkable phenomena in the final stages of capitalist development are interpreted as becoming depleted due to the non-capitalist market; accordingly, they are also interpreted as a harbinger of the imminent collapse of capitalism, which can be prevented by no force in the world.

In the period of relative stability after the First World War (hereinafter referred to as World War I), there was another discussion on the limits of capitalist development within the Marxist economics. Some of the main representatives of the Social Democracy Party have formed a united front against the collapse theory. Kautsky, writing in 1927, repudiated his own earlier theory of chronic depression from which capitalism would be unable to find an escape. Hilferding said it even more explicitly: "I have always rejected every economic collapse theory … after the war such a theory was championed chiefly by the Bolshevists who believed that we were now on the very verge of the collapse of the capitalist system. We have no reason to fear that. We have always been of the opinion that the overthrow of the capitalist system is not to be fatalistically awaited, nor will it come about through the workings of the inner laws of the system, but that it must be the conscious act of the proletariat."[13] The orthodox Bolsheviks still believed that capitalism will not encounter an automatic collapse due to economic reasons, for them only the proletarian revolution would perish it. Of course, some people still insist on the collapse theory, such as Fritz Sternberg who is one of the representatives, and in his book *Imperialism*, he systematically expounded his point of view.

Henryk Grossmann is also a supporter of the collapse theory. At the basis of Grossmann's reasoning for the development trend of the capitalist system is a reproduction scheme devised by Otto Bauer for use in his critique of Rosa Luxemburg's *Accumulation of Capital*. This scheme has the following structure and conclusions: the working population and the amount of variable capital both grow at the rate of 5 per cent per annum; the rate of surplus value remains always at 100per cent, so that the total quantity of surplus value grows also at a 5 per cent rate; the organic composition of capital rises – to bring this out it is assumed that constant capital grows at a rate of 10 per cent per annum. The way in which surplus value is divided into its three basic parts – capitalists' consumption, additional variable capital, and additional constant capital – is rigidly determined by these assumptions. So much must go for additional constant capital and so much for additional variable capital as to maintain the presupposed rates of increase; the remainder is left for capitalists to consume. Now it is obvious that if this scheme is pushed far enough it will lead to strange

---

13   Quoted by Paul Sweezy, *Theory of Capitalist Development*, pp. 231-232.

results, for the increments to constant capital, though themselves derived from surplus value, are assumed to grow more rapidly than surplus value. Bauer developed the scheme for only four years, which was not enough to bring out its potential curiosities. But Grossmann pushes resolutely ahead for thirty five years In the twenty-first year, the amount of surplus value left over for capitalists to consume begins to decline, and by the thirty-fourth year it is nearly all gone! From this point on, not only do the capitalists starve, but even by such heroic sacrifices they are no longer able to maintain the preordained rate of accumulation in the preordained proportions of constant and variable capital. The scheme, in other words, breaks down from a shortage of surplus value; given its assumptions, it is literally impossible to carry it beyond the thirty-fourth year.[14]

Bauer's scheme of collapse starts from the "shortage of surplus value". By a breath-taking mental leap Grossmann has concluded that the capitalist system will also collapse from a shortage of surplus value. Rosa Luxemburg's theory of an excess of surplus value is thus turned on its head. "The difficulty lies rather in the expansion of capital: the surplus value does not suffice for the continuation of accumulation at the assumed rate of accumulation! Therefore that is the catastrophe."[15] Despite certain qualifications and refinements, this "shortage-of-surplus value" theory, as derived from Bauer's scheme, remains throughout his work the essence of Grossmann's thinking on the collapse problem.

In reviewing the debate about the issue of collapse, Sweezy had given more evaluation on the theoretical derivation by Grossmann. He suspected the reliability of Grossman's derivation theory and what it means, considering that the reproduction schemes, including that of Bauer, are useful as method of making comprehensible the character of a certain set of relations. But to take any particular, and necessarily arbitrary, scheme and assume that it faithfully represents the essentials of the real process of capital accumulation is to invite theoretical disaster. Moreover, Sweezy also expressed his dissatisfaction with the theoretical assumptions by Grossman. He criticized Grossman's theory that: "So far as Grossmann's theory is concerned, we may regard it as sufficient to have shown, first, that the use made of Bauer's reproduction scheme is illegitimate; and second, that even if this were not so the conclusions which Grossmann draws are unwarranted. By denying the existence of a realization problem and by ignoring the real significance of the falling rate of profit, Grossmann in effect puts himself in the same school of thought with Tugan-Baranowsky. This is perhaps a harsh judgment to pass on one who spares no energy in castigating Tugan, but historical accuracy justifies no other."[16]

---

14 The number of years for which the scheme can run is naturally determined by the absolute size of the figures assumed for the first year as well as by the relative rates of growth of constant and variable capital. Bauer's first year is given by the formula 200,000c +100,000v+100,000s. The 34th year shows 4,641,489c+500,304v+500,304s. The quantity of s (500,304) is here less than 10% of 4,641,489 plus 5% of 500,304. Hence the scheme must come to an end with the 34th year.

15 Quoted by Paul Sweezy, *Theory of Capitalist Development*, p. 234.

16 Paul Sweezy, *Theory of Capitalist Development*, p. 237.

It is probably safe to assume that this is the reason why Marx did not concern himself with capitalist breakdown; he preferred to analyse the actual trends of capitalist development rather than to spin theories about a hypothetical outcome which would in any case never be reached. The incompleteness of his work is not to be found – as Rosa Luxemburg thought – in the absence of a breakdown theory, but rather in the unfinished analysis of capitalist tendencies.[17]

The reason that Sweezy believes that Marx did not concern himself with the breakdown theory is just because he is no less than an enthusiastic supporter of the consumer theory. He believes that capitalist production normally harbours a tendency to under-consumption (or overproduction), and it is inherent in capitalism. In principle this trend may manifest itself in a crisis or in stagnation of production. The tendency can apparently be overcome only by the partial non-utilization of productive resources. The partial non-utilization of productive resources is realized by forces counteracting the tendency to under-consumption. Sweezy argued that the counteracting forces can be attributed to two main categories: they are the forces based on those which can make consumption growth rate higher than the growth rate of means of production, as well as the forces that the disproportionate growth in the means of production will not cause devastating consequences in the economy. Those which belong to the former category are population growth, unproductive consumption and state expenditures, and those which belong to the latter category are the creation of new industries and faulty investment. In these counteracting forces, Sweezy argues that new industries, faulty investment and population growth have been weakening, and unproductive consumption and state expenditures have been growing stronger.

IV. The Collapse Theory of the Soviet Scholars – General Crisis Theory of Capitalism

In China, the issue of origin of the concept of "general crisis of capitalism" has been a hot topic and debate object for a long time in the academia. Soviet Scholars have argued that Marx used the term "full-blown crisis", "general crisis" including overproduction, trade, currency, credit and other aspects of the crisis.[18] The "general crisis theory", to be a system and to be expounded systematically, is finally formed based on the rich and the further development of the concept of Marx's "full-blown crisis" and "general crisis", and through the evolution and development of Lenin's uneven theory of the capitalist political and economic development. However, the first one who officially presented the concept of the "general crisis of capitalism" is the German Ernst Thälmann. On January 15, 1931, at the Plenary Session of the Central Committee of the Communist Party of Germany, Ernst Thälmann gave a report of the "Task of the German People's Revolution" and he mentioned: "The current crisis has the nature of the cyclical crisis within the scope of the general crisis of the

---

17   Ibid., p.240.
18   See Tao Dayong. *The Theory and Reality of the Capitalist General Crisis*. Shanghai: Shanghai People's Publishing House. 1984, p.85.

capitalist system in the era of monopoly capitalism, and we should understand the dialectical interaction between the general crisis and cyclical crisis. On the one hand, the cyclical economic crisis has the form of unprecedented acuity, because it occurs on the basis of the general crisis of capitalism, and is determined by the conditions of monopoly capitalism. On the other hand, the damage caused by the cyclical crisis deepens and accelerates the general crisis in the capitalist system."[19] In February 1952, Stalin accepted the formulation of the general crisis in the views on economic issues as mentioned in the textbook under discussion, and he believes that the general crisis in the world capitalist system "is a comprehensive crisis both economically and politically."[20] "The Second World War and the collapse of the all-encompassing world market in reunification, determined by the further deepening of the general crisis in the world capitalist system."[21] It was the Soviet textbooks that systematically elaborated this issue for the first time. Thereafter, economists had conducted the study on a large scale, and it went far beyond the borders of the Soviet Union as there were many participants, rich writings and wide influence. For example, some of China's well-known scholars also wrote books in early the 1980s to elaborate the creation, nature, characteristics, phase, trends and other aspects of the capitalist general crisis, but at this time, the Soviet textbooks have already deleted this content, from which its impact is apparent.

The proposal of the general crisis theory has deep historical roots, and it is a theoretical inference made by Stalin under conditions that there are many potential uncertainties in the capitalist development trend. The reason why the inference can be accepted and convinced by so many people in decades is because, in addition to the deification of leaders in the traditional socialist countries, the social reality after the Second World War (hereinafter referred to as World War II) was also very easy for people to accept this inference. After the impact of two world wars, capitalist forces had been severely weakened, and the world was divided into socialist and capitalist camps. The socialist camp has shown amazing opportunity for development: social progress, rapid economic growth, and rapid increase in the overall national strength. The capitalist camp has presented a comprehensive crisis: the cyclical economic crises still occur as scheduled; colonies broke away from the suzerain, and embarked on the path to independence; there has been a further sharp trend of the various contradictions in the capitalist world, and so on. This huge contrast between the two camps makes people seem to feel the demise of capitalism is accelerating its pace, and its doom is just not far away. Thus, on this basis, Stalin made a fundamental inference of the capitalist world system that this system has entered a phase of the general crisis. The general crisis that Stalin talked about means the crisis with the arrival of upsurge. Stalin believed that when it comes to the phase of the general crisis, the cyclical crisis will change the form. After the crisis there

264

---

19 Quoted from *Political Economy, Textbook*, Beijing:People's Publishing House, 1955, p.294.
20 *Selected Works of Stalin*, 2nd Volume, Beijing: People's Publishing House. 1979, p. 582.
21 *Economic Problems of Socialism in the USSR*, Beijing: People's Publishing House, 1961, p.23.

is no longer upsurge and prosperity in new industries. When Stalin accepted the concept of the general crisis, the Soviet theorists immediately launched a massive study and discussion. His comprehensive and representative research results first appeared in the *Political Economy, Textbook*. What is believed in the theory is that, it is the first stage of the general crisis of capitalism from World War I to World War II, and the second phase began after World War II. The first stage is characterized by: 1) the general crisis of capitalism is a full crisis throughout the world capitalist system, and it is characterized by war and revolution, and the struggle between the moribund capitalism and the growing socialism. The general crisis of capitalism includes all aspects of capitalism, both economically and politically. The basis of this crisis, on the one hand is the growing intensification of the collapse in the capitalist world system, and on the other is the growing economic power countries that have broken away from capitalism. 2) The general crisis of capitalism includes an entire historical period, the contents of which is the breakdown of capitalism and the victory of socialism in the world, the general crisis of capitalism began during the First World War, in particular after the Soviet Union has broken away from the capitalist system. 3) The Great October Socialist Revolution means the fundamental change of the human history of the world from the old capitalist world to the new socialist world. The world is divided into two systems – the capitalist system and the socialist system – and the struggle between the two systems is a basic feature of the general crisis of capitalism. As the world is divided into two systems, there have been two routes for economic development: The capitalist system is increasingly caught in the contradictions that cannot be solved; while the socialist system has been moving forward, and there are no crises and disasters. 4) The crisis of the imperialist colonial system is an integral part of the general crisis of capitalism. This crisis lies in the increasing development of the national liberation struggle, which has shaken the cornerstone of imperialism in the colonies. Those who lead the oppressed to have national liberation struggle are the working class. The Great October Socialist Revolution tapped the revolutionary enthusiasm of the oppressed, and opened the era of the colonial revolution led by the proletariat. 5) Under the conditions of the general crisis of capitalism, because individual countries break away from the imperialist system, the working people are poorer, as well as the colonial capitalism develops, market problems have become more acute. The characteristic of the general crisis of capitalism often reveals itself as enterprise running under their production capacity and often a large number of unemployment. Because of acute market issues, as well as business often running under their production capacity and often a large number of unemployment, the economic crisis is increasingly deepening, and the capitalist cycle has undergone major changes.

The second stage is characterized by: 1) During World War II, especially after the people's democratic countries in Europe and Asia broke away from capitalist system, it launched the second stage of the general crisis of capitalism. Since the formation of the two opposing camps on the international stage, the all-encompassing world market in reunification was collapsed and formed two parallel markets: the market of the socialist camp countries and the market of capitalist camp countries. The scope for the United States, Britain, France and other major capitalist countries to win resources of the world is suddenly narrowed. In capitalist countries, selling is more difficult, and enterprises are often running under their production capacity. 2) One of the most important results of the Second World War was a sharp intensification of the crisis in the imperialist colonial system. The new upsurge of the national liberation struggle in colonial and dependent countries makes the colonial system tend to collapse, so that China and some other countries broke away from the world imperialist system. 3) The uneven development of the capitalist countries further exacerbated the contradictions within the imperialist camp to be inevitably sharpening. U.S. imperialism embarked the road of unlimited expansion, trying to make the economies of other capitalist countries at its disposal. The militarization of economy intensified the disjointed state between the industrial production capacity and industrial sales capacity of the capitalist countries, thus brewing a new economic crisis and disaster. 4) The characteristics of the second stage of the general crisis of capitalism further deteriorated the material condition of the labouring masses sharply. This is manifested as the decrease of the real wages of the working class, the regular unemployment increases, and sweat wage system is widely used; it is also manifested as the inflation and the price rises, and the tax burden increases; it is manifested as the basic impoverishment of peasants and bankruptcy in the capitalist countries, as well as the intensification of colonial exploitation. Peace, democracy and the consolidation of the socialist camp, the weakening of the reactionary and bellicose imperialist camp, as well as the upsurge of the liberation struggle of the working class, farmers and people in colonial, all of which explains: the current era is an era of the breakdown of capitalism, and an era of communist victory.

After the generalization of the theory of general crisis in Political Economy, Textbook, the Soviet theorists had done a lot of in-depth studies on feasibility. For example, writings that have long been familiar with the theories, such as *The Theory and History of Economic Crises and Cycle* (by Stanislaw Mendelson), The General Crisis of Capitalism (by M.S. Dragilev), *Basic Economic And Political Issues Of Imperialism* (by Eugene Varga), *Modern Capitalist Economic Crisis* (by Gelchuk), are the results introduced in such a background.

Although Lenin did not explicitly put forward the concept of the general crisis, according to their description of the general crisis, Soviet scholars deduced such a conclusion from Lenin's writings: the general crisis theory "is an integral part of Lenin's theory of imperialism, and is the continuation of the theory under the condition of the immediate breakdown of capitalism." "Lenin revealed the essence of the general crisis, the premises it is created, and its most important manifestation."[22] Soviet scholars even found the basis of the discussion of the general crisis from Lenin's writings.

---

22 M.H. Rydina, *The History of Economic Thought*. Beijing: China Renmin University Press. 1987, p. 311.

"Lenin stressed that the general crisis of capitalism is a direct '… era of the complete breakdown of the entire capitalism and the birth of socialism'. When revealing the contents of the general crisis, he thinks that the general crisis is '… a time when it suffered enormous damage, implemented large-scale military force and full of crises', and he pointed out that in this era: '… it has begun, and we clearly see this era, but this is just the beginning'." "Lenin is certain that, the world capitalist crisis is an entire historical period, and the transition from capitalism to socialism is achieved through a series of countries breaking away in turn from the capitalist system. The premise of the general crisis of capitalism started from the era of imperialism, and is mature and accumulated with the development of imperialist contradictions. When talking about the starting point of the inevitable form when world capitalist crisis comes, Lenin pointed out that imperialism makes all contradictions of capitalism exceptionally sharpened, and when these contradictions have developed to the limit, the socialist revolution began."[23]

Soviet scholars have pointed out that the Bolsheviks have developed on Lenin's general crisis theory. In the early 1920s, the Bolshevik had identified the science-based prospect of the development and intensification of the general crisis of capitalism. At the Sixteenth Congress of the Bolshevik, they analyzed the essence and characteristics of the general crisis of capitalism, that is: the general crisis of capitalism is full economic crisis on the economy, politics and ideology of the capitalist system, and its basic and decisive sign is that the world is divided into two opposing systems. The general crisis of capitalism in the 1920s-1930s manifested features as: enterprise running under their production capacity and often a large number of unemployment, militaristic economy, inflation process, and changes in the development of capitalist cycle. Documents at the Sixteenth and Seventeenth Congress of the Bolsheviks also depicted the total picture of the world economic crisis movement in 1929–1933, scientists analyzed its features and devastating consequences, stressed that it was a special depression, and it did not lead to new industrial upsurge and development, but it will not make it back to the lowest point. In the first stage of the general crisis of capitalism, the crisis – depression part was prolonged and profound, while the recovery and upsurge phase is significantly shortened. After World War II, the resolution of almost every Congress of the Soviet Communist Party had made new conclusions of the general crisis, and those conclusions considered that the contradictions of capitalism are deepening and capitalist situation is deteriorating. Here, we take the main form and characteristics of the general crisis of capitalism described in the 22nd Congress of the CPSU as an example to illustrate it.

"More and more countries break away from capitalism; the imperialism is basically weakened in the economic competition with the socialism; the imperialist colonial system collapses; with the development of state monopoly capitalism and the growth of militarism, the contradictions of imperialism are getting

267

---

23   Ibid., pp. 311-312.

sharpened; with the intensification of internal instability and decay of capitalism, it is manifested in the inability of capitalism to take advantage of growing productivity (low production growth rate, cyclical crises, often enterprise running under their production capacity and often a large number of unemployment); the struggle between labour and capital is intensified, and economic contradictions of world capitalism is sharpened; the political reaction in all aspects is unprecedentedly strengthened, and abandoning the freedom of the bourgeois, many countries have established a brutal fascist regime; the profound crisis of bourgeois politics and ideology – all of this reflects the general crisis of capitalism."

Although there are some changes in the resolution afterwards, they are almost the same except slight differences. With the relative ease of the contradictions in the capitalist world after World War II, as well as with the rapid development of economy by the promotion of the new technological revolution, the general crisis theory is more and more away from the reality, becoming a purely political propaganda.

The general crisis theory can undoubtedly become part of political economics, but it can also be part of the scientific socialism or the history of the international communist movement and other disciplines. It studies the capitalist economic crisis less, and it focuses on the new features, new phenomena and trends of the crisis. The theory believes that when it comes to the general crisis, due to the establishment and expansion of the socialist camp, the sales market of capitalist camp is much smaller, and at the same time, the regular unemployment is increasing in numbers, which makes contradictions of capitalism so acute that the overproduction crisis is deepened and there are significant changes in the capitalist business cycle. These changes are mainly manifested in: the shortening of the length of the cycle, the result of which is that crises are more frequent; the increase in the depth and extent of sharpness of the crisis, which is reflected as a further decrease in the production with more unemployment, etc.; it is much more difficult to get rid of the crisis, because the crisis stage is longer, the depression stage is longer, and the upsurge stage is more unstable and shorter. Why do these changes occur? The proponents of this theory simply attributed it to the continuous intensification of the basic contradiction of capitalism.

Those who demonstrated the general crisis of capitalism are increasing in numbers, but basically they do not exceed the analytical framework that *Political Economy, Textbook* has developed.[24] Soviet scholar M.S. Dragilev is considered to have made a very typical study on the general crisis of capitalism, but what we can see from the results of his study is that his systematic elaboration on views in *Political Economy, Textbook*, and although these elaboration deepens and systematizes the theory, it seems to lack the contribution. The following paragraphs are the essence, premise and features of the general crisis of capitalism summarized by the author.

24   *Political Economy, Textbook* has absorbed discourse of Stalin's *Economic Problems of Socialism in the USSR*.

"The essence of the general crisis of capitalism is a historical process of world socialist revolution: the socialist revolution won the first victory of in one country, and the proletarian revolution in capitalist countries makes more and more new links break away from capitalism. The shock two world wars had on capitalism, the increasing collapse of the colonial system, the establishment of socialism in more and more emerging countries, the formation of the unified, all-encompassing world socialist system, and the final and complete victory of socialism within the range of the world."[25]

The premise of the general crisis of capitalism is: 1) On the basis of the rule of the monopolies and the pursuit of maximum profit, the contradiction between labour and capital is increasingly acute. 2) The contradiction between the colonial peoples and the imperialist suzerain is deepened. 3) The contradiction among the imperialist powers is deepened, and the struggle for the source of high profits of the monopoly among them is more acute.

The basic characteristics of the general crisis of capitalism are: 1) after the victory of the Great October Socialist Revolution, the world is divided into two opposing systems – the thriving socialist system and the decadent capitalist system. The world is divided into two systems, the coexistence, interaction; competition and struggle of the two systems are the decisive sign of the general crisis of capitalism, as well as the main content of the whole of human history after the Great October Socialist Revolution. 2) The crisis in the imperialist colonial system. 3) The sales market for commodities produced by capitalism is shrinking. 4) Capitalist enterprises are running under their production capacity. 5) The industrial reserve army becomes the regular large number unemployed troops.[26]

269

In addition to changing the angle of the presentation of the essence of the general crisis of capitalism, the other parts are almost repetition of the corresponding part in *Political Economy, Textbook*. If there is any development, it lists more new arguments for the relevant points.

Jürgen Kuczynski also accepted the view by Stalin, and at the same time he put forward some evidences. He pointed out that: after the crisis in 1921-1922, there were still significant production upsurges in many countries, which in the 1920s had brought very serious unemployment everywhere. After the crisis in 1929-1933, there were only some insignificant improvements of the production in many countries, so that the previous upsurge stage needs to be called special depression stage.

After World War II, with the rapid development of the state monopoly capitalism and the adoption of a series of improvement measures, the premise for the formation and development of the general crisis of capitalism – various conflicts under the capitalist conditions have been greatly eased. At the same time, the characteristics of the general crisis of capitalism gradually disappeared:

25 M.S. Dragilev, *The General Crisis of Capitalism*, Shanghai: Shanghai People's Publishing House. 1958, p.10.
26 Ibid.

the capitalist world has experienced decades of rapid economic development and prosperity, and the original "thriving" socialist system has disintegrated; neo-colonial system replaced the old colonial system; new international trade relations greatly increased the degree of free trade, so that the commodity sales market continues to expand; although enterprise running under their production capacity and industrial reserve army is still there, because of the establishment of the social security system and the implementation of the social welfare policy, the contradictions between labour and capital is greatly eased, and the living conditions of ordinary people has been greatly improved.

With the change in preconditions and characteristics of the general crisis of capitalism, the general crisis theory is also increasingly losing its foothold. In the early 1980s, the general crisis theory has been completely removed from the political economy textbooks. Moreover, some Chinese scholars also questioned if there is the capitalist economic crisis in the traditional sense. The following two paragraphs have certain significance:

"The world economic panic occurred in 1929-1932, followed by World War II, then Stalin stressed the general crisis of capitalism, it seemed that the capitalist economy is precarious, waiting for the impending doom. Yet half a century later, the fluctuation of capitalist business cycle, though more frequent, is relatively small, with the overall trend to be still slowly rising, let alone the crisis. Even on 'Black Monday 'in October 1987, securities prices in New York fell even lower than that in 1929; On 'Black Friday' in October 1989, there was once again slump in securities prices; neither of them had much impact on business, and the world economy was still running, equal to only having two nightmares. For crisis theory, these are the two most thought-provoking events." … "The characteristics of Western economic fluctuations since 1929 is that, in addition to that the cycle is much shorter, the vast majority of its recession rate is only a few percentage points, and only a very few is just over 10 percent, while the growth rate of the economy rise in years it is only three or four percentage points on average, but more than enough to offset the losses of the recession years. How can we call it the crisis? In the early and middle 19th century, people were not very familiar with or understood the cyclical fluctuations in the economy, and the recession rate of each fluctuation was often double-digit, so people paid more attention to the crisis and neglected the cycle, which is not surprising at all. The fluctuation of the modern cycle is not only short in time, but its rate of decline is generally only three or four percentage points, and if we still call it the crisis by using habit in the 19th century, it is not necessary. If we must study economic fluctuations of the modern capitalism, it is also closer to reality to call it the cycle theory rather than the crisis theory."[27]

To what extent is Mr. Hu Jichuang's questioning reasonable, the practice will further confirm it, although there are many who agree with him.

---

27   Hu Jichuang, *The Analysis of Differences in Political Economy*, Shanghai: Fudan University Press, 1991, p. 216.

VII. Conclusions

In the long debate on the breakdown theory and the modification theory, it forms the capitalist breakdown model and modification model. The basic logic structure of these two models is: Under the capitalist conditions, the degree of socialization of production is increasing, while the means of production is increasingly concentrated in the hands of a few, the basic contradiction of capitalism constituted by which is increasingly intensified, and the result is that it is bound to be manifested by the growing cyclical overproduction crisis. The cyclical economic crisis makes the contradictions of capitalism increasingly acute, and the capitalist system is unable to mitigate these conflicts, resulting in that after being hit by a series of the increasingly serious economic crises, the capitalist system finally failed to catch its breath in a crisis, and then broken down toward its opposite. The modification model added counterproductive factors in the logical structure of the breakdown model – decentralization of capital, monopolies, state intervention in the economy, etc., trying to prove that the capitalist system can escape the fate of breakdown by proving the modification of the basic contradictions. Whether it is the modification model or the breakdown model, it had far-reaching effects in the Marxist economists and even in the history of the international communist movement, but relatively speaking, before the 1970s the breakdown model was clearly in dominance, then after the 1970s the modification model got an advantage. Although there are many uncertain factors, the general trend is for sure, and that is that the two models will alternately prevail in the future development of history.

CHAPTER VIII

Tugan-Baranovsky's Three-Department Structure Model

I. Introduction

In the history of economics, Tugan-Baranovsky is a very controversial figure that, the Marxist economics camp called him the bourgeois economist, and the bourgeois economics camp called him the Marxist economist, because his theory was wandering between the two types of economic theory, especially when he used the principle of Marxist economics, he came to the same conclusion with bourgeois economics, for which he was accepted by the bourgeois economics. The orthodox Marxist economics camp criticized him to be a "complete eclectic", saying that he was "upholding a little bit of Marxism, a little bit of narodnik, and a little bit of 'marginal utility theory'".[1] "…And tried to be Marxists in 1899. Now they have all safely turned from "critics of Marx" into plain bourgeois economists."[2] As an economist, Tugan is one of those interested in academic discussion, and he made many spectacular views, which is an accepted fact. Like almost all economists in that era, Tugan had given high attention to "cyclical industrial crises", and he is one of the earlier

---

1   See Tugan-Baranovsky, *Cyclical Industrial Crises*, Publishing Instructions, Beijing: Commercial Press, 198, p. 3.

2   *Lenin Selected Works*, 3rd edition, Volume 1, Beijing: People's Publishing House, 1995, p.172 footnote.

authors that studied and elaborated the industrial crises from the perspective of the unity of history, theory and reality. In 1894, he published a book titled "The Industrial Crises in Contemporary England, Their Reasons and Effects on Public Life" which was a special study of the capitalist industrial crisis, and when the third edition was published in 1914, he changed the title to "Cyclical Industry Crises". In the book, inspired by Quesnay Economic Table and Marx's "two-department model" of the reproduction of social capital, he proposed a "three-department model," and derived the conclusion that "as long as there is proper proportion of social production, regardless of how the production expands or the consumption demand reduces, the total amount of supply of products on the market will not exceed the demand". On this basis, he examined the capitalist economy, considering that the characteristics of antagonism, the trend of unlimited expansion of production, and the unorganized economy of the capitalist system had determined that it was unable to maintain the proper proportion of social production, or to avoid economic collapse. It seems to Tugan that the root of the capitalist economic crisis is the poverty of the people, is the low level of consumption of the working class. In order to accumulate capital, capitalists always grab the maximum of surplus products. The smaller the share workers get, the greater the share capitalists have, and the faster the accumulation of capital will be, which would inevitably lead to shocks and crises.

Tugan's model was built on the basis of his intensive study of the history of the crisis. He carefully examined the developing details of the cyclical industrial crisis in England since the Industrial Revolution till the early 20th century, particularly those factors driving the economy into crisis, as well as their role in the crisis, changing trend, action mechanism, etc.. Of course, what is the most important thing is that he inspected the law, manifestation, and signs when the crisis occurs. Such work provides both a historical basis for the establishment of the model, and also determines the basic elements for the establishment of the model. The investigation of the real impact of the crisis is the real test of the model. His research achievements *Cyclical Industrial Crises* is also of the structure of trinity, namely, the history of the crisis in England, the economic crisis theory, and the social impact of the economic crisis, which was widely applauded by many theoretical writers of the economic crisis in the late 19th century and early 20th century. This structure explains an economic phenomenon, but it has different focuses, while the tasks done are different. In all, that is, it elaborated the capitalist economic crisis from three aspects of theory, history and reality. The study of the history of the cyclical industrial crisis can reveal the law of its occurrence through the detailed study of the details, symptoms, and factors in the process of crisis. The study of theory is to have systematic generalizations of the occurrence mechanism and the nature of the crisis. The study of the practical impact of the crisis is to assess its historical position, as well as its relationship with changes in the social system. Since history is the basis for the birth of the theory, a longitudinal theory; theory is a generalization of historical trends, a horizontal theory; the practical impact is the continuation of historical development, a test of the development of the theory. The unity of the three perspectives forms a comprehensive examination of the crisis, and compared with the dual perspective structure of the unity of theory and practice, it has obvious advantages, with a strong discourse effect. Of course, this is in terms of the structure of the analysis, and in the application of specific analytical tools, case and proof method is more typical. The strength of studying the history of the crisis is to find the phenomenon manifested in every crisis, to find regularities through comparison and analysis of these phenomena, and to reveal the real reason or the direct cause that lead to the crisis. However, in the process of understanding the crisis, only this is not enough but has to go deeper, and it needs to rise to up to the height of the theoretical understanding from the representation of understanding, achieving the object of understanding the nature, and then to return the understanding process to the real world. Tugan constructed the theoretical system in accordance with this method, which met the requirements of the thinking process, and thus it is self-evidently scientific. Compared with the method of Marxist economics, there are similarities on the fundamentals, which are influenced by the methodology of Marxist economics system. In addition, Tugan also used statistics, charts and graphs to describe changes in crisis. Statistical indicators used are the value of exports in England, the price of iron in England, metal reserve in Bank of England, and the number of corporate bankruptcies in England from 1823 to 1850. The graph shows that: the curve of export price and the curve of iron price fluctuated towards the same direction, while the curve of the number of corporate bankruptcies and the curve of the metal reserve in Bank of England fluctuated towards the opposite direction.[3] This fluctuation is the most evident one during the crisis.

In a very long time, the orthodox Marxist economists believe that the assertion by Tugan is anti-Marxist, because he not only said publicly that Marx did not complete his theory of reproduction, but also claimed that he has been transferred to the ranks of maintaining capitalism while destroying socialism. With the development of history, Tugan's assertion seems to have a more and more realistic basis, and the camp of Marxist economists has gradually been changing views on Tugan. They begin to re-examine Tugan's theoretical model, to figure out whether Tugan's theory negates the conclusion drawn by Marxist theory of reproduction, or develops it.

II. Core Issues of the Economic Crisis

The historical analysis of the capitalist economic crisis is a relatively boring thing, which Tugan had experienced himself. The reason is that every crisis has unique characteristics, because it is "as any historical event happening in a particular historical context... to point out that the direct cause of the crisis in the interpretation of the crisis"[4]... a relatively easy thing to do, and it also lies in

---

3   See Tugan-Baranovsky, *Cyclical Industrial Crises*, p. 37.
4   Tugan-Baranovsky, *Cyclical Industrial Crises*, p. 181.

those features common to previous crises, because these points are very similar. Because of these characteristics, each time when describing the process of each crisis, the words spoken on other crises will inevitably be repeated with almost no change at all. The explanation by Tugan is that on the one hand it describes how monotonous the described work is, and on the other hand it also shows the regularity of the capitalist economic crisis. It suggests that the crisis depends not only on accidental factors specific in a certain historical period, but also on the common factor inherent in modern civilization and economic system that often plays a role. To this end, Tugan stressed that in order to have a comprehensive interpretation of the modern industrial crisis; the task should never be completed if we only explain the cause of each crisis. We also need to clarify "the common factor rooted in the modern national economy that organizes, so that each industrial crisis is so similar and the commercial slump repeats itself and arrives on time."[5]

Therefore, what is the common factor? Tugan thinks it is a problem of sales or a problem of market of the capitalist product. To illustrate his view to be scientific, Tugan transformed Marx's formula on industrial capital cycle, and concluded after the transformation that: the sale of commodities is the most difficult part of the capitalist economy. Market is the main factor determining the whole capitalist economy, while the inadequate market that capitalist production often feels is the resilient bond that hinders the development of production.[6] In the capitalist market economy, it is the market that determines production, rather than the production determining the market. This conclusion is in line with Marx's original intent, and when he was elaborating the process of the industrial capital cycle, Marx also pointed out that in the stage of sales, the commodity will go through "the salto mortale", and whether it could make it or not, it is related to whether the capitalist is able to recover the prepaid capital and the surplus value, and thus it is related to whether the capital circulation as well as the fate of capitalists can run normally.

The importance of the market on production makes it become a focus of study on the economics. Studying the economic crisis must involve market issues, and Tugan saw it from the movement of capital. When his study went into this area, he did not forget the controversy surrounding this issue in the history of economics. Of course, the first to enter his field of vision is undoubtedly Say, whom he thought to be the worst political economy theorist that "the confusion and muddled logic is unimaginable" in "Say's Law".[7] In denying Say's Law, he also negates points of views of Ricardo, Mill and et al. who endorsed Say's Law, as well as the opponents of these people, such as Malthus, Sismondi, Chalmers and et al., thinking that their rebuttal is not convincing but some contradictory misunderstanding. When he made the critiques all way up to Engels, Tugan found basis for his theory. He found the topic that is in

5   Ibid., p.182.

6   Ibid., p.185.

7   Ibid., p.190.

favour of support for his views in a speech at Elberfeld by Engels titled *The English Ten Hours' Bill*. This passage describes the focus and its outcome of the competition between Germany and England. In order to avoid the fate of being defeated by England, Germany must implement the policy of high tariffs, which will cause the rapid development of the domestic industries. The rapidly growing industrial products will not be accommodated in the domestic market, so they have to find foreign markets, which in turn are bound to cause a deadly struggle between the German industry and the English industry. The struggle between the two can only have one outcome, and that is, the weakest one is to collapse, followed by a social revolution. If the collapse of capitalism occurs in one country, it is also bound to collapse in the remaining countries.[8]

Tugan believes the reason that Marx and Engels asserted the capitalism would break down inevitably is because the capitalist industrial products lack market. He illustrates the problem with the famous words in *Capital* Volume III on to, namely "[t]he conditions of direct exploitation, and those of realising it, are not identical. They diverge not only in place and time, but also logically. The first are only limited by the productive power of society, the latter by the proportional relation of the various branches of production and the consumer power of society. But this last one is not determined either by the absolute productive power, or by the absolute consumer power, but by the consumer power based on antagonistic conditions of distribution which reduce the consumption of the bulk of society to a minimum varying within more or less narrow limits. It is furthermore restricted by the tendency to accumulate, the drive to expand capital and produce surplus-value on an extended scale. ... This internal contradiction seeks to resolve itself through expansion of the outlying field of production. But the more productiveness develops, the more it finds itself at variance with the narrow basis on which the conditions of consumption rest. It is no contradiction at all on this self-contradictory basis that there should be an excess of capital simultaneously with a growing surplus of population. ... The real barrier of capitalist production is capital itself. ... that production is only production for capital and not vice versa, the means of production are not mere means for a constant expansion of the living process of the society of producers. ... The means—unconditional development of the productive forces of society—comes continually into conflict with the limited purpose, the self-expansion of the existing capital."[9] However, Tugan's perspective is opposed to this passage, although he did not directly refute this statement. It is in fact the key point that Tugan criticized, and he achieved the goal by criticizing people who agreed with this view.

277

Why should Marxists adhere to the view that the capitalist economic crisis is inevitable? Tugan believes that the key is that they recognize the problem from the following basis: "The market capacity of capitalism depends on the social consumption. If the production of products increases faster, there will be a part

8   Ibid., p. 208.
9   Ibid., p. 211.

of products that cannot be sold and a part of capital would be idle. Thus, the general overproduction of commodities occurs. Capitalism is bound to make this phenomenon of overproduction increasingly unable to be broken away, because social spending increases quite slowly under the capitalist economy, while production has grown quite fast. If this continues, someday the general overproduction of commodities will become a recurrent phenomenon, so the capitalist system will break down because the industrial products of capitalism cannot continue to be sold."[10] The above basis is precisely wrong. Because the view of Kautsky, Kunov, and et al. is also on this basis, that is they consider the root of the capitalist economic crisis lies in that the market cannot expand with the expansion of production, so they naturally became the object for criticism by Tugan. Anyway, those points of views that the capitalist production must be consistent with the demand, that consumer demand is the limit of the market, and that the market is the limit of the capitalist production resolutely opposed by Tugan.

III. Basic Structure and Theoretical Value of Realization Model of the Reproduction of Social Capital by Tugan

With the historical analysis, and the investigation of the history of doctrine itself Tugan drew the conclusion that the key for the capitalist economy to run smoothly lies in the market, and after that, the perspective was turning into the analysis of the abstract theory. Previously, he has clearly realized that: in order to solve the difficult market issues satisfactorily, one must first analyze the process of accumulation of social capital as a whole. However, when considering what means and what theories to use to analyze the problem, Tugan first thought about Quesnay's "Economic Table." He admired that "Quesnay regarded the social economy as a whole where commodities are transferring within his scope, and the part of the social products is engulfed in the process of consumption and production is recovered within its scope." Meanwhile, he also realized the importance of Marx's scheme of the reproduction of social capital for studying. He reminded himself, "only by using this method of Quesnay and Marx – the method to examine the social economy as a whole, can we scientifically analyze the process of capital accumulation and clarify the law of sales of social products."[11] However, he was not satisfied with Quesnay or the achievements by those who wanted to follow Quesnay's path and those who used his method to study the national economy for the past century and over. This also includes Marx's theory on distribution and accumulation of social capital, as well as on the sale of social products.

"Marx's analysis did not finish, and he did not use it to make any general conclusions. His scheme of writings was not completed in logic, and it seems

---

10   Ibid., p. 211.
11   Ibid., p. 217.

to have become a completely superfluous thing in thorough Marxism. It should draw a logical conclusion that Marx did not mention, which is apparently incompatible with the views Marx held when he had never listed these schemes, so no wonder that even school of Marxism unable to inherit their teacher's career, and so the market problem has not been resolved."[12]

Possibly he aimed to complete Marx's unfinished research, or perhaps he willed to transcend Marx's theory of reproduction of social capital, inspired by Marx's model of reproduction of social capital, Tugan established his own model. The assumptions and constituent elements of his model is basically the same as Marx's. For example, a society of only the capitalist class and the working class; rate of surplus value equal to 100%; production cycle of one year; a closed economy; the supply and demand of the social product being equal; etc. Tugan-did not explicitly mention these restrictive conditions, but the model is in fact subject to these constraints. He adopted the approach of Marx when modelling, but there are substantial differences between the actual model constructed and Marx's model, and the conclusion is true.

Conclusion I: Under the conditions that all surplus products are consumed, as long as the proportion of production is appropriate, the demand of all commodities is bound to be equal to the supply.

Conclusion I is based on:

The reproduction scheme of invariant scale of social capital:

Department I: the production of the means of production

$$720c+360p+360\pi=1,440$$

Department II: the production of workers' consumer goods

$$360c+180p+180\pi=720$$

Department III: the production of capitalists' consumer goods

$$360c+180p+180\pi=720$$

c is means of production, p wages, and π the surplus products. The organic composition of capital is 2:1; m' is 100%; the capitalists spend the entire surplus products on the consumption of personal life. If I, II and III are representing the productive sector of the means of production, the productive sector of workers' consumer goods and the productive sector of capitalists' consumer goods respectively, the realization conditions for reproduction of invariant scale of social capital extracted from the above scheme is:

$$I(p+\pi)=IIc+IIIc$$

$$II(c+p+\pi)=Ip+IIp+IIIp$$

$$III(c+p+\pi)=I\pi+II\pi+III\pi$$

12 Tugan-Baranovsky, *Cyclical Industrial Crises*, p. 211.

This set of realization conditions are substantially similar to the ones of the simple reproduction of social capital by Marx, and the only difference is that Tugan divided the sectors producing the means of subsistence into sectors producing workers' consumer goods and sectors producing capitalists' consumer goods. This division does not affect the investigation of the realization conditions, but is able to break down the correct realization conditions. In fact, Marx has made similar attempts, and in order to further investigate the internal realization issue of Department II, he further divided Department II into two sub-departments of IIa (necessary means of subsistence) and IIb (luxury means of subsistence). Products of IIa enter into the consumption of the working class, and also constitute part of the bourgeois consumption; Products of IIb only enter into the consumption of the bourgeois. Marx had a detailed description of the internal realization process of Department II. Social products are composed of three parts in the form of value, namely the value of the means of production, the value of labour, and the value of surplus products, which is also absorption of the findings by Marx. Therefore, in the realization issue of simple reproduction, Tugan's model is influenced by Marx's model, and the structure is clearly modelled on the structure of Marx's reproduction model. The reason that the realization process is not described in detail is also because Marx has done this work. Hence, from his simple reproduction realization model, Tugan has reached conclusions of high credibility. However, the three-department model is no better than the two-department model, but shows a more complicated character. The division of consumer goods and their production sectors lacks an objective basis, because it cannot determine the strict limit between capitalists' consumer goods and workers' consumer goods, and there is a cross-section between them. This extra division increases the difficulty of investigating the realization process. There are obvious omissions in the design of model itself.

Conclusion II: 1) The capitalist production will open up the market for itself. As long as there is enough productivity to expand production, and as long as the proportion of social production is arranged properly, demand can be expanded accordingly. The reason is that under such conditions, 2) the expansion in social production and the reduction in social spending will not cause an imbalance between social supply and social demand at all. 3) As long as the proportion of social production is appropriate, no matter how consumer demand is reduced, the total product supply in the market will not exceed the demand. Each piece of the newly produced goods is an emerging purchasing power, which can buy other commodities.

Conclusion II is based on:

The reproduction (capital accumulation) scheme of the expansion in scale of social capital:

In the first year:

Department I: the production of the means of production

$$840c+420p+420\pi=1,680$$

Department II: the production of workers' consumer goods

$$420c+210p+210\pi=840$$

Department III: the production of capitalists' consumer goods

$$180c+90p+90\pi=360$$

In the second year:

Department I: the production of the means of production

$$980c+490p+490\pi=1,960$$

Department II: the production of workers' consumer goods

$$490c+245p+245\pi=980$$

Department III: the production of capitalists' consumer goods

$$210c+105p+105\pi=420$$

In the third year:

Department I: the production of the means of production

$$1,143_{1/3}c+571_{2/3}p+571_{2/3}\pi=2,286_{2/3}$$

Department II: the production of workers' consumer goods

$$571_{2/3}c+285_{5/6}p+285_{5/6}\pi=1,143_{2/3}$$

Department III: the production of capitalists' consumer goods

$$245c+122_{1/2}p + 122_{1/2}\pi =490$$

c is means of production, p wages, π the surplus products, π/x the part of surplus products used for the personal life consumption of capitalists, and Y years. Obviously, the model sets: 1) the capitalists spend half of the surplus products for personal life consumption. 2) The ratio of the means of production, wages and profits in various sectors is 2:1:1, and stretches according to the same ratio.

If I, II and III are representing the productive sector of the means of production, the productive sector of workers' consumer goods and the productive sector of capitalists' consumer goods respectively, the realization conditions for reproduction of expansion in scale of social capital can be extracted from the above scheme, so as to analyze the internal composition of the scheme.

(1) $Y_n I (c+p+\pi) = Y_{n+1} I (Ic+IIc+IIIc)$ (n=1, 2, 3, ...)

(2) $Y_n II (c+p+\pi) = Y_{n+1} I (Ip+IIp+IIIp)$ (n=1, 2, 3, ...)

(3) $Y_n III (c+p+\pi) = Y_{n+1} I (I\pi/x+II\pi/x+III\pi/x)$ (n=1, 2, 3, ...)

In order to prove the correctness through the model that production opens up new markets for itself, Tugan intentionally sets up a model in which all products of the previous year are realized in the next year. That is, products of the physical form produced in the first year are the object of production and consumption in the second year; the product value in the first year is the purchasing power of production and consumption in the second year. However, the model only reflects that the value of the means of production in the following year is equal to that produced in the previous year, as well as wages in the next year are equal to workers' consumer goods produced in the previous year. It does not reflect that the profit for the capitalists to use for personal consumption in the next year is equal to capitalists' consumer goods produced in the previous year, but sets that the profit for the capitalists to use for personal consumption in the same year is equal to capitalists' consumer goods produced in the same year. This is inconsistent with his setting that "all products in the previous year are achieved in the next year". Different from Tugan's model, the realization condition of Marx's model of expanded reproduction is: the means of production produced in the same years is equal to the sum of the demand of the two departments for the means of production; the means of subsistence produced in the same years is equal to the sum of the demand of both workers and capitalists for the means of subsistence. Some dispute Tugan's model based on the differences between the two, which is quite reasonable.

The product of the previous year is realized in the next year, the extent of realization depends on the development of production in the next year. The more of production expansion, the more the means of production and the means of subsistence is needed to buy, and as long as there is enough productivity to expand production, the demand can be expanded accordingly; as long as the proportion of social production is arranged properly, the supply and demand for social products will remain balanced. It seems logical to draw the above conclusions through the deduction of the model.

Conclusion III: Even if there is a large decline in wages, sales of social products will not encounter any difficulty.

Inference: 1) There is not a risk for the capitalist economy to break down even under the condition that the national consumption reduces definitely and significantly. 2) Under the condition of arranging social production proportionately, regardless of how much consumer demand reduces, the total product supply will not exceed the total product demand on the market. 3) While the social wealth increases, the social income reduces, and social of supply and demand will remain balanced.

Conclusions and inferences are based on the following:

The reproduction (capital accumulation) scheme of the expansion in scale of social capital during the time of falling wages and capitalists' static consumption:

In the first year:

Department I: the production of the means of production

$$1,632c+544p+544\pi=2,720$$

Department II: the production of workers' consumer goods

$$408c+136p+136\pi=680$$

Department III: the production of capitalists' consumer goods

$$360c+120p+120\pi=600$$

In the second year:

Department I: the production of the means of production

$$1,987.4c+496.8p+828.1\pi=3,312.3$$

Department II: the production of workers' consumer goods

$$372.6c+93.2p+155.2\pi=621$$

Department III: the production of capitalists' consumer goods

$$360c+90p+150\pi=600$$

In the third year:

Department I: the production of the means of production

$$2,585.4c+484.6p+1,239\pi=4,309$$

Department II: the production of workers' consumer goods

$$366.9c+68.9p+175.5\pi=611.3$$

Department III: the production of capitalists' consumer goods

$$360c+67.5p+172.5\pi=600$$

c refers to the means of production, p wages, and π the surplus product. The author has made a description of the assumptions of the model in the footnote: In the first year, the means of production of various sectors of social production is twice larger than the value of wages, and profits and the value of wages are equal. From the second year, these two proportions have changed, where wages fall by %25 and profits increases correspondingly in the number. The total value of Department III remains unchanged. However, there is an important assumption with no explanation by the author, but is implicated in the model, which is under the conditions of technical change, the realization issue of reproduction of social capital. In addition, Tugan did not explain though, the scheme is clearly designed to test the correctness and universal applicability of the "scheme of invariant scale of reproduction" and the "scheme of expanded reproduction". By this argumentation, it is natural to come to the same conclusion once again from the model. But Tugan has taken a contrary path, on which he first has the conclusion before constructing the model, and by doing so he needs to cater to the model statistically, as well as to cater to the conclusions in the structure of the model. For example, he gave up the previous design of the "reproduction (capital accumulation) scheme of the expansion in scale of social capital", which to some extent is related to this. Originally, Tugan has long had a correct understanding of the changing trends of the capital structure under conditions of technological progress, that is, "as technology advances, workers are more and more replaced by the means of production, namely the machine in the production process. In an investment, the proportion of funds spent on wages is smaller and smaller, while the proportion of funds used in production is growing greater and greater".[13] However, in the model, he set that on the one hand there is a rising trend in the organic composition of capital, and on the other hand he also sets that there is a rising trend in the rate of profit (the three-year rate of profit in Department I is 25%, 33%, 40%), which is contradictory to the law of the tendency of the rate of profit to fall. The above defects of the model reduce the reliability of the conclusion to some extent. Tugan repeated that Marx's did not finish the investigation of the reproduction of social capital, and it means that he finished the job. If comparing Tugan's model with Marx's model, we will immediately find that the part which is beyond Marx's model is focused in here, that is, he examined the realization issue of social products under the conditions of the technological progress.

From the perspective of the realization condition of expanded reproduction, the scheme satisfies the conditions 1) and 2), namely:

(1) $Y_n I (c + p + \pi) = Y_{n+1} I (Ic + IIc + IIIc)$ $(n = 1, 2, 3, ...)$

(2) $Y_n II (c + p + \pi) = Y_{n+1} I (Ip + IIp + IIIp)$ $(n = 1, 2, 3, ...)$

However, it appears to be that the condition 3) cannot be satisfied, that is, except in the first year $Y_n III (c + p + \pi) = Y_{n+1} I (I\pi/x + II\pi/x + III\pi/x)$ $(n = 1, 2, 3, ...)$, from the second year, it is $Y_n III (c + p + \pi) < Y_{n+1} I (I\pi/x + II\pi/x + III\pi/x)$ $(n = 1, 2, 3, ...)$, and as for the difference, how to realize the value compensation and physical renewal, the scheme does not reflect it. As for how the additional capital comes from and where the reduction part goes, it is unknown. These facts explain in a way that that is an imaginary scheme suspected to be fabricated. Kautsky called it "unbridled absurd argument"[14], adding that: "Tugan's scheme proves that only when capital is turning from simple reproduction to expanded production, the reduction in consumption does not cause the crisis. Tugan regards this unique situation as the typicality of the reality of capitalism,

---

13   Tugan-Baranovsky, *Periodic Industrial Crises*, p. 225.
14   Ibid., p. 231.

but in fact, this situation probably will never appear."[15] Tugan argued that "the unique situation and which probably will never appear, as Kautsky called, is the general rule of the development of capitalism"[16].

In addition to the realization issue of social products under the conditions of falling wages and capitalists' static consumption, Tugan also inspected the realization issue of social products under conditions of continuous improvement in the organic composition of capital. He realized that the proportion of social products used for national consumption was increasingly smaller, while the part used for the production and consumption was increasing. There is a tendency that in a capitalist economy, because of technological progress while neglecting social consumption, the human consumption is relatively replaced by the productive consumption of the means of production. Will this trend happen to the surplus products that cannot find sales in the current market? Tugan thinks that this cannot happen. This is because, even if the working class is gone, it will not make the sale of capitalist industrial products any difficult. Capitalists will dominate a large number of consumer goods, so the total social products of a year will be swallowed up by the production and capitalists' consumption for the next year. Even capitalists seek to accumulate, and even they also want to reduce their spending, it is entirely feasible; then the production of capitalists' consumer goods will be reduced, and the means of production used for the continued expanded production will account for a larger portion of social products.

285

In order to find more evidence to conclusions, Tugan also repeatedly turned to the substance of capitalist production. He pointed out that in contrast to the production purpose under conditions of harmonious economy, in the capitalist economic system, "the principal of the economic cause is only part of people, and the rest is the economic object, so the direction of the economic process may be: The economy has turned from the means to meet the social demands to the means that neglects social consumption but to simply expand production." "There is a tendency that in a capitalist economy, because of technological progress while neglecting social consumption, the human consumption is relatively replaced by the productive consumption of the means of production". In a capitalist economy, it is not social spending that determines social production, but social production determines social spending, that is "it is not the capital for people, but the people for capital".[17] Tugan wanted to prove with these facts that: Even there are only capital and capitalists' consumption, capitalist production can also open up the market for itself, and there is no surplus products that cannot find the market, so the product can have unlimited development.

Since it can be drawn from the model and the essential relationship of the capitalist production that there is no problem of imbalance between production and demand in capitalism, or there would be never the risk of inadequate

15   Kautsky.Crisis Theory, in Die *Neue Zeit* (*The New Time*), 1902(4).
16   Tugan-Baranovsky, *Periodic Industrial Crises*, p. 228.
17   Ibid., pp.231-234.

market, but "why it is difficult for the capitalist enterprise to find a buyer for manufactures, and why the struggle for market has become a prominent feature of the capitalist economy."[18] Tugan raised such a question after drawing a series of conclusions from the model. It illustrates that what was built previously were some abstract models, and what was drawn were also some abstract conclusions. Some key factors on the capitalist mode of production have not been introduced into the model yet. As the theoretical explanations are becoming specific, the practical issues must have a reasonable explanation.

Here it is also the further and the most specific explanation made by Tugan. He believes that capitalism often feels the lack of market, which is not because there are too few consumers for the capitalist commodity, but because it will not work to arrange social production proportionately in the anarchy of capitalist production, and there is a great deal of trouble even it is close to the proportion of social production. This is the root of the difficult sales of products in the capitalist system. There is a huge capacity in the capitalist production, and it always strives to expand, but only under the conditions of right proportion of social production, these products can be sold out. Because of the anarchy of capitalist production, there is no way for it to arrange production proportionally, so as to maintain the proportion of social production. It plays role of a resilient bond in the capitalist economy, which often inhibits the capitalist production and prevents it from having full productivity. However, the resilient bond can only hinder but not halt the development of capitalism.

286

Hence, what is the root reason of the capitalist industrial crisis? Tugan excluded the following factors: 1) it is not caused by wheat, climate, or the cyclical and repeated reduction of output of other grains the nation produces. The explanation given for the reason of the crisis by W.S Jevons cannot be true. 2) Gold drain is a general sign of the industrial crisis rather than its reason. 3) The reason for cyclical industrial crises does not lie in fluctuations in the credit. Fluctuations in the credit are merely the reflection of more profound economic changes. 4) The reason the crisis does not lie in the underconsumption of a country, or in low wage levels. 5) Technical progress cannot be the reason of industrial crises. 6) The reason for the crisis to occur also does not lie in the shrinking of the proportion of the working class in the national product. 7) The reason for the crisis to occur also does not lie in the rampant speculation in the real estate sectors. The root reason of the capitalist industrial crisis lies in the anarchy and free competition of commodity production. With regard to the inevitability of capitalist economic crisis, Tugan believes that it is rooted in the three characteristics of the capitalist system: 1) Capitalism is an antagonistic economy, in which workers are the simple production tool of capitalist business leaders. 2) Different from other antagonistic economies, the capitalist economy has the trend of unlimited expansion of production. 3) The capitalist economy is an unorganized economy as a whole, in which all walks of life in social production lack planned arrangement. Sometimes Tugan also believes

18 Tugan-Baranovsky, *Periodic Industrial Crises*, p.235.

that the root of the capitalist economic crisis lies in the poverty of the people, and it is the low consumption level of the working class. In order to accumulate capital, capitalists always grab surplus products to the maximum. The smaller share workers get, the greater share capitalists have, the faster accumulation of capital is, and it would inevitably lead to shocks and crises.

As to why the capitalist economy is manifested in cycle? The realization mechanism Tugan described is: When the economy enters the period recession, due to lower prices which lead to the reduction in spending, there is an increasing trend in the "savings" of the rentiers and people with fixed income. The result that there are growing number of idle loan capitals in the financial markets. These capitals are accumulating, trying to find a way out but could not. On the one hand the industry refuses to accept the new capital; on the other hand the capital is crowding inside, and in the last the idle moneyed capital is piled up, so that the resistance of industry is overcome, which lead to the situation that the capital infiltrates into the industry and finds a way out, so the industrial upsurge period begins. During the period of upsurge, it creates a country's new fixed capital, and the demand for iron, machinery, tools, ships, construction materials and so on is increasing, the production related to which accelerates development. When the originally accumulated idle loan capital is exhausted, the expansion of fixed capital also comes to an end. With factories built and railways laid, the demand for all equipment used for manufacturing fixed capital is significantly reduced. Thus, the production gradually goes to disproportionality: the demand for machines, tools, iron, brick, and wood is less than before, because the newly established enterprises are less. Since the producer of the means of production cannot draw capital from his own business, and this capital is extremely large (such as buildings, machinery, etc.) so that the production must continue, resulting in the overproduction of production. As various industrial sectors are interrelated, local overproduction becomes a widespread general overproduction, and the price of commodities generally declines. The widespread slump appears. This phenomenon repeats itself periodically, and it is the cyclical capitalist industrial crisis.

Tugan-Baranovsky based his crisis analysis on the credit disorder or credit policies of the banking system and concluded: as long as there is an appropriate banking system and appropriate credit policy the crisis could be avoided.

Tugan-Baranovsky asserted that: The lack of capital is the reason of world crisis. In fact, in times of crisis, "… there is always a lot capital that cannot be converted into money." Capitalists have too many merchandise, but they cannot turn them into cash. The reason to have a serious difficulty is not the exhaustion of monetary funds, but the disruption of sales process is, the whole process of social reproduction tending towards chaos. When the crisis is particularly aggravated, it is the pursuit of cash, that is, the pursuit of money rather than the pursuit of additional capital. In depression, there is a lot of idle moneyed capital, and the production remains at a low level. At this time it clearly shows, in particular that, the argument that the lack of capital is the reason of the crisis is absurd. During this period, there is a lot of moneyed capital, which in itself is the result of the contraction of the reproduction process, part of the liquidity being idle, the stagnation of fixed capital due to compensation so that the depreciation fund increases. If in the overall conditions of reproduction and accumulation, there is no premise of upsurge, then no matter how much the monetary funds are or how large the expansion of credit is, it cannot cause industrial upsurge.

In addition to *Periodic Industrial Crises*, Tugan further elaborated his own point of view in a series of writings. From his illustration in the book *Theoretical Foundations of Marxism* published in 1905 and *Principles of Political Economy* published in 1909, we see that he was still taking all the trouble publicizing his views, and behaved more mature and refined than ever before.

"If all workers except one disappear and are replaced by machines, then this one single worker will place the whole enormous mass of machinery in motion and with its assistance produce new machines – and the consumption goods of the capitalists. The working class will disappear, which will not in the least disturb the self-expansion process of capital. The capitalists will receive no smaller mass of consumption goods; the entire product of one year will be realized and utilized by the production and consumption of the capitalists in the following year. Even if the capitalists desire to limit their own consumption, no difficulty is presented; in this case the production of capitalists' consumption goods partially ceases, and an even larger part of the social product consists of means of production, which serve the purpose of further expanding production. For example, iron and coal are produced which serve always to expand the production of iron and coal. The expanded production of iron and coal of each succeeding year uses up the increased mass of products turned out in the preceding year, until the supply of necessary minerals is exhausted."[19]

Not only that, he is still convinced of his theory to be the truth. "As truth naturally I do not mean the wholly arbitrary and unreal assumption that the replacement of manual labour by machinery leads to an absolute diminution in the number of workers (this hypothesis has only served to show that my theory, even if driven to the limit of unreality, does not break down), but rather the thesis that, given a proportional distribution of social production, no decline in social consumption is capable of producing a superfluous product."[20]

Marx concluded from his model that as long as the two departments can maintain the proportion, the aggregate social product is able to be successfully achieved, so social production can be carried out smoothly. Tugan concluded from his model that as long as the society can arrange social production proportionately, the supply and demand of production will not be imbalanced, and

19 Tugan-Baranovsky, *Theoretical Foundations of Marxism*, p. 230; Quoted by Sweezy, *Theory of Capitalist Development*, Beijing: Commercial Press, 1997, p. 188.
20 Ibid., p. 189.

there will be no surplus products that cannot find sales. Obviously it is just a different way of expression between the two. Marx attributed social production not to be able to run smoothly to the destruction of proportion of social production, and attributed the destruction of proportion to the basic contradiction of capitalism, to the contradiction between the organization of production of individual enterprises and the anarchy of production in the whole society, as well as the contradiction between the infinite widening trend of production and the reduced purchasing power of working people. Tugan attributed the capitalist economic crisis to that capitalism which is not able to arrange social production proportionately, attributed not to be able to arrange social production proportionately to the anarchy of capitalist production, attributed the anarchy of capitalist production to the social system of capitalist antagonism, that is, in the economic life, workers are the simple production tool of capitalist business leaders, and the purpose of production is for the production of capital, rather than for consumption. Marx attributed the cyclical outbreak of the economic crisis to the cyclical intensification of the basic contradiction, and considered that the renewal of fixed capital is the material basis for the economic crisis to occur periodically. Tugan attributed the cyclical outbreak of the economic crisis to the cyclical excessive investment. The final difference between the two shows that Tugan's crisis theory is different than Marx's. Because of this, in the history of the Western crisis theories, Tugan is known as one of the representatives of the "over-investment" school.

IV. Examination with Historical Facts

With different attitudes towards history, different theoretical guidance, different world outlook, and etc., the history in books is also different. Writing the history of the economic crisis, Tugan is different than his contemporaries as well as people before him. The investigation of the history of the crisis by Tugan is mainly focused on the evolution of the crisis elements, the signs and the consequences before the crisis, and he was more concerned with the regularity of occurrence and evolution of the crisis. This can be seen from his description of the history of every crisis. Since his motive and purpose to examine the history of crisis is to provide basis for modelling, therefore, import and export value, supply and demand in capital market, quotations from the exchange market, price changes, changes in metal reserves of the Bank of England, the outflow and inflow of gold are some of the important aspects that Tugan studied the history of crisis.

In the process of studying the economic history, Tugan found crises before the cyclical crisis were similar to the cyclical crisis in many respects, but there is a significant difference in one aspect, that is these crises are triggered by some special cases, mostly political events, without any regularity, with the time interval being very long. Tugan calls such crises the one "caused by external political factors", and called the cyclical crisis the one caused by internal factors. This distinction is to prove that: the cyclical industrial crisis is "organically linked with the industrial and commercial development" and the study of the economic crisis should be carried out through the study of commerce and industry.

Tugan realized that the economic fluctuations in 1825 and after appeared regularly, but brought confusions to the bourgeois economists, they could not see reasons directly from the phenomenon. For example, the British Parliament has set up a special committee to specifically investigate the reasons for the crisis. The Committee asked dozens of people of the financiers, bankers, businessmen and others, just to get some of the reasons in the form of the phenomenon. In a wide-ranging debate during the period, two famous factions were formed: one is the monetarism represented by Owlstone, Robert Torrens and et al., who think that the reason for economic fluctuations lies in the flawed currency circulation system; The other one is the Non-monetarism represented by Thomas Tooke, John Fullarton and et al., who believe that economic fluctuations and the currency circulation system are irrelevant. They tried to find the reason for economic fluctuations from a certain variable of the economy. Tugan saw the complexity in the reasons of economic fluctuations, and recognized that a single means could not give it a full explanation, so he had a wide range in studying the economic crisis.

The first one is the understanding of the phenomenon. With the upsurge of industry and commerce, exports increased, iron prices soared, metal reserves in the Bank of England declined rapidly, and gold stocks was almost swept away by the end of 1825. Then it came with a turning point, where credit began turmoil, financial crisis occurred, corporate bankruptcies increased significantly, exports reduced, iron prices fell and industrial crisis broke out. Soon, precious metal inventory in the Bank of England began to increase after the industrial crisis, followed by a fairly long period of business recession. Some phenomena in the process of the 1825 crisis in England have a typical significance in understanding the cyclical industrial crisis. The phenomena presented in 1836 and 1847 crises were almost the same of the 1825 crisis. So, Tugan's investigation of the history of the crisis has been firmly grasping and holding these clues, and found some regularity. From the perspective of method, it is reasonable without any doubt, because doing this kind of work is the basic part to study the economic fluctuations.

Understanding of economic phenomena and looking for changes in its regularity is to determine the business climate. To determine the business climate, it can first select changes in the amount of private loans of the bank as well as changes in the amount of the bank's gold reserves. The reduction in bank loans and the increase in reserves indicate a business downturn. The most prominent feature during the business downturn is that the loan market is flooded with capital, which cannot find a favourable place to invest in the country. Is it reliable to make judgment according to these phenomena? Tugan examined it with the historical facts of the 1825 crisis and several crises ever after. Among them, the evidence that the 1825 crisis provided is: Before the crisis, it is first

England where hot money was flooding, and could not find a better place for investment in the country. Later, with the opening up of new markets in South America, where there was a lot of money exporting, it stimulated England to have extreme debt speculation. Meanwhile, the production expanded rapidly, imports and exports increased significantly, the credit began to expand, commodity prices increased significantly, gold flew out massively, and metal reserves in the bank decreased. Then it came with a turning point, where the demand for commodities decreased suddenly, the exports decline sharply, speculators and businesses began to be bankrupt, followed by the credit crisis, the stock price slump, bank failures and the outbreak of industrial crises. The evidence that the1836 crisis provided is: England had agricultural harvest for several years from the 1833 onwards, causing the decline in agricultural prices and the increase in industrial consumption. Meanwhile, the United States raised a loan from England for the construction of railways and canals, so many shares of stock companies were being marketed in England, and as a result, large number of capital was pouring into the United States, which led to the establishment of a large number of new industrial enterprises. Some of the inflow capital entered the exchange market, fuelling speculation of various securities, and the flooded hot money led to the establishment of many new banks. The ample supply of capital, the booming industry and commerce, and the increase in the price of real and personal property, all of which combined are resulted in a great demand in the United States for European goods. This in turn made England have a substantial increase in exports, business booming, the prevalence of speculation, and a significant increase in prices. In 1835, speculators began to panic, and dumped foreign securities one after another, so that securities prices dropped quickly and the exchange crisis broke out. The excessive speculation in the United States caused a large number of gold to flow into the United States from England. The gold drain in England caused panic, and gold began to flow back into England. After November 1836, commodity prices began to fall, there were phenomenon of bankruptcy, reduced production and trade stagnation.

It is important to understand the general causes and the general phenomena manifested in every crisis, but this is built on the basis of understanding of the special reasons of every crisis. In order to make the specific reasons and phenomena of each crisis be fully demonstrated, Tugan put emphasis on the comparative analysis of various crises, and on the subtle investigation of differences and commonalities of various crises. The need to do this kind of work is obvious that it can discover problems that an isolated analysis of a crisis cannot find. In fact, through the comparative analysis of crises in 1825, 1837, 1847, 1857, and various crises after 1870s, Tugan found some common grounds as well as the regularities of these crises. What he has done led him to achieving this goal. That is: 1) every crisis has its own special reasons. 2) The crisis always occurs regularly. This result is what Tugan had been aware of beforehand, and when he made a systematic description of the history of the economic crisis in England in the 19th century, he expressed the necessity of doing so. He told the reader that the clarification of the economic conditions and the reasons for the crisis to occur in the British industry under different situations has a large number of repetition, which seems monotonous, but it is because of this monotony that is be able to clearly demonstrate "the regularity of the phenomenon that we've studied." Of course, it also shows that the crisis does not only depend on the specifically accidental factors in a certain period, but also on the inherent, recurring common factors of the modern civilization and economic system.

From the comparative analysis Tugan found that the 1825 and 1836 crises were caused by the artificial enlargement of the foreign demand for English products, and this demand was formed through a large number of capital flow out of England. In 1825 it flew to Central and South America and in 1836 to the United States. In 1836, the English speculation mania was pointing the finger of blame primarily to foreign enterprises, but to domestic enterprises. In 1825 and 1836, price changes were very similar. The collapse of the bank and the panic in the financial market occurred in the fall for both crises: October of 1825 and November of 1836. The reduction in the reserve fund of the Bank of England was due to gold drain abroad for both crises. Till 1936, the crisis had been developing in the exactly the same manner with that in 1825. The only significant difference is: the speculation mania in securities exchange and commodity exchange in 1825 is much more powerful than that in 1836, and it caused volatility in British financial market and even the entire British industry, which had serious consequences. In 1836, the British prices did not rise as rapid as it was in 1825, which affected the progress of British foreign trade. In 1825, the English output products were decreased in quantity, while the number of imports had increased significantly, and therefore, the number of gold drain in 1825 was much more than it was in 1836. The entrepreneurial fever in 1825 was greater than it was in 1836, so in a few months after 1825, many local banks went bankrupt in England, while in 1836 there was no English bank that stopped payment. In 1826 the total number of insolvencies in England increased by nearly 125%, and in 1837 it only increased by 64%. On the other hand, because the 1825 panic was serious, therefore it lasted shorter. In the early 1826, gold began to flow back to the Bank of England rapidly. In the years of 1837, despite gold drain, the reserve in the Bank of England was in a difficult situation to enrich itself until June, and the crisis lasted almost a whole year. In 1847, the crisis was neither the same as it was in 1825, nor like in 1836. In 1847, the British capital was not flowing to the foreign country but remained domestically, investing in the English rail companies. However, domestic demand for commodities was greatly increased initially, but was soon reduced. The reason is that: because of the poor harvests of two consecutive years in England, the massive importation of food prompted the rise in food prices and offset the effect of railway investment. In 1847, the British spent 40 million pounds on building the railway, which could have promoted the growth of the domestic trade, but the input of grain cost nearly 30 million pounds, as well as a few million pounds on cotton, because the price of cotton also soared due to the poor harvest. Therefore, the domestic market was not expanded but narrowed in 1847. The foreign market was also narrowed due to the poor harvest in countries that imported the English products. Indeed, if the English capital had not been invested in railways, it would inevitably have flown abroad; increasing the foreign demand for the English products, just like it was in 1825 and 1836. Thus, in a certain sense, the large-scale construction of railways hampered the increase in English exports. However, England did not suffer a disadvantage, had an advantage because the domestic market replaced the foreign market, and it was just because of the consecutive poor harvests in 1845 and 1846 that the national production was reduced in 1846 and 1847. The 1847 crisis occurred not because of the excessive supply, but because of the sudden decrease in demand. Therefore, the 1847 crisis manifested relatively unique signs: 1) In addition to the rapid rise in food prices initially and then rapid fall later, the price of most commodities did not rise. 2) the crisis was brewing slowly, and before it occurred, the English production was reduced with business depression. 3) It was accompanied by the financial crisis, but to a lesser extent. 4) The crisis was eliminated fast.

The evidence that the 1857 and subsequent crises provided is: in the early 1850s, countries that had trade with England launched a massive national railway network construction, and coupled with the increased production of precious metals, many European countries reduced tariffs on English goods, these factors had promoted the increase in the wealth in England. Especially the truce with Russia played a role of promoting the prosperity of the English economy. The economic prosperity and growth of wealth throughout Europe is also one of the reasons to promote the economic prosperity of England. The growth of wealth in Europe promoted the accumulation of capital, and a lot of excess capital flew continuously into the United States. These capitals first entered the stock exchange, and then flew into businesses. Stock companies were springing up and developing like mushrooms, speculative activities were also active, and railroad stocks, state-owned land was the focus of speculation. At the same time, the business was also booming that imports were more than exports, prices were rising, and the overstocking of commodities also increased significantly, with a large number of English goods piled up in New York Harbour. The English businessmen did not see the potential commercial crisis behind this prosperity, but provided a lot of commercial credit and bank credit to the Americans, carried on foreign discount bills, as well as lending loans to foreign businessmen, with these or those collaterals as security, or even without any collateral, as long as the borrower was honest and reliable, the credit could be provided. This in turn contributed to the speculation of commercial frenzy. In 1857, Europe had agricultural harvest, and food prices fell. Since food prices were the most important export goods of the United States, the decline in food prices caused a chain reaction in the U.S. economy. Some serious speculative companies, such as railway companies began to collapse and the stock began to fall sharply, there was a substantial increase in the discount rate in the Bank of America, and therefore a large number of English gold flew to the United States. In October 1857, the price in England plummeted, then the business and the financial panicked, and England raised the discount rate. In November, gold stopped flowing to the United States, but to the domestic market on a large scale, where companies began to go bankrupt and banks began to collapse. Overall, the 1857 crisis was the general crisis, and before the crisis, the price on the whole world market increased quite balanced. The torrent of commodities did not flow to one side unreasonably, but more uniformly dispersed in countries, and therefore, there was no outflow of gold in England. For the same reason, when the panic occurred in England, gold also failed to flow from other countries to England, because the panic spread to financial markets around the world. In the U.S., the panic came fiercer than it in England, and therefore gold flew to both the domestic market and England from the Bank of England. The reason that gold failed to flow into England from continental Europe was because the discount rate of important cities in Western Europe was as high as it was in England.

The historical study by Tugan on the economic fluctuations of decades in England after 1870s, which is mainly focused on the following two groups of indicators: the first group is exports, the exchange volume in the clearinghouse, and stock companies; the second group is the metal reserves in the Bank of England, iron prices, and bankruptcies. The changing movements of the first group of date on the graph are: accurate periodicity; four waves. (The first wave reached its highest point in 1873-1874, and then came a protracted industrial ebb until 1878-1879. The second wave soon reached the highest point – in about 1881-1883. After that, the tide fell, and in 1885-1886 it fell to the lowest point, while the third wave in the late 1880s descended after 1890. The first four years of the 1890s were the period of industrial ebb. From 1895 onwards, the industrial wave was rolling back.) Changes in the iron prices of the second group were similar to the first group. In the early 1870s, iron price jumped to the highest point, and also reached the highest point in 1880 and 1890. In 1894, it gradually recovered, and reached its highest point in 1896. The metal reserves in the Bank of England were moving inversely with the previous four curves. This shows that the industrial turmoil was associated with the credit turmoil during the period.

294

The various turmoils in the British industry after1870 were: In 1871-1873, commercial prosperity was rare in the Western Europe, and in the early 1870s, German and Austrian securities speculation prevailed (main the railway and land securities), forming the entrepreneurial fever, then the exchange crisis occurred immediately in Germany and Austria. The European entrepreneurial fever spread to the United States, during the 4 years from 1870-1873, the United States built railways of 23,406 miles[21]. The railway fever sparked speculation in securities, then the exchange panic, and the London Stock Exchange was also involved in the foreign debt boom. From 1870-1875, foreign bonds were

---

21   1 kilometer = 0.6214 mile

issued nearly 260 million pounds in London. Many of these foreign debts were issued extremely recklessly, and the reason it was able to obtain a temporary success is simply that the broker, exchange agents and financiers who are committed to promoting it played with an improper wrist. Many South American countries who had already been insolvent to debt and did not want to fulfil their own commitments to obligations, borrowed the debt in London just in this way.

After 1879, another railway construction fever is set of in the United States, and during 1880-1882, the railway network extended to 28,240 miles. The English exports to the United States surged, from 14.6 million pounds in 1878 to 31 million pounds in 1882. In 1884, the United States had the railroad collapse again. Since the 1880s, the price had been low, industrial downturn intensified, which the authors believe to be due to railway construction, it makes agricultural products to be transported out of the United States, Russia, India and other countries, giving a major blow to agriculture in Western Europe and England.

In 1886, the British industry ran high, and the iron industry and coal mining industry developed greatly. The export of iron increased from 21.8 million pounds in 1886 to 31.6 million pounds in 1890, the export of machinery from 10.1 million pounds to 16.4 million pounds, and the export of coal from 9.8 million pounds to 19 million pounds. After 1890, the British industry has entered a recession. In 1893, a serious industrial crisis broke out in Australia and the United States, and the direct reason of the crisis was "erecting en- terprises" and "speculation." During the crisis, massive gold flew out of the United States, gold reserves in the Treasury decreased from 120 million dollars in early 1893 to 90 million dollars in early June. The discount rate was 18%, with the corporate bankruptcies of 11,174. In 1895, the new industrial upsurge began. Tugan's interpretation of the 1866 crisis is an exception, that he not only explicitly expressed that the crisis was "not an industrial crisis but a credit crisis," and he also said that it was the accidental collapse of a major bank that triggered the 1866 financial crisis, thus avoiding the once impending industrial crisis.[22]

Since the end of the 19th century, the British industrial crisis had changed. Because of the prevalence of customized goods, the speculation of traders is reduced; since England lost its industrial dominance, the signs for the period of industrial upsurge are manifested as the increase in the export of the means of production, and the reduction in the extent of the crisis.

On the whole, through the investigation of the history of the crisis, Tugan has found some phenomena of regularity as follows, that is, the fluctuations before the 19th century were triggered by some special cases, mostly political events, without any regularity, with the time interval being very long. The fluctuations after 19th century had not only the regularity, but also caused by

---

22   See Mendelson, *Theory and History of the Economic Crisis and Cycle*, Volume I (2), Beijing: Joint Publishing, 1975, p. 781.

internal factors; the crisis came suddenly, with the consequences being often bankruptcy, unemployment, living in poverty of the underclass, and the reason for the crisis was mostly not clear. Moreover, almost before every crisis it was manifested as the commercial exuberance, followed by hard currency circulation, and then credit crisis. "Each time of upsurge ends with industrial crisis, followed by a fairly long period of business recession."[23] The crisis is basically due to the disproportionality among various industrial sectors.

V. Evaluation

As for whether Tugan's theory belongs to Marxist theory, there are many different opinions even in the era of Tugan. The reason that many Russian Marxists regarded it as Marxist theory is because they consider this theory as the one to demonstrate that the Russian capitalist production can continue to develop on the basis of the domestic market. Tugan himself also agrees to that, and it seems to him that his theory about solving the market problems "is indeed the completion in logic of the analysis of the cycle of social capital by Marx in *Capital* Volume II." But then, the vast majority of Russian Marxists changed their attitude, and excluded it from the orthodox Marxist theory. German Marxists most firmly denied of any point in common between Tugan's theory and Marxist theory, whether they are revisionists such as Bernstein and Schmidt or the orthodox Marxists such as Kautsky and Luxemburg, both of them held the same attitude. Kautsky had written articles and systematically refuted over Tugan's theory. Russian Narodniks have argued that Tugan's market realization theory was not part of the orthodox Marxist theory, but it was as good as, if not better than Marx's theory.[24]

Conrad Schmidt once had written reviews on Tugan's views and raised the question: "Tugan-Baranovsky believes that the entire overproduction is because of the unequal distribution of capital, and if this view is correct, then it cannot understand why capitalism, as Marx and Marxist inferred, is digging its own grave. If only the scourge of the crisis is rooted in the disproportionality of production, then before the shake of the whole existing economic system, it will not be inevitably aggravated with the development of capitalism. However, the actual situation is another thing, because the expansion of production is naturally (it has nothing to do with the so-called reason for the crisis to occur, the disproportionality of production) limited by consumer demand, even if the limit is elastic. From this point of view, we can use the simplest words to explain that the development of capitalism is destined to cause the total breakdown of the economy. Do not the capitalists, by their opposition to all wage increases, conduct a struggle which has the tendency to keep the income – hence also the purchasing power – of the masses as low as possible, while they, the capitalists, on the other hand, raise their own income – and

---

23   Tugan-Baranovsky, *Periodic Industrial Crises*, p. 38.
24   Ibid., p.245.

therewith the mass of accumulated capital seeking productive investment – in rapidly increasing progression? Will, under such circumstances, the increase in consuming power ... be able to keep step with tempo of capital accumulation? And if not, must not then the sale of commodities become always more difficult the more consumption demand, the basis production lags behind the rapidly increasing accumulation of capital and expansion of production – with only export, unproductive state expenditure, etc., to slow down the process? In this way, then, capitalism would tend to create in and of itself a steadily growing state of overproduction. ... The path of development of capitalist society would thus be likewise the path to its own bankruptcy, the transition to a new socialist order would be prescribed by a forced situation of society itself." "The purpose of production are purposes which in the final analysis and in one way or another proceed from the demand for consumption goods, purposes which are comprehensible only when taken in connection with and continuously referred back to consumption demand. Definitive or consumption demand is the enlivening force which, throughout the entire economy, keeps the huge apparatus of production in motion."[25]

Kautsky's review on Tugan's view is: "The capitalists may equate me and machines as much as he likes, society remains a society of men and never one of machines; social relations remain always relations of man to man, never the relations of men to machines. It is for this reason that in the final analysis human labour remains the value-creating factor, and it is for this reason also in the final analysis that the extension of human consumption exercises the decisive influence over the expansion of production ... Production is and remains production for human consumption."[26]

Lenin believes that Tugan does not properly understand what the schemes are intended for, because he assumes that they "prove the deduction". "Schemes alone cannot prove anything: they can only illustrate a process, if its separate elements have been theoretically explained. Mr. Tugan-Baranovsky compiled his own Schemes which differed from Marx's (and which were incomparably less clear than Marx's), at the same time omitting a theoretical explanation of those elements of the process that they were supposed to illustrate."[27]

Louis B. Boudin, known as the American orthodox Marxist theorist, called Tugan's theory "an utter absurdity" and "the veriest rot," and he claimed that "means of production ...are nothing more than means to the production of consumable goods ultimately to be produced by their means, their production is overproduction, and is so found to be when the ultimate test is applied."[28]

---

25 Quoted by Sweezy, *Theory of Capitalist Development*, Beijing: Commercial Press, 1997, p. 190.

26 Ibid..

27 *Lenin Collected Works*, Chinese Version 2nd Edition, Volume 4, Beijing: People's Publishing House, 1984, p. 48.

28 Quoted by Sweezy, *Theory of Capitalist Development*, p. 191.

As an important Marxist theorist in the Second International, Hilferding, also had dissenting views on Tugan's theory, and he said: "[Tugan] sees only the specific economic forms of capitalist production and therefore overlooks the natural conditions which are common to all production whatever its historical form; in this way he arrives at the strange notion of production which has nothing but production in view while consumption appears only as a troublesome accident. If this is 'madness' it still has 'method' and even Marxist method, since the analysis of the historical form of capitalist production is specifically Marxian. It is Marxism gone crazy, but still Marxism, that makes Tugan's theory so peculiar and so stimulating. Tugan feels this himself, though he does not realize it. Hence his sharp polemic against the 'common sense' of his opponents."[29]

Rosa Luxembourg, the queen of underconsumptionists, should have, of course scornfully rejected Tugan's reasoning, as was expected. The view that production of means of production is independent of consumption is naturally a vulgar economic fantasy of Tugan-Baranovsky "Tugan is wrong, not because he considers realization to be possible, but because he tears away the necessary connexion between production and consumption."[30]

Bukharin also believes that the essence of Tugan's consists "in cutting production off from consumption and completely isolating it." "If we had to do with a market which is emancipated from consumption, thus with a closed circle of production of means of production in which the branches of production mutually serve each other, in other words, if we had a stranger production system such as that pictured by the lively imagination of Tugan, then to be sure a general overproduction would be impossible... We reach entirely different results if, instead of the theory of Tugan-Baranovsky, we hold to the correct theory, the theory of Marx. We have then a chain of related industries providing each other with market which follow a certain definite order determined by the technical-economic continuity of the whole process of production. This chain ends, however, with the production of consumption goods which can ... only go directly into personal consumption ..."[31]

Sweezy pointed out that behind all these criticisms of Tugan's theory lays in one single idea, namely, that the process of production is and must remain, regardless of its historical form, a process of producing goods for human consumption. Any attempt to get away from this fundamental fact represents a flight from reality which must end in theoretical bankruptcy.

In the early 1940s, in his book *Theory of Capitalist Development* Paul Sweezy considers that like Bernstein, Tugan is also a 'revisionist' of Marxist economic theory. But he is said to contribute to theory of economics, "Tugan

298

29 Hilferding, *Finance Capital*, p. 355 footnote. Quoted by Sweezy, *Theory of Capitalist Development*, p. 191.
30 Bukharin, *Imperialism and the Accumulation of Capital*, Harbin: Heilongjiang People's Publishing House, 1982, 1925.
31 Ibid., p. 76.

also exercised a considerable influence on the development of modern business-cycle research, his work on the history of commercial crises in England being one of the pioneer pieces of empirical investigation in this field."[32] As for Tugan's viewpoint that, "If social production is organized in accordance with a plan, if the directors of production had complete knowledge of demand and the power to direct labour and capital from one branch of production to another, then however low social consumption might be, the supply of commodities could never outstrip the demand."[33] Sweezy had such review that: "Tugan's 'proof' of this statement is purely formal and rests on manipulation of the reproduction schemes."[34] As for Tugan's theory of reproduction, Sweezy argued that this theory was chiefly vulnerable on the grounds of its superficiality.

When Mendelson began to study the economic crisis, Tugan has been inconclusive as a completely bourgeois scholar, and he is the object of severe criticism by the orthodox. As Mendelson is considered to be the one who had the most thorough critique of the bourgeois theory of crisis, so there are many in his writings that was criticizing Tugan, and readers can learn from these to understand how their views became opposites.

Mendelson thinks that, Tugan's errors is mainly that he overlooked the contradiction between production and consumption, interpreted the disproportionality as the fundamental reason of the crisis, and in fact, he separated the phenomenon of the disproportionality of production itself from its root of the basic contradiction of capitalism. He pointed out that Tugan-Baranovsky admitted in 1825 that the English industry was badly damaged due to the crisis, but he really did not intend to explain the expansion of the crisis in the industrial aspects; he concentrated on analyzing the bankruptcy of speculation boom and the extension of currency crisis, denying that the 1825 crisis was a crisis of general overproduction, misinterpreting the interrelation of various phenomena in the process of brewing and expansion of the crisis, portraying the disorder of credit and the bankruptcy of speculation as the main reason for the industrial crisis, believing the alternation of various stages of the cycle is determined by the movement of money, considering that the reason for economic prosperity and the prevalence of all kinds of speculation is because of the excess moneyed capital, and thinking that the reason for the crisis is: "However strong the English capital is, it will finally be exhausted. The hot money on the lending market is gradually reduced significantly. The quiet period ... arrives, followed by the quick collapse of those papered unreal enterprises stuffed in London Stock Exchange."[35] Mendelson believes that these views are held by almost all bourgeois economists. Speculation is not the root reason for the eco-

---

32 Sweezy, *Theory of Capitalist Development*, p. 179.
33 Tugan-Baranovsky, *Commercial Crises*, p.33; Quoted by Sweezy, *Theory of Capitalist Development*, p. 186.
34 Sweezy, *Theory of Capitalist Development*, p.186.
35 Mendelson, *Theory and History of the Economic Crisis and Cycle*, Volume I (1), Beijing: Joint Publishing. 1975, p. 402.

nomic crisis of capitalism or the reason for overproduction, but the sign of overproduction. When talking about the role of speculation in the industrial cycle, Marx and Engels said: "Speculation regularly occurs in periods when overproduction is already in full swing. It provides overproduction with temporary market outlets, while for this very reason precipitating the outbreak of the crisis and increasing its force. The crisis itself first breaks out in the area of speculation; only later does it hit production. What appears to the superficial observer to be the cause of the crisis is not overproduction but excess speculation, but this is itself only a symptom of overproduction. The subsequent disruption of production does not appear as a consequence of its own previous exuberance but merely as a setback caused by the collapse of speculation."[36] On this basis, Mendelson made a description of recognition on the relationship between securities, commodities speculation and crisis. He pointed out, when capitalism was at the development stage where the industrial crisis did not have the foothold; it would result in the speculative boom of securities and trading in commodities, thereby causing bankruptcies and credit disorders of a large number of businesses. However, after the economic laws of capitalist crises of overproduction took effect, speculation had found a new foothold in the cyclical industrial turmoil, and took new effect. Speculation is essentially the most aggravated performance of the anarchy of capitalist production, which is the performance of the basic contradiction of capitalism. Therefore, the speculation in the prevalence of industrial upsurge is the reflection of the aggravation of the basic contradiction of capitalism, as well as a strong impetus for the aggravation of all the disproportionality phenomena that developed on the basis of such an aggravated contradiction and caused the outbreak of the crisis in the production process.

Tugan determined that the intensity of the crisis was based on the strength of the credit crisis. Mendelson held negative attitude towards it, and he believes "the strength of the crisis first manifested in the number of production and labour which the crisis made idle, manifested in the suffering of the working people caused by the crisis, and manifested in the duration of the crisis."[37] Therefore, Mendelson accused Tugan who was like Juglar and Wirth of always circling around the credit, attributing the crisis to credit disorders, and regarding the crisis merely as a currency crisis. Sometimes he turned to the field of trade, but to analyze the phenomenon of credit. Thereby, it is futile for the reader to find his analysis in his writings of the actual accumulation, production dynamics, overproduction and its manifestations of capital in the industrial aspect. He almost overlooked brewing and expansion of the crisis in the industrial aspect, and he did not regard production decline and business reduction as the most important manifestation of the crisis, but as a phenomenon that occurs before the crisis.

300

36　*Marx and Engels Collected Works*, Chinese Version 1st Edition, Volume 7, Beijing: People's Publishing House, 1957, p. 492.

37　Mendelson, *Theory and History of the Economic Crises and Cycles*, Volume I (2), Beijing: Joint Publishing, 1975, p. 481.

Tugan and Mendelson had very different angles in the interpretation of the crisis. Tugan mainly interpreted the crisis from the perspective of the banking and credit, and Mendelson mainly explained the crisis from the perspective of industrial production, i.e. the process of industrial production breaking away from the crisis, the elements that promote economic prosperity, and the general overproduction in the industrial sector – the investigation is conducted in such a procedure. In this confrontation, Mendelson always blamed Tugan to admit the property of crisis to be the "industrial crisis", and he was also aware of the facts of production reduction, factory closures, and unemployment, etc. However, in the description of brewing and expansion process of the crisis, he completely avoided taking about the reproduction, or the disproportionality in the industrial aspect, but just treated them as the derived phenomenon of the currency crisis.

Tugan and Mendelson are two important researchers in the same field in. As the study of the capitalist economic crisis by Mendelson is nearly half a century later in time, Tugan's viewpoints, theory, and thesis had become a natural theoretical reference and critical objects of Mendelson. Mendelson also did his best to play the critique down to almost every small part, almost pointing out all the argument that is antithetical to his views. Tugan regard the crises from 1780 to 1820 as the ones caused by purely political reasons, and the 1825 crisis as the one caused by the credit disorder and the bankruptcy of speculation, the1837 crisis was the result of credit disorder, the 1847 crisis was because of the poor harvest of grain and cotton, the 1857 crisis was currency crisis, the 1866 crisis was credit crisis, the 1873 crisis was the result of the bankruptcy of the exchange and the disintegration of credit, in 1882 there was no crisis of general overproduction, in 1890 it only appeared economic stagnation, and the 1907 crisis was due to the exhaustion and severe shortage of inactive capital. For Tugan's views on the various crises, Mendelson's assessment is that like the bourgeois economist, Tugan always tended to use the specific reason, that is, the coincidence of some cases and conditions to explain each economic crisis. Such explanation of crisis can be just a form of denying the regularity and inevitability of occurrence of crises in the capitalist system.

CHAPTER IX

Soviet Scholars' Analysis of Capitalist Economic Crisis

After the October Revolution, the study of the Marxist theory of economy encountered new opportunities – the base for the dedicated study and dissemination of Marxist economics; Marxist economics itself became the official economics in Socialism in the Soviet Union; in order to ensure the study to be carried out smoothly, the Bolshevik Party establish institutions for the special study of Marxist theory; a great many of important literatures by Marx and Engels were being collected across the Europe, and the Russian edition of *Marx & Engels Complete Works* had been published; a large number of dedicated researchers and theorists were gradually gathered; etc. All this created the conditions for the systematic study of Marxist economic theory. Throughout the Soviet period, the study of the capitalist business cycle has gone through three stages: the first stage is mainly represented by Lenin and Stalin, whose studies mainly aimed to defend and interpret Marx's theory of crisis, to further elaborate the specific forms of the basic contradiction, and to have a detailed analysis of the new changes in the capitalist economic crisis under conditions of monopoly. The second stage was mainly Eugene Varga, Jürgen Kuczynski, Stanislaw Mendelson, and some other representatives of the textbook authors, who proposed a standard analytical model based on their in-depth study of the theory, history and reality of capitalist economic crisis, which is the "textbook model." The third stage is mainly represented by Pakadaev, Shapiro, Stanislav

Menshikov, Martynov, Kuzminov, Rymalov, Alexander Ivanovich Gelchuk and et al., who had more writings, but with fewer breakthrough in theory. Gelchuk can be seen as one of the most typical representative scholars of this period, and his study and methods have made a breakthrough, developing the textbook model, which is called the modified textbook model and has stronger analysis capabilities than the textbook model to meet the need for normative and empirical analysis. Overall, there were studies of the capitalist economic crisis on a large scale in the Soviet period, with many study results being launched, but it still lacked creative results. This is very regrettable. Originally, after the Bolshevik controlled state power, with the improvement of the social system conditions and material conditions of the study, the theoretical study should have had more innovation and development, but due to some of the human factors, people's minds were detained, driving the Marxist theory into a dogmatic, absolute position, so that theory lost the due environmental innovation and vitality.

I. Reaffirmation of the Basic Method of Marx's Model

Lenin did not specifically study the writings on the problem of the capitalist business cycle, and he only had some fragments of discourse on issues of the business cycle when discussing other issues, but this did not prevent his influence. Throughout the Soviet period, there is no economists' business cycle theory can be compared with the theory of Lenin, and Lenin's theory of crisis is the criteria for other theories, that the study results of other people must be consistent with Lenin's theory. For example, after Lenin's opinion on the root reason of the economic crisis of capitalism was published, it immediately became a theoretical creed followed by Soviet scholars with consistency.[1] The studies afterwards were basically around the basic contradiction of capitalism, and to demonstrate the contradiction and conflict between socialized production and private ownership of the means of production is the core of the study. How does the basic contradiction of capitalism lead to the capitalist economic crisis? The basic idea of answering this question is that on the one hand there is the issue to analyze; the trends of continuously socialized production, and on the other hand to analyze the continuous development of and the continuous conflict with these two contradictory aspects with the improvement of capitalist possession of the means of production, where it is in cyclical process of intensification and becomes more and more serious than before. Specifically, on the one hand it is to have a full range of analysis of productivity, proving the development of socialized production; on the other hand it is to have an analysis of the relations of production, proving that the means of production is increasingly concentrated in the hands of a few people. The purpose of studying socialized production is to illustrate the development of the contradiction

304

---

1 Lenin's analysis of the root reason of the crisis inherited views proposed by Engels in Anti-Dühring, that is, the contradiction between socialized production and private ownership of the means of production.

between it and the form of capitalist possession, and to illustrate the results of such a development – the economic conflict has reached its zenith: in terms of economic benefits, it is manifested as the aggravation of the opposition between the proletariat and the bourgeois; In terms of production, it is manifested as a serious confrontation between the organization of production of individual enterprises and the anarchy of production in the whole society, as the mode of production against the mode of exchange, the productivity against the mode of production it had exceeded. Therefore, it often comes to this conclusion in the analysis of socialized production: the relations and the interdependent relations among all enterprises, production sectors, and countries are being expanded and strengthened; there is a certain unity between each other in the process of reproduction. The following is a description of the process of the socialization of labour by Lenin:

"The socialisation of labour by capitalism is manifested in the following processes. Firstly, the very growth of commodity-production destroys the scattered condition of small economic units that is characteristic of natural economy and draws together the small local markets into an enormous national (and then world) market. Production for oneself is transformed into production for the whole of society; and the greater the development of capitalism, the stronger becomes the contradiction between this collective character of production and the individual character of appropriation. Secondly, capitalism replaces the former scattered production by an unprecedented concentration both in agriculture and in industry. That is the most striking and outstanding, but not the only, manifestation of the feature of capitalism under review. Thirdly, capitalism eliminates the forms of personal dependence that constituted an inalienable component of preceding systems of economy. ... Fourthly, capitalism necessarily creates mobility of the population, something not required by previous systems of social economy and impossible under them on anything like a large scale. Fifthly, capitalism constantly reduces the proportion of the population engaged in agriculture (where the most backward forms of social and economic relationships always prevail), and increases the number of large industrial centres. Sixthly, capitalist society increases the population's need for association, for organisation, and lends these organisations a character distinct from those of former times. While breaking down the narrow, local, social-estate associations of medieval society and creating fierce competition, capitalism at the same time splits the whole of society into large groups of persons occupying different positions in production, and gives a tremendous impetus to organisation within each such group. Seventhly, all the above-mentioned changes effected in the old economic system by capitalism inevitably lead also to a change in the mentality of the population."[2]

---

2 *Collected Works of V.I. Lenin*, 2nd Chinese Edition, Volume 3, Beijing: People's Publishing House. 1984, *pp. 550-552.*

In terms of the relations of the specialization of production, division of labour and the socialization of labour:

"The socialisation of labour by capitalist production does not at all consist in people working under one roof (that is only a small part of the process), but in the concentration of capital being accompanied by the specialisation of social labour, by a decrease in the number of capitalists in each given branch of industry and an increase in the number of separate branches of industry—in many separate production processes being merged into one social production process. When, in the days of handicraft weaving, for example, the small producers themselves spun the yarn and made it into cloth, we had a few branches of industry (spinning and weaving were merged). But when production becomes socialised by capitalism, the number of separate branches of industry increases: cotton spinning is done separately and so is weaving; this very division and the concentration of production give rise to new branches—machine building, coal mining, and so forth. In each branch of industry, which has now become more specialised, the number of capitalists steadily decreases. This means that the social tie between the producers becomes increasingly stronger, the producers become welded into a single whole."[3]

The purpose of Lenin in studying the capitalist economic crisis is mainly to serve the revolutionary movement at the time, so to study the capitalist economic crisis, on the one hand is to continue to prove the inevitability that the capitalist mode of production is going from emergence, development and down to its doom, and on the other hand is to predict the revolutionary trends, because past history shows that the revolution is always caused by the crisis. In order to achieve the desired objectives, Lenin attaches great importance to explaining and defending Marx's theory of crisis, because he understands that the study of Marx's theory of economic crisis is to better study and explain the real crisis, e.g., what has been described in *A Characterisation of Economic Romanticism* is a good example of such efforts. Of course, Lenin also attaches great importance to the study of the real crisis; he predicted the development trend of the revolutionary movement from the development of the crisis. Therefore, in Lenin's discussion of the economic crisis, there are both critiques of the non-Marxist business cycle theory, as well as the studies on the real issues. In the analysis he used the typical basic contradiction analysis, that is, on the one hand to analyze the socialized trends in the development of productive forces, and on the other hand to analyze development trends the laws of capitalist possession, and by the description of the relationship of the unity of opposites between the two, to reveal the inevitability of the capitalist economic crisis. Because of Lenin's position and influence, people soon put his study and method together with Marx's theory of crisis, building an economic crisis analysis model, because in this model it analyzes the problem along two basic contradictions, so this model is called the "basic contradiction analysis model.

3　*Collected Works of V.I. Lenin*, 2nd Chinese Edition, Volume 1, Beijing: People's Publishing House. 1984, p. 145.

To analyze the economic crisis on the level of the basic contradictions, literatures in the 20th century mainly focused on the analysis of two contradictions, that is the contradictions between the infinitely widening trend of production and the reduced purchasing power of working people; the contradictions between the organization of production of individual enterprises and the anarchy of production in the whole society. Lenin once described the first contradictions as: "The contradiction between production and consumption that is inherent in capitalism is due to the tremendous rate at which production is growing, to the tendency to unlimited expansion which competition gives it, while consumption (individual), if it grows at all, grows very slightly; the proletarian condition of the masses of the people makes a rapid growth of individual consumption impossible....the growth of the national wealth proceeds side by side with the growth of the people's poverty; that the productive forces of society increase without a corresponding increase in consumption by the people, without the employment of these productive forces for the benefit of the working masses."[4] In addition to this description, Lenin also discussed the contradiction between production and consumption of capitalism on many occasions, which contain the following four propositions: 1) in the capitalist system, (individual) consumption is not able to adapt to the growth of production. 2) In the capitalist system, the expansion of markets in a way "do not rely on" the expansion of consumption. 3) In a capitalist society, the link between production and consumption is not straightforward. 4) The contradiction between production and consumption, as well as the disproportionality of various economic sectors are inextricably linked as two manifestations of the contradiction between social production and capitalist possession.

307

Lenin attaches great importance to the importance of the relationship between production and consumption, thinking that it cannot explain the crisis if overlooking the contradiction between production and consumption. ".. even with an ideally smooth and proportional reproduction and circulation of the aggregate social capital, the contradiction between the growth of production and the narrow limits of consumption is inevitable."[5] Under normal circumstances, the production of the means of production grows not only faster than the production of the means of consumption, but also shows the disjointing with the latter, that is, the tendency of going beyond the limits formed by lower level of consumption of the proletarian masses in the capitalist system. The disproportionality of the first department and second department of the social production periodically transformed into the disjointing between production and consumption. So it will be found that, production "does not rely on" consumption, which is relative, and there is a link between the two, although this link is not direct, it is very real. It will surely be punished if such a link destroyed. This is reflected in the crisis, because the crisis is the form in which it compulsorily connects the two factors that are intrinsically linked but "independent"

4 *Collected Works of V.I. Lenin*, 2nd Chinese Edition, Volume 4, Beijing: People's Publishing House, 1984, p. 139.
5 Ibid., p. 73.

on the surface of the capitalist system. The study of the contradiction between production and consumption of capitalism in political economy is not just to prove that the capitalist mode of production is unable to sell all of its products, or is able to sell all of its products, and Lenin said: "But it is no less clear that it is correct to draw one single conclusion from this contradiction—that the development of the productive forces themselves must, with irresistible force, lead to the replacement of capitalism by an economy of associated producers. It would, on the other hand, be utterly incorrect to draw from this contradiction the conclusion that capitalism must regularly provide a surplus-product, i.e. that capitalism cannot, in general, realise the product, and can, therefore, play no progressive historical role, and so on."[6]

The critique of non-Marxist theory of crisis is an important aspect of explaining and defending Marxist theory of crisis, because it can reflect the scientific nature of Marxist crisis theory from the opposite side. In the history of economics, the theory of underconsumption and the theory of disproportionality has been some of the highly controversial topics since the era of classical economics. As there is no systematic exposition of Marxist crisis theory, in those fragments of his discourse, some incomprehensible decrees confused many researchers for years –if Marx's theory of crisis is the "non-underconsumption theory", evidence can be found from his writings; if his crisis theory is "underconsumption theory", it seems to be able to find evidence as well. When refuting "underconsumption theory" in *Capital* Volume II, Marx pointed out, "[i]t is sheer tautology to say that crises are caused by the scarcity of effective consumption, or of effective consumers. The capitalist system does not know any other modes of consumption than effective ones, except that of sub forma pauperis or of the swindler....crises are always prepared by precisely a period in which wages rise generally and the working-class actually gets a larger share of that part of the annual product which is intended for consumption." "It is not alone the consumption of necessities of life which increases. The working-class (now actively reinforced by its entire reserve army) also enjoys momentarily articles of luxury ordinarily beyond its reach, and those articles which at other times constitute for the greater part consumer "necessities" only for the capitalist class...."[7] However, this increase in consumption does not eliminate the crisis. We can see from these discussions that Marx had negative attitude towards the "underconsumption theory". But in *Capital* Volume III when he was elaborating the credit problem, he unexpectedly made a point that seems completely opposite to the previous one, that "[t]he ultimate reason for all real crises always remains the poverty and restricted consumption of the masses as opposed to the drive of capitalist production to develop the productive forces as though only the absolute consuming power of society constituted their limit."[8] In this way, it seems that Marx held two contradictory views on the crisis. Marx

---

6 Ibid., p. 143.

7 *Capital*, Volume II, Beijing: The People's Publishing House, 1975, pp. 456-457.

8 *Capital*, Volume III, Beijing: The People's Publishing House, 2004, p. 548.

sometimes used "limited consumption" to explain the crisis, and sometimes also used disproportionality to explain the crisis. What is the relationship between them? Readers of *Capital* have long found the problem, and made any interpretations. When meeting this problem, Lenin had such an interpretation: "The two theories of which we are speaking give totally different explanations of crises. The first theory explains crises by the contradiction between production and consumption by the working class; the second explains them by the contradiction between the social character of production and the private character of appropriation... To put it more briefly, the former explains crises, by underconsumption, the latter by the anarchy of production. ... But the question is: does the second theory deny the fact of a contradiction between production and consumption; does it deny the fact of underconsumption? Of course not. It fully recognises this fact, but puts it in its proper, subordinate place as a fact that only relates to one department of the whole of capitalist production. It teaches us that this fact cannot explain crises, which are called forth by another and more profound contradiction that is fundamental in the present economic system, namely, the contradiction between the social character of production and the private character of appropriation."[9] Lenin's interpretation provides an idea for people to understand Marx's theory of crisis – to explain the contradiction between production and consumption, and to explain that the crisis must be subordinated to the contraction between the socialization of production and the private possession, so as to explain the crisis, because it is a concrete manifestation of the basic contradiction.

309

The frequent disproportionality is the characteristic of capitalism, and thus the equilibrium can only be a coincidence; it can only be close to the necessary and relative proportionality for the reproduction through constant destruction of proportionality and through cyclical crises. In this case, the disproportionality of the first department and the second department of social production is the leading and decisive disproportionality. Lenin expounded the second performance of the basic contradiction when he was refuting the disproportionality theory, but it was only a partial elaboration. For example, on the issue of the relations between the production of individual enterprises and the production of society as a whole, he had this explanation: "When, during the regime of small, isolated enterprises, work came to a standstill in any one of them, this affected only a few members of society, it did not cause any general confusion ... But when work comes to a standstill in a large enterprise, one engaged in a highly specialised branch of industry and therefore working almost for the whole of society and, in its turn, dependent on the whole of society (for the sake of simplicity I take a case where socialisation has reached the culminating point), work is bound to come to a standstill in all the other enterprises of society..." In addition, there have been no related discussions in Lenin's literature.

9 *Collected Works of V.I. Lenin*, 2nd Chinese Edition, Volume 2, Beijing: People's Publishing House. 1984, pp. 136-137.

Franz Brentano in *The Reason for the Collapse of Economy in Europe*, Eduard Bernstein in *Social Issues*, and Rudolf Hilferding in *Finance Capital* had raised the theory that monopoly organizations can eliminate the crisis, forming a theory of thought with the advocacy of their followers. Lenin had given the criticism at different times that monopoly only changed the form, order and scenarios of crisis, but did not change the inevitable trend of the crisis to occur because monopoly aggravated the anarchy of the capitalist production, so that the basic contradiction of capitalism became more aggravated. "The statement that cartels can abolish crises is a fable spread by bourgeois economists who at all costs desire to place capitalism in a favourable light. On the contrary, the monopoly created in certain branches of industry increases and intensifies the anarchy inherent in capitalist production as a whole. The disparity between the development of agriculture and that of industry, which is characteristic of capitalism in general, is increased. The privileged position of the most highly cartelised, so-called heavy industry, especially coal and iron, causes "a still greater lack of co-ordination" in other branches of industry. …"[10] Here, monopoly actually becomes a driving factor of the crisis.

In Lenin's era, the theory of the populists once posed a challenge to Marx's theory of crisis. They insist that the development of capitalism led to small producers' bankruptcy and proletarianization, resulting in a shrinking market; in a society of only the proletariat and the bourgeoisie, the surplus value cannot be achieved. To realize surplus value, there must be a "third person" that the demand of small producers or foreign market, otherwise capitalist countries will often fall into the attack of overproduction or the economic crisis caused by overproduction. Lenin put forward a series of his own ideas in the course of criticizing the populist: 1) the bankruptcy of small producers is an obstacle to capitalism and capitalist market development, and it is the performance of this development that the bankruptcy of small producers and the proletarianization expands the capitalist market.[11] 2) Even in a capitalist society with the existence of both classes, surplus value can also be fully realized, and even under the conditions that the organic composition of capital is increasing, the expanded reproduction and capital accumulation can be carried out. This accumulation is the characteristic of capitalism. 3) The issue of foreign markets and reality has absolutely nothing in common. The reason for capitalism to need the foreign market is because there is a trend of infinite expansion of capitalist production.[12] The reason that the "third person" leads to the expansion of the capitalist market is simply because they differentiate classes of capitalist society, so that these ideas that the demand for the "third person" is the factor of the expansion of the market are incorrect. Lenin's ideas defended Marx's crisis

10   *Selected Works of V.I. Lenin*, Version 3, Volume 2, Beijing: People's Publishing House. 1995, p. 595.
11   See *Collected Works of V.I. Lenin*, 2nd Chinese Edition, Volume 1, Beijing: People's Publishing House. 1984, pp. 81-82.
12   See *Collected Works of V.I. Lenin*, 2nd Chinese Edition, Volume 2, Beijing: People's Publishing House. 1984, pp. 131-135.

theory, and there are obvious developments – it specifies Marx's crisis theory. Since Marx's study focuses on a purely capitalist society – only two classes of capitalists and workers, Lenin investigated the realization issue of capital with the presence of small producers, and raised the above points of views which exactly negated the Narodnik populist ones, a field which was never studied by Marxist theory of crisis.

II. The Main Theoretical Contribution of Varga's Model

As a famous Soviet-era economist, Eugene Varga had a more outstanding performance in interpreting and defending the theory of Marx, Engels, Lenin and et al., and he raised many questions on the theory of "innovation" of Kautsky, Hilferding, Bauer and et al., giving systematic rebuttal. He insisted that the root reason of the economic crisis of capitalism is the contradiction between the attempts of the unlimited expansion of capital and the relative narrowing of social spending power, and the direct reason is the accumulation of capital. The material basis for the crisis to occur is the renewal of fixed capital. As a firm defender of Marx's theory of crisis, unlike his contemporaries, Varga had different understanding on Marx's theory of crisis that he took into account not only the background of Marx's theory of crisis, but also the characteristics of its methodology. Therefore, the Marxist theory of crisis that he saw is clearly unique: "1) In his analysis, Marx started consciously from the 'pure' capital- 311 ism that is the society composed of only two classes of the bourgeoisie and the proletariat. 2) Marx consciously regarded the whole capitalist society as 'one country', the capitalist market as a unified 'world market'; at this stage, he did not consider the fact that the capitalist society was divided into various independent national territories; he did not consider the difference between the domestic market and the foreign market as well. 3) Marx's general economic theory, especially his theory of crisis, is on the basis of the industrial capitalism, namely capitalism in the free competition of economy. Marx's theory of crisis is based on the capitalism in the ascendancy, that is, in the process of the rapid growth of the connotation and extension."[13] It should be said that, Varga strictly applied Marx's analytic model in the analysis of capital in the economic crisis in 1930s. The proportionality between the two major departments, the excessive growth of the production of the means of production, the expansion and contraction of iron and steel, machinery manufacturing, construction and others, rising and plunging in the stock market, changes in currency issuance, the storage conditions of products, changes in the price index, increase and decrease in the number of enterprises, the development of the credit system, etc., have become the basic elements of the analytic model of the economic crisis. By analyzing data associated with these elements, we can determine the time, extent and development trends of the crisis. Fundamentally, this analysis has

---

13 Eugen Varga, *Modern Capitalism and Economic Crises*, Beijing: SDX Joint Publishing, 1975, pp. 131-135.

provided more convincing evidence for Marx's theory of crisis. It should be noted that, Varga tried to explain all types of capitalist economic crisis with the basic contradiction of capitalism, and he believes that "the intermediate crisis" is also a crisis of overproduction, and like the "classical cycle", its root also lies in the basic contradiction of capitalism. If there are differences between them, it is that only when the intermediate crisis occurs, overproduction involves only certain sectors, and other sectors continue to rise. After the intermediate crisis ends, the rising phase continues, rather than the beginning of the depression phase.

Varga is one of the scholars who gave a systematic description of Marx's theory of economic crisis, since his early studies. He summarized some of the following propositions from Marx's theory of crises: The unplanned nature of commodity production, as well as anarchy is the prerequisite for the crisis; the contradiction between socialized production and capitalist possession is the basic cause of the crisis; private ownership, tenure of capitalism will inevitably lead to the situation of the masses being the proletariat, which is the ultimate reason of all the real crisis; the accumulation of capital is the driving force in the cyclical process of reproduction; the accumulation of capital can expand the capitalist market within certain limits, but it is also a direct reason of the crisis; the renewal of fixed capital is the material basis for production to be carried out periodically; the contradiction between socialized production of capitalism and the private ownership forces the capitalists to accumulate, which in turn leads to a reduction of social spending power, and it often is the same thing with the relative overproduction; under capitalist conditions, the disproportionality is not accidental, but inevitable; crisis is the starting point for massive new investment. These propositions are the core of Marx's theory of economic crisis, as well as the basic elements of Marx's analytic model of economic crisis.

To recognize the capitalist economic crisis, it is inappropriate to just stay in the form of phenomenon, and it is also not enough to just stay in the level of constitutive relations. One should strive to make the understanding not only of reflecting the constitutive relations, but also reflecting the form of phenomenon, so that the understanding of the fundamental reason and the specific reason will be in unity. Varga adheres to Marx's approach of understanding the economic crisis of capitalism from the perspective of the unity of "general" and "specific", insists that the root of the capitalist economic crisis lies in the basic contradiction of capitalism, but the general premise is not enough to describe each of the specific cycles and crises. Each cycle and each crisis has its own specific historic nature determined by a number of factors. The process of cycles and crises changes along with the development of the industrial capitalism of capitalist free competition to monopoly capitalism, and to the times of the general crisis of capitalism. The agricultural crisis has a great impact on both the cycle and the crisis. The "contingency" of economy such as poor harvests and finding a wealth of gold, etc., can cause changes in the cycle process. A number of factors caused directly by the non-economic reasons, such as plague, war, insurrection and revolution can destroy the process of cycle and crisis. That is to say, every cyclical crisis has a special place in the history of capitalism, and every crisis has its own characteristics different from the previous crises.

Varga insists on the role of accumulation in promoting reproduction, and role of consumption in constraining capitalist reproduction, and he thinks that the relative reduction in spending power caused by accumulation sooner or later is bound to terminate the expansion of production, and the phase of prosperity will inevitably lead to the crisis of the actual accumulation process to be temporarily interrupted. That is to say, as long as the actual accumulation process is in full swing, as long as the construction of new factories, blast furnaces and railroad continues, as long as old machines are replaced by new machines, prosperity will continue indefinitely. Once this process reaches a certain stage of completion, once the majority of new production facilities have been made, the demand for commodities of the first department will be reduced immediately and this will cause the reduction in demand for the means of subsistence, because workers of the first department began to become the unemployed. Meanwhile the supply of commodities increases because of new factories and renewed old factories begin to increase their marketing efforts. Overproduction already occurs, but the crisis does not appear obviously because those capitalists who are still optimistic and ignore the crisis possibility continue to reserve their commodities. As long as crisis remains covert and there are no open signals production always exceeds consumption.

Untill the Great Depression erupted in the 1930s, only few people were concerned about the capitalist agricultural crisis. Varga had done groundbreaking study work in this area. It was he who first suggested that the reason for the capitalist agricultural crisis and industrial crises is the basic contradiction of capitalism, that is, "the contradiction between the socialization of production and capitalist form of possession, as well as the resulting poverty and decline in the purchasing power of the masses."[14] The nature of the crisis is always the crisis of overproduction. The difference between the two is that the agricultural crisis lasts much longer than the industrial crisis without any sign of cyclical repetition. The reason why there is no crisis of cyclical repetition in agriculture is because production of simple commodity and the production of consumption by its own are dominant in agriculture. The reason why the agricultural crisis lasts much longer than the industrial crisis is because the capitalist development in agriculture is relatively low. As agriculture is backward, the agricultural production is not as reduced as industrial production in the case of crisis. Crisis does not have the form of the production to come to a standstill, but it is manifested in the form of accumulating a large number of reserves that cannot be sold under conditions of production which is not reduced. In the agricultural crisis of capitalism, rent plays a special role, because "rent is not the factor

14 Eugen Varga, *Modern Capitalism and Economic Crises*, Beijing: SDX Joint Publishing. 1975, p. 22.

of social production costs, but the factor of production cost of land renters or landowners. If the agricultural price falls when the production costs remain unchanged, well, land renters or landowners of the debt burden are unable to pay exorbitant rents or mortgage interest. Even the actual production costs he pays enables him to get the average profit, but if he is not able to settle the excessive rents as provided, he would go bankrupt."[15] In the interrelationship between agricultural crisis and industrial crisis, Varga tends to think they are mutually intertwined and promoted.

In terms of the insurmountable problem on the capitalist economic crisis, Varga provided a more illustrative viewpoint for Marx, Engels, Lenin and et al, he enumerated the ways that capitalism overcame the crisis: to exclude enterprises of competition by bankruptcy; to eliminate excess inventory by reducing the production below the shrinking level of consumption, by lowering prices, and by damaging or destructing commodities.; the necessity to replace the worn out fixed capital; low interest rate conducive to long-term investment, etc. and so on. He reiterates that these approaches are still, as Marx said, approaches that will lead to greater crises to overcome the crisis.

III. The Basic Interpretation of the Marxist Theory of the Economic Crisis by Mendelson

Mendelson also used the three-dimensional integrated structure of "theory, history, reality" to elaborate the crisis issue, and unlike the theoretical system of Tugan and Oelssneron in the order of the system, he belongs to the same type. Starting from resolutely defending Marx's theory of crisis, Mendelson listed systematically on Marx's theory of crisis, did a lot of empirical research work from a historical point of view, and gave a distinctive elaboration of Marx's theory of crisis.

In order for the possibility of the economic crisis to develop into a reality, it must meet a series of relationships. Marx pointed this out, but did not specify what these relationships are, which since then has become one of the difficulties that must carry out explorations in the political economy, there are many scholars who have tried to study in depth, to find strong evidences for solutions to the problem, and to make the reasonable explanation to it. Mendelson is one of them, and his study work involves almost all aspects of Marx's theory of economic crisis, putting forward his own evidence, or putting forward his views or conclusions. On the issue of the "intermediary" relations of the crisis to transform from the possibility to the reality, he realized that a set of relations that determines the inevitability of crisis develops along with the capitalist mode of production, and it resides in the basic contradiction of capitalism –the contradiction between the socialization of production and the capitalist private ownership. Specifically, this "a set of relations" is not only the relations of socialized production formed in the process of socialization of production, but

15 Ibid., pp.163-164.

also the relations of capitalist private ownership formed by the development of ownership relations. Once with the "relations of socialized production" and the "relations of capitalist private ownership," the possibility of crisis will develop into the reality. Socialized production "always means the relations and the interdependent relations among all enterprises, production sectors, and countries are being expanded and strengthened, there is a certain unity between each other in the process of reproduction."[16] It requires that the means of production is owned by the society objectively, and the society arranges production according to the needs of social members. However, the means of production is in the hands of the private, becoming a tool to maximize access to the surplus value. This antagonism is specifically manifested in the trends of unlimited expansion of production and "to limit the consumption of the masses in a low quantity"[17], as well as in the organization of production of individual enterprises and the anarchy of production in the whole society. Like all the orthodox Marxist economists, Mendelson's theoretical explanations are also under the premise that this antagonism is unable to be overcome in the capitalist system.

Mendelson endorses to attribute the root reason of capitalist economic crisis to the basic contradiction of capitalism, but he opposes to using a particular aspect of the performance of the basic contradiction to explain the reasons of the crisis. For example, it cannot simply and one-sidedly attribute the reason of the crisis to "underconsumption", "disproportionality", "difficult to achieve" and so on. Because, all the contradictions of capitalist society are the performance of the basic contradiction of capitalism; the basic contradiction of capitalism is the common basis of all contradictions of capitalism. There is a close relationship and interdependence between the various contradictions. The reason for the capitalist economic crisis could be anarchy, or the contradiction between production and consumption, or the contradiction between production conditions and realization conditions of the surplus value, because they are the performance of the basic contradictions of capitalism. Therefore, with a manifestation of the basic contradiction to explain the reasons of the crisis, while denying another manifestation of the basic contradiction to be also the reason of the crisis, this is a wrong approach. Mendelson's perspectives are coincident with Marx's understanding of the economic crisis, that the capitalist economic crisis is the result of all the contradictions of capitalism being fully developed.

Mendelson does not agree with the "disproportionality" theory, and he took out more convincing views of predecessors or contemporaries to illustrate the inevitability of the disproportionality of capitalist production. For example, he believes that the ongoing accumulation of capital that determines the

---

16 Mendelson, *Theory and History of the Economic Crisis and Cycle*, Beijing: Joint Publishing. 1977, pp. 29-30.
17 Whether "the consumption of the masses" here refers to "the desire for consumption" or "the consumption with the ability to pay", Mendelson and people before him, as well as his contemporaries were very clear, since they had noticed Marx's important comment "overproduction...without any consideration for the actual limits of the market or the needs backed by the ability to pay."

characteristics of capitalist reproduction is the expanded production, and what is needed for the smooth operation of the expanded reproduction is the proportionality, which is only shown as a trend under the capitalist system. Equilibrium is accidental, and the recurring disproportionality is absolute. Every time the expansion of production and the improvement of production in some sectors invalidate the old proportionality and forms the new one under the conditions of highly developed social division of labour and professionalization of labour. In the antagonistic relations of classes, the contradiction between production and consumption is bound to exist, which is the basis of the disproportionality between production and consumption. On this basis, it produced a fundamental disproportionality of capitalist production – the expansion of the market for personal consumption way behind the expansion of production.

Since the classical economics, the study of capitalist economic crisis and the exploration of the reasons for the crisis has been one of the main targets. In his writings, Mendelson almost quoted all fragments of Marx's remarks on the reasons of the economic crisis, but he did not summarize it as a whole. From his discourse, readers can see reasons that have not been summarized and are in levels, namely the reason in the first level or the most fundamental reason is "the basic contradiction of capitalism"; the reason in the second level is the "disproportionality" and "low level of consumption of the majority of the masses"; and the reason in the third level is the "sales difficulties" of commodities. The reason in the first level is the deepest, the most abstract theoretic reason, and the reason in the third level is the most direct theoretical reason. There should also be another reason fully consistent with the reality of economic life after the reason in the third level, which is the specific reason that triggers every crisis. The crisis of overproduction is caused by the sales difficulties of commodities, which in turn is not necessarily caused by overproduction. The reason for "disproportionality" is because the capitalist commodity production is the production to meet the desire for profit, which does not always lead to the "disproportionality."

Underconsumption theory and disproportionality theory have their own long development history. To interpret the economic crisis with underconsumption was advocated by Sismondi in the first 25 years of the 19th century, and it was repeated by Malthus and Rodbertus in one form or another. Ricardo and Say were the earliest advocators of the disproportionality theory; Tugan-Baranovsky, Hilferding and Bernstein were the main successors of the disproportionality theory. Mendelson even said that Hilferding had inherited and developed Tugan's idea. Since Kautsky used "underconsumption" to explain the crisis while Hilferding used "disproportionality", both of them have become the object of criticism by Mendelson. The underconsumption theory and the disproportionality theory are suspected to be able to overcome the economic crisis of capitalism without destroying the capitalist system[18], so for many

18 "Underconsumption theory" believes that the crisis can be overcome by raising worker's wages, while "disproportionality theory" believes that the crisis can be overcome through the power of monopolies.

years they have been regarded as the opportunist theory by the orthodox radical Marxist economists and gone through the punitive expedition. Mendelson also joined their ranks. In the middle of the 20th century, the Soviet mainstream theoretic economists had largely accepted the proposition that the basic contradiction of capitalism is the root reason of the crisis of overproduction, and used the dialectical movement of the basic contradiction to explain the business cycle, considering that every crisis was creating the premise to overcome itself, and creating the conditions for the next crisis to occur. Moreover, these economists also regarded the outbreak of the economic crisis as the destruction of the equilibrium, and the only possible means to restore the equilibrium forcibly, partially, and temporarily. This is not the development of Marxist crisis theory, but it means the political economists have increased the degree of cognition of Marx's crisis theory. Mendelson is one typical representative of such economists.

In the mid-20th century, another issue which was widely debated among Soviet economists is the "law of the capitalist economic crisis." Many economists, including Varga, made their comments. Mendelson seemed a step ahead of his colleagues in understanding the law of crisis, and he proposed a set of theories on the issue. He believes that the law of the crisis is the law of the capitalist reproduction. Its essence lies in the contradiction between the socialization of production and the private ownership of the means of production, which at every a certain point, it is inevitable to destroy the reproduction of social capital, manifested in the crisis of overproduction.[19] The form for the law of crisis to play a role is the periodicity of the capitalist reproduction, the material basis of which is the renewal of fixed capital. This explanation, in the sense of theory, obviously deepened and systematized Marx's theory of crisis. However, the performance of the capitalist economic crisis in the second half of the 20th century made people question Mendelson's theoretical explanation, since it is the law that its objectivity determines that the people can neither transform it nor create it, but the macro-control of the state monopoly capitalism not only changes the cyclical economic crises, even for those sporadic crises, the extent has greatly reduced, and the manifestations have undergone great changes. It is to some extent explains that capitalism does not seem to have the law of the economic crisis. Chinese scholar Hu Jichuang once stated that: "The mid-cycle of a period of 10 years or so, was repeatedly presented in the era of laissez-faire capitalism of the 19th century, but since the 1930s due to strengthening of the national intervention, the strong resistance of the transnational monopolies and other reasons, the fluctuation of the mid-cycle has been disrupted, often presenting a short volatility 3 to 5 years after World War II, with the economic revival sometimes while weakness in another. It is no longer presented in the regular fluctuations of the mid-cycle as in the past, but the overall trend seems to be that the capitalist economy continues to grow

---

19   See Mendelson, *Theory and History of the Economic Crisis and Cycle*, Beijing: Joint Publishing. 1977, p. 58.

slowly."[20] It is suggested that it is necessary to make a strict definition of "economic crisis" and "economic fluctuation" in the concept, because capitalism can weaken the cyclical economic crises, but cannot eliminate the economic fluctuations. The economic fluctuation can often occur, but the economic crisis can occasionally occur.

After World War II, with the confusion and disappearance in the frequency of the cyclical economic crises of about 10 years, people began to focus on the short-term, partial economic crisis, and found a suitable name from the writings of Marx and Engels – the intermediary crisis.[21] Except he disagrees that the intermediary crisis has cycle, Mendelson basically agrees with the views of Engels, but he just investigated and summarized it in the sense of the history of doctrine, without putting forward anything new. He put the intermediary crisis as the one that is not as universal and deep as the cyclical crises and a symbol that the market encountered specific difficulties. As for in what situation the intermediary crisis occurs, Mendelson believes that it occurs when factors of a strong reaction make it difficult for overproduction to be universal. The reason why Mendelson had fewer concerns about the intermediary crisis is mainly because the cyclical crisis of about 10 years at that time were more obvious, the movement frequency of its cycle has not been disrupted.

In the history of economics, the issue of whether the business cycle is consistent with the economic crisis is also a problem that experienced years of debate. Through the investigation of the economic crisis in1825-1900, Leschel drew the conclusions that the economic crisis had an "erratic pattern" and "non-crisis cycle" and etc. Mendelson accused Tugan-Baranovsky to be the advocator of "no-crisis cycle". Mitchell in his *Business Cycle*, Thorpe in his Business Yearbook, almost reached the conclusion of "crisis without the law" and "no-crisis cycle". Mendelson suggests that these people are the theory defenders, who announce that any fluctuation in the economy is the replacement of the various stages of the business cycle, thus concocting cycles of varying lengths and the indeterminate number. These so-called "cycle" is completely contrary to the fact, and there is no business cycle in England that does not end with a clear crisis of overproduction. "As long as the date of some crises is listed, it is enough to believe that the recurring crisis in the capitalist economy is regular", but it's only the interval of each crisis changes, showing a tendency to be shortened, which is completely in line with the regularity.[22] Mendelson claimed to have proved with the history of the economic crisis that: "Those places where there are no crises there are no cycles." "In places where the crisis is still partial due to the underdeveloped factory production, there is still

318

---

20   Hu Jichuang. *The Analysis of Differences in Political Economy*, Shanghai: Fudan University Press. 1991, pp. 211-212.

21   Marx called the intermediary crisis partial crisis and Engels called the crisis that occurred after a great crisis, as a more partial and particular economic crisis with a period of about five years.

22   See Mendelson, *Theory and History of the Economic Crisis and Cycle*, Beijing: Joint Publishing. 1977, p. 181

no cycle." "It is only the general overproduction that makes the movement of capitalist economy cyclical." "Every crisis is the start of a cycle and the end of another"[23]. This implies that where there are cycles, there are inevitably economic crises. In the field of political economy, modern people basically have accepted the view that the business cycle and economic crisis can be completely inconsistent. However, Soviet scholars accepted their inconsistencies only from one point of view.

Marx discovered and pointed out the material basis for the capitalist economy to be carried out cyclically, but he did not explain why the fixed capital could be concentrated and renewed on a large scale in the same time. Such a question that is crucial to explain the business cycle, in terms of the theoretical system, would a defect in any case if there is not a reasonable explanation. Mendelson had done a great work at this point. He believes that the reason why the fixed capital is able to be renewed spontaneously and on a large scale within a short period of time, showing the bouncing nature, the main reason is the capitalist economic crisis and the intangible abrasion of the fixed capital. Mendelson believes that the crisis creates premise for the renewal of fixed capital on a large scale, which in turn creates the conditions for the next crisis. Its realization mechanism is: The economic crisis reduces the price of commodities, so that enterprises with high production cost and technological obsolescence are destroyed, or on the verge of bankruptcy. Capitalists first adopt the direct approach of lowering wages to find a way out for themselves, but because of workers' revolt, as well as workers' standard of living coming down to a certain stage that would lead to the decline in labour productivity, and other reasons, so that lowering wages is subject to certain restrictions. In comparison, the adoption of the new machine can not only reduce labour costs, but also reduce the costs of production, lower costs, lower prices, and defeat opponents. During the crisis, the decrease in the price of the machine also makes the price of the machine reduced, which provides stimulus for the renewal of fixed capital in the sense of cost reduction. Under the blow of the crisis, companies whether they have advanced or backward technologies are looking to adopt new machines. Because the crisis also deteriorates those companies that have modern equipment, and the price decline caused by the crisis disqualifies these companies for excess profits, so in order to maintain their leading positions on the profits, they will adopt more competitive new machines. So, for capitalist production, the spontaneous renewal of fixed capital in the same time has the nature of forcible inevitability. In times of crisis, the renewal of fixed capital is usually down below its tangible abrasion, and at the same time, the intangible abrasion of fixed capital on a large scale occurs, so it needs to replace a large part in advance. As a result, at the end of a crisis, capitalism needs a lot of renewal of the obsolete equipment in practice and virtually. After the crisis, under the pressure of various conditions caused by the crisis, the scale of fixed capital renewal is much larger than the size of the renewal annually.

23   Ibid., p.183.

The renewal of fixed capital is the material basis of the crisis to be carried out cyclically. The argument about this proposition is caused by Marx's different versions at different occasions. During the first draft of writing *Capital* in 1858, Marx wrote to Engels and asked about the length of the renewal cycle in the plant equipment, and when Engels told him the figure of "13 years", Marx said, "it establishes a unit for one epoch of industrial reproduction", but he also pointed out that "the average time for the renewal of machines is an important factor to interpret the length of the cycle that industrial development has to go through"; or "in direct material premise of the great industry, it contains a factor of such a cycle. "This suggests that the renewal of fixed capital is only one factor of the large industry to be carried out cyclically, but not the one that later known as "the material basis for cyclical economic crises." This is confirmed by Marx's remarks when he investigated the prepaid capital turnover in *Capital* Volume II: "This much is evident: the cycle of interconnected turnovers embracing a number of years, in which capital is held fast by its fixed constituent part, furnishes a material basis for the periodic crises."[24] Here, "the cycle of interconnected turnovers embracing a number of years" should mean the "turnover of a number of years" of "a lot of capital" instead of "the renewal of fixed capital on a large scale." Therefore, from the question about the time of the renewal of plant equipment Marx inquired to Engels, it is difficult to draw the conclusion that "the renewal of fixed capital is the basis for the cyclical economic crises of capitalism". This debate ultimately focused on a question difficult to explain, namely: why the fixed capital is able to be renewed spontaneously and on a large scale. If the renewal of fixed capital is indeed the material basis for periodic capitalist economic crisis, what is the transmission mechanism? It is also a problem that needs to be clarified. From the description of Mendelson on the process of the renewal and expansion of fixed capital, we can see something. It is the renewal and expansion of fixed capital that improves the level of productivity, technology, and organic composition of capital, which in turn further causes a series of reactions: disproportionality, a serious deviation of the price of commodities from the value, fall in the rate of profits, acceleration of the intangible abrasion of the old enterprises, the imbalanced rise in the price of the means of production, the price of the means of subsistence, and the labour costs, it is inevitable to destroy the turnover of all social capital, and the whole process of social reproduction tends to disorder, so that the basic contradiction of capitalism becomes more and more aggravated, ultimately it can only be resolved through the crisis of the mandatory approach.

Why overproduction crisis is like an economic disaster, and like an explosion, to burst out suddenly? It is also known as an important problem of crisis theory. Hilferding raised the issue, but did not answer. Mendelson answered this question. He believes that the reason for the sudden outbreak is because that there has already been an incubation period for some time before the crisis, and during this period, factors of the crisis gradually accumulate, after reaching

---

24　*Capital*, Volume II, Beijing: The People's Publishing House, 1975, p.207.

a certain critical point, it bursts out in a sudden way. As to why there is an incubation period before the crisis, the reason is that: 1) when new plants that produce the material elements of fixed capital are in construction; they are not the source of supply of the material elements of fixed capital, but the root of the demand of these elements. Due to the high demand of new plants for material elements of fixed capital, the price rises. The rise in prices further stimulates the construction of new plants, and when these plants are put into operation the overproduction emerges. 2) The overstock of commodities. 3) Under capitalism, there is no direct link between production and consumption. Large overstock of commodities in the hands of middlemen causes an illusionary demand. 4) The effect of credit.

In the works studying the economic crisis after the 1940s, there is a considerable part of the Soviet scholars who made special arrangements of relevant sections in agricultural crisis, and ultimately formed a more mature analytic model. Mendelson's study on the issue of agricultural crisis made a better application of the model used in the analysis of the industrial crisis, but he is not limited to this model and according to the special nature of the agricultural crisis, he created a specialized model to analyze the agricultural crisis, making his study become groundbreaking in many ways. Mendelson divided the manifestation of capitalist overproduction crisis in agriculture into two forms: the cyclical overproduction manifested as the effect of the general cyclical crisis in agriculture; durable agriculture crisis. The basic reason for both is the same, namely, the contradiction between the socialization of production and the capitalist possession. The special contradiction of capitalism in agriculture – the contradiction of land rent and agriculture behind the law of industry – is demonstrated in the dynamic of both categories of crisis, but the performances are completely different. The cyclical overproduction begins with the second form in agriculture, and it is the result of the industrial crisis and the thereby reduction in the demand for agricultural products. The reason why the general crisis of overproduction takes this form to have effect in agriculture is because agriculture is behind industry; it is because in the stage of periodical upsurge, unlike the industry, agriculture will not have jump expansion of fixed capital on a massive scale and spastic expansion of production; it is because when the upsurge usually comes to an end, the phenomenon that agriculture is behind industry is intensified, and the disproportionality between industry and the demand of industrial population for agricultural products, and the supply of agricultural products occurs, which in many cycles has accelerated the outbreak of the general crisis of overproduction.

Agricultural crisis is incubated by more profound processes of lasting effect, and these processes have dramatically changed the conditions for the production and sale of agricultural products and destroyed the normal reproduction of agriculture. These processes had ever happened in the last 25 years of the 19th century, as well as between 1920 and 1940. Compared with the industrial crisis, agricultural crisis is lasting. Major factors for the everlasting agriculture crisis are: 1) A sharp and lasting particular conflict among the reduced value,

321

production price and market price that are fixed at a high level of rent; 2) The obstacle set by rent and backward agriculture to eliminate overproduction by reducing production; only the long-term and profound reduction in price drop will cause the decline in the seeded area and the destruction of part of the crop; 3) The obstacle set by rent and backward agriculture to get rid of the crisis by increasing investment, improving technology expanding specialization and other methods; 4) under the conditions of imperialism, the special form of monopoly oppression in agriculture caused by the agricultural backwardness also obstructs the escape of agricultural crisis; 5) It is a long-term process for the agricultural crisis to be unfolding, which is also why the agricultural crisis could not be relieved; 6) These processes are developed on the basis of the generally sharp conflict of reproduction in the whole capitalist world economy, which is also very important. Mendelson's main contribution to the capitalist agricultural crisis theory lies in his above interpretation of why capitalist agricultural crisis are protracted.

IV. The Examination of Marx's Analytic Model of Economic Crisis with Historical Facts by Mendelson

For the establishment of analytic model of economic crisis and the creation of the economic crisis theory, we must first study the history of economic crisis, which is almost the traditional procedure for studying the economic crisis issue. However, during the theory narrative, it is not necessary to adopt the part of the history of crisis, just as Marx did. Writers after Marx used the "trinity" narrative structure of a theoretical system, namely history, theory and reality, and "history" often account for a large portion. The description of the crisis before 1825 is sketchy while it is relatively detailed after 1825. This description of the facts, is the historical test of Marxist analytic model of the economic crisis with facts, and also provides the basis of historical facts for the development of the model, which has the importance for the promotion of the historic transformation of models and paradigms. When creating the analytic model of the economic crisis itself, Marx had studied crises before the cyclical crisis, and he also paid very careful attention, studied and analyzed a series of periodic world economic crisis occurring in 1825, 1837, 1847, 1857, 1866, 1873 and 1882, which is the process to establish and perfect the theoretical model, as well as the process to test the model. After Marx's death, corresponding to the development and improvement of Marxist analytic model of the economic crisis, the investigation and study of the history and reality of the economic crisis should also continue. Each step of the development of productivity and relations of production adds new elements; new contents and new features of both the capitalist economic crisis, and the model for analyzing the crisis should also be improved subsequently. In comparison, Mendelson had made a very typical study, as well as a comprehensive and detailed investigation on the facts. To see facts from Marx's model and to see Marx's model from facts is one of the basic methods that Mendelson studied the history of the economic crisis.

Verification of Marx's model with real facts

The logical sequence of Marx's analytic model of the economic crisis set by Mendelson is developed as: getting rid of the previous crisis–the formation and characteristics of the upsurge stage–the material basis of upsurge stage–erecting enterprises, entrepreneurial activity, speculation, credit expansion –the maturation of the crisis – the beginning of the crisis –sequence of countries to have crisis occurred – the status and struggle of the working class. As some later Marxist economists say, the purpose for the Marxists to study the capitalist economic relations is not to advise capitalism, saving its historical fate of the inevitable demise, but rather to reveal the historical trend of capitalism toward inevitable extinction. Therefore, the analysis of the crisis is not to provide solutions to problems in order to alleviate or overcome the crisis, but mainly to provide a theoretical weapon for the proletariat. Probably it is because of this reason, the study of capitalist economic crisis by Mendelson is based on the premise that the economic crisis of capitalism is inevitable and it is increasingly severe, and for every crisis he studied, he was trying to come to the conclusion that it is the crisis of overproduction, with universality, comprehensiveness and regularity. So, he put great emphasis on the accuracy of production cycle in time, as well as new features manifested. The policy implications of these conclusions contained that only by destroying the capitalist system can the crisis be overcome. The study of the capitalist economic crisis by Mendelson always only emphasized the inevitability of the crisis, focusing on general reasons, with little involvement of specific factors that affected the history of the crisis, which is largely ignored. This is one of the fundamental differences between him and the bourgeois economists at the capitalist economic crisis. He once pointed out: "The attempt to explain the crisis with each specifically historical kind of factors specified for a specific period has long been ridiculed by Marx; for characteristics that clarify each crisis, these factors are very important, however, the reason for all crises is the same, which is contained in the contradiction of antagonism of the capitalist reproduction."[25] Mendelson thinks that there is a significant difference between the crises in the late 18th century and early 19th century and crises after 1825, but the difference is only in the distinction of the same phenomenon and the same movement of the law of capitalism in the two different stages of the history of development. They are both the crisis of capitalist overproduction, subject to the same laws of capitalism, meaning that the market is flooded of merchandise, as well as of sales difficulties and production curtailments. It did not exhibit cyclical characteristics just before the crisis of 1825 only, and there are almost no rules to follow. It is only that machines and capitalist plants in their childhood have pressed commodities produced in accordance with the capitalist mode of production to flood in the market. These early crises are partial or localized, with little economic impact, but it is already the conclusive overproduction crisis.

---

25 Mendelson, *Theory and History of the Economic Crisis and Cycle*, Volume II (1), Beijing: Joint Publishing. 1975, p. 326.

So, Mendelson had negative attitude towards Tugan's insights, thinking that he made a mistake of metaphysics in the methodology. "Early in the late18th century, the development of the factory system has become the root reason of the overproduction crisis often caused by the intensified conflicts of capitalist accumulation. The root reason and the historical conditions of the crisis cannot be confused: The former determines the nature of the crisis, while the latter determines the characteristics of each crisis."[26] Wars, continental blockade and so forth are just some of the factors that exacerbate the crisis, rather than the root reason of the crisis. Due to the divergence in views, in Mendelson's opinion, two of the most important questions need to be addressed in studying the history of early capitalist economic crisis: What kind of historical conditions make overproduction crisis become inevitable; how they gradually developed into a regular and repeated cyclical general crisis of overproduction.

Mendelson insisted on approaching to history with the attitude of historical materialism, explaining the development process of the crisis in contradictory movement between productivity and relations of production, and when he described the history of the economic crisis, he always used the analytical method of contradiction. The elaboration is developing throughout two main lines: one is the main line of the development of productive forces; the other is the main line of the development of relations of production. The two main lines are developing contradictions in the unity of opposites, and continually forming the new unity of opposites in contradictions.

Firstly, in the main line, Mendelson has tried to prove that, the transformation from possibility to inevitability of overproduction crisis was gradually formed with the emergence and development of large-scale machine industry. Before the emergence of industrial machinery, there was not even the soil to produce the partial overproduction crisis. With the applications of machines, revolution in production methods and the emergence of capitalist factory system, it creates a premise for the rapid expansion of production. The economic conditions for the general law of capitalist accumulation and the antagonistic contradiction of capitalist reproduction to fully play the role are formed, and the contradiction between the socialization of production and capitalist private ownership also develop to a new stage. From this time, the capitalist economic crisis is inevitable. So, when inspecting the history of the periodic crises, Mendelson took the history of the economy in England as an example, with the emphasis on the investigation of the formation of large machinery production and its impact on the industrial revolution. He saw these facts from the historical facts: the use of the steam engine, the development of metal smelting and processing technology, and the improvement of transportation conditions, are the decisive factors for the industrial revolution to complete in the last; the invention, adoption and improvement of textile machinery promotes the rise of the factory system; the generalization of factory contributes greatly to the increase in productivity.

26 Mendelson, *Theory and History of the Economic Crisis and Cycle*, Volume I (1), Beijing: Joint Publishing. 1975, p. 356.

Mendelson sees these as the productive factors of capitalist overproduction. He had a very detailed description of the development of the plant industry in England, France, Germany, United States, Russia and other countries, trying to keep historical data used and quoted consistent with Marx and Engels, as well as the conclusions consistent with Marx and Engels. For example, through the study of the history of the crisis in England in the early 19th century, he had the following conclusion: "In the first quarter of the 19th century, the large factory production has played a major role in England, but still by no means it is dominant, but just the superstructure of the manipulatory manufacture and small handicraft production. The manipulatory manufacture and small handicraft production in England is basically organized in accordance with the capitalist household production system, and they provide most of the industrial products. Other countries and the whole capitalist world are even more so. This case determines the main features of the early industrial crisis."[27] The above conclusion is based primarily on the description by Engels on the development of large-scale machine industry in England, namely: "About the middle of last century England was the principal seat of the cotton manufacture, and therefore the natural place where, with a rapidly rising demand for cotton goods, the machinery was invented which, with the help of the steam engine, revolutionised first the cotton trade, and successively the other textile manufactures. The large and easily accessible coalfields of Great Britain, thanks to steam, became now the basis of the country's prosperity. The extensive deposits of iron ore in close proximity to the coal facilitated the development of the iron trade, which had received a new stimulus by the demand for engines and machinery. Then, in the midst of this revolution of the whole manufacturing system, came the anti-Jacobin and Napoleonic wars which for some twenty-five years drove the ships of almost ail competing nations from the sea, and thus gave to English manufactured goods the practical monopoly of all Transatlantic and some European markets. When in 1815 peace was restored, England stood there with her steam manufactures ready to supply the world, while steam engines were as yet scarcely known in other countries. In manufacturing industry, England was an immense distance in advance of them."[28] This consistency is further reflected in their understanding of the universal periodic crises of overproduction, where they both consider that the large industrial machine is not yet dominant, and it is the main reason for the cyclical economic crisis not to come yet.

In the second main line, Mendelson first examined the general law of capitalist accumulation. Because the law on the one hand manifests itself as an increase in the wealth of the capitalists, and on the other hand as intensified poverty of the labour people. Therefore, what the authors elaborated is to provide a historical basis for these two trends. During the industrial revolution, the British manufacturer obtained excessive profits with its monopoly position; the

325

---

27 Ibid., p. 295.
28 *Marx and Engels Collected Works*, Chinese Version, Edition 1, Volume 19, Beijing: People's Publishing House, 1963, p. 288.

British bourgeoisie, landed aristocracy and capitalist farmers made a fortune in the French wars, slave trade and the enclosure movement – these facts show the accumulation of wealth. The reduction in the nominal salary of the basic unit of the working class, the rising cost of living, the increase in tax burden, the bankruptcy of a large number of small farmers and artisans, the vast war spending, the tragic consequences by using machines to household industrial workers – the combined effect of these factors make masses of people fall into extreme poverty. The trend in these two areas can be summed up as "an unprecedented increase in the wealth of the exploiting classes, while the living standards of the masses and the average consumption calculated according to their population have greatly reduced."[29] This development contracts the domestic market, especially limits the scope of expansion in the social production sector of the second department. Thus, the bourgeoisie is compelled to seek foreign markets more perseveringly, but expanding in foreign markets is also full of contradictions. Overall, with the establishment of the capitalist rule, there is a large enough market for the universal law of capitalist accumulation to be effective. The contradiction between the socialization of production and the capitalist private ownership develops to a new stage, and manifests itself through various forms. The antagonism between the bourgeoisie and the proletariat, the contradiction between production and consumption, as well as the anarchy of capitalist production, is also manifested clearly for the first time in the history. Thus, the conditions for the overproduction crisis are formed. When he drew the above conclusions, Mendelson not only used the British historical facts, but also the historical facts of other countries.

The idea for Mendelson to study the crisis is not to summarize and generalize the theory, to build models based on the historical facts of the crisis, but to find the facts from the existing theoretical model – Marx's theoretical model of crisis. The meaning of doing such work is that: On the one hand to prove that Marx's theory of crisis has reliable historical basis, and on the other hand to prove Marx's theory of crisis can withstand the test of history and practice. However, it is easy to drive Marxist theory to the extreme for doing so, and shut itself up, losing the incentives for theoretical innovation.

The crisis itself is gradually developing from irregular occurrence towards regularity, and in this process, the number of common factors, the stage of development, and the phenomenon is more and more clearly demonstrated in the crisis, while the time interval is also becoming more and more regular, which is most typical in England. For example, Mendelson's historical description of the 1788 crisis includes such a sequence: large numbers of new enterprises emerge, the prevalence of speculation, technical performance of textile machinery improves, the increase in number, the increase in efficiency, a substantial increase in production, excess supply, the decline in prices which cause panic, the collapse of textile factories, the bankruptcy of capitalists and unemployment. The description of the1793 involves such elements in sequence: the application of

29   Mendelson, *Theory and History of the Economic Crisis and Cycle*, Volume I (1), p. 295.

new machines, the increase in exports, the entrepreneurial fever, the rise in stock price, credit expansion, the prevalence of speculation, the violent rise in prices, oversupply, falling prices and increased textile bankruptcy, financial collapse, and the breakout of the economic crisis. The description of the 1797 crisis involves such elements in sequence: the increase in cotton exports, wars, the development of heavy industry, the increase in production of woollen cloth, the decline in production, trade contraction, and the currency crisis. The description of the 1810 crisis involves such elements in sequence: wars and continent blockade, increasing production of pig iron, an increase in cotton imports, an increase in cotton textile exports, soaring raw material prices, poor harvests, soaring food prices, low purchasing power of the masses, the export reduction, raw material prices slump, bankruptcy surge, business crisis, credit crisis, industrial crisis (mainly textile industry).The description of the 1815 crisis involves such elements in sequence: the end of the war, the surge in exports of cotton textiles, new record for cotton yield, credit expansion, erecting enterprises, the prevalence of speculation, the rise in prices, flooding of commodities, prices slump, reduced exports, the breakout of crises, and in addition to the textile industry, ferrous metallurgy and coal industry are also suffered a heavy blow, the fixed capital of corporations is greatly devalued, currency crisis is very serious, a large number of bank failures, unemployment is severe. The description of the 1819 crisis involves such elements in sequence: abundant liquidity, gold drain, increased imports, exchange rate decline, bankruptcy of import speculation, the decline in textile exports and production, poor harvests, soaring food prices, the crisis, and the crisis hit almost all industrial centres of the textile and metal processing in England. Through careful description of each crisis, Mendelson found the crisis before the periodic crisis was in a process of gradual growth, extending gradually from a certain production department to all departments. A number of elements that play a role in the production area gradually extend to elements in all areas; there are some very fixed elements, as well as non-fixed elements. The worsening of the living condition of the working people is the low consumption level, as well as the intensification of the contradiction among classes are accompanied by the growth process of almost every crisis. The description of the growth trend of the crisis convinces the reader that in the capitalist society where the production is to maximize the profits, the economy is in anarchy, and consumption of the masses is very low, the tremendous growth in the large machinery production cannot avoid economic fluctuations caused by sales difficulties.

The investigation of the periodic crises is also to have the theoretical model in the first, and then to find historical basis. Mendelson had made strict definition of the object to be elaborated, and he thinks that the cyclical economic crises not only refers to inevitable repetition of crises, but also refers to the jump in the nature of the entire process of socialized reproduction. The so-called jump refers to the alternation of the spasmodic growth and decline stage is the form of changes in production, exchange, credit, price, accumulation and consumption. Only the general overproduction crisis that spreads to all major industrial sectors can become the basis of this sudden socialized reproduction. Compared with the previous crises, the cyclical economic crisis is mainly reflected in its periodicity, i.e., various stages of the cycle alternate regularly, and in addition to a few exceptions, the crisis repeats itself fairly and regularly. Each cycle consists of four stages of the crisis, depression, recovery, and upsurge. The crisis is both the starting point and end point. The renewal of fixed capital on a large scale is the material basis of crisis to occur periodically. The crisis deteriorates the living conditions of working people and intensifies the contradiction among classes. Mendelson described the economic crisis since 1825 in more strict accordance with this model, and came to some basic conclusions: "In the conditions that the machinery industry is predominant, the upsurge of periodicity depends on first of all the growth in fixed capital elements, and the open-up of the market depends on the accumulation of capital. The renewal of fixed capital and the expansion of the scale reduce badly during the crisis. It is the sectors of producing the means of production that play a leading role in the crisis, although the ultimate reason of the crisis is the limited consumption of the masses, which tightly restricted the development of production of the means of subsistence, thus limiting the production of the means of production."[30] The growing impoverishment of the masses is one of the basic elements of Marx's crisis model, and therefore in the historical elaboration by Mendelson, the relevant content always occupies larger space.

328   The 1825 Crisis:

Prosperity – price surge, imports surge, the soaring share price, the prevalence of speculation, the fever to start a business, industrial construction in full swing mostly by borrowings, increasing order of commodities sold to Central and South America.

Crisis – market flooded with commodities, the export reduction, bankruptcy of financial speculation, bank failures, prices slump, the rapid increase in bankruptcies, unemployment surge. Almost all of the major industrial sectors have been hit.

Depression – the further application of the steam engine, the automatic loom is in mass production and put into use, and many production sectors carry out a major technological innovation.

Recovery – a significant increase in steam looms and export volume, lack of workers, child labour increases.

Erecting companies, credit expansion, export volume of products, the purchasing power of the working people, food price fluctuations, fluctuations in major heavy industrial products, prices, changes in the quantity of building materials, changes in the quantity and quality of the machine, speculation, stock price volatility, currency crisis and etc., are some of the basic elements of the

---

30   Mendelson, *Theory and History of the Economic Crisis and Cycle*, Volume I (1), p.295.

Mendelson's examination of the crisis, as well as some elements brewing the crisis to be maturing. Of course, these factors play different roles in the formation process of the crisis, in which credit expansion, speculation, and founding companies play a relatively important role in the formation of the crisis. These elements can reflect the process and the performance of the development of various stages of the cycle, and also reflect the development trends of the basic contradiction. From these elements, the characteristics of the analytic model Mendelson used can also be inferred.

The cyclical crisis of overproduction matured in many countries simultaneously, and occurred in many countries through some transmission mechanism, which is the problem people encounter when studying the history of crises. Mendelson used more historical facts to describe it. On the basis of observing the facts, Mendelson found in the early days when the cyclical crisis of overproduction became a global crisis, the countries of higher degree of economic development tended to be the birthplace of the crisis, and the crisis gradually transferred from these countries to countries of relatively low degree of economic development. The flow of goods and capital between countries is an essential pathway of the crisis. Of course, there are exceptions. But with the establishment of the capitalist countries and their factory system, the root of the crisis was international, and the non-crisis followed it into a new era.

Mendelson disagrees with Tugan on the explanation of the cause of the 1825 and 1837 crises, he believed that the expansion of the market caused by the British capital exports to South and North America had some effects on the upsurge of the British industry; however, it is not the main effect, but just an external driving force. The internal impetus is mainly the expansion of UK's own fixed capital and technological progress, which causes the demand for building materials, machinery, and the means of subsistence. So, Mendelson was always trying to prove from a historical point that the renewal of fixed capital on a large scale is the material basis of capitalism.

If only England had the characteristics of general overproduction when the periodic crises occurred in 1825 and 1837, in 1847 the crisis finally developed to a new stage, becoming a real international crisis. At this time, no matter it was in England, France or Germany, the capitalist system and its factory system have been developed to such a stage – having all conditions for the general overproduction to occur. The root of the crisis is no longer just England, but every country has become the root of the crisis, thus the international causes of the crisis emerge. Therefore, it is not the textile industry but the railway construction that matures the 1847 crisis. This is one of the new features of the 1847 crisis. The large-scale railway construction means the industrial revolution has entered a new stage and spread to the transportation industry. Mendelson believes that the application of the machine in the transportation industry means the scope for the factory system to rule is further expanded, and with the increase in the proportion of heavy industry, the expansion and renewal of fixed capital on a large scale is for the first time fully and apparently shown as the material basis of the crisis. Another new feature of the 1847 crisis is that railway becomes a major field of speculation, and the development of the railway stock companies becomes a new form of speculative activity (founding new companies and stock trading speculation). These new forms have played a huge role in brewing and extending the economic crisis. Since the 1848 revolution occurred after the 1847 crisis, the Marxist economists including Marx considered that the revolution was basically caused by the crisis, and even some bourgeois economists admitted that the crisis was the cause of the revolution.

The 1857 crisis arrived on time, which further confirmed the cyclical characteristics of the crisis. Compared with the previous crises, this crisis spread to a wide range of fields including regions, countries, economic sectors, and etc., demonstrating itself as a more universal crisis. The crisis is greater than ever in the intensity, and a more violent crisis than ever before. Mendelson's investigation of the crisis is still focused on the issue of the implementation mechanism. The contradiction of capital accumulation, the development of the world market, the extensive involvement of countries in strengthening the world capitalist trade, the intensification of the interlinked among countries in the reproduction process, as well as the export of capital, the development status of these elements, as well as how they evolve and lead to the intensification of conflicts and cause the crisis. In 1857, the general cyclical crisis of overproduction occurred in Germany for the first time, and it is derived from the crisis within itself. Since around four-fifths of the world's factory industry is concentrated in England, France, the United States, and Germany. The interruption of the reproduction process in these four countries will enable the crisis of 1857 to be worldwide, like Russia, Sweden, the Netherlands, and Italy which are not purely involved in the crisis, but have a certain internal conditions for the crisis to occur. Some colonies have also suffered a blow of the crisis. Agricultural sector suffered a severe impact of the crisis, which is seen as a symbol of the crisis to expand the scope of impact and to enhance the striking force. Speculation, erecting enterprises are still seen as factors accelerating the crisis, and the state organs play a role in fuelling the crisis.

In the study of the 1866 crisis, Mendelson had found from the past crises the developing sequence of the industrial crisis in various sectors, those sectors to enter the period of crisis first are often sectors of absolute advantages, and the first to recover from the crisis are also these sectors. Compared with the previous crisis, the crisis of 1866 has the following characteristics: England has changed over the practice that the previous crises occurred in the cotton textile industry, but turns to the credit field, becoming especially aggravated, and when the crisis occurs, the conditions for the overproduction crisis in cotton textile industry did not mature. But this did not affect it to be a crisis of overproduction, because the crisis has taken place in major industrial sectors in England, and the cotton textile industry also fell into the crisis of overproduction in 1869. On the basis of analyzing a large amount of factual materials,

Mendelson confirmed that the crisis of 1866 was the similar to the crisis of 1857, which is in its nature the general crisis of overproduction, and on its scope the world crisis. As for the panic in the financial market of England, it is but a part and a performance of the crisis of overproduction.

In the previous crises before the 1873 crisis, the world industry and trade changed to upsurge, basically with its starting point and the birthplace in England. In England, this change had the starting point and the birthplace in the textile industry. The economic recovery after the crises of 1847 and 1857 is because the increase in output contributed to a rise in the production of the cotton textile industry. After the 1866 crisis, the situation has changed; the British textile industry delayed in entering the upsurge due to the sales difficulties, the time for other industrial sectors to enter the upsurge was also postponed accordingly. As a result, the huge capital cannot find new fields for investment, and the idle funds are filled with money market. These idle funds flow into the United States, greatly stimulating the American railroad speculative fever. American railway construction fever promotes the upsurge of steel, coal, transportation and other heavy industry sectors, thus creating a huge market for itself and other countries, particularly England, so that the appropriate British industrial sectors had upsurge. Since Germany got several hundred million dollars of war reparations, promoting the development of the speculative activity of founding enterprises, the increase in the speculation fever, and the accelerating maturity of the prerequisite for breakdown, thus the upsurge in industry becomes a huge scale frenzy. Overall, the expansion of the renewal of fixed capital is the material basis for the upsurge to arrive, which was very obvious in the brewing process of the crisis in 1873. The Railway construction frenzy in the United States being a source, it stimulates the development of a series of heavy industry sectors, which in turn stimulates the development of coal, oil and other energy industry sectors. Of course, the renewal of fixed capital is also carried out in those light industry sectors, such as the textile industry. Credit expansion, founding enterprises, exchange speculation is always accompanied by the cyclical prosperity. Before the crisis occurred in 1873, the above phenomenon is also shown fanatically. When the crisis occurs, the first to be hit is the heavy industry. It breaks the duration of the previous cycles and crises, emerging new features: in a number of countries the wave of two crises can be seen, many sectors or sometimes the entire industry experienced a decline twice. The first was in 1873-1874, and the second was in 1876 or 1878. These years are the two most acute periods in the world crisis, among which the one that plays a decisive role in the first stage is the overproduction in the U.S. and Germany, and it is the British overproduction in the latter stage. Overall, the crisis is of great destruction and long duration, exceeding any other previous crises. Mendelson believes that the main reason for the crisis to be extended lies in that: 1) the inconsistency of the crisis in time, the destruction of the traditional cycle, and the resulting extreme imbalance of it to be developed in various countries. 2) Further development of the industrial revolution and the imbalance of economic development in the major capitalist countries make the market issue and competition on the market extremely acute. This makes the market competitive conditions change radically. The crisis becomes more profound, the breakaway from the crisis is more difficult, and it lasts longer. There are signs of the transition from free competition to monopoly.

Since the whole capitalist world experienced a cyclical upsurge stage before 1882, fixed capital has undergone renewal and expansion on a large scale, the industrial production volume greatly exceeds the highest point before the crisis in 1873. Therefore, the 1882 crisis is a regular, universal, and cyclical world crisis of overproduction. For many people who said that the 1882 crisis was the continuation of the crisis and depression in 1870s, Mendelson reached the above conclusions through the analysis of a lot of facts and data. He had shown the facts that the conditions of the crisis in 1882 is very different from the crisis in 1873, it is developed under conditions that there is no apparent rise in commodity prices, the rate of profit tends to fall, the agricultural crisis, and the renewal of fixed capital is on a smaller scale. The expansion of production is realized strongly dependent on the production facilities built in the last cycle, and the upsurge period is generally short. Mendelson believes that these features indicate the aggravation of all contradictions in the capitalist economy. The reasons for this aggravation are: the market issue and the struggle for the market is greatly aggravated; the collapse of the British industrial monopoly; long-term agricultural crisis. Mendelson emphasized the impact of the agricultural crisis on the cyclical upsurge, and there are interaction relations between them: the agricultural crisis has become one of the decisive factors for the shortening of upsurge and extension of the cyclical crises, and the shortening of the cyclical upsurge and the abnormal extension of the general crisis of overproduction aggravates the agricultural crisis, and extends its duration. Unlike the crisis of the early 1870s, there is no frenzy in founding speculative companies in Germany in the 1882 crisis, and the credit expansion is at a slower speed in the United States. A number of stock companies are set up in England, but it is realized mainly through the reorganization of enterprises that belonged to the former individual capitalists into shareholding companies. In England, there is neither fever of erecting enterprises nor a lot of speculative credit expansion. The fever of erecting enterprises on a large scale only emerged in France. Except for France, when the crisis occurs, there is nowhere that has exchange crashes. Mendelson believes that this feature is just the proof that the bourgeois economists are wrong in interpreting the capitalist economic crisis. The credit and exchange crashes have an important impact on the crisis, but the factors that play a decisive role are the conditions of socialized reproduction. Credit affects the process of socialized reproduction, reflects and exacerbates the contradiction of the process of socialized reproduction. The 1882 crisis and the depression lasted for nearly four years or so, and Mendelson believes that this is the result of the intertwining of the cyclical crises with the agricultural crisis.

Mendelson believes that, compared to the crisis about a decade in the 19th century, the 1890 crisis comes 2 to 3 years earlier, which brings certain destruction to the cyclical crises. The crisis attacked Europe first, which, like the crisis of the 1870s, rapidly developed into the world economic crisis. Speculation had new forms: in pursuit of entrepreneurial profits, in addition to setting up new enterprises, a large number of solely funded companies are turned into stock enterprises; substantial capital is put out into the least developed countries like Argentina, Uruguay, Australia and others, fuelling speculation; The monopolies drive up the price of important industrial sectors, and these worldwide speculation intensified speculative boom. The background for the crisis to occur is the ongoing agricultural crisis. In the United States, the process of the crisis is quite unique, and it experienced the concussion of two crises: the partial crisis from 1890 to the first half of 1891, and the general cyclical crisis in 1893-1894. Thus, the cyclical upsurge of the U.S. economy came early but disappeared late, with the longest duration; the cyclical upsurge of the British economy came late but disappeared early, with the shortest duration. An important feature of this crisis is that it emerges in many poor countries, especially in Argentina and Australia, where the crisis has a very sharp form.

Due to the emergence of monopoly, there is a tendency of accelerated development in the capitalist productivity, and at the same time, there is also an imbalance of development shown among sectors and among countries, which further deepens the disproportionality in the capitalist economy. From the facts he saw, Mendelson reached the conclusions above, which was apparently to meet Lenin's conclusions, providing more evidences. Compared with the previous crises, new features of the 1900 crisis are: the cyclical upsurge of the production and the cyclical occurrence of the crisis in countries exhibit non-simultaneity; Historically, the global economic crisis first began in Russia; the crisis developed later in the United States than in Western Europe, but because of the effect of monopoly prices, it directly contributed to the development of the 1900 intermediary crisis in the United States; the 1900 crisis also spread to England, and has caused a lot of damage; through its monopoly price, monopolies frustrated and delayed the crisis, as well as the subsequent transition from depression to recovery and to cyclical upsurge.

From the beginning of the last decade of the 19th century until the Great Depression in the 1930s, the capitalist economic crisis had gradually undergone some significant changes, mainly in: the reproduction cycle was shortened, from 9-11 years to 7-8 years; in addition to the crisis of overproduction, there were also crises of inflation and production shortage during the war time; the scope that the crisis spread continued to be widened, and some of the colonial and semi-colonial countries were involved in the crisis; speculation in the exchange was even greater in size, and the ensuing financial crisis was more strongly; the intensity of the cyclical upsurge was weakened, and the increase in production and infrastructure was slow. Mendelson believes that the changes in the form of the cycle do not change the substance of the crisis, and the crisis is still the global economic crisis. It is rooted in the high price policy of monopoly capitalism and war, and it aggravates the contradiction of capitalist reproduction.

The description of the restrictive conditions for Marx's analytic model of economic crisis

Before the arrival of the era of industrial production based on the large scale industrial machinery, the local business crises and the currency crises have already occurred, but conditions for the crisis of overproduction are gradually mature in the era of the large industrial machinery. In the beginning of the era of the large industrial machinery, there were several local crises of overproduction, and also symptoms were exhibited like market flooding with goods, sales difficulties and production shrinking, with its roots also lying in that "the development of the factory system has become the contradiction of the capitalist accumulation and thus often intensified to cause the crisis of overproduction."[31] That is to say, the general crisis of overproduction and the local crisis are crises of two types but with the same economic nature, and are the results of the effect of the same capitalist movement law at different stages of the history. For the explanation of the crisis by Tugan and et al., Mendelson pointed out that "the basic cause and the historical conditions of the crisis cannot be confused: The former determines the nature of the crisis, and the latter determines the characteristics of each crisis." In terms of the cyclical problems of the economic crisis, Mendelson also has special instructions, and he said: "The periodicity not only refers to inevitable repetition of crises. The periodicity refers to the jump nature of the entire process of socialized reproduction, which refers to that the alternation of the spasmodic growth and decline stage is the form of changes in production, exchange, credit, price, accumulation and consumption. Only the general overproduction crisis that spreads to all major industrial sectors can become the basis of this sudden socialized reproduction (the 1825 crisis is the first of its kind), and it can become the foundation of such jump nature of socialized reproduction. Second, the periodicity refers to the regular alternation of stages of the cycle, and generally speaking, for a few exceptions, the crisis fairly repeats itself on a regular schedule."[32] Mendelson acknowledges that speculation may exacerbate the confusion in credit system, but it is not the root reason of the economic crisis, while the currency crisis is but a part of the industrial crisis, a form of expression. "Credit and credit-based speculation concealed and exacerbated overproduction, thereby increasing the intensity of the crisis. The crisis itself is caused by the actual accumulation process of capital, as well as the aggravation of the contradiction of capitalist reproduction process in such an accumulation process. Its inevitability is determined by the nature of capitalism and the contradiction of capitalism. Any credit policy cannot prevent the crisis, and it can only change the time of the outbreak and

---

31 Mendelson, *Theory and History of the Economic Crisis and Cycle*, Volume I (1), p. 375.
32 Ibid., p. 399.

expanded form of the crisis."[33] Or, any bank policy and government policy can only worsen the trend of cycles and crises, and it is absurd to go to these policies for the cause of the crisis.

Summary

From Mendelson's investigation of the history of economic crisis, the following elements are involved when he tested Marxist analytic model of economic crisis: the scope of the crisis, overproduction, cycle length, the renewal and upsurge of fixed capital on a large scale, credit expansion, erecting enterprise, speculation, and the living conditions of the working class when testing. As for Marx's model, he saw it as an absolute form, and he was more of testing the historical facts with the model than testing the model with facts. The conclusions are: Marx's analytic model of economic crisis is the only correct model to reveal the essence of the capitalist economic crisis, and despite it changes with changes in social and historical conditions and the crisis has some new forms, its essence has not changed, and the crisis always manifests itself as the inevitable trend of development and in a regular manner.

Throughout his verification process, Mendelson has resolutely opposed to explain each crisis based on "specific reasons" or based on "coincidence of some certain cases", so he considers what the bourgeois economists believe to be the main reason of the crisis as factors that accelerate the maturity of the crisis. Because it seems to him that he reveals "the main reasons that all crises of overproduction have in common," so he almost did not have any in-depth analysis of those "minor" factors. It is in these areas that Marxist theory of economic crisis and the bourgeois theory of crisis are in opposition.

335

The range of crisis fluctuation is an important criterion, and the Marxist political economy crisis only sees the crisis that spread to the major capitalist countries as the general crisis of overproduction. Those crises that do not meet this standard, but occurred in individual countries or local regions of the world, are generally regarded as the "intermediary crisis." Mendelson uses the reduction in exports, falling prices, the increase in the overstock of commodities, and other indicators to demonstrate the supply and demand conditions for various crises. In the 19th century, the economic crises in the natural state has the cycle length to be remained essentially between 9 to 11 years, while in 1873, the length was seven years, and Mendelson attributed it to the erecting enterprises on a large scale during the railway construction frenzy in the U.S. and German war reparations. Entering the monopoly period, the cycle of the crisis is reduced to 7-8 years, and Mendelson attributed it to the monopoly price that impacts the normal development of the upsurge period. The material basis of the breakaway from the last crisis and the arrival of a new crisis is, in Marx's analytical model of economic crisis, the renewal of fixed capital. Every investigation Mendelson had made crisis has highlighted the issue of the renewal of fixed capital, and there are cases or data regarding the relations between the

---

33 Mendelson, *Theory and History of the Economic Crisis and Cycle*, Volume I (2), p. 483.

renewal of fixed capital, economic recovery and the upsurge. Even in the monopoly capitalism period, it also can find sufficient factual basis.

When studying the economic crisis, Mendelson treated it as a peculiar phenomenon of capitalism, so his task is to explain the crisis is as something unavoidable, and with the aggravation of the inherent contradiction of capitalism, the intensity and destructive force of the crisis is increasingly greatly, which eventually drives the capitalist system to the grave. Throughout the testing process, he does not consider the impact of anti-crisis measures on the capitalist reproduction process, and it should be said that this is a large deletion in Mendelson's study. Mendelson's *Theory and History of the Economic Crisis and Cycle* Volume III was published in the early 1960s, and in the book it referred to the Great Depression of the 1930s, as well as the economic crises in the 1940s and 1950s. By all odds, during this period there was not only the anti-crisis theory in the capitalist world, but also the practice of anti-crisis for nearly two decades, the policy of which has achieved significant results in practice, playing a role of mitigating the fundamental contradiction of capitalism, as well as easing the crisis, Mendelson should have been aware of these changes occurring in the real world, and should have reflected it in his writings. So, from this perspective, the testing work by Mendelson is imperfect.

V. The Textbook Model

336

In the *Political Economy, A Textbook,* launched by Soviet scholars in the early 1950s, the study results are summed in an analytical model, with its logical structure as:

> The nature of the capitalist economic crisis – the crisis of relative overproduction.
>
> The root reason of the capitalist economic crisis – the contradiction between socialization of production and private ownership of the means of production, namely the basic contradiction of capitalism.
>
> The basic contradiction of capitalism is specifically manifested as: 1) the contradiction between the organization of production of individual enterprises and the anarchy of production in the whole society; 2) the contradiction between the infinite widening trend of production and the reduced purchasing power of working people.
>
> Conclusion: The crisis is the inevitable companion of the capitalist mode of production. To eliminate the crisis, the capitalist system must be destroyed.

The capitalist reproduction is cyclical. The cycle consists of four phases: crisis, depression, recovery and upsurge. Crisis is the basic phase of the cycle, and the starting point of a new cycle.

The renewal of fixed capital on a large scale is the material basis for the capitalist economic crisis to occur periodically.

Agricultural crisis.

The crisis aggravates all contradictions of capitalism.

This analytical model had a profound impact on analyzing the cyclical capitalist economic crisis, and it is widely accepted not only by the Soviet scholars, but also by scholars of many socialist countries. In the 1950s, the political economy textbooks in Eastern European countries almost invariably used this analytical model. Until now, in China's political economics textbooks, the above analytic model is still used to analyze the economic crisis.

VI. The Improved Textbook Model

The basic structure of the textbook model has not changed since the 1950s, but a number of new elements were added, which was more apparent especially in academic writings. The starting point to modify the model is the new changes in the post-war business cycle, and then regarding the explanation of these new features as the basic clue, the relations of the unity of opposites among factors that have counterproductive forces to the basic contradiction of capitalism are analyzed. The basic element that is added in the improved model is monopoly, and the adding of this element needs researchers to explain first the most basic question, such as what kind of impact the monopoly will have on the essential relations of capitalism. Brentano, Bernstein, Hilferding[34] et al. had proposed the theory that the monopoly can ease the crisis and thought world cartels would result in "longer..periods of prosperity" and shorter depressions. during the early days of the formation of monopoly, and flattered by the followers, it formed a theory of thought. Those who are called the orthodox Marxist economists have launched powerful counterattacks for several times, Kuczynski, Mendelson, Varga et al. are basically the main go-getters of this school. They believe that the monopoly aggravates the basic contradiction of capitalism, making the economic crisis extremely and inevitably deep, and the contradiction caused by the crisis is bound to be aggravated. Monopolization is the aggravation of the crisis.[35] Monopoly does not change the nature of capitalism, nor the fate of capitalism, but in the face of the new changes in capitalism during the monopoly stage, their counterattacks become increasingly feeble.

---

34 See Louis Brentano, *Reason for the Collapse of the European Economy*, Bernstein, *Social Issues*, and Hilferding, *Finance Capital*.
35 Jürgen Kuczynski, *Study of the History of the Capitalist World Economy*, Beijing: SDX Joint Publishing Company, 1955, p. 131.

With the changes in the conditions in the post-war capitalist economic growth, the capitalist business cycle has expressed itself in new forms, and Soviet scholars summarized these new changes as follows: 1) The crisis is not as profound as it was in the pre-war period, and the duration is relatively short. 2) The cyclical economic crisis does not occur with the significant decline in production of all the capitalist countries simultaneously. 3) The cycle of different countries has the non-synchronization in nature. 4) The intermediary crisis becomes a frequent companion of the cycle. 5) Economic stagnation becomes a frequent companion. 6) The rhythm for enterprise enthusiasm has changed. 7) The nature of price movement has changed. 8) Currency crisis is weakened. 9) The securities trading crisis has also changed. Soviet scholars have also attributed these changes to scientific and technological revolution; the deepening of international division of labour, as well as the strengthening of state monopoly capitalism to regulate the economic life, and in fact the Soviet scholars regard these elements as counterproductive forces to the basic contradiction of capitalism (The interaction of these elements with the basic contradiction makes economic crisis relatively mild. Relative to the textbook model, the analytical method has been improved, and from the analysis of the basic contradiction in two aspects as well as its conflicts, it has further been developed as the analysis of the unity of opposites between the basic contradiction and the counterproductive elements. Using this mode to analyze the capitalist business cycle, it seems simplistic in appearance, but in fact it is more complex than the textbook model with more factors to be considered. Scholars need to regard the pre-war crisis as a basic reference, to observe what new changes have emerged in the post-war crisis and to identify the causes of these changes, such as monopolies, state intervention in the economy, new technology revolution, the tertiary industry, etc. These factors are said to be the specific reasons for the crisis to have new changes in the form, and these specific reasons are also seen as factors that are counterproductive to the basic contradiction of capitalism.

Faced with the new changes in the post-war business cycle, Soviet scholars always adhere to the inevitability of the capitalist economic crisis. They insist that the general trend of the capitalist economy is the decline, and in addition to the economic crisis, there is no other means that can promote its self-transformation. The anarchy of capitalist production, the disproportionate development, and the contradiction between labour and capital lead to the destruction of the proportion of reproduction, and the latter is bound to reach the crisis point because under the conditions of the capitalist economy, there is no kind of inherent mechanism that can prevent in advance the movement towards the crisis point and solve the contradiction that emerged through another way. Any internal plan of a company, any economic program imposed by the bourgeois state, or even the international economic policy coordination are not able to change the situation fundamentally, because in the economy based on private ownership, most decision-making centres rest in the hands of private companies.

Since the normal rhythm of the post-war cyclical economic crisis is disrupted, there has been the situation of the primary cycle and the short cycle interweaving, with the limits in and out. In the course of paying attention to the primary cycle, Soviet scholars pay more attention to the study of the short cycle (also known as the intermediary crisis). Since the study of the intermediary crisis started from Engels, the researchers later have conducted studies in varying degrees, especially the work done by Soviet scholars Varga, and Mendelson the early post-wartime that laid the foundation for the further study. Till the 1970s, the intermediary crisis has manifested itself most fully in its characteristics, and there are a relatively complete statistical data, which makes the Soviet scholars have more favourable research conditions to build a new model. From the perspective of the history of the doctrine, Mendelson's study only focused on the characteristics of the intermediary crisis, and then A.H. Gelchuk mainly focused on the differences between it and the primary cycle, as well as the differences between the intermediary economic crisis and the local economic crisis. Many people, including Mendelson believe that the intermediary crisis is not the inevitable phenomenon accompanied by the primary cycle, and it is shallow in depth, largely confined within the scope of a country; the intermediary crisis can only interrupt the process of a certain phase of the industrial cycle, and cannot open up a new "circle spiral." A.A. Manukyan believes that "the intermediary crisis can be swept through a country's economy, but its size is smaller than the cyclical crises. They often come to be partial ... the feature of the intermediary crisis is that it is not a phenomenon regularly occurring in the world's industrial cycle, nor the beginning of a cycle or the beginning of another cycle." Gelchuk describes the intermediary crisis as: "The intermediary crisis or completed undone business of the cyclical crisis, or 'release the steam from the boiler' of reproduction when the conditions for the crisis of overproduction is not yet mature or part of the disproportionality has taken the form of conflict. In terms of its functions, the intermediary crisis is between the cyclical crisis and sectoral crisis. It not only affects the individual sectors, but affects a considerable part of the economy and sometimes even the most part, though the part and the depth affected is smaller than the cyclical crises. The intermediary crisis is different from the sectoral crisis which can be manifested both as overproduction and deficient production of certain commodities, and when it only occurs in overproduction, it is close to the cyclical crisis in this regard."[36] The localized crisis is the severe overproduction in an individual large sector, and it is not accompanied by a general decline in production. The supplementary crisis is a crisis occurring after the cyclical crisis, it can finish things that the cyclical crisis has no time to do, but it is not as profound as the cyclical crisis. Gelchuk believes that the localized crisis and the (periodic) general crisis of overproduction are different, and the localized crisis only covers part of the economy. It is reasonable to use the concept of localized crisis only in the sense of crisis sectors. The supplementary crisis is a special type of the

339

---

36 A.H. Gelchuk, *Modern Capitalist Economic Crisis*, Beijing: Oriental Press. 1987, p. 56, p.143.

intermediary crisis. In terms of the range, the intermediary crisis is shallower than the cyclical crisis, but it also can be involved in many areas. Gelchuk basically agrees with Mendelson's views on the intermediary crisis, but he believes that the criteria to determine the intermediary crisis are not quite precise. This is because there should be a unified standard system, a set of comparable indicators with a fairly broad range and a way to study the cycle interval so as to measure all forms of crisis.[37] Therefore, when constructing new models, many researchers consciously applied the quantitative analysis method.

Gelchuk advocates the use of a variety of indices to measure the crisis, which could increase the accuracy and reliability in investigating the economic crisis, and measure the magnitude of fluctuations more accurately. When he investigated changes in the U.S. economy, he used "index of industrial production", "duration of growth or drop in industrial production," "industrial production range that the crisis process swept", "fixed capital investment", "changes in reserves", "production capacity operation", "changes in the profits of private companies," "accepting the order", "the employment in the processing industry", "profit after tax", "stock market", "import" and other economic indicators. The aim is to examine and explain the crisis from different angles, because the crisis is always manifested in many ways, and if only one index is used, the problem reflected is likely to be one-sided, or even distorted. As for what the economic significance and function of every economic indicator is, the problems it can explain are naturally factors that should be taken into consideration. For example, the reason to select the "index of industrial production" is that the realization cycle is mainly the industrial cycle, and the material production with the industry as the base is the centre of economic fluctuations; index of industrial production is a more accurate barometer reflecting the economic conditions; statistics of industrial production is more accurate than the GDP statistics calculated at the constant prices. To select "accepting the order", "changes in reserves" and other indices, is because these indices are extremely sensitive to market changes and significant fluctuations, as well as the most obvious indicator in the economic development process. "Pre-tax profits" is not only a cumulative index that can reflect many aspects of reproduction comprehensively, but also an important motivation for entrepreneurs to have short-term, and especially long-term activity. "The employment in the processing industry" is a sensitive indicator of the industrial expansion and contraction. "Commodity import and export index" is closely related to changes in economic price, especially in imports. Overall, the indices selected are the indicator or barometer relatively sensitive to the economic development process. Some of scholars divided these indices into three categories, namely, forward index (order sources, reserves investment, stock quotes, and company profits), coincident index (industrial production, the employment of the processing industry), backward index (fixed capital investment, commodity imports). Different indexes provide different perspectives on the issue, with

---

37   See A.H. Gelchuk, *Modern Capitalist Economic Crisis*, Chapter II.

both backward observation and forward observation, as well as transverse observation, showing a full range of these indices.

To examine the issue of economic crisis with the index of the full range is an important development of Marxist analytical model of the economic crisis. Marx used the analytical method of contradiction to explain the nature, characteristics, forms, development trends and other aspects of the economic crisis. After Marx, Marxist economics used analytical methods of contradiction and the analytical method of history to examine the theory and history of the crisis, but in addition to that, before the 1970s, the focus of the study was also largely confined to the purely abstract theoretical level. Economic growth, employment, prices, changes in the number of enterprises, the output and input of money, and other indicators, are generally applied with the quantitative analysis tool. However, they do not primarily serve to examine the trend of changes in the cycle, but used to determine whether the economic crisis occurs, and to what extent. Marxist economics had excluded the analysis of economic quotation for a very long time, considering doing this kind of work is to replace the analysis of the essential relationship with the analysis of economic phenomena, an economic analysis that will never find the regularity. The short-lived characteristics of its achievements, as Marx said, are something very useful after the last crisis, but completely useless in the next one. In contrast with the traditional knowledge, Gelchuk used the economic indicator standard he selected to analyze the economic crisis in the United States from the post-war to the mid-1970s, proving that the 1948-1949, 1957-1958, 1969-1970, 1974-1975 crises are cyclical economic crisis, and the 1953-1954, 1960-1961, 1967 crises are the intermediary crisis. He also used the same method and means to analyze the economic crisis in Germany, Japan and the United Kingdom, drawing the analytical result of a clear boundary between the cyclical economic crisis and the intermediary economic crisis.

The new model also highlights its functionality of analyzing the world economic crisis. With regard to the formation and conduction mechanism of the world business cycle, Gelchuk believes that "the formation process of the world cycle can be realized through two ways in principle, 'evening up' the cycle of countries, and 'regarding' the domestic cycle of most capitalist countries as the most powerful source of volatility. In fact the process is mixed, but the main development direction is the adjustment of the world crisis following the economic fluctuations in the leading epicentre, bringing the economic process from one country to the other, mainly the system of international economic relations, and the first the foreign trade links. Once the unified world cycle emerges, it begins to reproduce itself on the basis of the internal law. In order to maintain the unity of the world capitalist cycle that has been formed, the intervention in foreign economic field is required. The extent of the foreign influence with each other depends on the status of the country or the group of countries in the international economic relations, and the sensitivity to the world market process depends on the effect of the external economic relations in a country's national economy."[38]

38   A.H. Gelchuk, *Modern Capitalist Economic Crisis*, p. 110.

Because of the dominance of the United States in the world economy, it has become the "generator" instead of "receptors" of the business cycle fluctuations to a greater extent. If the United States is free from the shock of serious crises, then the cyclical crisis of overproduction in the world will only occur in rare cases. Therefore, the development of the U.S. business cycle has become the decisive factor in the development of the world cycle; the staging of the world cycle is carried out based on the American model. Gelchuk regards this discovery as the given premise to classify the world cyclical economic crisis, and it is always the statistical data of the U.S. economy that is first adopted in the analysis of issues. As the intervention of state monopoly capitalism in the economy in the post-war era, there has been non-synchronization in the world business cycle. With this increases difficulty in classifying the global business cycle, Gelchuk believes that a methodological premise is required in solving this problem, which is the principle of the gradual increase in the synchronization of the cyclical fluctuations. In largest point of synchronization, it shows the typical characteristics of the world business cycle; during the crisis stage, the decline in the level of synchronization can be seen as a sign of the intermediary crisis; during the crisis stage, years of the growth in synchronization show the world business cycle, on the contrary it is in the intermediary crisis. By using these criteria, Gelchuk proved that there were three world cyclical economic crises before the mid-1970s, and the boundaries of these cycles are: 1948-1949, 1957-1958, 1970-1971, 1974-1975, where the elapsed time of the

first cycle is 1948-1949-1957-1958, the elapsed time of the second cycle is 1957-1958-1970-1971, and the elapsed time of the third cycle is 1969-1971-1974-1975. Gelchuk had detailed the analysis of these cycles, and came to the conclusion that: the development picture of the cycle is extremely complex, the depth and breadth of the crisis process is different even in the same country in different periods, where the number of crisis is different, the intensity of the cycle upsurge phase changes within the broad segment of the range, and in many cases the performance of various economic indicators is quite contradictory. The non-synchronization has taken a very different form: the crisis stage in some countries may be the recovery or upsurge stage in another; the cyclical crisis in different countries may coincide with the intermediary crisis. These differences have occurred in the second half of the 1940s and 1950s, but to the late 1960s, it was reduced.

From the first half of the 1970s, there was a new phenomenon in the world economy. On the one hand, it is the excess products in a lot of production sectors, and on the other hand it is the serious shortage of energy, raw materials, food and so on. There has been the situation of overproduction and underproduction combined, and the crisis is also exhibited correspondingly by the features of overproduction and underproduction, accompanied by currency crisis and ecological crisis, which are called the structural crisis. In terms of the reason of this type of crisis, the Soviet scholars believe that the aggravation of the food situation lie in the imbalance between the food production and the growth in food demand, which exists first in developing countries. In addition, there is another reason of the increase in the imbalance of the world grain market. The energy crisis and the raw material crisis, on the one hand, is caused because the developing countries fight for the control of the country's natural resources and change their status of being exploited in the capitalist world economy; on the other hand it is because of the relative increase in raw materials and fuel production costs. The ecological crisis is caused by the adverse effects of human economic activity on the surrounding environment, which has the nature of the conflict under capitalism.[39] This explanation by Soviet scholars is quite inconsistent with their interpretation of the capitalist economic crisis. They can attribute the crisis of overproduction, the intermediary crisis to the basic contradiction of capitalism, but separate the reason for the structural crisis to emerge from the basic contradiction of capitalism with an exception. In fact, from the perspective of Marxist economics, the serious shortage of energy, raw materials, food, etc. has a direct relationship with the unlimited expansion of the capitalist economy, and strong evidence can also be found from the contradiction of capitalism. A considerable part of a variety of ecological disasters is associated with the development of capitalism, and in the pursuit of surplus value to the maximum, capitalism always externalizes a large number of internal costs, causing ecological deterioration.

In terms of the intervention of the state monopoly capitalism into the economy which impacts the business cycle fluctuations, Soviet scholars believe that the bourgeoisie often has two sides of attitudes in state intervention into economic life. On the one hand, it recognizes the necessity to somehow intervene in the economy; on the other hand, entrepreneurs still want to be the "masters of their own home," and they try to turn this limited intervention to the minimum extent. Moreover, the country is still "the Bourgeois Affairs Committee ", which often seems to override the class, even the class it actually represents also gains some independence. In addition, a country's "excessive" intervention may be associated with some kind of socialist ideas for the association of compromise. As long as the mechanism of capitalist production is still working without a major disturbance, state is always playing the role as the maker and legal defender of the general "competitive rules". Within the scope of these rules, capital and private initiative, the inherent law of the capitalist production itself should play a role in determining the economic development. This view has described that the role of state monopoly capitalism is limited. Gelchuk has also asserted that the state regulation system that has been formed is no longer suited to the new conditions, because the nature of the state in the regulation means of the state monopoly contradicts with the internationalization of economic life. The regulation means resting in the hands of the bourgeois state has an almost absolute nature of the state, and their effect may even spread to the territory of countries concerned. The development of world economic ties leads to that all capitalist countries seem to be on the "same boat." On this boat, each passenger has his own steering wheel, and as long as the general

343

---

39   See A.H. Gelchuk, *Modern Capitalist Economic Crisis*, p. 151.

economic climate is not so dangerous, the in-coordination of the paddleman is not so dangerous. Once the storm comes with difficult sailing, the danger is severe. This is the limitation of the role of state regulation in the world economy.

After the 1980s, the structural crisis has become a hot topic for economists. The bourgeois economics and Marxist political economics have had many studies. From the writings of these researchers, there are significant differences in what the structural economic crisis is. Some people regard the long-wave phenomenon of the economic life as one of the manifestations of the structural economic crisis, while others regard the serious underproduction of some important products accompanied by overproduction as the structural crisis. The definition of the structural crisis given by Soviet scholar Gelchuk is: a persistent crisis in an important sector or in many similar sectors including the same economic field. The reason that causes the structural crisis is the basic disproportionality between production and consumption, between demand and supply, as well as the destruction of the functional mechanism of the link between suppliers and consumers of the product. The structural crisis is often accompanied by significant changes in the price scale. The structural crisis includes both the domestic economy, and the world economic relations of capitalist countries; it can either be the crisis of overproduction, or the crisis of underproduction.[40] The characteristics of the structural crisis are evidently shown in the comparison between it and the cyclical crises of overproduction. The structural crisis generally includes the overproduction or the underproduction in only one important key sector, while the cyclical crises are the mass overproduction in many or even most sectors. The structural crisis relates only to individual sectors, while the cyclical crisis covers all stages of reproduction, involving a wide range of sectors; in the structural crisis, the duration for underproduction or overproduction is generally longer, while in the cyclical crisis, the duration for overproduction is generally shorter; for the cyclical crisis of overproduction caused by disproportionality, the total overproduction is relative, which is just in terms of the comparison between income and price; The disproportionality of the structural crisis of underproduction is absolute, manifesting as the actual missing of products, and this disproportionality is difficult to restore equilibrium by raising prices; the structural crisis can also extend its influence into other economic sectors, but it is realized based on other rules and through other forms; the cyclical crisis of overproduction is essentially caused by factors within the range of the industrial cycle, so it appears within the scope of the industrial cycle, while the structural crisis is caused by factors beyond the range of industrial cycle, so it may appear at any stage; the root reason of the cyclical crisis is the basic contradiction of capitalism, while the reason of the structural crisis is more widespread, and there are economic, political reasons, as well as social, natural reasons. In short, these differences between the cyclical crisis of overproduction and the structural crisis suggest the basic characteristics and the nature of the structural crisis. These findings by the Soviet scholars have

---

40 See A.H. Gelchuk, *Modern Capitalist Economic Crisis*, pp. 184-185.

had a broad impact in the field of theory, winning applauses of a large number of advocates. However, its limitations are obvious, and since the structural crisis originates from the non-institutional factors of capitalism, which means that such crises can be overcome through artificial adjustment, as well as the invention and application of science and technology. Affected by the general crisis theory of capitalism, many Soviet scholars believe that the structural crisis is an integral part of the general crisis of capitalism, which occurs in the stage where capitalism turns into imperialism, then continues, with a trend of aggravation. Their views are related to their understanding of "structure" in the "structural crisis". The "structure" they understand is very extensive, including the relational structure between the two economies of socialism and capitalism, the relational structure between the developed capitalist countries and the developing countries, the relational structure among the developed capitalist countries, and the relational structure among different classes within the developed capitalist countries, etc.

Since the early 1970s, the price of energy, raw materials and food has soared sharply, and it seems to presage the arrival of a new crisis era. It was shrouded in a pessimistic warning: not only the natural environment will become increasingly worse, some of the important industrial raw materials will also be depleted in the near future, and the world food situation will worsen as well. In response, it calls for limiting industrial growth, controlling population growth, taking effective measures to protect the environment, and increasing food production. In Soviet economic circle, the related study has also become a hot topic. In their previous study models, there were elements of the raw material crisis, the energy crisis and the food crisis. Moreover, they believe that these factors and other factors are intrinsically linked, having the factor of consistency. Gelchuk regards the raw material crisis as a price phenomenon associated with the business cycle. The crisis of overproduction is often accompanied by the significant decline in the price of raw materials, while in the upsurge stage; the price of raw materials soars. The price volatility of raw materials is much greater in extent than other commodities. Even in times of inflation, the impact of cycle on the price of raw materials is still very obvious. Of course, the rise in the price of raw materials is also related to the enhancement of the role of developing countries in international economic and political affairs. The insufficient supply of raw materials is not the case in real sense. When raw materials appear to be lacking of the supply and the price increases significantly, the production of raw materials does not decrease, but increase substantially. Therefore, the rising price of raw materials is not the result of the deteriorating environment of raw material production and reduced production, but rather a phenomenon of price volatility caused by the business cycle. The role of technological progress and interest mechanism will automatically make adjustments to the supply of raw materials. A mineral raw material may be exhausted, but alternatives found through technological advances are unlimited.

In the late 1980s, the Soviet Union introduced the political economics text-book that used the research results of the structural economic crisis by Gelchuk and et al., agreeing that in capitalism, in addition to the cyclical crisis of over-production, there is the structural crisis due to severe disproportionality in some production areas or production sectors due, recognizing that the structur-al crisis has the nature of protraction and non-cycle, stressing that the structural crisis is intertwined with the cyclical crisis, dramatically expanding the size of the capitalist economic crisis shock and extending its duration.

VII. Conclusions

On the basis of inheriting Marx's theory of crisis, Lenin criticized the then prevailing non-Marxist theoretical thoughts of economic crisis, insisting that the contradiction between the socialization of production and the capitalist pri-vate ownership is the root of the capitalist economic crisis. Since the basic contradiction is specifically manifested in the contradiction between the orga-nization of production of individual enterprises and the anarchy of production in the whole society, as well as the contradiction between the infinite widen-ing trend of production and the reduced purchasing power of working people, and the analysis of the capitalist economic crisis is actually manifested as the analysis of the two contradictions. Many Soviet scholars including Lenin, such as Varga, Mendelson, Kuczynski, have adopted this model to analyze the capi-talist economic crisis, resulting in the formation of an analytical model of rela-tively stable structure, and suitable for the analysis of the capitalist economic crisis for the purpose of war and revolution, which is absorbed by the textbook in the 1950s, becoming the standard model of broad impact to analyze the capi-talist economic crisis. With the development of history, factors counterproduc-tive to the economic crisis start to appear, and correspondingly, the improved textbook model or the improved basic contradiction model is gradually formed. The focus of the analysis is gradually shifting from the analysis of the basic contradiction to the analysis of the contradiction between the basic contradic-tion and the counterproductive actors, with more diverse analytical methods, so the analytic range of the capitalist economic crisis is greatly expanded, that the model is not only suitable for the analysis of the essential relationship, but also suitable for the analysis of economic operation.

CHAPTER X

"Long-Wave" Model of Business Cycle

I. Introduction

The "long wave" phenomenon in the economic development is considered as one of the greatest discoveries in the economics of the 20th century, but until now, two of its most fundamental questions have still not been completely resolved satisfactorily: First, does the "long wave" phenomenon really exist? Second, what is the root reason for the "long wave" phenomenon? In the research of more than a century, there are many excellent economists of world class that have participated, who had spent almost all of the research means, with research and debate itself having experienced two world-scale climaxes, but there is still no substantive breakthrough, and the difference of economists remain as it was. After the worldwide contention in the 1980s, there has been no debate for nearly 20 years. In recent years, some of the Marxist economists once again raised the "long wave" theory, and they consider that the capitalist world economy is experiencing a new rise of the long wave. Of course, there are also people who hold negative attitude, considering that the issue of long wave has lost its practical significance, because the macro-control widely practiced in the post-war capitalist world has made economic fluctuations greatly alleviated, thereby disrupting the fluctuation frequency of various cycles. Not only the long-term economic fluctuation does not exist, and even the short-term fluctuation has lost the regularity. Debate continues, but the exploration of the issue does not stop. For the Marxist political economy, there still are many problems yet to figure out, and they are both old ones, but also new ones. For example, is there any scientific evidence for the "long wave" phenomenon exactly? What is the relationship between the "long wave" phenomenon and the business cycle that Marx had studied (the cycle of about 10 years in Marx's era)? What is the root reason for the "long wave" phenomenon to exist? Is the current world economy in the rising stage of the "long wave"? And so on. If these problems can well be solved, it will undoubtedly be significant to the political economy. Marx reveals the essence, fundamental reason, occurrence mechanism, transmission mechanism and the law of movement of the business cycle of about 10 years, and gives a convincing explanation with his economic theories. If Marx's theory can give "long wave" theory a reasonable explanation, it is also undoubtedly important to Marx's analytic model of economic fluctuation. Scholars from home and abroad have attempted, and written writings of great influence. In reviewing the "long wave" theory, the Chapter will have a basic assessment of the relationship between the "long wave" theory and Marxist analytic model of economic fluctuations, laying a further foundation for the study of the relationship between the two.

II. Proposal and Development of "Long Wave" Theory

348 The study of the "long wave" in the capitalist economic development can be traced back to the 19th century. In 1896, the Russian Parvus had discovered that there was a long-term fluctuation in the capitalist development of roughly every 50 to 60 years. Since then, J. G. K. Wicksell, Tugan-Baranovsky, V. Pareto, Aftailin, and Owen Fisher also independently discovered the long-term fluctuation phenomenon in a series of different indicators. In 1913, Dutch economist Jacob van Gelderen proposed the so-called "super cycle" in the economic development, with the cycle of about 60 years, and so on. However, the academia generally believes that the originator of the "long wave" theory should be the Soviet economist Nikolai Kondratieff, who made the assumption of long wave in 1919-1922. In the spring of 1925, Kondratieff wrote a monograph entitled *Long Cycle in the Economic Life*, which was published in the proceedings of *Economic Fluctuations* of Institute for Business Cycle. In the early 1926, he modified in this paper, and renamed it *Long Wave in the Economic Life*, published in German in the *Socio-Economic and Socio-Political Literature* magazine. In 1935, the article was translated into English and published in *The Review of Economics and Statistics*.

From the late 1920s when the "long wave" theory came into being until the outbreak of World War II, the exploration of the "long wave" phenomenon among theorists experienced its first active period, and the basic model for the analysis of the long wave phenomenon was formed during this period. (Herein referred to as long-wave analytic model).

In terms of the analysis methods, the majority of researchers have used empirical analysis, aiming to prove the existence of long wave and law of its motion. Some also have adopted qualitative analysis, aiming to prove the cause of the long wave. Of course, there are also many researchers who have combined these two methods; the founder of the "long wave" model has also used this method. Kondratieff discovered the existence of long-wave through empirical analysis of abundant economic data, that he chose the changing index sequence of statistics such as wholesale price, interest rate, wages, foreign trade, coal and pig iron production and consumption in England, France and the United States from the 18th century to the early 1920s. Kondratieff identified three long waves: rising from 1789 to a peak in 1814, then declining until 1848; rising to a peak in 1873, then declining until 1896; rising to a peak around 1920. He obtained his curves by using a 9-year moving average to smooth out the typical 7- to 11-year "intermediate cycle." As he wrote: "The long waves really belong to the same complex dynamic process in which the intermediate cycles of the capitalistic economy with their principal phases of upswing and depression run their course. These intermediate cycles, however, secure a certain stamp from the very existence of the long waves. Our investigation demonstrates that during the rise of the long waves years of prosperity are more numerous, whereas years of depression predominate during the downswing." Then he processed these data through statistical methods and represented them by a plane graph, which includes long-term fluctuations of about 50 years. On the other hand, Kondratieff concluded by deductive analysis that: the long-term economic fluctuations of capitalism is not originated from accidental, super economic environment and events (technical change, war and revolution, new countries incorporated into the world economy, fluctuations in gold production, etc.), but originated from the internal reasons of the capitalist system, this is the renewal major cycle of the major fixed assets.

349

Kondratieff discovered some of the features accompanied by the long wave through his analysis model: 1) The long-term fluctuation contains a movement of upsurge and depression stages in the middle; in the rising stage of the long-term fluctuation, there are more prosperous years, and in the falling stage, there are more depression years. 2) During the recession stage of the long-term fluctuation, the agriculture usually has particularly significant long-term depression. 3) During the recession stage of the long-term fluctuation, there are especially many major discoveries and inventions completed in production and transportation, but these are usually just applied on a large scale in the next long upsurge. 4) In the beginning of an upsurge stage, the gold production will usually increase, and because of the participation of new countries, particularly the colonial countries, the world (commodity) market has expanded to some extent. 5) During the rising stage of the long-term fluctuation, namely the period of high extended tension of the economic power, there would usually be catastrophic and widespread wars and revolutions.

When he first proposed the "long wave" analysis model, Kondratieff was not quite confident of the existence of the long wave, and he wrote with an uncertain tone: "We believe that according to the data referenced, the cyclical long-term fluctuation is likely to exist." Because "the opinion against the cyclical and regular long-term fluctuation is not convincing." Nevertheless, he seems to have realized the importance of studying and discovering the motion law of the long wave. "If this long-term fluctuation really exists, it is an extremely important fundamental element in the economic development, by which the whole main areas in the social and economic life will be affected."[1]

In the 1930s, Joseph Schumpeter accepted the long-wave analysis model and conducted a groundbreaking study, and achieved a series of opinions with great influence. In terms of the reasons of the long wave, the development stage of waves, and the internal structure of waves, Schumpeter almost put forward his own insights, and had a theoretical explanation systematically. In the analysis of the wavy-shaped movement existing in the economic life, Schumpeter emphasized that, "it is particularly necessary to combine the historical, statistical and analytic patterns," because by doing so it can "make the economics provide a very satisfactory, reasonable and thorough description of this phenomenon (economic fluctuation)"[2]. Since the analytic method by Kondratieff is more in line with his ideas, Schumpeter gave full affirmation of Kondratieff's research, and he agreed with Kondratieff's view that the long wave is generated in the "internal factors" the capitalist economic life, advocating that when observing the "wave operation" in economic life, it should not only "exclude factors like wars, revolutions, natural disasters, and institutional changes", but also exclude the external factors like "economic policy, banking and monetary management, payment habits, as well as changes in crop yields due to climate conditions or disasters and changes in gold production caused by the discovery of mineral deposits".

In terms of the origin of the long wave, Schumpeter and Kondratieff have fundamentally followed the same approach, trying to find reasons within the range of the productive forces, which they regarded as decisive. However, they have differences in the details: Kondratieff explains the origin of the long-term fluctuation with the renewal of the major fixed products which caused the damage and recovery of the economic equilibrium. Schumpeter considers that it is the entrepreneurs' "innovative activities" that cause the cyclical fluctuations in economic life. Schumpeter found that the "innovation activities" were cyclical in the exploration of innovative activities, and the specific realization process is: the implementation of "innovation activities" brings a huge profit to businesses and individuals – the whole economic field has set off the boom to follow the application of innovation – the advantage of "innovative activities"

1   Nikolai Kondratieff, *The Long Waves in Economic Life*. in *Selected Works of Modern Foreign Economics*, 10th series, Beijing: The Commercial Press, 1986.
2   *Selected Works of Modern Foreign Economics*, 10th series, Beijing: The Commercial Press, 1986.

gradually disappears–the economic downturn occurs – "innovative activities" appear again – ...... the "business cycle" forms again and again. Because of the breadth of economic fields and the diversity of economic sectors, "innovative activities" are also diversified. Moreover, because "different innovation requires different lengths of time to introduce new things to the economy", the innovation cycle manifests multiple-level cycle of mutual containing and unequal length. Thus, Schumpeter proposed three types of cycles naturally – cycles corresponding to different innovation periods, that is, in the cycle of economic movement, a number of Kitchin cycles make up Juglar cycle; a number of Juglar cycles make up Kondratieff cycle. Thus, he integrated the business cycle of different duration as a whole from the perspective of the innovative, so that the horizon of the business cycle is greatly expanded.

On the basis of normative analysis, Schumpeter confirmed the results of normative analysis with empirical analysis. According to the conditions he set, by long cycle was originated from the influential innovation of longer duration. Innovation cycles like this between the 1780s and the 1840s were originated from major innovation activities related to the industrial revolution; in 1842-1897, it was originated from major innovation activities related to "The Era of Steam, Iron Steel"; after 1898, from major innovation activities related to electrical, chemical and automotive activities. The innovation cycles composed of these major innovation activities are consistent with the analytic results of Kondratieff with statistical and historical methods. Some innovation activities of relatively limited influence and short realization duration are also basically consistent with Kitchin cycle and Juglar cycle. The research results by Schumpeter aroused great concern in the society, improved the people's interest in the social long-wave theory, and promoted the in-depth exploration of the long-wave theory.

In the study of the business cycle, Schumpeter accepted Marx's segmentation method of business cycle, and he also divided business cycle into four stages, namely prosperity, recession, depression and recovery. In addition, he further pointed out that the iterative business cycle "must always begin after the recovery and from the prosperity."

The "long-wave" analytic model experienced silence of more than 30 years after Schumpeter, and until the 1970s, with the deteriorating economic situation in Western countries, as well as it being difficult for Keynesians to explain the "stagflation", the "long wave" theory was once again concerned about. There has been the "resurgence" phenomenon of academic contention, and it ushered in a true period of "letting a hundred flowers blossom and letting a hundred schools of thought contend". In this debate, the American economist Walt Whitman Rostow first presented his question on the previous research achievements, and he believes that the interpretation of long wave by Kondratieff and Schumpeter has defects, lacking satisfactory explanations. Thus, Rostow tried another way, and explains the reason of long waves by using relative price. He found from a large number of data of changes in long-term price that the relative price of primary products and industrial products will affect the supply and demand of primary products, forming relative shortage or surplus of primary products. In the period of relative shortage of primary products, "the supply is relatively insufficient, ... the price rises; in order to expand the supply of primary products, investment is transferred to this sector", resulting in the overproduction of primary products, where prices began to fall immediately, the investment was turning to relatively high profitable sectors such as processing industry, consumer goods, urban public facilities, services and other industries. Due to the transfer of the investment, prices of primary products are recovering and rising gradually, entering a new round of circulation. From the relationship between changes in commodity prices and the "long waves", the period of price rising in primary products corresponds exactly with the rising phase of Kondratieff cycle, while the falling period also coincides with the decline phase of the cycle.

The exploration of the long-wave analytic model by Rostow did arouse widespread concern and recognition of his colleagues, which is mainly because his division of the long wave, especially the division of the fourth, fifth long wave differs quite a lot from the actual situation and the division by most scholars. He regarded the slow economic development in 1935–1951 as the rising wave of the fourth cycle, the rapid growth of capitalism in 1951–1972 as the falling wave of the fourth long cycle, the slow growth of the capitalist economy in 1973-1984 as the rising period of the fifth long cycle, and believed that this upward trend would continue. For such a division, some scholars believe that Rostow just provided a wealth of information for the further study of the capitalist long-term fluctuations.

In the late 1970s and early 1980s, in the research field of the analytic model of "long wave", a very compelling research activity was carried out. A dynamic model research team led by MIT professor Jay Wright Forrester analyzed the existence of "long wave" using computer tools, confirmed the presence of the "long wave" of about 50 years, and made new interpretations of the cause of long wave. Compared with the previous models using human intelligence for data processing, Forrester's dynamic model includes 36 exogenous variables related to economic long wave (including population growth, technological advance, per capita service given by government, occasional interference to economic growth and production), and the exogenous variables also include many subsidiary variables. For so many variables are included in the model and process using computer simulation, the results should be of greater authenticity and credibility. In addition, there are two creative achievements of Forrester's dynamic model in the methodology of long-wave analysis: 1) The model regards as the real capitalist economy as an unbalanced economy, which objectively reflects the true feature of the capitalist economy in understanding. 2) The model describes the transmission mechanism of economic long wave from the economic interaction in both macro and micro levels. The transmission mechanism of waves in the model is: When the demand of consumers and businesses at micro-economic level (individuals, companies, enterprises and other economic entities) increases, it will turn to the retailer or broker for orders, which are often greater than the actual demand. Receiving orders from the businessman, the factory will expand production capacity in order to fill the order, and it will thereby increase investment, increase investment in means of production, and stimulate the expansion of production sectors.

Thus, the increase of demand at the micro-economic level stimulates the excessive expansion of production sectors and promotes the long-wave curve to enter into rising phase through shocks occurring at the macroeconomic level – Forrester calls it "the magnifying effect".

When there is only a small amount of overstock at the micro-economic level, this magnifying effect will lead to further contraction of the demand through shocks in the system, thus driving the long wave curve into a descending phase.

Theorists believe that this analysis of the long-wave transmission mechanism by the model reflects the trend of the organization of production of individual enterprises in capitalist production while the blind development of the entire social production, or private enterprises blindly expand production, and cause serious macroeconomic imbalances. Thus, as the analysis is concerned, it is very close to Marx's analysis of the capitalist economic crisis. Some scholars made such comments on Forrest's model: The model applied the most advanced science and technology in the study of the economic long wave, and the result drawn is consistent with the some of the dissertation by classical Marxist writers. This shows on the other hand that the Marxist theory of economics is scientific; also on the other hand, it shows that advanced scientific methods can reflect the essence of capitalist economy more objectively. When it came to the 1970s, people who followed Schumpeter's ideas to continue the exploration of the long-wave phenomenon increase significantly, with more noticeable achievements, and there have been many variants of Schumpeter's theory of innovation. German-American economist Gerhard Mensch is one of them. 353

Mensch accepted Schumpeter's theory of long-wave technology, regarding the technological innovation as the main driving force of the economic growth and long-term fluctuations, and confirmed Schumpeter's theory with the use of statistical data. However, what Mensch had done is not simply to accept, but to inherit and develop Schumpeter's theory with a critical and developing eye. He believes that Schumpeter's theory is inadequate, who only emphasized entrepreneurial innovation, without mentioning environment and prerequisites needed in this innovation, and thus he failed to address the root reason for the periodic bursts of innovation. Out of the need for the theoretical expression, Mensch presented two unique areas of the economy, namely: "technology rigidity" and "unstable economic structure." He believes that "technology rigidity" is the premise of fundamental innovation, while "unstable economic structure" is the environment for fundamental innovation. In the relationship between the two, unstable economic structure is the reason of technology rigidity.

In Mensch's theory, "technology rigidity" means the dilemma that forces the society to seek a way out through innovation. Its formation mechanism is: the emergence of new fundamental innovation group always brings a whole new industrial sector. Corresponding to these industrial sectors, the huge new market will enable the rapid growth in these sectors and improve the production process of the products. The competition, rationalization and concentration improve the production capacity of new sectors. With the increase of the production capacity, first it is the gradual saturation of the domestic market, then the excess demand in the international market, and therefore the economy has entered an era of recession (or the era of Great Depression). During this time, only with the emergence of new fundamental technological innovation and new industrial sectors can the economy get rid of the crisis and get out of the plight. As can be seen, "technology rigidity" that Mensch referred is actually the long-term social and economic depression or crisis. The so-called "forces the society to seek a way out through innovation" refers to that the depression and major crisis will force governments and businesses to seek new technologies, and to get out of the plight. The emergence of the fundamental technological innovation lays the foundation for the next climax of economic development.

It seems to Mensch that the reason for "technology rigidity" is "unstable economic structure." Here the "unstable economic structure" refers to that the capitalist economy is composed of two levels—the micro and macro—which is connected by investment activity and innovation activity, forming an economic structure. In this structure, the economic movement is unstable and non-continuous. The instability is originated from the devaluation of a certain means of production at the micro level.[3] The instability promotes the development of economic structure towards two directions—the strengthening of economic structure and the weakening. During the period of the weakening of economic structure (period of major crisis), barriers for fundamental innovation are eliminated, providing a suitable environment for a large number of innovations to emerge, and as a result, a series of fundamental technological innovations emerge. Sectors that first completed fundamental technological innovation represent a new economic structure, and are centered round these sectors; innovative products and innovation process are further spread, so that the fundamental technology has been changing rapidly. Thus, the economic structure enters into the period of strengthening, and the economy also enters into an upward wave of the long cycle. After the spread of innovation reaches a certain stage, innovation of the production process replaces the innovation of products, thus promoting the industrial investment boom to peak, and the strengthening of economic structure is all lost. Then it enters into the period

354

3　These means of production have been produced by order, but at this time the production capacity of ordering sectors is excess. Therefore these means of production have devalued before being put into production. When these devaluated means of production continue to be put into the sector, the excess production capacity is further expanded to exacerbate the instability of the economic structure.

of the weakening of the economic structure ... Again and again, it forms long-term economic fluctuations.

In terms of changes in the shape of long waves, Mensch also made an original view. He believes that the long-term fluctuations in economy is not a continuous waveform but a discontinuous form of S-shaped cycles. The reason for this is: in the development of the industrial economy, especially in the marginal efficiency of capital, the continuous increase will be shown in sudden collapse, forming a sudden break or fall of the curve. In general, the sudden collapse of the industrial economy and the marginal efficiency of capital occurred during the Great Depression. The crisis then becomes the gestation period for innovation to emerge in large numbers. Thus, the crisis is overcome by the fundamental innovation, and the growth rises again.[4]Based on Schumpeter's paroxysmal technological innovation, Mensch proposed that the macroeconomic movement is paroxysmal and non-continuous. Its continuity and mutation is mainly reflected in technical impasse, namely recession and the Great Depression. The major crisis has become technological innovation, which is also a necessary precondition for economic growth.

British economist Christopher Freeman was another researcher who was inspired by Schumpeter's technological innovation theory of long wave. Based on Schumpeter's technological innovation theory of long wave, he regarded technological innovation as the main driving force of economic growth, putting more emphasis on the impact of technological innovation on the employment of labour and studying long wave from the perspective of the relations between technological innovation and the employment of labour, thus he formed the labour and employment theory of long wave. The theory can be summarized as: technological innovation has brought the emergence and development of new industries, and the development of new industries promotes the development of related industries. The development of these related industries increases employment opportunities. The demand for labour increases exponentially, and here, economic growth is in a rising wave. Large demand for labour causes wages to increase, resulting in the decline of marginal profit ratio, and thus a decline in investment. The decline in investment leads to a halt of the expansion of economic scale, and the economic movement goes into the decline phase of long wave. At this stage, not only the expansion of economic scale comes to a halt, and it is even further contracted. Therefore, Freeman believes that technological innovations determine the rise and fall of economic long wave, that is, technological innovations play a key role that impacts the economic long wave. In his view, the main driving force of technological innovation is not entrepreneurs at the micro level, but rather the specific science and technology

---

4   Recession and the Great Depression stimulates technological innovation, and is the major driving force for the innovation climax to emerge; the crisis will force companies to seek new technologies to solve the problem of the devaluation of capital; while a large number of technological innovations become the basis for the emergence of a new wave of economic development.

policies that the government takes at the macroscopic level. The specific science and technology policies that the government takes can effectively develop new technologies during the depression, and promote the economy to get out of recession and to regain development at high speed. Freeman even designed several specific projects related to scientific and technological development for Western governments. These projects contained such policies as technology selection, finance plan, strategies to encourage invention and innovation of the fundamental technology, strategies to introduce foreign advanced technology, and also proposed policies for dissemination and application of the new technology once it is produced.

I quite agree with those who criticize that Freeman laid extreme emphasis on governments' scientific and technological development policies, as the only policy that can save the economy from recession and crisis, which is inconsistent with the historical facts of capitalism. In the history of capitalism, the greatest two crises are the economic crisis in 1873-1878 and 1929-1933. In these two crises, the relevant economies relied on the expansion at the microeconomic scale and the extensive reforms in government's political and economic policies at the macroeconomic level; this was how these crises were transcended. In Schumpeter's view the reason behind his mistaken interpretation that because he advocates that the depression and crisis are products of exhaustion in technological innovation.

Based on Schumpeter's technological innovation theory of long wave, Dutchman named Van Dewing was also influential among those economists who regarded the innovation of the technology, especially the innovation of the fundamental technology as the main driving force of the long-term fluctuations. He proposed a long-wave theory based on innovation life cycle. The theory considers that any fundamental technological innovation will go through four stages, namely introduction, diffusion, maturity and decline. In the introduction stage of fundamental technological innovation, old technologies and old products are dying, and new technologies and new products begin to emerge; in the diffusion stage, new technologies and new products have been widely accepted by the society, and there are lucrative profits in the production of new products and the adoption of new technologies. The investment increases rapidly, forming a new industry group; in the mature stage, the development of new industries reaches the peak, and the creation matured; in the decline stage, the development of new industries is already saturated with products and production capacity is full, and the investment is shrinking. The theory also believes that in the national economy, there is a corresponding relation between the innovation life cycle at the micro-level and economic long-term fluctuations at the macro-level. The long-wave fluctuations are divided into four stages, namely prosperity, recession, crisis and recovery. The corresponding relation between these four stages and the four stages of the innovation cycle is: prosperity – diffusion; decline – maturity; crisis – decline; recovery – introduction. Each stage is characterized by: In the prosperity stage, the annual growth rate of GNP is high, the capital investment increases rapidly, and the demand for consumption in the various sectors is expanded. In the recession stage, the annual growth rate of GNP declines, capital investment reduces, and consumption in most sectors declines. In the crisis stage, the annual growth rate of GNP is very low or not growing, production equipment is excess, enterprises reduce demand and control investment, and various sectors and consumers spend past savings. In the recovery stage, the annual growth rate of GNP increases, enterprises need to renew equipment, investment increases, and the purchasing power of consumer demand also increases.

Japanese economist Shinohara Miyohei disagrees to explain the long-term economic fluctuation with a single braking factor. He believes that factors that halting the economic fluctuations are diversified, and there were even four main factors: 1) technological innovation; 2) currency supply; 3) energy resources; 4) war. Among these four factors, technological innovation is paramount. Technological innovation determines the cycle of the long-term fluctuation. Under the premise of emphasizing that technological innovation is the main driving force of long wave, Shinohara Miyohei illustrates the brake factors in the long-term economic fluctuation with empirical facts such as the peak of each long wave is associated with large-scale wars (such as the First World War, the Vietnam War), the expansion of currency supply, and price inflation of the primary commodity (such as oil prices soar in the 1970s). Shinohara Miyohei's interpretation of long wave has an outstanding colour of compromise. From the perspective of long-wave model development, he barely had anything new to be achieved. Shinohara Miyohei stressed the decisive role of technological innovation on long wave is but to follow Schumpeter; the impact of the rise in the price of the primary commodity on long wave is only identical with Rostow; diverse factors he stressed that brake to economic long wave are still within the Kondratieff's analytic model fundamentally.

In the late 1970s and early1980s, there were Western theorists who still explained the economic long wave with political factors and psychological factors. Those who explained economic long wave with political factors attributed the changes in the long wave purely to the expansion and contraction of government economic policies; those who explained economic long wave with psychological factors attributed to explain the movement of the long wave to changes in the psychological cycle of the two generations, or changes in the "confidence cycle" of technical staff. Academia considers that such an interpretation has the one-sidedness and limitations, that the explanation of the long-term economic fluctuation with political factors explains taking the branch for the root; while the explanation of the long wave with psychological factors is idealism.

After the 1970s, Marxist economists conducted in-depth exploration of the long-wave analytic model from the perspective of Marxist economics, and made some valuable insights. The one who is more influential abroad is the Belgian scholar Ernest Mandel, who made a general analysis of the cause of long wave from the point of view of Marxist economics. He recognizes that in the capitalist system, the expanded reproduction is driven by competition between capitalists; in order to obtain excess profits, capitalists will turn to new technology to reduce production costs. In order to obtain new technology, capitalists will invest capital into new areas of production on a large scale. The obtaining of new technologies promotes the renewal of fixed capital on a large scale and the formation of new industrial clusters, and therefore the rate of profit increases, the accumulation of capital accelerates, pushing the long wave into the rising wave; when the application of the fundamental technology reaches the peak, the rate of profit begins to decline, the accumulation of capital goes into the sluggish state, the renewal of fixed capital is reduced, promoting long wave into the falling wave. When the sluggish capital accumulated for decades is once again invested in the field of production on a large scale, a new round of long wave begins... these views of Mandel are affected from Schumpeter, but Mandel considered the issue from the perspective of Marx's economic theory, which is the same as Kondratieff's, who found that from the perspective of Marxist economic theory in the contraction stage of long wave, the reason why a lot of surplus value cannot be used for investment is because of the low economic rate of profit; while the application of new technologies suggests that investment is no longer non-profitable, and a lot of accumulated surplus value flew into new areas of investment opened up by the new technology, driving the whole economy towards prosperity and expansion. The emergence of new technologies can also transform the process, increasing the demand for capital goods and creating new consumer goods, thus increasing the demand for consumer goods, and so forth. Mandel placed the hope to interpret the issue on the emergence of new technologies, but the emergence of new technologies is not an external factor, which in itself is the result of the development of various factors within the internal economic system. These factors are changes in the rate of profit and in the rate of exploitation. Whether there is the emergence of new technologies or not depends on the rate of profit at the time. While the rate of profit itself is determined by some additional factors, such as whether the working class force is organized or not, how powerful it is, whether the international market is open or closed, as well as whether there is free competition or the oligopoly. Mandel also uses three major technological revolutions in the driving technology to explain the three long waves in the capitalist world.[5] As Mandel's long-wave theory well explained the long-term prosperity of the entire capitalist world after the Second World War, it enlightened some of the Marxist economics researchers who could not explain this long-term prosperity with the small cycle theory. In addition, as *Late Capitalism* was published in 1975 right after the expansion of the capitalist economy for 25 years since WWII, which was also faced with the first major recession, it further confirmed the correctness of the long wave theory. Mandel and his work thus also enjoyed reputation.

---

5   The steam technology emerged in 1848; the advent of electricity and the internal combustion engine after 1890; the development of electronics and nuclear power in 1940s.

In 1975, the publication of the English translation of Mandel's *Late Capitalism* has revived this theory that has been silent and untouched for nearly half a century. Since this theory well explained the prosperity for up to three decades in the post-war capitalist countries, it is accepted by the majority of economists, especially by the American radical economists. In the 1980s, there were some changes in Mandel's long wave theory, from the emphasis on technological innovation to the emphasis on the multifactor linked with the characteristics of the capitalist era. It adopted a brand new concept in the division of the long-wave cycle (the Industrial Revolution long wave, the free competition long wave, the heyday of imperialism, the declining era of capitalism, and it also consider a series of major non-economic factors in the division of long wave, such as the bourgeois revolution, the Napoleonic wars, the imperialist war, workers' movement, revolution and counter-revolution and so on. The academic community considers that this is a theoretical backwards.

The long-wave theory of "social structure of accumulation" proposed by David Gordon et al. is also worth mentioning that the theory emphasizes the decisive role of the formation and decay of a particular institutional environment in favour of accumulation of capital in the long-term economic fluctuations, and it believes that the formation and decay of specific social structures of accumulation is the endogenous economic process. What is accompanied by the alternation of different social structures of accumulation is the successive long wave, and it forms different stages of the development of capitalism. The school has also been profoundly impacted by the Marxist tradition.

359

The long wave theory pioneered by Kondratieff is not within the visionary field of the Western mainstream economists, but it is enduring research topic for the heterodox economists. There are sceptics, but a growing number of economists acknowledge that in the process of capitalist development, there is a long-term economic fluctuation for 50 years or so which is different from the classical business cycles, including the long wave upswing stage of rapid economic growth for more than 20 years and the long wave decline phase of relative economic stagnation for more than 20 years. The different interpretations of the internal mechanism of the long wave forms three long wave theories of greater impact. The first one is long wave theory of technological innovation pioneered by Schumpeter that mainly emphasizes the rising investment driven by the emergence of major technological innovation clusters in a certain period of time, and the investment decline caused by the exhaustion of the potential of technological revolution is the basic reason for the occurrence long-term economic fluctuations.[6] The second one is the long wave theory of Marxism structured by Mandel who believes that the rise and fall of the rate of profit constrained by a number of fundamental economic variables is a major force that causes the long-term economic fluctuation. He also stressed that the

6   For the review and development of Schumpeterian long wave theory of technological innovation, see Jacob van Duijn, *Economic Long Wave and Innovation*, Chinese Translation, Shanghai: Shanghai Translation Publishing House, 1993.

economic factors that promote the economy to transfer to the long wave downward phase are endogenous, but the transfer of the economy into the long-wave upswing phase must rely on the promotion of exogenous factors.[7] The third one is the long-wave theory of "social structure of accumulation" proposed by David Gordon et al., stressing the decisive role of the formation and decay of a particular institutional environment in favour of accumulation of capital (social structure of accumulation) in the long-term economic fluctuations, believing that the formation and decay of specific social structures of accumulation is the endogenous economic process. What is accompanied by the alternation of different social structures of accumulation is the successive long-wave, and it forms different stages of the development of capitalism. The school has also been profoundly impacted by the Marxist tradition.

The active mechanism stressed in the three long-wave theories is quite different. The theory of technological innovation mainly emphasizes technological variables, Mandel's theory mainly emphasizes the economic variables centered with the rate of profit, and "social structure of accumulation" school mainly emphasizes the institutional variables. But in our opinion, the three theories are not so much opposite of each other, but are complementary. The direct driving force of economic growth is investment, and the investment rate and the accumulation rate is the decisive factor that constrains the economic growth. The rapid economic growth in the long-wave rising phase is always associated with high investment, and the slow economic growth in the long-wave decline period is usually a direct result of low investment. This has been proved by numerous empirical analyses. Therefore, changes in the growth rate of investment and capital accumulation should be placed into the centre of the long-wave analysis. Once emphasizing the core of the change in the investment rate, then it easy to see that the three types of variables are directly related to the long-term changes in the rate of investment. The formation of higher investment rate and the rate of capital accumulation during the long-wave period requires at least three conditions. First, it is the strong investment momentum, which comes from the rising rate of profit and the resulting optimistically expected profit. The purpose of capital is the pursuit of profit, and without the stimulus of the increasingly growth of the rate of profit, capital owners will not invest a lot of capital in production and management. Second, it is the strong investment demand, which comes from a series of new production sectors formed with technological revolution and innovation cluster, as well as the profound technology transformation in the traditional production sectors driven by technological revolution. The production and construction of large-scale infrastructure and advanced production equipment is the material carrier of massive investment. Without this strong demand, it is very difficult to maintain high investment growth for more than twenty years. Third, it is the favourable investment environment, which means that some major changes in the institutional structure promotes certain fundamental economic variables to

7 See Ernest Mandel, *Late Capitalism*, Harbin: Heilongjiang People's Publishing House, 1983; *Long Wave of Capitalist Development*, Beijing: Beijing Normal University Press, 1993.

move in the direction of promoting the rate of profit, ensuring good and stable profit expectations and investment enthusiasm of investors. This particular institutional condition conducive to investment is also indispensable for any long-term investment upsurge. Conversely, the lower investment rate and the rate of capital accumulation during the decline stage of long-wave are due to the lack of investment momentum, investment demand and favourable investment environment. Thus, the internal mechanism of the economic long wave does not depend on a certain single factor that the three theories emphasize respectively, but is determined by the three basic factors directly related to the investment of social life.

The rising stage and falling stage of long-wave contains two to three consecutive cycles respectively. The rapid growth in the rising stage and the low growth in the falling stage are manifested respectively as the continuous movement of several moderate cycles or several intense cycles. The long-term fluctuation and the cyclical fluctuation have such contact though; their internal mechanisms are by no means identical. The cyclical fluctuation in economy does not necessarily require a radically technological change different from the technological advances, as well as major institutional change is different from the marginal adjustment of institutional relations. In economic operation, due to the influence of supply factors and demand factors, changes in the regularity of labour share, capacity utilization and relative prices of raw materials is able to lead to the rise and fall of the rate of profit, that is it can lead to the rise and fall of investment and the expansion and contraction of production. But for 361 the long-term fluctuation, there will be no strong investment demand of a longer period without the fundamental technological changes, and the long-term flourishing of investment demand is a necessary condition for rapid capital accumulation during the long-wave upswing stage; in the meantime, significant changes in the institutional structure which is not adapted to the requirements of accumulation will not promote long-term growth of the rate of profit, thus providing institutional guarantees for the higher investment rate during the long-wave upswing stage.

In short, the investigation of long-wave theory is not a trend of long-term economic volatility, but the trend of economic volatility throughout the capitalist world. The long-wave theory believes that there is a long period of recession and prosperity in every 50 years or so in the capitalist economy. This long period is composed of a number of small periods of 4 to 10 years. The latter is the crisis periodicity or the business cycle in the usual sense as stated earlier. In the period of the first 25 years or so, the international economy is in expansion and development stage. The above short business cycles manifest themselves as: the economy is strong during the prosperity stage, and declines a little during the depression. In the period of the second 25 years or so, the performance of the short period is opposite: the economy rises a little and falls steeply. What the long-wave theory argues is not the issue of the performance of such a cycle, but the cause of the cycle of recession and prosperity in every 50 years.

III. The Analysis of 'Long Waves' of Political Economy of Capitalism by Chinese Scholars

Chinese scholars started to study the long wave theories in the early 1980s. At the beginning, it mainly included the introduction and presentation of research results of foreign scholars. In the 1980s, Chinese scholar Zhao Tao published a book titled *The Economic Long Wave Theory: A Study on the Long-term Fluctuations of Capitalism*, which contained a systematic study of the theory and practice of the long wave, systematically interpreted the long-wave phenomenon of the capitalist economies from the perspective of Marxist economics.

When expounding on his theory of long waves, namely the long waves of economy and the long waves of technological innovations in tools, Zhao Tao has argued that all integrated statistical indicators reflecting the economic growth rate (such as the growth rate of the national economy, the annual growth rate of GDP, the growth rates of the GNP, the growth rate of industrial production, total consumption and total savings rate) and those individual indicators (such as investment growth rate, trade growth rate) are both statistical indicators which reflect the economic long wave. Both of these two types of statistical indicators perform wave form curves or approximate waveform curves of long waves when expressed through a statistical indicator graph. Indexes of prices, interest rates, unemployment, employment rates, and wages cannot be regarded as the major statistics to reflect the economic long wave, but only as the coordinating indicators. In the division of "long wave", Zhao Tao basically accepted Mandel's classification method, and she also divided the capitalist economic long wave into four long waves, namely "economic long wave of industrial revolution, economic long wave of the free competition capitalism, the economic long wave of the private capitalist monopoly, and the economic long wave of the state capitalist monopoly." She also statistically examined each economic long wave, and confirmed the existence of each economic long wave.

Zhao Tao analyzed the "long wave" phenomenon with the analytical method of Marxist political economy, and she thought, the "long wave" phenomenon was attributed to the cyclical movement of the internal contradictions of capitalist mode of production. This movement was shown as the periodic replacement of the capitalist working tool system in every a few decades. Because such replacement promotes the rapid development of productive forces, so that crises occurred in the capitalist relations of production on the adaptability of productive forces, and it forced capitalism to make local but major adjustments to its production relations, leading to morphological changes in the relations of production, in order to adapt to the development of productive forces. Capitalism of free competition, capitalism of private monopoly and capitalism of state monopoly are morphological changes of capitalist relations of production. In every form, the capitalist relations of production will go through a course from adaptation to obstacle on productive forces, that is, there will be a form of development and a form of shackle. Thus, the contradiction between the capitalist relations of production and the productive forces is manifested as: the cyclical movement of adaption – obstacle – adjustment – re-adaptation – re-obstacle – re-adjustment. This movement will continue until all the productive forces accommodated in the capitalist relations of production play out. Under the condition of no obstacle, the movement of productive forces shows the characteristics of continuous growth, and the ideal trend of its curve is gradually rising. However, relations of production are different. As its development and changes are the increase in the carrying capacity of productive forces, and this carrying capacity is increasing one step by another until it reaches the maximum. This specificity determines its movement to be shown as disconnection, and its changes are not shown to be incremental, but rather abrupt. The carrying capacity of relations of production on productive forces increases by every one level, it thereafter remains relatively stable in a relatively long time. When the development of productive forces exceeds the carrying capacity of the relations of production, the quantitative change in the relations of production is often blindly achieved through economic violence – major crisis. The major crisis pushes the capitalist system to the brink of collapse, and the rulers are forced to partially adjust the relations of production, resulting in the enhancement of the carrying capacity of the relations of production on productive forces, so that the relations of production adapts to the development of productive forces within a considerable period of time. When the development of productive forces once again exceeds the carrying capacity of relations of production, a major crisis will erupt... This is a cyclical development process, with each cycle of about 50 years or so, which happens to be an economic long wave. In a certain form of capitalist relations of production, the continuous movement of productive forces and the relatively stable carrying capacity of the relations of production will have contradictions, forming a cycle of the contradictory movement of capitalist mode of production. In each cycle, when the relations of production are in the adaption period to productive forces, the smooth development of productive forces makes the economic growth curve climb sharply, accelerating the pace of economic development. When the relations of production reach the maximum adaptation point, the economic growth rate is at the turning point. When the relations of production are at the shackle point, the economic growth is gentle or slow. When a major crisis occurs, the economic growth rate is zero or negative. Zhao Tao believes that the material basis for the capitalist reproduction to be carried out periodically is the renewal of fixed capital, and the material basis for the economic long wave is the periodical replacement of the working tool system.[8] The system of instruments of labour is replaced in a half-century or so, and has become the material basis for the movement cycle

---

8   Like the system of instruments of labour in the cycle of free capitalism is the steam power system; in the cycle of private monopoly capitalism it is the instrument of labour system of electricity and power; in the cycle of state monopoly capitalism it is the NC artificial intelligence labour system.

of the internal contradiction of capitalist mode of production, thus becoming the material basis for the economic long wave cycle. Therefore, the contradictory movement of the capitalist mode of production completes a cycle in about half a century or so, and correspondingly, the economic long wave is also experiencing a cycle in half a century or so. This cycle began after the industrial revolution, and after that, it went again and again, through the back rotation, so that the carrying capacity of the relations of production on productive forces is increasing at every step and piled larger. When all the productive forces that capitalist relations of production can accommodate are exhausted, this movement will end.

After presenting the above views, Zhao Tao had the empirical prediction of the forms of the relations of production and the development trend of long wave in the state monopoly capitalism. She believes that from the World War II to 1973, the long-term prosperity in Western economies constitute the rising curve of the long wave of state monopoly capitalism. The 1973-1975 world economic crisis has become a turning point in the economic long wave. After the crisis, the capitalist world economy went into "stagflation", and state monopoly capitalism has thus entered the descending curve of the long wave. Zhao Tao predicted that the falling wave of the fourth economic long wave will last until late 20th century and early 21st century, and then, there will be a major crisis more severe than the 1929-1933 crisis. The heavy blow to the capitalist system by the crisis will force the state monopoly capitalism to have major and partial adjustment of the relations of production in the international context, and this adjustment will cause the capitalist relations of production to develop from the form of the state monopoly capitalism to the form the international monopoly capitalism. Corresponding to the international monopoly capitalism, the capitalist economy will enter a fifth long wave.[9] She also predicts that the emergence of international monopoly capitalism will further expand the carrying capacity of capitalist relations of production on productive forces, including through international institutions, the intervention and regulation of the economy of all major capitalist countries, the intervention and regulation of the international production of transnational corporations, international capital flows in international financial markets and stock markets, partially to mitigate worldwide North-South confrontation and conflict between rich and poor, and gradually to make the global resource allocation and income distribution rationalized.

Entering into the 1990s, the number of the Chinese scholars who studied the 'long wave' has been greatly reduced, but the research continues. As can be seen from the results of their research, the existence of long wave seems to be an objective fact, and an economic phenomenon with regularity. However, the

9 Zhao Tao also believes that in the Great Depression of 1930s, the private monopoly capital had to offer the state the authority of intervention in the economy, and the Great Depression would force the capitalist state to offer the international organizations part of its authority of intervening in and regulating the national economy.

angle of understanding the long wave has changed, and the reasons for the long wave also have new claims. For example, Liu Chongyi, Li Dachang, Wang Xiaoqi, Chen Weihan and et al. regard the long wave as the structural economic crisis of contemporary capitalism, and believe that this crisis is a crisis of the productive sector, which arises after the establishment of the capitalist economy and is a crisis of wide range, strong destruction, and long duration. It often leads to the severe shock the entire national economy, and generally is an international or global crisis. The basic signs of this crisis are the poor economic conversion with a technological structure and industrial structure as the core, causing a devastating impact on socio-economic structure, and among them, the poor conversion of leading industrial sectors and basic industries sectors has the decisive significance. The form of this crisis is often manifested as overproduction in some sectors and underproduction in others. In the interpretation of the reasons of long wave, they are multi-element theorists, regarding only the technological innovation as the primary factor in the formation of long waves. They believe that the primary product innovation and the innovation in the basic industrial sectors leads to that new technology and the economic structure conversion with industrial and technological structure conversion as the core promotes the economic long wave to enter into the rising wave. With the advance of the rising wave, the organic composition of capital in these sectors continues to improve, the technology is reaching maturity and completeness, supply exceeds demand gradually. These sectors go into the falling stage, where the innovation spreads to other related industries, the excess profit is 365 reduced or even no longer exists, and the rate of profit becomes average and even falls. Capital in these traditional industrial sectors is often reluctant to timely comply with the needs of structure conversion and to transfer to the emerging industrial sectors, but is eager for a relatively stable income in the past, slacks in the old industrial sectors, by increasing the intensity of exploitation, to reduce the value of the constant capital, and to compress the supply and other channels, and therefore, within a certain period and a certain limit it slows or suppresses the decline in the rate of profit, resulting in the coexistence of the excess accumulation of capital in the old industrial sectors and the lack of capital accumulation in the new industrial sectors, i.e. the dislocation between the objective needs for the establishment of new industries and the rigidity of traditional industries, thus causing the structural destruction and depreciation of capital, as well as shocks and impacts to the national economy. The above explanation of the reason for the long wave is apparently the replica of Schumpeter's technology theory of long wave.[10]

---

10 Liu Chongyi et al. also believe that the structural crisis has the following manifestations: the long-term slow growth, and almost stagnation of investment, production and trade, enterprises running under their production capacity, idle equipment, high unemployment, prices and interest rates continued to fall, the international debt crisis marked with the shortage of international liquidity.

In addition to technological innovation factors, Liu Chongyi and et al. also believe that the rise or fall in the price of primary products, the budget deficit, inflation, balance of trade, the national industrial policy, the macroeconomic policy, the establishment of state monopoly capitalism, changes in the contrast between prices of raw materials and prices of finished goods, the rise in interest rates, world market conditions, foreign exchange rate, inflow and outflow of precious metals are motives for changes in the long wave. However, compared with other factors, these factors are the ones that cause the economic long wave phenomena and form, the ultimate reason that causes the economic long wave still lies in the ultimate contradiction of capitalist relations of production.

In the early 1990s, many Chinese scholars believe that the 1991-1992 crisis is the turning point of the transition from the fourth long wave to the fifth long wave. After the crisis, the capitalist economy will enter into the rising stage of fifth long wave, but the economic growth in 1990s was still relatively slow. The reason to determine the cause is that they found a law from the transition crisis of the long wave, that is, the transition crisis is the crisis that has the deepest extent and causes the maximum extent of the damage to the economy over a period, and before the crisis there is a longer period of continued growth, while after the crisis there is then a period of slow growth.[11] Li Cong confirmed this view in the end of 1990s, and he believes that in the early 1990s the rising stage of the fifth long wave began.[12] He said that although people had many debates on the reasons for the long wave, but it could be confirmed that the scientific and technological advances, capital investment, management innovation, the expansion of global market, etc. are some of the decisive factors for the existence of the long wave. The so-called long cycle is the cycle of the advances of science and technology and productive forces, the cycle of having capital investment on these new technologies, the cycle of reform and innovation of micro-and macro-economic management, the cycle of the backward countries rushing into the tide of world economy development. In this cycle, science and technology and productive forces are its driving force, capital accumulation and investment is its material basis, institutional innovation is its promotion factors, and the takeoff of the backward countries is the condition for it to expand the range. Of course, in the process of the long business cycle, it is inevitable that there are a number of unpredictable factors, including economic factors and non-economic factors, which play a certain role in the process of long cycle and its form of manifestation. These factors are that such as war, the upheaval, some critical resources (such as oil) in supply and demand as well as in the market price, bad and good harvests of grain, and so on. Currently, the capitalist economy has entered a phase of the fifth increase in long period. At this stage, the role of these various factors is very obvious. The high-tech

366

---

11   Yao Tinggang, *The Capitalist Economic Crises and Cycles in 1990s*, in *World Economy*, 1993(11); Zhang Yunling, *Transition and Long-Term Fluctuation in The Postwar Development of Western Economy*, in *World Economy*, 1982(10).

12   Li Cong, *New Development of Contemporary Capitalism*, Beijing: Economic Science Press, p. 384.

centered information technology is booming, the industrial economy continues to shift to an information economy, the investment of fixed assets continues to expand, the enterprise system undergoes new reform, the management system of the state over the economy is also under wide-ranging reforms, and the economy of more developing countries is recovering. According to the law of the development of long cycle, the ongoing economic rising stage will continue until the first 15 to 20 years of the 21st centuries. In 1990s, the United States experienced a record-breaking longevity of economic prosperity exceeding 10 years, with a substantial increase in labour's productive forces, "high growth, low inflation" in economy, low level of unemployment, and the continuous soaring of the stock price. This abnormal performance of the U.S. economy aroused a great concern in the academia, and many has argued that growth mode of the U.S. economy was changed, and attained new characteristics, which can be defined as the "new economy" distinct from the traditional economy, and therefore they put forward a set of theories related to the new economy.[13] Economist Gao Feng has argued that the abnormal performance of the U.S. economy is not the so-called "new economy", but an economic expansion driven jointly by the strong investment forces, strong investment demand, favourable investment environment and other economic variables. This expansion "means that the U.S. economy have walked out of the slow growth for nearly 1/4 of a century since 1970s, and start to enter into a new rising stage of long wave."[14]

IV. Conclusions

The long-wave theory was first proposed by Marxist economists, but it has created worldwide attention among economists of a variety of genres. Firstly because that they are able to apply their theories and methods and make reasonable explanation for the long-wave phenomenon; the second reason is that there are some differences in the findings from various angles, but the existence of the long-wave phenomenon is a universal conclusion, having become an accepted fact. The study on the long-wave phenomenon has been a history of more than a century, and experienced several worldwide high-level research and debate, but the study remains to be done, because there are still many mysteries in the long-wave phenomena. For example, the long-wave phenomenon existed in the world economy in the past two hundred years, and in the next two hundred years or even in a longer period, does the long-wave phenomenon still exist? Why cannot the existing research results reach a closer consensus in length of the wave? What is the root reason of the long-wave phenomenon exactly? And so on. Therefore, in future studies, with the cracking of a series of mysteries, the model itself will have a happy ending.

---

13   Huang Zhixian, *On the Formation and Debate on the US 'Theory*, in *Economic Review*, 2001(2).
14   Zhang Yu et al., *Advanced Political Economy*, Beijing: Economic Science Press, 2002, p.311.

Comparatively the existing literature of studying the long-wave phenomena, although it is difficult to bridge the differences, there are two advantages worthy of recognition: First, with the use of statistical data, statistical methods, and computer means it proves the existence of the long-wave phenomenon, indicating that the long-wave phenomenon is the result of empirical analysis; second, it reveals the reason for the existence of the long-wave phenomenon from the perspective of political economy, though it might be academic contention, it is still the result of using the principles of Marxist historical materialism to analyze the real economic relations.

Despite being not yet mature, the long-wave theory has become an effective analysis tool for many scholars to explain the history of the development of the world economy, to predict the development trend of the world economy and assists long term strategic decision-making. I suggest that the macroeconomic policy choices in many countries are also influenced by the long-wave theory.

CHAPTER XI

Contemporary Western Marxist Scholars' New Interpretation on the Economic Crisis

I. Introduction

After World War II, a group of Marxist scholars in the Western world had the in-depth study and exploration of the capitalist economic crisis from different angles by virtue of their more updated information advantages than their predecessors, used modern analysis tools, have done a lot of meaningful testing and demonstration work. In their works we can see both inheritance, development and improvement of Marx's analysis model of the economic crisis under modern conditions. As they chose various aspects to study the economic crisis, and considered different factors, they have formed different models. In the existing literature, models that we are able to see are: model of the rate of profit to fall, model of underconsumption, model of overaccumulation, model of disproportionality, model of three levels, model of crisis after the introduction of ecological factors, mode of crisis after the introduction of state intervention factors. These models are apparently classified in accordance with the single factor that plays a decisive role in the economic fluctuations, and we can call them single factor models. Among those scholars who study the economic crisis, not all of them consider that the crisis is caused by a single factor; some researchers have favoured a single factor, while others advocate the role of multi factors. Hence, according to their research mode or perspective chosen by the researcher there are both single-factor models and multi-factor models among various crisis theories. We can further classify them, because each theory involves different types of factors, the "single-factor" model is further divided into types of disproportionality, underconsumption, organic composition of capital increasing, wage increasing, government's fiscal crisis, and etc. In addition to early Tugan-Baranowsky, Otto Bauer, Fritz Naphtali, Josef Steindl, F. Sternberg, Kalecki, Bullock, Conrad Schmidt, Natalie Maszkowska, and et al. are active advocates of the "one-factor" model. The defender of the "two-factor" model is Paul Sweezy, who based his analysis on Marx's theory of crisis on two aspects as underconsumption and disproportionality. Joan Robinson outlined a "three-factor" model in the 1940s, based on 1) unemployed reserve army of labour; 2) the rate of profit to fall; 3) underconsumption combined with disproportionality. Hereafter, Vito outlined another "three-factor" model: 1) underconsumption; 2) investment reset; 3) overinvestment. While acknowledging the existence of the factors of the "investment reset type", Gaitan also proposed a "three-factor" model: 1) overinvestment; 2) underconsumption; 3) the tendency of the rate of profit to fall. The wording of the "three-factor" models is different, but the substance is basically the same. The proponent of the "four-factor" model is Makoto Itoh. In appearance, it seems that Makoto Itoh is also endorsing the "two-factor" model, but in fact after he made two categories of economic crisis, "capital surplus" and "commodity surplus", he further divided "capital surplus" crisis into two categories of crisis, "labour shortage" and "organic composition of capital ", and classified "commodity surplus" crisis further as "underconsumption" and "disproportionality". The chapter argues, to explain combining the two, it could both illustrate the realization mechanism of the crisis with the multi-factor effect, and explain the active mechanism of major factors that cause the crisis. But considering the issue from a narrative point of view, it will be more conducive to theoretical elaboration by sorting with the single-factor model.

II. Their Research Model on the Rate of Profit to Fall

Entering the 20th century, Western scholars paid increasingly more attention to the tendency of the rate of profit to fall in Marx's analytic model of the economic crisis, the profit model, and tended to strengthen the empirical study, with the purpose first to prove the reliability of the law itself, on the basis of which, to further prove the relations between the rate of profit to fall and the crisis. However, with respect to the root cause of the tendency of the rate of profit to fall, scholars had differences in understanding, thus forming different variants of the tendency of the rate of profit to fall. American scholar Thomas E. Weisskopf summarizes and analyzes the types of the theory of "the tendency of the rate of profit to fall", and depending on the different roots of the average rate of profit to fall, they are divided into three types: theory of the improvement of organic composition of capital, theory of the increase in labour's strength, and theory of realization failure. This chapter argues that what Weisskopf had done is meaningful, and it helps us have the in-depth and detailed understanding of the model of the tendency of the rate of profit to fall, as well as grasp the overall factor and structure.

The theory of rising organic composition of capital: The conclusion formulated as of "the model of the improvement of organic composition of capital" is derived with two steps: First, it is to deduce and show the mechanism that promotes the ever-increasing organic composition of capital; second, it is to illustrate the relations between the rate of profit to fall and the economic crisis. Large amounts of data on "theory of the improvement of organic composition" agree with this realization mechanism: With the rate of profit to fall companies of weak competitiveness go bankrupt, other companies stop investing, the demand for capital goods is reduced, capital goods sales are difficult, large numbers of workers are unemployed, and the economy goes into the crisis stage. The crisis also improves profitability once again by reducing wages, reducing the organic composition of capital, and eliminating production enterprises. Thus, the entire economy is driven into prosperity again. The cyclical economic crisis caused by the gradual decline in the rate of profit is more severe in extent than the last crisis. Investment is always insufficient, while there is long-term excess in production, which ultimately pushes the entire capitalist economy to the brink of collapse. Both analyses establish a link between the organic composition, the rate of profit to fall and the economic crisis.

371

The rate of profit to fall results in the intensification of the basic contradiction of capitalism, and the intensification of the basic contradiction causes economic crisis, which has been seen as orthodox model for Marxist economics to explain the crisis. Nevertheless, Marx himself did not use the model to analyze the crisis, but made an extremely abstract theoretical derivation of the model itself, especially with increasing organic composition of capital, the rate of profit to fall is a changing trend with the assumption that that the rate of surplus value remains unchanged, and its credibility has been one of the focuses of study and debate. In *Finance Capital*, Hilferding analyzed the realization mechanism of the capitalist economic crisis with the law of rate of profit to fall, but it is also a purely abstract theoretical derivation. The following are its logical expansion structure and the transmission mechanism: the capitalists continue having capital accumulation – the improvement of organic composition of capital – the tendency of the rate of profit to fall – conflicts between the self-expansion of capital and the rate of profit to fall emerges – new investments are reduced – product sales are sluggish – the outbreak of the crisis – the renewal of fixed capital on a large scale – prosperity – a new round of economic cycle – the role of credit in the economic cycle. Since Hilferding used the deductive and inductive analysis, focusing on the normative rather than the empirical analysis, therefore, its reliability is still questioned by many people, and compared to the explanation by Marx in *Capital* Volume III, it seems just to have done some systematic work. Before 1929, with regard to the argument on the tendency of the rate of profit to fall, the conclusion which is generally accepted is that the improvement of organic composition of capital driven by the technological advances is faster than the growth rate of exploitation, and it is also treated as a rigorous theory. Some orthodox Marxist economists generally acknowledge that Marx's analysis correctly reveals the consequences of technological changes, but do not connect it with the capitalist crisis, for example, Rosa Luxemburg is one of them. Hilferding did connect the rate of profit to fall with the crisis, but he did not emphasize this. Apart from a handful of economists, such overlook at the rate of profit to fall is common in the early 20th century, such as the Soviet economist Varga, who has been insisting this view in dozens of subsequent years.[1]

In terms of the issue of the rate of profit to fall under the condition of the improvement of the organic composition of capital, the debate has never ceased. Thus by 1918 it was a standard criticism of the falling rate of profit theory that "Marx had underestimated the effects of technical progress on the labour productivity; that these effects tended to reduce the value of constant capital and to increase the rate of exploitation; and that the rate of profit would not fall, but was likely to rise, as a result of technical change. Orthodox Marxists hedged, as indeed had Marx himself. Most, however, denied that the counter-acting tendencies would be sufficient, in the long run, to prevent the profit rate from falling, and few had any truck with the notion that technical change would actually increase the rate of profit. None saw the falling rate of profit theory as a very important part of Marxian crisis theory, nor (apart from George C. Stiebeling) made any reference whatsoever to empirical evidence."[2]

From the beginning of the 1930s, Marxists who used the law of the tendency of the rate of profit to fall to analyze the capitalist economic crisis are increasing in the number. On the one hand, this is partly because of the non-systemic exposition on the theory of economic crisis by Marx in *Capital*, and on the other hand, it is also because there are a lot of issues to be explored in the area. The aim of researchers has ultimately concentrated on the issue of the economic crisis, but the focus of the study is different. Some people tried to use empirical methods to provide more evidence for Marx's law of the tendency of the rate of profit to fall; some people regard the tendency of the rate of profit to fall as a strict theoretical assumption in order to derive the inevitability of capitalist economic crisis and its various manifestations. Many people connect the Great Depression with the rate of profit to fall for examination. German scholar Eric Pretzel stresses that the rate of profit to fall is the foundation of Marxist crisis theory, and it can be very successful in explaining overproduction and fierce market competition, which was later accepted by Henrik Grossman. Under the assumption of technological progress and a certain rate of exploitation, he used

372

---

1 See M. C. Howard, *A History of Marxian Economics (1929-1990)*, Beijing: Translation Publishing House, 2003, p. 6.
2 Ibid., pp. 132-133.

the mathematical model to prove that when the fixed capital increases at a rate of 10% in a cycle, the variable capital growth rate is only 5%, concluding that after 35 cycles the accumulation cannot be achieved ultimately due to the lack of surplus value. In his mathematical example, when the consumption of capitalists fell to zero, the crisis broke out. Subsequently, in some analyses of Marxist crisis theory, literatures the improvement of the organic composition of capital have occupied a very prominent position. Lewis Corey is a more prominent one, and he used official statistics to prove that the U.S. organic composition of capital was basically improving continuously, whether it was in the long term (from 1849 to 1914) or during preparation period of the Great Depression, where the rate of profit would not fall only in very exceptional circumstances. Among them, from 1923 to 1931, it dropped from 9.2% to a negative. This is an empirical result which had great influence.

In those scholars who disagree on the law of the tendency of the rate of profit to fall, there are many so-called "orthodox" Marxist economists and Natalie Moszkowska is one of them. She believes that the only fact of the rate of profit to fall cannot provide adequate argument for the analysis in *Capital* Volume III, because the rate of profit to fall may be caused by very different reasons. She also criticized that Marx's conclusions were unfounded, because the improvement of productive forces associated with technological advances will result in the rise in the rate of profit, unless the growth of real wages is sufficient to maintain the same rate of exploitation. In her view, it makes it the same thing when talking about "the law of the rate of exploitation to rise" and "the law of the rate of profit to fall". Marx himself had discussed the offsetting factor which is opposite to the rate of profit to fall. "The reduction in value of various factors of the constant capital" will reduce the organic composition, while the reduction in the necessary labour time will increase the rate of exploitation. It seems to Sweezy and M. Dobb that the capitalist economic factors make it impossible to draw any definitive conclusions about the long-term trends of the profitability. Hans Neisser pointed out more bluntly that even if Grossman's analysis was right, it still could not establish a link between the rate of profit to fall and the coming of the economic crisis, and even when the rate of profit declines, the accumulation will continue as long as the rate of profit remains positive. Moreover, the successful capitalists who improve their profitability at the expense of their opponents to, of course will continue to expand their production capacity.[3]

In 1936, Otto Bauer made a relatively reasonable explanation of the connection between the rate of profit to fall and the economic crisis. He believes that if the economy is in a slump period, and if there is a stimulation of the external force, the same plant equipment will produce more products, and the efficiency of the productive forces will be improved. At the same time, the number of employment will be increased, which will reduce the organic composition of capital, improve profitability, and it will lead to a new round of

---

3   See M.C. Howard, *A History of Marxian Economics (1929-1990)*, p. 146.

capital accumulation. With the economic recovery and prosperity, new investment is accelerated, and the organic composition of capital is raised. If this upward trend is sufficient for the capitalist to maintain the existing profitability, changes in the decline of wages with changes in profit could eliminate the crisis of underconsumption. If the rate of exploitation lags behind the organic composition, the rate of profit will decline. The response of companies to this situation is to cut their dividends or bonuses; the financial market will crash, directly resulting in the decline in investment and thus causing economic decline. Some commentators of economic theory believe that, "Bauer's analysis lacked both a formal model of the cycle and an endogenous mechanism to bring about the upswing, but it was the most convincing of a number of contemporary attempts to use the falling rate of profit in a theory of cyclical fluctuations, incorporating problems of effective demand."[4]Based on Marx's assumptions, Natalie Moszkowska established an analytical model, and drew the interdependence between the rate of profit and the rate of surplus value, that is: 1) when the rate of surplus value is constant, the rate of profit falls; 2) when the rate of profit is constant, and the rate of surplus value rises. Maurice Dobb also devoted himself to the issue of the rate of profit to fall, but he's just came to an ambiguous conclusion. He believes that the actual course of the profit rate depended on the relationship between technical change, productivity growth and the rate of exploitation. The rate of profit was likely eventually to decline, but this was contingent and might be long delayed. Joan Robinson's conclusion is more

374 affirmative, considering that one might as well talk of a rising rate of surplus value as of a falling profit rate. In 1956, H. D. Dickinson employed analytical tools taken from neoclassical economics to explore the relationship between the organic composition of capital and the rate of exploitation. Holding that the real wage constant, Dickinson used Cobb-Douglas production function to relate the growth of capital to that of output, and the result is that only if very special conditions held would the rate of profit fall continuously. Otherwise it would initially rise as the organic composition increased, decreasing only when capital accumulation had passed a crucial threshold. Thus any decline in the profit rate, Dickinson concluded, although eventually inescapable, might well be postponed until 'some distant future'. Critics believe that Dickinson made a wrong attempt, because the problem with Dickinson's argument is that he used neoclassical ideas which have since been shown to be seriously defective. Only very special types of technology can be represented in terms of an aggregate production function.[5] Since then, Ronald Meek avoided the defect of Dickinson, and his Research work avoided the necessary theoretical derivation, relying entirely on a series of plausible numerical examples. His conclusion is: If we start from a fairly low level of organic composition, then, I think it can possibly be said that on Marx's premises the "tendency" of the rate of profit is first to rise, and then some time afterwards to fall. The initial increase would be greater, and the pint of downturn later, the lower the initial rate of exploitation;

4   Ibid., p. 134.
5   Ibid., p. 139.

the greater the increase in productivity associated with a given rise in the organic composition; and the faster the growth of productivity in department II relative to department I. Since productivity growth in department I cheapen the elements of constant capital and thus work against the assumed increase in the organic composition. Some people think that this points to a defect in Meek's procedure. In response, Howard says: "In fact, technical progress may be associated with a decline in the organic composition if the unit value of constant capital falls fast enough."[6]

In the 1950s, using data from official U.S. sources for the later nineteenth and early twentieth century's Joseph Gillman found a clear break in trend around 1919, before which the organic composition of capital had been rising sharply, more than offsetting the increased rate of exploitation to give the expected decline in the rate of profit. After 1919 all three ratios of the organic composition of capital, the rate of exploitation, the rate of profit had remained roughly constant. Gillman therefore concluded that Marx's law must be reformulated. He was convinced that the "capital-saving" nature of technical change under monopoly capitalism, and more especially to the rapid growth of unproductive expenditures, such as sales and administrative costs, has a significant impact on capital savings. Ignoring variable capital, and denoting unproductive expenditures as u, the true rate of profit is $(s - u) / c$ rather than s / c. The profit rate depends not only on the rate of exploitation and the organic composition, but also on u / v, that is, the ratio between unproductive expenditures and the wages of productive workers. Re-estimated on this, Gillman argued, the rate of profit had indeed declined after 1919, but because of an increase in u/v rather c / v. In the 1970s, in his book *Late Capitalism*, Mandel made a new interpretation on the issue of the rate of profit to fall with the concept of long wave. For Mandel accumulation is function of the rate of profit. Upswings in the long cycle are initiated by 'triggering factors' which lower the organic composition or increase the rate of exploitation. The post-war boom was one such upswing, E. Mandel maintained, with characteristically prolonged and powerful surges of capital accumulation and short, weak depressions. The specific triggers which had operated after 1945 included major technical changes cheapening the elements of constant capital, and improvements in transport and communications which had reduced circulation time; both had offset the tendency for the organic composition to rise. Equally important was the substantial increase in the rate of exploitation resulting from the defeat of the European working class by fascism. As the 'third technological revolution' exhausted itself, and the working class recovered its strength and self-confidence, the long boom would give way to a new Kondratieff downturn, and capitalism would face renewed crises of the classic kind.[7]

---

6   Ibid., p. 140.
7   See Ernest Mandel, *Late Capitalism*, Chapter 4 to Chapter 8, Chapter 14, Harbin: Heilongjiang People's Publishing House, 1983.

In the 1970s David Yaffe published an article and pointed out, Marx had commenced his own analysis of capitalism, in Volume I of *Capital*, by focusing upon 'capital in general', or 'the inner nature of capital', abstracting from the effects of competition on the behaviour of 'many capitals'. From this perspective he had demonstrated that the increasing organic composition 'was not a mere assertion but flows logically from the concept of capital itself', since mechanization and the consequent replacement of living labour by dead labour are required to secure capital's domination over the process of production. Because there were counter-acting tendencies, Yaffe continued, the fall in the rate of profit was 'not linear but in some periods is only latent coming to the fore more or less strongly in other periods and appearing in the form of a crisis cycle'. Once 'absolute overaccumulation' occurs, so that further accumulation adds nothing to the mass of surplus value which is produced, growth comes to a halt. For David Yaffe, this is all that there is to Marx's theory of crisis. It is logically independent of competition and effective demand. In this sense the capitalist crisis can be regarded as the strongest counteracting tendency to the long-run tendency of the rate of profit to fall... The tendency towards "breakdown" and stagnation therefore takes the form of cycles due to effects of the countertendencies of which the actual crisis is an extreme case. The overaccumulation of capital is the cause of the over-production of commodities and the latter is not the limitation to the capitalist production process. It follows that the state activity cannot save off the tendency for the rate of profit to decline, since it is innately unproductive. The profits of capitalists who sell commodities (for example, armaments) to the state are acquired at the expense of other capitalists, since they represent only 'a redistribution of the already-produced surplus value'. Hence, 'the mixed-economy has not fundamentally changed the contradictions of the traditional capitalist system', which remains crisis-prone.

Unlike other Western Marxist economics researchers, Ernest Mandel, who gets a different evaluation, is seen as the best one. This is mainly because of two aspects: First, he used a lot of new materials and insights from other disciplines scholars to re-elaborate the basic economic theory of Marxism, including the economic crisis theory; second, it is basically close to the intent of Marx's economic cycle and the economic crisis theory. In the early 1960s, in his book *Marxist Economic Theory*, Mandel describes the basic Marxist theory of the economic crisis and his own basic views on the issue of the economic crisis, and in the late 1970s after the publication of *Late Capitalism*, he improved and expanded his idea.

Mandel regarded the capitalist economic crisis as the economic crisis of overproduction originating from the exchange value of underconsumption due to the lack of the ability to pay. Because this crisis is based on the generalization of commodity production as the premise, it is also universal. He believes that the transmission mechanism of the crisis stems from "cellars income and unproductive savings", and the active process is: "cellars income and unproductive savings can lead to the remaining revenue, thus causing a relative overproduction of certain commodities and forming the first reduction of employment. The reduction of employment can spread overproduction throughout the various sectors of the economy, and forms the second reduction of employment, following it in a circle incessantly."[8] Mandel regarded the "intermittent" between production and sale as the direct reason of cyclical fluctuations, and the improvement of the organic composition of capital and thus the decline in the average rate of profit led by it plays a role. The essence of capitalist production determines that the fluctuations in the average profit is the decisive criterion of the specific situation in the capitalist economy, and if we seize the fluctuation in the average rate of profit we are able to reveal the internal mechanism of the economic cycle. Acknowledging the regular renewal of fixed capital is the material basis of the cyclical economic crisis, Mandel also believes that the feverish expansion in every period of economic recovery is also one of the important factors.

Mandel attributes the root reason of the capitalist economic crisis to the basic contradiction of capitalism, and he also regards the movement of the rate of profit and the stretching in the actual market as two parallel conditions to cause the cyclical economic fluctuation. E. Mandel also regards the capitalist mode of production as a system composed of a series of variables. These variables should include: The total organic composition of capital; the distribution of permanent capital between fixed capital and circulating capital; the development of the rate of surplus value; the development of the rate of accumulation; the development of the capital turnaround time; the exchange relationship between the two departments. These basic variables can play a role of independent variables to some extent partially and periodically. Due to the interrelation and mutual influence between the variables, so we can infer the entire power of the capitalist mode of production from a single variable of the entire system. Specifically, from the combined result of the interaction of various factors, the average rate of profit should be seized as the clearest manifestation of this. As the improvement of the organic composition of capital and difficulties in sales is ultimately the economic crisis of overproduction occurring in shrinking in investment, economic recession or even market caused by the decline in the average rate of profit, and the re-expansion of the market and the restoration of the average rate of profit will re-stimulate investment, and thus promote the economic upsurge. Here, the rate of profit plays a role of the "seismograph", because the fluctuation in the rate of profit shows that the result of the interaction between factors is in line with the kind of logic of means of production based on the self-expansion of capital. In fact, in the industrial cycle, the production and accumulation of capital must fluctuate around the fluctuation of the average rate of profit. However, from the period of the industrial cycle, the fundamental factor affecting is the rate of profit, and the key factor is the turnover and renewal of fixed capital, which determines the length of the cycle and the foundation of the expanded reproduction.

---

8   Ernest Mandel, *Marxist Economics Theory*, Beijing: Commercial Press, 1979, pp. 361-362.

In Mandel's model, the renewal of fixed capital and technological revolution are also important factors. He considered each renewal to be a higher technical renewal. Especially under conditions of technological revolution, the renewal of fixed capital and the improvement of the organic composition prompt the capital accumulation and the accelerated expansion of investment, which has the practical significance in explaining the extension of cycle and scale expansion. From the historical facts, "for every time of an important technical invention, it seems to be a period of sudden acceleration of capital accumulation"[9]. For the underinvestment issue in the model, Mandel believes it has a dual role: it reflects that the average rate of profit is relatively low, and it curbs the rate of profit from continuing to decline; it creates a reserve fund of historical significance, and provides additional accumulation capacity for the expanded reproduction under the conditions of new technologies in the future. In normal circumstances, those values released at the end of the economic cycle of about 10 years are sufficient to adopt more and more expensive machines than those at the beginning of the cycle, but not enough to obtain the basic renewal of production technology, in particularly in department I. Only values released in a few consecutive cycles can have qualitative changes in the accumulation process. The business cycle during the underinvestment period releases capital necessary for the new technological revolution. From the perspective of the practical and necessary condition for capital accumulation, it must be the sudden increase in the average rate of profit, and only it can suddenly release a large number of investment behaviours of the remaining capital for years of stagnation. The reason for the sudden increase in the average rate of profit is: a sudden drop in the organic composition of capital; the sudden growth in the rate of surplus value; the price collapse of constant capital; the sudden contraction of the circulating capital turnover period. All of these are associated with the technological revolution. In order to illustrate the important influence of the technological revolution, he examined the influence of technical changes during the three technological revolutions on the renewal of fixed capital, expanded reproduction and capital accumulation, pointed out the possibility of the extension of capital accumulation cycle and concluded: the capitalist economy not only has a cyclical movement of about 10 years, but it also has a long cycle movement of about 50 years, which is also affected by the fluctuation in the average rate of profit.

378

Through this model Mandel aimed to prove that, "long wave cycle" and "classical period" together constitute the entire social crisis, including the crisis of the relations of production, and filled with an explosive, with a direct threat to the entire capitalist mode of production. As long as capitalism exists, the economic crisis will occur periodically.

Representatives of "theory of the improvement of the organic composition of capital" also include Dobb, Yaffe, Scheck, etc.. Based on the narrative in *Capital* Volume III, they have insisted that in the situation of the rate of exploitation to be constant, the improvement of the organic composition of capital

---

9   Ernest Mandel, *Late Capitalism*, p. 126.

will lead to the decline in the rate of profit, which will sooner or later lead to the decline in the rate of investment. The decline in the rate of investment will in turn lead to the decline in the rate of utilization of the production capacity. This trend has been made a detailed presentation by Yaffe. The law of the tendency of the rate of profit to fall sometimes is prevented by the counterproductive effects, and sometimes is manifested in the form of actual decline. When the rate of profit shows the downturn trend indeed, the crisis would be induced. The crisis temporarily overcomes the contradiction, but the tendency of the rate of profit to fall is just a manifestation of this contradiction. However, after overcoming the contradiction and removing the obstacle, the crisis brings the contradiction to a higher level. The economic crisis can be seen as a major reaction preventing the tendency of the rate of profit to fall. Yaffe also regarded the tendency of the rate of profit to fall as the law completely within the area of production, and the crisis can only be explained after the introduction of competition and activities in the field of exchange. In this way, the conditions that the crisis prevents the rate of profit to fall and restores accumulation include the recombination of production capital in the production area, the decline in the commodity prices in the exchange area, and some distribution phenomena. This analysis emphasizes the priority of production over exchange, and over the exchange-based distribution, indicating the crisis is the inevitable result of the accumulation of capital rather than by accident. Since Yaffe considers that the crisis depends on the competition between labour and capital as well as between capital and capital, resulting in the role of exchange and distribution to 379 be mechanically reduced to the logical needs of the law of production.

Theory of the increase in labour's strength: The representatives are Bodie, James Crotty, Andrew Glyn, Bob Sutcliffe and so on. Based on an assumption in "General Law of Capitalist Accumulation" in *Capital* Volume I, the capitalist accumulation process is bound to change the contrast of the political and economic power between capital and labour, so the working class can have wages in national income share increased, thereby reducing the share of profits in the national income, they proposed three propositions, namely: 1) The enhancement of the power of the working class enables them to make more successful negotiations for higher wages, thereby increasing the growth rate of money wages. 2) The enhancement of the power of the working class enables them to successfully resist the capitalists' attempts to improve the intensity of labour, thus reducing the growth rate of labour productivity. 3) With the acceleration of the growth rate of wages and the slowdown of the growth rate of labour productivity, it will sooner or later lead to an increase in the unit labour costs, while the increased labour costs would not be offset by a corresponding rise in price of the product, so the wage share will rise, resulting in the decline in the rate of profit, ultimately resulting in the economic crisis. Thomas E. Weisskopf considers that "theory of the increase in labour's strength" is based on the point of view of cyclical depletion of the reserve army of labour, so as to explain that labour demand is greater than supply so the political and economic power of workers is strengthened, improving their status of negotiations with the capitalists.

Theory of the improvement of wages: Like theory of the improvement of the organic composition, theory of the improvement of wages is a point of view to illustrate the economic crisis also through the decline in the rate of profit. In the specific argument, it is also divided into theory of cyclical crisis and theory of long-term crisis. Theory of cyclical crisis suggests that, with economic development, more and more workers are employed, and to a certain period, there is a shortage of labour, especially the lack of skilled labour. This makes the workers, especially skilled workers be improved in wages. In the stage of boom, the increase in wages has reached a peak, and the profit will fall to the bottom. The decline in profit has led to economic contraction, because capitalists do not want to invest. The existing production costs are too high, making a large number of enterprises overburdened and closed down. This in turn makes workers thrown again into the unemployed. Oversupply in the labour market decreases wages again, and the cut of production costs create good conditions for new investment and for the economy to get out of the crisis and go into prosperity. Theory of long-term crisis takes in the United Kingdom as an example, thinking that Britain is facing fierce international competition on the one hand, and on the one hand it is facing intense pressure from the domestic union. The powerful union makes the growth of wages exceed the growth of productivity and profits squeezed, and intense international competition makes the capitalists not able to compensate for the losses caused by the increase in wages through raising the price. This profit squeeze reduces the investment gradually, and the economy is at stagnation and recession phases for a long time.

380

Theory of realization failure. Representatives of "theory of realization failure" include Paul Sweezy. "Realization failure" refers to that there are difficulties selling commodities at profitable price, and the theoretic assumption is that the capitalist accumulation process will inevitably lead to the imbalance of demand for commodities lagging behind the production capacity. The lack of demand for commodities forces the capitalists either to suppress their standard of living, or to suppress the price of their products in order to avoid increasing the inventory of products difficult to sell. Because of the modern capitalist system of price limits, it forces the capitalists to deal with the underconsumption and undersupply relying mainly on reducing production and reducing the rate of utilization of production capacity. Therefore, "theory of realization failure" regards the decrease in the rate of utilization of production capacity as the root cause of the decline in the rate of profit, and the argument is also from underconsumption and underinvestment, with the central argument to be under-demand, the basic idea to be from the reduction in the wage share to the decline in the consumer demand, and then to the decline in aggregate demand relative to the production capacity. Thomas. E. Weisskopf believes that the essence of the theory of realization failure is ultimately the imbalance in sectors of demand and production capacity, rather than the lack of aggregate demand.[10]

10   See his article "Marxian Crisis Theory and the Rate of Profit in the Post-war U.S. Economy".

III. Model of Underconsumption

Model of underconsumption assumes that: the capitalist accumulation process is bound to have imbalance, in which the demand for commodities lags behind the production capacity. The lack of demand for commodities forces the capitalists either to suppress their standard of living, or to suppress the price of their products in order to avoid increasing the inventory of products difficult to sell. Generally, in the history of economic theories there are two theoretic models of underconsumption, derived from different classical economists. One of them can be traced back to Sismondi, who considers that capitalism produced and reproduced a large number of poor proletarians and a few wealthy capitalists, and the former has always lagged behind the supply in terms of the consumer purchasing power, which caused the overproduction, realization difficulties, economic stagnation and depression. This theory of underconsumption is based on such a passage in Marx's *Capital* Volume III: "The ultimate reason for all real crises always remains the poverty and restricted consumption of the masses as opposed to the drive of capitalist production to develop the productive forces as though only the absolute consuming power of society constituted their limit."[11] The other model of underconsumption can be dated back to Malthus, who suggests that the consumption of capitalists only accounts for part of their monetary income, which is a dangerous propensity to save, and it would cause underconsumption of commodities and realization crisis, because savings of capitalists turning into new investments will not eliminate these 381 crises, but will further expand the difference between supply and effective demand. Whether it is underconsumption caused by the excessive savings of capitalists, or underconsumption caused by workers due to poverty, they both can be manifested as the huge backlog of commodities, or as that of production capacity. The opening-up of new markets is recognized as a good mitigation measure by both models of underconsumption, and the export of commodities and capital is the specific practice of such mitigation. This once again associates the theory of underconsumption with the theory of the expansion of imperialism. Sherman once summarized viewpoints of the theory of underconsumption as follows: 1) in each economic expansion, the class struggle causes the improvement of the rate of exploitation, reflected in the decline of wages in the share of national income. 2) Workers have higher marginal propensity to consume than capitalists. Thus, 3) the decline in wage share causes the decrease in the average propensity to consume in the entire country. The capacity to produce exceeds demand, which is subject to the limitation of capitalist relations of production. Thus, 4) the investment falls, because the investment is merely a function of the increase in consumer demand. If consumption continues to grow, then the investment will decline. The reduction in investment would lead to a reduction in all production and employment, and then the crisis broke out.[12]

---

11 *Capital*, Volume III, Beijing: People's Publishing House, 2004, p. 548.
12 See Hu Daiguang, *Marx's Economic Crisis Theory and Reviews of Western Marxist Economists*, in *World Economy*, 1983(3).

Bernstein was the advocate of underconsumption theory, and he actually attributed the root of the crisis simply to the contradiction between the possibility of unlimited expansion of production and the limitation of consumer market, but did explain the issue from the perspective of the basic contradiction of the capitalist economy. Conrad Schmidt believes that Marx had a breakdown theory, which is based on underconsumption. He not only endorsed the crisis theory of underconsumption, but also made this description very beautifully: "do not the capitalists, by their opposition to all wage increases, conduct a struggle which has the tendency to keep the income – hence also the purchasing power – of the masses as low as possible, while they, the capitalists, on the other hand, raise their own income – and therewith the mass of accumulated capital seeking productive investment – in rapidly increasing progression? Will, under such circumstances, the increase in consuming power … be able to keep up with the tempo of capital accumulation? And if not, must not then the sale of commodities become always more difficult the more consumption demand, the basis of production, lags behind the rapidly increasing accumulation of capital and expansion of production – with only export, unproductive state expenditures, etc., to slow down the process? In this way, then, capitalism would tend to create in and of itself a steadily growing state of overproduction. Intensified competition on the market as a result of the growing difficulty of sales would have a tendency to manifest itself in a growing pressure on prices and therewith in a fall of the rates of return or of the average rate of profit, a fall in consequence of which the capitalist mode of production becomes even for the majority of private entrepreneurs ever more unprofitable and risky, while at the same time the labour market gets progressively worse for the workers, and the ranks of the industrial reserve army swell ever more terribly. The path of development of capitalist society would thus be likewise the path to its own bankruptcy, the transition to a new socialist order would be prescribed by a forced situation of society itself."[13] P. Sweezy endorsed not only the theory that the crisis is caused by the decline in the rate of profit, but also the theory of underconsumption. He also regarded imbalance between production and consumption as a special form of disproportionality, and the lack of aggregate demand caused by underconsumption itself is disproportionality. In order to illustrate that underconsumption is one of the reasons that cause the crisis, he cited many fragments of Marx's discussion in the relevant sections of his book *Theory of Capitalist Development*, among which there is a passage having been argued among Marxist economists for many years: "The ultimate reason for all real crises always remains the poverty and restricted consumption of the masses as opposed to the drive of capitalist production to develop the productive forces as though only the absolute consuming power of society constituted their limit."[14] Sweezy has argued, "it appears to be Marx's most clear-cut statement in favour

13   Conrad Schmidt, *Theory on Commercial Crisis and Overproduction.* Quoted by Paul Sweezy. *Theory of Capitalist Development.* Beijing: Commercial Press, 1997, pp. 218-219.
14   Marx and Engels, *Collected Works*, Volume 25, , Beijing: People's Publishing House, 1974, p. 548.

of an underconsumption theory of crisis."[15] Corey and Varga cited statistics in the United States and proved that the rate of unemployment was already in high at that time, and the real wage was in stagnation, finally resulting in the 1929 Great Depression. They proved the foundation of the Great Depression was under-consumption, rather than the over-accumulation.

The crisis theory of underconsumption by Moszkowska can be summarized as follows: the competition between capitalists either reduces real wages absolutely, or lowers the real wage relative to profits. And the rate of exploitation rises correspondingly, it is more and more difficult for the capitalists to find the sufficient consumer demand to realize the surplus value contained in their products. As long as the real wage lags far behind the growth of productivity, labour market will be imbalanced. This will lead to the imbalance in commodity market, and thus lead to the further development of the disproportionality between production and consumption. The result is that the distribution costs increase, because capitalists are helplessly trying to use a variety of promotions to create demand. Under monopoly capitalism, even if money wages are constant, due to the constraint of price competition, pressure of underconsumption will grow with the rise in the rate of exploitation. Moszkowska denies such a view that underconsumption will lead to stagnation rather than the volatility of economic activity. She believes that in the downturn phase of each cycle, the adjustment of production made for consumption is temporarily achieved through the effect of the three built-in stabilizers: to maintain the consumer spending of the unemployed workers and the non-bourgeois; fixed costs are more and more important, which means that productivity falls faster than the income and expenditure; to strengthen marketing and the corresponding increase in wages of unproductive workers. Otto Bauer presented a more mature underconsumption theory, and he has cleared many of the ambiguous parts in Moszkowska's analysis. Starting from the assumption that the propensity to save by capitalists is higher than that of the working class' propensity to save, he considers that the relationship between the development of mass consumption and the development of social production depends on the proportion between wages and profits. The slower growth in total wages, the faster growth total profits are; then mass consumption will grow more slowly, and the social productive sectors will grow faster. Therefore, all things are dependent on the relative share of wages and profits. If profits grow faster than wages, the rate of exploitation will rise, savings will grow more rapidly than output, while the growth of consumption will be even more slowly. When establishing the first ever mathematical model of underconsumption in the crisis studies of Marxist economics theory, Otto Bauer (1881-1938) has formalized these ideas. (see his book *Between the Two World Wars*.)

---

15   Paul Sweezy. *Theory of Capitalist Development*, Beijing: Commercial Press, 1997, p. 198.

He defined accumulation as the difference between net output and consumption. If the rate of exploitation rises, the growth of accumulation will be accelerated. This will bring real increase in production capacity. However, the increase in production capacity required is closely associated with the growth in consumption by a factor, but is not prompt to the acceleration factor in the Keynesian macroeconomic theory. Bauer concluded that, as long as the growth of consumption lagged behind the growth of revenue, the actual accumulation will exceed the necessary accumulation, because "the social growth will exceed the fixed capital required for the production in order to meet the growth of consumption; consumption lags behind production capacity", and in the end it is the outbreak of the crisis of underconsumption.

There are huge differences in the details of the contemporary Western Marxist theories of underconsumption, but there is a consensus on one point, which is thinking the wage increase for the consumption of the working class is too slow and cannot keep up with the pace of the expansion of output, thus resulting in the insufficient effective demand.

In the interpretation of the cases in the 1970s and the early1980s, theorists of underconsumption encountered two unexplained anomalies: 1) Either before the crisis in 1973 or at its initial stage, in the share of total net income wages and salaries were growing, which formed a stark contrast with the decline in the share of labour incomes during the 1920s; 2) Contrary to the drastic fall in the price level in the capitalist countries after1929, the crisis after 1973 was accompanied with an unprecedented high inflation rate. In the face of these two anomalies, after 1970s, the theory of underconsumption was strongly doubted. At this critical moment, Paul Sweezy has tried to deal with these anomalies. Although he still believed in underconsumption theory, he no longer regarded the "law of rising surplus" as the basic contradiction of monopoly capitalism, and instead favoured for Kautsky's over-investment model. Kautsky has argued that the investment by capitalists is the engine of economic growth, and it is true; the investment tends to cause over-accumulation of capital, which in turn leads to cyclical economic crisis, and it is also true. "Investment disaster" is that it simultaneously improves the effective demand and production capacity, that is strong motivation for investment makes it grow rapidly, and it in turn will destroy the motivation of investment. The recession after 1973 is such an "investment arrest", which is caused by old overaccumulation of the old industries, which were not able to be offset by the quick and effective expansion of emerging industries in the United States.

It is generally believed that if the crisis is explained by the contradiction between production and consumption and the basic reason of the crisis is attributed to underconsumption, the periodicity of the capitalist economy could not be explained fundamentally, and it would also inevitably come to a conclusion that the crisis is continuous, because underconsumption is not cyclical. As for how to overcome the crisis, theorists of underconsumption can only put the hope in external factors such as foreign markets, "third person", "existence of parasitic class," and so on.

IV. Model of Overaccumulation

The initial idea of overaccumulation is that, in the economic boom stage, because of the rise in real wages, the rate of exploitation may decline, which may decrease the rate of profit. Otto Bauer had rejuvenated this theory in 1913. He walked along the following lines, providing people with a clear and reasonable realization mechanism of cyclical fluctuation: In the beginning of the accumulation process, there was still a large reserve army of the unemployed, lower real wages, higher rate of exploitation and rate of profit; the accumulation of fixed capital is much faster than the accumulation of variable capital, but the demand for labour is still expanding; the reserve army of the unemployed is reduced, and real wages of workers begin to rise; real wages will soon exceed the growth of labour productivity, drive down the rate of exploitation, thus reducing the rate of profit; it in turn blocks the investment, so that the accumulation goes in stagnation; thus the unemployment increases, real wages decline, the rate of exploitation recovers, , and the rate of profit increases, so that the entire cycle can proceed in cycle. Sweezy and Dobb regarded the overaccumulation as the essential factor of Marx's crisis theory. Armstrong, Glyn, and Harrison described the theory of overaccumulation in their book *Capitalism since the World War II* as follows: "The basic idea is that overaccumulation is that capitalism sometimes generates a higher rate of accumulation than can be sustained, and thus the rate of accumulation has eventually to fall. Towards the end of the post-war boom, an imbalance between accumulation and the labour supply has led to increasingly severe labour shortage. The excess demand for labour generated a faster scrapping of old equipment. Real wages were pulled up and older machines rendered unprofitable, allowing a faster transfer of workers to the new machines. This could in principle have occurred smoothly: as profitability slid down, accumulation could have declined gently to a sustainable rate. But the capitalist system has no mechanism guaranteeing a smooth transition in such a circumstance. In the late sixties the initial effect of overaccumulation was a period of feverish growth, with rapidly rising wages and prices and an enthusiasm for get-rich-quick schemes. These temporarily masked, but could not suppress, the deterioration in profitability. Capitalist confidence was undermined, investment collapsed and a spectacular crash has occurred. Overaccumulation gave rise, not to a mild decline in the growth rate, but to a classic capitalist crisis."[16]

In his writings published in 1942, Paul Sweezy divided the crisis formed with the rate of profit to fall into two categories: 1) the crisis caused by the improvement of the organic composition of capital being faster than the growth of the rate of exploitation due to technological progress; 2) the crisis of the exhaustion of the unemployed, the increase in wages and the decline in the rate of exploitation due to the increase in the rate of capital accumulation. Sweezy agrees with the second type of crisis caused by the decline in the rate of profit.

---

16   Quoted by M. C. Howard, *A History of Marxian Economics (1929-1990)*, p. 321.

V. Model of Disproportionality

For a long time, Marxists have argued that the anarchy of capitalist production is the main reason leading to the economic crisis. Because the investments led by private capitalists independent of each other is decentralized, without a master plan which guides their decision-making or coordinating them, so overproduction in individual sectors is almost inevitable, and it is likely to spread to other industrial sectors, resulting in the overall overproduction. But the mechanism for causing this situation has never been made a special exposition. Marxist economists are like the orthodox theorists, who do not have any precise notion of the effective demand and the multiplier principle. However, they are closer to these notions than the previous orthodox Keynesian theorists, and the disproportionality also makes them aware of the function of crisis in the capitalist economy. The crisis has the function of regulating the economy, as well as the function of eliminating the irrational investments, forcibly recovering the imbalances (disproportionality) in the economy, and so on.

When elaborating their ideas on the rationalization of capitalism in the 1920s, Otto Bauer and Fritz Naphtali have also put forward some ideas on the theory of disproportionality. Fritz Naphtali and Fritz Sternberg associated it with the growth of monopolies, and further elaborated this view. In their view, further deterioration of the economic situation was due to the stimulus of over-investment in monopoly sectors of initial profitability, on the other hand due to the

shift of the entire burden brought by the necessary regulation to the competitive sectors. According to Friedrich Pollock's point of view, the state providing assistance to the troubled monopolists would further weaken the self-regulating capacity of the system. Here he introduced a form of "protected capitalism", in which, through the devastating loss of unsuccessful businesses, the competitiveness with rule could have a role to play. This is one of the most important reasons why the Great Depression was intractable. Pollock believed that this also indicates that there is a serious flaw in the "General Theory". Keynes had an overall analysis over sectors of investment goods and consumer goods, and ignored the disproportionality between different sectors, and thus made wrong judgments to the law of the capitalist economic chaos.

The explanation of the crisis by E.A. Preobrazhensky (1886-1937) is based on the proposition that the disproportionality is becoming more and more serious in the new monopoly stage of capitalism. Under competitive conditions, through the incentive of the price mechanism, resources can be quickly transferred from one economic sector to another, and the total production levels quickly responds to the growth of aggregate demand. However, under conditions of monopoly capitalism, the flow of resources is blocked, and changes in demand brought asymmetric consequences: the production declines with the reduced demand, while the rise in demand increase the price rather than production. When demand increases, the reasons why the growth of investment is especially slow are many. Monopolists control a large number of surplus production capacity, which will hinder new investment. Barriers to enter the market make it more difficult to create new businesses. It takes longer to eliminate inefficient production units, and the conservative bureaucratic trade union movement has more serious flaws, making the power of innovation weakened, which was provided by the increasing wages initially. Hence, compared with free competition stage in the history of capitalism, the crisis in the monopoly stage is more serious, and the recovery is slower. Even the room for temporary respite brought by non-capitalist demand growth (here Preobrazhensky quoted Rosa Luxembourg's point of view), will cease to exist under the conditions of monopoly capitalism.

However, since the beginning of the 20th century, the theory of disproportionality has caused intense debate among Marxist economists, which seems to have the colour of revisionist. If the crisis stems from anarchic individualism, it should probably be overcome through collective accumulation plan of capitalists themselves, which has either the private nature, or is associated with the government. The prospect that capitalism is largely getting out of the crisis first attracted Eduard Bernstein, followed by theorists of "organized capitalism" after 1914, but also boycotted perspectives from Varga and Luxembourg to Lenin and other revolutionary Marxists. The inconsistency in Moszkowska's view is that Moszkowska opposes to the theory using disproportionality to illustrate depression, as well as opposes to the view that under conditions of monopoly capital the enhancement of individual plans continue to play the role of effective regulation through the price mechanism; she even cited Hayek's point of view on the latter. Moszkowska compared the so-called old and new theories of disproportionality. The new theory emphasizes the imbalance between wages and profits, between consumption and savings, and between industries of investment goods and industries of consumer goods. If the old theory is said to find causes of the crisis in production, the new theory is turning to distribution... Low wages and high profits dampen the consumer ability and promote the accumulation. For Moszkowska, the disproportionality means underconsumption.

The model of disproportionality concludes: The production of capitalist society, on the one hand is in a state of anarchy, and whether sectors and enterprises expand or shrink the scale of production is up to capitalists to decide; and on the other hand, sectors and enterprises are inextricably associated, and the decision to produce in one sector or one enterprise will affect the production situation in other sectors. Thus, if the investment decision is dispersed in the hands of thousands of capitalists, there would often be some unforeseen imbalance. Although some imbalance is negligible, while others will lead to a series of cut in production by companies, thus it will spawn major economic crises in an economic system of mutual restraint. It can clearly be seen that, theory of disproportionality regards the capitalist economy as a hut of cards, and the anarchy produced and the blind decisions of investment will continue to cause unrest. When the unrest reaches a certain intensity, the whole building will be destroyed.

VI. Three-Level Model

In the early 1980s, David Harvey wrote several essays and books to examine Marx's theory of economic crisis. He refused those ideas that Marx did not have a theory of economic crisis, and made detailed descriptions on Marx's relevant ideas. For example, on the relationship between the accumulation, industrial reserve army and the rate of wages, he described the impulse of the cycles; he laid the foundation for the analysis of the explosive fluctuation with regard to yield and exchange in production sectors; he establish a general short-term dynamic model on the excessive accumulation and devaluation; the study of fixed capital cycle also revealed the cycle of innovation, expansion and devaluation, and so forth. However, he also believes that these insights have not yet become a system, and they need to be organized into a unified and dynamic representation in contemporary times. To accomplish this task, Harvey created a three-level system of the Marxist theory of the economic crisis: "The crisis theory of the first level" is a crisis theory expressed by Marx himself. This theory reviews and discusses the primary sources of the internal contradiction of capitalism, points out that the root of the crisis lies in the relations of production, once it is given that the unity of contradictions inevitably exists between production and exchange, the crisis is necessarily reflected in the exchange, and the tendency of the rate of profit to fall of capitalism has also been reflected."The crisis theory of the second level" strives to combine the finance with the initial analysis of forces that causes production imbalances, so as to examine the short-term dynamic volatility formed and adjusted through financial arrangements. The focus is to elaborate the effect of credit system and speculation, to consider capital as the capital of a whole class through credit cycle, and to look at the issue of the whole cyclical fluctuation through the interaction between the production cycle and the credit cycle. Since Marx just regarded the credit system as the conflict in the surface of the capitalist society, therefore, although Marx noted and refuted the theory of crisis caused by credit speculation, he only regarded credit speculation as economic bubble. "The crisis theory of the third level" refers to the theory of economic crisis that introduces the idea of "layout of productive forces" and the allocation of resources of geographically uneven development (the uneven geographical development of capitalism). Capitalist accumulation proceeds in a geographically differentiated context that, in virtue of its contradictions, contradictions assume sharply geographic forms and the accompanying conflicts take on territorial expressions. How is the uneven geographical development produced? Capital is always in motion and much of that motion is spatial: commodity exchange always entails change of location and spatial movement. The market is spatialized and how that spatiality works has consequences for uneven geographical development.

For Harvey the production, reproduction and reconfiguration of space have always been central to understanding the political economy of capitalism, he believes that only relying on the geographic expansion of the production space and resource allocation, can excess capital and labour be absorbed, thereby economic imbalance is adjusted. If it cannot be achieved, there would be a serious imbalance in economic development, and a full-blown crisis becomes inevitable. This is because the expansion of the geographical layout and the allocation of capital resources can provide a powerful basis for the sustained accumulation, and if the allocation of resources can be transferred in space, the world economy can have a balanced development, otherwise it will lead to economic fluctuations. Harvey considers that since Marx elaborated a closed economy, Marx's discussion could not reach the crisis theory of the third level.

Globalization consequently entails a geographical restructuring of capitalist activity across the face of planet earth, the production of new forms of uneven geographical development, a recalibration and even re-centering of global power and a shift in the geographical scale at which capitalism is organized.

For Harvey's three-level crisis theory, Chinese scholars believe that although there is a certain enlightening in it, this theory includes a certain misunderstanding on Marx's theory of crisis, and contains some erroneous aspects. The theory does not regard the crisis as the inevitable result of the basic contradictions of capitalism. And Harvey does not understand that, even there forms a balanced space configuration worldwide, as long as the fundamental relations in the capitalist economic conditions remain, the problem will not be solved.[17]

VII. Crisis Model after the Introduction of Ecological Ideas

It is also a prominent feature of Western scholars to treat Marxist crisis theory trying to break the traditional forms of Marxist analytic model of the economic crisis, and exploring the realization forms of capitalist crisis from different angles and dimensions. They think that Marx only analyzed the contradiction between productive forces and relations of production, as well as the economic crisis caused by the conflict and intensification of these contradictions. In fact, in addition to the contradiction at the capitalist mode of production level, there is also the contradiction between means of production and production conditions, and with the development of capitalist production, this conflict will gradually rise as a major form of contradiction, thus the crisis it causes will become the main form of the crisis correspondingly. One of the major holders of this view is James O'Connor, an American ecological Marxist, who believes that, the contradiction between productive forces and relations of production is the first contradiction of capitalist society, and the contradiction between means of production and production conditions is the second contradiction. In this model O'Connor designed, production conditions at both poles of the contradiction, refer to "things that are treated as commodities but are actually not produced as commodities." It includes: external nature, labour power, infrastructure and

---

17   See Hu Daiguang, et al., editor in chief, *Study of Marx's Capital by the Contemporary Western Scholars*, Beijing: China Economic Publishing House, 1990, p. 375.

space. The crisis triggered by the second contradiction is manifested as the crisis of underproduction, which belongs to the "liquidity crisis" or "structure of production conditions." Capitalism is not only full of crises, and is dependent on the crisis. The crisis is often committed to new social movements of changing production conditions (identity and family politics, feminism; urban movement; environmentalism), in specific: the physical process of the reproduction of production conditions; production process itself. The reconstruction of production conditions caused by such crises include: permanent-yield forests; land reclamation, regional land use and/or resource planning; population policy, health policy; toxic waste disposal planning. The crisis triggered by the second contradiction is the same with the first crisis in the ultimate direction, that is, to be transformed into more transparently social forms. O'Connor, an important proponent of "ecological Marxist theory", explains the contemporary contradictions and the study sphere of ecological Marxism as follows: "This exposition provides a point of departure for an 'ecological Marxist' theory of the contradiction between capitalist production relations and productive forces and the conditions of production; underproduction of capital and economic crisis; and the process of crisis-induced restructuring of production conditions and the social relations thereof, also into more transparently social, hence potential socialist, forms."[18]

Comparing the ecological crisis model constructed by O'Connor with Marx's crisis model of overproduction, there are two issues that need special notice, that is, what is the relationship between the first contradiction and the second contradiction of capitalism? Is their impact on changes in profit interacting with each other, or mutually offsetting? In O'Connor's description of the model, he believes that these two processes of overproduction and underproduction of capital are not mutually exclusive, but compensate for each other or complement each other, and thus creating a relatively stable appearance for the development of capitalism. In his opinion, in the first contradictions of capitalism, the rate of exploitation is both a sociological category, and an economic category. It reflects the social and political power of capital over labor, namely, the tendency of the crisis of overproduction. If the capital exercises more powers over labour, the rate of exploitation will rise, and the risk of facing a crisis will also increase in the dimension of realization; thus, the demand for a large credit system, aggressive marketing, continuous technological innovation and intense competition will also be enhanced. The first contradiction of capitalism is inherent in the system; it is not related to conditions of production (the conditions of production in both social and political dimension and economic dimension).

The second contradiction of capitalism requires a more complex terminology to analyze, which is actually embedded in the category of the use value: the share of spending and its value, the size of fixed capital and its value connotation, "the price paid for the natural factors to go into the field of constant

---

18 James O'Connor, *Natural Causes: Essays in Ecological Marxism*, pp. 158, The Guilford Press, A Division of Guilford Publications, Inc. 1998.

capital and variable capital", as the land rent deduced as the surplus value and all the various "negative external factors" (for example, costs paid for the urban congestion, and these costs will go into the cost of the individual capital).

In this second contradiction, no single term has the theoretical centrality that the rate of exploitation does in the first contradiction (This is one reason why there is a plurality of social movements today).Yet, all of the above terms are socio-political as well as economic categories (e.g. absolute rent reflect the power of landed capital over industrial capital; the costs of congestion reflect struggles over urban and regional transport systems; the cost of water reflects the power of ecology movements vis-à-vis capital; etc.).The point of listing these examples is to suggest that there is even less justification for an economistic-type theory of the second contradiction than there is for the traditional Marxist theory of the first.

The first contradiction strikes at capital from the demand side. When individual capitals lower costs with the aim of defending or restoring profits, the unintended effect is to reduce market demand for commodities, and thus to lower realized profits. The second contradiction strikes from the cost side. It states that when individual capitals lower costs – for example, when they externalize costs on to conditions of production (nature, labour power, or the urban) – with the aim of defending or restoring profits, the unintended effect is to raise costs on other capitals (and, at the limit, capital as a whole), thereby lowering produced profits. The first manifests itself in its purest form as a realization crisis; the second as a liquidity crisis. In the first case, there is no problem producing surplus value; hence for that reason there is a problem of realizing value and surplus value. In the second, there is no problem of realizing value and surplus value, hence for that reason there is problem of producing surplus value.

The basis cause of the second contradiction is capitalism's economically self-destructive appropriation and use of labour-power, urban infrastructure and space, and external nature or environment – "self-destructive" because the costs of health and education, urban transport, and home and commercial rents, as well as the costs of extracting the elements of capital from nature, will rise when private costs are turn into "social costs". In this account, capital and the state today can be interpreted as totally confused as to the new form of regulation that might provide a coherent framework for capital accumulation in the future. Individual capitals continue to lower costs in every imaginable way; by so doing they inadvertently tend to raise the costs of capital as a whole, at the same time threatening their own markets, as the first contradiction leads us to believe. Today, capital is faced with both rising costs and weak market demand, that is, with both the first and the second contractions. Is it any wonder that capital is thus obsessed with both process innovation and product innovation and market expansion? Any wonder that there occurs both a deterioration of the conditions of production and structures of equitable wage and salary income, as well as dangerously inflated credit structures? Any wonder that both Keynesian-type regulation and neoclassical, laissez-faire policies seems to be bankrupt?

VIII. Crisis Model after Introducing the Element of State Intervention

The emergence of the theory and practice of government intervention in the economy in the 1930s had eased the increasingly intensified trend of the basic contradiction of capitalism, disrupted the frequency of the traditional economic cycle, and promoted the relatively stable development of the economy. Changes in the real economy have aroused Marxist economists to focus on the role of the capitalist state. Differences in the academia are naturally divided into two types. One is called the "orthodox rule of habit", and people who hold such views still insist that the state is the "total capitalist", which is fundamentally serving the interests of capital. The exercising of the economic function of capitalist state does not change the nature of capitalism radically, but simply means that some qualitative changes in the capitalist system, and will not change the cyclical capitalist economic crisis. Critics believe that the country is simply asserted "to serve the interests of capital" is equivalent to not mentioning its decisive role or impact in economic activities. The other is called "new reformism", and people who hold such views acknowledge the positive role of the state to ease the basic contradiction of capitalism and promoting economic development, but they put much more emphasis in exploring the contradictions when the state performs the role of economic intervention, as well as the limitations in resolving these contradictions.

The emergence of reformism has its objective necessity. In the early 1970s, the nature and limitations of the state administration over economic crisis increasingly require further development of the state political economy. Some writings found that the expansion of the non-military spending of the government was conducive to promoting capital accumulation, especially spending in education, health care and social security provided by the state, which reduced the value of labour and promoted the accumulation of capitalists. As production becomes more and more complex, technological changes faster and faster, the social demand for skilled, healthy, flowable and flexible workers is growing day by day. Thus, the welfare state is interpreted to adapt to the demand of capital growth. However, this simple explanation of functionalists is not clever than the traditional Marxist viewpoint, and hardly plays a role in response to critics on the view that the state is only the prisoner of the ruling class of monopoly. Other Marxists are more radical, who believe that the state is the place for class conflict, and this view shows the prospects that: on the one hand the working class has won some kind of compromise in the struggle against capital interests, and on the other hand in these struggles the state itself has gained a certain degree of "relative autonomy". Thus, the power over the domestic structure of the state, its personnel composition, and its practices becomes important. The conflict of interests between capitalists, which is inevitable, must also be mediated by the state, and the government expenditures are antithetical to each other in many ways: by increasing the quality of labour force, it can improve labour productivity, so that the production activities in important areas are free from competition, encouraging waste while reducing labour productivity. By protecting inefficient capitalists and weakening the power of the masses of the unemployed, it stimulates economic recovery from the crisis, but at the same time undermines the internal mechanism of the economic recovery. Moreover, there is always a fixed tension between the accumulation demand – the higher disposable profits, the lower the corporate tax –and the legitimate demand. Workers have become accustomed to normal social welfare, and only make positive response to the continuous increase of the supply of commodities. This "ratchet effect" is the main cause of the pressures on the rising level of state spending, and also an important factor of "the state financial crisis". Compared with the manufacturing sector, the underdeveloped labour productivity in service industry is another important factor causing the financial crisis.

Nevertheless, there is still room for the discussion of many of the most important issues related to the state in the political economy. The first is to examine the issue of tax burden, and only assuming that the after-tax real wage has reached its lowest irreducible level, it will fall entirely upon the capital. As long as this is not the fact, the capitalists can, through the development of higher prices or paying lower wages, shift part of the tax burden to the working class, making their own money. But there is no theory for Marxist economics to explain, what proportion of the fortune can these methods shift within the class. When it comes to the effect of government spending, the situation is a little better. Some writings emphasize it is similar to the impact of "crowding out" effect in orthodox macroeconomics; others regard the state spending as the absorber of surplus capital, which weakens the tendency of underconsumption or the rate of profit to fall. To some extent, the state provides a "social wage", it can improve the overall living standard of workers without affecting the private wages paid by the employer; Or it allows wages to decline, but fully socializes the costs of education, children support, health and social insurance; finally, part of the government spending can directly or indirectly become the grants of private capital. The relative importance of these factors is controversial; and the question closely related to this is that which labour of the government employee can be seen as productive labour, and which is unproductive labour.

Views on these fundamental issues are not in agreement, so it is inevitable for Marxist economists to have disagreement on the issue of the effect and the potential impact of the state on the termination of long boom. Most people together with Ron Smith think that the sudden decline in the U.S. economic hegemony make it more difficult to have effective international management, which exacerbates the potential instability of the whole system and undermines capitalists' confidence in accumulation yield rate. Many people accept the evaluation of the crisis by Ron Smith in 1973, namely: "the impact of the economic system was eased due to the government intervention, and although coordination was inappropriate, it has proven valuable, thus the integrity of the international financial system was preserved in 1974–1975." If there had not been a timely intervention the panic in the 1929 crash could have occurred. Again, it also is correct for understanding the stock market crash in 1987. In either case, the misallocation of the financial market will provoke a huge real crisis. The exact significance of these developments is unclear. The government ensures that the financial system does not collapse, and therefore there would be no widespread deflation as a precursor of the Great Depression in the 1930s. What does it mean in the long run? This question raised by Paul Sweezy and Harry Magdoff awaits to be answered. It is noteworthy that, in Reagan's Administration term, full employment as the by-product of the increase in military expenses had occurred. This full employment was seen only in North America, but in other regions the situation was different. In most parts of Western Europe, governments have implemented tight fiscal and financial policies which aimed to reduce inflation, to weaken the power of the working class, to increase unemployment and to reverse the profit squeeze. The cut of welfare expenditures was at the heart of this policy, and it was increasingly accompanied by the privatization of state-owned enterprises, easing regulations over private enterprises, and retreat from progressive tax principle, and so on. No Marxist researcher could foresee the resurrection of economic liberalism in 1980s. For example, until 1978, Eric Olin Wright had predicted that government intervention would continue to expand and this process would cause the transformation of "state monopoly capitalism" into "mature state capitalism", Wright had also predicted the strengthening of the legitimization of the crisis of the capitalist system. Even Michel Aglietta[19] acknowledges that there is a possibility that the government will abrogate public goods and services, but he also points out that the continuous massive socialization of living conditions will destroy the private enterprise system based on liberal ideology, and create a centralized state capitalism.

The proponent of the government fiscal crisis theory explains the economic crisis with political (or regime) factors. O'Connor's book *The Fiscal Crisis of the State* in 1973 is a masterpiece of this concept. O'Connor believes that in order to solve the problem of employment and welfare of retirees, the government finances enterprises with government purchases, reducing tax rates and other measures, and follows the Keynesian policy of expanding government spending in times of economic decline. However, these expenses cannot be borne by enterprises, because the purpose of the government policy is to reduce their tax burden. The only one to bear the burden can be the government itself. Therefore, it asks the municipal, state, and federal government to provide services so as to meet the needs, and their financial expenses are increasing; on the other hand tax revenues cannot be increased. Caught in bankruptcy plight, all levels of governments can only rely on debts to survive. This is government's fiscal budget crisis, U.S' huge budget deficit is a typical example of it.

394

---

19   Michel Aglietta, founder of Regulation School in France.

IX. Speculation on the Crisis Theory through Marx's the "Six-book Structure" System

Some who thinks that Marx did not change the writing program of the "six-book structure" have tried to speculate the content, structure and system of his crisis theory according to the logic development order, the existing views and elaborations and tips of the writing system of Marxist economics. In the existing literature, the Japanese scholars Ryozo Tomizuka, Fumio Hattori, and Yoichiro Honma have co-edited the 10-volume book of *System of The Capital*, and explained the content of Marx's theory of crisis. Chinese scholar Tang Zaixin has co-edited *The Exploration of the Sequel of The Capital*, and he has done a similar job. While they have done excellent research on the same issue, but their contributions have different emphases.

The basis for Ryozo Tomizuka et al. to examine the Marx's theory of crisis is that: "The crisis does not show as a direct reduction of consumer demand, i.e. the direct reduction of the demand for the purpose of personal consumption, but as the reduction in the exchange of capital with capital, i.e. the reduction of the reproduction process of capital. The occurrence of this phenomenon is because of the completion of the conversion from commodity to currency – because of the world market and the credit system – and is irrelevant to whether the commodity is sold to the ultimate buyer; therefore, the advance and the completion of the conversion of commodity to currency do not depend – in certain limits – on real personal consumption process of these commodities. ...... in credit, the capitalist mode of production creates a necessary form suitable for the scale of their production process as well as to shorten the process of circulation, and the world market formed with this mode of production is conducive to covering up the action of this form on each individual occasion, and provides a very broad scope for expanding this form."[20] Here, Marx discussed the disconnection of the transformation of commodity to money with the ultimate consumption, and credit and the world market has become factors of the crisis. This is the foundation of Marx's theory of the world market crisis.

Ryozo Tomizuka et al. regard the transition of the crisis from possibility to reality as a multi-level structure from the abstract to the concrete, which is resulted from the scalability of capitalist reproduction. The possibility of crisis is just contained in the mutual separation of purchase and sale of in commodity exchange. In the reality of capitalist production, the movement of capital is not in direct conflict with the restrictions of consumption, but the movement of capital itself constantly stimulates the scalability of reproduction. Thus the condition for surplus production and excess trading is developed, and particularly to the level of credit and world market, the scalability of production is restricted, and the crisis has become inevitable. In their view, factor of the first level resulting in that there is scalability in the reproduction of capitalism, is

---

20 Marx and Engels, *Collected Works*, Volume 49, Beijing: People's Publishing House, 1982, p.292.

that the amount of capital invested in the production process is variable in playing a role. Specifically it is manifested in: production capacity of the existing fixed capital can be maximized in utility; when fixed capital is renewed, more productive equipment can be used with the application of science and technology; in the use of labour, the amount of labour is variable in terms of denotation and connotation. Factor of the second level is the saving of the circulation time, or "the abandoning of the circulation time." What has a major impact on this factor is the independence of the merchant capital and the development of foreign trade. Factor of the third level is the world market. The world market can cause "virtual trading", and the participation of commercial credit and bank credit in the world market will lead to a "virtual market", the phenomenon of which makes reproduction with greater flexibility, and ultimately leading to the cyclical world economic crisis. Ryozo Tomizuka et al. built a formation mechanism of the capitalist world economic crisis from credit relationship, i.e. the importer and exporter outputs and inputs the product, and obtains the commercial paper. They can also transform the commercial credit into the bank credit in the bank; the transaction between businessmen in the world market is also carried out through credit. As a result, it interweaves all aspects into a complex credit chain, so that when the actual production has a surplus, it is also reflected in a smooth trading situation on the surface, a boom. Therefore, the world market is manifested as the "virtual market" independent of the ultimate consumption. Once there are difficulties in a certain part of payment, it soon affects all aspects, and it is not as reliable to pay with bills as with cash, so the credit chain is interrupted, all are selling marketable securities for cash, and then sell the commodities. But then people feel overproduction, and the economic crisis is here. The economic crisis destroys part of the productive forces, so that the production is gradually recovered and further developed, and then it reaches boom. The capitalist production is conducted in this way periodically. Ryozo Tomizuka et al. also highlighted the role of central state, and they believe in the world market it has formed the central state with the overwhelming production capacity and the financial strength, as the centre of world trade and finance, the world market has greatly been improved in its role as a "virtual market". Thus, once the crisis breaks out, it will inevitably involve the whole world and also increases its size and severity. Therefore, the world market and credit is the most important factor in making the crisis occur.[21] It is clear that, Ryozo Tomizuka et al. have examined the issue mainly from the aspect of the foundation and the realization mechanism of the capitalist world economic crisis.

---

21   See Tang Zaixin, chief editor, *The Exploration of the Sequel of The Capital* (Appendix), Beijing, China Financial Publishing House, 1995.

X. Various Criticisms on Marx's Analytic Model of the Economic Crisis

In summarizing Marx's analytic model the economic crisis, Joan Robinson also turned to analyzing the validity of the model, with the purpose of illustrating Marx's theory of crisis to be an inaccurate and incomplete system. In her view, Marx regarded changes in the reserve army of labour and crisis to be consistent. Marx believes that employment depends on labour supply and demand. But, in fact, employment is dependent on the existing amount of capital and production technology. In reality, the real wage has the trend of increasing with the improvement of labour productivity, but employment level may remain constant or increased, so the crisis is not inevitable. The law of the tendency of the rate of profit to fall that Marx used to illustrate the paradox capitalist accumulation; because it assumes that the rate of exploitation is constant, "makes this proposition strikingly contradictory to the rest of Marx's argument."[22] Marx insists that the real wage is constant, but if the rate of exploitation is constant, the real wage will increase with the increase in labour productivity. Joan Robinson concludes: Marx's description of the rate of profit to fall, after all, does not illustrate anything at all. Because "Marx's theory cannot establish a presumption that if you do not consider the issue of demand, the rate of profits will fall".[23] In order to really explain the crisis, the problem of effective demand must be considered, and the issue of underconsumption will have to be involved. Although Marx had rejected the superficial theory of underconsumption which was quite popular in his era, his own analysis was clearly leading to the theory of underconsumption. In the eyes of Robinson, Marx sometimes accepted Say's Law, and sometimes denied it. By accepting Say's Law, the effective demand is favoured, and the ultimate reason for all real crises always remains the poverty and restricted consumption of the masses; by denying Say's law, the answer is negative. From the restricted consumption of workers and capitalists, he came to the conclusion that the two departments lacked the long-term trend of equilibrium, and he also found the reason for crisis in this trend. In terms of issue of 10-year business cycle, Robinson does not agree to explain it with the average length of the equipment life, because various equipments have different life spans, and it will inhibit the renewal cycle. In general, Robinson believes there is a contradiction in Marx's analytic model of the crisis theory, namely proposing the tendency of the rate of profit to fall when the rate of exploitation and real wages are constant; proposing the rise in real wages when the rate of exploitation is constant. He explained the reasons behind Marx's inconsistency as follows: 1) He did not notice the trends of the rise in real wages with the increase in labour productivity under capitalism. 2) Marx did not provide a theory of the rate of profit built on the principle of effective demand, he lacked a clear exposition of the lure investment. 3) Not

---

22   See, Joan Robinson's book *An Essay on Marxian Economics*, Beijing, Commercial Press, 1962, p. 34.
23   Ibid., p. 37.

understanding to what extent the orthodox bourgeois economics is consistent with Say's Law, Marx set himself a task of finding a crisis theory that can be used in case that Say's Law is both established and refuted. 4) Marx did not attach importance to the fact that the invention of high production efficiency which saves capital will reduce unemployment, prevent and overcome the falling profit. 5) Marx did not attach importance to the fact that the increase in the rate of labour production will cause real wages to rise.

From the perspective of theoretic development, Makoto Itoh investigated the change in Marx's analytic model of economic crisis. He found in Marx's *Economic Manuscripts (1857 – 1858)* that, Marx had developed the ideas of Malthus and Sismondi in the study of the development of the crisis, i.e., to explain the crisis spending with theory of underconsumption. In the *Theory of Surplus Value*, while continuing to explain the necessity of the crisis with the theory of underconsumption, Marx continues to emphasize that it is because of overproduction that the consumption of workers cannot reach the average number of life necessities, and the consumption lags behind the increase in production; on the other hand, Marx and used disproportionality to explain the economic crisis. This means that Marx has started looking for the causes of the crisis deep into the capital, but until *Capital* is published, Marx's crisis theory is only confined to the analysis of the process of circulation, hardly proceeding through the internal production process. Makoto Itoh called the crisis theory in this period "crisis theory of surplus of commodity." Makoto Itoh believes that

in *Capital*, Marx's investigation of the issue of crisis has turned from circulation to production, and he proved the inevitability of the economic crisis with the tendency of the rate of profit to fall. The falling rate of profit is the result of capital accumulation and the improvement of organic composition of capital, and the crisis caused by the falling rate of profit is seen as the manifestation of excess capital. Therefore, Makoto Itoh called it "crisis of capital surplus."Makoto Itoh tended to see "crisis of capital surplus" as Marx's mature crisis theory. Since the crisis theory of capital surplus suggests that the real obstacle for capitalist production is capital itself. Only through the crisis theory of capital surplus can the interpretation of the logical inevitability of periodic crises be improved. Makoto Itohis in favour of such an interpretation that the accumulation of capital is actually the expansion of productive forces and changes in the organic composition, and when such social productivity of broad expansion encounters limit of population size of workers, changes in such productive force cannot rely on one smooth type of technology to choose production. When there is overaccumulation of capital, the rise in wages advances the decline of the rate of profit, and the active mechanism of the credit system will inevitably lead to the rise in the rate of interest and shortages of lending capital. Without the analysis of the active mechanism of the credit system, the universality and the intensity of the cyclical economic crisis cannot be explained. Therefore, Makoto Itoh believes that Marx's theory of credit just proves the logical necessity of the universality and the intensity of the cyclical economic crisis here. However, it seems to Makoto Itoh that Marx's crisis theory is imperfect. Such imperfections are in particular manifested in: Marx's definition of the law of the population in capitalism overemphasizes the formation by incrementing the surplus population; forms of reserve army of labour include not only relative surplus population generated within the capitalist production, but also coming from small commodity producers and the surplus population in the process of the disintegration of farmers; the investigation of changes in mode of production in accumulation as well as its impact on the working class does not consider the special limit of fixed capital , which contradicts the theory; Marx's credit theory is far from being complete; the "money capitalists" tendency in credit theory is not only derived from the lack of theoretical generalization, but also from the theory of interest within this pattern in *Capital in General, The Critique of Political Economy*; Marx did not clarify why the speculating transaction was quite universal at the end of boom, and he also did not attempt to clarify the interrelations between the surplus of production and capital to the large-scale speculative climax. Makoto Itoh believes that if we want to improve Marx's crisis theory from a modern standpoint, it must start from the basis of typical cyclical crisis in the age of Marx. Meanwhile, the role of class struggle must be emphasized to the modern Western scholars in their study, rather than emphasizing to attach importance to changes in the labour market during the process of capital accumulation caused by the rise in wages, and the importance should be attached to the reality rather than the periodicity feature of the crisis. Makoto Itoh also believes that it is extremely difficult to infer the inevitability of the cyclical economic crisis with the law of the tendency of the rate of profit to fall, even the process of the rate of profit to fall includes the occasional, sudden, sharp forms, and we can only figure out the cause for the crisis to occur inevitably, but difficult to explain at what point that capital accumulation makes it feel "absolute overproduction." Therefore, Makoto Itoh advocates that Marx's such theory should be abandoned.[24] For those sayings by Makoto Itoh, Chinese scholars believe that he views on Marx's theory of economic crisis, in a way summed up or represented the major views of Western economists on Marx's theory of economic crisis after World War II. So they have common or similar errors, which misunderstand or misinterpret the methodolgy or content of the theoretical system of Marxist economics.

XI. Conclusions

Reflecting on the Western Marxist researches on Marx's analytic model of economic crisis we acknowledge both certain inappropriate approaches and creative breakthroughs in some aspects. In the abundant studies on the law of the tendency of the rate of profit to fall state of the art research methods and means, statistical and mathematical explanations and case studies were utilized, and have produced some meaningful conclusions.

24　See Makoto Itoh, *The Formation of Marxian Theory of Crisis*, in *Selected Papers of Modern Foreign Economics*, 3rd Series, Beijing, Commercial Press, 1982.

However, since they have absolutized this law, attempting to confirm the rise or the fall of the rate of profit by analyzing the long-term statistics, as well as some researchers repeatedly stressing that the law of the tendency of the rate of profit to fall is a contradictory movement, in which a downward trend and the counterproductive force finish its dialectical movement in the unity of opposites, but they still lack such understanding that the law of the tendency of the rate of profit to fall "is inevitable accompaniment of capitalist accumulation, but it must be understood as a trend, i.e. the trend of the falling rate of profit, so it is not the law of the actual decline in the anticipated rate of profit (based on the value or price)."[25]

Therefore, the misunderstanding of the law of the tendency of rate of profit to fall is an important reason that arouses people to obsess with the study of the actual changes in the rate of profit, which in turn is bound to lead such a study to a dead end, while also to push Marxist economic theory onto a vulgar road. Ben Fine's views on this issue is worth pondering, that he regarded the tendency of the rate of profit to fall as "an abstract tendency", rather than "an practical tendency", which should be in line with the intention of Marx on the concept of the law of the tendency of the rate of profit to fall. The law of the tendency of the rate of profit to fall should be understood as: "the law itself and a variety of reasons that play a role are the result of the continuous improvement of the technical composition of capital accompanied inevitably in the process of capitalist accumulation."[26] This result must be one of the interactions of a variety of complex contradictions between the tendency of the rate of profit to fall and various counterproductive factors. Among them, the economic crisis is one of the results of forcibly and temporarily easing the contradiction between the two.

400

Recalling the past literature of the "underconsumption" theory, people who had carefully studied and summarized views of the "underconsumption" theory basically had a clear preference, but the difference is that those who adhere to Malthus, Keynes' theory of "inadequate effective demand" are relatively greater in number. It is generally believed that Marx initially admitted the "underconsumption" theory, but then gave it up and became a strong opponent of the theory. For this reason, in Marxist political economy perspective, the mainstream is the explanation of how Marx abandoned and criticized the "underconsumption" theory, and those who believe that Marx had the idea of the "underconsumption theory" are only a very few. The reason Marx gave up on the crisis theory of single factor is because if not doing so, it would be in conflict with what he insisted that "contradiction is the root reason of the development of things." The root reason of the economic crisis of capitalism is the basic contradiction of capitalism, and this is no doubt a scientific thesis. But like any other contradiction, the basic contradiction of capitalism also has

---

25   Ben Fine, Lawrence Harris, *Rereading Capital*, Jinan: Shandong, People's Publishing House, 1993, p. 60.
26   Ibid., p. 63.

its own specific manifestations, as well as specific aspects of the contradiction. For example, the contradictions between the organization of production of individual enterprises and the anarchy of production in the whole society, as well as the contradictions between the infinite widening trend of production and the limited consumption of working people. Here, "the organization of production of enterprises", "the anarchy of production in the whole society", "the infinite widening trend of production", "the limited consumption of working people " etc., are manifested as the specific aspects of the contradiction, and they are also characterized by the capitalist mode of production. Every time when the contradiction is intensified, it will always show characteristics such as "severe disproportionality of production", "excessive economic prosperity", "general overproduction", "relative or absolute poverty of working people's living standard" and others. It is obviously wrong if these characteristics are regarded as the root reason of the economic crisis, because there are reasons of a deeper level behind them. Compared with the classical theory of underconsumption and the theory of underconsumption in the period of the Second International, the modern Western Marxist underconsumption theory had new progress in some areas, and they associated underconsumption with the relative decline in the share of workers' wages or the decline in real wages, which is something new and also valuable in related research. Those views that believe underconsumption is also one of the expressions of disproportionality are put forward by Lenin long ago. The theory of overaccumulation is essentially a replica of theory of wage growth. The analytic model of economic crisis after introducing factors like state, ecology and so forth has expanded the horizons of the Marxist theory of economic crisis, reflecting the theoretical development with the times. To speculate the structure and system of the Marxist theory of economic crisis from the angle of "six-book structure" is conducive for us fully and accurately understand and grasp the structure and content of Marx's analytical model of economic crisis, and the theoretical and practical implications of this research activity is obvious.

Western Marxist scholars have introduced new factors of crisis on the basis of Marx's crisis theory in order to analyze the capitalist economic crisis, which has greatly triggered world-wide academic contention. Their new exploration has expanded the horizons of Marxist economics in analyzing and understanding the capitalist economic crisis and benefits our deeper research. Some of them who denounce Marx's theory of crisis, obviously share the same error with the non-Marxist economics – that opposes the methodology of Marxist political economy with the methodology of vulgar bourgeois economics. Some of them even do not deserve a deep discussion, since they ignore the basic fact that the capitalist economic crises occur periodically.

CHAPTER XII

Review of the Marxist Analytic Model of Economic Crisis from the Perspective of Western Counter-Crisis Theory and Practice

I. Introduction

In the free competition period of capitalism and in the face of increasingly destructive periodic economic crises occurring one after the other, single capitalists were almost helpless. As the *official representative of capitalist society*, and capitalists, the capitalist states have tried to avoid crises and relieve them, but all relevant efforts have proved fruitless, hence Marx and Engels had asserted in the *Communist Manifesto*: "On the one hand by enforced destruction of a mass of productive forces; on the other, by the conquest of new markets, and by the more thorough exploitation of the old ones. That is to say, by paving the way for more extensive and more destructive crises, and by diminishing the means whereby crises are prevented."[1] However, when capitalism entered into the state-monopoly stage, the governments have adopted a series of counter-crisis approaches different from the past – macro regulatory policies and

---

1 *Selected Works of Marx and Engels*, 2nd Ed., Volume 1, Beijing: People's Publishing House, 1995, p. 278.

means, to strengthen the intervention of government in the economy internally, and to strengthen the international regulation of economic life abroad. These counter-crisis means did not eliminate the crisis radically, but effectively eased the crisis that it not only disrupted the natural cycle of the capitalist economic crisis, but also eased the strength of the cyclical fluctuation greatly, achieving long and rapid economic growth in the capitalist world. Marx's assertion of the development trend of the capitalist economic crisis is inconsistent with the real development of the crisis, and it gradually becomes a new subject that requires an in-depth study in the Marxist Theory of Political Economy. On one hand, it requires the researcher to make a reasonable explanation of Marx's conclusion, and on the other to explain the theory and practice of modern capitalist counter-crisis corresponding to the Marxist political economy. Previous studies have shown that each step of the in-depth study not only helps to deepen our understanding of the Marxist theory of crisis, but also helps this theory to accept new practice test under contemporary conditions, which provides new ideas and clues for the development and improvement of Marxist crisis theory.

II. Why the Counter-Crisis Approach is the One "Less and Less"

From the existing literature, we can acknowledge that Marx did not propose any statement denoting that capitalism had the function of counter-crisis, and even he completed all books he wanted to write, it is impossible for him to draw such a conclusion. This is because the conclusions in the *Communist Manifesto* are something that Marx ultimately wanted to prove in all his writings. In the *Communist Manifesto*, Marx and Engels derived the inevitability of capitalist economic crisis based on the principle of historical materialism, and they believed that, in the beginning when the capitalist mode of production replaced the feudal mode of production, productivity had enjoyed great development, but such development was more and more restricted by the capitalist mode of production, so that "for many a decade past the history of industry and commerce is but the history of the revolt of modern productive forces against modern conditions of production, against the property relations that are the conditions for the existence of the bourgeois and of its rule."[2] This resistance in the form of expression is the capitalist economic crisis, and economic crises are always but momentary and forcible solutions of the existing contradictions. The fundamental way to solve the opposition of capitalist productive forces against relations of production is to turn the capitalist private ownership of the means of production into common possession of "community of freely associated individuals", which means capitalism cannot complete this task within its own reach. Later in *Capital*, in the specialized anatomy of the capitalist relations of production, Marx elucidated a thorough analysis of the development and conflicts of the basic contradictions of capitalism, revealing the law of

404

---

2 *Selected Works of Marx and Engels*, 2nd Edition, Volume 1, pp. 277-278.

development of the productive forces under the condition of capitalist production relations, the law of the tendency of the rate of profit to fall. The basic contradiction of capitalism expounded as the contradiction between the production and realization of surplus value, between production expansion and value augmentation, as well as between excess population and excess capital by the law of the rate of profit to fall and the mass of profit to increase. The intensification of these contradictions is reflected in the outbreak of a crisis. The crisis can only temporarily overcome these contradictions, but make them more profound and expansive. For the inevitable result of the development of this law, Marx and Engels called it "an epidemic of an absurdity", and when it is reflected in the system of economic theory, it is the result of all contradictions of capitalism being a fully developed – the ultimate conclusion of all theories. When describing the subject of the study of political economy, Engels deliberately stressed that: "The task of economic science is rather to show that the social abuses which have recently been developing are necessary consequences of the existing mode of production, but at the same time also indications of its approaching dissolution, and to reveal within the already dissolving economic form of motion, the elements of the future new organisation of production and exchange which will put an end to those abuses."[3] The incurability of the capitalist economic crisis is still reflected on many specific theoretical levels in political economy. For example, in terms of one of the specific forms of the basic contradiction of capitalism – the contradictions between the organization of production of individual enterprises and the anarchy of production in the whole society, almost all textbooks on political economics believe that, under the condition of the private ownership of means of production of enterprises, for what to produce, how much to produce and how to produce their rights of owners of the means of production, the society cannot force him what to do or what not to do. In terms of the other specific form of a basic contradiction – the contradiction between the infinite widening trend of production and the reduced demand of working people, almost all textbooks on political economics believe that the income of the working people will not increase correspondingly with the expansion of production, and in order to have a good position in competition, the capitalists always want to maximize the accumulation and always depress the wages of workers below the labour value, which is determined by the nature of capital, and capitalism itself cannot change it. The reason why the capitalist socialized reproduction cannot be successfully carried out is because capitalism cannot solve the conflict between the realization condition and realization form of its socialized reproduction, as well as the contradiction between production and consumption, namely the operation of smooth socialized production requires the maintenance of proportion among and within various sectors of the national economy objectively, which can only be realized with the spontaneous effect of the market mechanism; the expansion of production also requires objectively the consumption to expand with a corresponding proportion, but

405

3 *Selected Works of Marx and Engels*, 2nd Edition, Volume 3, Beijing: People's Publishing House. 1995, p. 492. See. also Engels' Anti-Dühring.

the distribution relations of capitalism can only make workers get less and less share, and the only way to resolve these contradictions is to change the capitalist system, which is what capitalism cannot do. Therefore, in general, in the logical conclusion of Marxist political economics, the crisis of capitalist overproduction is not only "incurable" in capitalism, or even cannot be treated, because what capitalism uses to heal the economic crisis would be to prepare for a more comprehensive, more violent crisis, or that only by coping with the crisis so as tore solve the economic fluctuation.

From the counter-crisis practice in contemporary capitalism, the assumption for Marx and Engels to study the crisis phenomenon is not entirely reasonable. Perhaps constrained by historical conditions, they regarded some phenomena existing in the condition of liberal capitalism as an eternal attribute the phenomenon of capitalism, and regarded it as an established premise for studying the capitalist mode of production. For example, in a disorderly capitalist market economy, the state only plays the role of "night watchman", with neither the state macro regulation of the economy, nor the international regulation of the economy, and there is only antagonism between the capitalist class and the working class without cooperation, and the like. These realities in the era of capitalist free competition have gradually changed in the monopoly period. In his later writings, although there is the wording of "total capitalist" to safeguard the overall interests of the bourgeoisie, he did not think that the "ideal personification of the total national capital" (the state) would regulate the social economy through economic "plan", by the use of macro-economic policies, economic and legal means, administrative measures, and he either did not think the behaviour would ease the basic contradiction of capitalism in the long run, so as to alleviate the economic crisis of capitalism.

III. Quantum Equilibrium of National Economy in Marxist Economics and Modern Western Economics

The so-called anti-crisis, is to forcibly recover the equilibrium of the damaged equilibrium, so that the intensified basic contradiction of capitalism will be eased. At the operational level, it is that the public institution uses all kinds of policies and means to meet the conditions for the smooth socialized reproduction of capital, so as to realize the equilibrium of the total supply and the quantity, structure and value of the total demand of society, as well as the equilibrium of supply and demand of money. Marx had thorough and detailed exposition of the equilibrium on this level in *Capital*, and it is worth noting that when Marx revealed the equilibrium of the total supply and total demand of society, he also took into account the realization issue of the ultimate product (value) and the intermediate product (value) closely related (Department I is manifested as the constant capital of means of production in the physical form, and Department II is manifested as the realization issue of the constant capital of means of subsistence in the physical form).Comparing the Western macroeconomics that studies the equilibrium of the total supply and total demand from national income, it is more complete and scientific. On the total quantity equilibrium in macroeconomic regulation, we can find almost all theoretical basis in Marx's economics, such as the equilibrium of the total supply and total demand of society in value and quantity contained in the socialized reproduction model of capital as Marx suggests, as well as the composition and realization condition of the social total product. Let us look at the relationship between the total supply and total demand contained in the realization condition of the simple reproduction.

Basic condition: $I(v + m) = IIc$

Implied condition: (1) $I(c + v + m) = Ic + IIc$

(2) $II(c + v + m) = I(v + m) + II(v + m)$

Add the implied condition conditions, and we have:

$I(c + v + m) + II(c + v + m) = Ic + IIc + I(v + m) + II(v + m)$

m in the scheme can be further decomposed into profit (p) (income of enterprise plus interest) and rent (r), and the scheme can be further expressed as:

$I(c + v + m) + II(c + v + m) = Ic + IIc + I(v + p + r) + II(v + p + r)$

This scheme demonstrates more clearly the equilibrium condition for total supply and total demand in the form of income. The left hand side is the total supply of society among which $I(c + v + m)$ is the total supply of means of production, and $II(c + v + m)$ is the total supply of means of subsistence. The right hand side is the total demand of society, $Ic + IIc$ is the total demand of society for means of production, and as the sum of three incomes, $I(v + p + r) + II(v + p + r)$ constitute the total demand of society for means of subsistence in the condition of simple reproduction. Thus, $I(c + v + m) + II(c + v + m) = Ic + IIc + I(v + p + r) + II(v + p + r)$ reflects the equilibrium between the total supply and the total demand of society reproduction under the condition of the simple reproduction.[4]

Since the typical form of socialized production is expanded reproduction, the identity of the socialized reproduction of the total capital should be based on the realization condition of the expanded production. According to the realization condition of the socialized expanded reproduction of capital, the expression of the total supply and the total demand of society can be expressed as:

$I(c + v + m) + II(c + v + m)$

$= (Ic + IIc + I\Delta c + II\Delta c)$

$+ (Iv + IIv + I\Delta v + II\Delta v) + (Im/x + IIm/x)$

---

4   Tang Zaixin made a similar description in the book *From Marx to the Market Economy*.

Induce similar items:

$$(Ic + IIc) + (Iv + IIv) + (Im + IIm)$$

$$= (Ic + IIc) + (I\Delta c + II\Delta c) + (Iv + IIv)$$

$$+ (I\Delta v + II\Delta v) + (Im/x + IIm/x)$$

Simplify:

$$Im + IIm = (I\Delta c + II\Delta c) + (I\Delta v + II\Delta v) + (Im/x + IIm/x)$$

In modern Western macroeconomics, the expression that the total supply of society equals the total demand of society in the System of National Accounts is the basic formula of the national income composition. Elements and the fundamental equilibrium contained in the formula are: $C + I + G + (X - M) = C + S + T + K_r$ (C represents consumption; I investment; G government spending; $(X - M)$ net exports; T net income of government; K_r transfer of domestic residents on foreign residents). Since $I = S + (T - G) + (M - X - K_r)$, among them S represents private savings, $(T - G)$ government savings, $(M - X - K_r)$ foreign savings to domestic, so this formula is further described as "the savings investment identity". When the total savings equal to the total investment, the total supply equals to the total demand in the market, and the national economy is in an equilibrium. When the total investment is less than the total savings, there is surplus of products, and the production declines, with the reducing national income; when the investment is greater than the savings, the price of products rises, and the production increases with the increasing national income. If introducing the deciding factor of the rate of interest into "the savings investment identity", the equilibrium will be further expanded to the equilibrium between the money supply and money demand. In modern Western mainstream by economics, the above relationship is described as the IS–LM model (Investment Saving–Liquidity Preference Money Supply), which is used to illustrate the equilibrium between the product market and the money market, as well as interest and income when both markets reach equilibrium simultaneously. In modern Western economics, either the imbalance of IS (product market) is used to explain the business cycle, or the imbalance of IS–LM (money market) is used to explain the business cycle. Generally, the investment, savings, interest rates, income, and consumption are seen as the decisive factors affecting the business cycle, and the conscious control of the cyclical fluctuation in the economy is realized by affecting and changing these factors, thinking that the dynamic function of human can effectively control these elements, and thus it is able to avoid or moderate the cyclical fluctuation in the economy.

The macroeconomic equilibrium relationship in Marxist economics suggests that the basic equilibrium to realize the socialized expanded reproduction of capital is that the quantum of the total surplus value of two departments equals to the sum of the additional constant capital and variable capital, and the surplus value of capitalists used for personal life consumption, and the forcible recovery of the imbalance of this equilibrium relationship is the economic crisis. The additional total amount of means of production and the total amount of means of subsistence, as well as the total amount of means of subsistence consumed by the capitalists are the basic variables and affecting and constraining the equilibrium relationship. The nature of capital is to continue obtaining surplus value, and obtaining to the maximum. The basic approach to meet this requirement is to continue to expand the production scale and to ensure capitalists' consumption of surplus value, and the additional constant capital, variable capital and means of subsistence consumed by capitalists in expanded production equal to the sum of the surplus value. The basic premise for the expanded reproduction of social capital to be carried out in a given period is that, the total social product produced in the period can achieve value compensation and physical renewal. Specifically, the demand of replacement investment and new investment for means of production equals to the social total supply, and the means of subsistence consumed by workers and capitalists is equal to supply of the whole society for the means of subsistence. As the limit of capitalist investment is a certain amount of surplus value (maybe dividends, or the average profit), and if there is no satisfactory returns, the capital is likely to be idle. The income earned by workers during the effective sale time is used for the survival, development and enjoyment for life, so the income of workers is naturally spent in part in consumption, and another part is in idle. In the developed credit relationship, the idle capital and income becomes savings. If the capitalists cannot maintain a certain investment demand and consumption demand, and the workers cannot maintain a certain consumption demand, it is difficult to achieve the equilibrium between the total supply and the total demand. Since Marxist political economy fails to complete the theoretical elaboration from the abstract to the concrete, so the equilibrium model of the national economy in writings of Marxist economics is still very abstract, and there is also a distant gap between the realities of economic life. For example, workers only have wage income, and use it for consumption at the time one hundred percent; the media of trading is metallic currency; capital is coming from the idle funds in the surplus value and the process of production; there is no national macro control, and so on. Therefore, in general, Marx's economics virtually had no discussion that capitalism might have the macro control, but Marx had revealed the basic structure of the equilibrium relationship of social economy, the realization condition of the socialized reproduction of capital in the principle of Marxist Political Economy is actually the equilibrium relationship in the product market. When discussing the realization process of the socialized reproduction of capital in *Capital* Volume II, Marx had very carefully discussed the equilibrium relationship between money invested and its reflux because of the realization of the total social product, which is actually the equilibrium of money market in the operation of the national economy. For the perspective of anti-crisis theory and practice for nearly half a century in the capitalist world, the equilibrium relationship between the total social supply and total demand, the equilibrium of the product market, as well as the equilibrium of the money market that Marxist economics had revealed more than 100 years ago, no doubt has the groundbreaking status, and it also explains that Marxist macroeconomic theory is somehow connected with the modern Western macroeconomic theory.

State intervention is one of the most basic functions of the state, because the state is a product and a manifestation of the irreconcilability of class antagonisms, and a tool of the ruling class, which it uses to defend its interests. What to intervene in, when to intervene in, in what way to intervene in and the standard is whether it is in favour of the interests of the ruling class, as long as it is favourable to the ruling class, sooner or later it will be accepted. From a historical perspective, when it is favourable to the primitive accumulation of capital using the power of the state, the state will seize the opportunity to help the emerging bourgeois implement the enclosure movement, colonial trade, the slave trade and other activities. When laissez-faire is favourable to the development of capitalist mode of production, the state initiatively and consciously plays the role of night watchman. When the contradiction of the capitalist mode of production continues to intensify, and the imbalance of economic quantum and the excessive polarization threat to its survival and development, the state will intervene to have macro regulation, to prevent violent fluctuations in the economy, and to ease class contradictions. When the disorderly world capitalist system brings its own growing disasters, many countries are forced to come together on the same needs, and establish the international regulation and management system with regard to economy, politics, and military. The historical development of state intervention has suggested that, like other modes of production, the capitalist mode of production also has the ability to adapt to the large-scale socialized production in a certain range and to a certain extent, as well as out of the need for defending the interests of the bourgeoisie, by the use of the state's intervention function, to have macro regulation and management over the economic and social relationship to a certain extent, which can be carried out at both at the national level, and at the world level. To view the conclusions of Marxist economics from the necessity of state intervention, it demonstrates its highly abstract features. If we consider the functions of state intervention in the economy, the anti-crisis approaches of capitalism would not only be "by enforced destruction of a mass of productive forces", "by the conquest of new markets", and "by the more thorough exploitation of the old ones," it will have more means to prevent the crisis, but these measures cannot overcome the capitalist economic crisis fundamentally.

With the further development of socialized production, the capitalist mode of production gradually abolishes its previous relationship for partial adjustment of the economic relations. In Marx's time, the stock system of companies had offered a good performance in promoting the capital relationship. After Marx died, other new phenomena such as monopoly, state monopoly capitalism, international monopoly capital, and economic globalization in the capitalist economic life occurred, which are also called factors of "partial adjustment", and in fact, it is the changes in the ways of state intervention and the strengthening of intervention intensity, while the main form of intervention is the macro regulation of the economy. Below is the specific generalization of the state intervention in the economy by our domestic economics textbooks:

1) Using the huge capital that the state holds to invest in the process of re-production of social capital, huge emerging industrial enterprises that private monopoly capital is unable to set up and which meet the requirements of the development of new technologies can be set up, thereby partially overcoming the contradiction between socialized production and private monopoly capital. 2) As "ideal total capitalist", the bourgeois state overrides the interests of the individual private monopoly capital. It represents the overall interests of the monopoly bourgeoisie, and thus in the process of regulating the economic operation, it can break through the narrow limits of the private monopoly capital in simply pursuing the immediate profit within a certain range. 3) Using a variety of ways to intervene in the economy through the state, especially the "economic plan" to undertake a comprehensive regulation of the reproduction of social capital, which to a certain extent adapts to the development of the socialization of capitalist production, as well as the need for the economic restructuring, and has a certain mitigation effect on the anarchy of production in the capitalist society. So that the reproduction of social capital can be achieved in coordination in a certain period and to a certain degree, thus contributing to the social and economic development. 4) The state monopoly capitalism also temporarily mitigates the contradiction of labour and capital, as well as the contradiction between monopoly capital and small capital. The state of the monopoly bourgeoisie redistributes the national income through fiscal, and then redistributes the income of wage earners through "welfare state", which guarantees the basic livelihood of the working people to a certain extent, so that the family livelihood of no work, no labour and low income is somewhat improved, and the working people have some benefits, which has played a role in mitigating the contradiction between labour and capital, thus it is conducive to maintaining the capitalist system of wage labour. From the overall interests of the bourgeoisie, the state also formulates policies to protect and to support small and medium enterprises, and under the condition of monopoly capitalism, the existence of a large number of small and medium enterprises does not weaken the ruling of the monopoly, but is conducive to the interests of the large monopoly capital. 5) In the state monopoly capitalism, the state comes forward for international economic regulation, so that the contradictions between the capitalist countries also get some coordination, which is conducive to mitigating the contradiction.[5]

Consequently, the following measures have been taken for the macro regulation and control of the entire national economy: as "the ideal, total capitalist", the state is directly involved in the process of reproduction of social capital, to

5 See Wei Xinghua as editor in chief, *The Principles of Political Economy*, Chapter IX. Beijing: Economic Science Press, 2004.

regulate and manage the reproduction of the entire social capital through the normal operation of the reproduction of the state monopoly capital; for enterprises that the state holds the controlling stake, the state regulates and manages their business activities through government programs or policies, so that it can provide conditions and services for the normal operation of the reproduction of the entire social capital; for enterprise that the private monopolist holds the controlling stake, the state provides various kinds of favourable conditions for business activities for macro management and regulation; the state redistributes the national income through fiscal, monetary and other policy means to achieve the regulation of the private monopoly capital; and to regulate the social economy through the "economic plans".[6]

Facts in the above literatures demonstrate that the basic relationship of the capitalist mode of production is constantly being developed with the times, and in order to meet the needs of social production, in order to safeguard the interests of the entire capitalist class, they could and have the ability to reform and to adjust the mode of production it relies on, within a certain range and to a certain degree. That is to say, capitalist class is able to mitigate its contradiction through its own strength, to find ways to cooperate in its fight against the working class, and to meet the requirements of the development of productive forces through the socialization of capital relationship, so that the results of large-scale socialized production serve the growth of capital.

IV. The Practice and Limitations of Capitalist Counter-Crisis Measures

In terms of the relationship between new changes in contemporary capitalism and the capitalist economic crisis, on the one hand, the frequent outbreaks of the capitalist economic crisis, particularly the severely devastating consequences of the great 1929 – 1933 economic crisis, have forced the capitalist countries to strengthen the intervention in and the regulation of the economic life. In the measures taken against the crisis, the intervention and regulation is firstly manifested as the expansion of the administrative expenses and social welfare spending in the budget, which directly increases the demand for social spending, alleviates the imbalance of accumulation between two departments, reduces the overproduction of means of subsistence, and thus weakens the intensity of the capitalist economic crisis; secondly, it is manifested as the decentralization of the renewal of fixed capital, i.e. during the overheating stage before the crisis hit the economy, take austerity measures to curb excessive economic expansion. When the crisis comes, try to increase social spending, to stimulate private investment, to protect the financial system in order to maintain fixed capital investment of considerable size, thus reducing the production decline. These interventions and adjustment measures taken by the capitalist countries have reduced the intensity of the economic crisis. For example, in

---

6   Ibid.

the 1929–1933 economic crisis, the production in the United States fell by 46.2% in magnitude, with the unemployment rate of 24.9%;the production in Germany fell by 40.6% with the unemployment rate of 50%; the production in Japan fell by 32.9%; after the capitalist countries have taken intervention and regulation measures against the economic crisis, in the two economic crises erupting during 1973 – 1975 and 1979 – 1983, the production in the United States dropped by 15.2% and 11.8%, with the unemployment rate reduced to 10.8% and 9.1%; and the production in Germany declined by 12.2% and 12.9% with the unemployment rate dropped to 8.5% and 5.1%; and the production in Japan dropped to 20% and 4.1%. However, on the other hand, due to the state intervention and regulation, the economic crisis cannot be fully developed, and the crisis cannot be fully played to eliminate the excess production and in the forcible regulation of production so as to temporarily resolve the contradiction between production and consumption, which makes the excess production capacity become regular, deepens the crisis of overproduction, so that the economic crisis does not, as some people have imagined, disappear, or be transferred. However, it breaks out more frequent, with the interval between two crises reduced from once every 10 years in the mid-19th century to about once every four years in the 20th century.

Because of the special status of the U.S. economy in the world economy, this article uses it to illustrate the issue with its anti-crisis practice.

In the capitalist world, it should naturally be traced back to the New Deal when the anti-crisis measures truly became a targeted, mandatory, and conscious act by the government. Before the Great Depression in the 1930s, the economic crisis had occurred in the United States for many times, in spite of that, the government had never taken any targeted measures. The Great Depression in the 1930s was the starting time when the U.S. government took the targeted anti-crisis measures. In October 1929, the unprecedented severe economic crisis broke out in the history of the United States, the then U.S. President Hoover believed in the traditional laissez-faire policy, taking only a small number of measures such as increasing funding for public works and reducing the rate in order to mitigate the strike by the crisis, which had only limited effect. When Roosevelt became president in 1933, the major crisis had been four years, and with the strike of the crisis, the total value of the New York stock market lost 87.2%, almost close to collapse. The gross industrial production fell by 46.2%, retreated to the level in 1905-1906. Among them, the auto industry output fell by 95%, pig iron output fell by 79, 4%, steel output fell by 76%. 7,000 banks were destroyed in the run, and the currency circulation almost stopped. 14,000 businesses were closed down. The unemployment rate was as high as 25%, while the wage of workers declined by 40%. To early 1933, the total agricultural income was 60% lower than that in 1929, and about 1.19 million farmers went in bankruptcy. Millions of people lost their savings and real estate, hundreds of thousands of teenagers were dropped out of school, wandering around, and millions of young people did not have hope for jobs.

Such widespread unemployment, hunger and cold caught people unguarded, and the government were helpless in all this. A sense of despair filled the country, and people would think there must be something wrong with the social system. The evil and the general crisis of capitalism Marx prophesied were closer to the truth than ever. When he took office Roosevelt would have to declare: the national bank lagged the payment period. In the meantime he prohibited withdrawing and transporting gold, and began to take a series of legislative actions to "relieve, reform and recover" the U.S. economy which had been into recession. Thus began the so-called Roosevelt's "New Deal." The so-called "new" is that he abandoned the dogma that "federal government pursued the laissez-faire, and intervened as little as possible in economic affairs". He had bold attempt to relieve the economic crisis by state intervention, rather than relying on the run of the market mechanism to overcome the economic crisis automatically.

"New Deal" is divided into two stages: the first stage was from March 1933 to the end of 1934, focusing on legislation, with the Emergency Banking Act being passed, the gold standard abandoned; Acts like National Industrial Recovery Act (NIRA), Agricultural Credit Act and Agricultural Adjustment Act (AAA) were implemented, and the responsibility the government assumed in economic life was established. Meanwhile, a variety of laws and regulations had also been developed for the economic activity, so as to manage various activities of the economic group, and to promote the development of businesses and the entire economy, with some production activities being directly involved by the government. Roosevelt tried to prompt the falling price to rise so as to increase profits through the close coordination between the government and the private enterprises; the serious problem of unemployment was alleviated, and wages were rising, purchasing power increased, in order to restore the economy. The second stage was from 1935 to 1936, the government turned to the implementation of the legislation reform of long intervention in the economy, and National Labour Relations Act (NLRA) was adopted, affirming the legitimacy of trade unions and collective bargaining activities; Social Security Act (SSA) was adopted, establishing old-age insurance system and the unemployment insurance system jointly organized the federal and the state; in addition, raising the income tax rate and levying tax on the excess profits were used as a means of income redistribution. In this way, New Deal not only caused a revolution in the government management of the economy, but also completed such a revolution – a basic principle that the government cannot stand away from the economy, after the Roosevelt era, is no longer subject to serious challenge.

"New Deal" has brought two changes with profound meanings: First, the full intervention of the government in the economic life has become a reality, and there is a significant change in government functions. The government assumes many unprecedented functions, such as buyer and supplier of social goods, lender of capital, direct and indirect investor, manager of large enterprises, distributor of national income, and advisor of national economy. In short, as the "total capitalist", the government regulates and guides the economic life, and its legitimization ascertain new legal systems through the complex legislation struggle, having a long-term impact on the improvement of the anarchy of production. "New Deal" sought to eliminate the "excess" and to ease the crisis by expanding the effective social demand and promoting consumption, which had a new theoretical and practical significance. Second, the government directly intervened in the contradiction between labour and capital, recognizing the rights of labour and promoting the coordination between labour and capital, and it changed objectively from the defender of the interests of producers to the coordinator and equalizer of the interests of employers and employees. The labour legislation in the "New Deal" is the result of both workers' struggles and the impact of the Reformation Movement in American society. Overall, Roosevelt's anti-crisis policies alleviated the basic contradiction of capitalism through institutional innovation within the capitalist framework.

In the mid-1930s, Keynes tried to use "insufficient effective demand theory" to prove the cause for the economic crisis and the cycle, as well as the anti-crisis policy by the government. In fact in the early 1940s, American economist Alvin Harvey Hansen et al. clearly stated for the first time that based on the specific situation in the United States, the Keynesian theory could be treated as a policy basis. Hansen raised the "compensatory" fiscal policy, i.e. to revive the economy with the use of expansionary fiscal policy in times of crisis; during the economic boom, to curb the economic crisis with a tight fiscal policy; the deficits formed in times of crisis can be made up with the fiscal surplus in boom stage, in order to keep the budget balance within the entire cycle. The use of fiscal policy to counter the crisis, specifically, through increases or decreases in tax or in expenditure, results in a corresponding change in the purchasing power of the society or in the total demand, thus stimulating the economic expansion or economic contraction, in order to reduce the effect of cyclical fluctuations. In order to achieve the increase or decrease in the tax revenue or expenditure, the federal government can change the amount and sources of tax revenue, expanding or shrinking the government spending. When the total tax revenue is greater than the total government expenditure, the national income flow is reduced, social purchasing power compressed, the aggregate demand reduced, thereby the economic activity is slowing down or there is an economic contraction. When the total amount of government spending is greater than the total tax revenue, the national income flow is increased, the purchasing power of social income and aggregate demand expanded, so that the economy is expanded. In certain economic situations, for example, the economy will enter the crisis phase or will bottom out; the federal government deliberately takes reverse tax and spending measures against the economic activity, thus lagging the arrival of the crisis or accelerating economic recovery and upsurge. Since World War II, the use of fiscal budget to curb the cycle fluctuation of economy has, to a large extent, become a systematic economic policy accepted by the majority of the U.S. political, business, and academic circles. Until today, it is still a policy prior to the monetary policy.

The use of the monetary policy to counter the crisis is to indirectly affect the money supply, the scale of investment and other macroeconomic variables by changing the rate of interest, the statutory reserve ratio, the discount rate, the stock of government securities and some intermediate variables. In the expansionary monetary policy, the decline in the rate of interest promotes investment and expands the money supply, thus contributing to consumption and production, and if the economy is in crisis and depression, it can promote recovery and upsurge as soon as possible. In the tightening monetary policy, the rise in the rate of interest limits the investment, contracts the money supply, and reduces consumption and production. If the economy is in the upsurge stage, it can postpone the outbreak of the economic crisis.

In the anti-crisis measures during the "New Deal" era, it is the deficit fiscal policy that takes the important role. The monetary measures are mostly forced to take at the time of bank failures and the gold standard is difficult to maintain. From these flexible monetary and financial measures to the deficit fiscal policy regardless of the balance of payments is a major and unconscious policy change. For the U.S. government at that time, the emergence of the fiscal deficit was largely caused by the increasingly large fiscal spending, but with the stimulus of a significant increase in the budget deficit, it was showing some signs of recovery in the U.S. economy, which made the U.S. rulers strengthen the confidence in the expansionary fiscal policy. However, "New Deal" did not make the U.S. economy return to the pre-crisis level, and not until there was a large number of military spending caused by the outbreak of World War II and the U.S. arms expansion and war preparations did the U.S. economy get out of the "Special Depression" after the Great Depression in 1930s, rising gradually into a new upsurge stage. In fact, the war is more a powerful "anti-crisis" measure over fiscal policy and monetary policy. Because the stimulus of the war on the economy is a short external factor, in order to prevent the major crisis in the transition from a war economy to a peace period , as well as in order to maintain stable economic growth after World War II, shortly after the end of World War II, the U.S. Congress passed the Employment Act of 1946, declaring that "it is the continuing policy and responsibility of the federal government to use all practical means … to promote maximum employment, production, and purchasing power."In order to help the federal government policy makers achieve these objectives, The Employment Act of 1946 also provides for the establishment of Council of Economic Advisers (CEA), and the establishment of a U.S. Congress Joint Economic Committee under Senate and House of Representatives. With the support of Council of Economic Advisers, it forms the system of the annual Economic Report of the President. Therefore, it can be said that, for decades after World War II, a variety of "anti-crisis" policies and measures in the fiscal and financial aspects that the U.S. federal government adopted is basically based on The Employment Act of 1946.

From after World War II to the end of the 1950s, the effect of the proactive fiscal policy in the United States on stabilizing the economy played is often not targeting to stabilize the economy. For example in 1948 the Income Tax Reduction Bill was vetoed by President Truman initially. Truman was worried that tax reduction would expand the total demand of the society, and would therefore exacerbate inflationary trends that have emerged; while it also needed to have a greater financial resource to pay for the defence spending under the "Cold War". But the U.S. Congress overturned the President's veto, and the Bill was still passed. The actual situation shows that under the blow of the 1948 – 1949 crises, this tax reduction bill did play a role in stabilizing the U.S. economy. Then during the Korean War, the U.S. government took the measure of raising tax rates from the autumn of 1951 to 1952, so as to cope with the huge expense of the war, but it still caused a price rise. Subsequently, the Congress took measures initiatively to withdraw the excess profits tax, and reduced the general tax rate. Despite these measures were taken in 1953, a year before the economic crisis, but its implementation did help the whole economy go quickly into the recovery phase in 1954. In 1953–1960 during the tenure of President Eisenhower, the U.S. President was more worried about the development of inflation. Therefore, despite there was the outbreak of the 1957–1958 and the 1960 economic crises, the U.S. government continued to pursue a more contractionary fiscal policy.

From 1946 to 1952, the U.S. economy transited from the wartime economy to the peaceful economy. In addition to having a role to play in coping with the inflation, the monetary policy at that time also served the requirements of "supporting bond prices" and "government funding" in financial sectors. In the second half of 1948, there was the first post-war economic crisis, the index of industrial production continued to decline for more than a year. Federal Reserve System discontinued the practice of credit restrictions, and adopted a more relaxed monetary policy, reducing the statutory reserve ratio, lowering discount rate several times, in order to promote the economic recovery. During this period, compared with fiscal policy, monetary policy was not dominant in state intervention in the economy. From 1953 to 1960, there were three economic crises. Correspondingly, monetary policy and fiscal policy, prudent and flexible, constantly adjusted the direction, while maintaining a tight tone. From August 1953 to April 1954, i.e. during the period of the second post-war of economic crisis, the Federal Reserve System reduced the effect of the crisis on the magnitude of the production decline by reducing the discount rate, lowering the deposit reserve ratio, as well as purchasing the government bonds in the open market operations, etc., thus promoting the recovery of the economy. From 1955 to October 1957, the monetary policy was characterized by limiting the growth of the money supply, which prevented the excessive expansion of the economy and emergence of inflation. In the second half of 1957, the third post-war economic crisis occurred, which lasted till 1958. The monetary policy shifted from tightening to loosening from November 1957 on, but the economic policy shift was nearly three months later than the requirements of the objective economic situation. In fact, there has been an obvious sign of economic crisis since August 1957, but the U.S. government did not shift the policy objectives from "controlling and reducing the pressure of inflation" to "maintaining the economic growth"; in November, it reduced the discount rate, bought into government bonds, while reducing the statutory reserve ratio of demand deposits, and these monetary mitigation measures did not stop until August 1958, when the Federal Reserve changed its policy in favour of austerity measures, and the rate of interest also rose the highest level for 30 years. This is a so-called "wind" policy, and its purpose is not to increase the amount of money with the growing demand for money. After the first quarter of 1960, when the fourth post-war economic crisis arrived, the Federal Reserve System began turning to monetary easing policy, and implemented a moderately expansionary monetary policy.

Eisenhower served in office for 8 years, and although he achieved the target of a lower price growth, he paid the price for slow growth in the economy and a large number of unemployment. In 1961 when Kennedy took office as the President of the United States, in an attempt to reduce unemployment and to stabilize price, in the meantime to achieve a faster economic growth, Kennedy introduced the so-called "new economics" of a mobilized fiscal policy. In 1962, he implemented the investment tax reduction and accelerated depreciation rules in order to encourage private investment. In the meantime, with the government procurement as well as the increase in social insurance subsidies and unemployment insurance subsidies, it also stimulated the economy. In 1963, larger tax reduction legislation began brewing. In November 1963, after the assassination of John F. Kennedy, Vice President Johnson became President, and he signed the Revenue Act of 1964 in February 1964, the basic content of which is that individual income tax rates and corporate tax rates were reduced by over 20% and 80%respectively. This further stimulated the economic recovery. Shortly after the implementation of the large tax cuts bill, the United States expanded the war in Vietnam. A large number of military spending and war materiel consumption increased the domestic price rapidly. The consumer price index (CPI) in 1964 and 1965 increased by1.3% and 4.2% over the previous year. In 1961 –1965, with the stimulus of the expanding Vietnam War, the U.S. economy basically achieved the growth target, and by the end of 1965, the gap between the actual and the possible economic output value was gone, while the economy temporarily reached full employment with the unemployment rate of 4%, but it also paid a heavy price of inflation. In the situation of the increasingly serious inflation, industrial production had stalled for10 months from 1966 till August 1967, and the U.S. government had to implement the austerity of Revenue and Expenditure Control Act of 1968 in June 1968, which created a temporary 10 percent income tax surcharge on both individuals and corporations.

In 1966 after Nixon became the President of the United States, he declared to take a progressive policy to regulate aggregate demand and to mitigate the pressure of inflation, thereby promoting the long-term stability of the economy. Indeed, after Nixon administration adopted a restrictive fiscal and monetary policy, immediately the 1969–1970 economic crisis occurred. However, the economic crisis did not curb the development of inflation. Comparing the index of industrial production in December 1970 with that in December 1969, the figure dropped by 3.8% due to the hit of the economic crisis, the number of the unemployed increased by 6%, the unemployment rate increased from 3% to 6.1%, while the consumer price index increased by 2.2%. In December 1970, the U.S. economy started to recover, and by June 1971, the price started rising, which had proved that the progressive adjustment measures by Nixon administration did not achieve the expected results.

From 1961 to 1968, it was quite a long period of time for the continued growth of the U.S. economy, but also the period when inflation tended to be serious. The U.S. monetary authority advertised to implement the discretionary policy. The monetary and credit policy assumed "discretionary" refers to have the flexibility, and to react to the economic situation and economic changes immediately. "When the economy is in recession or beset by high unemployment and excess capacity, monetary policy should clearly be expansionary. How expansionary it should be depends very much upon the extent of the stimulus that the government budget is, and will be, giving to the overall demand. When demand is threatening to outrun the economy's production potential, monetary policy should be restrictive. How restrictive it should be depends, again, upon how much of the job of containing inflation is assumed by fiscal policy."[7] The discretion has two meanings: First, discretion over the economic situation; Second, discretion over the fiscal policy.

In the mid December 1968, the U.S. monetary policy began tightening, and the monetary policy had been tightening throughout 1969, with the rate of interest rising to the highest level in a hundred years; it strictly controlled the non-member banks to borrow reserves, fixed deposits and savings deposits of commercial banks were reduced, and the policy of high tightness accelerated the outbreak of the fifth post-war economic crisis. In November 1969, the economic crisis began, in the next year the U.S. government shifted the economic policy from tightness to expansion. Based on the principle that "a comprehensive stimulus of fiscal and monetary policy should be sufficient to ensure the expansion of the economy to meet the needs", the federal government increased spending and reduced taxes; while Federal Reserve System adopted stimulus expansionary policies, and paid more attention to indicators of the monetary aggregate than ever before. It is worth noting that although the monetary policy is somewhat tightening and it pays attention to controlling the quantity of money, during 1960 and 1970, the price was still rising fast, and

---

7 *Economic Report of the President*, Beijing: China Financial and Economic Publishing House, 1962, p. 85.

the price of consumer goods rose by 6.1% and 5.5%. After 1972, the tightening monetary policy began to shift to cautious expansion. From January to November 1973, it in turn became tightness. The tightening policy was not able to stop the overproduction, and in December the industry began to decline, the sixth post-war economic crisis occurred, thus the monetary policy was slightly relaxed. The economic crisis lasted till 1975, and the Federal Reserve System uses almost all monetary policy tools: reducing the statutory reserve ratio and the discount rate, and uses open market operations. After the second quarter of 1975, the economy began to recover, and in 1976, the process of economic recovery was accelerated, the inflation rate decreased.

The new economic situation forced Nixon administration to change course. Thus, in August 1971, the program of "New Economic Policy" was implemented, which reads: 1) under the coordination of the monetary authorities, fiscal stimulus measures are adopted. 2) Devaluation of the Dollar. The so-called "fiscal stimulus measures" include: the introduction of 7% tax breaks for private investment; the repeal of 7% license tax levied on automobiles and 10% license tax on light trucks; raising the personal tax credits and the minimum tax deductions in order to reduce the tax burden; levying 10% provisional surtax on imported goods that should pay tax and so on. It is estimated that these tax relief measures reduced the government revenue by 8.9 billion dollars in 1972. But at the same time, the social insurance base increased, reducing the spending on social insurance by 5.2 billion dollars. Thus, the net stimulus to the economy as a whole was 3.5 billion dollars. The measure of price freeze initially provided a 90-day period, as the first stage, and later for the regulation of the consecutive second, third and fourth stages, which was not terminated until 30 April, 1994.

In fact, during nearly three years, the U.S. consumer price and producer price index continued to rise, and during the rise in prices, from December 1973 to March 1975, it broke out an economic crisis of the longest duration and the largest decline magnitude for the 30 years after World War II. This economic crisis was throughout the capitalist countries. Therefore, in 1974, at the "Economic Summit Conference" for the capitalist countries, almost all economists were advocating taking policies to curb inflation and to curb economic "recession" at the same time. The U.S. government still focus on curbing the "recession", and on 4 April, the Tax Reduction Act of 1975 was implemented. That was the largest tax cut bill in U.S. history until then, which included reducing individual income tax, allocating grants for low-income workers, as well as expanding tax relief on private investment, and so on. It still provided that the federal government should increase grants for state and local governments, and it is estimated that these additional grants are sufficient to create 320 thousand jobs in public office. The above fiscal policies in total injected the revenue of 22.8 billion in the U.S. economy. Amended by Revenue Adjustment Act of 1975 and Tax Reform Act of 1976, part of the Act of tax relief of became unlimited measures; another part was extended to the end of 1977; there were 10% investment tax relief extended to the end of 1980.

After the 1974-1975 economic crisis, western economies generally had the situation of "stagflation", and the U.S. economy was suffering from it more seriously. In 1973 – 1980, the average annual growth of the real gross domestic product was only 2.4%, and the unemployment rate was often as high as 6% ~ 7%. In the meantime, the average annual inflation rate was often over 6%, of which it reached double digits in three years. In 1973-1979, the average annual growth rate was less than 1%. Facing the serious stagflation, the Keynesian demand policy could not balance it, and was caught in a dilemma. Stimulating the demand will cause the deterioration of inflation, and inflation will lead to more atrophy of the production. In order to get rid of this situation, the Keynesians were trying to implement revenue policies and human policies to supplement demand management policies, but it was not effective.

In 1977 when Jimmy Carter became the U.S. President, he signed the Tax Reduction and Simplification Act of 1977 and Economic Stimulus Appropriations Act of 1977, both of which continued to take provisions of expanding tariff reductions and exemptions, increasing spending and funding state and local government, so as to stimulate economic growth. In 1978, Revenue Act of 1978 was implemented to reduce and exempt tax, which made the tax relief in 1979 reach 18.9 billion dollars. In 1978, the Full Employment and Balanced Growth Act was also adopted, requiring the U.S. administration to achieve full employment and price stability as the two important objectives, and requiring to reduce total expenditures of the federal government to the limit of 20% of GNP, and the Act also provided for a deadline for achieving this objective. But President Carter addressed in the Economic Report of the President in 1979 and 1980 that because of the rise in oil price in 1979, these objectives were not achieved within the original deadline.

421

After 1981 when Ronald Reagan became the U.S. President, on the one hand following the advocate of the supplying school of economics, he reduced individual income tax and corporate income tax on a massive scale, in order to encourage individual "hardworking" and investment activities in the society; on the other hand pursuing the tradition of the new monetarism, the Federal Reserve Board continued to focus on controlling the money supply and the amount of reserves in banks, allowing the short-term interest rate to have free fluctuation in the market. The result of these policies was the continuous rise in the market interest rate. The prime rate of commercial banks grew from average 9.06% in 1978 to 18.9% in 1981, and 19.86% in 1982. Here it must be noted that during the last year of the Carter administration (1980) and the first two years of the Reagan administration (1981-1982), there had been two economic crises, but both administrations of the United States did not take any appropriate measures to address the decline in these two economies. This shows that in the wave of surging inflation, the U.S. authorities' attention has not been placed on these periodic economic fluctuations.

From 1977 to 1980 before the crisis, U.S. monetary policy shifted from expansion to contraction, and then from contraction to expansion. In April 1980, the economic crisis occurred, and the early austerity policy-centered anti-inflation had changed, from tightness to easiness. During this period, the basic task of monetary policy is to strictly control monetary growth, to oppose to inflation, and money supply has become a major target to control and index to regulate the monetary policy. The rate of interest is allowed to fluctuate freely with market supply and demand. The effect of the measure is not obvious on inflation, and in 1980 the Consumer Price Index rose nearly 30% higher than it in 1979.

Just a few months after the 1980 economic crisis, there was the 1981-1982 economic crisis, however, the Reagan administration did not adopt an expansionary monetary policy, but insisted on the implementation of tight money, not hesitating to curb the inflation at the cost of the falling production and rising unemployment. But in the context of "stagflation", the growth of money supply exceeded the pre-announced target.

From the early 1960s, in addition to fiscal and monetary policy, the U.S. government intermittently implemented Revenue Policy in order to deal with the rising price. Nixon's New Economic Policy announced in the early 1970s implemented the revenue policy of regulating wage and price. The main purpose of this kind of revenue policy is to combat inflation. Fiscal policy, monetary policy and revenue policy are usually from the perspective of the aggregate social demand to regulate the economy, that is, through the expansion or contraction of aggregate demand, eliminating the crisis (or preventing the arrival of crisis) and curbing the inflation. By the latter of 1970s, the stagflation occurred in U.S. economy, and the economic policy from the total demand aspect could not balance but became contradictory. It then resulted in the so-called Supply-Side Revolution in the guiding idea of the economic policy, and the federal government began to experiment the economic regulation from the total supply aspect, in order to curb inflation. Thus, the supply-side economic policy measures have gradually become the "new weapon" in the "counter-crisis" policy arsenal of the U.S's economic policies. The economic theory in opposition to big government, high taxes, high welfare expenses as the objective, known as the "Neoliberalism" in the United States and "Neoconservatism" in the United Kingdom, gained a high impact. The supply-side emphasized that in order to heal "stagflation", the stimulus of demand must be changed for the stimulus of supply, for which the tax rate must be reduced. They argued that as long as tax rate was reduced, investment and production would grow, supply would increase, and inflation would be suppressed. While the monetarist school emphasized to control the money supply, and they proposed that as long as the money stock is adjusted according to the economic growth or contraction, reducing the money supply when the economy was overheated, and increasing the money supply when the economy was in recession, the national economy could enjoy a healthy development. With the shift to "neoliberalism" or "neo-conservatism" from the policy, the typical one is the American "Reagan Doctrine", which is characterized by deregulation of the economy, tax cuts, cuts in government spending, deflation, etc. These policies had some effect in dealing with the recession in 1980s, reducing the debt burden of the country.

The Clinton administration implemented the economic policy and social policy later called the "third way", making efforts to look for the middle way among traditional liberalism, Keynesian, monetarism and etc., as well as adjusting means, field and intensity of government intervention. For example, in July 1993, Alan Greenspan, Chairman of Federal Reserve renounced the policy to regulate the economy with the increase or decrease in the money supply, taking the adjustment of the effective interest rate as the primary means of the macro-economic regulation. Clinton reduced the government expenditure, reduced the tax moderately, implemented a balanced and robust budget plan, and he also increased investment in health, education, environment, achieving good results. From April 1991 to August 2000, the U.S. economy has maintained a continuous growth for 114 months, with the rate of growth remaining at 4% or so, the inflation remaining low, and the unemployment rate falling below the accepted "full employment". In April 2000, the unemployment rate was 3.9%.

In terms of the actual development of capitalism from the end of World War II to 1990s, the intensity of the capitalist cyclical economic crisis and the extent of its damage to production and society indeed have been controlled . After the end of 1960s, apart from with few exceptions like having economic fluctuations more frequent in times there had been shorter intervals, smaller in crisis intensity, shorter duration, less distinct in the limit of recovery and depression phase. Capitalist countries continue to adjust their thinking, implementing the mixed tight and loose fiscal and monetary policy, limiting the excessive monopolies and the large gap in wealth, maintaining the environment for "fair competition" and basic social welfare state. In the supply and demand, the "visible hand" and the "invisible hand" interact with each other, using government intervention to deal with market failures, and using market mechanisms to limit the "government wrongdoing." It is noteworthy that the world has gradually strengthened the coordination in the international economic and monetary policy in order to jointly tackle the crisis.

Since the mid-1980s, the contemporary capitalism has undergone a series of important changes: First, changes in the production technology, industrial structure and productivity elements caused by the new technological revolution enabled the social production to have the characteristics and trends of "informationization". The macro model and micro organization of the economy have undergone a great deal of changes, because the government and the private sector are able to avoid blindness and to strengthen planning to the maximum through obtaining the information. The "flexible production" of small quantity and variety is widely implemented, and according to production orders it can even achieve "zero inventory". Secondly, the economic connection between nations and regions is increasing in breadth and depth, and the world has entered "an era of globalization." The flow and configuration of factors of production, as well as the allocation of resources are globalized, and the transnational corporations become the leader and the main beneficiaries of the international production. With the advantage of a mature market system, strong economic strength and the possession of information, the developed countries further intensify the unequal order of the international economy, and in the meantime, countries attach growing importance and take advantage of the cooperation and coordination mechanisms of the international economy for the sake of their own interests. Thirdly, the financial industry has become a relatively independent field, and there is a trend of "financialization". French scholar Jean-Claude Delaunay believes that the contemporary capitalism has entered from the state monopoly capitalism into stage of the financial monopoly capitalism, and the form of capital in the value has evolved from monetary capital in the industrial age to the binary structure of the monetary capital and financial capital, while the trading of financial derivative products has become increasingly important and direct way to profit. Financialization, of course, has provided a powerful impetus for promoting the development of new technology and the global economy, but also aggravates the separation of virtual economy and real economy. Financial liberalization policies that Western countries took the lead promote the formation of the international financial monopoly capital. The super-scale international capital was jaywalking and seeking the maximum profit. The financial speculation causes the unstable economy and continues to lead to a crisis, while the developing countries where the economic structure is flawed and there are loopholes in the foreign exchange control frequently become victims, such as the Mexican financial crisis in 1995, the Southeast Asian financial crisis and Russian financial crisis during 1997-1998. It should be noted that this type of financial crisis, including the debt crisis of the developing world in the 1980s, is not the same with the cyclical economic crisis as the founders of Marxism suggested, but essentially it can still be said to be the reflection of the basic contradiction of capitalism in a larger range and under the new historical conditions. The financial capitalism is still a concept being discussed, but it is one of the facts that cannot be ignored that the financial capital has the control over the global economy and thus has the double-edged effect.

From the end of World War II to the 1974-1975 crisis, the economic growth rate in Western countries was faster than it was during the interwar years. The severity of the cyclical economic crises arising due to overproduction is somehow eased. For the United States, the average annual growth of the real gross domestic product in 1929-1950 was 2.6%, and it reached 3.3% in 1950-1973. In the post-war period, there have been 7 economic crises occurring in the United States (not including the 1981 crisis), and changes in the magnitude of its major economic indicators is less great than the 1929-1933 crisis. Pattern of the economic development in the United States during this period is determined by many factors and specific conditions, in which the Keynesian demand management policies played a promoting effect. However, the result of the effect was only to reduce the extent of the crisis in a certain way, but did not change the objective necessity of the capitalist economic crisis to erupt periodically.

In general, the manoeuvre fiscal policies that the U.S. government implemented during 30-year period after World War II, and most of the measures aimed at expanding the total social demand and encouraging private investment, and thereby promoting the economic growth. But the results had inevitably led to inflation. Therefore, to the 1960s and beyond, the choice of the proactive fiscal policy cannot be free from the constraint of the anti-inflation, which in fact, had a certain contradiction of the "anti-crisis" or counter-cyclical effect. Moreover, from the selection to the implementation of the fiscal policy, it often takes some time. This period of time can be seen as the three time lags of the fiscal policy: The first one is the time lag in understanding, that is, a certain interval between the need for policy action and the practical recognition by the government of the need to take action. In general, from the changes in the objective economy to the recognition by authorities of the changes, it often will go through one or two quarters. The second one is the time lag in policy, that is, the time from which the relevant government departments recognize the need to implement fiscal policies and measures, to reporting to the higher departments for approval, and in all fiscal policies, government actions involving changes in financial revenue (such as tax change) should be approved by the U.S Congress. The time lag relative to such policies not only involves pure economic issues, but also involves the decision-making in policies. The third is the external time lag, that is, the interval between the implementation of the fiscal policy to its impact on the final performance of the economy. In addition, if comparing the fiscal policy with the monetary policy, not only both have the problem of the time lag, they also have differences in the operating mechanism: changes in financial procedures tend to go through the top, and some have to go through the formalities of legislation, which is not like the monetary authorities who have greater freedom, ready to intervene in the money market. Throughout the basic trend of the U.S. monetary policy in the post-war economic crisis, this basic conclusion can be drawn: Under normal circumstances, the monetary policy presents the "reverse" movements with the increase in production in the economic cycle, when economic stagnation and inflation coexist, tightness and easiness of monetary policy frequently alternate; while the rising inflation concentrated the main objective of monetary policy on the aspects of anti-inflation, rather than of anti-economic crisis.

V. The Capitalist Counter-Crisis Theory and Policy Advocates

In Western anti-crisis theories, the one that concludes with policy implications, proposes policy advocates, is adopted by the government, and has had an important influence on real economic life, should be no doubt the Keynesian theory and its policy advocates. When the Great Depression in the 1930s made

Say's creed that "supply creates its own demand" complete went bankrupt, Keynesian macroeconomics came into being, which answered the need for state intervention in the economy theoretically, and presented a model of macroeconomic regulation and a set of suggestions. Keynes admitted that capitalism would bring unemployment and crisis of overproduction, while he also recognized that it was concerned with the capitalist system, that it was the result of the "insufficient effective demand".

The "effective demand" that Keynes was talking about refers to the aggregate demand when the price of aggregate supply and the price of aggregate demand of the commodity in capitalist society reaches equilibrium. The aggregate demand in the form of commodity is manifested as the demand for the total amount of the product, and in the form is manifested as the monetary revenue. The "effective demand" and the national revenue are a reflection of the same content, and they are composed of two parts, consumption and investment. Keynes argues that the value of consumption depends on the propensity to consume; the value of investment depends on the rate of interest of the marginal efficiency of capital, where the marginal efficiency of capital depends on the expected return and the supply price of capital assets (or as a replacement), while the interest rate is determined by the quantity of money and the liquidity preference.

The aggregate demand constitutes investment demand (demand for means of production) and consumer demand (demand for means of subsistence). The inadequate "effective demand" includes both inadequate investment demand and inadequate consumer demand. Keynes used three "fundamental psychological laws" to illustrate the inadequate "effective demand". He believes that peoples' incomes are always divided into two parts, consumption and savings, and as incomes increase, the proportion of the spending would tend to reduce, and the proportion of the savings will tend to increase. This is called the psychological law of the diminishing marginal propensity to consume. Inadequate demand for consumption is derived from this law. Because of the diminishing marginal propensity to consume, the increasing share of income is turned into savings, resulting in the inadequate "aggregate demand". If savings are not turned into demand, unemployment and crisis of overproduction is inevitable.

CHAPTER XIII

Chinese Scholars' Study of the Capitalist Business Cycles

I. Introduction

After the death of Marx, the Marxist theory of economic crisis has always been faced with serious challenges, and the academic contention is focused on the following issues: 1) Is there the Marxist theory of economic crisis? If the answer is yes, then what should the structure, system, content of this theory be? 2) The reason, the material basis, the length, magnitude, characteristics of each stage for the cyclical capitalist economic crisis to occur. 3) Accumulation, investment, renewal of fixed capital, technological innovation, the improvement of the organic composition of capital, the falling rate of profit, and economic crisis. 4) Monopoly and capitalist economic crisis. 5) The world economic crisis and its simultaneity and non-simultaneity. 6) The capitalist agricultural crisis. 7) Economic crisis, business cycle, economic fluctuation and the real development of capitalist economy. 8) Standard of the capitalist economic crisis. 9) New development, new features of the post-war capitalist economic crisis, and reasons for the deformation of the business cycle. 10) The general crisis of capitalism, the intermediary crisis and the structural behaviour. 11) The anti-crisis measures and the phenomenon of "stagflation". 12) The capitalist Great Depression during 1929-1933. The exploration of these issues by Chinese scholars began after the Great Depression in the 1930s. Some Chinese scholars who have received training in Marxist theory overseas began a systematic study of the capitalist economic crisis, wrote books, introduced the Marxist theory of economic crisis to the Chinese scholars, and analyzed the real economic crisis of capitalism, in order to serve the needs of the development of Chinese revolution. However, due to restrictions by the war environment at the time, little progress was achieved both in theoretical research and researches on the reality of the economic crisis. On the other hand due to our learning from Soviet economic research and academic points of views, the academic evaluations on it were based on the mainstream economic theory in the Soviet Union. This practice has had a profound impact on Chinese economics, which to a certain extent restricted the desire for theoretical innovation among Chinese scholars, and even today we can observe traces of this influence. For example, the analytic model of capitalist economic crisis in the authoritative textbooks of political economics still possess essentially a simplified form[1] of the analytical model of *Political Economics, A Textbook*, which to some extent had influence over Chinese scholars' originality in the study of the capitalist economic crisis. Nevertheless, from the late 1950s, the Chinese scholars conducted extensive research and academic contention on major theoretical and practical crises in the capitalist economic crisis, and published thousands of scholarly books and articles, but because of the single topic, lack of depth in the research, narrow scope, abstractness and other reasons, those achievements with breakthroughs and carrying weights are rare. This chapter reviews the progress of Chinese scholars studying the capitalist economic crisis, and the important issues that are concerned over various periods, and makes a thorough analysis of some of the issues, showing the research achievements and academic value of the Chinese scholars in studying the issue of the capitalist economic crisis.

428

II. Research Progress

Despite the economic crisis of capitalism had a regular occurrence in the early 19th century, especially from the beginning of 1825, the capitalist economic crisis further evolved to the cyclical world economic crisis, and economists have almost invariably involved in the study of this economic phenomenon. At the same time, as China became a semi-feudal society step by step, of decadent and dark social system, occlusion, poverty, loss of national sovereignty, territory divided. Until the 1930s, a few earlier scholars who received Marxist theory began to study the capitalist economic crisis. Shen Guanlei, Shen Zhiyuan, Guang Mengjue and et al. are the typical ones among those few Chinese Marxist scholars. At the time, even though their work was preliminary, they started from a higher point, assuming the responsibility of sorting and establishing the Marxist analytic model of the economic crisis from the outset, and using this model to analyze the historical mission of the Great Depression

---

1 The model is actually a form of textbook used by Leontiev, Bukharin, Varga and et al. who analyzed the capitalist economic crisis with the model.

of the 1930s. Their findings demonstrate that they brilliantly accomplished this historic task.

Shen Guanlei published *The World Economic Crisis and the Armed Attack on the USSR*, in 1931, in which he used the principle of the relationship between the capitalist world economic crisis and the war in Marxism-Leninism to analyze the ongoing capitalist economic crisis and new trends of the political and economic development in the major capitalist countries. He was acutely aware that in order to extricate themselves from the shocks of the economic crisis, the major capitalist countries, especially Japan, Germany, Italy and others had embarked on the road of militarism, and they would launch a new world war, in particular, it was possible to launch the attack on the Soviet Union. He warned those peace-loving countries to be alert to the imperialist war.

In 1935, Shen Zhiyuan, a famous Marxist economist, who had studied in the Soviet Union for 5 years, participated in the translation and publication of the 6 Volume Set Chinese Version of *Selected Works of Lenin*, and compiled the Chinese Edition of the magazine *Comintern*, published his writings devoted to the analysis of a capitalist economic crisis, *The World Economic Crisis*, and he used more sophisticated Marxist theory of the economic crisis, to carry out the analysis in simple terms of the world economic crisis since 1825. In particular, his Marxist economics analysis of the Great Depression of the 1930s represented a high level of academic research at the time, and exerted a profound impact on development and dissemination of the Marxist economics in later times. Of course, for various reasons, in Shen Zhiyuan's description and analysis of the world economy, we are able to see traces that his doctrine was affected by the Soviet academia, especially by Varga et al. Shen Zhiyuan's expounded crisis theory maintained a high degree of consistency with the academia of the Soviet Union. Shen Zhiyuan also described the approach for the Marxist crisis theory to understand the capitalist economic crisis from the perspective of the general and the specific. In the most general sense, the root of the capitalist economic crisis lies in the basic contradiction of capitalism. But the premise of this general sense is not enough to describe each of the specific cycle and crisis. Each cycle and each crisis has its specific historicalness determined by a number of factors. The process of cycles and crises changes as the industrial capitalism of free competition develops into the times of the monopoly capitalism and the general crisis of capitalism. The agricultural crisis has a great impact on the cycles and crises. Shen Zhiyuan agreed on the conclusion that capitalism was on the way of collapse with more and more severe strike of the economic crisis, and he believed that outbreak of the cyclical economic crisis was not the mechanical repetition of the phenomenon with the same quality; each crisis pushed capitalism to a new phase much closer to its collapse. In the meantime, it is so not only in economic terms but also in social terms, because each crisis can accelerate the concentration of capital, thereby preparing a more intense crisis. Each crisis gives a fatal blow to the existence of many of the bourgeois, and each crisis reduces the number of people concerned about the maintenance of the capitalist system, making the contradictions between the proletariat and the bourgeoisie acute, in which the contradiction between social production and capitalist ownership is increasingly manifested acutely. Through his analysis of the crisis in 1929, he further confirmed the above conclusions. Shen Zhiyuan also insisted on the promoting effect of accumulation on reproduction and restrictive effect of consumption on capitalist reproduction. He asserted that the relative reduction in spending power caused by accumulation sooner or later would terminate the expansion of production, and in the phase of boom, it would inevitably lead to the crisis that interrupts the actual process of accumulation temporarily. Specifically, as long as the actual accumulation process is in full swing, as long as new plants, blast furnaces, and railways are constructed, as long as old machines are replaced with new machines, the boom will continue indefinitely. Once this process reaches a certain stage of completion, once the new production facilities are substantially made, the demand for goods of department I will be reduced immediately, which will cause a decrease in demand for means of subsistence, because workers of department I become the unemployed. In the meantime, the supply of goods will increase, because new factories and retooled old factories began to invest commodities into markets. Overproduction has already existed, but the crisis does not appear obvious because capitalists who never believe there is an end to the boom phase and they believe it will continue to reserve their commodities' reserves: As long as the crisis does not occur ultimately and publicly, production always exceeds consumption. Shen Zhiyuan also denied the statement that monopolies can overcome or mitigate the crisis, and he asserted that it was not only difficult for monopoly to alleviate the crisis, but to make the crisis prolong and deepen. Because monopolies may depress wages, below the value of labour wages, which further reduced the social spending power. Monopolies artificially maintain high prices of goods, which makes the abundant commodity reserves difficult to dissipate in times of crisis. They impede the restoration and expansion of fixed capital, thereby blocking the economic transition from recession to recovery. After World War II, the intervention in the economy by the state monopoly capitalism gradually became a regular behaviour of major capitalist countries, but in its infancy, and before its active role is fully manifested, many Marxist scholars basically cared nothing of its active role. Shen Zhiyuan also held a negative attitude towards intervention in the economy by the national monopoly capitalism. He believes that the bourgeoisie tries artificially prevent the crisis through economic and political measures, which is pointless. From the mid-1932, the crisis was eased, and was also improved slightly in individual countries, but in any case it cannot be said that it is successful for the bourgeoisie practices. In contrast, for example in the United States, these practices improved the trend of capitalist movement. Shen Zhiyuan also examined the history of the world economy, in addition to the falling prices, reduction in profits, unemployment, the collapse of the credit system, halt of the export of capital, halt of debt repayment, money devaluation, gold demand, shrinking in foreign trade, and fierce competition in the international market, the Great Depression of 1930s was more profound and widespread than ever, but there was the most profound agricultural crisis in the true sense in the history.

Before the founding of New China, Guan Mengjue also explored the issue of economic crisis, and in *The Preliminary Theory of Economic Crisis* published in 1940, he made a preliminary interpretation of Marxist theory of the economic crisis and the economic crisis in the imperialism. He also discussed with Fei Xi, Wu Feidan, Mei Bihua et al. the economic crisis in the United States, Japan, Britain and other countries, and although these explorations were still preliminary, it has played a role in promoting the understanding of capitalist economic crisis by the Chinese audience.

All in all, the early Chinese Marxist economists represented by Shen Zhiyuan studied the Marxist crisis theory in an extremely difficult and dangerous environment and analyzed the real economic crisis of capitalism, contributing to the development and improvement of Marxist crisis theory.

In the early days when New China was founded, with the improvement of academic criteria, the study of the capitalist economic crisis by Chinese scholars was gradually developed, and to the late 1960s, the number of published research results has been quite impressive, laying the initial material foundation for further commencement of the research. Judging from the type of research results, there are: 1) The introduction of foreign research results, especially the Marxist theory of economic crisis; 2) The general study of the capitalist economic crisis; 3) The case study on the U.S. economic crisis.

431

Introducing and building the Marxist theory of economic crisis and its analytical model, provides a strong theoretical support and an effective analytical tool for the research and it is one of the characteristics of this period. Before the new China was founded, the Marxist theory of the economic crisis had spread in China to a certain extent, but because of the environment of war and class attributes of Marxist theory, the scope of its spread had been greatly restricted. After the founding of New China, Marxist political economy had achieved the status of the official mainstream economics, becoming the guiding ideology and the theoretical basis of the Communist Party of China, and therefore it enjoyed an unprecedented propagation condition. The CPC Central Committee set up a special agency, and began a systematic translation and publication of works by Marxist classical writers. As a result, a number of literatures of foreign political economics in this period was quickly translated and published, hugely promoting the study of capitalist economic crisis by Chinese scholars. In the early 1950s, *The Marxist Theory of Crisis* by the British Marxist scholar Joseph Winternitz was translated and published, which increased a new angle and a new channel for Chinese scholars to understand the Marxist theory of the economic crisis – the interpretation of the Marxist theory of the economic crisis by Western Marxist scholars. Subsequently, *The Significance of Marxist-Leninist Crisis of Overproduction* (translated by Department of

Political Economics, Renmin University of China, 1952), *Capital* and *Political Economics, A Textbook* (USSR) was translated and published, which provides the raw data for Chinese scholars to study Marxist theory of the economic crisis, and also enables them to see a relatively mature Marxist analytic model of the economic crisis. *Capitalist Reproduction and Economic Crisis* (Trachtenberg, 1956), *Economic Crisis* Vol. I: *Pre-Monopoly Capitalism Crisis* (Fred Oelssner, 1956), *Economic Crisis* (A. Leontiev, 1957), *Discussion on the U.S. Economic Crisis* (Soviet magazine New Times, 1958), *World Economic Crisis: Comparative Information of the Historical Crises in Major Capitalist Countries in 1848-1935* (collective compiled by World Economics and Politics Institute of USSR Academy of Science, 1958), The U.S. Economic Crisis (compiled by Department of Economics, Liaoning University, 1961), *Proceedings on Capitalist Economic Crisis and Business Cycle* (translated and compiled by Translation and Compilation Office, International Relations Institute, 1962), *Critiques of the Bourgeois Economic Crisis Theory* (Song Chengxian, 1962), *Modern Capitalism and Economic Crisis* (Varga, 1964), and etc. These writings enriched the literature of Marxist crisis theory from the theory, history, reality and other aspects.

The study of the capitalist economic crisis in the general sense is mainly the investigation of the structure and system of the Marxist theory of economic crisis. What are involved include: the possibility and reality of the economic crisis; cyclical economic crises; commercial crisis; credit crisis; agricultural crisis; consequences of the economic crisis; economic crisis in monopoly period. Related writings are mainly the following: *Economic Crisis in Capitalist Countries*. (Xinhua Newsletter Collection Press, 1950), *The Economic Crisis and the Cold War* (James S. Allen et al., 1950) *Capitalist Economic Crisis* (Wu Chengxi, 1954), *Lecture on Political Economics, A Textbook (Lecture 18)*: *Economic Crisis* (Hong Jingming, 1956), *National Revenue, Reproduction of Social Capital and Economic Crisis under the Capitalist System* (Su Shaozhi, 1956), *Capitalist Reproduction and Economic Crisis* (Ji Taoda, 1956), *"Lecture on Political Economics, A Textbook (Lecture 5): Economic Crisis,* Capitalist Reproduction and Economic Crisis (Chen Zheng, 1957) *The Issue of Capitalist Economic Crisis after World War II* (Guang Mengjue, 1957), *What Is the Capitalist Economic Crisis* (Li Songke, 1957), *Economic Crisis* (Leontiev, 1957), *On Economic Crisis by Marx, Engels, Lenin and Stalin,* (Peking University, Department of Economics, 1958), *Capitalism's Terminal Illness – Economic Crisis* (Yao Tinggang, 1960), *The Capitalist Economic Crisis* (Shi Qiao et al., 1964). In order to facilitate the general reader to understand the Marxist crisis theory, Chinese scholars also excerpted and published *On Economic Crisis by Marx, Engels, Lenin and Stalin,* (Peking University, Department of Economics, ed., 1958), and in accordance with the logical structure of the analytic model in *Political Economics, A Textbook*, they laid out of the content.

After World War II, because of its special economic, political and military status, the United States has become the focus of world attention. The research on the issue of economic crisis often takes an example of the United States, and the development trends of the U.S. economy is the focus of attention, mainly because its large economies are enough to dominate the world economy and to impact the world business cycle. Chinese scholars are very serious in the study of the U.S. economy, and the effort put into and the achievements made are more than the study of other economies. In addition to articles published in academic journals, from the early 1950s to the mid-1960s, writings special-izing in the U.S. economy are mainly as follows: *The Economic Crisis is Fatal Weakness of the U.S. Imperialism* (compiled by Xinhua Bookstore, East China branch, 1950), *The U.S. Economic Crisis* (Jiang Xuemo, 1950), *Economic Crisis in Capitalist Countries* (Xinhua Newsletter Collection Press, 1950), *The U.S. Economic Crisis Perspective* (Xie Mu, 1951), *Capitalist Reproduction and Economic Crisis* (S. F Tokmalaev 1951), *On the U.S. Economic Crisis at This Stage* (Sun Zhizhong, 1955), *The Current U.S. Economic Crisis* (Ji Long, 1958), *Today's U.S. Economic Crisis"* (Shi Keming, 1958), *On the U.S. Economic Crisis: Proceedings* (compiled and translated by International Relations Institute, Academy of Sciences, 1958), *About the U.S. Economic Crisis* (Wu Dakun, 1958), *The Reproduction Process and Economic Crisis in the Postwar United States,* (Lu Zhaohuang, 1958), *The U.S. Economic Crisis and Capitalist World Economy,* (compiled and translated by International Relations Institute, Academy of Sciences, 1958), *The U.S. Economic Crisis* (Li Weiyi, 1958), *Keynesian and the U.S. Economic Crisis* (George Sisking, 1959), *About the U.S. Economic Crisis* (Mao Liqing, 1959), *State Monopoly Capitalism and the U.S. Economic Crisis* (Guan Mengjue, 1961), *The Capitalist Economic Crisis* (Shi Qiao et al., 1964).It has already been a very remarkable achievement given the condition of the shortage of information and the restric-tion of academic exchanges.

III. The Root Cause and the Specific Causes of the Economic Crisis

Before the 1990s, on the reason of the capitalist economic crisis, the un-derstanding of the vast majority of Chinese scholars was stuck at the level of essential relationship. They have preferred to inquire the fundamental reason rather than the specific reasons, and when they inquired the reason of the capi-talist economic crisis, it was linked to the basic contradictions of capitalism; when the basic contradictions of capitalism was inquired it was linked to its two specific forms; when its two specific forms was debated, it was generally suggested that the specific causes of the capitalist economic crisis lay in the "restricted consumption of the masses" and "disproportionality". When ana-lyzing the real capitalist economic crisis of capitalism, to determine the attri-bute of the crisis many scholars tend to think as whether these two causes can be educed, and if the answer is yes, then it is the capitalist economic crisis; if the answer is no, then either they will say there is an error in argumentation and analysis, or it is not the capitalist economic crisis. Moreover, if a crisis is considered to be the capitalist economic crisis, only the root cause can be discussed, while any other causes should not be educed. As long as others tend to believe that the crisis is caused by more specific reasons such as policy mistakes or due to excessive speculation, they will think such an analysis and conclusion is non-Marxist, which should resolutely be denied. They even think such a conclusion is the negation of the Marx's theory of the economic crisis. Due to such reasons, very few Chinese scholars have explored the specific reasons of the capitalist economic crisis, and in addition, on the issue of the root cause of the crisis, they haven't gone beyond persisting, defending and explaining the classical Marxist crisis theory.

For the root reason of the economic crisis of capitalism, the majority of domestic political economics textbooks have adopted such a form of expression: the reason of the capitalist economic crisis lies in the basic contradiction of capitalism. This contradiction manifests itself as the contradiction between the organized and planned character of production in individual enterprises and the anarchy of production in the whole society, as well as the contradiction between the trend of unlimited expansion of production and the limitedness of effective demand of the working people, the intensification of these two contradictions will inevitably lead to the outbreak of the economic crisis. In the mid-1980s, Lai Fengchen has questioned this argument. He has argued that such a statement is too ambiguous; he asked: "is it the simultaneous intensification of the basic contradiction in its two specific realization forms that leads to the outbreak of the overproduction crisis (theory of binary-combination)? Or is it the intensification in any one of the two forms that leads to the outbreak of the overproduction crisis (dualistic theory)? Or is it the intensification of the certain specific realization form that leads to the outbreak of the crisis of overproduction? An accurate answer to these should be given."[2]

Lai Fengchen suggested that: "the root reason of the capitalist economic crisis of overproduction, Marx has insistently advocated is neither based on dualism nor binary-combination, instead he regarded "the contradiction between the trend of unlimited expansion of production and the constrained effective demand of the working people" as the root cause. Therefore Marx wrote:"Then, a crisis could only be explained as the result of a disproportion of production in the various branches of the economy, and as a result of a disproportion between the consumption of the capitalists and their accumulation. But as matters stand, the replacement of the capital invested in production depends largely upon the consuming power of the non-producing classes; on the other side the consuming power of the workers is limited partly by the (development) laws of wages, partly by the fact that they are used only as long as they can

434

---

2 Lai Fengchen, *The Correct Understanding of Marxist Theory on the Root Reason for the Capitalist Economic Crisis to Occur*, in *Journal of Lanzhou University* (Social Sciences Edition), 1986(1).

be profitably employed by the capitalist class. The ultimate reason for all real crises always remains the poverty and restricted consumption of the masses as opposed to the drive of capitalist production to develop the productive forces as though only the absolute consuming power of society constituted their limit."[3] Engels, Lenin and Stalin have argued that the root reason for the outbreak of the capitalist economic crisis of overproduction is neither dualism nor binary-combination theory, but the contradiction between the unlimited expansion trend of production and the reduced effective demand of the working people.

The contradiction between the unlimited expansion trend of production and the reduced demand for the ability to pay of the working people is the root reason for the outbreak of the capitalist economic crisis of overproduction, in Lai Fengchen's opinion, this is because on the one hand there is an objective necessity of the trend of unlimited expansion of production in capitalism; on the other hand, it requires a growing market to achieve the purpose of capitalist production. The essential requirement that capital pursues the surplus value to the maximum, as well as the pressure from the competition among many capitals, forced the capitalists to do everything possible to develop production capacity and expand production scale. The effect of the law of rate of profit to fall also contributes to that fact that the capitalists are trying to expand production and to improve technology in order to get compensation, which in turn reinforces this trend, and in the same time, the development of the credit system and the application of new science and technology in production, also create objective conditions for the unlimited expansion of production. This requires addressing market issues, that market issues are not restricted by the consumption demand of the general society, but by effective demand in the society. That is to say, the effective demand is always restricted in an extremely narrow limit relative to the growth of production. This narrow limit is mainly the value of labour goods. Because the working class is mainly reflected as the purchasing power in the capitalist society, and the purchasing power of the working class does not depend on their consumption needs, but on the value of labour goods sold. The value of labour goods is the limit of the effective demand. The existence of a lot of relative surplus population has largely restricted the effective demand, and in addition, the competition of the relative surplus population with workers, which reduces the wage of workers sometimes, is also a factor that restricts the effective demand. In this way, it will inevitably lead to the contradiction between the unlimited expansion trend of production and the reduced the effective demand of the working people.

435

The contradiction between the organization of production of individual enterprises and the anarchy of production in the whole society will inevitably cause disproportionality, and when it reaches a serious proportion, the economic crisis of overproduction will erupt, but disproportionality can cause partial crisis in individual sectors without causing the widespread economic

---

3   Marx and Engels, *Collected Works*, 1st Chinese edition, Volume 25, Beijing, People's Publishing House, 1974, pp. 547-548.

crisis of overproduction in the society as a whole. Because the total quantity of social labour is an established quantity for a certain period of time, if there is disproportionality, it means that some sectors put too much labour, so that the production will be too much and it will lead to overproduction, while other sectors will correspondingly put less quantity of labour, so that these sectors will produce less due to the excessive production in some other sectors, and therefore it will not form the general economic crisis of overproduction in the whole society. As for the relationship between this contradiction and the economic crisis of overproduction, Lai Fengchen thinks that it mainly plays a role of accelerating the outbreak of the economic crisis and exacerbating the severity of the economic crisis. Because, 1) in the anarchy of production, the development of capitalist business and credit conditions often conceals the true purchasing power, resulting in a false demand, and when commodities in production have a large backlog, the capitalists are confused with the superficial economic prosperity, and still continue to expand production, which exacerbates the trend of unlimited expansion of production, 2) the disproportionality caused by the anarchy of capitalist production will lead to the formation of partial crisis in some sectors or certain individual sectors, the decline in the purchasing power to a certain extent caused by which, will also accelerate the eruption of the general economic crisis of overproduction and exacerbate the severity of the outbreak and crisis. However, it is not the reason for the widespread economic crisis of overproduction.

436

Wu Dakun insists that the common effect of "the contradiction between production and consumption" and "the anarchy of production" causes the capitalist economic crisis. It is first and foremost based on a passage from Lenin's *A Characterization of Economic Romanticism* written in 1897. Lenin said: "The two theories of which we are speaking give totally different explanations of crises. The first theory explains crises by the contradiction between production and consumption by the working class; the second explains them by the contradiction between the social character of production and the private character of appropriation. ... To put it more briefly, the former explains crises, by underconsumption, the latter by the anarchy of production. ... But the question is: does the second theory deny the fact of a contradiction between production and consumption; does it deny the fact of underconsumption? Of course not. It fully recognizes this fact, but puts it in its proper, subordinate place as a fact that only relates to one department of the whole of capitalist production. It teaches us that this fact cannot explain crises, which are called forth by another and more profound contradiction that is fundamental in the present economic system, namely, the contradiction between the social character of production and the private character of appropriation."[4] In the same article, Lenin also pointed out: the expressions of "anarchy of production" and "unplanned production" refers to the "the contradiction between the social character of production and

4   *Collected Works of Vladimir Lenin*, 2nd Chinese edition, Volume 2, Beijing: People's Publishing House. 1984, pp. 136-137.

the individual character of appropriation".[5] But these views of Lenin were later ignored by Stalin. In the Political Report of the Central Committee to the Sixteenth Congress of the C.P.S.U.(B.) in 1930, Stalin claimed: "the root reason of the crisis lies in the contradiction between socialization of production and the capitalist private ownership" and he identified the manifestation of this contradiction only as the contradiction between the huge growth in the capitalist production capacity and the relative reduction in the effective demand of the working people.[6] He did not mention the other manifestation of this contradiction pointed out by Engels and argued with emphasis by Lenin. This one-sided understanding of Stalin had a significant impact on the studies of capitalist economic crisis, including those in Chinese academy when studying economic crisis theory of the post-war capitalism they have only emphasized the contradiction between production and consumption, while completely ignored other contradictions, especially the contradiction of the anarchy of production.

Mr. Xue Jingxiao has argued that the direct cause of the business cycle is the contradiction between production and marketing, which is reflected in changes in the rate of profit through cost, price, sales and several other indicators, and the rate of profit is guiding production towards expansion and contraction, so that the economy is also in cyclical changes. Fluctuation in investment is more active than that in GNP. In general, the investment cycle and the business cycle are consistent, but the investment cycle sometimes takes precedence. Therefore, investment is one of the important factors that affect the business cycle. With the effect of the accelerator principle, the smaller changes in consumption can have a greater impact on investment, which lead to a series of chain effects of consumption to investment, investment to investment, investment to consumption, increase in consumption to further expansion and so on, so that consumption has an important impact on the development of the process of business cycle. Because of this, consumption has become an important factor affecting the business cycle, and its changes constitute an important part of the internal mechanism of the cycle. To this end, Mr. Xue Jingxiao further points out that the regular fluctuation of the capitalist economy is determined by its internal mechanism. Its internal mechanism refers to profitability, investment, consumption, industrial production, business, money credit and other factors, which have cyclical changes and interaction with its own laws, so that the capitalist business cycle exhibits the general regularity. In addition to the effect of its own force, the fluctuation in business cycle is also affected by many external accidental factors. These external accidental factors are: large-scale war, poor harvests, oil crisis, trade frictions, political events, government policy regulation, and etc. because of the impact of these external accidental factors on the operation of business cycle, the business cycle shows irregular and unique feature. This unique feature manifests outstandingly in the post-war

5   *Collected Works of Vladimir Lenin*, 2nd Chinese edition, Volume 2, p. 137.
6   See Political Report of the Central Committee to the Sixteenth Congress of the C.P.S.U.(B.), in *Collected Works of Joseph Stalin*, Vol. 12, Beijing: People's Publishing House 1955.

time. Due to the development of the state monopoly capitalism, government intervention in economics is strengthened, and especially with the implementation of a variety of counter-cyclical policies, the post-war capitalist business cycle operations have undergone many new changes and new features. This is the particularity of the business cycle. The capitalist business cycle is the unity of necessity and contingency, as well as of generality and particularity. For the cyclical fluctuation in the capitalist economy, each cycle roughly passes through the same process, which is the generality of the business cycle. The length, process, fluctuation of each cycle is not exactly the same, which is particularity of the cycle. Therefore, neither the capitalist business cycle is likely to disappear, nor it is possible to come as accurate as the clockwork, but increasingly profound. The study should focus on the general laws, and should pay attention to the analysis of specific reasons as well.

IV. The Transmission Mechanism of the Crisis

To reveal the transmission mechanism of the crisis is one of the important tasks when studying the capitalist economic crisis. Marx has revealed the most abstract, the most general form of the transmission mechanism of the economic crisis. But because he did not provide a systematic discussion of the state, foreign trade, world market, and other specific aspects, so he did not have the specific examination of the international transmission mechanism of the capitalist economic crisis. The study of the international transmission mechanism of the capitalist economic crisis is an important research topic in Marxism after the death of Marx. The classical transmission mechanism of the political economy is roughly developed along this path: economic prosperity (supply in short, strong price, high rate of profit) – a significant increase in business inventories – reduction in the stock of commercial sectors – increase in inventories of finished goods in department II – reduction in production in department II – increase in inventories of finished goods in department I – reduction in production in department I – unemployment and falling wages – decline in social purchasing power – further increase in stocks – occurrence of crisis of overproduction – business acquisition equal to sales – reduction in inventories – industrial recovery growth – increase in business inventories – increase in inventories of finished goods in department II – increase in production in department I – economy into boom stage… On this basis, Chinese scholars Xue Jingxiao has made a further study, and in *The Capitalist Business Cycle – Theory and Prediction*, he devoted a chapter (Chapter VI) discussing the international transmission mechanism of the business cycles through economic relations. Xue Jingxiao believes that this transmission mechanism enables the economic fluctuation of one country to have an impact on the economic fluctuation of another country, and in this process, the effect of a small number of core countries is particularly important, whose economic boom and economic crisis will spread to other countries, thus forming the world economic crisis. The author also analyzes that, the diffusion mechanism of the business cycle is the process of the interaction between national economies, and the economic expansion in these countries leads to the economic growth in other countries, while the economic expansion in other countries, in turn, stimulates and strengthens further economic expansion in these countries. Instead, the reduction in the investment in these countries will cause its economic contraction, which will spread to other countries through the transmission mechanism of international trade. The economic contraction in other countries also causes a reduction in their own national revenue and the decline in imports, and will further exacerbate their economic contraction or further recession. In other words, economic fluctuation in some countries gradually spread to other countries through changes in the import and export volume in the international trade of these countries, causing fluctuation in the economy of other countries, which in turn strengthens the economic fluctuation in these countries, and further strengthens the international proliferation of the economic fluctuation in these countries through the continuing effect of the trade mechanism. A country's international trade is affected by the changes in the world-wide demand, and in turn it will affect a country's business cycle. For those countries whose business cycle is just at the starting point of expansion and the end point of recession, the increase in exports caused by changes in the world market will become the external driving force of economic expansion in these countries. For those countries whose business cycle is already in the process of expansion or upswing, the changes in world market demand will slow the economic crisis and recessive pressures, and may even reverse its economic crisis and recession, thus changes the original track of the business cycle in this country. Conversely, if the changes in the world market demand lead to the reduction in exports in these concerned countries, then this change in the world market demand will have contractive effects on the original track of the business cycle. Because of this, during the crisis stage, the developed capitalist countries seek to increase exports by dumping goods, in order to pass the crisis to other countries. In the long term, the deterioration of trade condition will have contractive effects on a country's business cycle by affecting the balance of payments. Because the short-term excessive economic expansion caused by the deterioration in the trade condition will inevitably result in the deterioration of the balance of payments, which will force the government to adopt austerity policies and measures when it reaches a certain degree, causing a recession in the economy. With the expansion of the austerity policies and measures implemented, the economic recession becomes a cumulative process. Due to the inherent inertia of the business cycle in operation, the economy in the process of austerity will move toward crisis and depression. Tariffs and trade barriers have effects on the business cycle from both the international and domestic aspects. The implementation of tariffs and trade barriers will produce an expansionary force in the domestic economy, and can be used as a leverage as well. In the crisis and recession phases of the business cycle, it consciously raises tariffs and increases trade barriers; in the recovery and upswing phases of the business cycle, it consciously reduces tariffs and trade barriers. These measures will contribute to the normal operation of the national economy. Under certain conditions, the expansionary force to the economic system derived from tariffs and trade barriers could be an important factor for the business cycle to move from recession to prosperity. However, the implementation of tariffs and trade barriers is contractionary as the whole world is concerned. In terms of a country, if the development of the world economy undergoes ups and downs, it might be conducive to its economic operation to raise tariffs when the market condition deteriorates and to reduce tariffs when it gets better, in order to prevent external shocks. However, if all countries in the world implement such a policy at the same time, it will result in more severe depression in the world. Similarly, in the upswing phase of the business cycle, reduction of tariffs and of trade barriers would lead to excessive expansion of the economy. If all countries in the world implement such a policy at the same time, then the expansionary force of countries is subject to further stimulation. The transportation cost is also one of the transmission factors affecting the economic crisis.

The serious imbalance of international payments in capitalist countries and the dramatic changes in the national currency exchange rate it causes will cause fluctuations in the import or export of countries concerned, in turn this will cause changes in its domestic economy and in the business cycle. The adjustment of the balance of payments will promote a country's business cycle to transmit and spread to other countries. Mr. Xue Jingxiao describes the realization model and the realization mechanism of this process in his writings.

1. The Transmission Type of Surplus or Deficit in Balance of Payments

If a country's current account is in the state of surplus, on the one hand the accumulated trade surplus will bring pressure on the appreciation of the national currency, and on the other hand a lot of exports will bring greater economic expansion effects on the country. Out of the necessity to eliminate the adverse effects, the country must either increase imports or expand the export of capital, in order to adjust the balance of payments. However, the simple increase in imports or expansion in export of capital will bring contractionary effect on the economy, resulting in domestic economic recession. Therefore, in increasing the imports, the domestic demand must be expanded and the domestic investment must be increased correspondingly; at the same time, in expanding the export of capital, exports must be increased correspondingly. Thus, in the adjustment process of the surplus countries, on the one hand as the expansion of the domestic consumption and investment demand has driven the increase in imports of the country, thus it contributes to the economic growth of other countries in the world. On the other hand, the increase in the export of capital drives the expansion of the country's exports, and increases the supply of capital in other countries, becoming the factor of the falling rate of interest in other countries, thus it is in favour of the expansion of domestic investment and of the economy in other countries of the world. Therefore, surplus countries of the international balance of payments pass and spread their economic expansion to other countries and regions in the world through its balance of payments adjustment occasion, while ensuring their continued economic expansion. Conversely, if a country's balance of payments is always in a state of trade deficit, the economy will gradually be in contraction. In order to reduce the deficit of the balance of payments, the country will compress its domestic demand, reduce imports, and raise the rate of interest to attract foreign capital inflows. With the decrease in domestic demand, the investment is reduced accordingly, so the country's economy starts to shrink, with the reduction in imports, limiting the export of other countries, so that the economy of other countries tends to decline due to the reduction in exports. At the same time, with the increase in the domestic rate of interest, the domestic investment begins to shrink, aggravating the domestic economic contraction, which has attracted capital inflows from other countries, resulting in reduction in the supply of domestic capital of other countries accordingly, so that the rate of interest in other countries will also be improved, thus hindering their economic expansion. Thus the deficit countries in the balance of payments pass and spread their economic contraction or recession to other countries through the adjustment of their balance of payments.

2. The Transmission Type of Interest and Exchange Rates

Since each country has a different balance of payments structure, surplus countries will have excess funds with the rate of interest tending to fall, while deficit countries are usually in short of funds, thus the rate of interest tending to rise. Since the deficit in balance of payments pressures a decline in exchange rate, the surplus will lead to the rise in exchange rate. Therefore, the rate of interest will be affected by the changes in the exchange rate. In general, when a country's economy is in the late stage of upswing, due to the economic expansion and a substantial increase in imports in the previous stage, the balance of payments deteriorates, thereby resulting in a domestic shortage of funds, rise in the interest rates, and downward trend in domestic investment and consumption demand, namely the economy turns to contraction. The fast decline in the exchange rates further aggravates the economic contraction. With the economic contraction and recession, imports would be reduced and coupled with suppression of imports and stimulation of exports by devaluation, balance of payments will gradually be improved, thus forming surplus. Surplus in balance of payments will result in the excess domestic funds and the decrease in the rate of interest. The decrease in the rate of interest stimulates the domestic demand and the domestic investment to expand; while the rise in exchange rate formed with the surplus in balance of payments further stimulates the domestic demand, increases imports, increases the import supply of a variety of raw materials and energy, thus promoting the economy to expand.

Deficit in balance of payments will lead to economic contraction in deficit countries, the decline in the exchange rate of the country led by the deficit in balance of payments encourages the exports, discourages imports of the country and promotes the inflow of foreign capital, while passing the contraction tendency of the cycle to other countries by affecting the rest of the world so that there are exports reduction and capital outflows. On the other hand, surplus in balance of payments will lead to economic expansion in surplus countries, and transfer the expansion tendency of business cycle to other countries through the increase in imports and capital outflows caused by the increase in the exchange rate of surplus countries, so that exports and money supply of other countries increase. If the economy of countries in the world is in the different stages of the cycle respectively, then the effect of the international transmission on business cycle by changes in the exchange rate will be likely to change the progression of business cycle in the countries concerned, postponing or accelerating the operation of the business cycle of the countries concerned.

3. The Transmission Type of Hard Currency

When such a country employs the fixed exchange rate policy, it also means its currency can play key role in the world markets, this makes the cyclical economic fluctuation of this country cause a significant impact on the track of business cycles of the other countries. Namely, the cyclical expansion in this country's economy affects and spreads to other countries of the world. For example U.S.A. is such a country, when its economy is in the expansion phase of the cycle, this country increases the supply of dollars to other countries by increasing its imports, and this policy not only increases the foreign exchange reserves of other countries, but also brings expansionary impact on their economies. When the U.S. economy is in the contraction phase of the cycle, it reduces the supply of dollars to other countries by reducing its imports. This policy not only reduces the reserves of other countries, but also brings contractionary impact on their economies.[7]

Moreover, if a country's currency has the status of key currency, and faces external balance of payments deficits, a tightening monetary policy does not necessarily have to be adopted; instead this deficit can be narrowed by the expansion of money supply and by pouring more currency to the world markets. In a certain period of time and to a certain extent, this policy can cause an expansionary stimulation for the world economy. This policy not only causes inflation domestically but also spreads the inflation to other countries because of the expansion of the money supply and the output of the national currency. Under the floating exchange rate regime, the economic policy adopted is more flexible than before, and governments can implement capital management and adopt the monetary policy to influence the exchange rate through the official intervention in the foreign exchange market. It can either prevent or mitigate to some extent the short-term fluctuations in the exchange rate, so as to prevent the market chaos, or it can counteract the adverse long-term trends in changes

7   **Hard currency or strong currency** is any globally traded currency that is expected to serve as a reliable and stable store of value. Factors contributing to a currency's hard status might include the long-term stability of its purchasing power. Conversely, a soft currency indicates a currency which is expected to fluctuate erratically or depreciate against other currencies.

in the exchange rate, strengthening the adjustment effect of various economic policies on the domestic economy and balance of payments, thereby slowing the shocks of external forces on the national economy. Especially through joint intervention and regulation of the exchange rate, countries can stabilize the foreign exchange and prevent the international transmission of inflation to a certain extent.

4. The Transmission Type of International Capital

If a country's economy is in the expansion phase of the cycle, as the expansion progresses, domestic demand and investment becomes increasingly strong. However, when the progress of economic expansion reaches a certain moment, the domestic demand for capital is bound to exceed the domestic supply of capital in the country. Then if there is no foreign capital inflow, the strong domestic demand and investment in the country will inevitably promote the rise in the rate of interest. The rise in the rate of interest will dampen domestic demand and investment, thus inhibiting the further expansion of the economy. The foreign capital inflows increases the supply of capital in the country, mitigates the shortage of the domestic funds and the rise in the rate of interest in the country. Thus it is able to maintain strong domestic demand and investment, so as to further promote and strengthen the expansion of the domestic economy, until it reaches an upswing. Conversely, if a country's economy is in the contraction phase of the cycle, the domestic demand and investment is reduced with the contraction of the domestic economy, forming the excessive supply of domestic capital. On the one hand, excess capital will flow to other countries in seeking profits; on the other hand, since the supply of capital is greater than the demand for capital, the rate of interest falls. The falling rate of interest will stimulate the growth of the domestic demand and investment, which helps the economy out of crisis toward recovery. However, due to the impact of capital outflows, without capital flows the rate of interest decline is less , and the result is that capital flows to some extent hinders the economy moving toward recovery. Of course, if the international flows of capital are not because of changes in the business cycle progression in all countries of the world, but because of speculation or avoiding the risk, the international flows of capital will exacerbate the economic fluctuation around the world, will hinder or reverse the process of the business cycle around the world. In the case of massive speculative capital or capital fight, the world can easily adopt contractionary economic policies. In countries of capital outflows, in order to avoid large capital fight, the monetary authority will raise the rate of interest; in countries of capital inflows, in order to prevent inflation caused by large capital inflows, the monetary authority will also adopt contractionary economic policies. Thus, the international flows of capital have had a negative impact on the implementation of the macro-control policies. With acceleration of the pace of economic globalization, many countries have achieved financial liberalization, promoting the international flows of capital, and strengthening the international transfer and diffusion of the business cycle. Because, under the condition of bank credit and internationalization of banking business, the international capital, as an external force, has played a role of fuelling the cyclical fluctuation as well as the international transfer and diffusion. The international capital in the economy of the international credit system has a huge amount and rapid liquidity, and is extremely sensitive to changes in the rate of interest, exchange rate, risk and other factors. Any sign of trouble in the world economy will affect this part of the huge international capital to flow from one country to another or a country's currency to be converted into another country's currency, so that the rate of interest and the exchange rate of the relevant countries will have substantial changes. These changes will inevitably lead to changes in the money supply, so that the economy will have more serious fluctuation, and this economic fluctuation will spread to other countries in the world through trade transmission mechanism in the international economic relations.

5. Transmission Type of International Trade

Changes in the export or import of countries of strong economy will lead to the transfer and spread of the expansion or contraction of the business cycle from one country another. Assume that the economy of Country A is at the expansion phase, and that of Country B is at the contraction phase; due to the economic expansion, capital of Country A is in short supply, and due to the economic contraction, capital of Country B is in excess, so capital will flow from Country B to Country A, promoting and strengthening the original economic expansion in Country A. The investment demand, consumption demand and public spending of Country A will be further stimulated, and imports will continue to increase. In Country B, the increase in the import of Country A drives the export of Country B. The capital outflow from Country B ultimately promotes and drives the increase in its export. Thus, along with the capital export of Country B is the increase in export of Country B. The increase in export of Country B will slow the economic contraction of Country B, or promote the transition of Country B from the contraction process to the expansion process. So that the process of the economic expansion in Country A transfers and spreads to Country B. The result is that the process of business cycle in relevant countries tends to synchronize. If the economic ties between Country A and Country B are not close, with less amount of trade, the flow of capital from Country B to Country A will not be able to drive the increase in the export of Country B. Capital flows often accelerate the economic contraction of Country B, and abort the international diffusion and transfer of the international flows on business cycle. If the economic relations and trade in the world are restricted, such as in some countries, while it increases its trade barriers or tariffs with the input of capital, then the export of capital-exporting countries will not increase, the international transfer and diffusion effect of the international flow of capital on business cycle will also be weakened.[8]

8   See Xue Jingxiao, *The Capitalist Business Cycle – Theory and Prediction*, Beijing, People's Publishing House, 1992, pp. 252-273.

V. Intermediate Crisis, Structural Crisis

The capitalist production process is composed of large and small waves on the chart. It includes a few waves of ups and downs and many ripples in the middle of these waves. In the calculation of cycle length, leaving aside the tiny fluctuations in production, the key is to distinguish between the cyclical economic crises and the intermediate crises occurring in between. Originally, in theory, it is not a problem, because through the analysis and discussion of the capitalist economic crisis in the 19th century, it had already been found that, Marx and Engels did not consider every economic crisis occurring at the time to be the cyclical economic crisis, but drew a clear division between cyclical and the intermediate crises. In *Capital* Volume I Marx referred to "decennial cycle (interrupted by smaller oscillations" following each other "more and more quickly" as accumulation advanced. And Marx called some crises as "partial crisis", and suggested that "general periodic crises are always preceded by such partial ones."[9] Engels called some crises "intermediate crisis", considering that the intermediate crisis in which "some being of a more localised and some of a more specialised character"[10] is a powerful crisis of aftermath. According to the argument of Marx and Engels, periodic crises and intermediate crises both have similarities and differences, and the two cannot be equated. Their similarities are: both are produced by the basic contradiction of capitalism, and are in essence the crisis of overproduction. Their differences are: 1) The cyclical economic crisis is the end of the pervious business cycle and the beginning of the next business cycle, while the intermediate crisis is the one occurring in the depression, recovery or upswing phase of a cycle, where it is either the precursor of the cyclical crisis or the "aftermath" of the cyclical crisis, it is the "intermediate link" in the process of development of the business cycle. 2) The cyclical crisis is the universal crisis in the capitalist economy, and it is the "concentrated exposure" or total outbreak of all the contradictions in the capitalist production, while the intermediate crisis tends to be partial crisis.

445

The premise to accurately determine the cyclical crisis and the intermediate crisis is to accurately define the concept of the two. Is it the cyclical economic crisis, or the intermediate crisis? Chinese scholars generally looking at whether it experiences the renewal of fixed capital to decide, think that all economic crises associated with the cyclical renewal of fixed capital are the cyclical economic crisis, because the turnover of fixed capital is the material basis for the cyclical crisis. In the period of the outbreak of the crisis, the investment in fixed capital must decline substantially. The intermediate crisis has the following characteristics: 1) the intermediate crisis is shallow in depth and short in duration and it is the intermission of the recovery and upswing process in the industrial cycle. 2) The intermediate crisis is just a "partial crisis", involving

---

9   Marx and Engels, *Collected Works*, 1ˢᵗ Chinese Edition, Volume 33, Beijing: People's Publishing House, 1973, p. 609.
10   Marx and Engels, *Collected Works*, 1ˢᵗ Chinese Edition, Volume 35, Beijing: People's Publishing House, 1971, p. 259.

only part of the industrial sectors or part of the industrial areas, which is not universal. 3) The intermediate crisis is not necessarily connected with the periodical material basis of the renewal of fixed capital on a massive scale, and it is often triggered by certain accidental factors, such as war, political events, and oscillations in the financial sector caused by excessive speculation, and so on. 4) The intermediate crisis is not cyclical. However, in time of rapid development of the productive forces and the abnormally acute market issues, the intermediate crisis is prone to occur, and it is often an intermediate link of the cyclical crisis, or the aftermath of the cyclical crisis, or a precursor of the cyclical crisis. 5) The decline in a country's production does not synchronize with the decline in the production of other countries.

According to the above criteria, some scholars believe that the decline of production in the United States during 1953-1954 and in 1960-1961 should be evaluated as the intermediate crisis rather than the cyclical crisis. Because, in both crises, the decline in industrial production level, or the decrease in the fixed capital investment level was not large, and before both of the crises, there was no significant cyclical upswing; The 1953-1954 crisis was induced by the armistice of the Korean War, besides by the sudden decrease in the U.S. military production; when 1953-1954 and the 1960-1961 crisis had occurred in the United States, other major capitalist countries were not encountered with the cyclical economic crisis except for a few.

446 Since the 1970s, with the emergence of the "stagflation" situation in the capitalist economy, the protracted structural crisis situation has attracted people's attention more and more. One of the common characteristics of the 1974-1975 and the 1980-1982 world economic crises is that the structural crisis and the cyclical crises of overproduction are intertwined and mutually influence each other; consequently this combination not only deepens the economic crisis, but also exacerbates the structural crisis. Zheng Weimin suggests that the structural crisis in contemporary capitalism mainly refers to the crisis with an international dimension caused by significant changes in structures (including the structural relations between sectors and within sectors) of the material production sectors in the capitalist economy, as well as by the long term disproportionality between production and consumption, and between supply and demand. The structural crisis is a crisis of independent implication occurring within the capitalist economic system, and it is regarded as a manifestation that the crisis in the post-war capitalist world economic system has been deepened, but not vice versa. Except the cyclical economic crisis, all economic crises or crisis phenomena occurring within the scope of the capitalist world economy somehow possess the nature of structural crisis. The structural crises and the cyclical economic crises are both connected and distinct. Specifically, the differences are reflected as follows: firstly, the root cause of the cyclical economic crises lies in the contradiction between the unlimited expansion trend of production and the reduced effective demand of the working people. But the structural crisis can be caused by various reasons, such as significant changes in the economic

structure of capitalism, dramatic changes in the structure of consumer demand, external economic factors, etc., which can be a direct impulse causing a structural crisis. Second, the business cycle characterized by overproduction generally encounters four stages as the crisis, recession, recovery and boom, and the duration of crises as short as a year, or as long as three to four years, while the duration of the structural crises lasts much longer than the cyclical economic crises. Third, in any case, the cyclical economic crisis is always manifested as the crisis of overproduction, while in most cases the structural crisis manifests itself as overproduction, but in some cases it may demonstrate itself as underproduction. Fourth, when the cyclical economic crisis erupts, it tends to spread to most economic sectors, while the structural crisis spreads to a certain small number, and it only tends to affect one or a few sectors in the field of material production. Fifth, the time of the economic crisis hitting the capitalist countries is often not entirely consistent, and the time for the crisis to spread to all sectors follows a sequential order, while the structural crisis is narrow in its scope of spread, and the time for it to expand to countries is more consistent. When cyclical economic crisis occurs, the production declines from the highs before the crisis to lows, and after the crisis, in the new cycle, the production gradually recovers and exceeds the high point of the previous cycle again. When the structural crisis is developed, the production also declines, and sometimes because of the long sluggish demand, the production has remained stagnant. Some structural crises show that after the production drops from a high point, it is difficult to exceed the high point again. Sixth, the cyclical economic crisis is characterized by relative overproduction, and during the crisis, the capitalist countries tend to adopt a mandatory solution to the problem of excess production, including the destruction of surplus commodities, in order to achieve a temporary equilibrium between production and consumption, as well as between supply and demand. After the crisis, the contradictions are accumulated in other development phases of the cycle once again until the outbreak of the crisis of overproduction, and then a forcible solution is adopted to solve this conflict temporarily which cannot be fundamentally resolved in the capitalist system. The structural crisis is also manifested as a large number of overproduction, in some cases, especially when it is concurrently intertwined with the cyclical economic crisis, a mandatory approach will be adopted to deal with the excess commodities. However, as the structural crisis is mainly caused by significant changes in the capitalist economic structure, so that the proportion of production and consumption in certain sectors is long damaged, therefore, only when the existing economic structure is replaced by a new economic structure, or only when the damaged proportion of production and consumption regains equilibrium, the structural crisis in these sectors will be overcome. The structural crisis occurs mainly in the traditional industrial sectors, and is usually manifested in the form of the department crisis, but since these sectors are still the dominant sectors in the national economy, so the scope it spreads is not limited to one or a few sectors, but having direct and indirect effects on many sectors. A serious social consequence of the structural crisis in the capitalist world economy is that it has caused a serious structural unemployment phenomenon difficult to dissipate. An important feature that the structural unemployment manifests is that while some industrial sectors laid off large numbers of workers, other sectors could not find employees that could meet the technical and vocational training requirements.

VI. The Simultaneity and Non-Simultaneity of the World Business Cycle

The post-war world business cycle has both unity and non-unity, but the overall trend tends to unity. This is the conclusion drawn by Chinese scholars throughout their studies on the trend of the capitalist business cycles after World War II. The main purpose of discussing this problem is to explain that the capitalist business cycle not only still exists, but also gains a worldwide character; the capitalist economic system still evolves in accordance with its inherent law. Among Chinese scholars who discussed the issue of simultaneity and non-simultaneity, Mr. Xue Jingxiao's research achievements, who has published his papers in the early 1990s, offers a systematic discussion of the issue of the simultaneity and non-simultaneity, and has won greater authority, and acceptance. He believes that the simultaneity character of the economic crisis has emerged with the formation of dominant countries in the world economy. In the beginning of the early 19th century, with its great scientific and technological advances, and widespread adoption of machinery equipment, England has become the world's factory, established its dominant position in the world economy.[11]

448

In accordance with the law of regularity and particularity in the capitalist business cycle he made, Mr. Xue Jingxiao concluded that in any country, as long as the capitalist economy had considerably developed, its economy would fall into the cyclical fluctuation. In the meantime, as the international trade and the international financial transactions are playing an increasingly important role in capitalist economies, it is bound to promote the strengthening of economic ties in the world. Thus, a country's economic expansion or contraction will have a profound impact on the economy of other countries, so that the process of the business cycles of countries tends to come together, forming the world business cycle. After the formation of the world business cycle, there will be a phenomenon of the simultaneity and non-simultaneity in the business cycle of countries. The simultaneity is more a reflection of the commonness in the business cycle, while the non-simultaneity is more a reflection of the particularity in the business cycle. Therefore, the capitalist world economy is the unity of simultaneity and non-simultaneity.

We can see from Mr. Xue Jingxiao's interpretation of the simultaneity and non-simultaneity that, he regards the formation of the core countries as the prerequisite for the business cycle. In his opinion, in the entire 19 century, the

11 Xue Jingxiao, *History and Status Quo of the Business Cycles in Capitalist Countries*, (I & II), in *The Journal of Nankai Economic Studies*, 1991(1), 1991(2).

development of science and technology in England was the highest with the most developed productivity, and in terms of production or trade, compared to other countries, England had an absolute advantage to be the core country for granted. The English foreign output is mainly capital goods and manufactured goods, and the input is mainly raw materials and primary products. It is the largest exporter of capital. Thus, only the English economic fluctuation itself constitutes an important part of the fluctuation in the world economy, so that there are ups and downs in the world economy. England also affects the economic fluctuation in other countries through foreign trade, prices, and export of capital. In times of crisis, England dumps industrial products, lowers the price of primary products imported so as to reduce imports, and withdraws foreign investment. In times of boom, it carries out activities in the opposite direction. So that other countries will have the fluctuation consistent with the direction of England in market capacity, price, investment as well as production. As the scope of industrialization expands, after England, France, Germany, and the United States have become the industrial powers, but with the intensification of uneven development and internationally more intense competition. The unbalanced economic development is shown as the weakening of the simultaneity in the world business cycle when reflected in the field of economic fluctuation. During this period, the time for economic upswing and crisis of countries might not be entirely consistent, with different duration, and the depth of the business cycles is not the same as well. On the basis of Xue Jingxiao's discussion, Xue Boying[12] also had the in-depth discussion of core countries, as well as the 449 simultaneity of the economic crisis. He believes in the existence of state that dominates the world market; large-scale machine industry has occupied the dominance in the national economy; the economic dependence on the world market; the expansion of world market; many countries participate in the world market competition, these factors may explain the periodic recurrence of the business cycle, and are also able to explain the simultaneous outbreak of the crisis. In that year, when England occupied the absolute monopoly among all industrial countries and in the world market, the simultaneity of the business cycle was particularly prominent. First, the establishment of large-scale machine industry was in England, and then it spread to other countries as the sample. The English industry occupied a monopoly position in the world industry, and its industrial system had a great influence over other countries. Among them, in terms of the time limit of the renewal of fixed capital, under the technical condition at the time, other countries were roughly equal to England, and therefore, the renewal of fixed capital on a massive basis is both the material basis for the cyclical crisis, and also the material basis for the simultaneity of the crisis. In this pattern of the world economy, that countries were dependent on the world market is actually that countries were dependent on England, because England was the centre of the world market, and in a dominant position. In most cases, the expansion and contraction (especially contraction) in the

---

12   See Xue Boying, *Analysis of the Simultaneity of the Economic Crisis in the Post-War Capitalist Countries*, in *World Economy and Politics*, 1992(5).

English economy can quickly and relatively smoothly be transmitted to other countries through foreign trade and financial dealings. This transmission effect is very important regardless of the periodical or simultaneous occurrence of the crisis. The expansion of the world market and the increase in countries participating in competition is manifested as the expansion of the English influence and the enhancement of its monopoly in a considerable period of time. From the perspective of the formation of the simultaneity of the economic crisis, these are factors that play an important role. Of course, once these conditions are reversed, it will also repeat itself in the due period of the crisis and be reflected in the simultaneity. In the 19th century, the economic landscape was obvious, and thus the simultaneity was also very obvious. But entering the 20th century, the situation has changed. Compared with the period of Marx and Engels, the British monopoly in the world has been gradually replaced by the United States, however, in a considerable period of time, the United States does not have the kind of advantages that England once had, which has important implications of the development process, the length of the cycle and the simultaneity of the crisis in the capitalist business cycle.

In the early 1990s, examining the economic crisis data in the major capitalist countries since World War II, Xue Boying has asserted that the non-simultaneity of the capitalist economic crisis will be more inevitable, while the simultaneity will be more accidental. This trend will continue for a relatively long period of time. The reason is that the pattern of the capitalist world economy and factors that affect the reproduction cycle have undergone great changes, and only a few new important factors have emerged which could affect the simultaneity of the economic crisis.

First, in a considerable period of time after World War II, the monopolistic dominance of the U.S in the capitalist world economy has been greatly enhanced, and by virtue of its economic, political and military strength rapidly gained after its victory in World War II U.S has controlled many international economic organizations, besides it played a greater dominant role in the entire world economy through a variety of "aid" programs. However, this trend could not last forever, and at least since the beginning of 1970s, the world economic pattern has encountered significant changes, and economic multi-polarity has become an inevitable trend. In those days five poles has formed encompassing the whole world, and three of the poles were in the capitalist system, which meant that the sole American monopoly was broken, and its sole monopoly began to suffer relative decline. The trend of changes in the contest of strength does not favour the United States. In this case, the United States still has a strong economic strength on the one hand, but on the other hand it is increasingly stretched economically and faced with a dilemma. In the capitalist world, it has the most frequent crisis, and despite the U.S. trade and financial dealings with the major capitalist countries is the most practical, the crisis that it leads does not always have a strong impact on other countries. Second, the state monopoly capitalism was highly developed in all the major capitalist countries, and state intervention in the economy was unprecedentedly enhanced. All countries, without exception, were implementing measures of the Keynesian policy, but the objective of the macro-control and the policy system are not the same. This expands the differences in the development of the national economy, and exacerbates the effects of the law of the uneven political and economic development in capitalism on countries. Third, the impact of war is different on the economic development of countries. Fourth, the internationalization of the capitalist production and exchange has made great progress after World War II. However, it plays not only a catalytic role but also a destructive role in the simultaneity of the capitalist economic crisis. Finally, trade protectionism has been unprecedentedly developed in the post-war period, more refurbished in the pattern than the pre-war period. The result of these factors combined suggests that the alternating movement of expansion and contraction in the capitalist social production does not fully unfold, but will suffer greater distortion. Compared with the effects of factors that contribute to the formation of the simultaneity, factors that damage the simultaneity have greater effects.

After World War II there occurred five worldwide economic crises in Western countries; namely the 1948-1952, the 1957-1958, the 1964-1967, the 1973-1975, and the 1979-1982, and three of them have demonstrated obvious simultaneity. Before the 1960s, there was only one economic crisis in the major capitalist countries in around 1958, while two crises have erupted almost simultaneously after 1970. The other two crises were almost simultaneous in some countries when they erupted. For the economic downturn at the end of 1990, there was an obvious simultaneity. Of course, we also see that after World War II, there was also non-simultaneity between countries, especially between the United States and other countries. This is reflected in that the time of beginning and ending, as well as the duration of the crisis is not exactly the same in these countries. There are a lot of reasons for the non-simultaneity of the world business cycle. First, in the early post-war period, the economic base of countries was not the same, and the United States was not deeply affected by the War, and basically remained the normal business cycle. While Japan, France, Germany and other countries were severely destroyed by the War, and committed to the economic recovery for a long period of time after World War II. The contradiction of overproduction was accumulated slowly, which was the important reason that the simultaneity of the 1948-1952 global economic crisis was poor. Secondly, the economic environment and economic policy is different. In the mid-1960s, the United States managed to avoid an economic crisis with the expansion of Vietnam War and the expansionary policies. At that time, the United States occupied a large share in the world economy, and thus had a decisive impact on the world business cycle. Since the United States did not have crises but the post war boom in the mid-1960s, so it dramatically changed the economic environment of other countries, so that they all got through an economic crisis of non-simultaneity around 1966. In addition, we should also see that the regional economic grouping is also a factor that causes the non-simultaneity in the world business cycle, which is likely to be clearer in the future.

VII. Various Changes in Business Cycles and Its Reasons

Studying the issue of the capitalist business cycle with historical and dialectical attitude is one of the most prominent features of the Marxist theory of economic crisis. However, it is difficult for some people in reality, and they tend to regard this developing and changing theory as a perpetual creed. Under normal circumstances, the cycle of the capitalist cyclical world economic crisis should be about 10 years, and the crises occur simultaneously in the major capitalist countries. The economic crisis should be more severe in extent, and during the crisis, the economy and the price should fall. Once there are changes with new features in the real business cycle, the scholars are always reluctant to accept the reality, trying to prove that the cycle has not changed. This practice of maintaining the status quo has gradually formed a certain dogmatic standard in measuring the crisis. This situation largely confines people's thinking. As early as in the early 1960s, Wu Bannong has argued: "in order to break the shackles of some old formula related to crisis in people's thinking, we must respect the fact that the capitalist economic crises break out in about every 10 years, but in specific countries and specific crisis, the trend of the shortening cycle time trends has appeared as far as in 1880s. During the same cyclical world economic crisis, the time of beginning is not the same or consistent in different countries; the business cycle can be divided into four phases of crisis, recession, recovery and boom, but in specific countries, these four phases are not specified. Sometimes a certain phase is long in one country, but short in another; the world economic crisis does not necessarily extend to all capitalist countries, and it may not occur even in some of the major capitalist countries for exceptional circumstances; when we measure the crisis of overproduction, we regard the index of industrial production as a decisive indicator, which is unreliable; because the economic indicators of the major capitalist countries had declined by tens of percentages in the Great Depression in 1929, so when analyzing the crisis we have a tendency that the production index only fell marginally, or did not fall at all. Therefore, it should be the intermediate crisis rather than the cyclical crisis. This approach is also problematic. When we study the crisis, we must be good in grasping the overall situation, examine the contradictions from many aspects, and not rigidly or blindly follow the general idea of 10-year cycles and the idea of four phases, or be particular about whether the production has overall decline, or even be entangled in the dispute of the expression of the intermediate crisis and the cyclical crises."[13] We should carefully analyze their factual expressions to see if they are part of an intermediate crisis and the cyclical crises. These views of Wu Bannong have raised an issue worthy of reflection in the academic community: new changes in the capital business cycle should be treated dialectically.

---

13 Wu Bannong, *Some Questions about the Scale to Measure the Economic Crisis*, in *International Studies*, 1960(3).

The academic contention about the issue of changes in business cycles in the post-war era has basically formed four groups of theories, namely the theory of disappearing cycles, the theory of prolonging, the theory of unchange, and theory of shortening cycles. The renowned scholar Hu Jichuang who argues for the "theory of disappearing cycles" has written: "since the 1930s, due to the strengthening of the state intervention, the strong resistance of transnational corporations and other reasons, the fluctuation law of the mid-cycle has been disrupted. After World War II, it often presents the short wave of a period of 3-5 years, and economy is sometimes revived and sometimes weak, not showing the regular fluctuation of the mid-cycle in the past. But from the perspective of the overall trend, the capitalist economy continues to grow slowly. For example, the U.S. economy had been growing for 106 months during the Vietnam War, and since the end of 1982, it had been growing for another 80 plus months, which does not include the rapid economic growth of Japan, the former Federal Republic of Germany, and Four Asian Tigers. Faced with these facts, it poses some difficulties which cannot be overcome for the study of the western cycle theory. First, reasons that lead to each economic fluctuation are sometimes obvious and sometimes dull, but there is no common reason that dominates each economic fluctuation. If there is no such common reason, how can it form a cycle theory? Second, the period is too short to distinguish four phases, and it is even difficult to divide it into two phases of boom and depression, so some economists can only speculate whether it will turn better or worse next year subjectively, and they often estimate wrong. There is neither a peak nor a trough, let alone the crisis."[14] The above views by Mr. Hu Jichuang have received positive resonance in the Chinese academia. Those who argue for the theory of cycles prolonging generally believe that, from the historical comparative perspective, there was no sign of shortening or deterioration in the U.S. economy after World War II. On the contrary, there is a trend towards prolonging of the business cycles. In the 1970s the length of the cycle was slightly shorter, but after World War II as a whole, this period of time did not affect the overall trend. After World War II, the severity of the economic crisis in the United States was better than it was before World War II. The extension school also asserted that the capitalist economic crisis and the cycle had new changes after the 1980s. Specifically in: 1) The number of the economic crisis is reduced, but the duration is longer and more profound. 2) The business cycle restores the pre-war unity. 3) The economy grows slowly at a lower rate of inflation. 4) The interval of the economic crisis is significantly prolonged. Advocators and supporters of the extend theory are not so many.

The theory of cycles shortening is the most influential one, has many supporters who hold the same view. The first Chinese scholars who proposed the cycle theory of shortening are Xia Zhongcheng, Guang Mengjue, and they are subsequently joined by Wu Dakun. They basically hold the same viewpoint, with substantially similar basis. Xia Zhongcheng pointed out in an article

---

14   Hu Jichuang, *Analysis of Differences in Political Economy*, Shanghai, Fudan University Press, 1991, p. 212.

written in the 1950s[15] that to the eve of World War II, the interval of the industrial cycle in the capitalist world was not the usual 10-12 years, but reduced to 8 years or so; the four phases that the cycle usually has, was also disturbed by the "Special Depression" in 1930s, so that the capitalist world economy did not have time to recover and then turned to crisis. For this shortening trend of the capitalist business cycle, Guang Mengjue believes that its root reason lies in the military build-up and the development of the monopoly capitalism centered by the militarization of the national economy, so that the contradiction between the abnormal growth of production capacity and the relative reduction in the effective demand of the people has reached a very sharp extent, and therefore the cycle for the renewal of fixed capital is shortened, resulting in the shortening of the business cycle.

As the major author and the arguer of the shortening theory of the business cycle, in the early 1960s, by using the principle that the renewal of fixed capital is the material basis for the cyclical economic crisis set forth by Marx in *Capital* Volume II, Wu Dakun had the empirical studies of the renewal of fixed capital in the post-war United States. He found that there was a shortening trend in the cycle of the renewal of fixed capital, considering that he had found the basis for the U.S. business cycle to be shortened to 3-4 years in the post-war period, and had done a lot of argument in the subsequent research. Wu Dakun believes that there is a direct relationship between the capitalist cyclical economic crisis and the cyclical fluctuation in fixed capital investment, and he said that he checked all the economic crises available in the statistics of the history, and found that when the cyclical economic crisis occurred, the amount of investment in fixed capital was certainly declining in the society; more serious the crisis was, more dramatic the investment dropped. According to the principle that the renewal of fixed capital is the material basis for the cyclical economic crisis set forth by Marx in *Capital* Volume II, because he himself had studied the specific post-war development of fixed capital in the United States, the first conclusion he drew was to prove that all the post-war economic crises occurring in the United States were the cyclical crisis of overproduction, thus to prove the post-war business cycle in the United States had indeed been shortened to an average of 3-4 years, rather than the 10 years or so in the past. For the reason why the post-war business cycle in the United States had been shortened to the average 3-4 years, he asserted that the second conclusion drew from his study was that he found the case in which new machines were replaced within five years and which Marx and Engels found was not likely to occur, had become a possible reality in the United States after the Second World War. Because it was about replacement the fixed capital and a major plant can only rely on the provided rate of depreciation in the era of Marx and Engels. When it comes to the United States after World War II, the monopoly capitalists can change to the approach of "accelerated depreciation" to retake from the tax they should pay. He stressed that in *Capital* Volume II, Marx had attached great importance

15　Xia Zhongcheng, *On Several Issues of the Development of Capitalist Industrial Cycle in the Post-War Period*, in *Teaching and Research*, 1958(1).

to the different effects of the circulating component and the fixed component of capital utilized in production, namely different ratios between the two cause different capital turnover rates, and according to Marx's study, this replacement of fixed capital as value and the replacement of the elements of fixed capital in their natural forms or kind (such as machinery, tools, buildings) are inconsistent, process which is one of the contradictions of overproduction inevitably to occur in the reproduction process of the capitalist total social capital.[16] (See Marx's theory of compensation, in *Capital* Volume II.)

Because the simple reproduction of social capital is only possible under such conditions, that is, the total amount of fixed capital, which should be recovered from the natural form in a group of capitalists, equals the total depreciation of fixed capital in the form of money in another group of capitalists. The destruction of this replacement of fixed capital would make the simple reproduction of social capital impossible. But in the real capitalist society, this condition, like other conditions of the capitalist reproduction, is often destroyed. Thus in a capitalist society, there cannot always be that: on the one hand, it is a factor of the surplus fixed capital unavailable for production, and on the other hand, it is the consumer goods that cannot find a market. The difficulties and contradictions in process of the capitalist socialized reproduction as a whole, as Marx pointed out, caused by the inconsistency between the value-form and nature-form replacement of fixed capital, had reached the climax in the U.S. society after the Second World War, so that the value-form and nature-form renewal of fixed capital were completely disconnected. The monopoly capitalists who use "accelerated depreciation" have the advanced fixed capital all recovered within five years. However, for all of the fixed capital in physical form, the vast majority will continue to be used certainly after five years. Wu Dakun thinks that, the disconnection between the renewal of fixed capital in the form of value and the renewal in the physical form in the post-war United States that he studied and found, had seized the main characteristics of the reproduction process in the post-war U.S. society. After World War II, the reason why the crisis was frequent and the cycle is shortened in the United States is closely related to the main characteristics. Wu Dakun has also emphasized that the shortening of business cycles caused by the shortening turnover rate of fixed capital in the post-war United States, mainly refers to the turnover rate in the fixed capital renewals in the form of value, rather than in the physical form (in kind).

Wu Dakun also explained the reasons for the inconsistency between the renewal of fixed capital in the form of value and in the physical form in the post-war American industry. He believes that it is difficult to simply use the contradiction between the socialization of production and the capitalist private

---

16   A business executive who invests in fixed capital ties money funds in a fixed asset, hoping to make a future profit, since such an investment usually implies a risk, sometimes depreciation write-offs are also viewed partly as a compensation for this risk. Thus the wear in *value of fixed capital* is accompanied by the formation of a *compensation* fund which is called the amortization fund.

ownership to explain why in the capitalist society the economic crisis of over-production will occur periodically within a certain number of years. To clarify this issue, we need to go further, and concretely analyze the specific forms of the contradiction between the socialization of production and the capitalist private ownership. In accordance with the authoritative interpretation by Engels' Anti-Dühring, one of the specific manifestations of this contradiction is "an antagonism between the organisation of production in the individual workshop, and the anarchy of production in society generally." Because the production in the capitalist society demonstrates an anarchic nature, as Marx set forth in *Capital* Volume II that, when the total production of society is divided into two departments, the condition for the renewal of fixed capital in the two departments will certainly be destroyed periodically. As in the large industries, the turnover life of fixed capital in the most decisive sectors is certain (in Marx's time, it is ten years, and in large companies that implemented the "accelerated depreciation" in the United States after World War II, it has been reduced to five years), so in years of the economic crisis, with the premise that other conditions are the same, it is substantially constant and calculated alone by the turnover life of fixed capital, which is restricted within the range of the turnover life of the renewal of fixed capital. Because in the large industries in the United States in the post-war period, the turnover life of fixed capital in the most decisive sectors has been reduced to five years, so that in five years time, the condition for the renewal of fixed capital in two departments of the United States will certainly be destroyed once due to the development of the basic contradiction in the capitalist society, and in the one year of havoc, it is the year for the economic crisis to occur. That is the root reason why there is frequent economic crisis and shortened business cycle in the United States after World War II.

456

Evaluating the above explanations by Wu Dakun, Xue Jingxiao has argued that the explanation does not match the realities of the capitalist business cycle,[17] which led to a heated debate among them. Xue Jingxiao agreed with Wu Dakun on the view that under the condition of capitalism, the value turnover of fixed capital is inconsistent with the physical turnover, but he denied that this is the reason for the capitalist business cycle to be shortened, because the real turnover of fixed capital in capitalism follows the physical turnover rather than non-value turnover. Xue Jingxiao believes that Wu Dakun unilaterally equalizes the value turnover of fixed capital with the physical turnover, thus confusing the difference between the depreciation life and the physical renewal. The reality is that in the post-war period, except buildings, the depreciation of fixed capital apparently was duplicated, in which on the one hand, the depreciation of the majority of machinery and equipment accounted for of the most part of the depreciation of fixed capital, and the depreciation life is still an average of about nine years, while on the other hand, it is the part of fixed capital most likely to wear, represented by tools, as well as the part of

17   See Xue Jingxiao, *Renewal of Fixed Capital and Business Cycle*, in *Social Science Front*, 1984(4).

accelerated depreciation in the mechanical, both of which have accounted for a considerable proportion of fixed capital, becoming an inconsiderable part. Its durability is also not the same, with an average of about four years. Based on the depreciation duplication of fixed capital, a direct result is that the cycle of the equipment renewal is duplicated. The cycle of investment from low tide to high tide, and then from high tide to low tide, is closely interwoven with the cycle of economic crisis. The cycle of the economic crisis has become a required factor of the renewal cycle of fixed capital. The length of the renewal cycle of fixed capital is not exactly the same with the durability of fixed capital, but consistent with the business cycle. This phenomenon indicates that the renewal cycle of fixed capital on the one hand is provided by the durability of the equipment, and on the other hand is provided by the cycle of the economic crisis. The duplication phenomenon in the renewal cycle of fixed capital is bound to be reflected in the business cycle, resulting in the differences in the nature of the economic crisis. The renewal cycle of fixed capital in machinery and equipment of approximately 9 years is the material basis for part of the post-war economic crisis. This part of the post-war economic crisis erupts in around every 9 years. According to the definition by Marx, we still call them the cyclical economic crisis. Another part of the economic crisis is manifested in four or five-years' time. The renewal of fixed capital in equipment constitutes the material basis of this crisis. The increase in the short-term depreciation of fixed capital in the post-war period makes the duplication phenomenon of equipment depreciation evident, thus increasing the short-term turnover in the renewal of fixed capital correspondingly. That is to say, in the duplication phenomenon of the renewal cycle of fixed capital, for the proportion of short-term turnover and long-term turnover, the former is relatively on the rise, and the latter is relatively on the decline. This phenomenon will inevitably have an impact on the business cycle, so that the originally more evident duplication phenomenon of the business cycle becomes not so evident, and the gap between the cyclical economic crisis and the intermediate economic crisis is narrowed in depth, making it difficult to distinguish. This is because the increase in the short-term turnover in fixed capital strengthens the intermediate crisis, while the relative decline in the long-term turnover weakens the cyclical crisis.

For the issue why the capitalist economic crisis tended to be alleviated in the post-war era, Mr. Xue Jingxiao argues[18]: "it is largely the result of government intervention in the economy of the state monopoly capitalism. The reason why the state monopoly capitalism could be able to radically affect the business cycles in the post-war period is because the development of the state monopoly capitalism and its scale and functions. Firstly, the states began to control enormous economic resources, and the economic roles government assumed began to make occupy important effects in the national economy. Secondly, the bourgeois state had a relatively complete policy tool, "automatic stabilizers" policy, fiscal policy, monetary policy and income policy that could be

18 Xue Jingxiao, *History and Status Quo of the Business Cycles in Capitalist Countries*, (I & II), in *The Journal of Nankai Economic Studies*, 1991(1), 1991(2).

used upon consideration, until the international coordination, etc., so that it had a certain degree of manoeuvrability in the regulation of the total supply and the total demand. Thirdly, the development of Western economics, such as Keynesian, monetarism and supply-side economics provides a corresponding theoretical foundation for the policy measures of the state monopoly capitalism. When free competition and private monopolies are unable to grasp the capitalist economy, state monopoly emerges. One of its primary objectives is to maintain the economic stability, mitigate or even attempt to eliminate the economic fluctuation. As the total social capitalist, under the premise without changing the essence of the capitalism, the state monopoly capitalism adjusts the relations of production appropriately, which does mitigate and slow down the cycle in the post-war period. In times of crisis, by means of expansion to stimulate investment and consumption, so that production falls far less and the increase in unemployment is as small as possible, while in the upswing phase, by means of tightening to limit the growth of investment and consumption at the macro level, so that the growth in production is not excessive and the economic growth is free from overheating. As in the upswing phase, it limits the overheating of the economy and the economic growth is moderate, so that the crisis of the next stage will not come too fast, and it can be easily gone through by a certain expansionary policy.

Mr. Xue Jingxiao also affirms the role of scientific and technological development affecting the business cycle. He believes that the third scientific and technological revolution in post-war period has become the new source of the development of productive forces, and the adjustment of the relations of production and of the economic system by the state monopoly capitalism to some extent mitigates the contradiction between the productive forces and the relations of production, which provide a new impetus for the economic expansion. But the inherent contradictions of capitalism cannot be eliminated, and under the new historical conditions, not only the business cycle still exists, but the co-existence of high inflation and high unemployment has become a new phenomenon of the business cycle later the 1970s. In contrast, the post-war business cycle is gentler than it was in the pre-war period, the extent of the economic fluctuation is reduced, and the depth of the crisis is also shallower. The scientific and technological revolution and the improvement in labour productivity that it brings, helps to sustain the economic expansion for a long time, as well as helping the economy to recover from the crisis quickly. When the economic crisis comes, the rate of profit falls, the dynamic for economic expansion is weakened, while the invention and application of new technologies is able to improve labour productivity, reduce costs and enhance the competitiveness of enterprises, which enables enterprises to maintain the momentum of expanding the production. New technologies are applied to production, which is directly manifested in the investment in new plants and new advanced equipment, while the investment is the hub factor in the changes in cycle. In times of economic prosperity, the investment used in technological development constitutes one of the elements of economic expansion, and then forms a significant potential for economic development since then, while in times of economic crisis, the growth in investment in the new technology offsets the decline in investment in the traditional production, so that the crisis is eased. The development of science and technology is also reflected in the growth in research and development expenses, as well as in education expenses. In the short term, these costs are manifested as the expenditure of public and private consumption in the national revenue account, but in the long term, they are also an "investment." No matter from which point of view, they have played a role in maintaining the continuous growth of the economy and maintaining the confidence of investors.

VIII. Explanations on the "Stagflation" Phenomenon

Chinese scholars have made extensive studies on the "stagflation" phenomenon, but their focus is mainly concentrated in the nature and connotation of the "stagflation", besides on the reasons that lead to "stagflation", but failed to investigate the "stagflation" with the economic operation. The institutional analysis is its prominent feature. Results of the analysis also have great consistency, that is, it is believed that "stagflation" is a new phenomenon emerging in the development of modern capitalism, is an intensified form of expression of the basic contradiction of capitalism in the era of state monopoly capitalism, and its emergence has the objective necessity.

On the connotation of "stagflation", Chinese scholars have largely accepted the explanation by Western scholars who believe that "stagflation" is a state in which inflation and slow economic growth of the developed capitalist countries coexists. But there is also dissatisfaction that the concept of "stagflation" raised by Western scholars is only a better generalization in the phenomenon and in the shape, but does not touch the nature and the root. Therefore, the Chinese scholars believe that it is necessary to take the study further.

These are results to be considered as an in-depth study. In the 1980s, a typical view suggests that "stagflation" is a blend of economic stagnation and inflation, and its essence is a manifestation of the basic contradiction of capitalism under the condition of state monopoly capitalism, as well as a special manifestation of the economic crisis. Reasons for "stagflation" are partly the inevitability for capitalism to have the economic crisis, and partly are the negative consequences brought by the anti-crisis measures that the capitalist countries are pressing ahead.[19] Later, the study has made new progress that, some scholars believe that "stagflation" is a long and sustained economic phenomenon in the capitalist development of the state monopoly capitalism stage, rather than a short-term incidental or cyclical economic phenomenon; it is an overall and general economic phenomenon involving the developed capitalist countries."

---

19 See Wei Xun, chief editor, *Exploration on the Contemporary Capitalist Economy*, Shijiazhuang, Hebei People's Publishing House, 1988, p. 229.

It is not a superficial phenomenon, but a regular phenomenon essentially.[20] It differs from the cyclical economic crisis, being an economic law of the coexistence of the two. The inevitable "stagflation" depends on the inherent contradiction of the state monopoly capitalism: 1) the contradiction between counter crisis of the national macro-control of the economy and inevitability of the overproduction crisis; 2) the contradiction between the vast growth in expenditure and the limited revenue. The intervention in the "stagflation" phenomenon in Western countries can change the expression form of "stagflation", but cannot overcome it. When austerity policies are taken, "inflation" may be eased, but "stagnation" will become prominent; when expansionary policies are taken, "stagnation" can be eased, but "inflation" will become serious; when neutral fiscal policies are taken, it may be at the expense of something else in other aspects, but in a certain period it can improve the economic growth or lower the inflation level. However, as a general trend, in order to stimulate the economic growth, the government must carry out large-scale investment. Due to the limited financial revenue, the result is that it carries huge deficits. In order to cover the deficits, the basic approach is to raise taxes, to issue bonds and currencies, which are factors causing inflation. In order to prevent "inflation", the tight monetary policy has to be implemented, so that on the one hand the rate of price inflation is repressed, and on the other hand it leads to the direct rise in the rate of interest. The rise in the rate of interest is not conducive to business investment and production, nor conducive to consumption credit, thus–it prevent the economic growth. In order to prevent "stagnation", the tight monetary policy has to be loosened; in order to prevent "inflation", this looseness has to be cautious. When "stagnation" and "inflation" press on at the same time, policies will lose their effectiveness.

People who study "stagflation" almost ignore such a law in the economic development, that, with the increase in the total economy, the economic growth has a trend of gradual slow down, in which, while the absolute number is growing, the relative number has the trend of decrease. As a result, there is a misconception that the current economic growth rate is gradually reduced over the past, that is, the economy has the trend of stagnation. By using the longitudinal comparison approach of the economic growth index, it is demonstrated that the economic growth has slowed down or enters the state of stagnation. From today's perspective, the "stagflation" phenomenon after the 1970s is caused by the irrational use of fiscal policy and monetary policy, because entering the 1990s, the reasonable combination of the moderate fiscal and monetary policy helps the capitalist economy out of the "stagflation", with the momentum of high growth and low inflation, which has lasted for more than ten years. This transformation of the real economy many researchers withdraw from the study of the issue of "stagflation". Therefore, whether "stagflation" is an inevitable law in the period of state monopoly capitalism remains the topic to be tested by history and practice.

20   Qiu Qihua, *Preliminary Exploration on the Development and Changes of the Western Economic "Stagflation"*, in *The World Economy*, 1991(5).

IX. From Contempt for Counter-Crisis Policies to Attentive Studies

For a long period after the founding of New China, Chinese scholars had dismissed the counter-crisis measures and policies implemented in the capitalist world. They believed that the Keynesian counter-crisis measures paving the way for more extensive and more destructive crises, and by diminishing the means whereby crises were prevented. The capitalist anti-crisis activities were but simply the deathbed struggle before its demise. They insisted that all economic fluctuations under the capitalist conditions were caused by the basic contradiction of capitalism, which had the trend of continuous intensification, so any counter-crisis measures would not stop the occurrence of the capitalist economic crisis. The counter-crisis measures of the capitalist countries interrupted or eased the crisis process temporarily, so that the crisis was transformed, but these factors also provided conditions for the deepening of the capitalist economic crisis. Because: 1) in order to strengthen intervention in the economy, in the post-war period, the major capitalist countries stimulated economic growth, continuously expanded government spending, forming huge deficits, and they also vigorously promoted the consumption credit system. Therefore, the state, enterprises and individuals rely on borrowing to maintain their livelihood. Thus, although demand is temporarily expanded, purchasing power improved, economy prospered and crisis eased, it reduces the purchasing power in the future, intensifies the contradiction between production and consumption, and thus gives birth to a deeper crisis. 2) In order to compensate for the deficit, the capitalist countries long take the inflationary policy, and entering the 1970s, inflation was exacerbated, prices rose rapidly, which did not fall even in the phase of crisis. This leads to the mutual intertexture and influence of economic stagnation and inflation in the capitalist world. 3) With the new development of state monopoly capitalism in the post-war period, some measures were taken to ease the crisis and to stimulate the economic growth. These measures cannot eliminate all the inherent contradictions of capitalism, but make them even more acute.

Chinese scholars began to pay attention to the issue of anti-crisis a long time ago. At the end of the 1950s, Si Mu published an article and pointed out that state monopoly capitalism had taken a series of "anti-crisis" measures, such as: 1) arms expansion, increase in military spending and military orders; 2) increase public buildings, housing construction and other public works; 3) monetary easing, lowering the rate of interest and other measures. And so on. However, it is difficult for these measures to get rid of the blow of the cyclical economic crisis, but to aggravate the crisis. For example, in the United States, there have been further shortened cycle and the initial symptoms of the crisis are stretched; the overall deterioration of the economic situation, and the fixed capital investment fell again; the intertwined and concurrent economic crisis and inflation; the intertwined and concurrent crisis of overproduction and monetary and financial crisis. For these changes, some scholars[21] believe that the reason lies in the "anti-crisis" measures of the state monopoly of capitalism centered by the militarization of the national economy. Because, in times of crisis, the investment in fixed capital did not fall too much, but even continued to rise, so that the excess production capacity was not eased too much, but even further aggravated. In the meantime, the "anti-crisis" measures further weakened the purchasing power of the people, and further expanded the contradiction between the excess production capacity and the reduced effective demand. Thus, in the surface, the post-war crisis seems less intense than it was before World War II, and this is actually an illusion. Contradictions that lead to the crisis are only temporarily suppressed, which have not been resolved, but accumulated deeper. In the meantime, the growth of the investment in fixed capital was modest after the crisis, not enough to stimulate the capitalist economy to rise to a new upswing, so there was the shortened upswing phase and the lowered upswing amplitude of the cycle. There was a big gap between this thesis and the then reality of capitalism, because since the anti-crisis policy was adopted during the Great Depression in the 1930s, despite it failed to eliminate the capitalist economic crisis fundamentally, the extent of the crisis had been significantly reduced, in which case the completely negative attitude towards the capitalist anti-crisis measures was inappropriate in the methodology. Guan Mengjue also advocated to understand the issue of anti-crisis of the state monopoly capitalism from the dialectical perspective, and he believes that in a short period and under certain conditions, the anti-crisis measures stimulate the economic activity, create special markets, promote the growth of production capacity in deformity, and paralyze or delay the economic crisis, but on the long run and fundamentally, it also greatly increases the burden on the people and reduces the purchasing power of the people. The "anti-crisis measures" hinder the smooth commencement of the crisis, so that the contradiction between the excess production capacity and the relative narrowing of the effective demand cannot have the forcible solution temporarily, cannot restore the balance that has been destroyed through a good outbreak of crisis temporarily. Since the last crisis failed to unfold fully, the next crisis will come soon, and the deeper contradictions accumulate, the greater the severity of the crisis will be. One woe is past, and others come, which is "the inevitable result" of the "counter-crisis measures" in the U.S. state monopoly capitalism. The "anti-crisis measures" finally are converted to "measures" that shorten the cycle of crisis. Compared with Guan Mengjue, Wu Dakun had a higher evaluation on the positive effect of the capitalist anti-crisis measures, and he believes with the strengthening of the anti-crisis measures of the state monopoly capitalism, it has changed the generation mechanism of the capitalist economic crisis, and there is no longer the possibility of the outbreak of the vicious monetary and credit crisis similar to that in the 1930s. His view was strongly opposed in the academia. Some opponents argue that the strengthening of measures to intervene in economy by

---

21   Xia Jing, "*About the Characteristics of the Current Economic Crisis in the United States*", in *Journal of Literature, History & Philosophy*, 1975(3).

the state monopoly capitalism indeed played a significant role in suppressing the violent outbreak of the credit crisis, monetary and credit crisis, but the effect of the intervention in economy by the state monopoly capitalism, after all, has its limitations, and it will not be able to change the objective laws of the capitalist economy, it cannot solve the contradiction in the capitalist reproduction process fundamentally, but will make these contradictions be accumulated more and more acutely. The result of the objective laws of capitalist economy will lead to the outbreak of a Great Depression like the one that shocked the capitalist world in 1929-1933. The very scared 1929-1933 monetary and credit crisis will also be reproduced in our eyes.

Since China was in a special economic and political environment before the reform and opening up, the mainstream economics basically did not study the development laws of the socialized production and the market economy, and essentially no one discussed the positive impact of the capitalist anti-crisis measures on the macro economy. The primary issue that scholars are concerned about first is why the government spending and the unprecedented expansion of government purchases in the United States cannot stop the occurrence and development of the economic crisis. This tendency of the theoretical studies indicate that the main focus for Chinese scholars to the concern on the issue of the capitalist anti-crisis lies in the historical destiny of capitalism, rather than how socialized production runs. Taking Guang Mengjue's study for example, from his academic tendency we can see attitudes and perspectives of Chinese scholars to concern about the anti-crisis. It seems to Guang Mengjue that, the 463 reason why the anti-crisis measures of capitalism has not been able to stop the capitalist economic crisis is because the government spending and government purchases also have dual effect on the U.S. economy: on the one hand, it "creates" a special market for certain goods, supporting the economy to some extent; on the other hand, the huge amount of money needed by the government to "create" the "market" is still taken from the people and taken in the final analysis, thus greatly reducing the part of the market maintained by the masses. From this point, the government spending and government purchases have the damaging effects on the U.S. economy. "Creating" market and reducing market, supportive effects and damaging effects – in the effects of the two confronting forces, the former is partial, temporary and dependent, and the latter is fundamental, long-term, and leading; the effect of the former is gradually weakened until it disappears with the long sustained increase in the government spending and government purchases, while the effect of the latter is growing and always in an overwhelming advantage. Precisely because of this, in the long run, the increase in the U.S. government spending and government purchases centred by arms expansion and war preparations, as well as by the militarization of the national economy, cannot stop the occurrence and development of the U.S. business crisis, or extend the U.S. business cycle, but it promotes and intensifies the economic crisis in the United States, and reduces the U.S. business cycle.

With China's reform and opening up and the implementation of economic construction as the central strategy, Chinese scholars began to change gradually their one-sided understanding on the issue of the capitalist anti-crisis, and began to truly treat the positive and negative effects of the capitalist anti-crisis activities from the dialectical perspective. The reason for this shift is mainly because: first, the development strategy centered by economic construction requires objectively new modes to explore and develop the economy; second, it is the adoption of the commodity economy and the market economy which adapt to the development of the productivity. As the historical market economy of laissez-faire shows the growingly aggravated cyclical economic fluctuations often bring disaster to the society. Whether there is a possibility of the cyclical economic crisis occurring under the condition of China's socialism has repeatedly become the focus of the academic debate. China's socialist economic construction is in a growing need of a theory as a guide to ensure the smooth running of the economy, as well as in a need of having a successful experience for a reference to ensure the smooth running of the economy. In order to meet this requirement, Chinese scholars began to study the issue of the capitalist anti-crisis.

In order to adapt to the needs of the economic development and then to study the issue of the capitalist anti-crisis, the earlier scholars involving in this study include Xiong Xingmei, Xue Jingxiao et al., who launched their own book *Business Cycles and Crises under the Conditions of State Monopoly Capitalism after World War II* in the early 1990s, systematically elaborating issues of development stages, specific means, and the impact on the economy of the government intervention in the economy in the post-war period. The development and changes in the intervention in the economy of the Western developed countries since the end of World War II are divided into two periods: one is the period from recovery and boom to stagflation, which is manifested as strengthening of state intervention; the other one is the period from stagflation to gradually out of stagflation, which is manifested as the adjustment of the intervention policy. In the period from recovery and boom to stagflation, due to the social, economic and political differences in the capitalist countries, the specific forms of state monopoly capitalism are not the same. State intervention in the economy can be divided into three categories: demand management, industry promotion, and comprehensive regulation, namely represented by the United States, Japan and the Western European Economic Community. These different forms of intervention in the economy of state monopoly capitalism had a significant impact on the post-war capitalist reproduction cycle. First, the implementation of expansionary fiscal, monetary and credit policy, the nationalization, and welfare state policies stimulates the growth of effective demand, and can temporarily ease the contradiction between the trend of unlimited expansion of capitalist production and the relatively reduced effective demand of the labouring masses. Second, the implementation of economic planning, industrialization policy, international economic regulation have also played a role in easing the contradiction between the organization of production of individual enterprises and the anarchy of production in the whole society. The state intervention in the economy brings some of the following consequences: 1) Serious economic crisis like the one in 1929-1933 does not occur in the post-period. 2) Some crises are artificially delayed by the government intervention policies. 3) The short-term adjustment of the elastic fiscal and monetary policy results in that the alternation of the four phases in the reproduction cycle is not as significant as it was in the past; recession is shortened in the period, weakened in the extent, and there is no significant depression phase; economic stagnation and severe inflation coexist.

As the theoretical basis for the anti-crisis, the inadequate effective demand acknowledges the existence of the economic crisis and "involuntary unemployment", denies the basic contradiction in the capitalist economy, denies that the crisis and unemployment is the inevitable product of the capitalist system, and advocates that as to get out of the economic crisis, to eradicate unemployment, and to achieve steady economic growth the state intervention in the economy of the monopoly bourgeoisie, eliminate the so-called "underconsumption", "over-saving" and "underinvestment", so. For such a theory, Chinese scholars on the one hand assert that it is an absurd doctrine, and on the other hand admit that it is very useful for the monopoly capitalism. Because it provides a theoretical basis for the monopoly bourgeoisie to strengthen the rule of monopoly capital through the state "intervention" in the economy. From Roosevelt's "New Deal" in the 1930s, to Nixon's "New Economic Policy" in the 1970s, Keynesian theory was regarded as the primary means of the "anti-crisis" measures. The artificial stimulus of the investment in fixed capital, the organization of public works through government spending, bills and acts issued in favour of the increase in investment of the monopoly capital are all specific forms of implementation of the Western bourgeois "anti-crisis" measures in order to expand employment, to increase consumption, and to drive private investment.

In order to carry out the "counter-cyclical" policy successfully, the government establishes a set of systems and institutions, such as the financial system, the monetary system, the industrial restructuring institutions and so on to monitor and regulate the macroeconomic performance. These systems are improving, and form the macro condition for the West to implement the "counter-cyclical" policy. However, the implementation of the counter-cyclical policy is not easy. The fine tuning of the national economy from the aspect of demand is a severe test of the government's ability to manage the national economy, as well as of the effectiveness of a social and economic system. The successful counter-cyclical policies must also: 1) correctly grasp the trend of the national economy, and correctly predict the trend of the economy accordingly. This requires collecting and processing enough economic information of less distortion, and makes the aggregate analysis of the recent economic operation. This aggregate analysis usually requires the assumption that the established economic and political system remains the same. 2) have a certain amount in advance, in order to be timely and just right. This means that the counter-cyclical policies have strict requirements on time. Any policy always has a problem of "time lag" from finding out the conditions, making up the mind, to the policy being introduced and taking effect. If the "time lag" passed or is kept volatile, the counter-cyclical policies may have wrong effect in the wrong places and in the wrong time, thereby contrary to the original intention of the policy. 3) Have a suitable social and economic system. The counter-cyclical policies require precise and meticulous fine-tuning of the economy, which requires the formulation, practicing and implementation of the policy with high degree of flexibility and mobility, so that the direction and intensity of the policy implementation can be changed in a timely manner when needed, and thus it will not be subject to constraints. The condition for the successful implementation of counter-cyclical policies is very harsh, but in Western counter-cyclical theory and practice, we can see that the extent of fluctuation in the Western economies is indeed declined. In the America's post-war economic growth; it has been a long time to have a violent fluctuation since the Great Depression in the 1930s, which has to be attributed to some extent to the government macroeconomic regulation, namely the government's counter-cyclical policies.

In short, since entering the state monopoly capitalism, the most progressive part of capitalism is that it has done something in the fight against the crisis. The anti-crisis actions of state monopoly capitalism began with the "New Deal" during the Great Depression in the 1930s, and in this practice the bourgeoisie recognized that the government intervention in the economy could effectively alleviate the crisis, get out of the recession, and lead the economy to prosperity and recovery. Later, on the basis of summarizing the empirical experience in the 1930s, Keynes created the macroeconomics, and put forward a set of theories of government intervention in the economy. These theories became the main theoretical basis for government intervention in the economy in the post-war period. Since then, government intervention in the economy has become a regular policy. As government intervention in the economy had a profound impact on the post-war development of state monopoly capitalism, these countries achieved economic growth, alleviated the economic crisis and in general improved the livelihood. The new changes of the capitalism have offered a series of major research topics for the academic circles. Chinese scholars have also actively carried out the related research.

X. Presumed Marxist Theory of Economic Crisis in the "Six-book Structure" System

In the "six-book structure" system, Chinese scholars examined why Marx devoted himself to the issue of the crisis in the book *World Market*, how to discuss the crisis, what to discuss, as well as the elements, nature, characteristics and stages of development, etc. in the world trade crisis. They realized that the method of Marx's theory of economic crisis is the method that Marx used to analyze the capitalist economic relations. Since Marx believed that the crisis is the performance of all contradictions in the bourgeois economy, and the result of various contradictions of the bourgeoisie being fully developed. Chinese scholars speculated on that: "The crisis can only continue to lead to its provision in the gradually unfolding process of the basic contradiction of capitalism, from an abstract possibility to the presence of reality, and from the general crisis of individual countries to the world trade crisis". "The analysis of every contradiction of the bourgeois economy is to analyze the regularity that forms the crisis and determines the form of manifestation of the crisis. In this sense, the entire theory of Marx on the capitalist economy is the crisis theory."[22] Such a theory apparently cannot be completed in the narrative of *Capital* or even of the first few volumes of the "six-book structure" plan. In the later volumes, with the unfolding of the contradiction, the crisis theory is also deepened. When the capital is developed completely in the world market, when all conflicts are unfolded and concentrated in the exposure of the widespread world trade crisis, it is possible to carry out a comprehensive and integrated summary of the issue of crisis. Because Marx prompted the issue of the "world trade crisis" from the perspective of study, that is: "The world trade crises must be regarded as the real concentration and forcible adjustment of all the contradictions of bourgeois economy. The individual factors, which are condensed in these crises, must therefore emerge and must be described in each sphere of the bourgeois economy and the further we advance in our examination of the latter, the more aspects of this conflict must be traced on the one hand, and on the other hand it must be shown that its more abstract forms are recurring and are contained in the more concrete forms."[23] Therefore, Chinese scholars, in turn from the perspective of theoretical narrative, speculate in what way Marx might elaborate the theory of crisis in his book *World Market*. As the world trade crisis is the concentration of all the contradictions of bourgeois economy, it is also reflected as the general. To elaborate the crisis from the general sense, "horizontally, it should be elaborated of the conditions, factors, and the links that form the world trade crisis necessarily manifested in every area of bourgeois economy. Vertically, it should be elaborated of the development of the crisis from the simplest regulations to the increasingly complex regulations, and elaborated of the process in which the crisis is developing to a rich and specific world trade crisis with the entire harvest in every phase of its continuous development."[24] According to Marx's prompt and the practical economic relations, Chinese scholars made the speculative elaboration on the issue of the crisis that might be elaborated in the volumes after *Capital*, which is an in-depth discussion on the basis that Marx has laid.

22　Tang Zaixin, chief editor, *Exploration of the Sequel to Capital*, Beijing: China Financial Publishing House, 1995, p. 537.

23　Marx and Engels, *Collected Works*, 1st Chinese edition, Volume 26 (II), Beijing: People's Publishing House, 1973, p. 582.

24　Tang Zaixin, chief editor, *Exploration of the Sequel to Capital*, China Financial Publishing House, Beijing, 1995, p. 539.

XI. Conclusion

The course to study the capitalist business cycle and the major issues explored by Chinese scholars suggest that they have essentially basically done the job of both adhering to the basic principles in the Marxist theory of economic crisis to analyze and to understand the capitalist economic crisis, and keeping pace with the times, actively observing the new changes in the capitalist economic crisis, and interpreting the new phenomena and new features in compliance with the Marxist economics; both adhering to the in-depth study of the general principles of the Marxist theory of crisis, and adhering to promoting the academic contention of the new and major issues; both adhering to the basic method in the Marxist economics to analyze and to understand the capitalist economic crisis, and adhering to positive innovation, introduction and absorption of new scientific methods to enhance the theoretical analysis and argumentation ability. Overall, the Chinese scholars have realized abundant valuable research efforts to deepen the Marxist theory of economic crisis and the grasp the new development trends related to recent economic crises. However, it should be noted that they have paid too much emphasis on the study of the essential links of the capitalist economic crises, but ignored studies of the new phenomena, facts and forms; too much emphasis was placed on the discussion on the root reason of the capitalist economic crisis, but systematic study of the various nonessential causes were ignored; they have one-sidedly focused on the negative effects of the crises on the capitalist system, ignoring its positive effects; too much emphasis was placed on the relationship between crisis and revolution and war, and ignored its relationship with the socialized production, and with the market economy; they laid too much emphasis on the impact of the social institutional factors on the economic crisis, but ignored the impact of non-institutional factors; they laid too much emphasis on logical deductions and normative research, but ignored mathematical analysis. For these reasons, in general, their study of Marx's theory of business cycle has been short of creative results, basically failing to arrive breakthroughs on many important theoretical issues, with few successful fruits achieved in the study of the new phenomena and new features, which seems incongruous compared to the Marxist mainstream economics.

CHAPTER XIV

Re-visiting the Theory of Socialist Business Cycle in the New Era

I. Introduction

Since the late 1950s, Chinese scholars have gradually broken through the forbidden zones throughout their researches on the economic growth trends of China, Soviet Union, Eastern Europe and other socialist countries. They have soon discovered that socialist economies are also faced by cyclical economic fluctuations which obviously meant that Marxist economics was challenged by a series of new questions. If the cyclical economic fluctuations are an essential concomitant of a capitalist system, then how could the same phenomena occur in socialist economies? If the cause leading to cyclical fluctuations in the capitalist economy could be explained by the theory of periodic intensification of the basic contradictions of capitalism, then which theoretical frame could grasp the cyclical fluctuations in the socialist economy? Is the cyclical economic fluctuation an ordinary feature of the large-scale socialized production, or is it a phenomenon accompanying a certain social system? Faced with these new questions, notable scholars of the era have tactfully achieved a certain consensus, that there were essential differences between the cyclical economic fluctuations of the two opposed systems, errors in planning work, or variable input and variable in action of certain production factors were the immediate causes of the economical fluctuations occurring in socialist planned economy, and all these analyses have led them to the most basic reason at the root: the law that society moves (if it advances at all) in a spiral line. In the mid-late 1980s, when they resumed their studies of socialist economic fluctuation, the scholars insisted on the Basic Principle of Marxism for interpretation, but they essentially stayed on the sideline of the Marxist theory. In this era the traditional approach of contradiction analysis was generally abandoned, instead studies have mainly turned to statistics, measurement, comparative analysis and other methods, which in the first place aimed to explain and affirm the existence of cyclical economic fluctuations, transmission mechanisms causing fluctuations, counter policies to ease fluctuations, etc. besides some researches sought to transcend the classical theory on the root cause of fluctuations. Certainly, these changes in the analysis approaches or methods were related with the uncommon economic reforms initiated, thus the changes in the nature of the research object. In the early 1980s, studies focused on proving the existence of business cycles in China, describing the track of cycles, and exploring the cause of cycles and the coordination of reform in the economic system and cyclic fluctuations of economy.[1] Afterwards, the subject of research was averted to rather detailed questions such as how to tackle the economical fluctuation in the situation of deepening reform and speeding up the process of economic transition and how to deal with inflation and deflation, etc. After entering the 21st century, the subject of research was further averted to how to actively make the most of circumstances to guide relative extension of the rising phase of business cycles and seek to relatively compress the sliding phase. After all these transformations, the nature of research has already become similar to the traditional research of prosperity by and large with substantial differences from the Marxist theory of business cycle and no more emphasis on researches of the irresistible trend of the socialist business cycle.

470

Mr. Liu Guoguang once pointed out at a seminar about issues of economic fluctuation: "The issue of cyclical fluctuations of economy is an important research subject of significance as well as a very complicated one. It is also concerned with a series of major issues of economic theories. For instance, in his days, Marx profoundly analyzed the cyclic fluctuation of the capitalist economies, and also predicted that once the capitalist form of production was abolished, there would still be fluctuation for updating of fixed capitals and development of production. However, Marx didn't indicate that there would still be issues of cyclical fluctuation for the socialist economies. What significance does Marx's prediction about fluctuation for updating of fixed capitals and development of production impose on the research into the cyclical fluctuation of the socialist economies? What are the objective conditions and internal mechanism of the cyclical fluctuation of the socialist economies? What are their differences from and connection with the cyclical fluctuation of the capitalist economies? What guiding role does Marx's theory about the cyclical fluctuation of the capitalist economies play on our current studies of socialist issues?

1   See Liu Guoguang, *Three Questions for the Current Economic Situation,* in *Journal of Quantitative & Technical Economics,* 1997(6).

All these require us to do serious researches and give the answers."[1] When looking back now, we can find great progress has been achieved in researches of the subject, but there are still parts needing to be solved.

II. Initial Studies

Faced with violent fluctuations of the state economies during the period of the first and second five-year plans, Chinese scholars began to reflect on and demonstrate the issue whether there are fluctuations in the socialist economies, which were considered breaking through "the forbidden zone" on that historical condition because the studies were regarded as "heterodoxy" of the Marxist economics theory. Therefore, one can imagine the difficulty in carrying out the research work. When they found and firmly believed there are also cyclical fluctuations in the socialist economies, their answer to its root became a very difficult problem for political sensitivity. In order to avoid conflicts with political issues, scholars participating in the research of this issue almost simultaneously stated that there were substantial differences between fluctuations of the socialist economies and those of the capitalist economies. Based on the law of non-balanced development of the subject they thought in the development of the socialist economies there is also the unity and opposition of balance and imbalance and its development mode is also wave-like and in a spiral line.[22] The first sponsor of the discussion was Yan Nai, who issued an article on *Jiefang Daily,* pointing out that wave-like advance is the irresistible trend for quick development of the socialist economies. His idea brought in a lot of enthusiastic dis- 471
cussants, one of whom was Yin Shijie. Being an active participant, Yin Shijie's discourse generated great impacts. Inheriting the core contents of the Marxist crises theory, he held that the relation of continuity and equilibrium was the basic condition for development of the socialist economies, and regarded cyclical fluctuations of economy as the continuous and discontinuous, balanced and unbalanced movement of the economic relation. In terms of continuity, he thought each sector and each facet of the national economy is interdependent and inter-constraint, thus forming an organism converging and gripping with each other. The development of any segment, on one hand, depends on the adaptable development in many other segments, on the other, also influences the development of many other segments. In terms of equilibrium, among sectors and facets of the national economy, some develop a little fast while others develop a little slowly, always causing contradictions between balance and imbalance as well as those in proportion and out of proportion. In a certain period, while the proportional relation coordinates new imbalance and incongruity of the proportional relation appear in another period. This requires adjustments of proportion for temporarily relative equilibrium. For instance, as for production and requirement on the socialist condition, they may coordinate with each other in a period while they may not coordinate in another period, thus needing the establishment of a new equilibrium relation. When the new equilibrium

2   Fang Zhong, *Review of Issue about Wave-like Advance of the National Economy,* in *Plan and Statistics,* 1959(10).

relation is established, a new contradiction appears. This circle from balance to imbalance and again to a new and superior balance goes round and round until eternity. Each circle helps the national economy reach a higher level. Because there are constantly contradictions between balance and imbalance in the national economy to continuously break the old balance and establish a new one, this determines that speeds of development of the national economy in different years are various. The speed of development in some years is high while that in other years is low, taking on a wave-like development state. Besides, Yin Shijie also attributed the root for imbalanced development of the socialist economy to its basic contradiction—the law of contradiction between the productive forces and the relations of production, i.e. revolution of the social production relation is a process from quantitative change to qualitative change. When the production relation is in the phase of quantitative change, its facilitation to productivity is quite balanced, while when it is in the phase of qualitative change, it will cause a qualitative leap in productivity. He also connected fluctuations of the socialist economies with technological advance, and held that technological advance is also an imbalanced development process from quantitative change to qualitative change on the socialist condition and that each technological breakthrough is always followed by large-scale investment in capital construction, which multiples the production.

On that historical condition, discussion of fluctuations of the socialist economies means stepping into the political "forbidden zone", so some scholars were unwilling to connect fluctuations of the socialist economies with its basic contradictions. They held that factors determining the wave-like advance of the national economy were complicated, such as situation of natural conditions, scale of capital construction and situation of its impact, the amount of labour forces input in production, changes of the productive relation and changes of people's attitude towards labour. The non-equilibrium changes of these conditions and factors in years influence production in varying degrees.[31] Later on, Luo Gengmo also thought wave-like development of the socialist economy is related to the following factors, i.e. great changes in natural conditions, disequilibrium in the amount of new enterprises running production annually, invention and application of new and great science and technology, alternating effect of "development and strengthening" in the evolution of matter, etc. He also specifically pointed out that the socialist economies will inevitably develop at a high speed but that there must be some adjustments after a great development for consolidation, repletion and improvement followed by another great development. That's because after a great development, quite a number of new matters and issues will appear in the socialist production and construction. Those will need adequate adjustments to help people know new matters and tackle new issues, thus creating conditions for the next development process.[42]

472

3   See Wang Xiangming, *Correct Understanding of Wave-like Development of the Socialist Economies*, in *Economic Studies*, 1960(1).
4   See Luo Gengmo, *On Issues of Durability and Wave-like Advance in the Great Leap*, in *China Youth*, 1961(9).

As of 1960s, people have already began to think that the "advance of national economy in waves is determined by the inherent objective laws of the economy itself rather than being affected or changed by people's will." "The advance in waves is the development law of the socialist economy to develop at the highest possible pace". "This advance in waves reflects the objective development process of the socialist economy to develop – strengthen – re-develop, expand – improve – re-expand, leap – adjust – re-leap." Propositions as such had become the consensus among scholars.[53]

In addition, they unanimously held that compared with cycles in the capitalist economies, cycles of the socialist economy are rising fluctuations, except that the cyclical fluctuations in the socialist economy is caused by non-antagonistic economic relations. Without leading to crises or suspensions, business cycles of the socialist economies actually followed the development in waves while socialist economy advanced in a fast pace.

Reviewing the studies of cycles of the socialist economies from the late 1950s to the early 1960s, one can find important qualitative contributions though there were not many achievements and researching participants. The research achievements of this period have basically laid the foundation for the establishment of the theory of the socialist business cycle and their research have made a great impacts on the deeper researches realized in the period in the1980s.

For instance, they have shaken and changed people's belief that there could $\underline{473}$ be no economic fluctuations in the planned socialist economy, they have argued that the wave-like advance is the objective basic development law of the socialist economies and that its existence cannot arbitrarily be omitted by will. The arguments and explanations related to their nature and motion were supported by the basic tenets of Marxism and have successfully applied the methodology of the Marx's theory of business cycles. Researchers of this period have clearly stated that studies and deeper knowledge on socialist business cycles and their formation mechanism could enable control and checks over them and thus finally promote sound and fast development of the socialist economy. I can comfortably agree that their theories arguing that society moves (if it advances at all) in a spiral line, realistically reflect the law of the socialist economic development in China, which are also consistent with the farther three-step development strategy proposed by Deng Xiaoping and others in 1980s. I can also say that compared with the Real Business Cycle Theory, the Political Cycle Theory and the Technology Cycle Theory in the contemporary West, the researchers of this era have produced earlier sprout of their ideas.

5   See Yin Shijie, *Preliminary Analysis of Factors Forming the Wave-like Advance of the National Economy*, in *Jianghan Tribune*, 1961(5); Li Zixin, Bu Lu: *Wave-like Fast Advance is the Objective Law of the Socialist Economies*, Published in *Shijian*, 1961(8), (9).

III. The Emancipation of Minds and Theoretical Innovation

Along with the violent fluctuations faced by China's economy after the foundation of New China, it meant a mental emancipation for Chinese scholars to courageously claim that economic fluctuations are the objective development law of the socialist economy in the late 1950s and the early 1960s. Although they had repeatedly emphasized that those fluctuations occurring in the socialist economy are different from the capitalist business cycle and regarded those greater economic fluctuations as the specific form for growth of the socialist economies, they were in fact attempting to enter into the "forbidden zone", which is proven by the later controversies and debates around the "wave-like advance of the socialist economy". In the 1980s, when the studies on the issue of economic fluctuations of socialism could be realized in a relatively liberal environment people have generally affirmed the bold breakthrough achieved by the researchers of the 50s and early 60s who have challenged the traditional ideas. In the relatively favourable academic environment of the 80ies, researches and debates have developed faster and in a little while the term "socialist business cycle"[6] was put forward and various other challenging ideas have appeared one after the other almost all vigorously suggesting to achieve the better management of the national economy by grasping —the motion mechanism and pattern of the cycles, and pinpointing "to control the invest-

474　ment scale and develop initiatives for the integrated and coordinated development of the national economy."

Practically, after super-speed growth in the early 1980s, China's economics began to experience downturns, and then suddenly there were heated discussions about cyclic fluctuations of China's economics in the academic circles, thus breaking through the forbidden zone once again after many years. In 1985, Wu Jiapei and Liu Shucheng issued articles,[7] firstly putting forward the idea that there are "cyclic fluctuations" for the socialist economic growth. Afterwards, Liu Shucheng issued several articles continuously, in which, with the periodicity of fixed-asset investment in our country, he explored its characteristics and causes and how to master this periodicity to gain the initiative for mastery of the investment scale and control of the development of the whole national economy.[83] It's necessary to explicate that: From the beginning, researches in the 1980s treated violent economic fluctuations as the disastrous factor for the development of the national economy, and further treated understanding and control of the patterns of economic fluctuation and achieving long-term stable

---

6　In 1987, Lu Jian directly used *Analysis of Features, Cause and formation Mechanism of the Country's Business Cycle* as the article title.

7　See Wu Jiapei, Liu Shucheng: *30 Years' Studies of Quantitative Relation in Economy*, in *Economic Studies*, 1985(6).

8　See Liu Shucheng, *Initial Exploration of the Cycles of Fixed-asset Investment in Our Country, Second Exploration on the Cycles of Fixed-asset Investment in Our Country—Analysis of Each Phase in the Cycle*, published on *Economic Studies*, 1986(2), (6).

development of the national economy as the objective to study economic fluctuations. Such research angles were different from those in the late 1950s and the early 1960s to a great extent. The researches into economic fluctuation at that time were not only intended to explain that wave-like advance of economy is a normal phenomenon of the socialist economies but also to explain that such economic fluctuations around "the great leap" period are also objective laws for the socialist economic development.

Since Marx did not specifically mention or expound on the possibility of cyclical economic fluctuation in socialism, the attempt to explain the cause of economic cyclical fluctuation in China based on Marx's elaborations and analyses related to cyclical economic crises of capitalism requires a creative theoretical effort of deepening and developing all Marxist theories related to economics based on current realities.

Because to accomplish such analytic work, one has to have a thorough understanding of the actual conditions of socialism, and find these necessary and sufficient conditions required to meet the theoretical analysis from the actual economic life. It was in this flexible way that scholars achieved their explication of the socialist economies by utilizing Marxist economics. They thought that although the establishment of socialist economic system fundamentally eliminated the contradictory cause for dominant economic relation, traces of the basic contradiction of capitalism still existed—the existence of multiple economic sectors and faultiness of economic plans made it hard for the national economy to develop according to rather measured plan and ratio to some extent. Driven by profit maximization, enterprises constantly carry out capital accumulation, and update technology to raise labour productivity while consumption is restricted at a very low level. The contradiction and conflict of these elements will inevitably lead to economical fluctuations, sometimes even violent ones. The reason why scholars saw things at this angle is that they already separated economic fluctuation from social system, and thought that it was the universal law of the market economy, belonging to representation of effects of market mechanisms. As long as the market economy exists, there will inevitably be cyclical fluctuations of economy. This is undoubtedly a brand new angle for Marxist economics to have an understanding of the socialist business cycle. Because with connection of economic fluctuations and the market economy, one can not only conceive the inevitability of cyclical fluctuations in China's economies, but also the possibility for economic crises to happen. Some scholars drew the following conclusions based on this understanding: economic crises are not phenomenon exclusive to the capitalist economies, and there are also economic crises in the socialism. And the mechanism for economic crises to happen is not in the socialist economic system but in the market economy. After separating the economic fluctuation from the social system, some other scholars systematically utilized the modern western theory of business cycles. They held that the unified political system of China made the economic policies of each leader subjective to the overall objective of the national economic development with no existence of policy fluctuation caused by election. However, because of participation of the government in prosperity adjustment, at the premise of the internal contradiction between full employment and price stability within the economy, periodical political movements in China may also impose great impact on the economy, causing it to cyclically fluctuate with political movement. They deliberately drew the time intervals in all the business cycles since foundation of New China, and corresponding policy adjustments, political events, political movements, political mobilization and unveiling of great strategic measures. These arguments can neatly explicate the immediate cause of fluctuations from a certain angle.

Consistent with the vigorous reform course of China, the researches into China's socialist business cycle have always been a hotspot. Before China determined its reform objectives for the market economy, some scholars did researches into finance, currency and other macro-control policies as the contra-cyclical policies, and put forward countermeasures and advice suitable to China's national conditions. Other scholars advocated the establishment of the statistical system and cycle pre-warning system of China's business cycle, and put forward systematic plans and operation schemes, hoping to increase their capabilities to control the cycles with these efforts. As for this, they did extensive and in-depth researches into how to drive business cycles, and developed a whole set of pre-warning system, and put forward what reform scheme should be released in different periods of the economic fluctuation cycle. All these could both help reform measures to comply with fluctuations, and also help to "iron out" the violent economic fluctuation. Still some scholars admit that there are business cycles on the socialist condition is not a bad thing, because the existence of some economic cyclical fluctuation can actually bring into full play the market mechanism of survival of the fittest, and make those low-quality enterprises eliminated in the economic fluctuation and high-quality ones thrive, thus achieving the optimal allocation of resources and optimization of the economic structure. There are still other scholars who hold that the fluctuation of China's national economy is formed with combined action of its internal transmission mechanism and external impact mechanism. And the violent fluctuations among them existed mainly because of the more powerful non-viability of its external impact mechanism, especially the main impacts from irregular operation of finance, currency and investment policies. They drew conclusions from theories and empirical analysis that the self-impetus of economy determined by the internal transmission mechanism of China's economic activities is periodical, so one can conceive that there is inevitability in the cyclical fluctuation of China's economies. Considering there is also the issue of economic fluctuations on the socialist condition, some scholars thought that the cyclical fluctuations of economy derives from the periodical inconformity of aggregate supplies and aggregate demands, and that the reason for inconformity is mainly the instability of aggregate demands, which is caused by some features of the system itself, therefore, the root of business

476

cycles is in the economic system itself. Along with the popularity of the Real Cycle Theory abroad, some scholars applied this theory to observe and study China's business cycles.

In terms of studies, analysis, description and measurement of the business cycle, Chinese scholars generally achieved the transformation from domination of traditional methods to integration of traditional methods and modern ones by combining the attitudes of insistence, introduction and innovation. Some scholars, especially those young and middle-aged ones, actively advocated the application of modern statistical and measurement methods in describing the business cycle, analyzing the cause and internal operation mechanism of the business cycle, and predicting the business cycle. They held that the focus on traditional methods like statistical observation, induction and analysis will not be able to analyze the deep relationship and operational mechanism of the business cycle, nor will it be able to make economic predictions. So, modern methods should replace those traditional ones to study the business cycle. Undoubtedly, the theorist of traditional methods thought that although there is some regularity in the business cycle, cycles are different from each other. So that method to treat a business cycle as accurate reproduction of cycles and to use the econometric model for accurate description is wrong, and emphasis should be laid on researches into traditional methods.

Chinese scholars regard the realization mechanism of the socialist economic fluctuation as an important research subject and have gained striking achievements after many years of supports in the way of rolling stimulation. Studies of the realization mechanism of the socialist economic fluctuation are essentially studies of the dynamic mechanism and transmission mechanism of economic fluctuations. Scholars found in studies that although business cycles are a common economic phenomenon in modern society, the formation mechanisms are different in different economic systems or institutions. In the planned economic system, the economy will automatically present the system of aggregate demands over-sizing aggregate supplies at set intervals, making the actual output higher than the potential output and the appearance of positive gap of output. When the economy develops on its wave crest and the high growth of economy cannot sustain owing to severe imbalance between economic aggregate and the economic structure from the superheat state, the economy will come into recession and depression. Even though the government does not execute deflation policies to restrain economic overheating, the process will occur sooner or later. Economic recession and depression is actually a voluntary adjustment towards overheating economy. After the economy drops to the bottom and develops for a while, this mechanism inherent in the planned economy will again propel the economy to revive and prosper with quite sufficient structural adjustments and energy accumulation and here comes a new round of demand inflation and overheated economy. There is a mechanism different from the planned economic mechanism in the market economy, which does not automatically propel the economy firstly to demand inflation and overheated economy but automatically propel the economy to the state of aggregate demands fewer than aggregate supplies, i.e. in the state of insufficient effective demands, which makes the actual output lower than the potential output and the appearance of negative gap of output. When the economy develops to the wave hollow, over-cold economy will appear. After structural adjustment and power accumulation for a while in the over-cold state, the economy will slowly enter into the period of recovery and prosperity. During this process, even though the government does not adopt any expansionary economic policies to intervene in the over-cold economy, economic recovery will also occur but with a lower speed and higher social costs for people to endure. After the economy sustains for a while in the prosperous period, the mechanism inherent to the market economy will again propel the economy to recession and depression and here comes a new round of insufficient demands and over-cold economy. In the planned economic system, publicly owned enterprises are in the absolutely dominant position, and whether they are enterprises of state ownership or those of collective ownership, actually they are all enterprises with "government ownership". With the paternalist protection of the government at different levels, publicly owned enterprises all have the features of soft budget constraint, among which the soft budget constraint for state-owned enterprises are the most severe. On the condition of soft budget constraint, because all the costs of enterprises for investment and consumption demands are independent of their business state, investment hunger and consumption comparison prevalent in enterprises will inevitably propel the investment and consumption demands of the whole society to the inflation state, ultimately causing inflation of aggregate demands and shortage of aggregate supplies and the planned economy to become shortage economy. When the inflating aggregate demands propel the economic operation to the wave crest, the economic operation will come into recession and depression, and then fall into the valley bottom sooner or later because of resource shortage and structural imbalance. After the economy operates at the valley bottom for a while with quite sufficient structural adjustments, the mechanism inherent in the above-mentioned planned economy will eventually propel the economy to recovery and prosperity again and the economy will demonstrate an over-heated state. The circle goes round, thus it forms the demand-featured business cycle in a planned economy. However, in a market economy based on private ownership, enterprises possess the features of hard budget constraints, with which there is the mechanism propelling the economy to the over-cold condition rather than the one firstly propelling the economy to the over-heated condition in the economic system. Because hard budget constraint means that enterprises have to assume sole responsibility for its profits and losses, on which condition they have to compensate for all the costs in demands with their own incomes and ultimately gain profits so that they can survive and develop in the market economy. Therefore, seeking profit maximization is the natural instinct of enterprises. Seeking profits makes enterprises inevitably limit consumption of labour forces to a relatively narrow scope, so there is insufficient consumption demand in the economy at intervals.

Consumption demands are the ultimate demands of an economic society, so insufficient consumption demands will necessarily cause insufficient investment demands, and ultimately insufficient aggregate demands, thus propelling the economy to recession and depression. Likewise, after adequate adjustments and energy accumulation at the valley bottom, the economy will eventually come into recovery and prosperity slowly. However, the instinct of enterprises in pursuit of profits will finally propel again the economy into insufficient aggregate demands and over-cold condition. It goes round and round and here forms the business cycle featured with insufficient effective demands on the condition of the market economy. The socialist market economy is established on the basis of public ownership. To establish the market economy on the basis of the socialist public ownership, its core is to establish the enterprise system of hard budget constraint, i.e. the enterprise system of independent management, responsibility for their profits and losses, self-development and self-constraint. This kind of enterprise system is the premise to establish the market economy. In this enterprise system, the survival and development of enterprises depend on whether the enterprise can gain profits and to the magnitude of their profit. Therefore, there are inevitably the same characteristics between the formation mechanism of the business cycle in the socialist market economic system and the formation mechanism of the business cycle in the market condition. This means that even though on the condition of the socialist public ownership, business cycles featured with insufficient effective demands is also inevitable once the enterprise system with hard budget constraint is formed. The phenomenon of severe product surplus and unemployment manifested each time the economy develops at the low ebb ever since China decided to establish the socialist market economy.

The analyses above have laid the micro-foundation for analysis of the socialist business cycle, and have great theoretical value.

IV. Types and Features of China's Business Cycles

Many scholars urge to strictly distinguish between cyclical economic crisis, cyclical economic fluctuation, economic fluctuation and other concepts. Because in their view, if economic fluctuations are random and irregular, they will not be able to be called cyclical economic fluctuation but only economic fluctuations. If there is no negative growth in the cyclical fluctuations of economy, which causes destructive consequences to the national economy, they will not be able to be called economic crises, or even cyclical economic crises. Crisis is just a severe economic imbalance and an abnormal fluctuation. Nowadays, a very popular statement goes that cyclical economic crises mainly exist in the period of laissez-faire capitalism, and evolved into cyclical economic fluctuation in the period of state monopoly capitalism; and then evolved into economic fluctuation along with the age of economic globalization. Why China's economic growth is called as cyclical fluctuation? Because there is indeed periodicity in the frequent fluctuations of China's economy in years with the cycle length at 4-5 years. Counted from the economic recovery in 1952 and entering the industrialization in 1953, supposing regarding fluctuation of the economic growth rate as the main study object, China's economic growth altogether experienced 10 cycles as classified by the "trough-trough" method, among which 5 took place after the implementation of the reform and opening up. Before 1978, China's economy experienced three crisis-level cyclical fluctuations: The first great cycle (1953-1962) reflected China's winding course from large-scale planned socialist construction in 1953 to the successful accomplishment of the First Five-year Plan, and to "the Great Leap" Movement and severe impacts hereby brought about; the second great cycle (1963-1968), reflected the achievements made in "the three-year adjustment period" and the following destructive consequences brought by outbreak of "the Great Cultural Revolution;" and the third great cycle (1969-1976) overlapping the middle and late periods of "the Great Cultural Revolution", reflected the tortuous development of China's economy in this period. Though there was negative growth of economy in the above-mentioned three cycles, they were caused by insufficient supply rather than insufficient demand. So some scholars call it the "economic crisis of underproduction" exclusive to the condition of planned socialist economies.

As for whether there are cyclical fluctuations in China's socialist economies, scholars have for years carried out more elaborate and multi-angle description and heated academic controversies. After the 1980s, the description process began with *Initial Review of Fixed-asset Investment Cycles in China* published by Liu Shucheng on Economic Studies. The author compiled China's total amount of fixed-asset investment and the chart of its growth speeds from 1952 to 1984 by the time sequence, and then drew the plane graph. The graph visually and clearly displays seven investment cycles with the length of 4-5 years. The investment fluctuations are generally parallel to the five-year plans of the national economy, with its peak phases corresponding to the investment peak, and the trough phases corresponding to the end of the five-year plans. The changing tendency of these cycles also shows that the amplitude for rise or fall of the growth speed for fixed-asset investment in each cycle is gradually alleviated, and the trough years with negative growth speed of fixed-asset investment is gradually moving forward in the position of each five-year plan. In the following studies for over 20 years, Liu Shucheng also drew the graphs of economic growth fluctuation according to the time sequences (GNP, GDP) of economic growth after the foundation of New China. The following is the graph drawn by Liu Shucheng in 2006 (See Graph 14-1).

Graph 14-1: Curve of the Fluctuation in China's Economic Growth Rate

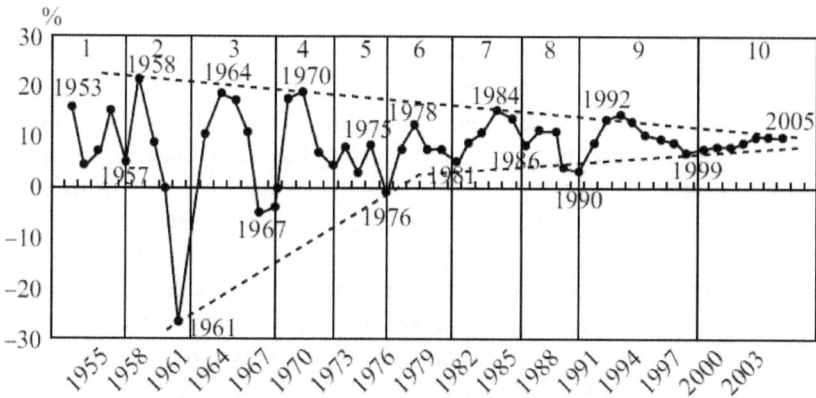

Source: *China Statistical Yearbook* 1953-2005

Seen from Graph 14-1, China's economic fluctuation has experienced a radical transformation after 1976 with economic contraction speed turning slower and the contraction period evidently becoming longer. So here came the short-expansive business cycles sustaining longer with shallower contraction depth, higher trough level and alleviated economic fluctuations, simply put it as –transforming from "the radical change" type to "the high position–flatness" type. As for this development tendency, scholars think that China's economic development had left back the classical business cycle for the growing cycle, and the economic growth has displayed the tendency of smooth development in high orders. That's mainly because the transformation of micro-foundation of economic cyclical fluctuations, i.e. the process of marketization of micro-economic unit with budget constraint hardening in state-owned enterprises and optimal configuration of scarce resources in state-owned and non-state-owned sectors as the main content was also implemented correspondingly. Changes in micro-foundations have caused mature market economic fluctuations gradually showing themselves, on the other side weakened re-tracking fluctuations.[9]

481

According to the changes mentioned above, scholars generally think China's business cycles since the reform and opening up have entered a new stage. Why did such a transformation occur in China's economic fluctuation? Liu Shucheng thought [10] that the reason can be classified into two types: one is

9   Ju Guoyu, Lan Yi, Transformation of Micro-foundation of Cyclical Fluctuations in China's Economies, published on Social Sciences in China, 2005(1).
10   Liu Shucheng also thinks that the cyclical fluctuation of economy consists of two parts: one is the endogenous fluctuation, i.e. basic waves generated by the internal structure of an economic system. The internal structure of the economic system determines the periodicity of fluctuation, also determines the basic condition of fluctuation, i.e. determining the wave amplitude, height, depth, position and length in a certain period of time. Two is the exogenous fluctuation. It refers to the overlaying waves generated when the impact outside the

the internal changes in the economic structure, and the other is the alleviation effect provided by the macro-control policies as the external impact. In terms of the economic structure, its endogenous stabilizing effects become stronger, shown in dramatic expansion of the overall scale of economy.[11] Ever since the implementation of reform and opening up, the proportion of China's first industry has continued its falling trend, that of the second industry has generally remained stable, while that of the third industry has risen quickly. In the gross industrial output value, the proportion of output values of state owned enterprises have seen radical decreases, while that of the non-state-owned enterprises have risen remarkably. Feeling fewer administrative interventions of the state, non-state-owned enterprises have strong budget constraints and can react sensitively to changes in demand and supply. In the expansion period of cyclical fluctuation, non-state-owned enterprises have very strong growth capacity, while in the contraction period of cyclical fluctuation, they also have very strong capacity to counter recession. Non state-owned enterprises have become the main growth source of our country's industrial production and the main vibration wave in industrial fluctuations. In terms of changes in foreign trade dependence, ever since the implementation of policies of reform and opening up, the scale of import and export in our country has expanded rapidly with a significant rise in foreign trade dependence. With great domestic demands, the increase of import can benefit the increase of supplies in economy, ease the bottleneck restriction of agricultural produce, resources, raw materials, transport facilities and other important materials, and support the sustainable growth of domestic economy. Increase in export can benefit mobilizing the growth of domestic economy. When the growth of domestic demands becomes mild or descends, excessive economic slide can be prevented as pulled by the export demands.[12]

As for phase classification of cycle and characteristics of each phase, Liu Shucheng has made rather elaborate description of his study achievements in Second Review of the Periodicity of Fixed-asset Investment in Our Country.

482

---

economic system affects the endogenous fluctuation. The external impact does not determine the periodicity of fluctuations, but imposes impacts on the wave amplitude, height, depth, position and length in every specific period of time, thus make basic waves transform. The macro-control of the government is a very important factor for external impact.

11   The industrial fluctuations are characterized by: The industrial-based secondary industry has the largest fluctuation. The primary industry or agriculture has the smallest fluctuation, but it is unstable. When the primary industry accounts for a larger proportion of the national economy and light manufacturing mainly takes agricultural products as raw materials, the fluctuation has larger impact on the whole economic fluctuation. The tertiary industry has smaller large fluctuation, and it is more stable. Within the secondary industry, the light and heavy industrial fluctuation is characterized by: the fluctuation in light industry is smaller than it is in heavy industry, but when the light industry mainly takes agricultural products as raw materials, affected by the instability of agricultural production, the fluctuation is slightly larger. Heavy industry is closely linked with investment which has an even larger fluctuation. – The above is also the research by Liu Shucheng.

12   Liu Shucheng, *On the New Stage of Economic Cyclical Fluctuation in China*, in Economic Studies, 1996(11).

And he classified the cycle into four phases—the recovery phase, the peak phase, the sustainable growth phase and the trough phase. Characteristics of each phase are shown as: (1) The recovery phase. Investment growth production growth→chained prosperity of various demands→investment growth in a larger scale→optimistic attitude at different levels. (2) The peak phase. Diverse idle productive capacities and productive potentials are made most of and brought into full play, and production develops rapidly to reach the upper limit of production capacity. The expansive effects of investment on production become alleviated. The facilitation of production on investment pushes the investment to the peak, and exceeds the upper limit of the production capacity and relevant capacity of material supply. Production, investment and consumption reach the comprehensive expansion. (3) The sustainable growth phase. With the restriction of resource shortage growth slows down→various demands contract in chains→investment drops→shortage further aggravates. (4). The trough phase. Severe imbalance in great proportional relations→the total social demands largely exceed the total social supplies→the government put forward mandatory deflation policies yet with great flexibility for its duration.

Compared with the business cycles abroad, China's economic growth was in the phase dominated by the classical business cycle before 1976. After 1976, China's economic growth turned into the phase dominated by the growth cycle. In this new phase, economic expansion was actually growth expansion, and economic recession was actually growth recession. Economic growth has become the theme of economic fluctuation. The average length of China's economic cyclical fluctuation has been around 7 years; sometimes their duration was five years or nine years. Lu Jian thinks that before the reform and opening up, China's economic fluctuations were basically not synchronized with the cyclical fluctuation of the global economies, and listed as non-diffused fluctuation; After the reform and opening up, with significant rise in correlation coefficient with the economic fluctuation in the western industrially developed countries, there was a tendency to fluctuate simultaneously with the global economies. According to the length of business cycles, Li Yining has classified the socialist business cycles as short phase, medium phase and long phase. He held that the short phase is mainly related to changes in investment amount caused by increase and decrease of enterprise inventory, and that the medium phase is mainly related to changes in investment structure and investment amount caused by the industrial structure and its changes. Besides, the long phase is mainly related to changes in investment structure and amount caused by changes of citizens' living environment, lifestyle and living habits and a series of relevant concepts.

Scholars also find that there are some regular trends of change in China's economic growth——Each time the economy booms, the inflation rate rises and the national revenue increases rapidly, the government will adopt deflation policies; while each time the economy declines, the growth rate of national revenues drops and the fiscal revenue decreases, the government will relax the deflation policies and adopt certain stimulating policies. The other way round, the deflation polices cause economic recession, and relaxation of deflation polices causes economic boom. According to this correspondent relation, some scholars think that China's business cycle distinctly has the features of "political–business cycle", i.e. because changes of cyclical policy make the economic development in the alternative transformation of the expansion phase or the deflation phase, and the economic development display itself in different development cycles with changes in cyclical policies. The reason for repeated changes of policy lies in the contradiction and conflicts between reality of restriction factors of China's national condition and subjectivity of the leader's development objective. The most important lesson concluded from China's economic development for over forty years is the tendency to detach from the national conditions and go beyond the national power with eagerness for success and radical changes.

In the 1990s, China explicitly brought up the direction for reform of the economic system—to establish the socialist market economy system and prompt the progressive reform to continue its in-depth advance with the reform pace obviously speeding up and the market playing primary functions in resource allocation. Meanwhile, the enforceability of traditional plans gradually weakens, and the regulatory effects of planned targets and means on the economy begin to turn to guidance, predictability and flexibility. The profound transformation in the economic system and the operating environment of macroeconomics leads to new features in tracks of China's economic cyclical fluctuation and the formation mechanism of fluctuations. The economic overheating at this time has already transformed from "overheating from expansion impulse of the central government" in the planned economy to "overheating from expansion impulse of enterprises" in the market economy.

484

Some scholars think that because the state commands the ownership of assets in state-owned enterprises, these state-owned enterprises must be endowed with multiple non-profit goals, mainly referring to the achievement of full employment and strategy of heavy industry priority in the planned economic period, and undertaking employment, pension and other social insurances to provide a stable social environment for the development of diverse economic elements in the transition period. Because there are various targets of state-owned enterprises, profits are only one facet of enterprise performance. As long as state-owned enterprises can have some effects while achieving other goals, sustaining their survival will be important and worthwhile to the government. Therefore, in a very long period, the national economy also has the soft budget constraint. In the meantime, owing to proceeding of the reform, state-owned enterprises gain their independent profits and investment power, which will inevitably make state-owned enterprises repeatedly carry out extensive investment expansion driven by its intrinsic "investment impulse", infringe upon owners' equities with soft budget constraint and achieve utility maximization of insiders. Because of this, the growth rate of investment and GDP rapidly rises at the beginning of each cycle, and fiscal expenditures also rapidly ascend for fiscal appropriation is an important source of the investment funds of state-owned sectors. The investment of state-owned sectors cannot gain its self-control from the inside on account of soft budget constraint; it shall only be regulated by the state from the outside. As a large developing country, China holds social stability and economic growth as the vital development goals of the state, and for inflation and material shortage caused by over-heated investment; the state will execute economic contraction. As for state-owned sectors, constraint is usually carried out through administrative measures and quantity control of credits, therefore, there will be more violent decline of actual investment and rapid decrease of currency supply until the economic growth rate becomes so low that the government thinks it necessary to again accelerate the development rate of the economy. Such a behavioural pattern explains the asymmetry of economic cyclical fluctuations in our country. It also describes the normal pattern of transitional economic fluctuation, i.e. such a circle from initiation of economic growth, to inflation of investment demands, quantity bottleneck of resources and transportation, appearance of inflation and braking of the government.

Economic transition and advance of reforms bring about consistent changes to the economic structure and behaviours. To state-owned enterprises, their budget constraint becomes hardened constantly. Especially after implementation of the shareholding reform, there are great changes in the ownership structure of state-owned enterprises, the main-supplement separating project and establishment of the social security system improve the issue of information asymmetry in the principal-agent relation. To the non-state-owned economy, it reflects in rapid expansion in number, becoming dominant investment subject from being insignificant. Because the non-state-owned economy naturally has stronger budget constraints than the state-owned economy, it will not form unlimited demand inflation for funds and materials like state-owned enterprises in the process of expansion. Meanwhile, because the banking system dominated by state-owned banks has not changed its institutional arrangement to non-market-oriented interest rate to provide subsidies to state-owned enterprises, non-state-owned enterprises have difficulties in gaining necessary funds from banks, they mainly depend on self-accumulated funds, thus alleviating the pressure on currency supply and inflation; on the other hand, the non-state-owned economy holds pursuit of profits as its objective and the speed for its investment transformed into production capacity is high, so the effective supplies can be formed quickly, weaken transitional economic fluctuations from demands and supplies. As a matter of fact, these are all connected to the weakening process of economic volatility in our country. Moreover, since 2001, investment of the non-state-owned economy has exceeded that of the state-owned economy with the tendency of increasingly enlarging gaps. It cannot be denied that the change in conditions of resource allocation is the potential reason for a new round of relatively steady growth.

It can be expressed that ever since the policy of reform and opening up, the primary reason for China's economic cyclical fluctuations lies in the interaction between the economic subject with "investment hunger" and the government's macro-control behaviours with promoting rapid economic growth and maintaining stability as the objective, while the state-owned sectors affected by soft budget constraint are the micro-basis of this economic fluctuation. However, with the advance of the reform course, the micro-basis of economic fluctuation is gradually changing, mainly reflected in continuous hardening of budget constraints in state-owned enterprises and rapid development of non-state-owned sectors, as well as scarce resources constantly changing the allocation conditions while gradually transferring from state-owned sectors to non-state-owned ones. This change reflects marketization of the micro subject of economic activities, while the marketization of the micro subject is the main force for economic fluctuation with features of transitional economy to gradually decrease, and after the marketization of the micro subject reaches to a certain level, it will inevitably cause changes in features of economic fluctuation, thus making transitional fluctuations transferred into ones of the mature market economy.

V. Inevitability of the Fluctuation in Socialist Business Cycle

As one of the universal laws of economic development, advance in waves and spiral escalation will not be transferred at people's will, nor will it be changed with impacts of social systems, and this is the negation of theory of no-fluctuation in the socialist economies. Therefore, whether there are economic cyclical fluctuations in the socialist economies has become a worthless topic. We can only say that economic fluctuation is an inevitable phenomenon in economic activities. Although economic fluctuations in different systems have different features, fluctuations are unavoidable. Even on that condition, people cannot or should not "smooth" fluctuations, and the correct practice is that they should utilize fluctuations to grasp opportunities and seek development. The environment is not always favourable to economic development, so when favourable opportunities come, relevant authorities should lead citizens to grasp the opportunities and seek rapid development for several years. With gradual loss of opportunities, the authorities should make timely adjustments to the economic structure, industrial structure, product structure and relevant polices to greet the arrival of new development opportunities. The speed of economic development at the adjustment phase will dramatically drop, but this is the "preparation for starting a race" necessary to a new round of rapid development. Hence, economic fluctuations should be treated dialectically with slight fluctuation as the normal condition of economic development while radical changes as the abnormal condition. The studies of economic fluctuation are mainly to find those reasons for abnormal fluctuation of the social economy and then take measures to "desalinate" fluctuations. There are natural and human factors. Because natural factors cannot be resisted by manpower in most cases, what interests people are mainly those human factors causing abnormal economic fluctuations. Li Yining also treats the cyclical phenomena in the socialist economic development as the normal ones in the course of socialist economic activities. Because economic cyclical fluctuation can be regarded as the temporary "intermission" in the course of economic growth, and a "rest and consolidation" in the advance process. The "intermission" in the short phase is mainly to guarantee the inventory structure and amount adjustment in the market as well as the time required for inventory structure and amount adjustment of enterprises, while the "intermission" in the medium phase is mainly to protect product structure, adjustment of industrial structural adjustment and the time required for relevant investment structure adjustment. As long as there are no interventions of non-economic factors, the economy will advance as usual after the "intermission", while the "rest and consolidation" is only to make preparation for the next round of economic growth.[13] This view is not only the inheritance to the research achievement in the late 1950s and the early 1960s, but also consistent with the three-step development strategy put forward by Deng Xiaoping in the 1990s. In order to prove prevalence of the socialist economic cyclical fluctuation, Du Hui, Liu Shucheng and others respectively investigated the phenomenon of economic fluctuation in the former Soviet Union, former Yugoslavia, and Hungary, etc., and found that they are very similar to the economic fluctuations in China.

On the condition that the national economy is overall reflected in the aggregate supplies fewer than the aggregate demands, enterprises are likely to expand production capacity to gain more potential profits, thus causing inflation of fixed asset investment and structural imbalance, so the cyclical movement of economy is the inexorable outcome resulting from excessive investment demands in the period of socialist economic development. Making the production structure and industrial structure reasonable by adjusting the investment structure is one of the basic ways to "desalinate" cycles.[14] Generally speaking, the aggregate supplies exceeding the aggregate demands is a general feature of the market economy, and the cyclical deviation of the aggregate demands with long term aggregate supplies can only find its root in instability of the aggregate demands. But why do the aggregate demands have instability and even cyclical instability? The answer can only be found in the economic system itself.

As for whether there is objective necessity of economic fluctuation, in the socialist economy different voices come out. And Hu Jichuang is one of them. He is not only denies the existence of economic crisis in modern economies, but even denies the existence of business cycles. He thinks that made up of numerous activity factors, any socio-economic system will inevitably generate some kind of economic fluctuation. Many reasons exist for economic fluctuations in our country, such as high investment, renewal of fixed assets,

---

13 See Li Yining, *"Assumptions of the Socialist Business Cycles"*, in *Economic Studies*, 1987(9).
14 Ibid.

technological innovation and mechanism of economic self-regulation, etc. which are all likely to incur economic fluctuations, but not necessarily forming regular cyclical fluctuations. The human errors in our country's planning department will "inevitably cause economic chaos", and too much human intervention will cause new fluctuations and chaos. As the reform of the economic system deepens in our country, the theory of traditional consumption and accumulative proportional relation as well as planned settings cannot impose any realistic guiding significance. On such a condition of opening up, the investment shares occupied by foreign enterprises and private enterprises become bigger and bigger, and quite a part of the investment funds are not from domestic accumulative funds, so the central planning organization cannot make plans for aggregate private investment at home and abroad, and the ratio of consumption and accumulation planned according to the national gross income hasn't had any guiding significance. In the western economic theory, the social gross consumption depends on employment and income level of citizens, and consumption mainly depends on personal consumption tendency and market interest rate. The amount of consumption and accumulation and their proportion relation can be counted when the national income distribution in a certain period of time is calculated afterwards.

Now that business cycles are rooted in the economic system itself, there will inevitably be a business cycle relevantly related as long as there is the planned economic system or the market economic system. The government of any country cannot eliminate business cycles. Faced with business cycles, what the government can do is forwardly utilize policies of business cycle to "cut peaks and fill valleys", reduce the range of economic fluctuations and maintain long-term stable growth of economy.

VI. Root of the Socialist Business Cycle

Where is the socialist economic cyclical fluctuation rooted? Different theories have existed with divergences among them up to now. It's because of this that the Theory of Natural Fluctuations and the Theory of Factors have their space of existence. In the late 1950s and the early 1960s, restricted by the premise of traditional socialist consumptions, people attributed the reason for socialist economic fluctuations to one of the general laws of matter's development, and also attributed the direct reason for fluctuations to natural disasters, technological advance, errors in planned work and other factors.

Within the analytical framework of historical materialism, Marx revealed out that the root for the capitalist business cycles lies in the basic contradiction of capitalism. As it is the most profound findings, scholars also tried with Marx's methodology for solutions when they were studying the socialist business cycle. For example, Liu Shucheng, one of the pioneering researchers of China's socialist business cycles after the1980s, would always quote some of Marx's expositions of the business cycle in the very fundamental part of his works, and then he would put forward his own theoretical proposition on such a ground. He used to attribute the root of the socialist economic and cyclical fluctuation to the contradiction between the ever-growing material and cultural needs of the people and the backwardness of social production, i.e., the principal contradiction of socialism. This is because it shows itself as the contradiction between large-scale economic construction and the shortage of material force. Afterwards, he again attributed the cyclical fluctuation in the socialist economies to "the result of contradictory movement of two mechanisms", i.e. "the mechanism of interaction between large-scale investment and large-scale industrial production; restraining mechanism of supply and demand". Among them, the interaction and expansion of large-scale investment and large-scale industrial production is the leading mechanism materially and "the primary reason" to form the economic cyclical fluctuation; the equilibrium between supply and demand is the restraining mechanism materially and "the ultimate reason" to form the economic cyclical fluctuation.[15] After more than ten years, along with the development of commodity economy and the establishment of the market economic system in China, Liu Shucheng turned to the contradiction between production and consumption, and the contradiction between the proportionality of socialized production and the blindness of investment expansion for the interpretation of the cyclical fluctuation in China's economy. He put it like that: "In terms of the general principle in the market economy, on one hand, the internal impetus for enterprises to seek profits and the external pressure from violent competition in the market will make them expand investment and production at any risks, however, on the other hand, enterprises will lower the payroll costs by all means in order to achieve relative shortage of consumption demands from purchasing power. Therefore, in general, in the market economy, the market expansion can never catch up with the expansion of investment and production, and then comes the periodically relative surplus in production capacity. " "In the market economy, enterprises will have expansion impulse due to internal impetus for pursuit of profits and face external pressure of strong competition in the market; however on the other hand, the reforms about the function of government are still ongoing. Besides we see strong expansive efforts initiated by the local governments. For example, there are provinces where we see oversized "vanity projects" and "image projects" which are being carried out vigorously consisting of exaggerated urban construction projects and there are cases where arbitrary authorizations/ permissions for development zones, are issued. Whether it is the expansive impulses by enterprises in the mainstream market economies, or the expansive impulses by the central government in the socialist planned economy, and whether the expansive impulses by enterprises or the local governments in the current system of our country, they all will lead to economic overheating."[16]

489

---

15 Liu Shucheng, *Economic Cyclical Fluctuations in China*, p. 40-43, Beijing, Economic Science Press, 1989.
16 Liu Shucheng, *"Characteristics of Background for a New Round of Business Cycles"*, in *Economic Studies*, 2004(3).

This interpretation returns to Marx's theory of the business cycle, because the contradiction here between production and market is consistent with one of the concrete forms of the basic contradictions of capitalism: "The contradiction between the tendency towards unlimited expansion of production and the restrictions capitalism imposes on the individual and social consumption of the workers."; and the contradiction between proportionality of the socialized production and blindness of the investment expansion is consistent with one of the concrete forms of the basic contradictions of capitalism: "The contradiction between the increasingly planned and conscious organisation of production within each capitalist firm resulting from the socialisation of labour, and the unplanned, anarchistic nature of capitalist production as a whole."[17]

On the whole, Liu Shucheng interpreted the socialist business cycle in a common sense. Because he "relinquished the issue of social cause between investment and production when interpreting fluctuations through "the mechanism of interaction between large-scale investment and massive industrial production", and "relinquished the social system and social material conditions" when interpreting fluctuations through "the restriction mechanism of supply and demand".[18] Therefore, in his works, he always attributes the cyclical fluctuation of economy to the socialized mass production and the market economy, and holds that the economic cyclical fluctuation is the common phenomenon of socialism and capitalism, and that whether in the planned economic system or the market economy system; there are certain uniform mechanisms for economic cyclical fluctuations. For example, he regards the cyclical fluctuation as common phenomenon of the socialized mass production, and thinks that on the condition of the socialized mass production, the interaction between large-scale investment and production is significantly brought into play, which makes the cyclical fluctuation of investment turn from possibility to come into reality to inevitability. Because Liu Shucheng has always acted as the "leading figure" in the studies of the socialist business cycle ever since 1980s, under his influence, there is some market for "the Theory of Neutrality of the Business cycle" and some schools are formed, in which some people put forward a serried of challenging ideas. For instance, some people think the socialist business cycle is basically the same with the capitalist business cycle in occurrence mechanism, manifestation pattern and economic nature. Other people say that whether in the market economy or the planned economy, the general mechanism for rise and fall of the economic operation is the same, and the differences lie in different features of the specific formation mechanism (e.g. initiation mechanism, constraint mechanism) and the specific manifestation pattern (e.g. amplitude) owing to different economic systems.

---

17   Marx's theory of Economic Crisis, quoted in International Socialist Review(32).
18   Liu Shucheng, "*Economic Cyclical Fluctuations in China*, p. 40. (The China Economy Yearbook, Volume 5: Chief Editor Chen Jiagui).

In the theory of China's economic cyclical fluctuation, the Theory of Investment Cycle is the most influential, which was put forward by Liu Shucheng and enjoys prestigious recognition in the theoretical circles. I should also note that in addition to the detailed demonstration of this theory by Liu Shucheng, Lu Jian also did a lot of important demonstrative work. He thinks that the cyclical fluctuation of investment will inevitably lead to the cyclical fluctuation of the whole national economy, but in different historical periods, the formation of investment cycle and the occurrence mechanism of the business cycle are not the same. In a simple planned economy, the formation of investment cycle can be basically attributed to cyclical changes in the executive decisions of the highly centralized government; while in a planned commodity economy, there is a diversified tendency for the decision-making powers of production and the investment.

Why will investment cause violent fluctuations in the traditional system? The reasons lie in: (1) Driven by quantity indexes, enterprises strive to seek the rapid growth of production value with no emphasis on revenues in the growing process; In the course of seeking quantity indexes, enterprises tend to select methods that are the easiest to expand. Increase of investment amount and expansion of the scale of enterprises undoubtedly become the factors which the enterprise gives priority to, and also the methods to achieve economic growth most easily. Because the attraction of investment is far larger than the production value gained by enterprises through internal potential tapping and innovation, that's not only because enterprises will not have to undertake the responsi- bility and risks related to this part of investment while gaining the investment, but also because in the actual course, investment can bring about accelerated growth of production value and other quantity indexes in a short time. (2) In the traditional system, the expansion impulsive of enterprises will ultimately converge into the desire of each economic sector to vigorously increase their investment, and each sector is very eager to require the change in the former investment pattern and the structure of investment shares. Therefore, the growth performance brought about by the last round of investment has already become the premise for seeking more investment for the next round. In order to gain "work achievements" and result in "self-actualization" in a faster way, all that each sector requires is increasing investment. (3) In the industrialization process, the development in different areas is always unbalanced. With early starting, the industrialized level in the advanced areas is relatively high and the investment demands are relatively large; while tempted by the objective to catch up with the advanced areas, those backward areas strive for more investment allocations. On the general conditions, the new investment demands of the original enterprises in the backward areas cannot be satisfied easily, therefore, the pursuit of more new project to be allocated in the areas will become the alternative for pursuit of investment increase. The investment demands in the three levels mentioned above show that: the relative attraction of investment to achieve economic growth most quickly and no responsibility and risks to be undertaken by investment is the root for the appearance of such surplus demands.

The mechanisms for economic fluctuation in socialist countries are basically the same, which was proven by the research conclusion of business cycles made by economists in the eastern European countries in those years. The time for them to start the researches into the socialist business cycle was generally the same with that of the Chinese scholars. The difference lies in that they maintained the continuity of research work on the whole before "the great revulsion", so there are certain reference values to researches into fluctuations in China's economies in their research results. Kornai, one of the famous economists, once thought that the economic cyclical fluctuations in the period of the socialist planned economy are the "inflation—recession" fluctuation phenomenon caused by "the expansion impulsive" while constrained by resource shortage.[19] This conclusion happens to coincide with the research conclusion of Chinese scholars, which supports the research work of Chinese scholars to a great extent. Based on the research achievements of scholars in the Soviet Union and East Europe, some scholars think that there is internal expansion impulsive in the socialist economies, established on the basis of shortage. Investment fluctuation is the main force for the cyclical fluctuations in the socialist economies. Various factors from outside the economy intensify the range of the cyclical fluctuation in economic operations.

Moreover, along with deepening of the researches, some scholars think the economic cyclical fluctuation is the common features of the market economy, owned by the capitalist society and the socialist society. Because on the condition of the market economy, the interactions of supply-demand relation and prices will always cause the expansion and constraint of investment, which further influences the rate of economic growth. Liu Shucheng holds that although there is some difference in the detailed formation mechanism and manifestation pattern of the economic cyclical fluctuation between the market economy and the planned economy, the basic mechanism for the economic cyclical fluctuation is the same, both with economic overheating and radical changes from great rises to great falls. Economic overheating, economic cyclical fluctuation, and great rises causing great falls are originally the phenomena in the market economy and the industrialization process, so whether in the market economy or the planned economy, the general mechanism for rise and fall of the economic operation is the same, and the differences lie in different features of the specific formation mechanism (e.g. initiation mechanism, constraint mechanism) and the specific manifestation pattern (e.g. amplitude) owing to different economic systems. In terms of the basic mechanism, the multiplier principle and the acceleration principle in the economics tell us that there is internal accumulative amplification in economic expansion. An initial expansion of the demand (demand for articles of consumption or investment) will result in a multiple (multiplier) amplification effect of production; and the expansion of production will also result in a multiple (multiplier) amplification

---

19   Wu Jinglian, *Economic Fluctuation and the Dual System*, in *Finance & Trade Economics*, 1986(2).

effect of investment; and then expansion in investment will in turn further promote the expansion of production. Especially when the economic expansion approaches and surpasses the potential economic growth rate, the economic operation tends to be over-heated and the proportional imbalance will accumulatively happen in the economic structure, and ultimately the business cycle will turn to the falling phase from the rising phase. The bigger the rise is, the more severe the proportional imbalance in the economic structure which will cause greater falls As for proportional imbalance in the economic structure, the most important are two large types of imbalance: one is the proportional imbalance between rapid expansion of investment and production and the resource supplies. Resource supplies mainly refer to the supplies in finance, human power and materials. The shortage of resource supplies will inactivate the economic expansion. The other one is the proportional imbalance between rapid expansion of investment and production and the consumption demands. This can be reflected collectively in the overall proportional imbalance between investment and consumption, and can also be reflected in regional proportional imbalance between the overdevelopment of investment and production and the consumption demand of some leading sectors with over-speed expansion. The overall proportional imbalance and the regional proportional imbalance between investment and consumption will both lead to cut in the whole economic expansion. In the market economy, initiation of the economy is mainly market activities. The subject in the market economy—enterprises, have the expansion impulsive because of the internal motivation for pursuit of profits and the external pressure from violent competition in the market, or as Keynes put it, this kind of expansion impulsive is a "spontaneous""impulsion of vigour". In the former planned economic system of our country, the initiation of economy is mainly governmental behaviour. The subject of the planned economy—the government, especially the central government, is always eager for success or in pursuit of work performance. Along with soft budget constraint, they will generate strong expansion impulsive. Nowadays, the socialist market economic system has preliminarily established in our country and the transformation of governmental functions is still ongoing. Especially much of the transformation for functions in the local government has not been achieved. Although the automatic growth capacity of enterprises is being enhanced, the expansion impulsive of local governments is still very strong. There are places where "the vanity project" and "the image project" are carried out vigorously with oversized scale and overtop standards of the urban construction and arbitrary authorization or construction of the development zone, etc. Whether it is the expansion impulsive of enterprises in the market economy, or the expansion impulsive of the central government in the planned economy, or else the expansion impulsive of enterprises and the local governments in the current system of our country, they will all lead to economic overheating." While in the former planned economic system of our country, the strong power of the central government for impulsive of arbitrary expansion will always make the economic fluctuation display features of more expansion of amplitude in specific

493

manifestation patterns. In the market economy, the factors restricting economic expansion include financial resources, man power and materials, etc. However, financial resources and man power are always more prominent, and reflected on the rise of capital costs (interest rate) and the rise of man power costs (remuneration), which will force enterprises to stop the expansion with the hard budget constraint. In the former planned economic system of our country, the factors restricting economic expansion also include financial resources, man power and materials, but the frequently prominent one is materials rather than financial resources (because of soft budget constraint, non-marketization of interest rate) or man power (because of numerous surplus labour in rural areas, non-marketization of remuneration). Restriction of the economic development level and lack of vitality in the supply side will frequently cause energy, important raw materials and communications to become the bottleneck restricting the economic growth.[20] Li Chong also subscribes to the cause of market economy for the economic cyclical fluctuation. He thinks that the business cycle is actually caused by the market economic system, and that the capitalist economic system strengthens weaknesses of the market economic system in different degrees while the socialist economic system can compensate for the weaknesses of the market economic system in different degrees. Now that the fundamental cause for the occurrence of business cycles lies in the market economic system, then in the socialist economic system, the business cycles will still occur with the implementation of the market economic system. In the actual socialist economic system, the national ownership, the collective ownership, the individual ownership and other ownerships co-exist while commodity producers are independent from each other, which carry out production for profits. Therefore, their response to the market is very sensitive, and they will adjust the output quantity according to signals of the market prices. The spontaneity and blindness of the regulatory mechanism of prices still exist and business cycles will still occur. Even though there are only public ownership forms of state ownership and collective ownership, there is only the independent relation of commodity exchanges among commodity producers and the regulatory mechanism of prices still function voluntarily with occurrence of business cycles.[21]

As one of the universal laws, the cyclical fluctuation of the capitalist economies is rooted in the contradictory movement of productivity and the productive relation, i.e. the special manifestation pattern of this contradiction in the capitalism—the contradiction between socialization of production and personal occupation of means of production. The socialist business cycle is also rooted in the contradictory movement of productivity and the productive relation, but the special form of this contradiction is not only different from that of capitalism, but there are different manifestation forms of it in different transformation periods of the socialist economic system of China: In the period of the planned

20   Liu Shucheng, *"Features of the Background of a New Round of Business cycle"*, in *Economic Studies*, 2004(3).
21   Li Chong, *"Re-visiting the Causes of the Business Cycle"*, in *Contemporary Economic Research*, 2005(8).

economy, it is the contradiction between socialized mass production and the imperfect planning work in the national economy; in the market economy, it is the contradiction between socialized mass production and diversification of economic sectors. Empirical researches for many years show that violent economic fluctuations in China's planned economic period are mainly caused by errors in planning work, while the economic fluctuation in the market economy period is mainly caused by contradiction between production anarchy caused by the pursuit of interest subject for maximization of its interest and limitation in the macro-control capacity of the state. Scholars think that the material basis for the socialist business cycle also lies in large-scale renewal of fixed assets, i.e. large-scale investment in fixed assets. The empirical researches of Liu Shucheng provide potent evidence for this idea. And there are no great divergences in the issue of material basis of cycles in the later researches. Scholars are mainly devoted to studies of the formation mechanism of wave-mode investment of the government and enterprises. In the free market economy, the anarchy of production can easily stimulate all the capitalists' desire for the uttermost pursuit of surplus values to the utmost, and force them to make excessive risk-taking investment decisions collectively, thus causing radical changes in economy. In the socialist market economy, influenced by the dominant position of public ownership, impulsive of the governmental officials at every level for work performance and impulsive of enterprises for maximized benefits, and other factors, investment impulsion will occur periodically, thus causing radical changes in economic growth.

As for the nature of China's business cycles, we can almost find the traces of all the modern theories of business cycles in quite a number of theoretical interpretations. One may interpret the business cycle in China with the Theory of Real Business Cycle (technological impulsion), another may interpret the business cycle in China with the Theory of Actual Business cycle (impulsion of currency supply), and still another interpret the business cycle in China with the Theory of Political Business cycle. In general, introduction of western theory of modern business cycles to make new interpretation of China's business cycles can be regarded as one of the features for the current socialist business cycle researches in China. However, this is not the mainstream of the socialist business cycle researches in China. When based on the Marxist Theory of business cycles and with combination of the Marxist contradiction analysis method and the modern statistical approach, the theory of socialist business cycle formed hereby is the mainstream.

The Theory of Inner and Outer Factors is one of the important forms to interpret the socialist business cycle and accepted by many people. The owner of this analysis method thinks that the actual economic fluctuations are neither the natural process of voluntary effects of inner factors of a single economy, nor the social process with only effects of outer factors. It's the result of common effects of two kinds of factors in the same historical sequence. Surely enough, the features of the factors will be more significant with more effects coming out. As for natural fluctuations determined by inner factors, their fluctuation amplitude is generally quite small, while for natural fluctuations determined by outer factors, their fluctuation amplitude is generally large. The endogenous factors refer to some variable fluctuations inside the economy, such as increment of the national income, accelerators, inducing investment and resetting investment, etc. The exogenous variables refer to exogenous factors, such as natural disasters, political events, policy changes, etc. The opponent of the idea holds that the economic impact of some factors outside the economic system can only be used to interpret random economic fluctuations; it does not interpret the cause for the business cycle formation . It cannot be the stable solution for the cause of business cycles formation.

Among the proponents of the Theory of Multiple Factors, some scholars cannot distinguish the primary and secondary reasons, and think that they are the result of additive effects of multiple factors. For example, Wu Chunzhi thinks that the cyclical fluctuation of the socialist economic growth is the result of common effects of multiple factors: the first factor is the contradiction between balance and imbalance of the social economic development, the second is the contradiction between the aggregate supply and the aggregate demand in the society, the third is the contradiction between large-scale infrastructure and renewal of fixed assets, the fourth is the limitation of economic growth or decline, and the fifth is the outer impulsion of non-economic factors.[22] Some scholars think the socialist economic fluctuation is the result of the additive effects of the following factors: impulsion of the planner, soft constraint competition, agricultural harvest, investment (large-scale renewal of fixed assets) cycle, consumption, conditions of foreign trade, currency supply and fiscal expenditure, etc.

Some scholars have strict classification of reasons for economic cyclical fluctuations, and think that the renewal of fixed assets, investment cycles are the general reason for formation of cyclical economic phenomena of the modern commodity economy. On the special condition of socialism, the most basic reason for formation of the economic growth cycle is the basic contradiction of socialism. In addition to these reasons in the economic field, there are fluctuations caused by the factors stemming from the other spheres, such as nature, science and technology, policy and politics, etc.[23]

Some scholars argue that the business cycles in China can be classified as political cycles, because economy is closely connected to politics in China, and in most of the time, the political system and the economic system are in a union. The government is the most authorized and effective representative of the owners of assets in the system of public ownership. As the sole representative of the state-owned enterprises, the government at every level dominates

22 Wu Chunzhi, *"On Socialist Business Cycle"*, in *Journal of Sichuan Normal University* (Social Science), 1999(1).
23 Zha Peixuan, *"Studies of Features and Reasons for the Socialist Economic Growth Cycle"*, in *Journal of Humanities*, 1992(2).

the overall tendency of investment demands, and it's the government to release or tighten the rein. And as one of the main means for the government to regulate the economy, the economic policies specially impose profound and lasting significance on the economic fluctuation. The practical advance of economic fluctuations propels people to do theoretical thinking. Especially the obvious features of "radical changes" displayed in China's economy before the reform and opening up gradually draw the emphasis of the theoretical circle on policy factors. After comprehensive consideration of the factors influencing economic fluctuation, the theoretical circle gradually brings the cyclical fluctuation of policy into the important variables influencing economic fluctuations. Starting from the view whether policies can form the factor of economic fluctuation, some scholar thinks that economic policies should be generally listed in the internal factors influencing the economic cyclical fluctuation. Starting from the view of effects of polices on the economic fluctuation, another scholar thinks that governmental policies have the effects of strengthening, hindering and initiating effects on the general condition of economic operations, and further thinks various polices of the government have the double effects of easing or strengthening fluctuations. And starting from the view of the relation between cyclical fluctuations of policies and the economic fluctuation, another scholar thinks that the root for China's economic fluctuation mainly comes from external impulse caused by cyclical changes of policies. These show that the theoretical circle in our country has already regarded the cyclical fluctuation of policies as one of the important variables generating effects on the economic fluctuation. 497

The analytical results show that the transformation impulse of China's economic system (institution) has great determining effects on the direction and degree of the economic cyclical changes. In China, those important reform measures promulgated with the influence of political background impose massive and profound influence on the development of economies. Surely enough, on today's condition with gradual perfection of the market economic system, the economic system with dependence on political changes of so cannot replace the effects of economic laws. However, there are significant correlation between changes in the economic system (institution) and the economic cyclical fluctuation. This correlation was displayed very significantly before the 1990s, i.e. changes in institution can have "instant" effects on the economy, and "the hard landing" method should be used each time for regulation to cause "sudden braking" in the course of the overall economic operation, which further caused violent economic fluctuations. One scholar once utilized the second-phase auto-regression dynamic equation to imitate the impact of political mobilization, and his conclusion held that there are strong effects of political mobilization in the congress of party representatives, and the expansion of economy has the corresponding relationship with each session of the congress of party representatives, and also the corresponding relationship with congress of people's representatives. Of course, one of the purposes of progressive reforms in the economic system (institution) is to avoid violent fluctuations of the economic operation. However it can't be denied that implementation of every great reform measure will inevitably cause corresponding economic fluctuations. This shows that the system reform itself will generate the effects of expansion and recession; therefore, investigations must be carried out first about the conditions of economic cyclical fluctuation and fluctuation tendency at that time, and the inverted operation between the fluctuation effects in the system reform and the cyclical fluctuation. The correct practice is to timely issue reform measures with large cost burdens in the rising phase of economy to eliminate costs in growth; while timely issuing reform measures with expansion effects in the declining phase. Because it's better to advance system measure than to withdraw them, the government also should bring into its consideration the changes in the system environment caused by system reform and the macro-economic effects generated by the system reform, and treat the transformation of system as the internal factor of the economy to draw up cyclical policies. When the measures for system reform already have the effects of expansion and recession, the counter system policies should reduce its intensity accordingly. The policies for system reform and the policies for counter-cycle in the government should coordinate with each other to jointly achieve the objective of ironing the business cycle and maintaining the steady operation of economy.[24] Shi Wei demonstrated the effects of policy factor and currency factor on the influence of China's economic fluctuation, and specifically listed the corresponding relationship between them.[25] After over ten years, Du Ting, Pang Dong and others utilized the economic quantitative method to test the system impact and changes in features of our country's business cycles, and test their relativity with China's economic cyclical fluctuation through three system impact variable through degree of marketization, level of denationalization and the opening degree. And the result showed that great reform of the economic system issued while China was influenced by political background impose massive and profound influence on the economic development. The impact of system changes has very large determining effects on the direction and degree of the economic cyclical changes.[26]

Some scholars think that the reasons to make the stability of China's business cycles stronger are generally the following several facets: the first facet lies in more matured economies in our country with the proportional structure of each facet more coordinated while the fluctuation degree of economy is always inversely proportional to the coordinated degree of the structure. The second lies in that the marketization degree becomes enhanced and the government alleviated its degree of economic intervention while the investment

24   Du Ting, Pang Dong, Yang Can, "*Analysis of the System Impact of China's Economic Cyclical Fluctuation*", in *Journal of Finance and Economics*, 2006(4).

25   Shi Wei, "*Policy Factors and Currency Factors in the Economic Cyclical Fluctuation*", in *Research on Financial and Economic Issues*, 1994(6).

26   Du Ting, Pang Dong, "*System Impacts and Cyclical Fluctuation of China's Economies*", in *the Journal of Quantitative & Technical Economics*, 2006(6).

behaviours advanced and amplified at each level and governmental behaviours were weakened. Therefore, though the main target of investment growth ever since the 1990s investment subject was not the government but the enterprises dominated by non-governmental enterprises, so it's an act of enterprises, and the result was the devolution of administrative power to lower levels by the central government (project examination and approval). The third one lies in the intensified degree of opening up and relevantly intensification of adjustment of foreign trade. This effect will smooth the degree of economic fluctuations. This is not only one of the important reasons for easing of recession degree in the last cycle, but one of the important reasons for relative fatigue from economic expansion in this cycle. The fourth one lies in that the government utilizes active fiscal measure to stimulate the economy to make the decline degree of the investment scale in the recession period lighter than previous scale.. This is not the only important reason for soft rising degree of prices in recent years, but the main reason for rather stable growth of the investment amount in the expansion period of business cycles.[27]

VII. Transmission Mechanism of the Fluctuation in China's Business Cycle

As for the issue of transmission mechanism of China's business cycle, some scholars think that the whole national economy is a large system, and the system, structure, total quantity and other multiple factors jointly determine that there are growing expansion and constraint mechanism in the process of economic operations itself. They also think that it's not the case for macro control (including the selection and execution of economic policies) to lie outside the economic system and influence the process of economic operations from the outside. Macro-control itself is one of the components in the operation process of the economic system. Fan Mingtai analyzed the internal transmission mechanisms (mainly including the multiplier-accelerator mechanism of investment, the correlative mechanism of industry, the buffer mechanism of upper limit-lower limit) and the external impact mechanisms (the impact mechanism of currency policy and the impact mechanism of financial policy) of the economic fluctuation in our country, and then established measurement models to carry out empirical analysis of these two mechanisms. And the conclusion was drawn as follows: The economic fluctuation in our country is the result of joint effects of the internal transmission mechanism and the external impact mechanism. Classification of the internal transmission mechanism and the external impact mechanism provides possibility for better convergence of the theory of economic fluctuation and experience estimation. The internal transmission mechanism reflects the internal evolution process of the economic system (i.e. structural equation) starting from the initial state. The nonlinearity is introduced into the model of cycle theories indirectly and the limited cyclical

499

---

27 Yang Wenjin, *"Review of the Current Economic Situation and Tendency through the Relations of Cycles"* in *Journal of Statistical Research*, 2004(8).

fluctuation is self propelled by the economic activity itself. And the external impact mechanism makes the economy achieve actually recurrent fluctuations. Seen form the economic empirical analysis, only by classifying the external impact mechanism and the internal transmission mechanism can the random structure equation be sued to replace the determinant structure equation to make the simulation result more adaptable to the actual economic fluctuation of statistical observations. Fang Jiachun thinks that on the condition of foreign trade and economic opening up, the economic fluctuation of a country can possibly impose impacts on the domestic economic system of that country and then incur economic fluctuations through foreign trade, interference in the foreign trade of countries with open economy, convergence of the latent defects in domestic distribution of resources on the condition of the open economy. The national economy will also be impacted through changes of prices in the world market, channels for international capital flow and international talents flow and the scale of foreign debts, etc. Li Yining once thought that like any social economy, the socialist economies are not only the development course of fluctuations, they are also one of the self-regulatory mechanisms to prevent oversized expansion and shrink. The macro-control of government refers to the measures adopted to enhance the functions of mechanism regulation and recovering the balanced growth of the economy when the self-regulatory mechanism of economy cannot restrain the excessive imbalance of economy.

Seen from the investment supplies, what actually determines the increase or decrease of investment amount is the organization of planning and decision. For areas, sectors, enterprises and non-profit units, the demand for investment amount is almost hard to satisfy. However, the amount of supplies provided to this vigorous investment demand in the economic course is controlled in the "sluice gate" of the organization of planning and decision on control of investment amount, while the more profound influence naturally comes from the highest decision-making sectors. Seen from this sense, "the main switch" for control of planning and decision in the operational system of socialism determines the overall level of economic growth. The fluctuations incurred in growth of the social gross output, the national revenues and per capita GNP are inevitably related to the rise and fall of the "main switch". In this way, we will naturally connect the economic fluctuation with the "policy factors" of the organ of decision making.

The main basis for organs of planning and decision is the judgment to the economic situation. Specifically speaking, the first one is evaluation of the changeable amount in the national revenues in the last year; the second one is the evaluation of conditions for investment demands. If the economy is in the rising phase, the national revenue will grow very rapidly, and the organ of planning itself will generate strong impulsion to increase investment. In this way, the gate for supplies is opened to meet the ever-lasting excessive investment demands. If the economy is in the phase of depression, the national revenue will slow down and the organ of planning will reduce the amount of investment supply for planning arrangement according to common practices. However, this process is very slow in actual reality. One is because of the rigidity in the growth of investment amount, and the decision made by the organ of planning cannot lower the tendency for increasing the investment supplies in a short time, which will affect the contrast for benefits and power of all parties, unless the top organ of decision determines to reduce the supply amount. The other is because the growth of short-term output values generated by rapid investment growth in the rising period will prolong the effects, which will bring about an illusion that the economic situation is in the "prosperity" period and this therefore induces new investment impulsions. In order to protect the growth scale, investment must be accelerated. At that time, even though the economic growth slows down, the investment demand is always in the activated state, thus propelling investment supplies to grow in an unrestrained type, which will continue until the national economy has difficulty in bearing it. On the one hand, the increase of national revenues has already had difficulty to support the bigger and bigger "construction situation"; on the other hand, the short-term restraint for resources and investments has reached the limit. The investment supplies have to slam the brakes with the "main switch" dropping suddenly because the urgent compression of excessive investment demands and the overall adjustment of the national economy. It can be clearly seen that the radical changes in policies of investment supplies made by the organ of planning and decision is one of the main causes that result in violent fluctuations in investment growth.[28]

501

Seen from the macro-background to propel the economic cyclical growth each time, though there are some differences in specific manifestation for the power source of the first four economic cyclical growths ever since the reform and opening up, there are few divergences on the whole, and they all go round the big framework of "investment promotion–resource restraint". In the early stage of the economic transformation, the normal state for economic operation is economic expansion impulsion–aggravation of bottleneck restraint – inflation–temporary economic regulation of the government–alleviation of the bottleneck shortage in the macro-economy–a new round of economic expansion. Because of the introduction of market mechanism, the capacity for macro aggregate supplies will increase greatly for the increase of efficiency of resources allocation and the micro efficiency. Besides, because of the reform and opening up, the introduction of foreign funds can make up for shortage in capital, technological innovation and management factors in the macro-economy of China, and will greatly increase China's capacity for aggregate supplies with combination of the input foreign capitals and rather abundant labour forces.

28 See Wang Yongzhi, Zhang Xinhua: *Analysis of the Promotion and Constraint Mechanism of Business Cycles in Our Country*, in *Journal of Quantitative & Technical Economics*, 1987(11).

Through empirical analysis, Lu Jian proves the formation theory of currency fluctuation, the formation theory of consumption fluctuation, the formation theory of price fluctuation, and the formation theory of transformation of the industrial structure cannot ultimately interpret the general cause for cyclical fluctuations in China's economy. So he put forward the conclusion assumption of "cyclical fission" to demonstrate the decisive effects of the fission process in the industrial cycles and agricultural cycle as well as the industrial cycle on the business cycle, i.e. industry is the main engine for the economic growth in China. The expansion and contraction, as well as the prosperity and depression of the industrial production impose decisive influence on the cyclical fluctuation of the national economy. Based on this, he further attributed the endogenous factors of China's business cycles to investment of fixed assets, increment of the national revenues in the last period, induced consumption, accelerator, induced investment and reset investment; and then attributed the exogenous factors to political events, administrative decisions, changes in the social economic system, etc. and then revealed their transmission mechanism. Lu Jian thinks that the endogenous factors to propel cyclical fluctuation of China's investment will ultimately be attributed to changes in levels of national revenues in the early stage. The cyclical fluctuation of the growth level of national revenues in the last phase basically determines the general rhythm of the investment cycle. And the political economic system, administrative decisions and other exogenous factors indirectly influence the fluctuation amplitude, length of expansion and contraction of the investment cycle, the turning point, and bring forward or retard the arrival of peak or trough of investment. In general, the endogenous factors and transmission mechanism of China's business cycles are reflected in: changes in the level of national revenues in the last phase will incur changes in the consumption levels in this phase, the changes in consumption levels in this phase will incur changes in the investment levels in this phase, and the changes in the investment level in this phase will in turn incur changes in the level of national revenues in this phase. It goes round and round, thus forms the cyclical changes of the national revenues-investment-national revenue, i.e. the business cycle.

502

Lu Jian thinks that in different historical periods, especially before the reform of the socio-economic system and after the reform, the exogenous factors have different transmission mechanisms for influence and effects on the economic system. In a single planned economic period, the formation of China's business cycle is always greatly influenced by administrative policy changes of high centralization. In this period, what to produce, how many to produce and for whom to produce are not be decided independently by enterprises but depend on the superior organ of administrative decision with high concentration of these three production powers. However, the functions of administrative organs are not only making decisions for production objective, more importantly making decisions for the political objectives in society. The decision for production objective serves the decision for political objective. Political objectives are always reflected in high indexes for idealized economic growth. Because three great productive powers are highly concentrated on the organ of administrative decision, the power for investment decision is also highly concentrated on the organ of administrative decision. The important reason for incurrence of substantial fluctuations lies in that the organ of administrative decision violates the objective economic laws and rashly makes decisions for substantial expansion of economic and investment scales in order to achieve some direct political objective or idealize high indexes for economic growth. Based on this, the planning sector draws up and issues the specific plans for expansion of investment scale and high growth of economy. In order to achieve the objective put forward by the organ of administrative decision, party and governmental departments also politically demand and call upon sectors at different levels and local areas to over-fulfil the national plan indexes. Local areas and sectors have to improve safety risks in order to ensure the accomplishment of the superior planned indexes. Hence, the growth indexes gradually accumulate and the investment scale expands at each level, and here comes the "acceleration principle" exclusive to the planned economy. This enlarged effect of investment in the execution process of plans will rapidly push the economy to the peak, and ultimately cause the economic expansion to cross the potential border of production and proportional imbalance of the national economy. Meanwhile, the economic expansion is restricted by the "bottleneck" of shortage of domestic resources and the hard constraint of shortage of foreign exchange, and troubled by the imbalance of the national economic structure, so the organ of administrative decision will have to stop the economic expansion and turn to the adjustment of economic structures and make decisions for contraction. Based on this, the planning department formulates and issues the plan objective to cut down investment scale and clear up projects on construction. At this time, the party and government departments will once again require and call on departments and local areas at each level to strive for the accomplishment of constraint tasks. So, "the acceleration principle" of the planned economy militates in the opposite direction. Local areas and departments at each level have to raise the safety risks to ensure the accomplishment of constraint tasks. Therefore, the contraction indexes are raised gradually, and the investment scale receives more pressure at each level. The progressive effects of investment in the adjustment process will have to push the economy to depression, and ultimately cause the production department to run below capacity, and severe structural resource idling comes out. Such severe phenomenon of waste of social productivity is definitely unbearable in politics. Therefore, the organ of administrative decision will make decisions again to take expansive measure to make the national economy return to peak and enter the planned commodity economic period with diversified tendency of the decision-making power of production and the decision-making power of investment. Nowadays, enterprises have gained certain autonomous right for production and investment along with accomplishment plans by the administrative organs at each level. The investment cycle and the business cycle are now influenced by two factors.

503

On the one hand, they still depend on the investment decision made by organs of administrative decision; on the other hand, they depend on the investment decision of enterprises, i.e. the anticipation of enterprise for off-plan production benefits according to the price signal in the market. With high anticipated benefits, the growth rate for enterprises' off-plan investment will rise; while with low anticipated benefits, the growth rate for enterprises' off-plan investment will fall. Now that the planned investment of the state is still the leading force, changes in planned investment demands will still be the important factor to influence the economic fluctuation. However, the price changes affected by the dominant investment demands will cause relevant fluctuation of off-plan production anticipation and investment. Therefore, the fluctuation of off-plan investment will inevitably impose cumulated influence on the economic fluctuation. But now the fluctuation dominating investment itself has already tended to be relatively placid, at least not so violent like the single planned economic period. This is mainly because along with introduction of market mechanism and increase of monetization levels, price control and wage control gradually ease and the supply amount of currency, total wages of staff and workers, inventory of commodity and price index, etc have already sensitively reflected the condition of economic inflation and depression. The inflation of investment demand will inevitably cause excessive supply of currency, push the economy to over-expansion, and result in excessive employment and inflation of consumption demands with decline of commodity inventory and rapid rise of price index. Otherwise, excessive contraction of investment demand will inevitably cause shortage of currency supply and economic recession, and result in employment stagnation and slack consumption demands with rise of commodity inventory and decline of price index.

504

The multiplier principle and the acceleration principle in economics tell us that economic expansion has the internal accumulative amplification. An initial expansion of demands (demand for article of consumption or demand for article of investment) will cause the amplification effect of production by a multiple (multiplier); the production expansion will cause the amplification effect of investment by a multiple (multiplier); and the investment expansion will in turn further stimulate the expansion of production. Especially when economic expansion approaches or surpasses the potential economic growth rate, the economic operation will tend to be over-heated and the economic structure will accumulatively experience proportional imbalance, and ultimately cause the business cycle turn from the rising phase to the declining phase. The greater the rise is, the more severe proportional imbalance the economic structure will experience, which will cause greater decline. As for proportional imbalance in the economic structure, the most important ones are two kinds of imbalance: the first one is the proportional imbalance between rapid expansion of investment, production and resource supplies. Resource supplies mainly refer to the supply of financial power, human power and materials. The shortage of resource supplies will cause turns in the economic expansion. The second lies in the proportional imbalance between rapid expansion of investment, production and consumption demands. This can be collectively reflected in the overall proportional imbalance of investment and consumption, and can also be reflected in regional proportional imbalance between the excessive development of the investment, production of some leading sectors with over-speed expansion and the consumption demands. The overall proportional imbalance and regional proportional imbalance between investment and consumption will both cause turns in the whole economic expansion. Seen from the view of industrial growth, expansion and contraction of investment and labour employment determines the expansion and contraction of the industrial production, and the cyclical fluctuation of investment and employment level will result in cyclical fluctuation of the industrial production level. When comparing these principles with the above-mentioned ideas of the Chinese scholars, one can see their contributions neat and clear.

VIII. Gradual Development in Steps and Business Cycle

It's fair to say that there is the significant relationship of inheritance and development between Deng Xiaoping's idea of "gradual development in steps" and the "wave-like development of the socialist economy put forward by Chinese scholars in the late 1950s and the early 1960s. This is mainly reflected in that Deng Xiaoping's idea of "gradual development in steps" has extensive theoretical and practical basis, abundant historical basis and realistic pertinence, and it puts more emphasis on development.

After summarizing the experience and lessons of socialist economic construction work since the foundation of New China, Deng Xiaoping has suggested that the three-step development strategy is the development pattern suitable to China's national economy.

This idea was developed on the basis of repeated summarization of past practical experience. In August, 1991, Deng Xiaoping pointed out after summarizing the development experience of China since the 1980s, "It seems that our economy tends to develop in waves, moving rapidly ahead for a few years, reaching a higher stage, after which we pause to solve the problems that have arisen, and then moving on again."[29] Around January-February, 1992, Deng Xiaoping has made a further suggestion: "It seems to me that, as a rule, at certain stages we should seize the opportunity to accelerate development for a few years, deal with problems as soon as they are recognized, and then move on." "Judging from what we have accomplished in recent years, it should be possible for our economy to reach a new stage every few years." "In developing the economy, we should strive to reach a higher level every few years." "It is now both possible and necessary for us to bring about, in the prolonged process of modernization, several periods of rapid growth with good economic returns.

505

29 *Selected Works of Deng Xiaoping*, Vol.3, Beijing, the People's Publishing House, 1993, p. 368.

We must have this ambition." The economic development is restricted by multiple factors, and when favourable factors come in numbers, the fast economic development will last for several years if opportunities are grasped. And when unfavourable factors dominate, vicious recession of the economy can be avoided for timely adjustments. And powers are accumulated for the concentrated arrival of favourable factors, when leaping development of the economies can be achieved after several years. This process will repeat itself non-stop and cause the economic development for wave-like advance and spiral escalation. Conforming to the general law of the development matter, this pattern is used by Deng Xiaoping to guide the practices of China's economic development. He repeatedly emphasized that opportunities must be grasped for the socialist modernization construction. And efforts must be made to achieve several periods of fast development and good benefits while development is speeded-up in pursuit of a step forward in economic development every few years.

The thoughts mentioned above show that expansion and contraction, and the wave-like advance with interactions between the peak and trough act as the objective laws for economic development. See from people's control of the law, the economic development is advancing in the cyclical process of "leap – adjustments – further advance, another leap" rather than linear growth by a fixed percentage annually. One step forward can be achieved once every few years rather than non-stop advance without any time for breath. Expansion is the critical phase for cyclical fluctuations. In this phase, economic activities are very vigorous with interactions between investment, consumption, production, and circulation, which will provide objective potentials for achievement of leaps in the national economy to reach a new step. Expansion is followed by contraction, which serves as the second phase of cyclical fluctuation. In this phase, the economic life is in the state of whooping, and the development speed for investment, consumption, production, circulation and the whole national economies to facilitate the adjustment relation, accumulate power, and prepare conditions for new steps. The advance will continue after contraction and adjustment, and comes into a new round of expansion and leap.

Matter develops from quantitative changes to qualitative changes with partial qualitative changes in the middle. The periodical quality leap, presented in terms of economic development, refers to leaping to a step in the last few years. Moreover, the movement and development of matter do not always advance linearly but in a zigzag wave-like way. That's because they are restricted by multiple factors with wave-like advance as its economic manifestation. In this sense, Deng Xiaoping's three-step development strategy reveals the objective law for the economic cyclical development in our country. Therefore, the three-step development strategy is an important component of Deng Xiaoping's thought for construction of socialism with Chinese characteristics. It reflects Deng Xiaoping's scientific attitude and ambition to start from objective laws and active control and initially utilize the cyclical economic fluctuations. The three-step development strategy breaks the forbidden zone of traditional theories, reveals the objective laws for the economic cyclical development in our country, help us have a deeper, more detailed and realistic knowledge of the socialist economy, and further enriches and develops the socialist economic theory.

IX. Control of Cycles

When Chinese scholars began to study the socialist business cycle, they set the motivation and objective as the objective to control cycles and facilitate fast and sound development of the national economy. At the early stage of researching the business cycle, they pointed out that although wave-like development of the national economy is the inevitable result affected by objective factors, the size of waves is closely connected with people's subjective factors. Through people's subjective efforts, the wave-like laws for development of the national economy can be correctly understood, and the negative effects of various factors can be alleviated while the positive effects can be played, ultimately seeking orderly wave-like balanced development of the national economy along the spiral curve.[30] Once the state is able to master the laws of economic fluctuations, it "will possibly organize various work of the national economy according to changes in the objective economic conditions. When the objective conditions ripen, it can bring favourable conditions into full play, and organize production peaks with mobilization of all positive factors. After gaining the great achievements from the Great Leap and the Great Development, it can adjust the development speed for consolidation, enriching and improvement, and prepare conditions for organization of new leaps."[31] If we change "the Great Leap", "adjustment, consolidation, enrichment, improvement" and other nouns reflecting that age into the ones used since the reform and opening up, we will find that they are consistent with Deng Xiaoping's three-step development strategy. However, it should be pointed out that because scholars didn't realize the hazard for radical changes in economic growth in the late 1950s and the early 1960s, they did not have the recognition to strive to avoid violent economic fluctuation, but strove to achieve economic leaps through radical changes. Since the 1980s, the objective to study the business cycle has been fundamentally changed and determined as "clipping peaks for valley filling", i.e. to realize the economy's maintenance of long-term stable growth and slight fluctuation in the moderate growth section, transform the business cycle from violent fluctuations with great gaps between peak and trough to steady fluctuations with small gaps between peak and trough, prolong the rising phase of economy, boost the growth quality, maintain steady economic growth and ultimately achieve the objective of mastering cycles. The so-called mastery of business cycles refers to "clipping peaks for valley filling" while improving

507

---

30   Fang Zhong, "*Studies on the Issue of Wave-like National Economic Development*", in *Planned Economy*, 1959(10).
31   Yin Shijie, "*A Tentative Analysis of the Factors Forming the Wave-like Advance of the National Economy*", in *Journal of Jianghan University*, 1961(5).

the occasion according to the tendency of economic fluctuations, and achieve the smoothing of the economic cyclical fluctuation at moderate altitude. The government should emphasize economic growth rather than focus on economic fluctuations. This is the consensus of almost all the economists.

Socialist countries can only choose to master the business cycle, because socialism cannot eliminate the cyclical fluctuation of economy but "iron" the fluctuation or make it smooth, which is the consensus formed earliest in the 1980s. Ever since his initiation of researches of business cycles, Liu Shucheng has positioned the research subject on cognition and mastery of the business cycle. He explicitly pointed out in his article of initiating significance published on Issue II of Economic Studies in 1986, "As long as we continue to cognize and master the periodicity of fixed-asset investment, we will be able to reduce blindness, increase consciousness to voluntarily master it and utilize it to serve us." He also put forward very specific countermeasures and advice to utilize the fixed-asset investment cycle in China; (1) In the years with positive growth of investment, efforts will not be taken at one token for loss of after-effect. (2) When investment continues with the growth, some leeway should be left properly each year to avoid too steep investment peak and reduce the amplitude to prolong the years with positive growth of investment and expand cycles. (3) When the trough years is about to come with negative growth of investment, timely contraction should be carried out to voluntarily reduce the investment wave. (4) For the years of trough, effective control and supervision should be carried out to shorten the adjustment period to the utmost and avoid excessive dropping in the trough. (5) The economic system reform and reforms of other kinds are promoted to improve scientific levels of economic plans, management, prediction and decision-making, give full play to the effects of various means and economic levers to ultimately achieve effective macro-regulation and control. In the following exposition, Liu Shucheng further pointed out that the objective existence of investment periodicity provides diverse environmental conditions for the introduction of various measures in the economic system reform. We should consider the situation and utilize various favourable conditions to introduce the reform measures requiring great support of financial resources and materials in the recovery period and peak period; while in the periods of sustainable development and the trough, consolidation, digestion, supplementation and improvement shall be carried out. The reform measures without any requirement of support of large financial resource and materials can be taken in the sustainable growth period of investment and the period of trough, and work should be done to promote them to develop their effects in the recovery period and the peak period.[32] Lu Jian, who put forward the concept of the socialist business cycle, studies the business cycles with his strong purpose to serve the actual economic development, specially speaking, on one hand to seek the economic policies coupled with the business cycle through

---

32   See Liu Shucheng, "A *Second Study on the Cycles of Fixed Assets Investments in Our Country*", in *Economic Studies*, 1986(6).

understanding the objective laws and internal mechanism of the business cycle, and to reduce the frequency and amplitude of the economic fluctuation and avoid frequent and violent fluctuations from causing severe interference and hazards; On the other hand, to seek the preferred solution coupled with the operation of economic reform and cycles through mastery of the operation rhythm and features of the business cycle in our country to enhance the capacity of the economic system reform to counter cyclical disturbance and gain rather realistic reform achievements.

Because Liu Shucheng carried out the follow-up research into China's economy for many years, he not only has distinctive cognition of the nature of fluctuations, and forms a whole set of systematic and high-operational ideas after summarizing and generalizing the experience and lessons for mastering the business cycle. According to him, China's economic operation from foundation of New China advanced in the fluctuations of interactions between expansion and contraction. Generally speaking, in the period of contraction, the whole economic life is in the state of slow development and adjustment, therefore it does not have the objective conditions to help the national economy step up further .While in the period of expansion, the whole economic life comes alive again with mutual promotion of investment, production and consumption, and positive growth of the effects of the multiplier and acceleration, which provides actual possibility for the economic development to climb a new step. However, in order to turn this possibility into reality, right decision guidance is still needed. Upon arrival of the period of economic expansion, blind advance or missing a golden opportunity is prohibited. Opportunities should be grasped with the attitude to positively master the business cycle and with utilization of the tendency of economic expansion work should be done to positively promote the economy to a new step. As for radical changes in economies, the key lies in big rise. Rising too high will inevitably cause very deep falls. That's because by rising too high, the excessive consumption of materials, financial resources and human power seriously break the various orders and balanced relationship for normal economic operation, and it will cause the great falls. In order to maintain fast and sustainable development of economy, special attention should be paid to control of peak position and peaks should be clipped timely to avoid great rises and iron fluctuations in the rising period of the business cycle. Only in control of the peak position will the sustainability and stability of the economic growth be guaranteed and the microwave feature of economic fluctuation will be promoted. Only with sustainable, fast and steady development of economy there will be a good macro-environment for deepening of various reforms and normal operations of enterprises.[33] Liu Shucheng's idea mentioned above will always impose influence on the state's macro regulation.

509

---

33 See Liu Shucheng, "*Commemorating the Experience and Lessons of the Great Historical Rise and Fall at Home and Abroad*, in *Journal of Tianjin Normal University (Social Sciences Branch)*, 2004(4).

Because the research objective is to serve the mastery of business cycle, the research work has become deeper and more elaborate since the mid-late 1980s, and conclusions and relevant countermeasures and advice have also become more operational. Scholars study the methods for supervision and prediction of China's macro-economy and then use prosperity index and the system of early warning signals to carry out supervision and prediction of China's macro-economy, and actively promote these methods, which some functional departments of the state have already used to supervise the tendency of macro-economy operation. Under such a background, the studies of economic fluctuation also gradually evolved into prosperity studies, which is one of the specific forms to master the business cycle. Prosperity studies have the thoroughly different significance from studies of the nature, root, and transmission mechanism of the economic fluctuation. The service object of prosperity studies can be various market subjects of investment, production, consumption and other specific economic activities. And the research objective is to carry out supervision, analysis and prediction of the economic cyclical fluctuation so that measures can be timely adopted to reduce the cost to the lowest according to the changing tendency. Specifically, with supervision over macro-economy, once can clearly find changes in every level of the macro-economy and understand changes in the economic structure that would lead investors for rational investment and in the decision-making level the government could timely adopt steady policies, and promote the steady and fast development of economy. Therefore it has great practical significance. As for the economics, though its final objective is to reveal its nature through phenomena of the business cycle, the investigation of phenomena cannot be ignored. Because phenomena are the reflection of nature and people have to start with phenomena to recognize the nature, and reveal the connection between some phenomena and nature through researches. Once mastered by people, those phenomena reflecting their relation with nature will help people to conclude the development tendency of the matter according to changes in phenomena. To research various phenomena manifested in the economic cyclical fluctuation, is to understand the nature of business cycles, and to know the corresponding morphological forms of phenomena reflecting the nature relation. As the omen of the economic fluctuation, these phenomena provide basis for people to carry out supervision, analysis and prediction of change tendencies of the business cycle.

510

With regard to the theoretical basis of how political economy controls the socialist business cycle, the essential practice in the theoretical circle during the planned economy was to leave aside capitalist factors in Marx's theory of the reproduction of social capital, and concluded that socialism should achieve steady growth of economy through spontaneous management of national economic plans in terms of the planned and proportional development in the large-scaled socialized production. When it came to the socialist market economy, people have gradually realized that, in order to control the business cycle, they have to understand the laws of the market economy apart from the knowledge of the basic equilibrium of the national economy. This means there is necessity to do research into the prosperity of the national economy. In Marx's time, the capitalist world already did prosperity researches, but the objects they serve then were mainly for single capitalists with the objective to help a single capitalist timely adopt precautions to reduce losses according to the development tendency of the social economy. However, cyclical outbreak and increasing severe economic crises almost made these efforts become post-mortem pity. Then in the period of state monopoly capitalism, such researches became the basis for the state to interfere with the economy, the position for prosperity researches has been greatly elevated ever since, and some researchers of the economic cyclical theories set foot in this field, and made the integration of theories of business cycle and prosperity researches to have mutual improvement. So it has become the genuine "crutch" for the government to carry out macro-control. For a very long historical period, the Marxist Economics has not regarded prosperity researches as one of its field. With revelation of the objective economic laws as its duty, the Marxist Economics mainly studies the nature, manifestation pattern, transmission mechanism, development tendency and other theoretical issues of the capitalist business cycle, rather than those theories or countermeasures serving the capitalist anti-crisis demands. Because Marx thinks that capitalism cannot overcome the cyclical outbreak of crises within its own scope, its anti-crisis methods is to bring about more violent crises. In the period of socialism, especially for the establishment of the basic state policies centred by the economic construction after the reform and opening up, the socialist economics not only serves the state's ideology form, 511 but more importantly serves the economic construction of the state. For this, relevant subject researches cannot only stay in the system level; researches into the social economic operation are also needed.

As for researches into the economic operation, it can be avoided to carry out prosperity researches, because prosperity researches can effectively support the formulation and adjustment of short-term policies, and serve as one of the general bases for micro regulation of the national economy, which is proven by the macro-control experience of the western countries after the World War II and the tendency for economic development. Besides, it can also be proven by the experience and economic development trends since the reform and opening up in China. However, research work cannot only stay on this level, because the research route for the Marxist Economics has to ascend from details to abstraction. That's because only in this way can one know the nature of the matter and reveal the objective economic laws to fulfil the research tasks. Therefore, the Marxist Economics emphasizes prosperity researches but without treating it as its destination. Work should also be done to finish theoretical summarization on the abstract and rational level and then treat the final utilization of it to guide prosperity researches as the ultimate objective.

Macro-control is the basic form for the state to master the business cycle. Nowadays, there have been great changes in China's macro-control, which has gained the capacity to drive the business cycle at a very high level. It is mainly shown in: (1) Change in the guiding thought of macro-control —-Macro-control emphasizes the control of peak position. (2) Change in functions of macro-control. Before the reform and opening up, in the system of planned economy, the government is both the subject and the object of macro-control. Therefore, in the whole expansion period of the economic cyclical fluctuation, the function for macro-control of the central government is the single "complying cycle" advance. In this way, from the central government to local governments, from each sector to each enterprise, in the expansion period, they were marching together, got going and went all out in a confusing manner, which easily caused the peak of fluctuation to reach high to the sky until being forced to stop for difficulty to sustain. After the policy of reform and opening up, the subject of economic activities tend to be diversified with the central government becoming the subject of macro-control and local governments, each sector and enterprise becoming the object. In this way, in the economic cyclical fluctuation, the "conversion period" regulation is added to the functions of the macro-control of the central government. When the economic expansion reaches a certain degree, the central government can initiatively adopt moderately conversed contraction measures in good time to prevent blind expansion. (3) Change in signal mechanism of macro-control. In the system of planned economy, prices are uniformly determined by the government, mainly as the tool for economic measurement. With the economic overheating, prices will not rise accordingly. The imbalance of economic operation will not be reflected by price rises but

512 only by the shortage of goods. However, the shortage of goods is a kind of "soft" signal. Especially under the condition of shortage characterized economy, the shortage of goods case is a kind of ordinary state, and will not arouse people's special attention. After the reform and opening up, along with the liberation of prices, once potential and hidden inflations go public, and make goods shortage reflected in price rise. Economic over-heating is followed by rapid rise of good prices. Price signals replace signal of quantity shortage to deliver the message of economic imbalance. Prices, as the barometer of economic operation conditions, which plays a crucial role in determining resource allocation, begin to impose effects. This is beneficial to the central government to implement macro-control policies timely and accurately according to price signals. In conclusion, before the reform and opening up, blind pursuit of the government for high speed used to cause violent economic fluctuations. And in the course of reform and opening up, the macro-economic control capabilities of the government has greatly improved. Due to certain effects caused by the newly established market mechanisms and due to the internal high growth tendency during the middle period of industrialization, our economic cyclical fluctuations have started to demonstrate a relatively steady tendency in high level.[34]

34　See Liu Shucheng, "*On the New Phase of China's Cyclical Economic Fluctuations*", in *Journal Economic Studies*, 1996(11).

As for the conclusion; "cyclical fluctuation of fixed asset investment is one of the direct dominant factors influencing the economic cyclical fluctuation"[35] Liu Shucheng thinks that control of cyclical investment fluctuation, and prevention of great rises and falls of investment is one of the important conditions for long-term steady development of the national economy. Through his researches into seven business cycles from 1953 to 1985, Liu Shucheng summarized the following experience and lessons: the principle for best effort within one's capabilities; the principle to firstly arrange agriculture and consumer markets, then arrange the current industrial production and finally arrange capital construction investments; the principle for looking back and looking ahead, the principle of short-term balance; the principle of leaving adequate margins; the principle for enough retreat for adjustments. In 1996, he acquired new understanding of the business cycle researches, and said: "The deepest experience and lesson I learned from the cyclical fluctuation in our country's economies after the foundation of New China are: control of peak position, prevention of great rise, clipping peak to fill valley, ironing out fluctuations. As long as the peak position is controlled, the decrease of the overall fluctuation range will be guaranteed"[36]. Some scholars think that the implementation of macro-control policies should consider both the short-term factors and the ones of medium and long terms; there should be control of total amount and strengthening of structural adjustment to seek a market mechanism based on a regulatory way to effectively maintain the steady and coordinated growth of the economy. Other scholars pointed out that there are two levels of significance to prevent excessive expansion of investment and the whole economy in the rise phase of the business cycle; one is to prevent goods prices to evolve from regional rise to thorough inflation along with the excessive investment expansion and the excessive expansion of the whole economy; and the other is to prevent some leading sectors or industries with super speed growth to evolve from relative production surplus and decline of goods' prices, even related occurrence of thorough inflation when encountering periodical changes in demands. And still other scholars emphasized that the following wrong tendencies should be avoided with efforts for exploration of the economic fluctuation: Regarding economic fluctuation as abnormal phenomenon, and advocating adoption of strong measures to avoid economic fluctuations. The phenomenon of cyclical fluctuation existing in the course of our country's economic growth is an objective existence not transferrable by anyone's subjective value judgment. Only by formulation and implementing relevant economic policies, measurement with detailed analysis and profound understanding of laws for the economic cyclical fluctuation can we lower the range of economic fluctuation, weaken its hazardous degrees, and thus guarantee the sustainable and steady economic growth. Now that the economic growth and development in China is achieved in the

513

35 Liu Shucheng", "*Influence of Investment Cyclical Fluctuation on the Economic Cyclical Fluctuation*", in *Journal of Quantitative & Technical Economics*, 1987(10).
36 Liu Shucheng, "*On the New Phase of China's Cyclical Economic Fluctuation*", in *Economic Studies*, 1996(11).

cyclical fluctuation, the cycle concept and counter-cyclical awareness should be established with cooperation of the economic cyclical policies and the business cycle to effectively reduce the fluctuation frequency and amplitude and increase the growth rate of economy; the design, selection and implementation of various economic reform schemes must coordinate with the contraction and expansion periods of the business cycle to decrease social friction and resistance and guarantee the smooth implementation of new schemes.

In order to timely detect the fluctuation situation of the macro-economy and aiming to provide necessary information inputs to enable effective government macro-control policies, the Department of Comprehensive Statistics of the National Bureau of Statistics designed the system for supervision, early warning and forecasting which suits to China's specific conditions in 1990. The system includes three parts: First, 12 supervision indexes for the macro-economic development are designed. They are: 1. the gross value of industrial output; 2. sales revenues of independent accounting enterprises; 3. the total volume of retail sales; 4. the total value of net purchases of domestic goods; 5. the total value of purchases of domestic industrial products; 5. currency circulation; 7. narrow money M_1; 8. industrial loans; 9. national salary and other individual costs; 10. Total cash (payments) disbursement in banks; 11. Nation-wide investment in capital construction[37]; 12. National general retail price index.

The second component part of the above system is to set five signal zones to signify different conditions of the economic prosperity, i.e. zone of blue light (contraction); zone of green light (stable); zone of yellow light (Tendency for stability); zone of red light (quite hot); zone of double red lights (overheated). And the third component part includes a comprehensive rating system. When the total scores for the rise of economic indices surpasses 20, it shows the economy tends to enter the green light zone, and leaves back the blue light zone; over 32 scores shows that the economy is entering the yellow light zone, over 40 scores shows that the economy is entering the zone of red light; and over 48 scores shows entering the zone of double red lights. When the economy falls in the opposite direction, the limit for rating will not be changed. According to the introduction of relevant department, the system runs well and the information of economic trends regularly issued by it has provided scientific basis for the State Council to make economic resolutions. The objective of economic early warning is not to eliminate fluctuations but to forecast according to the regularity of economic fluctuations, and then adopt necessary precautionary measures according to the possible influence or risks incurred by fluctuations to reach the objective of alleviating its unfavourable influence. This is one of the general motives for China to carry out prosperity researches. Along with development of China's market economy, increase of the economic aggregate

---

37 Capital construction refers to the new construction projects or extension projects and the related work of the enterprises, institutions or administrative units mainly for the purpose of expanding production capacity or improving project efficiency covering only projects each with a total investment of 500,000 RMB and over.

and complication of economic relations, researches into economic warning have become one of the important bases for the state's macro-control.

Nowadays, researches into business cycles have become more and more practical, and some researchers combine the production and operation activities in designing enterprises and the development tendency of the business cycle to determine the right development strategies. Just as predicted by scholars, the cyclical fluctuations of China's economy will increasingly display the new tendency of "softened rise and decline". The arrival of this situation means that the supplies of enterprise will become loose and the supply restrictions will be relieved somehow. However, no great changes will happen in demands of the market with quite tightened restrictions of demands. This also means that the "market opportunities" of enterprises will be reduced, and the "investment opportunities" will also be reduced with more violent competition in the market. This broad environment will not only create opportunities and conditions for sound development of enterprise, but also impose challenges and tests on them.

X. Reflection on Methodology

The history of socialist economic development indicates that, unlike the theoretical deduction made by the founders of Marxism, there're not only drastic fluctuations in the economy but also business cycle and crisis in socialism. And no in-depth study made and consensus reached on how to analyze these phenomena in the field of Marxist political economics. As Marx's theory of economic crisis is established during the analytical process of capitalist economic relations, the specificity of the analysis paradigm make people naturally apply it to the analysis of capitalist economic crisis or cycle. In the meanwhile, theories for analyzing socialist business cycle are basically gained by scholars through a direct introduction, digestion and absorption of the analysis paradigm for western business cycle. So the analysis of socialist business cycle as mainstream has been gradually integrated with western theory of business cycle, and the theoretical models, analysis tools, statistical method and descriptive approach tend to be more and more similar to the analysis paradigm of western business cycle. The traditional theory of Marxist political economics for the analysis of business cycle tend to be marginalized as we can hardly see any traditional Marxist analysis paradigms on economic crisis in documents about the analysis on socialist business cycle in recent years. In this regard, Marxist researchers should rethink and figure out the reason behind this, whether it is because the Marxist analytical genre on economic crisis fell behind the times or it is because Marxist workers lacked the ability to apply the Marxist analytical mode on economic crisis to the analysis of socialist business cycle or for any other reasons. This chapter holds that it is feasible to use Marxist analytical mode on economic crisis to analyze socialist business cycle but based upon theoretical innovation.

Marx analyzes capitalist business cycle through the method of contradiction analysis. The advantage of this method is that it deems capitalist economy whose growing trend is periodic economic crisis as a dialectical process of development. During this process, the contradiction between socialization of production and privatization of means of production plays a decisive role in development trend. Which method is appropriate for analyzing socialist business cycle? Scholars from the late 1950s to the early years of 1960s explained socialist economic fluctuation with the basic contradiction in a given society and the law of wave-like development. And this is undoubtedly a cognitional breakthrough at a time when the mainstream economics regard socialist economy as a right ascension. However, if this explanation is only limited to the level of the basic contradiction in a given society and the law of wave-like development, it would lose its practical significance. While some scholars after the 1980s still stick to the method of contradiction analysis, they have quite misunderstood the concept of contradiction. Here we may take Shu Liu as an example. He attributed the root cause for socialist economic fluctuation to the principal contradiction in socialism which is the contradiction between the people's growing material and cultural needs and the backward social productive forces. He held that this reflected the contradiction between a need for large-scale economic construction and a lack of material strength in terms of fixed asset investment. He also deemed the cycle fluctuation of socialist economy as the result of paradoxical movement between two mechanisms-the interaction

516   mechanism between "large-scale investment and mass production; mechanism of supply and demand." However, there're gaps in his knowledge about contradiction, as the principal contradiction in a socialist society in traditional sense has already changed dramatically in the market economy. The overall relative overproduction has transformed from advanced needs to demand lag, the main aspect of contradiction between production and consumption has transferred into demands and the stimulation effects of consumption on large-scale investment has been largely weakened. As to the contradiction movement between the "two mechanism", the relationship between the two is not like that between "purpose" and "means" to the purpose, therefore they're not the principal contradiction of the society and their subordinate status prevents them from dominating the business cycle fluctuation. Caihong Chen also thought that, the primary cause for business cycle is the contradictory but integrative contradiction movement between social production structure and demand structure. And obviously this point of view is a little one-sided.

Economic cyclical fluctuation is the essential link between phenomenon and essence in economic performance, so we should not limit our views on economic fluctuation cycle solely to phenomena and forms. We should see through the appearance to perceive the essence to really grasp the regularity of economic fluctuation cycle so as to make full use of regularity. The way to understand the capitalist economic cyclical fluctuation is the same as that to understand the socialist economic cyclical fluctuation. In the era of Marx, there were many people who loved to explain the phenomena and forms of business cycle. Marx at that time criticized harshly on this kind of behaviour. He said that, "The superficiality of Political Economy shows itself in the fact that it looks upon the expansion and contraction of credit, which is a mere symptom of the periodic changes of the industrial cycle, as their cause."[38] The superficiality of theory determines that such theory can only explain economic crisis that has already happened and when it was to face up with a new crisis, it would pale into insignificance and become outdated. Today, as we try to understand and control the socialist business cycle, we should not be content with the degree of understanding and describing phenomena but should recognize its nature as our basic task as well.

Since in *Capital*, Marx wrote that "In this work I have to examine the capitalist mode of production, and the conditions of production and exchange corresponding to that mode."[39] The capitalist economic cyclical fluctuations, in Marx's point of view, mainly refer to fluctuations caused by economic relation, those drastic economic fluctuations caused by social institution. The purpose of Marx's study on capitalist mode of production is not to offer advice on eliminating capitalist business cycle but to reveal the rules of generation, development and final doom of capitalism. Therefore, Marx's task is not to study those normal fluctuations during the process of capitalist economic development but those drastic fluctuations that occur in abnormal economic operation brought great disaster to the capitalist system-financial crisis. As socialist system is not an antagonistic social form established in the wake of fundamental negation of the capitalist system. Theoretically predicted, the establishment of socialist public ownership economy, planned economy and distribution system according to one's performance, etc. has fundamentally avoided economic disasters caused by overproduction while at the same time maintained normal economic fluctuations as this obeys the objective laws of the development of things. In order to safeguard their own interests to the utmost, the bourgeoisie created a social institution composed of adversarial economic relations. In the primary stage of the system-the contention of free period, the growing degree of production socialization as one side of the basic contradiction in a given society, and the other side, the ownership structure with absolute ownership and full expression of the will of Property owners as its core extremely emphasize the absolute right to control one's own property, resulting in an intensified cyclical conflicts between organized production of individual enterprises and the whole social production, between the unrestrictive expansion of production and relatively decreased purchasing power as well as the drastic cyclical fluctuations of the social economy. Entering the era of national monopolistic capitalism, capitalist countries have undertaken a series of innovations on property right system, including" those to change the property right system with absolute individual ownership as its core into checked relative individual ownership as

38 *Capital*, Vol. 1, Beijing: People's Publishing House, 1975, p. 694.
39 *Capital*, Vol. 1, Beijing: People's Publishing House, 2004, p. 9.

its core, to empower the state the right to conduct macro control over national economy and to establish a mechanism that mitigates the basic contradiction of capitalism so as to avoid a devastating economic crisis arising from cyclically intensifying basic conflicts of capitalism. And this is the reason for the gradual fading out of the crisis since the World War Two. Accordingly, the focus of research has gradually shifted from "prosperity" and "depression" that are linked with economic crisis into normal economic fluctuations and cycle.

Due to the limits of historical conditions, business cycles on which Marx studied refer specially to capitalist cyclical economic crisis that is the cyclical fluctuations of production resulted from capitalist system. Therefore, logical reasoning based on Marx's business cycle can't predict the possibility that cyclical overproduction occurs in socialist society as a form of product economy characterized by a highly-developed productive forces, single public ownership, distribution according to work and planned and proportional economic development. Today, when we have to understand the rule of economic development by proceeding from the national conditions of the primary stage of socialism, we should not deduce in total accordance with Marx's theory on business cycle as the hypothesis but should instead, revise assumptions before deducing conclusions. Take China's primary stage of socialism as an example. The revised basic hypothesis should be: the foundation of capitalist economy has yet to be replaced by a newly established social system. For instance, at the primary stage of socialism of China today, one part of the conflict is socialized mass production, the other part is coexistence of various economic elements. And this has not only resulted in anarchy in the whole social production but also overproduction on the rise caused by oversupply. These factors showcase that there's still possibility that cyclical economic crisis of overproduction occurs at the primary stage of socialism. And the reason for the inevitability of the cyclical economic crisis of capitalism is that there's an antagonistic contradiction coexisting with basic system in capitalism-the principal conflicts in capitalism, and the crisis can't be avoided forever if this kind of conflict were not to be removed. Of course, there are two possibilities: if capitalism aggravates the basic contradiction, cyclical economic crisis would aggravate too; if capitalism can ease the basic contradiction, economic crisis can also be de-escalated.

In fact, with the establishment of the public ownership and the primary stage of socialism dominated by distribution according to work, the basic social contradiction has evolved into the conflict between socialized production and underdeveloped average plan. Although the social appropriation of the means of production has been established as required by socialized production, facing up to the socioeconomic realities of multiple stakeholders, information imperfections and planning failure, etc, national organization and management agencies can't maintain a balance between supply and demand of the total social product. On the contrary, in order to solve the major contradiction, the one between the ever-growing material and cultural needs of the people and the low level of social production, there's always a strong expansion drive for developing production in socialist society at its primary stage while the finance is constrained by soft budget. And this resulted in the hard constraints on investments arising from resource shortage due to ceaseless expansions, causing a large number of on-the-construction project suspended, unable to go into operation or reach design capacity and a sharp decrease in economic growth rate. And with innovation and establishment of the principle of socialist economic system with the public sector remaining dominant and diverse sectors of the economy developing side by side, this situation has been improved quite a lot. However, the government still owns and controls the huge amount of the most important resources in the society. Local governments also have a strong impulse for expansion and investment in pursuit of work performance. Officials tend to take the pursuit of projects and investments as their administration goals and when there's a collision between expansion impulse and national plans and arrangements, they would rather take the risk of being punished to launch new projects, bring about strong impacts on the country's macro-control work. As an economic entity, a main body of market competition as well as a legal entity, corporate decisions making is decentralized.

We can attribute the root cause for socialist economic cyclical fluctuation to its principle contradiction, as the basic contradiction of socialism is non-confrontational. And this is the most challenging dilemma we've ever met in explanation of socialist business cycle fluctuation: not accepting cyclical fluctuation of the economy as the economic laws of socialism means ignoring reality; and even if we recognize cyclical fluctuation of the economy as the economic laws of socialism, we still don't know specifically what the reason behind this is. Therefore, for a long period of time, we have to generally attribute the economic development in waves to the contradiction movement between productive force and production relations, attribute the sharp fluctuation in a planned economy to work faults made by the planning department as a practical and accurate economic plan could make the economy develop at a steady and rapid pace, rather than vice versa.

We can't understand the economic fluctuations of socialism without materialistic dialectics, as neither can we deny that the root cause for movement and development of things lies in the internal contradiction nor we can deny that the combination between conditional and relative identity and unconditional and absolute belligerence plays a decisive role in the existence of things and drive development of all the things. We can only say it in this way; the root cause behind wave-like development of national development is the internal contradiction of economy. The cyclical wave-like movement of economy is consistent with the high summarization of the development laws of things by materialistic dialectics and it conforms to the universal laws of development of things. And economic development can only be a combination of progress and setbacks, ascendency and reversibility, and these are what a scientific materialistic dialectics reveals for us about universal rules of development of things.

The cyclical fluctuation of economy as a phenomenon is the external expression of internal contradiction movement, that is to say, there's no cyclical fluctuation of economy in the real world without contradiction, any form of cyclical fluctuation of economy always corresponds to relevant contradiction movement. Therefore, inspection is always limited to phenomena and forms of cyclic economic fluctuation or research activities focusing solely on direct cause can't reveal the real reason and laws for the cyclical fluctuation of economy, not to mention controlling the business cycle. As any contradiction movement is a combination of universality and particularity, so does economic fluctuation. Cyclical economic fluctuations at any development stage or under any social system fall into the category of normal economic fluctuation or the so-called "normal business cycle". And only cycle that occurs at specific stage of socio-economic development and under particular social institution falls into the category of special economic fluctuation and can be called "special business cycle". Generally speaking, business cycle is a reflection of the basic contradiction of human society, the contradiction movement between productive forces and relations on the fronts of economic performance; specific business cycle is a reflection of basic contradiction movement of society (i.e. basic contradiction of capitalism) from the view of phenomenon. Under capitalist circumstances, the special form of basic contradiction in a given society is the contradiction between production socialization and private possession of production means. And in socialism, this could turn into the contradiction between production socialization and imperfect means of resource allocation. Lacking of effective national macro-control measures, capitalist economy would periodically meet with increasingly huge economic crisis for overproduction while planned economy in socialism would also fall into victim of dramatic economic fluctuation. With the improvements in resources allocation mechanisms and efficient macroeconomic control tools cyclical overproduction crises of the capitalist society and drastic violent economic fluctuations in the socialist society have gradually eased and both systems have evolved into a quality of milder cyclical fluctuations. The history of world economic development during the state monopoly capitalism and China's socialist economic development have made this point clear.

520

Theoretically, planned economy can certainly avoid the anarchic state of social production at large. Yet as the prerequisite to achieve this aim the planning needs to be fully scientific and perfect. Besides since both the building of socialism and the building of the economic institutions of socialism are still in their primary stage of development and the current constraints and limitations in the deeper cognition of planned economic development, plus the imperfectness of planning means and tools. Planning work can hardly meet the objective requirements of rational allocation of total social labour to be realized throughout the entire production sectors and reproducing links of the national economy. Since people's understanding on the essential aspects of the vast national economic system and its complex development process can advance and enrich only gradually, thus incomplete, consequently planned allocation of social labour forces for social reproduction based upon people's knowledge (especially economics) will most probably fail to meet objective requirements of economic development. Understandably this reality has constituted the inevitability of cyclical economic fluctuations in the planned economies.

It's an important progress to attribute the general reason of economic fluctuation of market economic system as it break out the chains of Marxism's traditional theory on business cycle that is, the theory is only suitable to explain business cycle of capitalism but not that of socialism. Meanwhile, the market economic system made a theoretical breakthrough by differentiating systemic factors from instructional factors that affect business cycle fluctuations. And I think it's necessary to restudy the reason for business cycle once we have proved both theoretically and practically that economic systems and economic structure are two different economic forms. Economic system is a production and distribution system based upon the system of ownership of the means of production while economic structure is the regulation method and mechanisms of social resources. In history, capitalist economic system and market economy are twin brothers. And the capitalist private ownership is the premise of the development and prosperity of all kinds of market. After the establishment of capitalist economic system, market economic system was used to allocate social resources. For a long time, people have always believed that market economic system is only feasible for capitalist system, making capitalism and the market economy system closely linked to each other. In addition, in history, an obvious business cycle hadn't occurred until capitalism and market economic system developed to some certain extent. Therefore, it's a right direction for Marxist economists to search for the reason of business cycle from economic system of capitalism itself. Nonetheless, during the limited period of commodity production and exchange, will the business cycle disappear even if capitalist private ownership is replaced by state-owned or collective ownership? If we say monitory's function as means of circulation and payments make the occurrence of economic crisis possible, then the formation of market economy will make the economic crisis a reality. Western economists have long known the phenomenon of market failure in regulating economy. But they have noted that such kind of a failure only happens in the field of micro economy. When there's an economic monopoly, due to incomplete market information and negative external effects, the market would lose its role of regulation in the field of public goods production. However, the regulation failure not only occurs in the area of micro economy but also happens in the field of macro economy. Karl Marx pointed out a long time ago that: the law of value as an inherent law, is suitable for a single individual as a blind natural law and maintain the social balance of production in a variety of accidental changes. Later, Marxian economists also pointed out the spontaneous and reckless role of market economy. In market economy, allocation of social resources is realized via the adjustment of price mechanism. However, the price regulation is on the one hand, of low cost and efficiency, while on the other hand it is spontaneous and blind. When there're commodity production and exchange, individual producers are independent and they produced for their own profits. If some products are in short supply, the commodity markets would send signals to producers through price rise. Driven by profits, producers will increase production of this commodity. But without coordination between producers, once the producer overreacted, excess production of such merchandise would happen. If many cases in this kind happen, then there will be overproduction. And economic contraction tends to happen after expansion, resulting in the business cycle.

As market economy system runs under a certain economic system, economic system will enlarge or narrow the weakness of market economic system. In the capitalist economic system, production processes tend to attain increasing social nature, but the ownership of the means of production essentially remains to be private. Profit first, the supreme drive of capitalism compels social production to a more chaotic state of anarchy. Capitalists gathered more and more wealth in their hands and working people's demand for payment capacity is undermined. All these added to blindness of the price regulation, making cyclical changes of the economy more and more drastic. The Great Depression occurring in the capitalist world in the 1930s has delivered a powerful example. It has vividly illustrated that combination of traditional capitalism and market economy could lead to more severe drastic economic fluctuations. The capitalist economy will suffer constant drastic economic turmoil unless adjustments have been made either to the capitalist economic system or to the market economy system. It is in this case that "Keynesian revolution" has appeared in Western economics. Although Keynes did not realize that the basic reason for business cycle is the market economy system and the capitalist economic system intensified the market economy's weakness, undeniable facts of the Great Depression made Keynes realize that it was impossible for capitalism to maintain national income equilibrium in the premise of full employment. From the overproduction phenomenon, Keynes got the reason for "lack of demand" which is tautological to "overproduction" and attributed further the low demand to people's psychological features. Theoretical explanation can be vague but policy proposals must be feasible. Although Keynes's explanations of causes of depression are superficial, but economic reality made Keynes aware that, demands from private sector are insufficient; government should intervene to stimulate aggregate demand. Based on this understanding, Keynes proposed macro-monetary policy and macro-fiscal policy. He suggested that government can adjust its demands and private consumption and investment demand through the adjustment of macro financial policy of fiscal spending and revenues, it can also adjust the money supply to modify interest rates so as to further affect private consumption and investment demand. That is to say, the government uses this kind of "visible hand" to make up for the weakness of the market, this "invisible hand". After World War II, the capitalist countries made certain adjustments in both economic system and the economic structure.

Such adjustments played a certain role in easing the drastic fluctuations of the business cycle. Progressive income tax system and the social welfare system have to some extent eased the contradiction between the rapid expansions of production and relatively narrow social needs. Governments' macro-economic policy to some degree eases the conflicts between organized production of corporations and anarchy of social production. Thanks to these measures, there are no more serious economic recessions occurring after the Second World War like that in the 1930s. However, capitalist countries simply adjusted the economic system and the economic structure; the basic features of the capitalist economic system and the market economy system have yet to be transformed. The blindness of price adjustment mechanism has been checked, but it still played a major role in the economy. The role of capitalist economic system in intensifying the weaknesses of price regulation mechanism has been weakened, but it still remained. Therefore, after the Second World War, the business cycle occurred again and again. Since the basic cause of business cycle is the market economy system, then in the socialist economic system, as long as there's market economy system, the business cycle will still occur. In the real socialist economic system, state ownership, collective ownership, individual ownership and other ownerships coexist and producers are independent from each other as they produce for their own profits. Therefore, they are very sensitive to the market as they will adjust production output according to market price signal. In the socialist economic system, the spontaneity and blindness of the price regulation mechanism continues and the business cycle still occurs. As the market economy system can effectively allocate social resources and inspire the enthusiasm and creativity of commodity producers, China selected market economy system according to its own long-term economic practice. However, any economic decision brings about benefits and costs and any economic system has pros and cons. Market economy system would not be perfect even though it is combined with socialist economic system in our country. Since China's reform and opening up, the establishment of market economy step by step has stimulated economic vigour and vitality and has promoted the long-term and rapid growth of China's economy. However, the business cycle is just beginning to emerge. Business cycle has become an inevitable fact of life. If the capitalist economic system plays a role of intensifying economic weakness, then what about the role of socialist economic system? State-owned enterprises are the key sectors and play a leading role in the economy in the socialist economic system. Therefore, in socialist economic system, apart from macro-monetary policy and macro-fiscal policy, government can also adjust the economy through expansion and contraction of output of state-owned enterprises. This means that in socialist economic system, the effect and efficiency of government's regulation on economy are better than that of the capitalist economic system and socialist economic system plays a role in mitigating the weakness of the market economic system.[40]

523

40　Li Chong, *Re-visiting the Causes of the Business Cycle*, in *Contemporary Economic Research*, 2005(8).

Some scholars have classified socialist business cycles into two categories as "natural cycles" and "man-made cycle." The assumed natural cycle refers to the wave-like self-motion of the socio-economic development, while the man-made cycle refers to those fluctuations caused by man's irrational behaviours or those fluctuations caused by macro-economic management failures. They called those small cyclical fluctuations causing no devastating impacts on society and economy as natural cycles; and for cyclical fluctuations that are quite volatile and may have serious impacts on society and economy, they called them as the man-made cycle. Although this view is yet to be discussed, it is a reasonable creation to divide the socialist business cycle into "man-made cycle" and "natural cycles" as it can not only explain the law of economic development with the general laws of development but can explain people's economic behaviour's impact on economic development. In laissez-faire market economy, either the capitalism or the socialism would inevitably suffer drastic economic fluctuations and cyclical overproduction crisis; a less developed planned economy would also confront economic fluctuations and cyclical resources shortage crisis. No matter whether it is cyclical overproduction crisis or production shortage crisis, they are epiphenomenon in economic development in the natural state, so they are called "natural cycle". In market economy with macroeconomic regulation and control, the economic fluctuation is checked within certain limits, as this cycle has been controlled by people, disastrous impacts of the economic crisis on society have been avoided. So it is called as "man-made cycle." The world economy today has entered into the stage of market economy with macroeconomic regulation, "natural cycle" during the process of economic development has been basically replaced by "man-made cycle", small economic fluctuations and stable economic performances have become the ordinary state of economic development. This situation shows that it is necessary for us to reinterpret a series of problems related to business cycle.

The periodic economic fluctuation originating from the fundamental contradiction of capitalism is in essence, given the capitalism environment, a result of contradictory movement between productive forces and productive relation. The contradiction between socialization of production and the privatization of means of production under the capitalist environment is a special form of that between productive forces and productive relation. Why does privatization contradict with the trend of socialization of production? Socialized production requires an economic form in which social resources are distributed according to social needs, guided by the social authority or by the social institution administering the national economy, whereas under the condition that ownership of the means of production is private, this authority for distribution is placed in the hands of scattered means' owners, who seek to maximize their profit and allocate resource as their wish, leading to a social chaos in distribution. This theory indicates that the reasons that resource distribution conducted freely by means' owners set off social disorder in production is the absolute authority on

524

the capital they own. They have paramount decision making power on which department to invest, what product to manufacture and how many of them should be produced. As age of the national monopoly capitalism came, the country gradually took over this decision-making power on macroscopic scale, which restrained that power of private owners, who can only now conduct decision within the restraint of resource allocation imposed by national power. This power transition enables the nation to adjust the distribution of resource on a social scale, fulfilling the demand of socialized production and stabilizing in a reasonable status. Although the ability of this adjustment is limited, neither could it eliminate the impacts on economy originating from the fundamental contradiction of capitalism, it relieves the contradiction and thus allows the society to avoid drastic economic periodical fluctuation.

Either from the theoretical aspect or the practical one, the economic fluctuation experienced in the primary stage of socialism is in essence the result of contradictory movement between productive forces and productive relation, particular form of which, in highly centralized planned economy, reflects the contradiction between the impulses yearning for investments and the restraint on resource, whereas in socialist market economy, it reflects the contradiction between the market entity's tendency to maximize the production scale and the relatively downsizing social payment ability as well as the contradiction between proportionality of socialized production development and the insufficiency of macro-control. Those explanations claiming that the periodical economic fluctuations occurring in the capitalist economies and China's socialist economy is essentially different, that the fluctuation in capitalism originates from its basic contradictions whereas that in socialism is caused by errors in economic work, can barely justify the fact.

The economic fluctuation caused by the economic activity originated from the pursuit of material interest. In capitalism, capitalist's pursuit for maximum surplus value forces him/her to choose different investment strategies in different times. In the prospective time, the desire for investment and the growth of prospect upgrade simultaneously and interact on each other positively until both of them reach their maximum. In the period of downswing, their large scale capitals gradually drive the economy into recovery and booming. Investment and economic fluctuation is in essence the particular active form of the fundamental contradiction of capitalism, that is, on one hand, the maximum capital accumulation and the uttermost investment activity satisfy capitalists' demand to maximize the surplus value, on the other hand, however, the decrease of profit exposes the various kinds of contradiction and intensifies periodically. When the factors leading to this intensification are not controllable, as the quantity changes usually accumulates to a certain bound, they end the extreme prospective economy by means of quality changes and start a new periodical fluctuation. When factors are under control, social management institutions will spontaneously control quantity changes within a certain range, releasing energy by partial quality changes in order to avoid the drastic ones. After World War Two, the reform of property right system in the capitalist society has, to some extent, transformed some factors which are able to aggravate the fundamental contradictions into a more controllable status and thus prevent the economic crisis from arising periodically. There is causality between economic fluctuation and investment in socialism, indicating that this fluctuation originates from the material interest in economic life as well in socialism and has connection with its fundamental contradiction. People are not willing to connect the fluctuation and contradiction because of political concern rather than economical one. In the contradiction of people's ever increasing material and social demands and the low social productivity, the later one is the main restraint. Consequently, to solve this contradiction we mainly need to develop productivity, yet to develop productivity we need to invest. The history of planned socialist economy showed that the desire for investment is a general characteristic in this system. The impulse of economic expansion is constrained periodically by insufficient resource, which is the economic inflation and deflation respectively.

Due to the fact that economy always belongs to a certain economic relation and develops in certain circumstances, its development is inevitably affected by multiple factors, impact of which presents as fluctuation to a different extent. Therefore, the economic fluctuation in modern society is not caused by one single factor, rather is a result of overlaying effect of multiple factors. To specify, along with the inherent wave-like development tendency, economy will be influenced by anthropic factors such as the social system, economic relation, economic behaviour, economic policy and technology development, which provide several overlaying driving forces on the natural fluctuation of the economy. These forces are divided into two types, positive one and negative one. The former amplifies the volatility of the fluctuation and the later dampens. Due to the inconsistency of these forces in time, direction and form, they may counteract against each other. When the overlaying factors and natural factors impose impact on the economy with the same direction and on the same time, the outcome will lead to a drastic fluctuation of the economy; when these factors have different directions and act in different times, as long as some of them greatly surpass their opposite impact, though dampened, can cause fluctuation with high volatility. In the time of capitalist free market, because of the decisive influence of its fundamental contradiction, its intensifying periodic fluctuation factors create an impact that overweigh and counteract its opposite forces and thus result in periodic fluctuation with high volatility, not to mention that other overlaying factors were constrained and dominated by the fundamental contradiction, impose force with the same direction as that from fundamental contradiction.

As it is the general rule that any object develops wave-like and spiral manner so does the economy regardless of different social systems, which could also be regarded as a natural fluctuation. Natural fluctuation is an inevitable tendency in economic development, change of which would only be different in volatility. Economic natural fluctuation is caused by natural factors apart from human economic activity, such as natural disaster and sunspot, which directly influence the agriculture and impose collateral effect on other industries causing economic fluctuation that is characteristic to agricultural society. When discussing industrial society, market economy has become the main form of resource allocation, adding market system, technical innovation, credit and debit scale, multiplier and accelerating effect and speculative activities as overlaying factors that result in economic fluctuation. These factors influence the motion of economy in different ways, sometimes combine and drive the economy to boom or to shrink, sometimes counteract and eliminate the effect, relieving the economy from inflation or deflation. Because such factors are restrained by the fundamental contradiction of the society to some extent, the fundamental contradiction is a more basic overlaying factor contributing to the society and economic fluctuation, having a paramount impact on fluctuation. Those who are enthusiastic about seeking the reasons why fluctuation occurs from particular a phenomena tending to regard a particular overlaying factor as the cause of fluctuation has made a mistake that they take a part for the whole from the aspect of epistemology. In socialism, the contradiction of antagonistic interests has no longer been the fundamental one for the society, yet it still influences the progress of social reproduction as an overlaying factor. As for random factors like technical innovation, policy changing, system innovation and the fluctuation of supply and demand relation, they are regular factors that cause economic fluctuation.

527

The fundamental social contradiction in capitalism renders as the contradiction between socialization of production and the privatization of means of production, as that between the organized individual corporations and anarchic status of social production and as that between the infinite development tendency of production and the shrinking payment ability of labourers. Under the condition of free market in capitalism, the periodic intensification of fundamental contradiction can effortlessly combine factors of every aspect and drive the drastic periodic economic fluctuation. The history of free market has proved this. By the time of national monopoly capitalism, with the establishment, optimization and increasingly effective operation of the national macro-control system, the fundamental contradiction of capitalism has been relieved to some extent and thus the combined forces of factors that lead to economic fluctuation have been dampened. To radically eliminate the economic crisis of capitalism is a total denial of capitalism and the establishment of socialism, such as the establishment of unitary public ownership, the unitary mode of distribution, which is according to one's performance, and the consummate planned economy. Yet this is a level where no socialism in reality can achieve, especially like the primary stage of socialism in China, where capitalistic economic relations are still remaining. Under such circumstances, although the fundamental contradiction of capitalism is not dominating, it still exists and imposes its influences. For example, the mutualism of multiple economic constituents does not only build the entity of diversified interest, but also the antagonistic interest relation between some interest entities. The surplus value rule dominating the behaviour of private corporations' owners and the rules regarding the capital accumulation are still applicable. The profiteering nature and blind development tendency of the private company have a constant impact on the macro-control aim of national economy and the proportion that allows national economy to develop normally, acting as an important factor leading to the fluctuation of national economy.

Marx has a profound explanation on the development period of capitalist economy, indicating that the characteristic process of modern industry includes intermediate active stage, prospective stage, crisis stage and stasis stage. Engels has summarized the economic period of capitalism into four stages of stasis, prospection, overproduction and crisis. Marx has also foreseen once the reproduction of capitalism is abolished, there will still be a fluctuation in the economic development. However, whether this fluctuation is periodical, Marx and Engels did not further explain. Consequently, is there any periodic rule in the economic development in socialistic country? China during its planned economic stage and the ex-Soviet Union had denied the periodical characteristic and even the fluctuation of economic development, regarding such fluctuation and economic crisis as same, and as the later one was characteristic in capitalism, so was the fluctuation and the period, in spite of the periodical economic development was an actual fact in the world. Deng Xiaoping was aware of this, stating that "It seems that our economy tends to develop in waves, moving rapidly ahead for a few years, reaching a higher stage, after which we pause to solve the problems that have arisen, and then moving on again."[41] His view has a crucial meaning toward advancing the study on socialistic economic period and led to the theoretical liberation. After that, Marxist Political Economics does not only believe that socialism can control the development of its fundamental contradiction, so can capitalism. Considering this, the essence of the problem is no longer relevant to whether fluctuation has a relation with the fundamental contradiction, since the fluctuation must have been caused by and rendered as the movement of fundamental contradiction. Regardless of capitalism or socialism, drastic economic fluctuation results from the excessive and blind investment of the economic entity.

Since 1980s, the analysis methodology applied by the Chinese scholars has improved and developed greatly. The normative analysis in the past has been substituted by empirical analysis. Apart from applying a spectrogram for describing the curve in periodical economic fluctuation, it is usual to use mathematical statistics for examining the economic period.

The economic development since the foundation of our nation is uprising with fluctuation, moving forward in a wave-like and spiral manner. Admitting this periodic fluctuation and learning the socialist economic periodic development

---

41 *Selected Works of Deng Xiaoping*, Volume 3, p. 368.

rules so as to control and utilize such rule concords with the basic viewpoint from Marxism. Learning and unveiling the periodic economic development rules is an act of enriching and advancing on the Marxist economic theory.

We believe that whether the periodic economic study is scientific depends on the methodology and the narrative approach applied. Therefore, this is the main viewpoint of ours.

XI. Concluding Remarks

Guided by the Marxist theory of business cycle, Chinese scholars have developed a brand new research field, the study of Chinese socialist business cycle through free research and theoretical innovation. Since it is the practical need of economic development to study the fluctuation of socialist economy, the study well serves practice by concentrating on managing business cycle in its motive and goal from the start. In the initial stage of research, scholars proved the objectivity of socialist economic cyclical fluctuation by basic principles of Marxism. As the research work has advanced scholars, they made innovation in both methods and theories of the research and adopted methods including modern statistics, measurement and quantitative analysis while adhering to method of contradiction analysis, which has greatly enhanced theoretical innovation and the capacity to analyze and explain the business cycle. Deng Xiaoping's "gradual development in steps" approach thought has played an important supporting role in constructing the theory of socialist business cycle. 529 At present, a mature method of research has been established, that is, methodology research, description of fluctuations, explanation of fluctuations, theoretical construction, practical detection, methodology modification, and revising the previous explanation and analysis of fluctuations. Before 1960s, research on both capitalist and socialist business cycles was carried out on the following three questions: what is the nature of business cycle, what is the reason for the cycle to emerge, is it feasible to reduce economic fluctuation and how to do so? Researches on these questions are consistent with the study on the capitalist business cycle, so that it could distinguish the capitalist business cycle from the socialist one, help scholars find the special features of the socialist business cycle, and the research can better adapt to the needs of those opposing to capitalism at that time. Until the 1980s, to accommodate the requirement of shifting the basic guideline of socialism, focuses of the research have been changed to questions such as, what are the fundamental roots of the economic fluctuation, what is the transmission mechanism of economic fluctuations and how to manage them? In this process, researchers gradually refrained from the impact of the social system on business cycles, applied modern analytic methods of the business cycle to carry out a detailed investigation over the fluctuation in the economy since the founding of New China, drew a diagram of economic fluctuations, and analyzed various factors restricting the business cycle. At the same time, they also launched the study on the business cycle and growth cycle in the national economy.

Main References

I. Books

(Poland) Feliks Młynarski, *Credit and Peace: a Way Out of the Crisis*, Shanghai: Commercial Press, 1936.

Xu Dixin, *General Political Economics Beijing*: Joint Publishing, 1948.

Shen Zhiyuan, *New Economics Outline*. Life Bookstore, 1935 first edition, *Outline of Political Economy*, 1953 edition, published by Joint Publishing.

Shen Zhiyuan, *The World Economic Crisis*, Shanghai: Zhonghua Book Company, 1935.

Guang Mengjue, *The Preliminary Theory of the Economic Crisis*, Chongqing: Life Bookstore, 1940.

(United Kingdom) Winternitz, *The Marxist Theory of Crisis*, Shanghai: World Affairs Press, 1950.

(Soviet Union) Tramayev, *Capitalist Reproduction and Economic Crisis*, Beijing: Joint Publishing, 1951.

Department of Political Economics, Renmin University of China, translated, *The Significance of Marxist-Leninist Theory of Crisis of Overproduction*, Beijing: China Renmin University Press, 1952.

Su Shaozhi, *National Revenue, Reproduction of Social Capital and Economic Crisis under the Capitalist System*, Shanghai: New Knowledge Press, 1956.

USSR Academy of Sciences, Institute of Economics, compiled, *Political Economy, A Textbook*, Beijing: People's Publishing House, 1955.

(Soviet Union) Trachtenberg, *Capitalist Reproduction and Economic Crisis*, Beijing: People's Publishing House, 1956.

531

(Soviet Union) Leontiev, *Economic Crisis* Beijing: China Renmin University Press, 1957.

Shi Keming, *Today's U.S. Economic Crisis*, Shenyang: Liaoning People's Publishing House, 1958.

International Relations Institute, Academy of Sciences,compiled and translated, *On the U.S. Economic Crisis: Proceedings*, Beijing: World Affairs Press, 1958.

Wu Dakun, *About the U.S. Economic Crisis*, Beijing: Workers Press, 1958.

World Economics and Politics Institute of USSR Academy of Science, collective compiled, *World Economic Crisis: Comparative Information of the Historical Crises in Major Capitalist Countries in 1848 – 1935*, Beijing: World Affairs Press, 1958.

(Soviet Union) M. S. Dragilev, *The General Crisis of Capitalism*, Shanghai: Shanghai People's Publishing House, 1958.

(U.S.) Hansen, *Economic Policy and Full Employment*, Shanghai: Shanghai People's Publishing House, 1959.

Stalin, *Economic Problems of Socialism in the U.S.S.R.*, Beijing: People's Publishing House, 1961.

(U.S.) Joan Robinson, *An Essay on Marxian Economics*, P34, Beijing, Commercial Press, 1962.

(France) Althusser, *For Marx*, London: Irene Ranney, Penguin Press, 1969.

(France) Althusser, *Reading Capital*, Beijing: Central Compilation and Translation Press, 2001.

Marx and Engels Collected Works, Chinese Version 1st Ed., Volume 1, 4 - 8, 15 - 16, 18 - 20, 22, 26 - 32, 34 - 37, 39, 42, 46, 50, Beijing: People's Publishing House, 1956 – 1985.

Marx, *Capital*, Volume I, II, III, Beijing: People's Publishing House, 1975, 2004.

(Soviet Union) Varga, *Modern Capitalism and Economic Crises*, Beijing: SDX Joint Publishing, 1975.

(British) M. Blaney, *Underconsumption Theory*, London: *Monthly Review* Press, 1976.

(Soviet Union)Mendelson, *Theory and History of the Economic Crisis and Cycle*, P58, Beijing: Joint Publishing. 1977.

(U.S.) Baran, Sweezy, *Monopoly Capital*, Beijing: Commercial Press, 1977.

Selected Works of Joseph Stalin, Volume 2, Beijing: People's Publishing House, 1955.

(U.S.) Galbraith, *Economics and the Public Purpose*, Beijing: Commercial Press, 1980.

Xiao Dezhou, Du Houwen et al., *The Development of the Basic Economic Features of the Post-War Imperialism*, Nanning: Guangxi People's Publishing House, 1980.

(U.S.) Gunnar Myrdal, Monetary Equilibrium, Beijing: Commercial Press, 1982.

(Russia) Tugan-Baranovsky, *Cyclical Industrial Crisis*, Beijing: Commercial Press, 1982.

(U.S.) Ernest Mandel, *Late Capitalism*, Harbin: Heilongjiang People's Publishing House, 1983.

(Germany) Ludwig Erhard: *Prosperity Through Competition*, Beijing: Commercial Press, 1983.

(Russia) Bukharin, *Imperialism and World Economy*, Beijing: China Social Sciences Press, 1983.

Tao Dayong, *The Theory and Reality of the Capitalist General Crisis*, Shanghai: Shanghai People's Publishing House, 1984.

(U.S.) Edward Shapiro, *Macroeconomic Analysis*, Beijing: China Social Sciences Press, 1985.

Foreign Economics Research, Papers in Economics *Selected Works of Modern Foreign Economics*, the 10th series, Beijing: Commercial Press, 1986.

(Soviet Union) M. H. Rydina, *The History of Economic Thought,* Beijing: China Renmin University Press. 1987.

(U.S.) Charles K. Wilber, Kenneth Jameson, *An Inquiry into the Poverty of. Economics*, Beijing: Commercial Press, 1987.

(U.S.) Paul Craig Roberts, *Supply-Side Revolution: An Insider's Account of Policymaking in Washington*, Shanghai: Shanghai Translation Publishing House, 1987.

(Soviet Union) Gelchuk, *Modern Capitalist Economic Crisis*, Beijing: Oriental Press, 1987.

Qiu Qihua, *Modern Monopoly Capitalist Economy*, Beijing: Central Party School Press, 1987.

(U.S.) Arthur Lewis, *Growth and Fluctuations*, Beijing: China Press, 1987.

(Poland) Binyamin Mintz, *Modern Capitalism*, Beijing: Oriental Press, 1987.

Wei Xun, editor in chief, *Exploration on the Contemporary Capitalist Economy*, Shijiazhuang: Hebei People's Publishing House, 1988.

Zhao Tao, *The Economic Long Wave Theory: a study on the long-term fluctuation of capitalism*, Beijing: China Renmin University Press, 1988.

The Collected Works of Vladimir Lenin, Chinese Edition Version 2, Volume 1, 3, 4, 6, 21, Beijing: People's Publishing House, 1984.

Liu Shucheng, *Fluctuation in Chinese Business Cycle*, Beijing: China Economic Publishing House, 1989.

Hu Daiguang et al., *The Study by Contemporary Western Scholars of Marx's 'Das Kapital'*, Beijing: The Economic Press of China. 1990.

Liu Shucheng, Bi Dachuan, *Business Cycle and Early Warning System*, Beijing: Science Press, 1990.

(Japan) Ito Makoto, *Value and Crisis: Essay on Marxian Economics in Japan* Beijing: China Social Sciences Press, 1990.

Bi Dachuan, *Business Cycle and Early Warning System*, Beijing: Science Press, 1990.

Hu Jichuang, *The Analysis of Differences in Political Economy*, Shanghai: Fudan University Press, 1991.

(U.S.) Joseph Schumpeter, *The Theory of Economic Development: An inquiry into profits, capital, credit, interest and the business cycle*, Beijing: Commercial Press, 1991.

Wu Dakun editor in chief, *The Contemporary Capitalism: structure, characteristics, and trend.* Shanghai: Shanghai People's Publishing House, 1991.

Zhu Zhongdi, *The Study of Western Scholars on the Marxist Theory of the Economic Crisis*, Shanghai: Shanghai People's Publishing House, 1991.

Xue Jingxiao, editor of chief, *The Capitalist Business Cycle – Theory and Prediction*, Beijing, People's Publishing House, 1992.

(Germany) Roman Rosdolsky, *The Making of Marx's Capital*, Jinan: Shandong People's Publishing House, 1992.

(U.S.) Jesse G.Schwartz, *A Critique of Economic Theory*, Jinan: Shandong People's Publishing House, 1992.

(Japan) Tsusaburo Sato et al., *100 Questions for Capital*, Jinan: Shandong People's Publishing House, 1992.

(U.S.) Paul Samuelson, *Economics*, Beijing: China Development Press, 1992.

(Germany) Dennis Muller, *Public Choice*, Beijing: Commercial Press, 1992.

(U.S.) Ernest Mandel, *Long Waves of Capitalist Development*, Beijing: Beijing Normal University Press, 1993.

Tian Guang *The Logic of Capital*, Jinan: Shandong People's Publishing House, 1993.

(Dutch) van Dewing, *Economic Long Waves and Innovation*, Shanghai: Shanghai Translation Publishing House, 1993.

Selected Works of Deng Xiaoping, Volume 3, Beijing: People's Publishing House, 1993.

Tang Zaixin, *Studies of the Manuscripts of Marxist Economics*, Wuhan: Wuhan University Press, 1993.

(Germany) Günter Gabisch and Hans-Walter Lorenz, *Business Cycle Theory: A Survey of Methods and Concepts*, Shanghai: Shanghai Joint Publishing, 1993.

Ma Jianxing et al., *General Monopoly Capital*, Jinan: Shandong People's Publishing House, 1993.

(U.S.) Ben Fine, Lawrence Harris, *Rereading Capital*, P60, Jinan: Shandong, People's Publishing House, 1993.

(Germany) Hilferding, *Finance Capital*, Beijing: Commercial Press, 1994.

Liu Peixian, Ma Jianxing, *The Study of Thought in the Second International*, P66. Beijing: China Renmin University Press, 1994.

Tang Zaixin, editor in chief, *The Exploration of the Sequel of The Capital* (Appendix), Beijing, China Financial Publishing House, 1995.

(U.S.) Gottfried Von Haberler, *Prosperity and Depression: A theoretical analysis of cyclical movements*, Beijing: Commercial Press, 1995.

Hu Jichuang, *Hu Jichuang Anthology*, Beijing: China Financial and Economic Publishing House, 1995.

(Germany) Mechael Heinrich, *Is There Marx's theory of Crisis?*, Marx and Engels' Studies (Berlin), 1995 New Series.

Chen Daisun, *From Chinese Classical Economics to Marx*. Beijing: Beijing University Press, 1996.

Liu Shucheng, *New Stage of Fluctuations in China's Business Cycle*, Shanghai: Shanghai Far East Press, 1996.

(U.S.) Sweezy, *Theory of Capitalist Development*, Beijing: Commercial Press, 1997.

Liu Chongyi, *The Structural Economic Crisis in the Contemporary Capitalism*, Beijing: Commercial Press, 1997.

(U.S.) Robert Joseph Barro, *Modern Business Cycle Theory*, Beijing: Commercial Press, 1997.

Michael R. Krätke, *Capitalism and Crisis*, Marx and Engels' Studies (Berlin), 1998 New Series.

He Bingmeng, Liu Shucheng, editor in chief, *The Asian Financial Crisis: Latest Analysis and Countermeasures*, Beijing: Social Sciences Academic Press, 1998.

Yuan Mu, Yang Deming, Sun Xuewen, *The Asian Financial Crisis that Shook the World*, Beijing: Contemporary China Publishing House, 1998.

Li Cong, *New Development of Contemporary Capitalism*, Beijing: Economic Science Press, 1998.

Dai Jinping, Sheng Bin et al., *Out of the Crisis: The Economic Perspective of the East Asian Financial Crisis*, Guiyang: Guizhou People's Publishing House, 1999.

(U.S.) Joseph Schumpeter, *Capitalism, Socialism and Democracy*, Beijing: Commercial Press, 1999.

(England) John Maynard Keynes, *The General Theory of Employment, Interest and Money*, Beijing: Commercial Press, 1999

(U.S.) Robert E. Lucas, Jr., *Studies in Business-Cycle Theory*, Beijing: Commercial Press, 2000.

Liu Shucheng, *Prosperity and Stability: Studies of Chinese Economic Fluctuations*, Beijing: Social Science Academic Press, 2000.

Gao Feng, *"New Economy", or New "Long Wave"?* See Zhang Yu et al., editor in chief, *Advanced Political Economy*, Beijing: Economic Science Press, 2002.

Wang Luolin, Li Yang et al., editor in chief, *Financial Structure and Financial Crisis*, Beijing: Economy & Management Publishing House, 2002.

Wei Xinghua, *Wei Xinghua Economics Anthology*, Volume 1, Beijing: Economic Science Press, 2002

Wei Xinghua, *Wei Xinghua Economics Anthology*, Volume 2, Beijing: Economic Science Press, 2002

Zhang Yu et al., editor in chief, *Advanced Political Economy*, Beijing: Economic Science Press, 2002.

(England) M. C. Howard, *A History of Marxian Economics (1929 – 1990)*, Beijing: Central Compilation and Translation Press, 2003.

(U.S.) James O'Connor, *Natural Causes: Essays in Ecological Marxism*, Nanjing, Nanjing University Press, 2003.

Yang Guochang, editor in chief, *Inheritance and Innovation of Marxist Economics System*. Beijing: Beijing Normal University Press, 2004.

536

Liu Shucheng, *Business Cycles and Macro-Control*, Beijing: Social Sciences Academic Press, 2005.

Liu Chongyi, *Business Cycle Theory*, Beijing: People's Publishing House, 2006.

II. Papers

Karl Kautsky. *Theory of Crisis*, in *Die Neue Zeit*. 1902 (4).

Hiroshi Kobayashi. *Introspection of the Postwar "Economic Crisis"*, in *World Economic Papers*, 1957 (5).

(Soviet Union) Izrail Grigorevich Bliumin, *The Theory of "Non-Crisis Capitalism" at the Service of Monopoly Capital*, in *World Economic Papers*, 1957 (11).

Xia Zhongcheng, *On Several Issues of the Development of Capitalist Industrial Cycle in the Post-War Period*, in *Teaching and Research*, 1958 (1).

Si Mu, *The U.S. Economic Crisis and Its Impact*, in *Journal of Finance and Economics*, 1958 (4).

(Germany) Jürgen Kuczynski, *Studies of Intermediate Crisis*, in *World Economic Papers*, 1958 (5).

(U.S.) Henry Claudel, *Analysis of the Current Economic Crisis in the United States*, in *World Economic Papers*, 1958 (5).

Yao Nai. *On the Rapid Development of the Socialist Economy and the Trend in Waves*, in *Jiefang Daily*, 1959 – 08 – 07.

(Japan) Ishihara Naganana, *Key Issues in the Study of the World Economic Crisis*, in *World Economic Papers*, 1958 (5).

(Germany) Schmidt, *New Issues in the Economic Crisis Theory*, in *World Economic Papers*, 1958 (6, 7).

Hong Junyan, *The Unstable U.S. Economy*, in Journal of Peking University, 1959 (4).

Wu Dakun, *On Postwar Business Cycles and Inflation in the United States*, in *Teaching and Research*, 1959 (6).

Fang Zhong, *Speed and Waves*, in *Plans and Statistics*, 1959 (10).

Fang Xing. *A Brief Analysis on the LAW of the Socialist Economic Development in Waves*, in *Theoretical Front*, 1959 (11).

Wang Xiangming. *Correct Understanding of the Waves in Socialist Development*, in *Economic Research Journal*, 1960 (1).

Yin Shijie, Liu Guangjie, A Brief Analysis on high speed development of the national economy in waves and in sustained leap. In *Journal of Wuhan University*, 1960 (1).

Wu Bannong, *Some Questions about the Scale to Measure the Economic Crisis*, in *International Studies*, 1960 (3). 537

Wu Dakun, *More on the U.S. Economic Crisis and Inflation*, in *Teaching and Research*, 1961 (2).

Wu Dakun. *On the Impact of the Postwar U.S. capital exports on the Current Economic Crisis*, in *Economic Research Journal*, 1961 (4).

Wu Bingyuan, *Development Is the Advance in Waves*, in *Guangming Daily*, 1961 – 04 – 21.

Yin Shijie, *Preliminary Analysis of the Factors Forming the Development of the National Economy in Waves*, in *Jianghan Journal*, 1961 (5).

Liu Gugang, *A Brief Analysis of the Form of Motion in the Development of Socialist Economic in Waves*, in *Ta Kung Pao*, 1961-06-02.

Guang Mengjue, *State Monopoly Capitalism and the U.S. Economic Crisis*, (Volume 1 & 2), in *Economic Research Journal*, 1961 (5, 6).

Li Zixin, Bu Luo, *High Speed Development in Waves is an Objective Law of the Socialist Economy*, in *Practice*, 1961 (8, 9).

Luo Gengmo, *On the Issue of Persistency and Waves in the Great Leap Forward*, in *Chinese Youth*, 1961 (9).

Song Chengxian, *Western Bourgeois Economic Crisis Theory*, in *Academic Monthly*, 1961 (9).

Wu Bannong, *Some Questions about the Postwar Capitalist Economic Crisis*, in *International Studies*, 1962 (1).

Wu Dakun, *Discussion on the Issue of the Renewal of Fixed Capital and the Contraction in the Postwar U.S. Business Cycle – An Answer to Comrade Song Zexing*, in *Economic Research Journal*, 1962 (3).

Su Shaozhi, *A Brief Analysis on the Capitalist World Economic Crisis (Volume 1 & 2)*, in *Economic Research Journal*, 1963 (4, 5).

Core Group of Theory, *The 1929 - 1933 Capitalist World Economic Crisis*, in *Journal of Northeast Normal University (Philosophy and Social Sciences)*, 1975 (1).

Huang Zhixian, *Monetary and Financial Crisis in Present Capitalist World*, in *Journal of Fujian Normal University (Philosophy and Social Sciences)*, 1975 (1).

Tong Chou, *Ins and Outs of the 1929-1933 Capitalist World Economic Crisis*, in *International Trade Journal*, 1975 (1).

Xue Zhixian, *Refutation of the Fallacy that "Oil Price Increases Caused the Crisis"*, in *Journal of Shaanxi Normal University(Philosophy and Social Sciences)*, 1975 (1).

Hang Qin. *The Current Capitalist World Economic Crisis*, in *International Trade Journal*, 1975 (1).

Marxist-Leninist Teaching and Research Group, *The Major Manifestations of the Current Capitalist World Economic Crisis and Its Roots*, in *Journal of Northeast Normal University (Philosophy and Social Sciences)*, 1975 (1).

The Three-Department Research Team of "Economic Crisis Issue", *Several Features of the Current Capitalist World Economic Crisis*, in *International Trade Journal*, 1975 (2).

Zhong Jin, *Refutation of the Fallacy that Monopoly Can Eliminate the Economic Crisis*, in *Hunan Normal University Social Science Journal*, 1975 (3).

Wang Huaining, *Inflation in the Major Capitalist Countries and Its Impact on the Economic Crisis*, in *World Economy*, 1979 (1).

Hong Dalin, *Why Cannot Say "Socialist Society May Have Economic Crises"*, in *Social Sciences*, 1979 (3).

Liu Chuanyan, *the U.S. Economy in the "Stagflation"*, in *Jilin University Social Science Journal*, 1979 (3).

Su Min. *Another Form of Economic Crisis May Emerge in the Socialist Country*, in *Social Science Front*, 1979 (3).

Qi Hua, Xue Xiao. *Is the Postwar Economic Crisis More Frequently in Capitalist Countries?*, in *World Economy*, 1979 (4).

Zhang Zhongmin. *The Socialist Society May Also Have the Economic Crisis*, in *Journal of Nanchang University*, 1979 (4).

(U.S.) R. Wolf, *Marx's Theory of Crisis: Structure and Connotation*, in *Foreign Social Science*, 1979 (4).

Da Yijin, *The Postwar Capitalist Business Cycle Transformation and Crisis*, in *Journal of Fudan University*, 1979 (6).

Lu Hongde, *The Postwar Capitalist Economic Crisis and the Features of the Cycle*, in *World Economy*, 1979 (6).

Guo Ding, *Two Humble Opinions about the Postwar Capitalist Economic Crisis and Cycle*, in *World Economy*, 1979 (6).

Zhou Maorong, *On the Issue of the Frequent Economic Crisis in the Postwar United States and the Shortening of the Cycle*, in *World Economy*, 1979 (9).

He Ming. *Several Opinions on the Current U.S. Economy*, in *World Economy*, 1979 (10).

Wu Dakun, *On the Postwar U.S. Economic Crisis and the Nature of Business Cycle*, in *World Economy*, 1979 (11).

Han Shilong, *About the Shortening of the Postwar U.S. Business Cycle from Intermediate Crisis*, *Journal of Sichuan University (Philosophy and Social Sciences)*, 1980 (1).

Liu Diyuan, *The Comparative Analysis of the Sixth Economic Crisis in the Postwar United States with the Great Depression in the 1930s*, in *World Economy*, 1980 (1).

Shen Huasong, *Analysis on the Essence of the Energy Crisis*, in *World Economy*, 1980 (1).

Wu Jixian, *Few Questions about the Post-War Capitalist Economic Crisis and Cycle*, in *World Economy*, 1980 (1).

Dai Zhixian, *Review of the Roosevelt "New Deal"*, In *Hunan Normal University Social Science Journal*, 1980 (1).

Yao Tinggang, *The Issue of the Post-War U.S. Economic Crisis and Cycle*, in *Journal of Wuhan University (Philosophy and Social Sciences)*, 1980 (2).

Ye Yicai, *The U.S. "Stagflation" and the Bankruptcy of Keynesian Doctrine*, in *Finance and Trade Research*, 1980 (5).

Wu Dakun, *The U.S. Economic Crisis and the Business Cycle in the Past Thirty Years*, in *Teaching and Research*, 1980 (5).

Liu Chuanyan, *Observation of the Effect of State Intervention in the Economy from the Sixth Post-War Economic Crisis in the United States*, in *Jilin University Social Science Journal*, 1980 (6).

Wu Dakun, *Some Views on the Current World Economic Crisis*, in *World Economy*, 1981 (1).

Li Yizhi, Inflation and Economic Crisis of Capitalism, in *Journal of Zhongnan University of Economics and Law*, 1981 (1).

Wang Zhuo, Huang Jubo, *Theory of the Constraint of the Disproportionality of the National Economy Must Be Studied*, in *Academic Research*, 1981 (4).

Wang Hongru, *The Evolution of the Postwar U.S. Monetary and Credit Policy*, in *Foreign Economics and Management*, 1981 (1).

(Soviet Union) C. Ivanov, *Characteristics of the Contemporary Capitalist Business Cycle*, in *Foreign Economics and Management*, 1981 (2).

Li Cong, *The Observation the Reagan Administration's Economic Policies from the Practice of the Post-War U.S. Government Intervention in the Economy*, in *World Economy*, 1981 (5).

(Soviet Union) K. Moisuc, Conflicts and Crises in the Contemporary World Economy. In *Foreign Social Science*, 1981 (8).

(U.S.) M. Carstairs. *Economic Crisis and the U.S. Society: Dusk of the U.S. Capitalism?*, in *Foreign Social Science*, 1981 (11).

Li Cong, *The Capitalist World Economic Crisis in the Current Historical Conditions*, in *World Economy*, 1982 (1).

Jiang Minguang, *Supply Economics and Say's Law*, in *Journal of Huazhong Normal University*, 1982 (1).

Lu Lijun, *Marx's Theory of the Capitalist Economic Crisis*, in *Journal of Henan Normal University (Philosophy and Social Sciences)*, 1982 (2).

Wang Hongding, *Planning and Monopoly Capitalism in France*, in *Foreign Economics and Management*, 1982 (5).

Zhang Yunling, *Transition of the Post-War Economic Development in the West and Long Fluctuation*, in *World Economy*, 1982 (10).

Zhou Jianping, *New Features of the Postwar Capitalist Economic Crisis and Its Causes*, in *Economic Research Journal*, 1982 (10).

Xie Yao, *Looking Ahead the Western Economic Trends from the U.S. Economic Crisis*, in *China International Studies*, 1983 (1).

(Soviet Union) II. M. Grigoryev, *Capitalist World in Times of Crisis*, in *Financial Theory and Practice*, 1983 (1).

Lv Fangju, *The Formation and Development of Marxist Theory of the Economic Crisis, and Its Scientific Nature*, in *Journal of Finance and Economics*, 1983 (1).

Wu Dakun, *The Economic Crisis in the Post-War Capitalist World and Material Basis for the Business Cycle*, in *Economic Research Journal*, 1983 (1).

Tao Dayong, *Theory and Reality of the General Crisis of Capitalism: Commemorating the Centenary of the Death of Karl Marx*, in *Journal of Beijing Normal University (Social Sciences)*, 1983 (2).

Ma Jianxing, *The Initial Formation of Marx's Theory of the Capitalist Economic Crisis: Notes of the Economics Manuscript (1857 - 1858)*, in *Economic Theory and Business Management*, 1983 (2).

Zhu Mutang, *The Systematic Assortment of the Possibility of the Economic Crisis in Capital to Develop to the Practical Theory*, in *Financial and Trade Management*, 1983 (2)

Wang Wanglie, *The 1981 - 1982 Global Economic Crisis and Prospects of 1983*, in *International Trade*, 1983 (2).

Hu Daiguang, *Marx's Theory of Economic Crisis and Comments of Western Scholars*, in *World Economy*, 1983 (3).

Wang Huaining, *The Current Economic Crisis in the Capitalist World*, in *Economic Research Journal*, 1983 (3).

Li Dachang, *The Economic Crisis Theory in "Capital" and the Reality of Contemporary Capitalism*, in *Social Science Research*, 1983 (5).

Ma Jianxing, *The Initial Formation of Marx's Theory of the Capitalist Economic Crisis*, in *Teaching and Research*, 1984 (2).

Li Wusi, Kong Xiangguan, *Review of the Rise and Fall of Keynesian from the Capitalist Economic Crisis*, in *Journal of Shanxi Finance and Economics University*, 1984 (3).

Xue Jingxiao, *The Renewal of Fixed capital and Business Cycle*, in *Social Science Front*, 1984 (4).

Zhang Chi, *The Contemporary Capitalist Structural Economic Crisis and Its Performance*, in *World Economy*, 1985 (3).

Song Baoxiang, *Characteristics of the Economic Crisis under the Condition of the Fourth Technological Revolution*, in *World Economy*, 1985 (11).

(Canada) Frank Faisal, *The World Economic Crisis in the 1986 – 1990*, in *World Economy*, 1985 (11).

Wu Jinglian, *Economic Fluctuation and the Dual System*, in *Finance & Trade Economics*, 1986 (6).

Lai Fengchen, *The Correct Understanding of Marxist Theory on the Root Reason for the Capitalist Economic Crisis to Occur*, in *Journal of Lanzhou University(Social Sciences)*, 1986 (1).

Liu Shucheng, *Preliminary Exploration in China's Investment Cycle in Fixed Assets*, in *Economic Research Journal*, 1986 (2)

Du Hui, *A Brief Analysis of the Cycle of the Economic growth in Soviet Socialism*, in *Nankai Economic Studies*, 1986 (2).

Liu Shucheng. *Further Exploration in China's Investment Cycle in Fixed Assets*, in *Economic Research Journal*, 1986 (6)

Liu Shucheng. *Third Exploration in China's Investment Cycle in Fixed Assets: The Historical Analysis of Each Cycle*, in *The Journal of Quantitative & Technical Economics*, 1986 (9).

Du Hui. *On the Cyclical Pattern of China's Economic Growth*, in *Nankai Economic Studies*, 1987 (1).

Lu Jian, *Analysis of Characteristics, Reasons and Mechanism of China's Business Cycle*, in *Economic Research Journal*, 1987 (4).

Li Yining, *Assumption of the Socialist Business Cycle*, in *Economic Research Journal*, 1987 (9).

Chen Caihong. *Investment and Business Cycle*, in *Economic Research Journal*, 1988 (2).

Zhou Yongxue, *Rethinking of the "Economic Crisis"*, in *Seeking Truth*, 1987 (2).

Liu Shucheng, *Impact of Cyclical Fluctuations of Investment on Cyclical Fluctuations of Economy:Third Exploration in China's Investment Cycle in Fixed Assets*, in *The Journal of Quantitative & Technical Economics*, 1987 (10).

Wu Jixian, Tang Shaoyun, *Analysis of the Fluctuation in the U.S. Business Cyclein 1980s*, in *World Economy Study*, 1988 (4).

Ye Xianming, *A Personal Perspective of the Development Law in the Thinking of Marx's "Mature" Time*, in *Journal of Tsinghua University (Philosophy and Social Sciences)*, 1988 (4).

Cui Xiangyang, *Capital and the Asian Financial Crisis*, in *Contemporary Economic Research*, 1988 (6).

Wang Tongxun, *Characteristics and Development Trend of the Postwar Capitalist Economic Crisis*, in *Journal of Beijing Normal University*, 1989 (6).

Ma Jiantang, *A Brief Analysis of Changes in the Industrial Structure in China's Business Cycle*, in *China Industrial Economic Research*, 1990 (1).

Zhuang Qishan, *Several Reflections on the General Crisis Theory of Capitalism*, in *World Economic Papers*, 1990 (3).

Yao Tinggang, *The Capitalist Economic Crisis and the Cycle in the 1990s*, in *World Economy Study*, 1990 (4).

Hu Guocheng, *The U.S. Economic Crisis in the 1930s and its Reasons for Continuation*, in *World History*, 1990 (4).

Zhang Yin, *Dialectical Thinking of the Universality and Particularity of "Economic Fluctuation"*, in *Probe*, 1990 (6).

Xue Jingxiao, *History and Status Quo of the Business Cycle in Capitalist Countries*, (I & II), in *Nankai Economic Studies*, 1991 (1), (2).

Kang Youshu, *The Historical Evolution and Its Essential Characteristic of Bourgeois Business Cycle Theory*, in *Journal of University of International Business and Economics*, 1991 (3).

Lu Jian. *Empirical Analysis of China's Business Cycle* (Volume I, II, III), in *Management World*, 1991 (4, 5, 6).

Sun Gang, *On Changes in the U.S. Business Cycle after World War II*, in *World Economy*, 1991 (12).

Feng Jinju. *The Theory and View that Socialism has Business Cycle Should Be Denied: and on the Characteristics of China's Economic Fluctuation*, in *Journal of Renmin University of China*, 1992 (1).

Niu Desheng, *Discrimination of Reasons for the Capitalist Economic Crisis*, in *Journal of Henan Normal University (Philosophy and Social Sciences)*, 1992 (4).

Liu Shucheng, Fan Mingtai, *Actively Manage Economic Fluctuation*, in *Economic Research Journal*, 1992 (5).

Shi Liangping. *Theoretical Thinking on Warning Methods of Business Cycle*, in *Journal of Finance and Economics*, 1992 (5).

Xue Boying, A Brief Analysis of the Simultaneity of the economic crisis in the postwar capitalist countries, in *World Economics and Politics*, 1992 (5).

Zhou Fang. *Aggregate Demand, Aggregate Supply and Economic Fluctuation*, in *The Journal of Quantitative & Technical Economics*, 1992 (6).

Fan Mingtai, *Formation Mechanism and Pattern of Chinese Economic Fluctuation*, in *Economic Research Journal*, 1992 (12).

Zhang Sai, *On the Law of Business Cycle and the Practice of macro-Control*, in *Statistical Research*, 1994 (2).

Zhang Rui, Dia*lysis of the Structural Crisis in the Contemporary Capitalist Countries*, in *Teaching and Research*, 1994 (5).

Shi Wei, *Policy Factors and Monetary Factors of the Cyclical Fluctuation in China's Economy*, in *Research of Financial and Economic Issues*, 1994 (6).

Yang Wenjin, *The Internal Mechanism of the Cyclical Economic Fluctuation*, in *Contemporary Finance & Economics*, 1994 (8)

Li Jingwen, Liu Shucheng, *Actively Manage and Actively Use Fluctuations in Business Cycle*, in *Studies on Mao Zedong and Deng Xiaoping Theories*, 1995 (1).

Fan Mingtai, *Comparative Analysis of Chinese Economic Fluctuation Mechanism Before and After Reform*, in *Management World*, 1995 (5).

Ma Jiujie, Kong Xiangzhi, *Economic Fluctuation and Agriculture during the Transition Period of China's Economy*, in *Management World*, 1995 (6).

Liu Shucheng. *On the New Stage of Cyclical Fluctuation in China's Economy*, in *Economic Research Journal*, 1996 (11).

He Wei, *Preliminary Exploration of Prospects of the Business Cycle Theory*, in *Contemporary Finance & Economics*, 1997 (2).

Zhang Tongyu, *Comparative Analysis of Two Kinds of the Business Cycle Theory*, in *Nankai Economic Studies*, 1997 (5).

He Keng, *Fluctuation of Business cycle Is Not the Inherent Economic Law of the Socialist Economy: And on Issues of Socialist Macroeconomics*, in *Journal of Zhongnan University of Finance and Economics*, 1998 (4).

Wen Qian, *On Economic Fluctuation and Policy Regulation*, in *Social Sciences in China*, 1998 (5).

Qi Guanyi, Miao Pei, *Does Business Cycle Still Exist in Developed Countries?: Thinking over the Sustained Economic Growth in the United States*, in *Journal of International Trade*, 1998 (9)

Dai Fengli, *Analysis on the Positive Role of the Business Cycle*, in *Teaching and Research*, 1998 (9).

Dai Renxiang, *Analysis of the Morphological System in the Business Cycle*, in *Journal of Central University of Finance and Economics*, 1998 (10).

Wu Chunzhi, *On Socialist Business Cycle*, in *Journal of Sichuan Normal University (Social Science)*, 1999 (1).

Liu Jinquan, Wang Jun, *Characteristics of Economic Impact in China's Economic Fluctuation*, in *Jilin University Social Sciences Journal*, 1999 (3).

Liu Zhibiao, *Marx's Social Structure Theory of Accumulation and Contemporary Economic Crisis*, in *Jiangsu Social Sciences*, 1999 (5).

Liu Shucheng, *On the New Trend of China's Economic Growth and Fluctuation*, in *Social Sciences in China*, 2000 (1).

Li Lianzhon, *Long Wave Theory and the World Economic Development*, in *Probe*, 2000 (3).

Liu Shucheng, Fan Mingtai, *Analysis of China's Economic Fluctuation*, in *China Industry Economics*, 2000 (5).

Zhao Jianqiang, Yi Dinghong, *Counter-Cyclical Policies and the Sustained and Steady Growth of China's Economy*, in *Research on Economics and Management*, 2000 (6).

Liu Hangang, *The Prevention of Marx's Labor Theory of Value on Fictitious Economy*, in *Contemporary Economic Research*, 2001 (2).

Zhai Zhicheng, *Business Cycle Theory and Trend of China's Current Macro Economy*, in *Economist*, 2001 (2).

Yang Tianyu, *Studies of Marx's Theory of Effective Demand*, in *Contemporary Economic Research*, 2001 (4).

Luo Wendong, *On Motivation and Trends of the Development of Contemporary Capitalism*, in Contemporary World and Socialism, 2002 (5).

Zhang Liancheng, *On Institutional Reasons of Economic Fluctuations and Policy Choices of the Government*, in *Research on Economics and Management*, 2002 (5).

Liu Guirong. *Causes and Enlightenment of the Financial Crisis in Argentina*, in *Shanghai Economic Review*, 2002 (8).

Cui Youping. *Business Cycle Theory and Its Practical Significance*, in *Contemporary Economic Research*, 2003 (3).

Zhang Haitao, *New Development of the U.S. Economic Crisis*, in *Economic Review*, 2003 (3).

Liu Heng, Chen Shuyun, *New Situation of the Cyclical Fluctuation in China's Economy*, in *Management World*, 2003 (3).

Liu Shucheng, *New Track of China's Economic Fluctuation*, in *Economic Research Journal*, 2003 (3)

Liu Jinquan. *Analysis on the Relevance between Investment Volatility and Business Cycle*, in *China Soft Science Magazine*, 2003 (4).

Dong Zhongqi. *Analysis of Marx and Engels' Understanding of the Capitalist Society in the Late 1840s*, in *Journal of Sichuan University (Philosophy and Social Sciences)*, 2003 (5).

(U.S.) Robert Brenner, *The Emerging World Capitalist Economic Crisis: from Neoliberalism to Recession*, in *Marxism & Reality*, 2003 (5).

Men Shulian, Cheng Qiufen, *Neoliberalism and the Economic Crisis in Argentina*, in *Research of Financial and Economic Issues*, 2003 (12).

Wang Zaikun, *Capitalist System Root of the Ecological Crisis: an Explanation from the Perspective of Ecological Socialism*, in *Journal of Fujian Provincial Committee Party School of CPC*, 2004 (3).

Liu Shucheng, *Background Characteristics of the New Round of the Business Cycle*, in *Economic Research Journal*, 2004 (3).

Qian Shichun, *Empirical Analysis of China's Macroeconomic Fluctuation: 1952 - 2002*, in *Statistical Research*, 2004 (4).

Wang Lin. *On Economic Fluctuation of Enterprise Warning*, in *Reform of the Economic System*, 2004 (3).

Gao Suying, Wang Jing, Jin Hao. *Measurement and Calculation of the Cycle of China's Economic Fluctuation*, in *Nankai Journal (Philosophy and Social Sciences)*, 2004 (3).

Research Group of Macroeconomic Monitoring and Early Warning, *Empirical Analysis of Changes in Characteristic of fluctuations in China's Business Cycle*, in *Jilin University Social Sciences Journal*, 2004 (5).

Song Dianqing, Li Bihao. *New Exploration of the Cyclical Economic Crisis Theory*. In *Academic Exchanges*, 2004 (11).

Ju Guoyu, Lan Yi. *Transformation of the Micro-Foundation of the Cyclical Fluctuation in China's Economy*. In *Social Sciences in China*, 2005 (1).

Guo Baohong. *Reflections on Productive Forces and Relations of Production of the Contemporary Capitalism*. In *Socialist Studies*, 2005 (5).

Du Hui. *Witness the Study Course of Fluctuations in China's Business Cycle*. In *Economic Research Journal*, 2005 (7).

Yang Yingjie, *Analysis of Deep-Seated Causes of Fluctuations in China's Business Cycle*, in *Contemporary Economic Research*, 2005 (10).

Liu Shucheng, *To Achieve Smoothing of Fluctuations in the Business Cycle in the Moderate Height*, in *Economic Research Journal*, 2005 (11).

Liu Shucheng, Zhang Ping, Zhang Xiaojing, *China's Economic Growth and Cyclical Fluctuations*. In *Macroeconomics*, 2005 (12).

Jin Chengwu. *Frontier Research of Fluctuations in China Business Cycle*, in *Economic Research Journal*, 2006 (1).

Yang Jiansheng, *Review of the U.S. Underconsumption Theory*. In *Contemporary Economic Research*, 2006 (2).

Sun Guangsheng, *Economic Fluctuation and Industrial Fluctuation (1986 – 2003)*, in *Social Sciences in China*, 2006 (3).

Pang Dong, Yang Can, *Analysis of the Effect of the System Impact of Fluctuations in China's Business Cycle*, in *Research on Financial and Economic Issues*, 2006 (3).

Wang Yuanzhang, You Yong. *Marxist Economic Crisis Theory and Its Development in the Contemporary Time*. In *Journal of Zhongnan University of Economics and Law*, 2006 (5).

Huang Like. *Comparison between the Marxist Theory of Economic Crisis and the Western Theory of Business Cycle*. In *Contemporary Economic Research*, 2006 (5).

Liu Xiaohua. *The Comparison Study of Marx's "Capitalist Reproduction Cycle" with the Western "Long Business Cycle"*, in *Economic Review*, 2006 (6).

Dong Jin. *Measurement of the Macroeconomic Fluctuation Cycle*. In *Economic Research Journal*, 2006 (7).

Wang Yue. *Review of Western Business Cycle and Economic Fluctuation Theory*. In *Probe*, 2006 (10).

Peng Xuenong. *Production Conditions and the Second Contradiction: on O'Connor's Theory of Ecological Marxism*, in *Studies in Dialectics of Nature*, 2007 (2).

Liu Shucheng. *On Good and Fast Development*. In *Economic Research Journal*, 2007 (6).

III. Foreign References

Alcaly, R. "An Introduction to Marxian Crisis Theory", in URPE, *The U.S. Capitalism in Crisis.*

Althusser, L. and Balibar, E. (1970), *Reading "Capital"*, London.

Alberro, J. "The Simple Analytics Falling Profit Rates", Okishio's Theorem and Fixed Capital, *Review of Radical Political Economics*, 11, 1979.

Bleaney, M. (1976), *Underconsumption Theories*, London.

Cogoy, M (1973), "The fall in the rate of profit and the theory of accumulation: a reply to Paul Sweezy", *Conference of Socialist Economists Bulletin*, vol. 2, no. 7.

Dickinson, H. D. (1956), "The Falling Rate of Profit in Marxian Economics", *Review of Economic Studies*, 24.

Dobb, M. (1940), *Political Economy and Capitalism*, London.

Foley, D. (1986), "Money, accumulation and crisis". New York: Harwood Academic.

Friedman, M. 1968. "The Role of Money Policy". American Economic Review: 72 (January),1 - 24.

Friedman, M 1982. *Capitalism and Freedom.* Chicago: University of Chicago Press.

Harrod, R. F. 1950. *The Business Cycle.* Oxford: Oxford University Press.

Hicks, J. R 1950. *A Contribution to the Theory of the Trade Cycle.* Oxford: Oxford University Press.

Itoh, m. (1978a), "The formation of Marx's theory of crisis", *Science and Society*, vol. 42.

Lucas, M. 1981. *Studies in Business Cycles Theory.* Oxford: Basil Blackwell.

Lebowitz, M. A. (1976), "Marx's Falling Rate of Profit: A Dialectical View", *Canadian Journal of Economics*, 9.

Mandel,E. (1967),"An Introduction to Marxist Economic Theory", New York: Pathfinder Press.

Mandel, E. (1975), *Late Capitalism*, London.

Mattick, P. (1969), *Marx and Keynes*, London.

Mitchell, W. C. 1913. *Business Cycles.* Berkeley: University of California Press.

Mitchell, W. C. 1951. *What Happens During Business Cycle.* New York: National Bureau of Economic Research.

O'Connor, J. J. (1984), "Accumulation crisis", Oxford: Blackwell.

Robinson, J. (1967), *An Essay on Marxian Economics*, London.

Roemer, J. (1977),"Technical change and the 'tendency of profit to fall'", *Journal of Economic Theory*, vol. 16.

Roemer, J. (1978),"The effect of technological change on the real wage and Marx's falling rate of profit*", Australian Economic Papers,* vol. 3.

Roemer, J. (1979), "Continuing controversy on the falling rate of profit: fixed capital and other issues",*Cambridge Journal of Economics,* vol. 3.

Roemer, J. (1980), "A general equilibrium approach to Marxian economics",*Econometrics,* vol. 48.

Robinson, J. "The falling rate of profit: A comment", *Science and Society*, 23, 1959.

Schumpeter, J. (1939), *"Business cycles"*, New York.

Sweezy, P. "The Economic Crisis in the United states", *Monthly Review*,33, December 1981.

Sherman, H. (1967), "Marx and the business cycle", *Science and Society*, vol. 31.

Sherman, H. (1971), "Marxist models of cyclical growth", *History of Political Economy*, vol. 3.

Shibata, K. "On the law of decline in the rate of profit", *Kyoto University Economic Review*, July 1934.

Sherman, H. J. 1991. *The Business Cycle.* Princeton University Press.

Van Parijs, P. (1980), "The falling-of-profit theory of crisis: a rational reconstruction by way of obituary", *Review of Radical Political Economics*, vol. 12.

Weisskopf, T. E. (1979) "Marxian Crisis and the Rate of Profit in the Postwar U.S. Economy", *Cambridge Journal of Economics*, 3.

Yaffe, D. S. (1973), "The Marxian Theory of Crisis, Capital and State", *Economy and Society*, 2.

Postscript

Professor Ma Jianxing once said: compared with the study of the history of thought of Marxist philosophy, the study of the history of Marxist economic thought is very inadequate, still lacking a comprehensive, in-depth, and systematic study. And there are also some studies with a utilitarian color, lacking objective, fair and reasonable theoretical evaluation. In the study of the Marxist theory of the economic crisis for the past a few years, I deeply appreciate that Professor Ma Jianxing's assessment is fair and realistic. Promoting Marxist economics is a systematic project, and it is undoubtedly an important part to have a comprehensive, in-depth, systematic and systematic assortment and exploration of the Marxist economic thought, as well as to carry out a reasonable, fair and objective academic evaluation.

In the process of the study of Marxist theory of economic crisis, Professor Ma Jianxing gave me a lot of support and encouragement. As the well-known expert in the history of Marxist economic thought, he had the research spanned almost the whole field of the history of Marxist economic thought, from *The History of the Creation of "Capital"*, *The History of the Formation of Imperialism Theory*, *The History of the Socialist Economic Thought in the 20th Century* to *The History of the Formation of the Socialist Economic Theory with Chinese Characteristics*, which have recorded his scholarship and research trajectory. As his student, I was fortunate to consult him on many issues, and to discuss with him in an unfettered manner, listening to his academic teaching is always inspiring and helpful, which is one of the reasons why I have been able to uphold the study of the Marxist theory of economic crisis for a long time. Taking this opportunity, I am grateful to Professor Ma Jianxing for his concern and help for years, and sincerely wish him good health and longevity.

In the theoretical research and writing of this book, I was also supported and helped by Qiao Yuhua, Wang Yuliang, Niu Yiping, Lu Huiyun and others. As entrepreneurs, they have deep feelings and a more professional sensitivity over the relations between production, operation, strategic investment decisions of the enterprise and business cycles, perhaps it is for these reasons that they are interested in the subject I have studied in this book, thus held exchanges and discussions with me on relevant issues, during which I have learned a lot. Again, taking this opportunity, I am very grateful that they have friendly contributed to my academic endeavor and wish them full success in managing their business cycles, making their companies greater and stronger!

In the process of writing and publishing the book, I was also supported and encouraged by Prof. Zhang Yu, Prof. Chen Xiangguang, Prof. Yao Kaijian, so my deep gratitude also goes to them!

www.ingramcontent.com/pod-product-compliance
Lightning Source LLC
Chambersburg PA
CBHW031136020426
42333CB00013B/398